POLICE COURTS IN NINETEENTH-CENTURY SCOTLAND, VOLUME 1

CW01497158

Police Courts in Nineteenth-Century Scotland, Volume 1

Magistrates, Media and the Masses

DAVID G. BARRIE AND SUSAN BROOMHALL
The University of Western Australia

Routledge
Taylor & Francis Group

LONDON AND NEW YORK

First published in paperback 2024

First published 2014 by Ashgate Publishing

Published 2016
by Routledge
4 Park Square, Milton Park, Abingdon, Oxon OX14 4RN

and by Routledge
605 Third Avenue, New York, NY 10158

Routledge is an imprint of the Taylor & Francis Group, an informa business

Publisher's Note
The publisher has gone to great lengths to ensure the quality of this reprint but points out that some imperfections in the original copies may be apparent.

British Library Cataloguing in Publication Data
A catalogue record for this book is available from the British Library

The Library of Congress has cataloged the printed edition as follows:
Barrie, David G., author.
    Police courts in nineteenth-century Scotland. Magistrates, media and the masses /
    by David G. Barrie and Susan Broomhall.
        pages cm
    ISBN 978-1-4094-4245-5 (hardcover : alk. paper)
    1. Courts of first instance--Scotland--History--19th century. 2. Police magistrates--Scotland--History--19th century. 3. Justices of the peace--Scotland--History--19th century. 4. Criminal justice, Administration of--Scotland--History--19th century.
    I. Broomhall, Susan, author. II. Title. III. Title: Magistrates, media and the masses.
    KDC860.B373 2014
    347.411'02--dc23
                                                                                2014026176

ISBN: 978-1-4094-4245-5 (hbk)
ISBN: 978-1-03-291897-6 (pbk)
ISBN: 978-1-315-60102-1 (ebk)

DOI: 10.4324/9781315601021

Contents

List of Figures and Illustrations

List of Tables

List of Abbreviations

BPP	British Parliamentary Papers
DCA	Dundee City Archives
DCL	Dundee Central Library
DI	Dick Institute, Kilmarnock
ECA	Edinburgh City Archives
ECL	Edinburgh Central Library
GCA	Glasgow City Archives
GUL	Glasgow University Library, Special Collections
NAS	National Archives of Scotland, Edinburgh
NLS	National Library of Scotland
PKCA	Perth and Kinross Council Archives
Police Intelligencer	*The Police Intelligencer, or Life in Edinburgh* (These can be found in Edinburgh Central Library)
Police Reports	*Police Reports of Causes tried before the Justices of Peace, and the Glasgow, Gorbals and Calton Police Courts* (These can be found in Glasgow City Archives)
The Detective	*The Detective: or, A Journal for the Exposure and Suppression of Crime*

Acknowledgements

Collaboration can be a risky business. It can also be extremely fruitful and rewarding. While working with someone who thinks about things differently, prioritises different questions, and has a different writing style can be challenging and a little frustrating, any angst is vastly offset by the benefits that collaboration brings. Inevitably, working on this project over the last few years has resulted in (fairly minor) compromises in argument, style and research direction, but, thankfully, not in the respect we hold for each other as co-author. Our first acknowledgment therefore goes to each other.

We have benefited from the assistance of two first-rate research assistants. Iain Hutchison was his usual unselfish and helpful self in responding to (usually urgent) emails to visit archives and photocopy and digitise sources in Scotland (invaluable, and somewhat inevitable, support when we are 9,000 miles away with limited opportunities for research travel). Our friend and colleague, Joanne McEwan, provided excellent research and editorial support at various stages of the project. A great debt is owed to both, not least for putting up with our many requests and demands. Sarah Finn also helped to proof some drafts and provided efficient and friendly administrative support. Thanks to W. Hamish Fraser for meeting to discuss aspects of the project and for pointing us in the direction of the fascinating and richly rewarding periodical, *The Bailie*. Thanks also to Irene Maver for responding to a query and for providing helpful advice. David Lemmings, and the editors at Ashgate, kindly let us have advanced access to *Crime, Courtrooms and the Public Sphere in Britain, 1700–1850* (Farnham, 2012). A special acknowledgment is owed to our peers in the wider academic community. The pioneering work of scholars in criminal justice first stimulated our interest in this topic and provided invaluable research frameworks – both theoretical and methodological – in which to locate our own work. So, too, did that of historians of Scottish, urban and cultural history. Without question, our study would be much poorer had it not been for their labours. The anonymous referees who reviewed our proposal provided helpful insights and advice which we have done our best to address.

We also owe a large debt of gratitude to the staff working in the following libraries and archives: Glasgow University; Glasgow University Special Collections; The Mitchell Library, Glasgow; Glasgow City Archives; Edinburgh Central Library; Edinburgh City Archives; The National Library of Scotland, Edinburgh; The National Archives of Scotland, Edinburgh; Dundee Central Library; Perth and Kinross Council Archives; and The University of Western Australia Library. Financial assistance with this project was provided by a small research grant from The University of Western Australia (RA/1/989/188); a teaching relief grant from The University of Western Australia (00120/70240019); and a Discovery Grant from the Australian Research Council (DP130104804). We are especially grateful to the editorial team at Ashgate for their patience and understanding – and above all, for allowing us to develop our project into two companion volumes and to submit our manuscripts over a year late and 250,000 words over the original contracted word limit. We can only imagine how thankful they are that nineteenth-century police courts rarely kept detailed written records ....

Sue would like to thank David for his patience, adaptability and flexibility over the inevitable shifts and changes that occur in such a long-term project, including chapter themes, general structure, and more than one deadline. She also thanks Tim, Fionn and Cai for their continued interest in hearing tales from the dark side of Scotland's past, which, one finds, sometimes turn out to double as excellent moral lessons for young children contemplating less than admirable actions and behaviours.

David thanks Sue for the unselfish support she has provided with this project and a range of others over the last few years. Hopefully, like myself, she will have taken something from this collaboration ... at the very least the recognition that 'outwith' is actually a word and not another mispronunciation on my part. Above all, I would like to thank my family in Australia (Lorraine, Paul and Oliver) and Scotland (mum and Colin). My contribution to this project would not have been possible had it not been for the love, support and encouragement they have provided over the years.

Introduction

I. Introduction

This two-volume companion represents the first comprehensive investigation into the workings of police courts in Scottish towns in the nineteenth century. Introduced in the early 1800s, these courts had a greater impact on the lives of ordinary people than the much more widely studied higher courts. Whether for non-payment of police rates, breaching local bye-laws, committing criminal acts, or seeking legal redress and advice, police courts were the places of justice in which urban inhabitants were most likely to experience and interact with the law. By the end of the nineteenth century, they dealt with approximately 85 per cent of all crimes and nearly all offences and contraventions prosecuted in Scotland's largest towns and cities.[1] Sometimes referred to as magistrate courts, these centres of civic and criminal justice were integral to the growth in municipal administration, the expansion in summary procedure and the development of the modern Scottish criminal justice system.[2] As the principal place of summary jurisdiction in many towns, police courts allowed for a speedy form of criminal justice, facilitated the prosecution of a larger volume of legal cases, and were symbolic of a growing willingness on the part of local officials and the general public to bring forward prosecutions in the public interest.[3]

Drawing on extensive new research derived from a wide array of sources, both volumes blend social, institutional, urban and cultural history to uncover the workings and delivery of magisterial justice, the ways in which police courts attempted to extend control over citizens and the physical structure of towns, and how communities were affected by, and engaged with, this layer of judicial authority. Our analysis adopts an innovative approach in that it is concerned not only with crime, summary jurisdiction and how these were represented in

[1]   See Chapter 5 and the 'Report on Judicial Statistics of Scotland, 1898', *British Parliamentary Papers (BPP)*, 1900 (cd. 28), CIII.447, p. 38.

[2]   David G. Barrie and Susan Broomhall, 'Public Men, Private Interests? The Origins, Structure and Practice of Police Courts in Scotland, 1800–1833', *Continuity and Change*, 27/1 (2012): pp. 83–123.

[3]   Lindsay Farmer, *Criminal Law, Tradition and Legal Order: Crime and the Genius of Scots Law, 1747 to the Present* (Cambridge, 1997), pp. 70–82; and David G. Barrie, *Police in the Age of Improvement: Police Development and the Civic Tradition in Scotland, 1775–1865* (Cullompton, 2008), pp. 151–3.

contemporary texts, but also police courts' wider significance in society and the urban infrastructure. This involves examining their role in the spatial and social ordering of burghs, their efforts to create and sustain communities, and their function in controlling citizens of different sexes and ages as well as social, religious and ethnic backgrounds. It also includes addressing police courts' capacity to provide platforms to participants such as victims, criminals and witnesses to express and impose their views and enact identities.

II. Historiographical Context

In the early 1990s, Anne Crowther noted, rather tongue-in-cheek, that Scotland was 'a country with no criminal record'.[4] This clever play on words was not an attempt to claim the absence of criminality in Scotland, but rather to highlight the dearth of historical research into Scottish criminal justice history and to encourage further research in this field. In recent years, more scholars have begun to recognise the unique and rich criminal justice history of Scotland and its value to the social, legal and cultural historian.[5] Growing scholarly interest in Scottish crime, policing and the courts has produced exciting studies and stimulated new lines of inquiry.[6] In addition to addressing a major gap in Scottish history, works on these topics have often drawn revealing contrasts with English, Welsh and Irish experiences and have helped to shed light on criminal justice matters beyond Scotland itself.[7] They have been invaluable in highlighting what

---

[4]   M.A. Crowther, 'Scotland: A Country with No Criminal Record', *Scottish Economic and Social History*, 12 (1992): p. 82.

[5]   For the value of crime and police records, see M.A. Crowther, 'Criminal Precognitions and their Value for the Historian', *Scottish Archives: The Journal of the Scottish Historical Records Association*, 1 (1995): pp. 75–84; David G. Barrie, 'Scottish Police Records and their Value for the Historian', *Scottish Archives: The Journal of the Scottish Records Association*, 16 (2010): pp. 51–69.

[6]   The most significant monographs to be published in recent years in these areas include Anne-Marie Kilday, *Women and Violent Crime in Enlightenment Scotland* (Woodbridge, 2007); Barrie, *Police in the Age of Improvement*; and Farmer, *Criminal Law, Tradition and Legal Order*.

[7]   Carolyn A. Conley, *Certain Other Countries: Homicide, Gender, and National Identity in Late Nineteenth-Century England, Ireland, Scotland and Wales* (Columbus, 2007); M.A. Crowther, 'Crime, Prosecution and Mercy: English Influence and Scottish Practice in the Early Nineteenth Century', in S.J. Connolly (ed.), *Kingdoms United? Great Britain and Ireland since 1500: Integration and Diversity* (Dublin, 1999), pp. 225–38; W.W.J. Knox and A. McKinlay, 'Crime, Protest and Policing in Nineteenth-Century Scotland', in Trevor Griffiths and Graeme Morton (eds), *A History of Everyday Life in Scotland, 1800 to 1900* (Edinburgh, 2010), pp. 196–224; and David G. Barrie, 'Anglicisation and Autonomy: Scottish Policing, Governance and the State, 1833 to 1885', *Law and History Review*, 30/2 (2012): pp. 449–94.

the Scottish dimension can offer to a wider historiography that has been largely preoccupied with developments in other parts of the United Kingdom.

However, despite the importance of these studies, the research focus on Scottish legal history is still fairly limited. Scholarship on the Scottish summary courts has largely centred on modern legal or sociological rather than historical studies,[8] or on the role of justice officials in Scottish counties.[9] What work has been carried out on Scottish law enforcement in the eighteenth and nineteenth centuries has concentrated mainly on police development,[10] governance,[11] typology,[12] and masculinity,[13] not police courts *per se*.[14] Similarly, studies on criminality have tended to concentrate on indictable crime and trials in the justiciary courts,[15]

---

[8] See, for instance, Z.K. Bankowski, N.R. Hutton and J.J. McManus, *Lay Justice?* (Edinburgh, 1987); Susan R. Moody and Jacqueline Tombs, *Prosecution and the Public Interest* (Edinburgh, 1982).

[9] Johan Findlay, *All Manner of People: The History of the Justices of the Peace in Scotland* (Edinburgh, 2000); Anne E. Whetstone, *Scottish County Government in the Eighteenth and Nineteenth Centuries* (Edinburgh, 1981).

[10] Barrie, *Police in the Age of Improvement*; David G. Barrie, 'Patrick Colquhoun, the Scottish Enlightenment and Police Reform in Glasgow in the Late Eighteenth Century', *Crime, Histoire & Sociétés/Crime, History & Societies*, 12/2 (2008): pp. 59–79.

[11] David G. Barrie, 'Police in Civil Society: Police, Enlightenment and Civic Virtue in Scotland, 1780–1833', *Urban History*, 37/1 (2010): pp. 45–65; G.S. Pryde 'The Burgh Courts and Allied Jurisdictions', in *An Introduction to Scottish Legal History* (Edinburgh, 1958), p. 384; and David M. Walker, *A Legal History of Scotland* (7 vols, Edinburgh, 1988), vol. 1, ch. 8.

[12] David G. Barrie, 'A Typology of British Police: Locating the Scottish Municipal Police Model in its British Context, 1800–1835', *British Journal of Criminology*, 50/2 (2010): pp. 259–77.

[13] Susan Broomhall and David G. Barrie, 'Changing of the Guard: Governance, Policing, Masculinity and Class in the Porteous Affair and Walter Scott's *Heart of Midlothian*', *Parergon: Journal of the Australian and New Zealand Association for Medieval and Early Modern Studies*, 28/1 (2011): pp. 65–90; David G. Barrie and Susan Broomhall, 'Policing Bodies in Urban Scotland, 1780–1850', in Susan Broomhall and Jacqueline Van Gent (eds), *Governing Masculinities: Regulating Selves and Others in the Early Modern Period* (Farnham, 2011), pp. 263–82; and Susan Broomhall and David G. Barrie, 'Making Men: Media, Magistrates and the Representation of Masculinity in Scottish Police Courts, 1800–1833', in David G. Barrie and Susan Broomhall (eds), *A History of Police and Masculinities, 1700–2010* (London, 2012), pp. 72–101.

[14] Some, though, do look briefly at the workings of police courts. The most detailed study carried out so far is by John McGowan, *Policing the Metropolis of Scotland: A History of the Police and Systems of Police in Edinburgh and Edinburghshire, 1770–1833* (Musselburgh, 2010), passim.

[15] See, for instance, Kilday, *Women and Violent Crime*; Anne-Marie Kilday, 'The Barbarous North? Criminality in Early Modern Scotland', in T.M. Devine and Jenny Wormald (eds), *The Oxford Handbook of Modern Scottish History* (Oxford, 2012), pp. 386–404; Anne-Marie Kilday, 'Desperate Measures or Cruel Intentions: Infanticide in Britain', in Anne-Marie Kilday and David Nash (eds), *Histories of Crime: Britain 1600–*

prosecutors and punishment,[16] morality offences in the church courts,[17] and urban order and protest.[18] Much less attention has been given to the petty offences, assaults and misdemeanours that dominated the business of police courts and to how urban inhabitants used these courts to settle disputes and shape their communities.[19] A few studies and unpublished theses, in assessing the impact of industrialisation on Scottish society, have correlated police court criminal returns over short periods (rarely stretching beyond a few weeks).[20] Other works have made brief reference to the expansion in nineteenth-century summary prosecution procedure,[21] to institutional developments within the courts themselves, and to the significance of these for the evolution and operation of the Scottish legal system[22]

2000 (Basingstoke, 2010), pp. 60–79; Peter King, 'Urbanization, Rising Homicide Rates and the Geography of Lethal Violence in Scotland 1800–1860', *History*, 96/323 (2011): pp. 231–59; Michael T. Davis, 'Prosecution and Radical Discourse during the 1790s: The Case of the Scottish Sedition Trials', *International Journal of the Sociology of Law*, 33/3 (2005): pp. 148–50; and Ian Donnachie, '"The Darker Side": A Speculative Survey of Scottish Crime during the First Half of the Nineteenth Century', *Scottish Economic and Social History*, 15/1 (1995): pp. 5–24.

[16]   Paul T. Riggs, 'Prosecutors, Juries, Judges and Punishment in Early Nineteenth-Century Scotland', *Journal of Scottish Historical Studies*, 32/2 (2012): pp. 166–89.

[17]   See, for example, Leah Leneman and Rosalind Mitchison, *Sin in the City: Sexuality and Social Control in Urban Scotland 1660–1780* (Edinburgh, 1998).

[18]   For recent works, see Christopher A. Whatley, 'Order and Disorder', in Elizabeth A. Foyster and Christopher A. Whatley (eds), *A History of Everyday Life in Scotland, 1600 to 1800* (Edinburgh, 2010), pp. 191–207; and David G. Barrie, 'Urban Order in Georgian Dundee, c.1770–1820', in Charles McKean, Bob Harris and Christopher A. Whatley (eds), *Dundee: Renaissance to Enlightenment* (Dundee, 2009), pp. 216–42.

[19]   For studies that draw upon statistical trends in crime produced by the police in the second half of the nineteenth century, see Knox and McKinlay, 'Crime, Protest and Policing'; W. Hamish Fraser and Irene Maver, 'The Social Problems of the City', in W. Hamish Fraser and Irene Maver (eds), *Glasgow, Volume II: 1830 to 1912* (Manchester, 1996), pp. 352–94.

[20]   Christopher A. Whatley, *Scottish Society 1707–1830: Beyond Jacobitism, Towards Industrialisation* (Manchester, 2000), p. 287; and T.M. Devine, 'Urbanisation and the Civic Response: Glasgow, 1800–30', in A.J.G. Cummings and T.M. Devine (eds), *Industry, Business and Society in Scotland since 1700: Essays Presented to Professor John Butt* (Edinburgh, 1994), pp. 191–4. A few theses also make brief use of court records. See, for instance, Maurice C. Golden, 'Criminality and the Development of Policing in Dundee 1816–1833', unpub. MPhil thesis (University of Dundee, 2003); and A. Goldsmith, 'The Development of the City of Glasgow Police 1800–1939', unpub. PhD thesis (University of Strathclyde, 2002).

[21]   Barrie and Broomhall, 'Public Men, Private Interests', is the only study to give this serious attention.

[22]   Crowther, 'Crime, Prosecution and Mercy'; Farmer, *Criminal Law, Tradition and Legal Order*.

and the built environment as a whole.[23] Recent publications have also examined newspaper and journal reports of police court business in exploring how magistrates dealt with domestic violence and reflected and reinforced concepts of masculinity in passing moral commentaries on those brought before them.[24] Nonetheless, this area of Scottish criminal justice history remains very much in its infancy and much more needs to be done. Scotland may no longer be 'a country with no criminal record' as far as the experience of its higher courts is concerned,[25] but its summary centres of justice have often been overlooked or given insufficient attention in studies in which greater focus might have been expected.[26]

In seeking to fill this void, we hope to make a significant contribution not just to Scottish criminal justice history. Our study also facilitates a broader understanding of summary jurisdiction, and adds new insights to social and urban history. It broadens and deepens knowledge of summary justice in a wider British context, especially by exploring the institutional workings of police courts, people's experiences of them, and their relationship with the media. This is important, as until fairly recently historians of crime in England were largely preoccupied with examining high-court indictments rather than summary jurisdiction. Fascination with England's infamous eighteenth-century 'Bloody Code', allied to a number of influential seminal studies on property, authority and the criminal law, resulted in much scholarly attention being devoted to the workings and experiences of the high courts, assizes or quarter sessions, the discretionary nature in which justice was administered, and the often brutal punishments which were inflicted.[27] Moreover, the often incomplete and fragmented nature of summary records further influenced the direction of historical inquiry. Sources for the inferior courts, especially up

---

[23] Even then, the bulk of attention has focused on police commissioners and public health rather than police courts themselves. See, for instance, Christopher Hamlin, 'Environmental Sensibility in Edinburgh, 1839–1840: The "Fetid Irrigation" Controversy', *Journal of Urban History*, 20/3 (1994): p. 311.

[24] Leah Leneman, 'A Tyrant and Tormentor: Wifebeating in Scotland in the Seventeenth and Eighteenth Centuries', *Continuity and Change*, 12/1 (1997): pp. 31–54; Annemarie Hughes, 'The "Non-Criminal" Class: Wifebeating in Scotland, c.1850–1949', *Crime, Histoire & Sociétés/Crime, History & Societies*, 14/2 (2010): pp. 31–54; and Broomhall and Barrie, 'Making Men', pp. 72–101.

[25] Crowther, 'Scotland: A Country with No Criminal Record', p. 82.

[26] David M. Walker, *The Scottish Legal System: An Introduction to the Study of Scots Law*, 7th edn (Edinburgh, 1997).

[27] The historiography on this is too exhaustive to list in full. See, for instance, Douglas Hay, Peter Linebaugh, John G. Rule, E.P. Thompson and Cal Winslow (eds), *Albion's Fatal Tree: Crime and Society in Eighteenth-Century England* (London, 1976); V.A.C. Gatrell, *The Hanging Tree: Execution and the English People, 1770–1868* (Oxford, 1994); Michael Ignatieff, *A Just Measure of Pain: The Penitentiary in the Industrial Revolution 1750–1850* (London, 1978); John H. Langbein, 'Albion's Fatal Flaws', *Past and Present*, 98 (1983): pp. 96–120; and Peter Linebaugh, *The London Hanged: Crime and Civil Society in the Eighteenth Century* (Cambridge, 1992).

to the mid-nineteenth century, have not been as well preserved, and are not as detailed, as those for the higher courts, largely due to the fact that summary cases were usually heard without formal written evidence in order to speed up judicial process and reduce legal costs.

Yet, despite these barriers, scholars of criminal justice history in England have made important strides in this field in recent years. A small, but growing, number of historians have increasingly put summary courts at the centre of historical inquiry.[28] Those scholars looking at the eighteenth and early nineteenth century have, for instance, analysed the character and extent of summary justice and its institutional workings,[29] how far magistrates traded in justice,[30] the extent of

---

[28]   See, for instance, Drew D. Gray, *Crime, Prosecution and Social Relations in London: The Summary Courts of London in the Late Eighteenth Century* (Basingstoke, 2009) which deals with many of the themes referred to in this paragraph; and Joanne Turner, 'Summary Justice for Women: Stafford Borough, 1880–1905', *Crime, Histoire & Sociétés/Crime, History and Societies*, 16/2 (2012): pp. 55–77.

[29]   Robert B. Shoemaker, *Prosecution and Punishment: Petty Crime and the Law in London and Rural Middlesex, c.1660–1725* (Cambridge, 1991); Cynthia Herrup, *The Common Peace: Participation and the Criminal Law in Seventeenth-Century England* (Cambridge, 1987); and Faramerz Dabhoiwala, 'Summary Justice in Early Modern London', *English Historical Review*, CXXI/492 (2006): pp. 796–822. For the standard whiggish study, see Leon Radzinowicz, *A History of English Criminal Law and its Administration from 1750, Volume 2: The Clash between Private Initiative and Public Interest in the Enforcement of the Law* (London, 1956), pp. 388–94 & 503–6; Leon Radzinowicz, *A History of English Criminal Law and its Administration from 1750, Volume 3: Cross-Currents in the Movement for the Reform of the Police* (London, 1956), pp. 123–31. For the options available to various parties within the prosecution process, see J.M. Beattie, *Policing and Punishment in London, 1660–1750: Urban Crime and the Limits of Terror* (Oxford, 2001); J.M. Beattie, *Crime and the Courts in England, 1660–1800* (Oxford, 1986); Douglas Hay and Francis Snyder, 'Using the Criminal Law, 1750–1850: Policing, Private Prosecution and the State', in Douglas Hay and Francis Snyder (eds), *Policing and Prosecution in Britain, 1750–1850* (Oxford, 1989), pp. 3–52; and Peter King, *Crime, Justice and Discretion in England, 1740–1820* (Oxford, 2000), passim. For the ways in which summary proceedings dispensed with procedural and evidential problems, see Bruce P. Smith, 'The Presumption of Guilt and the English Law of Theft, 1750–1850', *Law and History Review*, 23/1 (2005): pp. 133–72. For a critique, see Norma Landau, 'Summary Conviction and the Development of the Penal Law', *Law and History Review*, 23/1 (2005): pp. 173–89. For Smith's response, see 'Did the Presumption of Innocence Exist in Summary Proceedings?', *Law and History Review*, 23/1 (2005): pp. 191–9. For the distinction between the justice administered by judges and professional lawyers in high courts involving juries and the lesser magistrates' courts, see Douglas Hay, 'Legislation, Magistrates, and Judges: High Law and Low Law in England and the Empire', in David Lemmings (ed.), *The British and their Laws in the Eighteenth Century* (Woodbridge, 2005), pp. 59–79.

[30]   Norma Landau, 'The Trading Justice's Trade', in Norma Landau (ed.), *Law, Crime and English Society, 1660–1830* (Cambridge, 2002), pp. 46–70.

plebeian involvement in local courts,[31] and the significance of summary courts in maintaining social relations[32] and in arbitrating in disputes involving interpersonal violence.[33] Much academic attention has focused on the emergence and expansion of prosecution and summary justice in London following the introduction of paid magistrates and magistrate courts in 1792,[34] the institutionalisation of the police court as a public forum, its legal and social implications, and its impact on trends in indictable crime.[35] The neutrality, or otherwise, of magistrates in administering

---

[31]   Jennifer S. Davis, 'A Poor Man's System of Justice? The London Police Courts in the Second Half of the Nineteenth Century', *Historical Journal*, 27/2 (1984): pp. 309–35.

[32]   Peter King, 'The Summary Courts and Social Relations in Eighteenth-Century England', *Past and Present*, 183/1 (2004): pp. 125–72; Drew D. Gray, 'The People's Courts? Summary Justice and Social Relations in the City of London, c.1760–1800', *Family and Community History*, 11/1 (2008): pp. 7–15; Gwenda Morgan and Peter Rushton, 'The Magistrate, the Community and the Maintenance of an Orderly Society in Eighteenth-Century England', *Historical Research*, 76/191 (2003): pp. 54–77.

[33]   Drew D. Gray, 'The Regulation of Violence in the Metropolis: The Prosecution of Assault in the Summary Courts, c.1780–1820', *London Journal*, 32/1 (2007): pp. 75–87; and Drew D. Gray, 'Settling Their Differences: The Nature of Assault and its Prosecution in the City of London in the Late Eighteenth and Early Nineteenth Centuries', in Katherine Watson (ed.), *Assaulting the Past: Violence and Civilization in Historical Context* (Cambridge, 2007), pp. 124–40.

[34]   Bruce P. Smith, 'The Emergence of Public Prosecution in London, 1790–1850', *Yale Journal of Law and the Humanities*, 18/29 (2006): pp. 29–62; and Ruth Paley, 'The Middlesex Justices Act of 1792: Its Origins and Effects', unpub. PhD thesis (University of Reading, 1983).

[35]   Thomas Sweeney, 'The Extension and Practice of Summary Jurisdiction in England, c.1790–1860', unpub. PhD thesis (Cambridge University, 1985); Jennifer S. Davis, 'Prosecutions and their Context: The Use of the Criminal Law in Later Nineteenth-Century London', in Hay and Snyder (eds), *Policing and Prosecution in Britain*, pp. 397–426; V.A.C. Gatrell and T.B. Hadden, 'Criminal Statistics and their Interpretation', in E.A. Wrigley (ed.), *Nineteenth-Century Society: Essays in the Use of Quantitative Methods for the Study of Social Data* (Cambridge, 1972), pp. 336–96; David Philips, '"A New Engine of Power and Authority": The Institutionalization of Law-Enforcement in England, 1780–1830', in V.A.C. Gatrell, Bruce Lenman and Geoffrey Parker (eds), *Crime and the Law: The Social History of Crime in Western Europe since 1500* (London, 1980), pp. 155–89; V.A.C. Gatrell, 'The Decline of Theft and Violence in Victorian and Edwardian England', in Gatrell, Lenman and Parker (eds), *Crime and the Law*, pp. 238–370; V.A.C. Gatrell, 'Crime, Authority and the Policeman-State', in F.M.L. Thompson (ed.), *Cambridge Social History of Britain, 1750–1950* (Cambridge, 1992), pp. 243–310. For a more recent study, see David Taylor, *Hooligans, Harlots, and Hangmen: Crime and Punishment in Victorian Britain* (Santa Barbara, 2010). Still useful studies are David J.V. Jones, *Crime in Nineteenth-Century Wales* (Cardiff, 1992); David J.V. Jones, *Crime, Protest, Community and Police in Nineteenth-Century Britain* (London, 1982); David Taylor, *Policing the Victorian Town: The Development of the Police in Middlesbrough, c.1840–1914* (Basingstoke, 2002); David Philips, *Crime and Authority in Victorian England: The Black Country,*

the law in areas in which they had a vested interest, has also been keenly debated.[36] Studies of the Victorian police courts, meanwhile, have examined the continuing importance of community values to law enforcement,[37] the treatment of sexual violence against women,[38] and the construction and representation of media narratives about courtroom trials.[39] More recently, attention has focused on the police's role in the prosecution process and their impact on crime trends and domestic violence from the second half of the nineteenth century,[40] as well as the

---

1835–1860 (London, 1977); and Clive Emsley, *Crime and Society in England, 1750–1900*, 3rd edn (Harlow, 2005).

[36]   Studies that argue that the summary courts in the nineteenth century represented the interests of the propertied class include David Philips, 'The Black Country Magistracy, 1835–60: A Changing Elite and the Exercise of its Power', *Midland History*, 3/3 (1976): pp. 161–90; D.C. Woods, 'The Operation of the Master and Servants Act in the Black Country, 1858–1875', *Midland History*, 7 (1982): pp. 93–115; Roger Swift, 'The English Urban Magistracy and the Administration of Justice During the Early Nineteenth-Century: Wolverhampton 1815–60', *Midland History*, 17 (1992): pp. 75–92. However, David Taylor argues that magistrates in Middlesbrough, despite being drawn from the dominant trades of the town, were less inclined to use the law to protect their interests. Taylor, *Hooligans, Harlots, and Hangmen*, pp. 107–10 & 223. Similarly, rather than viewing the local courts as an instrument of the ruling class, the following have stressed their flexibility and autonomy: Jones, *Crime, Protest and Community*, pp. 23 & 111; Carolyn A. Conley, *The Unwritten Law: Criminal Justice in Victorian Kent* (Oxford, 1991), p. 41; Davis, 'Prosecutions and their Context', pp. 379–426; and Louise A. Jackson, 'Women Professionals and the Regulation of Violence in Interwar Britain', in Shani D'Cruze (ed.), *Everyday Violence in Britain, 1850–1950: Gender and Class* (London, 2000), pp. 119–35.

[37]   Conley, *The Unwritten Law*.

[38]   Shani D'Cruze, *Crimes of Outrage: Sex, Violence and Victorian Working Women* (London, 1998); and Shani D'Cruze, 'Sex, Violence and Local Courts: Working-Class Respectability in a Mid-Nineteenth-Century Lancashire Town', *The British Journal Of Criminology*, 39/1 (1999): pp. 39–55. See also the essays in D'Cruze (ed.), *Everyday Violence in Britain*. For a wider study of violence that looks at magistrate courts, see Rob Sindall, *Street Violence in the Nineteenth Century: Moral Panic or Real Danger?* (Leicester, 1990).

[39]   See, for instance, Joanne Jones, '"She Resisted with all Her Might": Sexual Violence against Women in Late Nineteenth Century Manchester and the Local Press', in D'Cruze (ed.), *Everyday Violence in Britain*, pp. 104–18; and Judith R. Walkowitz, *City of Dreadful Delight: Narratives of Sexual Danger in Late-Victorian London* (Chicago, 1992).

[40]   Barry S. Godfrey, 'Changing Prosecution Practices and their Impact on Crime Figures, 1857–1940', *British Journal of Criminology*, 48/2 (2008): pp. 171–89. For more on the role of the victim in the prosecution system, see Tony Kearon and Barry S. Godfrey, 'Setting the Scene: A Question of History', in Sandra Walklate (ed.), *The Handbook of Victims and Victimology* (London, 2011), pp. 17–36; and Paul Rock, 'Victims, Prosecutors and the State in Nineteenth-Century England and Wales', *Criminology and Criminal Justice*, 4/4 (2004): pp. 331–54. Studies of domestic violence which make use of police records include Nancy Tomes, '"A Torrent of Abuse": Crimes of Violence between Working-Class Men and Women in London 1840–1875', *Journal of Social History*, 11/3

extent to which the police and the courts were able to 'civilize' local populations and safeguard urban order.[41]

However, as Clive Emsley has pointed out in a recent review of criminal justice history in Britain, more research needs to be carried out on summary jurisdiction, especially in the nineteenth century.[42] Many of the studies which chart the rise of summary justice in England focus not on police courts *per se*, but instead connect it to wider developments within the criminal justice system following major judicial reforms from the 1840s onwards.[43] Moreover, the majority of works which give attention to magistrates' courts are, with some notable exceptions,[44] London-centred and, like studies of indictable crime,

---

(1978): pp. 328–45; and Anna Clark, *Women's Silence, Men's Violence: Sexual Assault in England 1770–1845* (London, 1987).

[41] Manuel Eisner, 'Modernization, Self-Control and Lethal Violence: The Long-Term Dynamics of European Homicide Rates in Theoretical Perspective', *British Journal of Criminology*, 41/4 (2001): pp. 618–38; J. Pratt, *Punishment and Civilization: Penal Tolerance and Intolerance in Modern Society* (London, 2002); Pieter Spierenburg, 'Violence and the Civilizing Process: Does it Work?', *Crime, Histoire & Sociétés/Crime, History & Societies*, 5/2 (2001): pp. 87–105; and Martin J. Wiener, 'The March of Penal Progress?', *Journal of British Studies*, 26/1 (1987): pp. 83–96. For more on violence, see J.S. Cockburn, 'Patterns of Violence in English Society: Homicide in Kent, 1560–1985', *Past and Present*, 130 (1991): pp. 70–106; Robert B. Shoemaker, 'Male Honour and the Decline of Popular Violence in Eighteenth-Century London', *Social History*, 26/2 (2001): pp. 190–208; Robert B. Shoemaker, 'The Taming of the Duel: Masculinity, Honour and Ritual Violence in London, 1660–1800', *The Historical Journal*, 45/3 (2002): pp. 525–45; Robert B. Shoemaker, *The London Mob: Violence and Disorder in Eighteenth Century England* (London, 2004); Clive Emsley, *The English and Violence since 1750* (London, 2005); John Carter Wood, *The Shadow of Our Refinement: Violence and Crime in Nineteenth-Century England* (London, 2005); Clark, *Women's Silence, Men's Violence*; Barry S. Godfrey, 'Counting and Accounting for the Decline in Non-Lethal Violence in England, Australia and New Zealand, 1880–1920', *British Journal of Criminology*, 43/2 (2003): pp. 340–53. For the influence of gender on sentencing patterns, see Barry S. Godrey, Stephen Farrall and Susanne Karstedt, 'Explaining Gendered Sentencing Patterns for Violent Men and Women in the Late Victorian and Edwardian Period', *British Journal of Criminology*, 45/5 (2005): pp. 696–720. For an interesting study on the police court as a form of theatre, see Barry S. Godfrey, 'Sentencing, Theatre, Audience and Communication: The Victorian and Edwardian Magistrates' Courts and their Message', in Benoît Garnot (ed.), *Les témoins devant la justice* (Rennes, 2003), pp. 161–71. For a contemporary portrayal, see H.T. Waddy, *The Police Court and Its Work* (London, 1925).

[42] Clive Emsley, 'Filling in, Adding Up, Moving On: Criminal Justice History in Contemporary Britain', *Crime, Histoire & Sociétés/Crime, History & Societies*, 9/1 (2005): pp. 118–19.

[43] Gatrell and Hadden, 'Criminal Statistics and their Interpretation', pp. 336–96; and Gatrell, 'The Decline of Theft and Violence'.

[44] Although focusing primarily on assize courts and quarter sessions, an interesting study of crime in provincial England is provided by Gwenda Morgan and Peter Rushton, *Rogues, Thieves, and the Rule of Law: The Problem of Law Enforcement in North-East*

focus mostly on the eighteenth and early nineteenth centuries.[45] This is, to some extent, understandable given London's importance in an English context, the development of the Bow Street Magistrates' Court from the 1750s,[46] and the employment of paid magistrates under the 1792 Middlesex Justice's Act.[47] But it has left notable gaps in historians' understanding of the development of summary jurisdiction in other parts of the United Kingdom, especially in Scotland, and in the nature, purpose and significance of the expansion in summary jurisdiction as the nineteenth century progressed. Indeed, it is noticeable that the rich historiography on nineteenth-century police development which has evolved over the last few decades has said very little about the police courts that were responsible for imposing and administering justice – a fact that has only recently begun to be addressed.[48] This is surprising, as the wide-ranging discretionary and regulatory powers that magistrates enjoyed made them as important in shaping the regulatory role and impact of nineteenth-century law enforcement as the police itself.[49] Moreover, studies that have drawn upon police court records tend to adopt fairly narrow approaches by focusing on selective crimes[50] and social groups[51] rather than the workings, business and experiences of courts as a whole. They have, in other words, used police court records and trial reports as

---

England, 1718–1800 (London, 2004). For a broader history, see David J. Cox and Barry S. Godfrey (eds), *Cinderellas and Packhorses: A History of the Shropshire Magistracy* (Almeley, 2005). A fuller listing of studies that look beyond London is provided at footnote 36. See also Clark, *Women's Silence, Men's Violence.*

[45]   In addition to many of the references noted throughout the above footnotes, see also Ruth Paley (ed.), *Justice in Eighteenth-Century Hackney: The Justicing Notebook of Henry Norris and the Hackney Petty Sessions Book* (London, 1991). There are also recollections from magistrates in the early twentieth century. See for instance, C.M. Chapman, *The Poor Man's Court of Justice: Twenty-Five Years as a Metropolitan Magistrate* (London, 1925).

[46]   J.M. Beattie, 'Sir John Fielding and Public Justice: The Bow Street Magistrates' Court, 1754–1780', *Law and History Review,* 25/1 (2007): pp. 61–100.

[47]   Paley, 'The Middlesex Justices Act of 1792'.

[48]   Godfrey, 'Changing Prosecution Practices and their Impact on Crime Figures', pp. 171–89. Barry S. Godfrey recently led a British Academy research project entitled 'Prosecuting and Sentencing Processes in International Perspective, 1880–1940' (June 2007–May 2009), which examined the police and magistrate court records in towns and cities in the United Kingdom (including Scotland and Wales), United States, Canada, New Zealand and Australia.

[49]   Davis, 'A Poor Man's System of Justice?', p. 313.

[50]   Police and summary court records have been especially popular for historians studying domestic violence. In addition to those mentioned above, see also Elizabeth A. Foyster, *Marital Violence: An English Family History, 1660–1857* (Cambridge, 2005).

[51]   Irish migrants were often the subject of police attention and have featured prominently in police histories, albeit with most attention focusing on police policy rather than court proceedings. See, for instance, Roger Swift and Sheridan Gilley (eds), *The Irish in the Victorian City* (London, 1985); and Roger Swift, 'Urban Policing in Early Victorian England, 1835–86: A Reappraisal', *History,* 73/238 (1988): pp. 211–37.

a means of exploring wider social and cultural issues such as sexuality, violence and media representations of courtroom discourse rather than making police courts the focal point of the study *per se*. A detailed history of police courts – as civic institutions for regulating behaviour and imposing justice, as places where communities were forged and environments shaped, and as vehicles for expressing and imposing contrasting values, cultures and mores – remained, therefore, to be written. It is the purpose of our study to do this.

III. Urban Scotland in the Nineteenth Century

Urban Scotland provides a fascinating case study in which to examine the expansion of police court summary justice in the nineteenth century. Scotland had, and continues to have, a separate legal system and distinct administrative structures, traditions and customs from elsewhere in the United Kingdom, which produced a different course of police development and summary procedure. Its experience was, in many ways, unique in a British context, and was to have significance beyond its own borders. Indeed, Scotland was at the forefront in pioneering developments in policing and summary procedure that would later be introduced in England. From the early 1800s, the police in some major Scottish urban centres were responsible for bringing before police courts publicly-funded prosecutions in the public interest. Although, as has been recently argued, public officials in London played an important and under-acknowledged role in prosecuting misdemeanours in the city's lower courts from the late eighteenth century,[52] it would be decades before the police in provincial England mirrored their Scottish counterparts by taking the lead in prosecuting crimes and almost a century before public prosecution was officially recognised in England with the establishment of the Public Prosecution Office in 1879. Examining the proceedings of police courts in Scotland from the early nineteenth century not only allows for comparisons in the administration of summary justice in different parts of the British Isles to be drawn, it also uncovers the formative development of summary police court procedures and prosecutions that came to characterise local justice throughout the British Isles. This is important, as attention to such developments in England has, with some exceptions, understandably focused on the latter half of the nineteenth century as police involvement in this sphere of the criminal justice system grew. Moreover, the 'police' concept in urban Scotland continued to be more broadly defined as a form of civic governance for much longer than other parts of the United Kingdom, which gave the officers, magistrates and the courts responsibility for overseeing a wide array of public order issues and municipal services. Our analysis, therefore, covers the period from 1800, when the first major burgh police act was introduced in Glasgow, to the passing of the Burgh Police Scotland Act in 1892, which superseded all

---

[52]   Smith, 'The Emergence of Public Prosecution in London', pp. 29–62.

previous general police acts.[53] This will enable the study to assess the changes in the life of the city that are reflected in and shaped by the courts' work, and will allow us to explore continuities and changes in the perception, activities and experience of the court over a century of great change.

The Scottish experience is important in other ways too. Scotland in the nineteenth century had a number of major urban centres which are of particular significance for criminal justice history. The Glasgow Police Court was amongst the busiest in the United Kingdom, dealing with more cases than any other city outside of London for much of the nineteenth century. Along with local police legislation in general, the court was an important cog in Glasgow's construction of a formidable 'municipal machine' – a machine which, by the turn of the twentieth century, was amongst the largest in Britain.[54] The court's role was very much in keeping with the city's interventionist history in the public sphere that underpinned its longstanding commitment to the tradition of civic virtue.[55] However, despite the city's achievements there was a paradox at the heart of its administration. The city, which was at the forefront in pioneering police reform and municipal improvement in Scotland with the 1800 Glasgow Police Act, was also described as being amongst the dirtiest, most crime-ridden cities in the Western World. As J.C. Symons, assistant handloom weaving commissioner, famously stated in 1839:

> I have seen human degradation in some of its worst phases, both in England and abroad, but I can advisedly say, that I did not believe, until I visited the wynds of Glasgow, that so large an amount of filth, crime, misery, and disease existed on one spot in any civilized country.[56]

Rapid urban and industrial expansion had transformed Glasgow into an economic powerhouse but it came at a tremendous human cost.[57] According to contemporary governmental perceptions, the city which boasted it was the 'Second City of the Empire' was unrivalled when it came to crime, squalor and environmental social problems – problems with which, crucially, the police

---

[53]   Glasgow Police Act, 1800 (39 & 40 George III, cap. 88) and The Burgh Police Scotland Act, 1892 (55 & 56 Victoria, cap. 55).

[54]   J. Lindsay, *Review of Municipal Government in Glasgow* (Glasgow, 1909), p. 31. See also W. Hamish Fraser and Irene Maver, 'Tackling the Problems', in Fraser and Maver (eds), *Glasgow, Volume II*, p. 395.

[55]   Irene Maver, 'A (North) British End-View: The Comparative Experience of Municipal Employees and Services in Glasgow (1800–1950)', in Michèle Dagenais, Irene Maver and Pierre-Yves Saunier (eds), *Municipal Services and Employees in the Modern City: New Historic Approaches* (Aldershot, 2003), p. 179.

[56]   'Reports on the Sanitary Condition of the Labouring Population in Scotland: in Consequence of an Inquiry directed to be made by Poor Law Commissioners', *BPP*, 1842 (008 House of Lords), XXVIII.I, p. 71.

[57]   T.M. Devine, 'The Urban Crisis', in T.M. Devine and Gordon Jackson (eds), *Glasgow, Volume 1: Beginnings to 1830* (Manchester, 1995), pp. 402–16.

courts were charged with dealing. With Glasgow undergoing amongst the fastest rates of urban growth in western Europe in the first half of the nineteenth century – as thousands of migrants from rural Scotland, the Scottish Highlands and Ireland flooded into the city – its experience provides an intriguing case study not only of urban social problems, but also of how the city fathers sought to control people of different social, religious and cultural backgrounds, and how the latter used police courts to build their own communities. Police court records also help uncover how inhabitants experienced such cities and illuminate their stories about, and perceptions of, the places in which they lived.

Edinburgh faced similar challenges to Glasgow, albeit on a slightly smaller scale. But unlike its industrial powerhouse neighbour to the west, Edinburgh was a 'City of Lawyers' in the nineteenth century. It was home to the High Court of Justiciary, the Court of Session, and the Lord Advocate (the government's chief legal representative in Scotland), was the main hanging centre for Scottish capital offenders and had a sizeable number of legal professionals. The city was also at the epicentre of Scottish legal and Enlightenment inquiry and, like its west-coast rival, had a well-developed and thriving press in which crime reports were often published. In 1805, Edinburgh authorities set up Scotland's first police court under a statutory local police act which laid the foundations for subsequent reform in summary jurisdiction in other parts of the country.[58] Edinburgh was also at the forefront in Europe in terms of city planning and the spatial ordering of the built environment with the staged development of its famous 'New Town' between 1765 and 1830. Along with Glasgow, it provides an important case study in which to locate the research, not just because of its status as Scotland's capital and the urban pressures it faced, but because of the influence that senior legal and government figures, most notably the Lord Advocate, played in the legal construction and workings of its police court.

Much of the focus of our study is on these two great cities. This reflects their social, economic and demographic standing and significance,[59] as well as the fact that they established police courts earlier than most Scottish cities and have generally the best preserved and most detailed records in the country. However, scholars have recently called for the need to counterbalance the heavy urban history emphasis on these centres, and to contextualise their experiences, with examination of a range of other, smaller Scottish burghs at this period.[60] We therefore also examine police courts in other towns in order to provide a fuller picture of summary jurisdiction across the country as a whole. These include the flourishing commercial ports and trading centres of Aberdeen, Greenock, Leith and Dundee (which went on to become a major centre of industry from

---

[58]   Edinburgh Police Act, 1805 (45 George III, cap. 21).

[59]   Devine and Jackson (eds), *Glasgow, Volume I*; and Fraser and Maver (eds), *Glasgow, Volume II*.

[60]   Ewen A. Cameron, 'Glasgow's going Round and Round: Some Recent Scottish Urban History', *Urban History*, 30/2 (2003): pp. 276–87 suggests this.

the 1820s), the rapidly expanding textile towns of Paisley and Gorbals, and the important judicial centres of Perth and Inverness.[61] Collectively, these centres accounted for the majority of the Scottish population, and the overwhelming majority of its urban inhabitants, in the late nineteenth century.[62] They have been selected for a number of reasons: firstly, because of the primary source materials that have been preserved; secondly, on account of their contrasting economic and social profiles; and thirdly, because they were home to the main police courts in Scotland (with other towns often relying on sheriff courts, and to a lesser extent, burgh courts to administer criminal affairs). This broad focus ensures that as representative a picture of summary jurisdiction for the country as a whole is advanced as far as possible. It will also add to the emerging integration of Glasgow and Edinburgh with other centres, in a rich comparative analysis of the role of police courts in social and physical urban development. Part of our assessment is thus both comparative analysis of the distinctions between cities and change over time.

IV. Analytical Themes

Taking the form of two companion volumes, *Police Courts in Nineteenth-Century Scotland* explores diverse, but complementary, themes relating to judicial practices, relationships, experiences and discourses through the lens of the police court. This volume, subtitled *Magistrates, Media and the Masses*, provides an institutional, social and cultural history of the establishment, development and practice of police courts. It explores their rise, purpose and internal workings, and how justice was administered and experienced by those who attended them in a

---

[61]   For local histories and local studies of particular aspects of these towns, see R. Tyzack, "'No Mean City'"? The Growth of Civic Consciousness in Aberdeen with particular Reference to the Work of the Police Commissioners', in Terence Brotherstone and Donald J. Withrington (eds), *The City and its Worlds: Aspects of Aberdeen's History since 1794* (Glasgow, 1996), pp. 150–67; E. Patricia Dennison, David Ditchburn and Michael Lynch (eds), *Aberdeen Before 1800: A New History* (East Linton, 2002); W. Hamish Fraser and Clive H. Lee (eds), *Aberdeen, 1800–2000: A New History* (East Linton, 2000); Bob Harris, 'Towns, Improvement and Cultural Change in Georgian Scotland: The Evidence of the Angus Burghs, c.1760–1820', *Urban History*, 33/2 (2006): pp. 195–212; McKean, Harris and Whatley (eds), *Dundee: Renaissance to Enlightenment*; Louise Miskell, Christopher A. Whatley and Bob Harris (eds), *Victorian Dundee, Images and Realities* (East Linton, 2002); Aileen Black, *Gilfillan of Dundee, 1813–1878: Interpreting Religion and Culture in Mid-Victorian Scotland* (Dundee, 2006); and Wendy M. Gordon, 'The Demographics of Scottish Poverty: Paisley's Applicants for Relief, 1861 and 1871', *Journal of Scottish Historical Studies*, 30/1 (2010): pp. 25–42.

[62]   Richard Rodger, 'Employment, Wages and Poverty in the Scottish Cities 1841–1914', in George Gordon (ed.), *Perspectives of the Scottish City* (Aberdeen, 1985), pp. 25–63.

variety of roles. Special attention is given to examining how courtroom discourse was represented in print culture, the role of the media in providing a discursive commentary on summary justice, and the ways in which magistrates and the police engaged in a law and order dialogue with the press. Throughout, consideration is given to uncovering the relationship between magistrates, the courts, the police and the wider community, and to charting the implications of the rise of summary justice and the 'police-man' state for the urban masses (as evidenced through prosecution, conviction and punishment patterns). Volume 2, sub-titled *Bodies, Behaviours and Boundaries*, explores, through themed case studies, how police courts shaped conceptual, spatial, temporal and commercial boundaries by regulating everyday activities, pastimes and cultures.

Ever since Douglas Hay argued that the legal system in eighteenth-century England was an ideological instrument for securing the hegemony of the ruling elite, class has been an important conceptual framework for historical analysis in criminal justice history.[63] While scholars have contested Hay's hypothesis,[64] the importance of social background has been widely acknowledged as influencing people's treatment within the judicial system, including access to legal redress, sentencing and punishment.[65] More recently, a burgeoning literature has contended that confessional allegiance, ethnicity and, in particular, gender underpin how criminal justice systems function.[66] As Deirdre Palk has argued, for instance, the law and the courts embodied and applied patriarchal assumptions in their day-to-day business.[67] Indeed, gender expectations have been shown to have been at the centre of the decision-making process, shaping the experiences of both men and women who interacted with, and participated in, the legal system.[68] Throughout

---

[63]   Douglas Hay, 'Property, Authority and the Criminal Law', in Hay, Linebaugh, Thompson and Winslow (eds), *Albion's Fatal Tree*, pp. 17–63.

[64]   These are explored more fully in Chapter 2.

[65]   See, for instance, Beattie, *Crime and the Courts*; Shoemaker, *Prosecution and Punishment*; and Kilday, *Women and Crime*.

[66]   Studies that stress the gendered nature of criminal prosecutions, courtroom experience and sentencing are cited widely throughout this chapter (see, for example, footnote 68). Those that identify the importance of religion and ethnicity include Roger Swift and Sheridan Gilley (eds), *The Irish in Britain 1815–1939* (London, 1989); David Mayall, *English Gypsies and State Policies* (Hatfield, 1996); and Norma Myers, 'The Black Presence Through Criminal Records, 1780–1830', *Immigrants and Minorities*, 7/3 (1988): pp. 292–307. For the Irish experience in Scotland, see Martin Mitchell (ed.), *New Perspectives on the Irish in Scotland* (Edinburgh, 2008); and Tom Gallagher, *Glasgow, The Uneasy Peace: Religious Tension in Modern Scotland* (Manchester, 1987).

[67]   Deirdre Palk, *Gender, Crime and Judicial Discretion 1780–1830* (Woodbridge, 2006), p. 13.

[68]   For studies of the gendered nature of the law and crime see Robert B. Shoemaker, *Gender in English Society, 1650–1850: The Emergence of Separate Spheres?* (London, 1998), pp. 291–304; J.M. Beattie, 'The Criminality of Women in Eighteenth-Century England', *Journal of Social History*, 8/4 (1975): pp. 80–116; Lucia Zedner, *Women,*

our study, we adopt social and cultural historical approaches that imply particular attention to specific presentations of and assumptions about identities, especially those of class, ethnicity and gender. We do this by exploring four cross-cutting analytical themes that run throughout both volumes.

(i) Media Representations of Magisterial Justice and Courtroom Discourse

The press has become a fertile source of investigation for scholars of criminal justice history in recent years.[69] Indeed, given its widely recognised importance, newspaper coverage of crime has increasingly become central to academic inquiry of criminal justice history. As Peter King has pointed out, the press was the most widely consulted printed source of information on crime and justice in the eighteenth and nineteenth centuries and was instrumental in shaping social perceptions of crime and the measures needed to control it.[70] Newspaper reports helped to raise anxieties and moral concerns about crime, constituted middle-class opinion concerning law and order, and influenced both the production of stringent criminal law legislation and prosecution and sentencing patterns.[71] They also had

---

Crime and Custody in Victorian England (Oxford, 1991), p. 27; and Maeve E. Doggett, *Marriage, Wife-Beating and the Law in Victorian England* (Columbia, 1993), pp. 34–99. For studies on the relationship between gender and law breaking and gender and judicial decisions, see Kilday, *Women and Crime*; Peter King, 'Female Offenders, Work and Life-Cycle in Late Eighteenth-Century London', *Continuity and Change*, 11/1 (1996): pp. 61–90; J.I. Kermode and Garthine Walker (eds), *Women, Crime and the Courts in Early-Modern England* (London, 1994); and Conley, *The Unwritten Law*. Although much of this scholarship has focused on women, there have been some notable studies that examine the impact of masculinity on men's experiences. As Angus McLaren has shown, the criminal has been shown to be an arena in which normative heterosexual masculinities were reflected, reinforced and challenged. Angus McLaren, *The Trials of Masculinity: Policing Sexual Boundaries, 1870–1930* (Chicago, 1997). For the ways in which changing ideas about manliness affected decision-making within the criminal justice system, see Martin J. Wiener, *Men of Blood: Violence, Manliness and Criminal Justice in Victorian England* (Cambridge, 2004). For the representation of masculinity in police court media reports in Scotland, see Broomhall and Barrie, 'Making Men'.

    [69]   Most of the studies discussed in this section are historical, but for modern-day ones which explore the relationship between the media and the criminal justice system see Chris Greer (ed.), *Crime and the Media: A Reader* (London, 2009); Chris Greer, *Crime News* (London, 2011); Ian Marsh and Gaynor Melville, *Crime, Justice and the Media* (London, 2009); and Paul Mason (ed.), *Captured by the Media: Prison Discourse in Popular Culture* (Cullompton, 2006).

    [70]   Peter King, 'Newspaper Reporting and Attitudes to Crime and Justice in Late-Eighteenth- and Early-Nineteenth-Century London', *Continuity and Change*, 22/1 (2007): p. 76.

    [71]   Robert B. Shoemaker, 'The Old Bailey Proceedings and the Representation of Crime and Criminal Justice in Eighteenth-Century London', *Journal of British Studies*, 47/3 (2008): pp. 559–80; Elizabeth A. Foyster, 'Introduction: Newspaper Reporting of

the potential to quell public concerns about crime,[72] and influence structures of law and governance.[73] The press was a crucial vehicle for transmitting the day-to-day business and lessons of courts,[74] as well as an important instrument for critiquing civic policy on law and order issues.[75] By sensationalising trials, newspapers helped to portray criminal trials as emotionally charged clashes between criminals and victims.[76] Moreover, as Émile Durkheim pointed out, press coverage of the 'deviant' criminal enabled nineteenth-century society to test the limits of its tolerance, define acceptable behaviour, provide diversion from the dullness of day-to-day life, and allow separation of those deemed deviant as 'others'.[77] Indeed, Jeff Ferrell and Neil Websdale have argued that the interrelations between media, crime and crime-fighting are such that 'policing can in fact hardly be understood apart from its interpenetration with media at all levels'.[78]

Particular scholarly attention in recent years has focused on the role of the media in representing the administration of justice and detective work.[79] E.P.

Crime and Justice', *Continuity and Change*, 22/1 (2007): pp. 9–12; Peter King, 'Newspaper Reporting, Prosecution Practice and Perceptions of Urban Crime: The Colchester Crime Wave, 1765', *Continuity and Change*, 2/3 (1987): pp. 423–54; and David Lemmings, 'The Dark Side of Enlightenment: *The London Journal*, Moral Panics and the Law in the Eighteenth Century', in David Lemmings and Claire Walker (eds), *Moral Panics, the Media and the Law in Early Modern England* (Basingstoke, 2009), pp. 150–51.

[72] King, 'Newspaper Reporting and Attitudes to Crime', pp. 95–9 & 102–3; and Esther Snell, 'Discourses of Criminality in the Eighteenth-Century Press: The Presentation of Crime in *The Kentish Post*, 1717–1768', *Continuity and Change*, 22/1 (2007): pp. 34–5.

[73] Lemmings and Walker (eds), *Moral Panics, the Media and the Law*; Judith Rowbotham and Kim Stevenson (eds), *Behaving Badly: Social Panic and Moral Outrage – Victorian and Modern Parallels* (Aldershot, 2003); and Judith Rowbotham and Kim Stevenson (eds), *Criminal Conversations: Victorian Crimes, Social Panic, and Moral Outrage* (Columbus, 2005).

[74] Davis, 'A Poor Man's System of Justice?', p. 317.

[75] Barrie, 'Urban Order', pp. 232–4.

[76] Donna T. Andrew and Randall McGowen, *The Perreaus and Mrs. Rudd: Forgery and Betrayal in Eighteenth-Century London* (Berkeley, 2001), ch. 3.

[77] Émile Durkheim, *The Rules of Sociological Method and Selected Texts on Sociology and its Method*, ed. Steven Lukes, trans. W.D. Halls (New York, 1982), pp. 50–59.

[78] Jeff Ferrell and Neil Websdale (eds), *Making Trouble: Cultural Constructions of Crime, Deviance, and Control* (New York, 1999), p. 15.

[79] Haia Shpayer-Makov, for instance, has argued that the press was the most important factor in shaping the dominant view on police detectives over the course of the second half of the nineteenth century. Detectives, she contends, have experienced a reciprocal, and at times uneasy, relationship with the press in late Victorian and Edwardian England. Sometimes critical, sometimes supportive, the press ultimately proved to be 'instrumental in ending the public's opposition to the existence of plain clothes officers, and later in entrenching a positive image of them as protectors of society and of the empire'. Haia Shpayer-Makov, 'Journalists and Police Detectives in Victorian and Edwardian England: An Uneasy Reciprocal Relationship', *Journal of Social History*, 42/4 (2009): p. 980; Haia

Thompson pointed out many years ago that the criminal justice system had to be seen to be legitimate: 'The essential precondition for the effectiveness of law, in its function as ideology, is that it shall display an independence from gross manipulation and shall seem to be just.'[80] In late eighteenth-century London, the city authorities used the *Proceedings of the Old Bailey* – reports of trials at London's main criminal court – to promote a positive image of justice. Simon Devereaux and Robert B. Shoemaker have both argued that the *Proceedings* presented a carefully selected image of justice which, by favouring the prosecution's case to the detriment of the defence, served to justify the workings of the court and its verdicts.[81] Similarly, a number of essays in a recent publication contend that press coverage of eighteenth- and nineteenth-century criminal trials helped to legitimise the law through selective trial reporting and by affording opportunities for informed criticism.[82] As Lemmings concluded in his study of the press in the early eighteenth century, newspapers were 'generally deferential to the courts and their decisions, for the rule of law ideology was just too strong to challenge court decisions directly'.[83] Authorities 'had an interest in constructing a "law and order" dialogue through the press that might legitimize their mandate to rule'.[84] Similarly, according to Anne-Marie Kilday, Scottish newspapers in the pre-modern period [up to the end of the Napoleonic wars] were very much 'the

---

Shpayer-Makov, 'From Menace to Celebrity: The English Police Detective and the Press, c.1842–1914', *Historical Research*, 83/222 (2010): pp. 672–92; and Haia Shpayer-Makov, *The Ascent of the Detective: Police Sleuths in Victorian and Edwardian England* (Oxford, 2011), passim.

[80]   E.P. Thompson, *Whigs and Hunters: The Origin of the Black Act* (London, 1975), p. 63.

[81]   Shoemaker, 'The Old Bailey Proceedings and the Representation of Crime', pp. 559–80; Simon Devereaux, 'The City and the Sessions Paper: "Public Justice" in London, 1770–1800', *Journal of British Studies*, 35/4 (1996): pp. 466–503; and Simon Devereaux, 'The Fall of the Sessions Paper: The Criminal Trial and the Popular Press in Late Eighteenth-Century London', *Criminal Justice History*, 18/1 (2002): pp. 57–88.

[82]   See, for instance, David Lemmings, 'Introduction: Criminal Courts, Lawyers and the Public Sphere' in David Lemmings (ed.), *Crime, Courtrooms and the Public Sphere in Britain, 1700–1850* (Farnham, 2012), p. 7; Esther Snell, 'Trials in Print: Narratives of Rape Trials in the Proceedings of the Old Bailey', in Lemmings (ed.), *Crime, Courtrooms and the Public Sphere*, pp. 23–42; Robert B. Shoemaker, 'Representing the Adversary Criminal Trial: Lawyers in the Old Bailey Proceedings, 1770–1800', in Lemmings (ed.), *Crime, Courtrooms and the Public Sphere*, pp. 71–92; and Rosalind Crone, 'Publishing Courtroom Drama for the Masses, 1820–1855', in Lemmings (ed.), *Crime, Courtrooms and the Public Sphere*, pp. 193–216.

[83]   David Lemmings, 'Negotiating Justice in the New Public Sphere: Crime, the Courts and the Press in Early Eighteenth-Century Britain', in Lemmings (ed.), *Crime, Courtrooms and the Public Sphere*, p. 144.

[84]   Ibid., p. 143.

mouthpiece of the Scottish courts'.[85] Kilday argues that 'Scottish newspapers merely reflected the dominance of this powerful voice' [of judicial and religious authority] and by relying on courtroom propaganda 'they played a key part in the burgeoning misconception surrounding crime and criminality in the pre-modern era'.[86] While some scholars have stressed the mere entertainment and commercial purposes of courtroom trial reports and literary representations,[87] or questioned the extent to which the media in the eighteenth and nineteenth centuries advanced a dominant message on crime that was supportive of the work of the courts,[88] it is widely acknowledged that press trial reports contributed, in the words of Esther Snell, 'to a popular discourse on crime, criminals and criminal justice affairs that may have influenced popular perceptions'.[89] They could also determine popular perceptions of victims. As Shani D'Cruze has pointed out, in trial reports of cases involving women who brought charges of sexual violence, newspapers constructed narratives that often put the complainer's reputation and integrity on trial more than that of the accused.[90] Moreover, in publishing everyday acts of violence as news, they

---

[85]   Anne-Marie Kilday, 'Contemplating the Evil Within: Examining Attitudes to Criminality in Scotland, 1700–1840', in Lemmings (ed.), *Crime, Courtrooms and the Public Sphere*, p. 158.

[86]   Ibid., p. 159.

[87]   See, for instance, Gerald J. Baldasty, *The Commercialisation of News in the Nineteenth Century* (Madison, 1992), which looks at police court reports.

[88]   Peter King, for instance, concluded of crime reporting in late eighteenth- and early nineteenth-century London: 'the newspapers' lack of in-depth accounts, their collage-like style and their multi-vocal nature ... forced readers to forge their own sense of the degree to which printed discourses might offer them any real insights into, or strategies for understanding, both the prevalence of crime and the effectiveness of the authorities' reactions to it'. King, 'Newspaper Reporting and Attitudes to Crime', p. 77. Andrea McKenzie, in her study of Old Bailey *Select Trials* argues that 'The picture which emerges is of a robust legal culture preoccupied less with justifying past verdicts or silencing criticism than with illustrating the complexities of weighing evidence. It is not so much as if the consent and approval of the reading public is solicited, as their complicity in the legal system ... is taken for granted.' Andrea McKenzie, '"Useful and Entertaining to the Generality of Readers": Selecting the *Select Trials*, 1718–1764', in Lemmings (ed.), *Crime, Courtrooms and the Public Sphere*, p. 49. Allyson May claims that police magistrates had been under fairly consistent attack in literary representations and the radical Sunday papers in the 1830s: Allyson N. May, 'Fiction or "Faction"? Literary Representations of the Early Nineteenth-century Criminal Courtroom', in Lemmings (ed.), *Crime, Courtrooms and the Public Sphere*, pp. 167–92.

[89]   Esther Snell, 'Trials in Print: Narratives of Rape Trials in the Proceedings of the Old Bailey', p. 25.

[90]   As D'Cruze argues, 'judges, magistrates and newspapers not infrequently repackaged these narratives as moral tales for broader public edification in ways that might undermine working-women's own agendas within the context of their own neighbourhoods and communities'. D'Cruze, *Crimes of Outrage*, p. 155.

also, as Joanne Jones has stressed, constructed narratives that 'invoked wider concerns of perceived disorder within working-class neighbourhoods and, in doing so, spelt out the case for regulation and reform'.[91]

With some notable exceptions, the bulk of this scholarly attention has focused mainly on the media's relationship with higher courts and crime in the eighteenth century and from the mid-Victorian period,[92] and less on police courts in the first half of the nineteenth century.[93] Yet, as is explored below, it was in the 'unstamped era' of the late 1820s and 1830s that a number of periodicals covering police court reports were published, adding an invaluable insight into the workings of police courts and the social, gender and cultural mores that underpinned them. As Schiller has noted, crime news based on police reports 'led to … the growth of a cheap urban culture' in which crime reporters were afforded the opportunity to develop a storytelling style and to make news from villains and heroes.[94] Moreover, Scottish police courts provide a particularly apt case study in which to examine the representation of criminal justice affairs as, unlike most cases in England in the early nineteenth century, prosecutions were led by a legally trained professional in the form of the procurator fiscal. This is particularly significant as recent research has suggested that lawyers could exercise considerable influence not only on courtroom trials (creating their perception as species of theatre)[95]

---

[91]　Jones, '"She Resisted with all Her Might"', p. 104.

[92]　See, for instance, Hughes, 'The "Non-Criminal" Class', pp. 31–54; Sindall, *Street Violence in the Nineteenth Century*; Jennifer S. Davis, 'The London Garroting Panic of 1862: A Moral Panic and the Creation of a Criminal Class in Mid-Victorian England', in Gatrell, Lenman and Parker (eds), *Crime and the Law*, pp. 190–213; and Judith Rowbotham and Kim Stevenson, '"For Today in this Arena …" Legal Performativity and Dramatic Convention in the Victorian Criminal Justice System', *Journal of Criminal Justice and Popular Culture*, 14/2 (2007): pp. 113–41.

[93]　Broomhall and Barrie argue that nineteenth-century Scottish journals tended to endorse the masculinity performed by police judges in their interactions with others. Broomhall and Barrie, 'Making Men', pp. 72–101. What work has been done on police courts, though, has tended to be fairly fleeting and submerged within wider studies on media representations of crime and the courts *per se*. See, for instance, Rosalind Crone, *Violent Victorians: Popular Entertainment in Nineteenth-Century London* (Manchester, 2012), pp. 219, 220, 228–30, 234–5, 238, 243, & 245; Crone, 'Publishing Courtroom Drama for the Masses', p. 204; and May, 'Fiction or "Faction"', pp. 169–77.

[94]　Dan Schiller, *Objectivity and the News: The Public and the Rise of Commercial Journalism* (Philadelphia, 1981), pp. 68–9.

[95]　John H. Langbein, *The Origins of the Adversary Criminal Trial* (Oxford, 2003), ch. 5; J.M. Beattie, 'Scales of Justice: Defense Counsel and the English Criminal Trial in the Eighteenth and Nineteenth Centuries', *Law and History Review*, 9/2 (1991): pp. 221–67; David Lemmings, 'Criminal Trial Procedure in Eighteenth-Century England: The Impact of Lawyers', *Journal of Legal History*, 26/1 (2005): pp. 76–80; David Lemmings, *Law and Government in England during the Long Eighteenth Century: From Consent to Command* (Basingstoke, 2011), passim.

but also on the construction of media crime narratives from court proceedings.[96] Indeed given, as will be shown in Chapter 4, that it was extremely unusual for the accused to have legal representation in Scottish police courts, it is possible that the existence of a public prosecutor not only put the accused at a disadvantage in courtroom proceedings, but also influenced how magisterial justice was reflected in the press and police court periodicals. At the same time, the fact that police courts, unlike the higher courts, were conducted without written proceedings[97] meant that there was less scope for journalists to regurgitate official courtroom transcripts. Journalists had to attend court themselves, listen to proceedings, and construct their own narratives. This potentially made police court reporters even more autonomous, powerful and influential in conveying the messages of the court than their high court counterparts, where official records and a stronger presence of defence counsel might have helped to reduce journalists' capacity for personal commentary, though clearly not their ability for selective reporting.

A key theme of the book is to examine how courtroom discourse was represented in print culture. We explore how the media reported on magisterial justice and law and order issues through its coverage of police court trials and assess what the selection of trials reported on reveals about the culture and *mentalité* of the media. At the same time, the book considers the concerns of magistrates and senior police officers about public image. As Elaine McFarland has noted, the police in Scotland were media-aware and often interacted with newspapers, providing tip-offs to support their investigations.[98] We consider how and why magistrates and the police engaged in a law and order dialogue with the press.[99] Our study also examines the changing role of the press in the reporting of courtroom trials in an era when popular participation and attendance in the courtroom was reported to be in decline.[100] Did, for instance, media coverage of police court trials represent the growth of discursive commentary on criminal justice matters?

---

[96]   See, for instance, Simon Devereaux, 'Arts of Public Performance: Barristers and Actors in Georgian England', in Lemmings (ed.), *Crime, Courtrooms and the Public Sphere*, pp. 93–118.

[97]   Police court proceedings were conducted without written pleas. As Irons points out, this meant that 'no record shall be kept of the proceedings except the complaint, the plea, the names of the witnesses examined, and the judgement pronounced'. James Campbell Irons, *The Burgh Police (Scotland) Act, 1892* (Edinburgh, 1893), p. 700.

[98]   Elaine W. McFarland, 'A Reality and Yet Impalpable: The Fenian Panic in Mid-Victorian Scotland', *Scottish Historical Review*, 77.2 (1998): pp. 199–223.

[99]   Lemmings argues that authorities 'had an interest in constructing a "law and order" dialogue through the press that might legitimize their mandate to rule': David Lemmings, 'Conclusion: Moral Panics, Law, and the Transformation of the Public Sphere in Early Modern England', in Lemmings and Walker (eds), *Moral Panics, the Media and the Law*, p. 143.

[100]   Crone argues that long working hours and court attendance fees made it difficult for the masses to attend courtroom public galleries: Crone, 'Publishing Courtroom Drama for the Masses', p. 195.

(ii) Accessing and Experiencing Justice

Once regarded as ideological tools of the ruling elite,[101] criminal courts are now viewed in a growing body of historical scholarship in recent years as fluid and participatory spaces that empowered participants and could serve as arenas in which competing views, ideals and identities were discussed and negotiated.[102] With a few notable exceptions,[103] the bulk of this work has focused on the high courts or the eighteenth-century summary courts in England, so by looking at the Scottish police courts in the nineteenth century our study contributes to historical understanding of the function and ideological underpinnings of the criminal justice system. It explores the ways in which the police courts functioned as a discursive space where different social actors had the opportunity to voice their views, identities and aspirations, and aims to uncover the voices and experiences of those subjected to or acting within this branch of summary jurisdiction. This involves looking at how police courts provided institutional spheres in which legal participants, including police officials, victims, witnesses, offenders and prosecutors, were given an avenue to address grievances, articulate opinions, and advance values. Moreover, our analysis assesses the responsiveness of the court to various forces and voices, determining the urban (or indeed other) influences with which procurators and magistrates interacted. Throughout, we also consider how participants shaped the legal system by exposing court personnel to the ways in which other urban inhabitants lived, and analyse how the court responded to these voices.

(iii) Policing the Populace

Police courts were also part of the new, nineteenth-century bureaucratic police machine and an important instrument of power, control and repression. They were, in theory, separate from the police forces that were introduced in Scottish towns in the nineteenth century, but the relationship was complex and the level of judicial separation often questionable. The magistrates who served in Scottish police courts also served as *ex-officio* police commissioners, who were responsible in most towns for appointing and directing chief constables and shaping police policy. As members of town councils, magistrates never ceded their longstanding position as guardians of law and order, a fact which in

---

[101] For the classic view of the law being an ideological tool of the propertied elite, see Hay, 'Property, Authority and the Criminal Law'.

[102] Beattie, *Crime and the Courts in England*; King, *Crime, Justice and Discretion*; King, 'The Summary Courts and Social Relations'; Drew D. Gray, 'The People's Courts?'; and Morgan and Rushton, 'The Magistrate, the Community and the Maintenance of an Orderly Society'.

[103] See, for example, Davis, 'A Poor Man's System of Justice?', pp. 309–35; and Gray, *Crime, Prosecution and Social Relations*.

the police's formative years sometimes brought them into conflict with newly established police commissions.[104] Moreover, as magistrates were drawn from civic rather than legal backgrounds, the administration of magisterial justice in police courts had the potential to become politicised and entangled in wider issues of civic government. As is explored throughout the book, magistrates had many roles to fulfil in the nineteenth century, which could, and on occasion did, have implications for how police courts functioned. The nature of public prosecution in Scotland further muddled the boundaries between the judicial and the executive branch of law enforcement. As the century progressed, the police became more and more involved as public prosecutors for contraventions, offences and less serious offences – all of which were charged and dealt with in police courts. It is, therefore, impossible to divorce police courts from the wider legal and municipal administration in Scottish burghs and how these impacted on those who experienced the law.

Police courts were primarily municipal and criminal courts, but not civil courts. As Chapter 3 shows, the boundaries were sometimes blurred for criminal cases in which property was damaged,[105] with magistrates, on occasion, instructing the accused to pay damages to complainers, especially in rare cases brought by private complaint. But, for the most part, prosecutions were led by the public prosecutor, thereby ensuring that the police would play a central role in the administration of justice in police courts. The police, along with the courts, were at the forefront in enforcing local police and bye-laws relating to behaviours deemed deviant – including vagrancy, drunkenness and prostitution – exemplifying, in the words of V.A.C. Gatrell, 'the developing range and potency of the policeman state'.[106] Much police and, indeed, court time was devoted to dealing with the non-criminal pursuits of the urban poor.[107] At the same time, in framing local police laws, magistrates helped to construct definitions of crime

---

[104]   See David G. Barrie, 'Epoch-Making Beginnings to Lingering Death: The Struggle for Control of the Glasgow Police Commission, 1833–46', *Scottish Historical Review*, 86.2/222 (2007): pp. 253–77.

[105]   In the eighteenth-century summary courts in England, the lines between criminal and civil offences were also sometime blurred, with assault often being treated as a civil offence in the criminal justice system. P. King, 'Punishing Assault: The Transformation of Attitudes in the English Courts', *Journal of Interdisciplinary History*, 27/1 (1996): p. 48.

[106]   Gatrell, 'Crime, Authority and the Policeman–State', p. 245.

[107]   The accused could be prosecuted under municipal, police and Scots criminal law depending on the severity of the offence and the nature of the charge. The latter, for instance, included assault and theft, although such cases would be remitted to a higher court than the police court if the violence, or the value of the property stolen, exceeded a certain level. See Chapter 1 for more on this. As the century progressed, police legislation increasingly embraced aspects of Scots criminal law (although not serious crimes, such as homicide and rape, which continued to be prosecuted in higher courts). Generally, police and courts records made no specific reference to the laws under which prosecutions were brought.

and deviant behaviour.[108] Police courts were, therefore, very much part of a new municipal and legal machine which, for the most part, disciplined the sprawling lower orders by using newly acquired, and sometimes loosely-defined, police powers. As Gatrell has written:

> The history of crime, accordingly, is largely the history of how better-off people disciplined their inferiors; of how elites used selected law-breakers to sanction their own authority; or of how in modern times bureaucrats, experts and policemen used them to justify their own expanding functions and influences. ... Historians might profitably remind themselves that the history of crime is a grim subject, not because it is about crime, but because it is about power.[109]

By examining against whom the law was mainly directed, our analysis advances our understanding of the courts and the impact of the policed society. The police was, to some extent, an instrument of coercion, with much of its time in the nineteenth century being devoted to regulating the behaviour of the lower orders, the supervision of working-class political activities and the suppression of trade unions. Therefore, it is intriguing to consider how the ideological underpinning of police courts might have impacted the ways in which people used and experienced the law.

Moreover, although the focus of the study is primarily on the courts themselves, we also explore the complex relationship between the courts and the police discussed above and how it played out in practice.[110] This is important, as too often the forces of law and order in an institutional, judicial capacity and as a body of men on the ground have been viewed in isolation from one another. While a plethora of studies have examined the role of magistrates in 'policing' and law enforcement in the eighteenth century,[111] their part in promoting, and opposing, police reform in the early 1800s,[112] and their ongoing links with police

---

[108]   As King points out, 'All definitions of crime are, of course, social constructions changing over time and between different societies, social groups and individuals': King, *Crime, Justice and Discretion in England*, p. 6.

[109]   Gatrell, 'Crime, Authority and the Policeman–State', pp. 245–6.

[110]   There have, of course, been studies that briefly engage with both (see, for instance, Ibid., and Godfrey, 'Changing Prosecution Practices and their Impact on Crime Figures'), but few which make this a key focal point.

[111]   See, for instance, Beattie, *Policing and Punishment*; and Beattie, *Crime and the Courts*.

[112]   See for instance, Philips, '"A New Engine of Power and Authority"', pp. 155–89; David Philips and Robert D. Storch, *Policing Provincial England, 1829–56: The Politics of Reform* (London, 1999); J.M. Beattie, *The First English Detectives: The Bow Street Runners and the Policing of London, 1750–1840* (Oxford, 2012); David Philips, 'A "Weak" State? The English State, the Magistracy and Reform of Policing in the 1830s', *English Historical Review*, CXIX/483 (2004): pp. 873–91; and Francis M. Dodsworth, '"Civic"

management throughout the nineteenth century,[113] less attention has been devoted to police–judicial relations in the courtroom,[114] especially in those settings where the magistrates continued to have a role to fulfil in police governance. In the few British histories which have briefly addressed this issue, Jennifer S. Davis and Wilbur Miller have questioned the extent to which the London police courts could be relied upon to function in tandem with police forces.[115] Davis, for instance, argues that while magistrates and police forces were concerned with maintaining social stability and the unequal distribution of property and power in society, each had different views on how best to achieve these ends. Indeed, according to Davis, magistrates enforced the law in a manner which brought them into conflict with the police.[116] Miller, meanwhile, claims that magistrates were initially resentful of the new police in London, and the threat it posed to their own position, status and authority, and could not be relied upon to convict. Although accepting that conviction rates and relations between the judiciary and the police improved over the course of the century, Miller contends that relations between policemen and magistrates were sometimes strained and that the courts were a check on police prosecution practices and interview techniques.[117] Similarly, Carolyn Conley has argued that although magistrates were largely supportive of the police, they were likely to sympathise with those

---

Police and the Condition of Liberty: The Rationality of Governance in Eighteenth-Century England', *Social History*, 29/2 (2004): pp. 199–216.

[113] K. Carson and H. Idzikowska, 'The Social Production of Scottish Policing, 1795–1900', in Hay and Snyder (eds), *Policing and Prosecution in Britain*, pp. 267–97; Chris A. Williams, 'The Sheffield Democrats' Critique of Criminal Justice in the 1850s', in Robert Colls and Richard Rodger (eds), *Cities of Ideas: Civil Society and Urban Governance in Britain, 1800–2000* (Aldershot, 2004); Shane Ewen, 'Managing Police Constables and Firefighters: Uniformed Public Services in English Cities, c.1870–1930', *International Review of Social History*, 51/1 (2006): pp. 41–67; and Shane Ewen, 'Power and Administration in Two English Cities, 1870–1938', unpub. PhD thesis (University of Leicester, 2003).

[114] Studies, in a European context, which look at the historical relationship between the police and the judiciary include Réné Lévy, 'Police and the Judiciary in France since the Nineteenth Century: The Decline of the Examining Magistrate', *British Journal of Criminology*, 33/2 (1993): pp. 167–86; Jacqueline Hodgson, 'The Police, The Prosecutor and the Juge d'Instruction: Judicial Supervision in France, Theory and Practice', *British Journal of Criminology*, 41/2 (2001): pp. 312–61; and Clive Emsley, *Crime, Police and Penal Policy: European Experiences, 1750–1940* (Oxford, 2007).

[115] Unlike most other parts of Britain, the police in London were subject to direct central control in the form of two police commissioners, accountable to the Home Secretary, which meant there was less scope for conflict of interest between the police and the summary courts than in many provincial towns where magistrates often served on council watch committees.

[116] Davis, 'A Poor Man's System of Justice?', pp. 328–9.

[117] Wilbur Miller, *Cops and Bobbies: Police Authority in New York and London, 1830–1870* (Chicago, 1977), pp. 74–103.

charged with offences that violated accepted community norms and customs as defined by middle-class men.[118] Studies of police in North America, on the other hand, have shown how some members of the public and even officers perceived police courts not as centres of justice but as administrative quarters of the police itself,[119] even though, as Childress points out, senior police officials frequently complained that the courts failed to back up the testimonies of arresting officers.[120] In some parts of the British colonies, meanwhile, scholars have pointed out that the independence of the judiciary was highly questionable. Although the nature of police governance could be fractious,[121] magistrates were sometimes dispatched to frontier lands to direct police policy and administer justice to a predominantly indigenous population.[122] Yet, despite the contribution of such studies, much more needs to be done on how police–magistrate relations impacted on judicial outcomes, especially in British provincial towns, where magistrates, unlike in London, often continued to have a say in police management throughout the nineteenth century.[123] While a detailed examination of police–judicial relations is outside the scope of our study, we do explore how those at the forefront of law

---

[118]   Conley, *The Unwritten Law*, pp. 23–34.

[119]   R.C. MacLeod and David Schneider (eds), *Police Powers in Canada: The Evolution and Practice of Authority* (Toronto, 1994). See also John C. Weaver, *Crimes, Constables and the Courts: Order and Transgression in a Canadian City, 1816–1970* (Montreal, 1995); Michael Grossberg and Christopher L. Tomlins, *The Cambridge History of Law in America, Volume II: The Long Nineteenth Century, 1789–1920* (Cambridge, 2008), p. 154; and Mark R. Ellis, *Law and Order in Buffalo Bill's Country: Legal Culture and Community on the Great Plains, 1867–1910* (Lincoln, 2007).

[120]   Morton O. Childress, *Louisville Division of Police: History and Personnel, 1806–2002* (Paducah, 2005).

[121]   For more on police governance in Australia, see Mark Finnane, 'Police Rules and the Organisation of Policing in Queensland, 1905–1916', *Australian and New Zealand Journal of Criminology*, 22/2 (1989): pp. 95–108; and Mark Finnane, *Police and Government: Histories of Policing in Australia* (Oxford, 1994). For police governance in Tasmania, and how this affected the independence of judicial decision making, see Stefan Petrow, 'Tolerant Town, Model Force: The Launceston Municipal Police, 1858–98', *University of Tasmania Law Review*, 16/2 (1997): pp. 235–62; and Stefan Petrow, 'Economy, Efficiency and Impartiality: Police Centralisation in Nineteenth Century Tasmania', *Australian and New Zealand Journal of Criminology*, 31/3 (1998): pp. 243–66.

[122]   Amanda Nettelbeck and Robert Foster, *In the Name of the Law: William Willshire and the Policing of the Australian Frontier* (Kent Town, 2007); Chris Owen, '"The police appear to be a useless lot up there": Law and Order in the East Kimberley, 1884–1905', *Aboriginal History*, 27 (2003): pp. 105–30; and Lisa Ford and Lauren Benton, 'Magistrates in Empire: Convicts, Slaves, and the Remaking of the Plural Order in the British Empire', in Lauren Benton and Richard J. Ross (eds), *Legal Pluralism and Empires, 1500–1850* (New York, 2013), pp. 173–98.

[123]   For more on provincial policing and magistrates' role in it, see Philips, 'The Black Country Magistracy, 1835–60', pp. 161–90; and Taylor, *Policing the Victorian Town*, passim.

enforcement – magistrates, procurators fiscal and police officers – interacted in court and the implications for courtroom participants.

We also consider whether civic communities and urban landscapes were rendered more coherent or divided through the work of the court. Our analysis asks whether courts were forces for unifying urban communities or ones that divided people (by class, gender, religion or other identities). In this era of civic interventionism, scholars have already examined the role of town councils and some court structures, such as the dean of guild courts, in creating spatial boundaries in the city, urban planning and development, and community leisure facilities.[124] R.J. Morris has recently argued that police courts too helped to define modern urban space through their work to maintain public order, protect health and safety, and resolve local disputes.[125] We study how the work of the police courts unified the physical space of the city or acted to render urban spaces socially, morally and economically distinct from each other.

(iv) Pride, Prejudice and Posturing in the Age of Discretionary Justice

While scholars have widely recognised the impact and significance of the expansion of summary jurisdiction in the nineteenth century, the extent to which it was a fundamental departure from eighteenth-century practices has been contested. Some historians suggest that the eighteenth-century English criminal justice system – with its defining characteristics of informal, discretionary justice, informal local sanctions, and exemplary state punishments[126] – gave way to a more systematic, centralised, impersonal system, based on greater certainty of prosecution and formalisation in legal procedure following sweeping reforms to the criminal law, procedure and policing.[127] This was part of wider attempts to control and discipline more effectively the expanding urban masses in line with industrial, capitalist needs, to ensure the status quo and to safeguard private property.[128]

---

[124] Richard Rodger, 'The Law and Urban Change: Some Nineteenth Century Scottish Evidence', *Urban History*, 6 (1979): pp. 77–91; Richard Rodger, 'The Evolution of Scottish Town Planning', in George Gordon and Brian Dicks (eds), *Scottish Urban History* (Aberdeen, 1983), pp. 71–91; and Irene Maver, 'Glasgow's Public Parks and the Community, 1850–1914: A Case Study in Scottish Civic Interventionism', *Urban History*, 25/3 (1998): pp. 323–47.

[125] R.J. Morris, 'New Spaces for Scotland, 1800 to 1900', in Griffiths and Morton (eds), *A History of Everyday Life in Scotland, 1800–1900*, p. 228.

[126] Hay, 'Property, Authority and the Criminal Law', p. 19; and Thompson, *Whigs and Hunters*, p. 266.

[127] Philips, '"A New Engine of Power and Authority"', pp. 155–89; Ignatieff, *A Just Measure of Pain*; and Michel Foucault, *Discipline and Punish: The Origins of the Prison* (Harmondsworth, 1978).

[128] Robert D. Storch, 'The Policeman as Domestic Missionary: Urban Discipline and Popular Culture in Northern England, 1850–80', *Journal of Social History*, 9/4 (1976): pp. 481–509.

Others, however, contend that 'the continuities between eighteenth- and nineteenth-century law enforcement were at least as important as the contrasts',[129] with the nineteenth-century stipendiary magistrate dispensing justice, handing out advice and assuming a role that was similar to his eighteenth-century counterpart.

Our study explores the importance of discretionary justice to magisterial governance, status and authority, as well as to wider civic efforts to control Scotland's rapidly expanding urban population. It addresses the role that individual magistrates and other court personnel had to play in terms of leeway, how they applied it over time and how, in Glasgow, this changed with the introduction of a stipendiary magistrate in the late nineteenth century. We bring into focus the importance and impact of those other court personnel, such as the fiscal, superintendent and policemen, whose work was integral to the functioning of the judicial system at a summary level. Moreover, our study explores the ongoing influence of religion in the life of this secular court, in terms of the moral positions taken by its personnel and advanced through the court, the relationship of this court to the church courts and their personnel, and also the varied perceptions held by media and legal participants about the moral, pastoral and parochial role of the court in nineteenth-century urban life.[130]

V. Sources

Our analysis draws upon a variety of police, court, media, parliamentary and miscellaneous records. This section traces the emergence of such sources throughout the century and how they provide different lenses through which to view the business of police courts, how people experienced the law, and how magisterial justice was represented in print. We explore in greater depth throughout the book the challenges and difficulties involved in using these sources where those issues are most relevant.

Police Court Records, Council/Magistrates Records and the Statistical Turn

As with any study of criminal justice history, the 'official' records produced by the police and the courts form an important source for our analysis.

---

[129]   See, for instance, Davis, 'A Poor Man's System of Justice?', p. 309; and Conley, *The Unwritten Law*, passim.

[130]   Ivo MacNaughton Clark, *A History of Church Discipline in Scotland* (Aberdeen, 1929); G.D. Henderson, *The Scottish Ruling Elder* (London, 1935); Callum G. Brown, *The Social History of Religion in Scotland since 1730* (London, 1987); Peter Hillis, *The Barony of Glasgow: A Window onto Church and People in Nineteenth-Century Scotland* (Edinburgh, 2007); Stewart J. Brown, 'Beliefs and Religions', in Griffiths and Morton (eds), *A History of Everyday Life in Scotland, 1800–1900*, pp. 116–46.

Unfortunately, though, police court records for Scotland are not as complete as those for the summary courts in some parts of England (especially London). The majority of Scottish court records appear to have been destroyed. Handwritten police court minute books/records have been preserved for just two Scottish burghs – Glasgow and Edinburgh – although information on court business in other towns is sometimes included in police and magistrates' records.[131] Moreover, the Glasgow and Edinburgh records are incomplete and cover only short periods of time. Edinburgh Police Court records, for instance, run only from 1805 to 1807 and provide only the briefest summary of information. Each case is afforded just one line of information, in which is recorded the prosecutor (although usually only the procurator fiscal is noted), the accused, the offence, the judgement and the punishment.[132] Similarly, handwritten Glasgow Police Court diet books cover the period 1813–1824 and provide little more than a short paragraph of information on how the accused was brought to court and the outcome of the case.[133] 'Official' court records provide almost no information on what actually went on in court, the degree of negotiation that occurred, the workings of judicial process, and the voices or experiences of those who used and encountered the law. The summary nature of police court proceedings meant that neither court transactions nor evidence was recorded. This leaves a significant gap in the historical record, forcing historians to look to a variety of other 'official', and non-official, judicial records to gain an insight into police court proceedings and transactions.

From the 1820s onwards, information about the business of police courts was recorded in a variety of statistical surveys produced by local council officials,[134]

---

[131] See, for instance, Glasgow City Archives (GCA), H-HIL/12: Burgh of Hillhead Police Court Book, 31 October 1870 to 12 September 1871; and GCA, H-SH1/14 and 15: Pollokshields Police Court, 1888–1890. Both, however, are extremely short and contain scant information.

[132] Edinburgh City Archives (ECA), ED006/8: Edinburgh Police Court Abstract of Processes, 1805–07.

[133] GCA, B3/1/1-10: Glasgow Police Court Diet Books, 1813–1824. The Glasgow City Archives also holds the fiscal's accounts for prosecutions – which contain a list of fines imposed in the police court – for the period 1807 to 1819: GCA, B3/1/5: Fiscal's Accounts for Prosecutions, 1807–1819.

[134] In 1820, for instance, the local council statistician James Cleland produced the *Enumeration of the Inhabitants of the City of Glasgow*, in which he compiled a short, statistical survey of the city's local courts. James Cleland, *Enumeration of the Inhabitants of the City of Glasgow and its Connected Suburbs; together with Population and Statistical Tables, relative to Scotland and England* (Glasgow, 1820), p. 29. This was followed three years later by James Cleland, *Statistical Tables relative to the City of Glasgow, with other Matters therewith connected*, 3rd edn (Glasgow, 1823), p. 91.

police court clerks,[135] the police themselves,[136] and parliamentary inquiries.[137] Aimed mainly at those in civic, and then legal and government, circles, these surveys were part of a wider trend towards gathering statistical information on Scottish cities which had begun in the late eighteenth century with the *First (Old) Statistical Account of Scotland* (1791–1799) – a nation-wide social survey conducted by parish ministers of the Church of Scotland covering geographical, population, agricultural and social information.[138] *The Second (New) Statistical Account of Scotland* (1833–1834), initiated by the General Assembly of the Church of Scotland in 1832, included more information gathered from community leaders such as doctors and school teachers, reflecting its broad civic orientation, and the emerging society that it was measuring.[139] These accounts did not isolate crime and policing as a specific interest, but did detail various punitive options, such as houses of refuge, magdalene asylums and bridewells, among other forms of social support for disadvantaged populations.[140] In the earliest records, police court data was part of wider statistical surveys into urban life and was extremely limited in focus, usually recording only total trends in recorded crimes over a small number of years, or providing a periodic breakdown of cases dealt with by magistrates.[141] Moreover, such information was produced intermittently rather than on a consistent basis, often following requests from senior police officials, and, in some cases, in response to parliamentary inquiries about the workings of law courts in Scotland.[142] However, from 1859 onwards, chief constables' criminal returns published annual statistical returns of crime, offences and contraventions in

---

[135]   'Fourth Report by Her Majesty's Law Commissioners, Scotland, 1839', *BPP*, 1840 (241), XX.115, pp. 251–339.

[136]   See, for instance, GCA, M.P.24, D–T.C.14/1/24, 23: H. Miller, Superintendent of Police, and City Marshal, *Papers Relative to the State of Crime in the City of Glasgow, with Observations of a Remedial Nature; and an Appendix of Tables* (Glasgow, 1840).

[137]   'Fourth Report by Her Majesty's Law Commissioners, Scotland, 1839', pp. 251–339.

[138]   This was followed a few decades later by *The Second (New) Statistical Account of Scotland* (15 vols, Edinburgh, 1845) which included information from other community leaders such as doctors and school teachers, reflecting the broader civic orientation it was seeking to track and reflect, and of the emerging society that it was measuring.

[139]   Charles W.J. Withers, 'Scotland Accounted For: An Introduction To The "Old" (1791–1799) And The New (1834–1845) Statistical Accounts Of Scotland', *EDINA: Statistical Accounts of Scotland*, http://edina.ac.uk/stat-acc-scot/reading/intro.shtml; and R.J. Morris, T.C. Smout and Charles W.J. Withers, 'Scotland, Statistics and Happiness', *EDINA: Statistical Accounts of Scotland*, http://edina.ac.uk/stat-acc-scot/reading/shortintro. shtml.

[140]   As the example of Aberdeen in *The Second (New) Statistical Account of Scotland* demonstrates.

[141]   GCA, *Papers Relative to the State of Crime in the City of Glasgow*.

[142]   'Fourth Report by Her Majesty's Law Commissioners, Scotland, 1839', pp. 278, 304, 323, 332, 335, 336 & 338.

Scottish cities. The returns provide statistical breakdowns of offences known to the police, arrests, cases prosecuted, conviction rates and sentencing and are extremely wide in range and detail.[143] These were produced for public consumption by the police themselves, were part of a national trend towards collating and publishing criminal returns, and were indicative of the growth in state bureaucracy.

However, as has been widely pointed out, crime returns need to be handled with care.[144] Police court documents recorded only crimes that were brought before the courts, or were known to police, not the actual number of crimes committed. They were often affected by changes in policing policy and legal and administrative reforms. Moreover, as Chapter 5 examines, chief constables' annual reports became increasingly concerned with portraying police forces in a good light as the second half of the century progressed, which needs to be borne in mind when interpreting the information they presented. Nonetheless, the value of such records greatly outweighs their limitations. They are an invaluable resource for uncovering the perceptions and fears of the city fathers, as well as power relations and class conflict in urban environments. The statistical returns came to offer an analysis of character in Scotland's cities, and were widely drawn upon to justify and mould civic policy. Although not without their problems, they are a rich repository of social, cultural and legal history and provide invaluable insight not just into the nature of police business, but also the nature of urban law-breaking for which prosecutions were brought and complaints lodged.

As it is impossible to divorce police courts from the wider legal and municipal administration in Scottish burghs, we examine police, council and magistrates' records to provide important insights into civic and legal workings of police courts. In addition to the richly detailed minute books that the civic authorities created, the police and magistrates also produced a wide array of miscellaneous material on policing and law enforcement in Scottish cities and the discussions and debates that surrounded policing, judicial and civic policy.[145] All are extremely useful in uncovering how police courts functioned and how they related to other civic institutions and municipal power structures.

Newspapers

Given the paucity and nature of Scottish police court records, and the study's interest in print culture, the press is an extremely important resource for these volumes.

---

[143]   Edinburgh Central Library (ECL): *Return of Crimes, Offences and Contraventions and Cases of Drunkenness within the Bounds of the Edinburgh Police, by Thomas Linton, Superintendent of Police* (Edinburgh, 1855).

[144]   Philips, *Crime and Authority in Victorian England*, p. 20.

[145]   See, for instance, the *Report on the Moral and Physical Character of the Watching Force*, which criticised the practice in the first few years of the Court of rewarding officers for bringing cases as it could lead to corruption: ECL: *Report on the Moral and Physical Character of the Watching Force* (Edinburgh, 1846), p. 10.

Media sources not only fill in periodic gaps in knowledge and information, they also represent police court trials and magisterial justice. From Scottish police courts' inception, local and national newspapers reported on court proceedings. That they did so is testament to the importance of police courts to urban life.[146] Given the enormous volume of cases processed by the courts, newspaper coverage was necessarily short and selective, which should caution against drawing conclusions on how representative they were of the bulk of court business.[147] Typically, only three or so cases, out of upwards of 20 that were processed on an average day, were selected for publication. Journalists chose stories deemed to be in the public interest or for supposed edification. These were often sensational crimes and offences, or as sensational as the jurisdiction of the police courts could offer, and included those that were violent, sexual, involved alcohol or played to readers' fears about the insecurity of the urban environment.

Although press reports had the potential to skew the impression of police business and urban safety for both reader and historian, their coverage was extremely significant. They opened up new insights into the activities of, and interactions within, the police courts, and offered their own opinions of urban criminality and the work of the courts. Moreover, in the early nineteenth century, newspapers sometimes published statistical data on police court convictions, providing a window into the business of police courts long before official crime returns were published by the police themselves. The press also performed a vital role as a key conduit for knowledge about the police courts and assessment of their efficiency and 'success' in controlling urban crime. The *Aberdeen Journal* willingly reproduced the comments of E.L. Bulwer that the newspaper was 'the chronicle of civilisation'. He had argued at the inquiry into the state of public journals in 1824 that

> The newspaper informs legislation of the public opinion, and it informs the people of the acts of legislation. And this is not all. The newspaper teems with the most practical morality; in its reports of crime and punishments you find daily warnings against temptation; not a case in a police court, not a single trial of a wretched outcast or a trembling felon, that does not preach to us the awful lesson how imprudence leads to error, how error conducts to guilt, how guilt reaps its bitter fruit of anguish and degradation. ... The

---

[146] Davis, 'A Poor Man's System of Justice?', p. 317.

[147] For example, in the early nineteenth century *Glasgow Herald* reports often made the point of highlighting how unusual or important a case was. See, for example, 'A case of a very extraordinary nature was brought before the police court on Tuesday', *Glasgow Herald*, 4 December 1820; 'On Thursday last, a case of some importance to tenants was decided in the Police Court [Edinburgh]', *Aberdeen Journal*, 9 July 1823; 'A case of fraud came before the Police Court [Edinburgh] on Friday, which is of importance to the public, as it may tend to prevent a species of swindling that appears to be easily practiced', *Aberdeen Journal*, 12 April 1826.

newspaper is a law-book for the indolent, a sermon for the thoughtless, a library for the poor. It may stimulate the most indifferent, it may instruct the most profound.[148]

As the above quote makes clear, the press's capacity to influence public opinion and public image was widely recognised in civic circles in the nineteenth century – a fact that was not lost on magistrates and the police. Indeed, as is explored throughout the book, the press gained an important role in the proceedings of police courts, serving as an extension of the discursive and participatory nature of judicial transactions.

As William Donaldson has argued, nineteenth-century newspapers gave public visibility to the language and expression of ordinary Scots. Indeed, this was an era, he contends, in which 'the Scottish vernacular as a medium of written communication' flourished.[149] Throughout our study, we have retained the Scottish (and Irish) dialect as it was recorded in both newspapers and other media forms. As has been widely recognised, language is an important form of cultural expression and empowerment that can shed light on people's experiences in court.[150] Although represented through the mediating filter of the court reporter, retaining the voices of courtroom participants provides echoes of the views, values, mores and, in some instances, motivations of marginalised social and ethnic groups.[151] Moreover, printed literature which represented offenders in first-person narratives also allows the historian to uncover which voices court officials and reporters deemed worthy to listen to, and record, and which were silenced.

The study draws upon three online databases that contain local and national Scottish mainstream newspapers: *The British Newspaper Archive*;[152] *19th Century British Library Newspapers*;[153] and *The Scotsman Online Digital Archive*.[154] Five major newspapers were selected for cities in different regions of Scotland that had police courts: the *Aberdeen Journal* (under various titles), the *Caledonian Mercury* (Edinburgh), *The Scotsman* (Edinburgh), the *Glasgow*

---

[148]   *Aberdeen Journal*, 9 October 1850. See Charles Henry Timperley, *A Dictionary of Printers and Printing* (London, 1839), p. 724.

[149]   William Donaldson, *Popular Literature in Victorian Scotland: Language, Fiction and the Press* (Aberdeen, 1986), p. 71.

[150]   For more on language and discourse in the courtroom, see Anne Wagner and Le Cheng (eds), *Exploring Courtroom Discourse: The Language of Power and Control* (Farnham, 2011); and John M. Conley and William M. O'Barr, *Just Words: Law, Language and Power*, 2nd edn (Chicago, 1998).

[151]   See, for instance, Robert B. Shoemaker 'Print and the Female Voice: Representations of Women's Crime in London, 1690–1735', *Gender and History*, 22/1 (2010), pp. 75–91.

[152]   *The British Newspaper Archive*, 2013, http://www.britishnewspaperarchive.co.uk.

[153]   'British Newspapers, 1650–1900', *Gale Cengage Learning*, 2013, http://gale.cengage.co.uk/product-highlights/history/19th-century-british-library-newspapers.aspx.

[154]   The Scotsman *Digital Archive*, 2013, www.archive.scotsman.com.

Herald and the *Dundee Courier.* As the scope of police court reporting in all the newspapers selected was immense – running to tens of thousands in total – a variety of approaches were adopted.[155] Keyword searches for 'police court' and its variants were conducted for all police court reports in these newspapers in the early nineteenth century, and then at periodic intervals within each decade as the century progressed and the number of relevant articles increased significantly.[156] This gave a general overview as to how and where police court business was reported over the century and how reporting evolved in its presentation and interest qualitatively and quantitatively. Further sampling was then carried out, with between 10 and 15 cases per month for the years chosen being randomly selected to obtain a general spread and sense of seasonal variation. In addition, many more targeted keyword searches pertinent to specific issues, crimes, offences, court personnel and specific individuals were carried out across the entire digital databases of nineteenth-century newspapers in Britain, and where applicable were followed across several editions. Depending on the number of relevant matches per issue, articles were read across the time span and across diverse journals to see how the same matter might be dealt with differently across time and location. In total, several thousand relevant articles were examined.

All of the newspapers consulted were 'mainstream' newspapers and subsequent references throughout the book to 'newspapers' relate to such publications only. These include newspapers with conservative leanings, such as the *Glasgow Herald,* and liberal leanings, such as *The Scotsman.* The first half of the nineteenth century witnessed a proliferation of usually short-lived 'radical' and Chartist newspapers, but such presses consulted in this study did not report on police court issues to anywhere near the extent (and often not at all) of the mainstream press. However, as is explored below, periodicals produced in the post-1819 'radical' era of publication that followed the introduction of the 1819 Stamp Act did provide more opportunity for political commentary. These periodicals were not necessarily radical, but they did provide other insights into the business and practice of police courts.[157]

---

[155]   The *Aberdeen Journal,* for example, had 11,450 such entries, although many related to London over the course of the nineteenth century. The *Caledonian Mercury* had 3,523 entries on 'Police Court', the last one in 1867. In the 1860s, the *Caledonian Mercury* had typically between 150 and 200 entries per year.

[156]   The number of 'hits' for 'police courts' and its variants was huge, which made a case-study approach unavoidable. All of the entries for *The Scotsman* (between 1805 and 1825), the *Caledonian Mercury* (between 1805 and 1817) and the *Aberdeen Journal* (between 1800 and 1805) were checked. Thereafter keyword searching was carried out at five-year intervals for each. On strategies for reading nineteenth-century media, see James Mussell, *The Nineteenth-Century Press in the Digital Age* (Basingstoke, 2012).

[157]   For more on radicalism in Scotland in this era, see Gordon Pentland, *Radicalism, Reform and National Identity in Scotland 1820–1833* (Woodbridge, 2008); Gordon Pentland, 'The Challenge of Radicalism to 1832' in Devine and Wormald (eds), *The Oxford Handbook of Modern Scottish History,* pp. 439–54; Catriona M.M. MacDonald,

Periodicals

By the end of the 1820s, police court reporting began to reach new levels and new audiences. The 1819 Stamp Act was introduced to prevent radical presses by raising the stamp duty on journals published less frequently than monthly, but its effect was to increase the underground media.[158] By 1830, a new breed of printers and journalists began to publish hundreds of unstamped periodicals to voice political views and signal their demand for franchise and media freedom.[159] Between 1830 and 1836 (when the stamp duty was reduced from 4d. to 1d.),[160] a proliferation of voices found expression through print culture, including many assessing police and legal activities. In Scotland, a series of titles published in the late 1820s to early 1830s focused on crime, policing, and the courts in Edinburgh and Glasgow, and later in Dundee from 1841 to 1851.[161] Many of the publications appearing at this period lacked obvious numbering. They also changed titles frequently, and their printers and publishers adopted pseudonyms to avoid definition as a regular periodical (though not so completely as to lose their readers in the process) and thus, prosecution.[162] Their publication appeared to vary from daily to twice weekly and weekly. Those that reported on the business of police courts included *Police Reports of Cases Tried before the Glasgow, Gorbals and Calton Police Courts* (1829); *The Police Intelligencer, or Life in Edinburgh* (1831–1832); *Bawbee Bagpipe* (Edinburgh, 1833); and *The Dundee Police Gazette or Weekly*

The Radical Thread: Political Change in Scotland: Paisley Politics, 1885–1924 (East Linton, 2000); Catriona M.M. MacDonald, '"Their laurels wither'd, and their name forgot": Women and the Scottish Radical Tradition', in Edward J. Cowan and Richard J. Finlay (eds), *Scottish History: The Power of the Past* (Edinburgh, 2002), pp. 225–52.

[158]   Joel H. Wiener, *A Descriptive Finding List of Unstamped British Periodicals, 1830–1836* (London, 1970), p. vii.

[159]   Joel H. Wiener, *The War of the Unstamped: The Movement to Repeal the British Newspaper Tax, 1830–1836* (Ithaca, 1969), p. xiii.

[160]   Wiener, *A Descriptive Finding List of Unstamped British Periodicals*, p. viii.

[161]   Based on analysis of John S. North (ed.), *The Waterloo Directory of Scottish Newspapers and Periodicals, 1800–1900* (2 vols, Waterloo, 1989). The dates of publication are as listed in North's survey. For Glasgow, these are *Police Reports of Causes tried before the Justices of Peace, and the Glasgow, Gorbals and Calton Police Courts* (*Police Reports*), 18 July–3 October 1829. For Edinburgh, *Report of the Interesting Proceedings in the Police Court*, February 1829–November 1831; *The Police Intelligencer, or Life in Edinburgh* (*Police Intelligencer*), August 1831–June 1832; *Police Recorder*, September 1832–October 1832; *Life in Edinburgh, Police Intelligencer and Dramatic Review*, May 1833–1833. Later, for Dundee, *The Dundee Police Gazette or Weekly Reporter*, October 1841–c.1851.

[162]   Some publishers could argue that a single edition was a pamphlet, rather than a periodical, incurring only the lesser pamphlet duty. See Wiener, *The War of the Unstamped*, pp. 153 & 157.

Reporter (1841–1851).[163] These publications give lucid, sometimes amusing, and sometimes disturbing, descriptions of selected cases before the police courts, often accompanied with a moralistic social commentary. Although, as Joel Wiener has pointed out, the sensational and journalistic turn in criminal reporting through cheap prints and seeking big sales for dramatic stories must surely have influenced court coverage in the press over the century,[164] these particular publications provide very little detail in general about any one case and appear rather as, at times, a prosaic list of a range of the weekly cases before the court, with some flavoursome details of speeches, events and characters where these occurred. They did not report all cases before the court and are therefore not used in a quantitative capacity as representative of the entirety of court business. As John Brownlie, the author of the 1829 *Police Reports*, writes for one week: 'No case of importance till the 13th',[165] or 'On the 6th July, there were twenty-two cases before the court, generally uninteresting.'[166]

According to Wiener, the proliferation of unstamped periodicals was stimulated by the French Revolution of July 1830 and represented 'a form of pre-chartist agitation'.[167] However, while this hypothesis might be relevant to wider reforming periodicals, it does not explain those which were concerned with police courts and urban crime specifically. Not only did police court periodicals pre-date the 1830 French Revolution, they were not necessarily radical in their politics. It is possible that the timing of these publications might have been influenced by the introduction of the 1829 Metropolitan Police Act in London, which helped to stimulate interest in, and to some extent politicise, the issue of law enforcement beyond the immediate confines of England's capital, but this is unlikely. As has been argued elsewhere, the impact of this statute was far greater in shaping law enforcement arrangements in England than in Scotland, where it appears to have passed with little notable impact.[168] Significantly, the local Scottish police court periodicals made no reference to the Metropolitan Police whatsoever. It

---

[163]   *Police Reports*; and *The Police Intelligencer*. The *Bawbee Bagpipe* was published by William Smith, an active publisher of penny chapbooks and at least two illegal periodicals during the 1830s. Both – the *Bawbee Bagpipe* of 1833, lasting 12 numbers, and the *Advocate* of 1834, consisting of six numbers – were concerned with issues of law and order combined with 'amusing and instructive' songs, stories and images. See John Bulloch (ed.), *Scottish Notes and Queries*, II (1906): p. 5; and *The Dundee Police Gazette or Weekly Reporter*, October 1841–1851. For additional information, consult North (ed.), *The Waterloo Dictionary of Scottish Newspaper and Periodicals*.

[164]   Martin J. Wiener, 'The Victorian Criminalization of Men', in Pieter Spierenburg (ed.), *Men and Violence: Gender, Honor and Rituals in Modern Europe and America* (Columbus, 1998), p. 207.

[165]   *Police Reports*, 13 July 1829, p. 11.

[166]   *Police Reports*, 25 July 1829, p. 15.

[167]   Wiener, *The War of the Unstamped*, p. xiii.

[168]   Barrie, 'Anglicisation and Autonomy', p. 446.

is much more likely that the emergence of police court periodicals in Glasgow and Edinburgh reflected a wider growing local interest in crime and urban social problems. These publications seem to have appeared after the widely reported, sensational Burke and Hare case of 1827–1828,[169] which may have stimulated publishers to address the market for readers of crime, playing on their heightened anxieties about urban safety. Indeed, Philippe Chassaigne has argued that this case spawned fears about a new uniquely urban crime, 'burking'; an indiscriminate, anonymous and unpremeditated violent attack.[170] The first issue of *Remarkable Scottish Crime*, published in Glasgow in 1834, justified its accounts of crime, saying:

> It is a mistaken notion that the recital of crimes tends to injure the morals of youthful readers, we believe, on the contrary, that like the romance, or the Eastern tale, it acts as stimulus, or preparatory step, to more refined matter; and many a one but for such would never have become what is called readers at all. Under this impression, we offer no other apology for the appearance of Remarkable Scottish Crime.[171]

Other publishers used periodicals, meanwhile, to promote personal interests and campaigns aimed at moral reform. As the authors of *Remarkable Scottish Crime* would later do, Brownlie justified his publication of the business of the police court as primarily instructive and frequently emphasised alcohol as a major cause of criminality: 'Keeping in view this principle, the author trusts that these Reports, while they may have the effect of wounding some, they may have the tendency of warning others.'[172]

The era of the unstamped periodicals ushered in a new kind of reporting. Unlike pre-1829 newspaper reports, the police periodicals displayed a more overt tendency towards inflammatory reporting, a distinct curiosity about the 'way others live' and definite moralising, making police court clients more akin to the subject of fiction and anthropological investigation than fellow inhabitants of a shared urban environment. As Chapter 4 explores, they also tended to highlight court dialogue and report it in direct speech that is amongst the earliest occasions we see the (mediated) voices of magistrates and accused together, which creates an impression that the clientele of the court was in dialogue with another (hitherto

---

[169] William Burke and William Hare were Irish migrants and notorious murderers in Edinburgh. A series of murders over several months in 1828, after which corpses were sold to Dr Robert Knox for dissection, are attributed to them.

[170] Philippe Chassaigne, *Ville et Violence: Tensions et conflits dans la Grande-Bretagne victorienne (1840–1914)* (Paris, 2005), p. 39.

[171] *Remarkable Scottish Crime: Murder of Buchanan the Lanark Carrier*, no. 1 (Glasgow, 1834), p. 1, cited in North (ed.), *Waterloo Directory of Scottish Newspapers and Periodicals*, vol. 2, p. 1087.

[172] *Police Reports*, p. 1.

the mainstream newspapers had done this only occasionally and not to any great extent).

While it cannot be conclusively proved that their presentations accurately represent the spectrum of courtroom positions, it seems unlikely that the quotes of statements made in court could have been fabricated without disciplinary action – perhaps especially regarding the speech of the police magistrates and officers. Indeed, the introduction of the 1829 Glasgow *Police Reports* made a specific point of noting:

> In publishing POLICE REPORTS, a strict adherence to Truth must be observed, because, in most instances, Truth itself, in police matters, eventually gives many cause of offence, and surely much greater grounds of disapprobation can consistently be urged, when a just and true Report is not given, or ridiculously embellished, at the risk of injuring the feelings of the unfortunate.[173]

Significantly, civic leaders did not complain about the accuracy of the reports that appeared in the periodicals in this era. This was in contrast to some newspaper coverage of police court trials in the second half of the nineteenth century following the proliferation of weekly newspapers aimed at lower middle and working classes that specialised in sensationalising stories (see Chapter 4 for more on complaints in civic circles about the accuracy of newspaper reporting).[174] Moreover, there is no evidence that the reports that appeared in the periodicals were censored, although it is possible that magistrates were able to exert indirect influence over their content.

Both the Glasgow *Police Reports* and Edinburgh's *The Police Intelligencer* included more cases – and more detailed reports – than newspaper court reports, the latter likely to have been perceived by the reader as more openly selective in what they reported, although they were still extremely picky in the types of cases and voices included. As Chapter 4 explores in more depth, the number of cases covered typically numbered between three and 12 in any given edition, with the opinions of the court clientele (magistrates and procurators fiscal) being more commonly recorded than those of witnesses and, to a lesser extent, the accused. Nonetheless, although the cases and the transactions chosen for publication should not be regarded as representative of police court business in general, the periodicals provide an intriguing qualitative insight into police court transactions that other sources do not provide. They constitute an extremely rich source for our analysis and reveal a great deal about social and cultural values and how these were represented at the time.

Towards the end of the century there emerged a number of periodicals with yet another style of reporting on police courts in Glasgow. In 1850 the unstamped

---

[173] Ibid.

[174] For more on the publication of police court trial reports in the 'weeklies', see Crone, *Violent Victorians*, pp. 209–56.

conflict was reactivated, and with the 'taxes on knowledge' between 1852 and 1861, including Stamp Duty in 1855, a new popular journalism emerged. This challenged the established media with cheap penny dailies and weeklies aimed at appealing to, and developing, a wide readership and covering news of all kinds.[175] Although not directly reporting on police court cases in the same way as the above journals, these publications provided commentary on police courts, magisterial authority and public prosecution. In 1885, for instance, *The Detective, or Criminal and Historical Gazette* provided weekly representations of crime and police in Glasgow, criminal trials, and, in one edition, an intriguing description of the Glasgow Central Police Court on a typical Monday morning.[176] Published from 1872 through to the early twentieth century, *The Bailie* provided political and satirical commentaries on leading men in Glasgow's public life, including magistrates,[177] procurators fiscal[178] and chief constables.[179] The periodical's title, *The Bailie*, in itself alluded to its concern with matters of law and order and civic governance. The weekly commentaries and reports on civic personalities and governance provided intriguing features as to whether or not stipendiary magistrates should be introduced in the city's police courts, the reliability of police evidence in court, and the relationship between magistrates, procurators, the police and the media.[180] Although often tongue-in-cheek, *The Bailie* provided information about, and analysis of, Glasgow's police courts that is rarely found in other sources and is an invaluable resource for scholars interested in the leading personalities who helped to govern and administer justice in Scotland's largest city in the late nineteenth century. All of the periodicals cited above were examined in their entirety.

---

[175] Wiener, *A Descriptive Finding List of Unstamped British Periodicals*, p. viii; Chassaigne, *Ville et Violence*, p. 267. See also James Curran and Jean Seaton, *Power without Responsibility: The Press and Broadcasting in Britain* (London, 1997); and Donaldson, *Popular Literature in Victorian Scotland*, p. ix.

[176] On 17 September 1885 the journal changed its name to *Thistle or Detective* and appears to have run until 5 November 1885. It is not clear whether the latter was the last date of publication, or merely the last edition held in Glasgow University Library (GUL), Special Collections: *The Thistle, Literary, Theatrical and Police Reporter*. See, for instance, the following articles: 'A Monday Morning at the Central Police Court', no. 7, vol. I, 23 May 1885, pp. 1–16; 'Detective Sketches of Dangerous Characters', no. 9, vol. I, 6 June 1885, pp. 1–16; 'Sunday on Glasgow Green', no. 10, vol. I, 13 June 1885, pp. 1–3; 'Sauchiehall Street after Dark', no. 14, vol. II, 9 July 1885, pp. 1–2; 'Midnight Scenes in Glasgow', no. 16, vol. II, 23 July 1885, pp. 1–2; 'The Shadow of Crime', no. 25, vol. II, 24 September 1885, pp. 1, 4–5.

[177] See, for instance, *The Bailie*, no. 2, 30 October 1872, p. 1; no. 4, 13 November 1872, p. 1; and no. 10, 25 December 1872, p. 2.

[178] See, for instance, *The Bailie*, no. 9, 11 December 1872, pp. 1–2.

[179] We are grateful to W. Hamish Fraser for bringing this periodical to our attention. *The Bailie*, no. 19, 26 February 1873, pp. 1–2.

[180] These are explored throughout the book.

While several studies have focused on particular aspects or periods of dynamic media activity in Scotland during this century, examining the elite end of intellectual publishing such as *Blackwood's Magazine, The Edinburgh* and *Quarterly Review*,[181] and the political machinations of editors and politics of the mainstream press,[182] one of the challenges of these sources is that we still lack detailed knowledge about the extent and composition of nineteenth-century Scottish media readership.[183] Literacy rates in urban Scotland, though, were extremely high by the 1830s. A report on Scottish millworkers published in 1833 claimed that of the 28,000 workers sampled, 96 per cent could read and 53 per cent could write, compared with respective figures of 86 per cent and 43 per cent for England.[184] Although reading levels were often extremely basic, and there was considerable social and regional variation in standards of literacy throughout Scotland,[185] it is clear that a significant proportion of the population from different social backgrounds would have been able to read the published trial reports for themselves. Wiener estimates that popular English police gazettes such as the *People's Hue and Cry, People's Police Gazette, Weekly Police Register* and *Weekly Police Gazette*, ran to estimated weekly circulations as high as 30,000 to 40,000.[186] However, Mark Hampton has emphasised the challenges of linking newspaper circulation numbers to readers, since more people may have heard the news than read it. This suggests that estimated readerships based on circulation

---

[181]   John O. Hayden, *The Romantic Reviewers, 1802–1824* (Chicago, 1969); Joanne Shattock, *Politics and Reviewers: The Edinburgh and the Quarterly in the Early Victorian Age* (Leicester, 1989); David Finkelstein, *The House of Blackwood: Author–Publisher Relations in the Victorian Age* (University Park, 2002); David Finkelstein (ed.), *Print Culture and the Blackwood Tradition, 1805–1930* (Toronto, 2006); Jonathan Cutmore (ed.), *Conservatism and the Quarterly Review: A Critical Analysis* (London, 2007); Jonathan Cutmore, *Contributors to the Quarterly Review, 1809–25: A History* (London, 2008).

[182]   See, for example, William Stewart, *The Glasgow Press in 1840* (Glasgow, 1921); and R.M.W. Cowan, *The Newspaper in Scotland: A Study of its First Expansion, 1815–1860* (Glasgow, 1946).

[183]   Much analysis has focused upon the readership implied or targeted through such media. For Britain broadly, see such studies as Alvar Ellegård, *The Readership of the Periodical Press in Mid-Victorian Britain* (Göteborg, 1957); Aled Jones, *Powers of the Press: Newspapers, Power and the Public in Nineteenth-Century England* (Aldershot, 1996); and Laurel Brake and Julie F. Codell (eds), *Encounters in the Victorian Press: Editors, Authors, Readers* (Basingstoke, 2005).

[184]   Helen Corr, 'An Exploration into Scottish Education', in W. Hamish Fraser and R.J. Morris (eds), *People and Society in Scotland, Volume II: 1830–1914* (Edinburgh, 1990), p. 292.

[185]   See, for instance, Donald J. Withrington, 'Schooling, Literacy and Society', in T.M. Devine and Rosalind Mitchison (eds), *People and Society in Scotland, Volume 1: 1760–1830* (Edinburgh, 1988), pp. 163–87; and R.A. Houston, *Literacy in Early Modern Europe: Culture and Education, 1500–1800* (London, 1988), pp. 43–9, 132 & 139; and Corr, 'An Exploration into Scottish Education', pp. 292–4.

[186]   Wiener, *The War of the Unstamped*, pp. 176–7.

numbers may substantially underestimate the population's access to print media.[187] Donaldson has proposed that a sizeable range of weeklies which combined news with popular miscellany were popular with lower and middle-class readers in Victorian Scotland.[188] This attention to a wide readership aligns with other studies of nineteenth-century media. As Guy Reel has recently argued, sensationalism 'helped build readership – mostly notably among men from the lower to middle classes'.[189] Jon Klancher observes that periodicals of this era 'deliberately smudged social differences among their readers'. However, although prices were not typically printed on the texts themselves, he argues that most English quarterly and monthly magazines represented prohibitive sums to working-class readers, at 4s.–6s. and 2s.–3s. respectively per issue.[190] Our analysis of the media not only assesses its capacity to present the work of the police courts to these broad audiences but also how its publications demanded the attention also of the literate urban elite who were anxious to maintain the esteem of the court and their own work within it.

Miscellaneous Sources

The above sources have provided the bulk of information for this book, but others have been drawn upon to elucidate different themes. Church records and annual reports from organised religious missions provide additional insights into the perceived criminality of Scottish burghs and success of the police courts in managing it.[191] A myriad of book publications such as William Tait's *Magdalenism* (1840), Thomas Ferguson's *The Dawn of Scottish Social Welfare* (1848), Robert Buchanan's *The Destitution of the Masses in Glasgow* (1851), and William Logan's *The Moral Statistics of Glasgow* (1864) shed light on urban criminality and police work as well as published collections of speeches such as those of Glasgow's medical officer of health, James Burn Russell.[192] These texts have

---

[187] Mark Hampton, *Visions of the Press in Britain, 1850–1950* (Urbana, 2004), pp. 26–9.

[188] Donaldson, *Popular Literature in Victorian Scotland*, p. x.

[189] Guy Reel, 'Of Tabloids, Detectives and Gentlemen: How Depictions of Policing helped Define American Masculinities at the Turn of the Twentieth Century', in Barrie and Broomhall (eds), *A History of Police and Masculinities*, p. 183.

[190] Jon P. Klancher, *The Making of English Reading Audiences, 1790–1832* (Madison, 1987), p. 50.

[191] Extant records include: the *First Report by the Commissioners of Religious Instruction, Scotland* (1835) and *Second Report by the Commissioners of Religious Instruction, Scotland* (1837); The Free Church of Scotland's *Proceedings*; The Church of Scotland's *Assembly Papers* and *Acts of the General Assembly*; and archives of specific congregations such as W.J. Couper, *A Century of Congregational Life: History of Great Hamilton Street United Free Church, 1819–1919* (Glasgow, 1920).

[192] Archibald K. Chalmers, *Public Health Administration in Glasgow: A Memorial Volume of the Writings of James Burn Russell* (Glasgow, 1905).

been used to provide discursive contexts and contemporary commentary on the role of police courts in managing crime and the burghs. Similarly journalistic were the documentary-style visual commentaries of Shadow in *Midnight Scenes and Social Photographs: Sketches of Life in the Streets, wynds, and dens of the city* (1858) and Thomas Annan in his *The Old Closes and Streets of Glasgow* (1868 to 1871).

Broadsides, ballads and other chapbook literature have also been examined to shed light on (or be sympathetic to) the views of a range of social groups including the working class.[193] Forbes, among others, has argued that music is an important and socially sensitive feature of nineteenth-century urban culture that could be instrumental to social improvement agendas or be used to parody them.[194] We examine such sources as complementary to civic agendas of policing or potentially subversive to these.

A range of diaries and memoirs have also been consulted to offer further individual perceptions on the activities of the police court and the changing environment in which these were undertaken. By the end of the nineteenth century a more diverse range of memorialists were able to have their views recorded in print,[195] although like other sources their generic contexts must be kept in view.[196] Finally, a wide range of legal and civic tracts have been drawn upon to chart the changing powers of police courts and the rules, regulations and procedures that governed them.[197]

VI. Structure

We have broken Volume 1 into 7 chapters that reflect distinct areas of investigation and advance key arguments. The first chapter, 'Evolution and Expansion',

---

[193]   Donaldson, *Popular Literature in Victorian Scotland*. The role of such sources in elucidating migrant group experiences and views has already been suggested by Busteed for Manchester: Mervyn Busteed, 'Little Islands of Erin: Irish Settlement and Identity in Mid-Nineteenth-Century Manchester', *Immigrants & Minorities*, 18/2–3 (1999): pp. 94–127.

[194]   Simon Gunn and R.J. Morris (eds), *Identities in Space: Contested Terrains in the Western City since 1850* (Aldershot, 2001).

[195]   Henry Cockburn, *Memorials of His Time* (2 vols, Edinburgh, 1856); Archibald Alison, *Some Account of My Life and Writings: An Autobiography* (2 vols, Edinburgh, 1883); William Thom, *Rhymes and Recollections of a Hand-Loom Weaver* (London, 1844); Thomas Guthrie, *Autobiography* (2 vols, London, 1875); William Cameron, *Hawkie, The Autobiography of a Gangrel* (Glasgow, 1888); James Myles, *Chapters in the Life of a Dundee Factory Boy, Written by Himself* (1850, republished Dundee, 1951); Robert Bruce, *William Thom: The Inverurie Poet – A New Look* (Aberdeen, 1970).

[196]   A broader analysis across the genre can be found in James R. Simmons (ed.), *Factory Lives: Four Nineteenth-Century Working-Class Autobiographies* (Peterborough, 2007).

[197]   See chapters 1–2.

explores the establishment of police courts by analysing the economic, social and intellectual influences that underpinned legal and legislative changes. It pays particular attention to the challenges men of property faced in bringing forward prosecutions under the old burgh court system, and their shared private commercial, social and cultural interests in effecting the expansion of police court summary justice. Chapter 2, 'Dignity and Discretion', examines the role of magistrates in the newly formed court structure, the importance of judicial discretion and the role of 'community values' to how the law was administered. It analyses the identities of those expected to adjudicate in police courts, including their roles, beliefs and relationships to civic, including the police, and moral elites. The third chapter, 'People's Courts?', examines the function of the police court in Scotland as a legal instrument to resolve disputes, seek legal redress and acquire justice. It analyses access to complaint and settlement and the significance of court personnel in determining which cases were brought to, and were resolved, in court. Chapter 4, 'Public Theatres?', explores the experience of the courtroom from the eyes of diverse legal participants (including the fiscal, the policemen, the accused, witnesses, journalists and the public gallery). It also considers media representation of courtroom activities, behaviours, emotions and speech.

In the fifth chapter, 'Practices, Patterns and Perceptions', we examine the business of the court, how it changed over time, and the influence of the police and contemporary sources in shaping statistical patterns. Chapter 6, 'Legal, Social and Cultural Convictions', considers what factors influenced and determined conviction patterns over the course of the nineteenth century. Consideration is also given to the role of the media in legitimising magisterial judgements. Chapter 7, 'Punishment and Protection', looks at the diversity of punishments not only for those convicted of distinct crimes, offences or contraventions, but also for those of different age, gender, religious and social status. The role of the media in naming and shaming, and the extent to which it could function as an extra-judicial resource, is also considered.

In addressing these issues, and the detailed case studies explored in Volume 2, we uncover a fascinating history of the lives, identities and communities of nineteenth-century Scottish cities and how police courts came to shape Scottish life in ways that are still evident today.

Chapter 1
Evolution and Expansion

I. Introduction

> Every public outrage, every theft, robbery or depredation, every obstruction,
> nuisance, or breach of cleanliness, and every imposition or overcharge in articles
> under the cognizance of the police act, are deemed public offences, and are
> prosecuted by the inspectors of the wards [under the authority of the police
> judge]. The examination of the offender and witnesses are in this [Edinburgh
> police] court taken *instanter*, and *viva voce*; and the sentence pronounced is
> immediately executed.[1]

Writing in *Picture of Edinburgh* (1806), local author John Stark paid homage to
the efficiency and scope of the city's recently established police court. Edinburgh's
example was quickly followed by other major urban centres, which, like Scotland's
capital, established police courts under local police legislation.[2] These courts came
to be integral to the smooth running of towns, the maintenance of magisterial
concepts of urban order, and the development of the Scottish criminal justice
system. From their inception, police courts dealt with more business, prosecuted
more cases, and punished more offenders than any other centre of justice in the
country. They were the principal local courts before which people were likely to be
summonsed and to interact with the law, and were instrumental in bringing about
a massive increase in the number and type of crimes, offences and misdemeanours
that were dealt with and punished in a summary manner. It was in this era that
summary legal procedure emerged as the cornerstone of the criminal justice
system and police courts were at the forefront of this transition.[3] They helped
change how Scots criminal law was administered over the course of the nineteenth

---

[1]   John Stark, *Picture of Edinburgh; Containing a History and Description of the City,
with a particular Account of Every Remarkable Object in, or Establishment Connected
with, the Scottish Metropolis* (Edinburgh, 1806), p. 179.

[2]   The first, and most significant, of these acts was introduced in the rapidly expanding
industrial and commercial centres of Glasgow (1800), Edinburgh (1805), Paisley (1806),
Calton (1819) and Dundee (1824): Glasgow (39 & 40 George III, cap. 88); Edinburgh (45
George III, cap. 21); Paisley (46 George III, cap. 116); Calton (59 George III, cap. 3); and
Dundee (5 George IV, cap. 129).

[3]   Lindsay Farmer, *Criminal Law, Tradition and Legal Order: Crime and the Genius of
Scots Law, 1747 to the Present* (Cambridge, 1997), pp. 74–5; Thomas Trotter, *The Summary
Jurisdiction (Scotland) Act 1908* (Edinburgh, 1908), p. 3; James Fitzjames Stephen,
'Suggestions as to the Reform of the Criminal Law', *The Nineteenth Century*, 2 (1877): pp.

century, as proportionately fewer cases were prosecuted in higher courts in favour of local centres of justice that could process cases in a fairly quick, cheap and, on occasions, informal manner.[4]

Scholars of criminal justice history in England have in recent years given greater attention to chronicling the summary courts' rise to prominence in administering the criminal law. Explanations for this phenomenon in the eighteenth century have identified the important role played by Sir John Fielding in the Bow Street Magistrates' Court, mounting concerns with crime held by men of property, and the perception that lay magistrates were corrupt and 'trading in justice'.[5] Historians have also identified the impact of the 1792 Middlesex Justices Act, which authorised the appointment of stipendiary justices and the establishment of seven police offices in the metropolis, and the growing challenges of securing convictions in higher courts following the introduction of defence counsel, in making summary justice more attractive.[6] Although often not examining police courts *per se,* studies have also connected the expansion in summary jurisdiction in the nineteenth century to wider developments within the criminal justice system following major judicial reforms from the 1840s onwards.[7] Scholars have pointed to legal and administrative changes to improve the efficiency of court procedure, the re-classification of what constituted

---

123–4; and Edwin R. Keedy, 'Criminal Procedure in Scotland', *Journal of the American Institute of Criminal Law and Criminology*, 3/5 (1913): pp. 728–53.

[4] Henry Brown defined summary procedure in the following way: 'The Law of Scotland commits summary criminal jurisdiction to all Inferior Judges ... [They] try by virtue of it the whole of the minor crimes recognised by the common law and most of the punishable offences created by Acts of Parliament. The number of persons affected by procedure of a summary character thus exceeds by many times the number of those arraigned before the more solemn tribunals.' Henry Hilton Brown, *The Principles of Summary Jurisdiction according to the Law of Scotland* (Edinburgh, 1895), p. xix.

[5] See, for instance, Drew D. Gray, *Crime, Prosecution and Social Relations in London: The Summary Courts of London in the Late Eighteenth Century* (Basingstoke, 2009); J.M. Beattie, 'Sir John Fielding and Public Justice: The Bow Street Magistrates' Court, 1754–1780', *Law and History Review*, 25/1 (2007): pp. 61–100; Bruce P. Smith, 'The Emergence of Public Prosecution in London, 1790–1850', *Yale Journal of Law and the Humanities*, 18/29 (2006): pp. 29–62; and Norma Landau, 'The Trading Justice's Trade', in Norma Landau (ed.), *Law, Crime and English Society, 1660–1830* (Cambridge, 2002), pp. 46–70.

[6] Ruth Paley, 'The Middlesex Justices Act of 1792: Its Origins and Effects', unpub. PhD thesis (University of Reading, 1983); Bruce P. Smith, 'The Emergence of Public Prosecution in London'; and Bruce P. Smith, 'The Presumption of Guilt and the English Law of Theft, 1750–1850', *Law and History Review*, 23/1 (2005): pp. 133–72.

[7] Jennifer S. Davis's investigation into the London police courts is the main exception to this, but this is largely concerned with the workings of the courts and people's experiences of them rather than their evolution. Jennifer S. Davis, 'A Poor Man's System of Justice? The London Police Courts in the Second Half of the Nineteenth Century', *Historical Journal*, 27/2 (1984): pp. 309–35.

indictable crime, and the removal of juveniles from the higher courts.[8] The evolution and expansion of summary justice has also been viewed as a product of the emergence of the 'police state', changes in middle-class perceptions of violence and appropriate masculine conduct, and the judicial system's growing preoccupation with 'civilising' the lower orders and safeguarding urban order.[9]

Unfortunately, the expansion of Scottish summary justice has not received the same level of attention as the English model. As Clive Emsley points out, Scots legal history has traditionally been backward rather than forward looking, 'glorifying a mythical past in which Scots Law is said to have originated and established its defining characteristics' during the Enlightenment rather than

---

[8] See, for instance, V.A.C. Gatrell and T.B. Hadden, 'Criminal Statistics and their Interpretation', in E.A. Wrigley (ed.), *Nineteenth-Century Society: Essays in the Use of Quantitative Methods for the Study of Social Data* (Cambridge, 1972), pp. 336–96; V.A.C. Gatrell, 'The Decline of Theft and Violence in Victorian and Edwardian England', in V.A.C. Gatrell, Bruce Lenman and Geoffrey Parker (eds), *Crime and the Law: The Social History of Crime in Western Europe since 1500* (London, 1980), pp. 238–370; David J.V. Jones, *Crime in Nineteenth-Century Wales* (Cardiff, 1992); David Philips, *Crime and Authority in Victorian England: The Black Country, 1835–60* (London, 1977); and Leon Radzinowicz and Roger G. Hood, *A History of English Criminal Law and its Administration from 1750, Vol. V: The Emergence of Penal Policy* (London, 1986), ch. 19.

[9] The literature is too extensive to list in full. Amongst the most significant studies on the police are V.A.C. Gatrell, 'Crime, Authority and the Policeman–State', in F.M.L. Thompson (ed.), *Cambridge Social History of Britain, 1750–1950* (Cambridge, 1992), pp. 243–310; David Philips, '"A New Engine of Power and Authority": The Institutionalization of Law-Enforcement in England, 1780–1830', in Gatrell, Lenman and Parker (eds), *Crime and the Law*, pp. 155–89; and Barry S. Godfrey, 'Changing Prosecution Practices and their Impact on Crime Figures, 1857–1940', *British Journal of Criminology*, 48/2 (2008): pp. 171–89. For violence, gender ideology and masculinity, see Martin J. Wiener, *Men of Blood: Violence, Manliness and Criminal Justice in Victorian England* (Cambridge, 2004); Shani D'Cruze, *Crimes of Outrage: Sex, Violence and Victorian Working Women* (London, 1998); J.S. Cockburn, 'Patterns of Violence in English Society: Homicide in Kent, 1560–1985', *Past and Present*, 130 (1991): pp. 70–106; Robert B. Shoemaker, 'Male Honour and the Decline of Popular Violence in Eighteenth-Century London', *Social History*, 26/2 (2001): pp. 190–208; Clive Emsley, *The English and Violence since 1750* (London, 2005); John Carter Wood, *The Shadow of Our Refinement: Violence and Crime in Nineteenth-Century England* (London, 2005); Anna Clark, *Women's Silence, Men's Violence: Sexual Assault in England, 1770–1845* (London, 1987); and Barry S. Godfrey, Stephen Farrall and Susanne Karstedt, 'Explaining Gendered Sentencing Patterns for Violent Men and Women in the Late Victorian and Edwardian Period', *British Journal of Criminology*, 45/5 (2005): pp. 696–720. For the civilising process more generally, see Pieter Spierenburg, 'Violence and the Civilizing Process: Does it Work?', *Crime, Histoire & Sociétés/Crime, History & Societies*, 5/2 (2001): pp. 87–105; and Martin J. Wiener, 'The March of Penal Progress?', *Journal of British Studies*, 26/1 (1987): pp. 83–96.

seeking to chart its modern development in the nineteenth century.[10] In most histories of Scots Law, the 1747 Heritable Jurisdiction Act – which abolished heritable jurisdiction following the failed Jacobite rising in 1745–1746 – is held up as having laid the foundations for the modern criminal justice system by sweeping away local feudal courts in favour of a more structured, uniform and centralised system.[11] Only recently have scholars explored the important role that fiscal concerns, legal technicalities associated with common law, and the rise to prominence of a new class of businessmen played in the development of summary procedure in the first few decades of the nineteenth century.[12] But much more needs to be done.

This chapter aims to address this by examining not just legal and legislative changes, but also the economic, social and intellectual influences that underpinned them. In doing so, it reveals how men of property reconceptualised urban order and intertwined civic imperatives in line with their own moral and economic interests in order to effect reform and defend their own position, status and influence. Nineteenth-century police legislation, it contends, was at the forefront in extending the local state's influence over the urban population through new police laws and in facilitating major reform within the criminal justice system through the expansion in summary procedure. Although parliament in London exerted influence in passing statutory police legislation, it is shown here that it was local elites who were central to shaping police laws, regulations and legislation with central government playing a less important role in the development of criminal justice history than was once believed. Mirroring recent work in England and, indeed on Scottish policing, this chapter demonstrates that it was urban elites, not politicians in London, who laid the foundations for the reform of what was to become the busiest and, arguably, the most important branch of the criminal justice system.[13]

----

[10]   Clive Emsley, 'Review of Lindsay Farmer, *Criminal Law, Tradition and Legal Order: Crime and the Genius of Scots Law, 1747 to the Present* (Cambridge, 1997) and Radhika Singha, *A Despotism of Law: Crime and Justice in Early Colonial India* (Oxford, 1998)', *Crime, Histoire & Sociétés/Crime, History and Societies*, 4/1 (2000): pp. 138–41.

[11]   Stephen J. Davies, 'The Courts and the Scottish Legal System 1600–1747: The Case of Stirlingshire', in Gatrell, Lenman and Parker (eds), *Crime and the Law*, p. 120.

[12]   Farmer argues that summary justice arose not just as a means of 'avoiding the legal technicalities and formalities associated with common law', but also as a desire to move from a system concerned with local territory and sovereignty to one preoccupied with procedure and order: Farmer, *Criminal Law, Tradition and Legal Order*, p. 97. Barrie and Broomhall, meanwhile, have recently explored how civic tensions and the rise to prominence of a new class of businessmen contributed to the evolution of Scottish police courts and their institutional structures between 1800 and 1833. David G. Barrie and Susan Broomhall, 'Public Men, Private Interests? The Origins, Structure and Practice of Police Courts in Scotland, 1800–1833', *Continuity and Change*, 27/1 (2012): pp. 83–123.

[13]   This supports the conclusion by Peter King who argues that in England, justice was often remade from the margins by local magistrates, judges and others. Peter King, *Crime*

II. The Local Courts and Magisterial Justice in the Late Eighteenth and Early Nineteenth Centuries

In the early 1700s, the Scottish criminal justice system was characterised by multiple jurisdictions and a lack of centralised legal and national control.[14] The High Court of Justiciary and the Court of Session were the country's most senior central criminal and civil courts, but the majority of courts were in the hands of individuals unconnected with the state. Scottish society was supervised and controlled by an elaborate and extensive system of private, local courts – royal, seigneurial and ecclesiastical – with wide-ranging variations between them in terms of judicial authority, day-to-day business and legal procedure.[15] In the Highlands and counties, judicial power was either purchased or inherited and was firmly under the authority of landowners and clan chiefs in seigneurial and sheriff courts.[16] In urban centres, it was predominantly in the hands of magistrates in burgh and guildry courts. There were also justice of the peace courts scattered throughout the country, although these were much less common and important than was the case in England. The lines of judicial authority were often determined by perceived spatial boundaries, specific local needs and interests, and the economic and social status of parishes, whilst judicial powers were based on local statutes and charters rather than a uniform principle of application.[17] Similarly, Scots Law was largely a collection of local practices, usages and conventions.[18] There was little consistency in decision-making or sentencing, and little regulation of procedure in a system 'founded on custom and convention rather than precise statutory codification'.[19]

---

and the Law, 1750–1840: Remaking Justice from the Margins (Cambridge, 2006), passim. See also J.M. Beattie, *Policing and Punishment in London, 1660–1750: Urban Crime and the Limits of Terror* (Oxford, 2001); and David G. Barrie, 'Anglicisation and Autonomy: Scottish Policing, Governance and the State, 1833 to 1885', *Law and History Review*, 30 (2012): pp. 1–41.

[14] For an outline of the Scottish courts and their jurisdictions, see R. Scott, 'The Politics and Administration of Scotland, 1725–1748', unpub. PhD thesis (University of Edinburgh, 1982), pp. 217–46.

[15] Davies, 'The Courts and the Scottish Legal System', pp. 120–54.

[16] Anne-Marie Kilday, *Women and Violent Crime in Enlightenment Scotland* (Woodbridge, 2007), p. 26.

[17] Farmer, *Criminal Law, Tradition and Legal Order*, p. 67. For more on the relationship between judicial boundaries and the perception of space, see R.A. Houston, *Social Change in the Age of Enlightenment: Edinburgh, 1660–1760* (Oxford, 1994), ch. 2. For summaries on the inferior courts in nineteenth-century Scotland, see Henry James Moncreiff, *A Treatise on the Law of Review in Criminal Cases* (Edinburgh, 1877), chs 1 and 2; and W.C. Spens, *Jurisdiction and Punishment of Summary Criminal Courts (with special reference to the Lash)* (Edinburgh, 1875).

[18] Davies, 'The Courts and the Scottish Legal System', p. 121.

[19] Kilday, *Women and Violent Crime*, p. 27. See also Davies, 'The Courts and the Scottish Legal System', pp. 120–54.

Justice was often administered informally to suit private and religious interests, and criminal prosecutions – especially in the inferior courts – were rare.

The second half of the eighteenth century, however, brought significant change to the local criminal courts throughout Scotland. The 1747 Heritable Jurisdiction Act streamlined the Scottish court structure. The statute aimed to extend central control over Scottish jurisdiction: firstly, by weakening, and in some cases, breaking the feudal structure of authority that tied local courts to landowners and clan chiefs; secondly, by laying down regulations regarding court sittings, duties and justice qualifications; and, thirdly, by extending the influence and jurisdiction of the High Court of Justiciary in Edinburgh.[20] Although there was no desire to break completely with the old feudal structure, especially in towns where some ancient powers survived well into the nineteenth century, the statute limited feudal jurisdiction when it challenged sovereign power.[21] Widely regarded as laying the foundations for the modern Scottish criminal justice system,[22] the abolition of heritable jurisdiction 'brought about the demise of a complex and distinctive legal system' in favour of a more structured and uniform one.[23] It signified a move towards greater centralised control by abolishing many old feudal courts and the jurisdiction of others.[24]

By the late eighteenth century, the number of Scottish criminal courts had been significantly reduced and their roles and powers clarified. More serious criminal cases – which included serious assault, rape, grand larceny and murder – were tried under solemn procedure[25] before juries in either sheriff courts or the High Court in Edinburgh (or one of its circuit courts). Less serious offences – which included petty theft, assault and breach of the peace – were brought primarily before either justices in sheriff courts or magistrates in burgh courts, both of which had become the principal local courts for dealing with statutory and common law crimes. Barony courts and admiralty courts also dealt with criminal matters, but their jurisdictions were limited to a narrow category of offences and their roles within the criminal justice system were fairly minor.[26]

---

[20]   Farmer emphasises that there was no desire to break completely the old feudal structure. Farmer, *Criminal Law, Tradition and Legal Order*, pp. 63–4.

[21]   Ibid., p. 64.

[22]   Ibid., p. 59.

[23]   Davies, 'The Courts and the Scottish Legal System', p. 120.

[24]   This included burgh courts. See Irene Maver, 'The Guardianship of the Community: Civic Authority before 1833', in T.M. Devine and Gordon Jackson (eds), *Glasgow, Volume I: Beginnings to 1830* (Manchester, 1995), pp. 254–5.

[25]   Solemn procedure is the formal legal process used in serious cases involving High Court or sheriff court trials before juries.

[26]   For an overview of Scottish criminal courts in the eighteenth and nineteenth centuries, see Davies, 'The Courts and the Scottish Legal System', pp. 120–54; Johan Findlay, *All Manner of People: The History of the Justices of the Peace in Scotland* (Edinburgh, 2000); Anne E. Whetstone, *Scottish County Government in the Eighteenth and Nineteenth Centuries* (Edinburgh, 1981), ch. 2; and David M. Walker, *A Legal History of*

Similarly, justice of the peace courts dealt with petty offences committed within the jurisdiction of the county shire and generally performed the same role that police courts would fulfil for urban centres, but the number of cases with which they dealt was relatively small.[27] Whether a case was brought before burgh courts or sheriff courts was determined by judicial boundaries and the seriousness of the charge. Burgh courts traditionally had wide-ranging powers, including capital ones until the seventeenth century, but by the late eighteenth century their judicial scope had been reduced to dealing with quite mundane crimes. By this point, magistrates in many towns were more than content to let sheriffs with concurrent jurisdiction deal with more serious crimes (although not serious enough to warrant jury trial in a justiciary court).[28]

In addition to these criminal courts, church courts held an extremely important position in Scottish parishes. Indeed, the Church of Scotland had an integral role to play in the everyday lives of Scots and was a vital mechanism for maintaining urban order and social stability in the eighteenth century.[29] Elders – who along with the minister made up the kirk sessions – performed important religious and public duties that were akin to a parish state.[30] As Anne-Marie Kilday has argued, church figures worked with legal authorities to curb bad behaviour.[31] Although elders had no judicial powers to deal with serious

Scotland (7 vols, Edinburgh, 1988–2003), vol. 4, p. 473 and vol. 5, pp. 494–7. For church courts, see Leah Leneman and Rosalind Mitchison, *Sin in the City: Sexuality and Social Control in Urban Scotland 1660–1780* (Edinburgh, 1998).

[27] Justice of the peace courts were introduced in 1578 in order to remedy some of the deficiencies of other criminal courts. They dealt with criminal and civic cases, but their powers were subordinate to those of sheriff courts. Albert V. Sheehan and David J. Dickson, *Criminal Procedure: Scottish Criminal Law and Practice Series*, 2nd edn (London, 2003), p. 11.

[28] Ibid., p. 10; G.S. Pryde 'The Burgh Courts and Allied Jurisdictions', in *An Introduction to Scottish Legal History* (Edinburgh, 1958), p. 384; and David M. Walker, *A Legal History of Scotland*, vol. 1, ch. 8.

[29] T.M. Devine, *The Scottish Nation, 1700–2000* (London, 1999), p. 84. See also Bruce Lenman, 'The Limits of Godly Discipline in the Early Modern Period with particular Reference to England and Scotland', in Kaspar von Greyerz (ed.), *Religion and Society in Early Modern Europe, 1500–1800* (London, 1984), pp. 134–9; and Leah Leneman, 'The Kirk Session and Social Control in the Early Modern Scottish Cities', in *Popular Religion and Society* (St Andrews, 1991), pp. 78–89.

[30] Elders were chosen according to gender, piety, judgement and knowledge. Stewart J. Brown, 'Beliefs and Religions', in Trevor Griffiths and Graeme Morton (eds), *A History of Everyday Life in Scotland, 1800 to 1900* (Edinburgh, 2010), p. 127. See also Christopher A. Whatley, *Scottish Society, 1707–1830: Beyond Jacobitism, Towards Industrialisation* (Manchester, 2000), p. 149.

[31] Anne-Marie Kilday, 'The Barbarous North? Criminality in Early Modern Scotland', in T.M. Devine and Jenny Wormald (eds), *The Oxford Handbook of Modern Scottish History* (Oxford, 2012), p. 400.

crimes,[32] they were expected to police the morals of parish congregations and were responsible, as Leah Leneman and Rosalind Mitchison have pointed out, for prosecuting and punishing a wide array of misdemeanours and minor offences.[33] Most related to moral crimes and included fornication, adultery and Sabbath breaches, but they also extended to assault, theft, domestic violence, drunkenness, sexual offences and dishonest business practices.[34] Calvinist doctrine, from which the Church's teachings were derived, preached moral restraint and godly discipline, and those found to have breached the kirk's moral codes were publicly rebuked before the congregation. Unlike local justices, elders had no legal right to imprison or fine offenders. Punishment took the form of public penance and fines (kirk dues) which would be used to provide parish poor relief and other forms of assistance. Indeed, popular eighteenth-century texts, reprinted into the early nineteenth century, mocked the authority of the church courts over people's sexual behaviour and suggested that they functioned as little more than a revenue raiser.[35] This was, in effect, not just a form of religious censure, but also community justice. Kirk sessions would impose religious authority, but whether an offender was reconciled within the parish was also, in practice, at the discretion of the wider public. As David Nash and Anne-Marie Kilday have shown, shame and community sanction

---

[32] Nonetheless, local ministers and kirk officials also often worked hand-in-hand with burgh magistrates and crown officials to regulate public morality. Witness testimonies before the High Court of Justiciary reveal that kirk elders, along with local justices, 'regularly helped to interrogate suspects bound for the higher criminal courts of the country' and 'provided a strong moral, criminal and cultural investigative framework within Scottish society'. Kilday, *Women and Violent Crime*, p. 28. A similar point was made by Davies, 'The Courts and the Scottish Legal System', p. 120; and Ian D. Whyte, *Scotland before the Industrial Revolution: An Economic and Social History, c.1050–c.1750* (London, 1995), p. 215.

[33] For more on godly discipline in Scottish towns, see Leneman and Mitchison, *Sin in the City*, p. 2.

[34] Devine, *Scottish Nation*, p. 84; and Peter Hillis, *The Barony of Glasgow: A Window onto Church and People in Nineteenth-Century Scotland* (Edinburgh, 2007), pp. 129–40.

[35] See, for example, *The Ancient and Modern History of Buck-haven in Fife-shire ... the noted sayings of Wise Willy in the Brae, Witty Eppie the ale-wife, and Linle-tail'd Nancy* (Glasgow, 1806). There were at least two further editions: one undated and the other an abridged edition in 1817, which appears in *Collected Writings of Dougal Graham, "Skellat" Bellman of Glasgow*, ed. George Mac Gregor (2 vols, Glasgow, 1883), vol. 2, pp. 226–7. When Wise Willie's daughter Janet is brought to the kirk court for bearing an illegitimate child, the elders insist on both fine and public penance: 'Come, come, say they, pay down the kirk-dues, and come back to the stool the morn, four pound, and a groat to the bell-man.' To this Janet responds, 'The auld thief speed the dearth o't stir, for less might sair you and your bell-man baith, O but this be a hard warld indeed, when poor honest fouk maun pa for making use o' their ain a'–'.

were important parts of godly discipline with religious values underpinning attitudes towards much criminality.[36]

In pre-industrial Scottish society, it was extremely difficult to evade the ubiquitous influence and prying eye of godly discipline and Scots were much more likely to be brought before a church court than a burgh, sheriff or justiciary court.[37] As Table 1.1 shows, the volume of criminal cases prosecuted in burgh and sheriff courts was extremely low – mirroring male prosecutions and male committals to trial per head of population in higher courts which were much lower than in England in the late eighteenth and early nineteenth centuries.[38] Procurators fiscal tended to prosecute in burgh courts only the more serious cases for which magistrates had jurisdiction, especially property crimes (often involving violence) and 'social' or 'protest' crimes that were deemed serious enough to threaten social stability and question magisterial capability to govern.[39] Thus, in 1802, the Perth Town Council issued a handbill, entitled 'Thefts and Depredations in the Town's Wood', in which it was stated that 'the magistrates and other proprietors have determined to repress such practices by prosecuting offenders to the utmost rigour of the Law' and offered a reward of three guineas for information which might lead to conviction.[40] Tellingly, their resolve for prosecuting more mundane crimes that did not threaten private property was less strong. Just 17 cases are listed in the 'Criminal Papers' archival records for Perth in 1797.[41] Throughout the country, a major priority for magistrates was to ensure the supply of the meal market in order to allay the threat of meal riots. Thus, in 1791, magistrates in Kilmarnock agreed to contribute whatever was necessary to prosecute the 'lawless mob' who attacked James Tod. Tod, a farmer, stood accused among the community of hoarding grain in order to inflate

---

[36] David Nash and Anne-Marie Kilday, *Exploring Crime and Morality in Britain 1600–1900* (Basingstoke, 2010), passim.

[37] Bruce Lenman and Geoffrey Parker, 'Crime and Control in Scotland, 1500–1800', *History Today*, 30 (1980): p. 16.

[38] Scotland had lower rates of male committals to trial – which accounted for the overwhelming majority of all committals – than in England in the nineteenth century, although female committals were higher. M.A. Crowther, 'Crime, Prosecution and Mercy: English Influence and Scottish Practice in the Early Nineteenth Century', in S.J. Connolly (ed.), *Kingdoms United? Great Britain and Ireland since 1500: Integration and Diversity* (Dublin, 1999), p. 231.

[39] See, for instance, Perth and Kinross Council Archives (PKCA), PE/47 Series: Perth Town Council Posters/Handbills 1709–1914, 30 November 1802, for a handbill from magistrates offering a reward of thirty guineas after a merchant's shop was broken into.

[40] PKCA, PE/47/18: Thefts and Depredations in Town's Wood, 6 December 1802.

[41] PKCA, PE/51/1 to 318 bundles: Perth Town Council Legal Papers 1753–1866, 'The Criminal Papers'. Bundle 48, 'Bills for Criminal Prosecutions', accounts of the Town Clerk for Perth, show that between November 1800 and November 1801, a total of just £10, 12s., 9d. was spent for writings relative to criminal prosecutions.

Table 1.1   Return of the Number of People charged with Criminal Offences and Committed to Gaol in Scotland, 1810 to 1823†

1800	'10	'11	'12	'13	'14	'15	'16	'17	'18	'19	'20	'21	'22	'23
Aberdeen:														
Summary*	31	29	29	43	39	100	65	79	56	42	63	101	101	110
Trial														
Ayr:														
Summary	7	8	14	18	12	33	17	12	8	18	22	18	16	20
Trial	18	22	19	24	41	46	37	35	29	24	71	33	39	48
Dumfries:														
Summary	13	26	30	30	36	55	27	60	47	64	60	45	53	42
Trial	9	18	12	14	15	29	11	27	25	31	16	18	24	15
Edinburgh:														
Convicted Returns**	294	283	499	792	875	1,265	1,436	1,604	1,490	1,663	1,266	1,554	1,669	1,637
Glasgow:														
Summary*	724	643	589	503	704	944	1,043	1,021	1,016	1,323	1,221	1,190	1,150	845
Trial														
Greenock:														
Summary	31	40	2	51	72	92	116	79	133	151	99	133	84	77
Trial		32	18	11	5	21	13	15	16	28	36	27	24	34
Leith:														
Summary	13	9	15	10	8	17	16	25	14	12	19	29	37	35
Trial	6	7	12	6	8	9	7	15	11	7	10	20	26	24

Summary: In execution on summary process

Trial: For trial before Jury.

* The summary and trial returns appear to be one and the same. Summary returns include cases before the sheriff and burgh courts.

** Edinburgh's returns listed the convicted criminal returns only. These returns included prisoners sent to Edinburgh for trial in the High Court of Justiciary.

The above returns cover committals from sheriff, burgh and high courts.

† 'Return of the Number of Persons charged with Criminal Offences in England and Wales, Ireland and Scotland, 1822–23', *British Parliamentary Papers* (BPP), 1825 (197), XXIII.523, pp. 1–36.

the price at market (despite the civic fathers complaining of a shortage of funds for criminal purposes which had kept the level of prosecutions for other crimes extremely low).[42] These examples were indicative not just of the influence that magistrates could exert over burgh procurators as to whether to prosecute crime, but also both how community and magisterial attitudes could differ about what constituted crime, and the selective and self-interested way in which the law was often administered.[43]

Formal legal action was often the last resort for those in position of governance. Summary justice in burgh courts was frequently administered informally and consisted of non-custodial punishments such as whipping and banishment, both of which were popular because they were cheap and did not incur legal or aliment costs.[44] It was common for local procurators and magistrates not to prosecute suspects in custody so long as the latter agreed to leave the burgh, which ensured that the level of recorded crime and offences was much lower than the level committed.[45] Parish discipline was frequently exercised face-to-face rather than through bureaucratic means, with neighbours and magistrates often relying upon the ancient form of civil protection known as 'lawburrows' to settle disputes.[46] Indeed, magistrates appear to have employed a variety of extra-judicial means as an alternative to criminal prosecution. During the Napoleonic Wars, the press gang – an impress service which would seize able-bodied men to serve in the navy – was utilised as a mechanism for removing offenders. In Dundee, many debtors and petty criminals, who might otherwise have been formally dealt with by the courts, appear to have 'volunteered' to enlist, presumably on the recommendation of

---

[42]   Dick Institute, Kilmarnock (DI), BK/1/1/2/1: Kilmarnock Town Council Minute Book, 30 July 1791.

[43]   For key studies on social crime, see E.P. Thompson 'The Moral Economy of the English Crowd in the Eighteenth Century', in *Past & Present*, 50 (1971): pp. 76–136; John G. Rule, 'Social Crime in the Rural South in the Eighteenth and Early Nineteenth Centuries', *Southern History*, 1 (1979): pp. 135–53; and John G. Rule and Roger A.E. Wells, *Crime, Protest and Popular Politics in Southern England, 1740–1850* (London, 1997). For social crime and popular protest in Scotland, see Christopher A. Whatley, 'Order and Disorder', in Elizabeth A. Foyster and Christopher A. Whatley (eds), *A History of Everyday Life in Scotland, 1600 to 1800* (Edinburgh, 2010), pp. 191–216; and Whatley, *Scottish Society*, passim.

[44]   The Dundee lawburrow minute books between 1775 and 1799, for instance, record 221 banishments, with the returns showing an increase up until the outbreak of the Napoleonic Wars. Dundee City Archives (DCA): Lawburrows Books of Dundee, 1775 to 1799 (no reference numbers).

[45]   PKCA, PE/51/1–7: Perth Town Council Legal Papers 1753–1866. See especially bundles 1 to 7 for cases in the second half of the eighteenth century.

[46]   Lawburrows was a form of civil action which arose when two parties were in dispute, resulting in one pursuing a lawsuit to procure legal security that the other would not harm the petitioner or petitioner's family and property under financial penalty: *Encyclopaedia of the Laws of Scotland, Volume IX: Land Tax to Midwives* (Edinburgh, 1930), p. 53.

magistrates, rather than face criminal prosecution.[47] The *Return of the Number of Persons charged with Criminal Offences in Scotland*, published in 1825, illustrates both the pragmatic, cost-effective approach taken by magistrates and procurators and the limitations of summary jurisdiction under the unreformed burgh court structure. Produced by parliament and reflective of London's growing interest in criminal justice matters in the United Kingdom as a whole, the return shows that between 1810 and 1823, 580 suspects were charged with criminal offences and committed to the local gaol for trial in the burgh of Dundee. Of these, almost half were liberated by the order of magistrates without having been being tried.[48] Just 82 were tried in a summary manner by magistrates and convicted. The remainder were either transmitted to other gaols to await trial, disposed of according to law, or liberated on finding caution.

Culture and tradition were important, too, in explaining the low level of recorded crime.[49] Even though heritable jurisdiction had been abolished, Scots, according to Cameron, continued to have a mindset that was geared towards informal, local, 'rough' justice which privileged ministers over justices.[50] Furthermore, the geographical challenges that victims in Scotland had to face in bringing forward a prosecution were greater than in most parts of England and are likely to have deterred many from reporting crimes. With the exception of the larger burghs, Scottish communities were more isolated and often had inferior infrastructure to that of English towns, which made getting access to procurators, magistrates and the courts difficult and potentially costly if the time involved in doing so resulted in the loss of pay.[51] The chances of legal redress were further hampered by the fact that magistrates in many small burghs did not hold regular criminal courts and were often fairly inactive in dealing with criminal affairs. As evidence presented to the 1839–1840 Law Inquiry revealed, magistrates in such instances would hold burgh criminal courts only when they believed it was needed – with many not having held one for over a year![52] As in England, such men were

---

[47]   For more on this, see David G. Barrie, 'Urban Order in Georgian Dundee, c.1770–1820', in Charles McKean, Bob Harris and Christopher A. Whatley (eds), *Dundee: Renaissance to Enlightenment* (Dundee, 2009), p. 228; and DCA: Customs and Excise Records, 14 October 1790, 25 November 1770, 1 April 1803, 24 April 1808 and 1 June 1808. Thanks are owed to Malcolm Archibald for these sources.

[48]   'Return of the Number of Persons charged with Criminal Offences in England and Wales, Ireland and Scotland, 1822–23', p. 26.

[49]   See Crowther, 'Crime, Prosecution and Mercy', p. 234.

[50]   Joy Cameron, *Prisons and Punishment in Scotland from the Middle Ages to the Present Day* (Edinburgh, 1983), p. 57.

[51]   Alexander Lambert, Procurator Fiscal of Oban, for instance, lamented the fact that the procurator fiscal of the county resided at Inverary, 32 miles from Oban, where the nearest gaol was for that area: 'Fourth Report by Her Majesty's Law Commissioners, Scotland, 1839', *BPP*, 1840 (241), XX.115, p. 299.

[52]   John Mitchell, Interim Town Clerk of Kirkwall, reported that 'A burgh criminal court has been very rarely held in this town. Proceedings generally laid before the sheriff';

conscientious in administering the law when they believed it was required, but were often fairly casual about doing it on a regular basis when social relations were harmonious.[53] Furthermore, most Scottish towns relied upon a few town officers, part-time, unpaid constables and, during periods of heightened tension, the ancient system of watching and warding to deal with day-to-day law and order.[54] With the exception of Edinburgh, full-time, salaried watch forces were not introduced in Scottish towns until the late eighteenth and early nineteenth centuries. This was later than in most English provincial centres, so the chances of a victim bringing an offender to court were slim unless he or she knew who the alleged offender was and could convince the fiscal that there were sufficient grounds for bringing forward a prosecution.

The fiscal's role in explaining the low level of criminal prosecutions in Scotland was crucial. In giving evidence to the 1854–1855 Select Committee on Public Prosecutions, James Moncreiff, Lord Advocate of Scotland, outlined the key principles of the Scottish criminal prosecution system:

> The system proceeds upon the principle that it is the duty of the State to detect crime, apprehend offenders, and punish them, and that independently of the interest of a private party. The Scotch system acknowledges the right of a private party to prosecute; but the duty of the public prosecutor is altogether irrespective of that.[55]

The overwhelming majority of criminal prosecutions were undertaken by the public prosecutor – the procurator fiscal – under the authority of the Lord Advocate in the Crown Office in Edinburgh (usually for indictable crimes tried before the High Court and circuit courts) and under the authority of magistrates

---

Alexander Mackenzie, Joint Town Clerk of Perth, reported that 'There has been no Burgh *Criminal* Court held in Perth for the last fifteen years or so. Since then all the cases which have happened within the burgh have been taken up by procurator fiscal of the county and tried before magistrates.' 'Fourth Report by Her Majesty's Law Commissioners, Scotland, 1839', p. 292 (first quote) and p. 303 (last quote). Italics in original.

[53] For a wider study of how summary just worked in practice, see Peter King, 'The Summary Courts and Social Relations in Eighteenth-Century England', *Past and Present*, 183/1 (2004): pp. 125–72. Paul Langford makes a similar claim. He notes that although rural justices were 'committed, conscientious men', many were 'at best casual in the carrying out of their duties': Paul Langford, *Public Life and the Propertied Englishman: 1689–1798* (Oxford, 1991), p. 401. For the commitment of magistrates in Scotland to law enforcement before burgh reform in 1833, see David G. Barrie, *Police in the Age of Improvement: Police Development and the Civic Tradition in Scotland, 1775–1865* (Cullompton, 2008), ch. 2; and Maver, 'The Guardianship of the Community', pp. 239–77.

[54] Barrie, *Police in the Age of Improvement*, ch. 2.

[55] 'Report from the Select Committee on Public Prosecutors; Together with the Proceedings of the Committee, Minutes of Evidence, Appendix and Evidence', *BPP*, 1854–1855 (481), XII.1, p. 17.

and sheriffs in the respective local courts.[56] These were all professionally trained legal men of significant social status and influence – and, in the case of the Lord Advocate, the government's chief legal officer in Scotland. However, financial considerations and constraints often deterred procurators and justices from pursuing formal, legal action. Although magistrates could exert influence over burgh procurators, not least because they appointed them, prosecutions in local courts were very much at the discretion of procurators who would often base their decision about whether or not to bring charges upon the likelihood of conviction or payment of legal fees.[57] Burgh procurators were extremely cautious of bringing forward criminal prosecutions in the inferior courts as it could take many months for their expenses to be reimbursed.[58] The cost of criminal prosecutions in the High Court and circuit courts, and criminal prosecutions involving juries in sheriff courts, were met by the crown, but those which were dealt with in a summary manner (without juries and formal written pleadings) in burgh courts were to be defrayed from local funds which were often inadequate. As a result, local burgh procurators and magistrates prosecuted only a small number of crimes so as not to burden the public purse with legal costs.[59] Indeed, the capacity of many burghs to finance criminal prosecutions in the late eighteenth and early nineteenth centuries became especially strained given the heavy tax burden that had been imposed on them to finance the Napoleonic Wars. This was a frequent gripe for Scottish authorities and a significant reason why a number of them started to look seriously at finding new ways of financing municipal services in this period, as is explored further below.[60] In a number of instances, legal costs had to be met by men of property through voluntary subscription due to a paucity of burgh funds.[61] In 1784, a 'Memorandum from Glasgow Magistrates relative to the Expense of Maintaining and Trying Criminals when Committed to Prison on different Warrants from Different Judges', revealed that:

---

[56]   In Scotland, private criminal prosecutions were extremely rare. William Reid, 'The Origins of the Office of Procurator Fiscal in Scotland', *Juridical Review*, 10 (1965): pp. 154–60. See also Crowther, 'Crime, Prosecution and Mercy', p. 226.

[57]   In some burghs, procurators fiscal received an allowance with further remuneration from fees. 'Eleventh Report of the Commissioners Appointed for Inquiring into the Duties, Salaries, Fees and Enrolments, of the Several Officers, Clerks, and Ministers of Justice, of the Courts in Scotland. Burgh Courts', *BPP*, 1822 (558), VIII.117, p. 69.

[58]   'Fourth Report by Her Majesty's Law Commissioners, Scotland, 1839', pp. 251–339. For the role of money in shaping prosecutions and the administration of justice in England, see Landau, 'The Trading Justice's Trade', pp. 46–70.

[59]   See complaints from citizens about this in the *Dundee, Perth and Cupar Advertiser*, 29 December 1815 and 29 November 1816.

[60]   DI, BK/1/1/2/2: Kilmarnock Town Council Minute Book, 26 October 1796.

[61]   DI, BK/1/1/2/2: Kilmarnock Town Council Minute Book, 8 December 1801: The Council agreed that 'an association should be formed and a subscription raised for the prosecution of offenders within the town and parish'. A scheme was drawn up.

In Edinburgh the ordinary funds have proved inadequate and therefore a voluntary contribution has for sometime taken place under the direction of the Sheriff who raises from one to five shillings from most if not all the householders in the Town of Edinburgh including not only those within the royalty but also those in the suburbs.[62]

That money weighed heavily on the minds of local officials was illustrated in the 1830s by John Dunlop, Sheriff of Lanarkshire, who claimed that 'the burgh fiscal … in Paisley, has not a sufficient interest to burden his constituents with the expense of criminal prosecutions within the burgh, where no fine can be expected'.[63]

There were also legal, institutional and procedural constraints within burgh courts which kept the level of criminal prosecutions fairly low. Although burgh courts had the judicial authority to deal with many offences in an informal and summary manner, criminal prosecutions for more serious offences often had to be conducted according to formal criminal procedure.[64] In criminal cases before the Glasgow Burgh Court, procedure was, according to the 'Eleventh Report of Commissioners of the Courts in Scotland' in 1822, 'conducted in writing and under the superintendence of their [magistrates'] legal assessors'.[65] To pursue a criminal prosecution was expensive, convoluted and time-consuming: it consisted of a whole raft of written pleadings, including libels, summonses, warrants, declarations and proofs.[66] In an era when few towns had full-time paid watchmen or police officers, gathering evidence and following judicial procedure was a slow process which placed a great burden on the time of town officers, part-time constables, procurators and magistrates.[67] Many local

---

[62] Besides this, a sum amounting to £1,250 was raised annually from the citizens within the royalty called 'watchmoney' in order to defray the expense of a Town Guard. Glasgow City Archives (GCA), A2/1/1: Glasgow's Town Papers, Volume 1, 1726–1794, 27 April 1784.

[63] 'Fourth Report by Her Majesty's Law Commissioners, Scotland, 1839', pp. 251–339.

[64] There does not appear to have been obligatory national or uniform rules on criminal procedure in the local courts before the passing of the Act of Adjournal in 1827. The only definite forms of criminal procedure concerned jury trials in the High Court. See Farmer, *Criminal Law, Tradition and Legal Order*, p. 70. However, procedure was often governed by local charters and statutory laws. See 'Eleventh Report of the Commissioners Appointed for Inquiring into the Duties, Salaries, Fees and Enrolments', passim. Also, the inferior courts often adopted the legal guidelines of the higher courts for more serious crimes.

[65] 'Eleventh Report of the Commissioners Appointed for Inquiring into the Duties, Salaries, Fees and Enrolments', p. 56.

[66] 'Eleventh Report of the Commissioners Appointed for Inquiring into the Duties, Salaries, Fees and Enrolments', p. 9.

[67] The stages involved in bringing a criminal prosecution are revealed in PKCA, B59/26/2/1, Bundle 5 (1a): Burgh Court of Perth Criminal Processes, December 1797.

courts simply did not have the judicial capacity to dispose of a high number of criminal cases and infringements of local bye-laws in a fast, efficient and cost-effective manner. In 1807, a 'Committee of Police Commissioners' in Edinburgh revealed the difficulties involved in securing convictions prior to the establishment of the local police court in 1805:

> the great evil complained of in the old system under the magistrates was, that the most worthless vagabond, who could raise a few shillings to advocate his cause, might escape punishment; as it must be obvious that the funds, even of the city of Edinburgh, might have been inadequate to the daily and enormous expense attending the discussion of every suspension and advocation that might be offered of their sentences; and your committee are well informed, that the delay and trouble of bringing offenders to justice is reckoned the greatest error of the [1800] Glasgow Police Act.[68]

Coming just two years after the establishment of the local police court, their sentiments are likely to have been influenced by the raised expectations and standards that accompanied reform, as well as perhaps being advanced as a way to validate the change in judicial practice. Nonetheless, they highlighted the problems courts faced in dealing with crime and the changing mindset of civic leaders.

Similar concerns were echoed both in other parts of the country and in higher courts. As William Davie, Assessor of the Glasgow Police and Burgh Courts, informed the 1839–1840 Law Inquiry, there was an 'aversion to commit for trial, in order to avoid a higher punishment, unless the case is of serious amount, or attended with some aggravation'.[69] Even with serious cases, the challenges involved in securing convictions were major obstacles to legal action. In the higher courts – to which procurators and magistrates had to remit more serious cases – judges stringently adhered to formal process. In the early nineteenth century, between 10 and 20 per cent of cases before the justiciary courts were dropped because of irregularities and insufficient evidence – a costly disincentive to criminal prosecution for all but the strongest cases.[70]

The challenges involved in bringing offenders to justice were further exacerbated by the fact that magistrates were unpaid and, according to local council records, unable to devote sufficient time and energy to criminal justice matters.[71] Unlike London, where stipendiary magistrates were introduced in 1792, in Scottish towns they were all unpaid throughout the first half of the nineteenth century. This followed the long-held tradition of civic duty –

---

[68]   Edinburgh Central Library (ECL): *Reports of the Committee of Commissioners of Police and Minutes of General Meetings Thereto* (Edinburgh, 1807), 23 February 1807.

[69]   'Fourth Report by Her Majesty's Law Commissioners, Scotland, 1839', p. 327.

[70]   Farmer, *Criminal Law, Tradition and Legal Order*, p. 107.

[71]   GCA, C1/1/36: Glasgow Town Council Minute Book, 2 March 1779.

espoused most famously in Adam Ferguson's *History of Civil Society* (1767) – which endorsed public service as a key aspect of male virtue.[72] However, the ideal did not always match the reality. In 1779, in discussing whether or not to introduce police reform, councillors in Glasgow complained that

> it has of late years been found not only difficult to get respectable citizens to accept the office of magistracy, but also that those in that office cannot give that close attention to the police of the city for the detection of persons guilty of crimes and offences therein as is requisite.[73]

Most magistrates came from business backgrounds and in reality often could not give their full intention to hearing pleas, determining disputes and administering statutory and criminal laws in their local courts, as they admitted in the same council meeting.[74] Even if they could, there was the further problem of accommodating and paying for the maintenance of those in custody and prisoners. Gaol and bridewell accommodation was extremely limited in Scottish towns and greatly restricted magistrates' capacity to prosecute crime. In 1785, the magistrates in Glasgow highlighted this, complaining that 'it has hitherto been impracticable to put the law in execution for want of a proper place of confinement'.[75] A year earlier magistrates had drawn up a 'Memorandum Relative to the Expense of Trying Criminals' which emphasised not just the numerous steps that had to be taken to apprehend suspects and prepare cases for trial, but also the cost involved in maintaining prisoners whilst they awaited trial.[76] Not surprisingly, very few offenders convicted in burgh courts were imprisoned for long periods of time. Evidence presented to the 1839–1840 Law Inquiry revealed that it was rare for the convicted to be sent to gaol or bridewell for more than fourteen days.[77] The Glasgow burgh criminal court by this point

---

[72]   David G. Barrie, 'Police in Civil Society: Police, Enlightenment and Civic Virtue in Scotland, 1780–1833', *Urban History*, 37/1 (2010): pp. 45–65.

[73]   GCA, C1/1/36: Glasgow Town Council Minute Book, 2 March 1779.

[74]   Ibid.

[75]   R. Renwick, *Extracts from the Records of the Burgh of Glasgow, Volume VIII: 1781–95* (Glasgow, 1913), 29 June 1785, pp. 172–3. This was a common complaint to the 1839 Commission on the Law Courts. See, for example, 'Fourth Report by Her Majesty's Law Commissioners, Scotland, 1839', p. 303: William Alexander, Town Clerk of Peterhead, 'As we have no gaol in Peterhead … our magistrates not having the means of carrying their warrants into execution, do not hold a criminal court.'

[76]   GCA, A2/1/1: Glasgow Town's Papers, Volume 1, 1726–1794, 27 April 1784. Reports great expense in maintaining criminals either before or after trial, and in 'taking those steps which are necessary prior to the trial for apprehending criminals taking precognitions'.

[77]   'Fourth Report by Her Majesty's Law Commissioners, Scotland, 1839', pp. 251–314.

could imprison for up to six months,[78] but magistrates' powers of punishment in most other burghs were much more modest and rarely exercised in full.[79]

Underlying such constraints was the ethos of the early modern Scottish criminal justice system. As in other parts of the United Kingdom, it was not the intention of the legal system to prosecute all offences. Civic elites and the Scottish legal profession adopted a pragmatic approach to administering the law – increasing the number of criminal prosecutions and taking a tough stance against offenders during periods of heightened unrest, and adopting a more informal, lenient approach when anxiety waned and social relations improved.[80] This was a system of discretionary justice that procurators, judges, magistrates and sheriffs valued as it was cost-effective, strengthened their control over the judicial system and society, and helped buttress their status and position as governing men.[81] However, it was also a system that was unsuited to rapidly expanding urban centres and the needs and interests of commercial elites. As the next section examines, the expanding business classes were looking for greater certainty of prosecution and legal protection in the late eighteenth century in response to wider intellectual, social and economic changes.

III. Towards Reform, c.1780 to 1833

Unsurprisingly, it was in the larger, expanding towns such as Glasgow that discontent first emerged about the level of protection for private property that the burgh courts provided. Much of this emanated from those in business and commercial circles who were on the fringes of, or were excluded from, council office and who used the issue of law and order to discredit the self-selecting nature of civic representation and magistrates' handling of municipal affairs.[82] In Glasgow, local landowners, burgesses and the Merchants and Trades Houses – who represented the city's mercantile and manufacturing classes – conducted a sustained campaign for the introduction of a police system in the late eighteenth century.[83] This was prompted in part by a perceived rise in property crime

---

[78]   However, this was very unusual, with a mere 131 people convicted in Glasgow's burgh court between 1833 and 1835 being imprisoned for between three and six months. Ibid., pp. 321–4.

[79]   Some had the power to, or dealt only with cases for which they could, imprison for a week or two. See burgh of Annan, ibid., p. 253.

[80]   Crowther, 'Crime, Prosecution and Mercy', pp. 233–5.

[81]   Ibid.

[82]   For more on this, see Barrie, *Police in the Age of Improvement*, chs 3 and 5.

[83]   See, for instance, GCA, T-TH1/1/8: Trades' House Minutes, 17 April 1789 and 15 October 1789; GCA, T-MH/1/3: Merchants' House Minute Book, 11 February 1790; GCA, C2/1/1: 'Answers to Proposals of Committee of Heritors and Burgesses relating to Police Bill', 19 February 1790, pp. 174–90; and GCA, C1/1/38: Glasgow Town Council Minute Book, 18 August 1790.

and urban disorder,[84] but it was also indicative of the business communities' growing preoccupation with better protecting commercial transactions and private property. Glasgow was a thriving centre of commerce and industry in the late eighteenth century and its business leaders were seeking to introduce new ways to safeguard their interests. Testament to this was the establishment in the city of the world's first Chamber of Commerce in 1783, which, interestingly, was pioneered by the famous London police magistrate and reformer, Patrick Colquhoun, who served as Lord Provost (chief magistrate) in his native Glasgow between 1782 and 1783.[85] However, business leaders could not agree upon who should control the new police model: the emerging middle ranks and trade incorporations refused to concede further power and money to unaccountable councillors; and civic leaders resisted the establishment of an independently elected police commission that would rival their own authority. As magistrates noted, giving commissioners police powers would be 'of most dangerous consequence to the liberty of the citizens ... [as it would equate to] creating forty-eight new magistrates with a jurisdiction equal if not superior to what the present magistrates have right to exercise'.[86] What was at stake, however, was the principle of magistrates' authority as guardians of law and order. As in other Scottish cities, political infighting among men of property would paralyse police reform for many years.[87]

Nonetheless, the discourse which emanated from the ensuing debates highlighted that businessmen were increasingly looking to seek legal redress through criminal prosecution and no longer perceived existing arrangements to safeguard their needs.[88] In discussing a 1792 Police Bill, the business leaders of the Trades' House requested that a clause be inserted into the bill that made provisions for the refund of expenses from successful private prosecutions. It argued that new ways were needed to ensure that more public resources would be made available to prosecute offenders to guarantee that delinquents would

---

[84] In 1793, magistrates claimed that 'street robberies, shop and house breakings, thefts and other crimes are more frequently committed there in proportion to the extent of the place, than in any other city in Britain'. GCA, A2/2/1: Process Papers of the City of Glasgow before the Court of Session, 11 April 1793: 'Answers for James Montgomery and the Deacon Convenor and the Trades' House of Glasgow to the Petition given in the Name of the said Trades' House, but without their Authority', pp. 1–2.

[85] For more on this, see David G. Barrie, 'Patrick Colquhoun, the Scottish Enlightenment and Police Reform in Glasgow in the Late Eighteenth Century', *Crime, Histoire & Sociétés/Crime, History & Societies*, 12/2 (2008): pp. 59–79.

[86] GCA, 'Answers to Proposals of Committee of Heritors and Burgesses relating to Police Bill', p. 190.

[87] Barrie, *Police in the Age of Improvement*, ch. 5.

[88] In 1801, councillors in Kilmarnock resolved that 'an association should be formed and a subscription raised for the prosecution of offenders within the town and parish' in response to a perceived rise in crime. DI, BK/1/1/2/2: Kilmarnock Town Council Minute Book, 8 December 1801.

'be brought to justice upon the public expense'.[89] It complained that 'inhabitants have in past times been put frequently to great trouble and expense in searching for goods stolen from them and in bringing delinquents to punishment'.[90] In the ensuing debates, the merits of 'preventative policing' were espoused – which, significantly, was deemed to involve bringing more offenders before the courts to deter others.[91] It was symbolic of a wider intellectual change in favour of certainty of prosecution that would come to define the modern criminal justice system which evolved in the nineteenth century.

Similar views were expressed in other towns and resulted in new approaches. Aberdeen's 1795 Improvement Act made provisions for 'defraying the charges of apprehending, prosecution and subsisting criminals'.[92] Glasgow, however, did not acquire a police act until 1800 – and even then, it retained its existing burgh court structure with fairly limited summary powers. More serious criminal cases were tried in the Town Clerk's Office (the burgh court) according to formal criminal procedure. Minor offences – usually involving those in which small fines of 1s. to 5s. or short prison sentences, were likely to be imposed – were dispensed with in a summary manner in the police office.[93] However, in the subsequent local police acts of 1807 and 1821 the police office's summary powers were expanded significantly and it quickly established itself as the busiest centre of justice in Scotland.[94] Increasingly, the term 'police office' gave way to 'police court',

---

[89]   In discussing a proposed police bill in 1792, the Trades' House called for the 'Intendent of Police' to take cognisance of the investigation and detection of crime at the public's expense, provided that when stolen goods were recovered and criminals brought to justice, the owner should pay towards expenses a sum not exceeding 5 per cent of the goods' value. GCA, T-TH1/1/8: Trades' House Minutes, 23 March 1792.

[90]   Ibid. The difficulties local traders faced were highlighted in 1785 when two merchants in Port Glasgow unsuccessfully petitioned the Glasgow Chamber of Commerce requesting that financial assistance be given to victims intent upon pursuing a criminal case against suspects: GCA, TD1670/4/series: Glasgow Chamber of Commerce Correspondence and Other Papers, letter dated 8 July 1785.

[91]   For the influence of this on the framing of the 1805 Edinburgh Police Act, see *Edinburgh Advertiser*, 27 August 1805.

[92]   42 George III, cap. 47.

[93]   Glasgow University Library (GUL), Special Collections: *Vindication of the Observations on the Heads of a New Police Bill for the City of Glasgow: and on the Report of the Commissioners of Police, to the Magistrates and Town Council, respecting the proposed alterations to the Present Law* (Glasgow, 1807), p. 4.

[94]   The 1800 Glasgow Police Act stated that magistrates' existing judicial rights were to be safeguarded, but made no specific reference to summary justice. The 1807 Glasgow Police Act stated that all prosecutions against police offences were to be carried out in a summary manner, so long as punishment did not exceed 30 days' confinement in bridewell and/or a fine of more than £2. The Glasgow Police Act, 1807 (47 George III, cap. 29), clause 56. The 1821 Glasgow Police Act extended summary powers to cover fines up to £5 and imprisonment to 60 days, which ensured that a greater range of offences were covered by the police courts' jurisdiction. GUL, Special Collections: John Scott, *Abstract of the*

highlighting the court's growing role and status in civic affairs.[95] Its capacity to deal with volume of cases was further facilitated by the appointment in 1804 of advocate James Reddie to the position of town clerk. Unlike clerks in other towns, he was to devote his energies full-time to municipal affairs, which was symbolic of the strengthening resolve of the civic elite – defined here as councillors, magistrates and town procurators – to improve the local burgh machine's capacity to deal with criminal affairs.[96]

Similar initiatives were introduced in other large towns and were underpinned, and to some extent fuelled, by press reports of a perceived rise in property crime and a growing determination among men of property to protect their own interests. In 1805, manufacturers in Dundee successfully prosecuted 18 offenders in the burgh criminal court for stealing and resetting linen. According to the local newspaper, the convictions had encouraged the manufacturers 'not to compromise with such criminals in the future'.[97] Instead, they resolved to form an association and create a fund for the protection and punishment of all offenders.[98] This was indicative of a growing intolerance among employers to the customary practice of workers appropriating goods as part of their income.[99] What was once widely tolerated as a perquisite was from the late eighteenth century onwards increasingly criminalised.[100] This tougher stance, and reformulation of employer–employee relations, on the part of the former not only symbolised a slackening of ties between worker and

Police Acts of Glasgow, with a Summary of the Powers and Duties of Special Constables (Glasgow, 1821), p. 67.

[95] Interestingly, the 1800 Glasgow Police Act – or, indeed, the subsequent acts of 1807 and 1821 – made no specific reference to the establishment of a police office or police court. There were, however, a few contemporary sources that referred to these. For example, GUL: *Report of the Committees appointed by the Merchant Company, Incorporations, and Several other Public Bodies in the City of Edinburgh, to Consider the Effects of the Act Lately Passed for Regulating the Police of the Said City* (Edinburgh, 1806), pp. 16–18; and Scott, *Abstract of the Police Acts of Glasgow*, p. 29. As in many other towns, the police court evolved from police legislation and the expansion in summary powers which local police acts conferred upon magistrates.

[96] The business of the burgh court also soared, especially in the post-Napoleonic period amidst growing concerns with crime and disorder. The number of criminal cases prosecuted by the fiscal rose from 464 in 1812 to 1,028 in 1820, with a further 90 cases being remitted for trial in the High Court of Justiciary. 'Eleventh Report of the Commissioners Appointed for Inquiring into the Duties, Salaries, Fees and Enrolments', p. 56. However, their role in handling criminal cases diminished considerably in the 1820s as the powers of the police court were extended under the 1821 Glasgow Police Act and a resident sheriff was acquired to serve the city. Maver, 'The Guardianship of the Community', pp. 254–5.

[97] *Dundee, Perth and Cupar Advertiser*, 12 July 1805.

[98] Ibid.

[99] For more on this, see Christopher A. Whatley, 'The Experience of Work', in T.M. Devine and Rosalind Mitchison (eds), *People and Society in Scotland, Volume I: 1760–1830* (Edinburgh, 1988), pp. 234–9.

[100] Barrie, 'Urban Order in Georgian Dundee', pp. 228–34.

manufacturers in the industrial city,[101] it also suggested a growing unwillingness to settle cases outwith the judicial system. Men of property were now looking to the courts rather than informal sanctions as a means of deterring and punishing offenders and validating their position for future employment relations.

This collective action on the part of employers was followed by a plethora of voluntary law enforcement initiatives by manufacturers, merchants and shopkeepers to better safeguard shipping interests and commercial goods in the economically depressed post-Napoleonic years, as fears of a rise in property crime escalated.[102] Criticism of magisterial management of civic affairs became more frequent from men who could not access representation on the town council. These highlighted the concerns of a new group of middle-rank men about their experience of justice as complainers and their capacity to rely on the law to reflect their concerns. According to many reports and letters in the *Dundee Advertiser*, it was extremely difficult to secure a criminal prosecution in the burgh.[103] The cries for change were firmly embedded in, and linked to, growing demands for a new system of police administration, which included municipal provisions funded by a wider group of urban inhabitants for lighting, paving and cleaning, as well as the appointment of full-time watch forces to relieve middle-class male householders of their traditional obligation of watching and warding. As in Glasgow and Edinburgh, there was a sustained and bitter campaign by the middle ranks and the local press for the establishment of a directly elected police commission with tax-raising powers to oversee the management of a wide array of municipal services, including a police force and court.[104] Middle-class media spoke for their readership, echoing their self-interested preoccupations with certain types of crimes and victims. As the *Dundee Advertiser* commented in 1815: 'Some of the most respectable and inoffensive citizens have been knocked-down, cruelly beat, and plundered, at an early hour in the evening, and sometimes at their own doors.'[105] Middle-rank concerns highlighted a perceived rise in property crime, theft from the local port, and public safety fears that affected them.[106] In 1823, magistrates called for the introduction of a local police act with powers for a summary police court on the basis that:

---

[101]   Emsley makes a similar point in relation to England in the late eighteenth century: Clive Emsley, *Crime and Society in England, 1750–1900*, 2nd edn (London, 1996), p. 32.

[102]   See, for instance, *Dundee, Perth and Cupar Advertiser*, 29 December 1815; 24 May 1816; 22 November 1816; 14 November 1817; 8 December 1820; and 7 November 1822.

[103]   *Dundee, Perth and Cupar Advertiser*, 29 November 1816 and 21 May 1819.

[104]   As has been examined elsewhere, the *Dundee Advertiser* used the issue of law and order to discredit the unpopular, self-selecting town council's handling of civic affairs. Barrie, 'Urban Order in Georgian Dundee', p. 233.

[105]   *Dundee, Perth and Cupar Advertiser*, 29 December 1815.

[106]   Interestingly, most law enforcement initiatives were established by merchants and shopkeepers to protect their own property rather than the people of the burgh as a whole. Some employed watchmen to sleep in their shops, whilst others erected iron bars to stem

the increase in crime in the burgh and its suburbs rises in a great degree from the inefficiency of the police; from the want of power in the local magistracy for the suitable punishment of the lesser crimes; and from the expense and delay attendant on the judicial procedure. … It would tend very much to the advantage of the burgh and the surrounding district, and to the preservation of peace and good order, if an Act of Parliament were passed for removing the evils before referred to, and more especially for establishing a Court of Police, having the powers necessary for the suitable and summary punishment of the lesser crimes, and appointing Commissioners for raising and applying the funds necessary for the proper watching, paving, cleansing and lighting the burgh and suburbs.[107]

This view was typical of the way in which the justification for reform was portrayed as being synonymous with the common good. The following year, the 1824 Dundee Police Act made provision for both an elected police commission and a police court.

The introduction of police courts in Glasgow (1800), Edinburgh (1805) and Dundee (1824) was matched by similar developments in other burghs, including Paisley (1806), Greenock (1810), Calton (1819) and Aberdeen (1829). The nature of adoption, however, was not uniform. Some cities, such as Glasgow and Aberdeen, established new police courts which were distinct from, but continued to co-exist with, burgh criminal courts, with the latter playing an increasingly restricted role in criminal affairs. The judicial lines between them were often blurred – with the seriousness of the offence determining whether a case was dealt with in the police court or in the burgh court, the latter of which had stronger powers of punishment in some of the larger burghs such as Glasgow. Most police courts could imprison for between 30 and 60 days, depending on the terms of the local police act, which, although representing an increase in sentencing power in most towns, was shorter than the lengths of imprisonment that magistrates in the most populous cities had traditionally had at their disposal.[108] In other towns, including Leith and Inverness, burgh criminal courts assumed responsibility for prosecuting and punishing breaches of statutory regulations enshrined in police legislation. Such burgh courts, however, were increasingly referred to in contemporary reports as, and effectively became, police courts given that the bulk of their day-to-day business, judicial powers and, in some cases, authority was constituted under police legislation.[109] By the 1830s, police courts had effectively replaced burgh courts as the main centres of urban justice in all of the major Scottish cities (see Figure 1.1).[110]

---

the growing tide of burglaries. Moreover, a few years later a harbour watch was established to protect shipping interests. See *Dundee, Perth and Cupar Advertiser*, 29 November 1816 and 4 March 1824.

[107] DCA: Dundee Council Minute Book, vol. XVII (1821–1824), 7 August 1823.
[108] 'Fourth Report by Her Majesty's Law Commissioners, Scotland, 1839', pp. 321–4.
[109] Ibid., pp. 283 & 296.
[110] See the evidence and criminal returns presented to ibid., pp. 252–339.

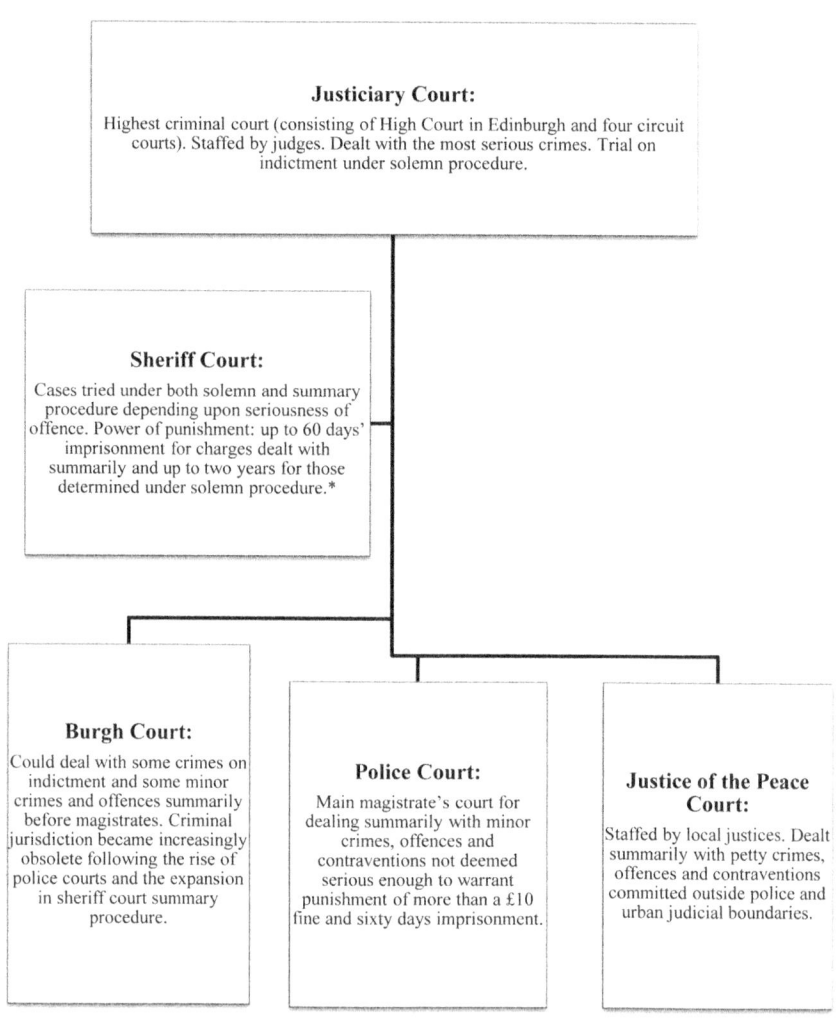

Justiciary Court:

Highest criminal court (consisting of High Court in Edinburgh and four circuit courts). Staffed by judges. Dealt with the most serious crimes. Trial on indictment under solemn procedure.

Sheriff Court:

Cases tried under both solemn and summary procedure depending upon seriousness of offence. Power of punishment: up to 60 days' imprisonment for charges dealt with summarily and up to two years for those determined under solemn procedure.*

Burgh Court:

Could deal with some crimes on indictment and some minor crimes and offences summarily before magistrates. Criminal jurisdiction became increasingly obsolete following the rise of police courts and the expansion in sheriff court summary procedure.

Police Court:

Main magistrate's court for dealing summarily with minor crimes, offences and contraventions not deemed serious enough to warrant punishment of more than a £10 fine and sixty days imprisonment.

Justice of the Peace Court:

Staffed by local justices. Dealt summarily with petty crimes, offences and contraventions committed outside police and urban judicial boundaries.

Figure 1.1   Hierarchy of Scotland's Main Criminal Courts, c.1833

*   Based on information presented to 'First Report of the Commissioners Appointed to Inquire into the Courts of Law in Scotland, together with Minutes of Evidence', 1868–1869 (4125), XXV.29, p. 7. Sentencing powers in the first half of the century were subject to local variation.

In some towns, the case for reform was given added stimulus by the Act of Adjournal in 1827.[111] Introduced by central government, and applying to the whole of Scotland, the statute standardised rules for the trial of petty delinquencies in sheriff and burgh courts, obliged procurators to follow detailed and costly legal procedure and set a minimum period between citation and trial.[112] Under the Act, all cases tried in burgh criminal courts were to be under criminal libel, which further increased the time, trouble and expense involved in prosecuting offenders. As D.D. Black, Town Clerk of Brechin, noted in 1835:

> The necessary expenses of trying petty offenders under the Act of Adjournal is so heavy that the magistrates acting under it find themselves in the awkward situation of either awarding a fine disproportionate to the crime or to the circumstances of the offender, or of charging the town's funds with pounds of expense incurred in fining a criminal a few shillings. ... so many questions have been mooted since the Act ... came into operation, that the magistrates of Brechin have latterly declined trying almost any case: and for the last two years no criminal cause has been tried in the Bailie [Magistrate] Court of Brechin, except the paltry summary cases alluded to.[113]

Indeed, the 1829 Aberdeen Police Act introduced clauses regarding the creation and constitution of its police court. In the words of A. Cadenhead, the local fiscal, this was for the express purpose of circumventing the 'tedious nature of procedure pointed out by the Act of Adjournal'.[114]

However, there were other motivations behind reform. In all the major urban centres which established a new court structure, the justification was presented by public men as moral, economic, civic and personal, often intertwined. Much of the discourse surrounding reform centred on the benefits it would bring to whole communities and the better ordering of the built environment. Magistrates argued that they needed greater powers to enforce new, and in many cases, existing police regulations that sought to safeguard and improve the physical structure and public health of towns. Many burghs had acquired improvement legislation in the late eighteenth century, but few had made provision for the more effectual disposal of cases in a summary manner.[115] Magistrates frequently complained about the

---

[111] Act of Adjournal, 1827 (6 George IV, cap. 23).

[112] Ibid. Under this, libels had to be drawn as far as possible in the form of criminal letters. This meant that warrants and petitions had to be served, precognitions taken, witnesses cited and proofs written – all of which combined to delay and increase the cost in bringing forward criminal prosecutions.

[113] 'Fourth Report by Her Majesty's Law Commissioners, Scotland, 1839', p. 257.

[114] Ibid., pp. 252–3.

[115] John McGowan, *Policing the Metropolis of Scotland: A History of the Police and Systems of Police in Edinburgh and Edinburghshire, 1770–1833* (Musselburgh, 2010), pp. 58–63.

problems involved in keeping streets lit, clean and safe without a quick and efficient mechanism for disposing of offenders.[116] Establishing police courts to ensure that offenders who breached municipal bye-laws would be summonsed before magistrates was therefore presented as a response to the limitations of the existing municipal machine and its capacity to meet the raised expectations of comfort, safety and security of civic leaders in the early 1800s.

There was a degree of paternalistic moral projection about the benefits of summary justice for offenders. Local justices argued that it would reduce the likelihood that those who were accused of crimes would suffer hardship by being confined in gaols while they awaited trial. Archibald Alison, Sheriff of Lanarkshire, captured this sentiment in 1833:

> Jury trial is of inestimable importance in all political cases, and in all cases whatever where a grave sentence, decisive of the prisoner's fate ... is to be pronounced; but in small cases, where imprisonment only, or fine, is to be the result ... it may well admit of doubt, whether a privilege introduced for his benefit does not too often practically become an aggravation of his sufferings.[117]

Civic authorities presented the benefits of summary justice as a moral responsibility in their role as civic fathers and protectors of the weak.[118]

However, underlying the rhetoric of the common good were middle-class concerns about the urban poor, the industrial 'godless' masses and the financial implications of trying to control them. The first few decades of the nineteenth century were an era of great demographic change, strained industrial and social relations, cyclical high unemployment and escalating concerns with crime.[119]

---

[116] Police regulations had to be frequently reiterated, but abuses continued to go unchecked. For a council's effort to enforce police regulations and the problems encountered, see DCA: Dundee Council Minute Book, 24 May 1770 and 25 May 1803. In 1819, the Council sought to address the problem by appointing a committee 'to superintend the police of the town in so far as may be requisite for directing legal proceedings to be taken for preventing and removing nuisances and prosecuting persons guilty of breaches of the peace or other crimes committed within the burgh'. DCA: Dundee Council Minute Book, 11 August 1819.

[117] Archibald Alison, *The Principles of the Criminal Law of Scotland* (Edinburgh, 1833), p. 58.

[118] William Davie, Assessor of the Glasgow Police and Burgh Courts, argued for an extension in summary procedure on the basis that the speed at which cases were disposed reduced the likelihood that the accused would suffer great hardship. He also argued it would make it easier to ensure witnesses attended court. 'Fourth Report by Her Majesty's Law Commissioners, Scotland, 1839', p. 325.

[119] For more on this, see W.W.J. Knox and A. McKinlay, 'Crime, Protest and Policing in Nineteenth-Century Scotland', in Griffiths and Morton (eds), *A History of Everyday Life in Scotland, 1800 to 1900*, pp. 196–224; Barrie, *Police in the Age of Improvement*, pp. 96–104; Christopher A. Whatley, 'Roots of 1790s Radicalism: Reviewing the Economic

The transition to a free-market, capitalist economy resulted in widespread misery for many workers. Scottish urban economies simply did not have the capacity to absorb in regular employment the thousands of migrants who poured into cities at a relentless rate.[120] Living standards for many of the poorest deteriorated markedly.[121] Outbreaks of political radicalism and popular protest became more common and crime was widely reported and perceived to be on the increase.[122] The number of cases prosecuted in the High Court of Justiciary rose steadily up to the 1840s, although whether this represented a real increase in crime or simply a growing willingness to prosecute is impossible to say, such are the vagaries of criminal statistics.[123] What is more certain is that middle-rank perceptions of crime and the urban poor had changed. Both were increasingly perceived as a threat to social stability unless disciplined and controlled. In *Commentaries on the Laws of Scotland Respecting Crimes* (1844), Baron Hume linked calls for the expansion of summary procedure specifically with wider societal efforts to discipline unruly urban populations: 'Such a privilege of sharp and summary coercion had been thought material to the quiet of those places, and the safety of their inhabitants, otherwise so much exposed to the evil practices of the many dissolute and profligate persons, who have their haunt and resort in towns.'[124]

Other commentators attributed the need for summary justice more directly to industrial and commercial expansion and the growing needs of the employing and propertied classes. In the 1839 'Fourth Report by Her Majesty's Law Commissioners' – one of a series of law reports commissioned by the government over the course of the nineteenth century to look into the workings of the Scottish courts and legal system – George Thompson, Town Clerk, and Thomas Lees, Procurator Fiscal, both of Musselburgh, called for magistrates to be given additional summary powers 'because from the increase of

---

and Social Background', in Bob Harris (ed.), *Scotland in the Age of the French Revolution* (Edinburgh, 2005), pp. 23–48; W.W.J. Knox, *Industrial Nation: Work, Culture and Society in Scotland, 1800–Present* (Edinburgh, 1999), passim; Whatley, 'The Experience of Work', pp. 234–9; W. Hamish Fraser, 'Patterns of Protest', in Devine and Mitchison (eds), *People and Society in Scotland, Volume I*, pp. 280–81; and W. Hamish Fraser, *Conflict and Class: Scottish Workers, 1700–1838* (Edinburgh, 1988), p. 102.

[120]   T.M. Devine, 'Urbanisation', in Devine and Mitchison (eds), *People and Society in Scotland, Volume I*, pp. 27–52; and Devine, *The Scottish Nation*, pp. 220–21.

[121]   N. Murray, *The Scottish Handloom Weavers, 1790–1850: A Social History* (Edinburgh, 1978), pp. 89–93.

[122]   For radicalism during the French Revolution, see Harris (ed.), *Scotland in the Age of the French Revolution*; and Bob Harris, 'Scottish–English Connections in the British Radicalism of the 1790s', in T.C. Smout (ed.), *Anglo-Scottish Relations from 1603 to 1900* (Oxford, 2005), pp. 189–212.

[123]   See Chapter 5 for more discussion on this issue.

[124]   Baron David Hume, *Commentaries on the Law of Scotland Respecting Crimes*, 2nd edn (Edinburgh, 1844), p. 149.

manufactories in the burgh, instances of dissipation and rioting are considerably on the increase'.[125] In the flourishing port of Greenock, magistrates acquired additional police powers largely to safeguard private property and commercial transactions. As the local fiscal reported: 'it will at once be perceived that the Acts in which the police clauses have been introduced have been constructed more with a view to advance the commercial interests of the town than to frame a comprehensive code of Police Law.'[126] This was very much in line with Scottish Enlightenment rhetoric, much of which was preoccupied with how jurisprudence could be employed to better safeguard private property and economic transactions.[127] Indeed, in legal and government circles, there was a growing body of opinion that saw economic progress, industrial expansion and crime as going hand in hand.[128]

Urban, industrial expansion not only brought changing work practices, strained social and employer–employee relations and changing middle-rank perceptions of the poor,[129] it also weakened the influence that church courts had over large sections of society.[130] These courts continued throughout the nineteenth century to impose godly discipline on congregationalists,[131] but growing numbers of the urban population were effectively excluded from religious control due to demographic, fiscal and cultural pressures. In 1792, Robert Heron, on a visit to Glasgow, noted that the city had lost 'much of its ancient piety'.[132] An unprecedented rate of urban expansion in the first few decades of the nineteenth century exacerbated the problem. In 1827, the governors of the Glasgow City Mission reported the following in their annual report:

> No one passing along our streets on the Lord's Day, and seeing the crowds of
> people going to and from the places of public worship, would ever imagine that

---

[125]   'Fourth Report by Her Majesty's Law Commissioners, Scotland, 1839', p. 296.

[126]   Ibid., p. 399.

[127]   For more on this, see Barrie, 'Police in Civil Society', pp. 45–65.

[128]   As Frederick Hill, Inspector of Prisons in Scotland, noted in 1850: 'there cannot, of course, be an increase in wealth in the country without an increase, other things being equal, in the temptations to crime.' Frederick C. Hill, *Crime: Its Amount, Causes and Remedies* (London, 1853), p. 134. For more on property crime in industrial society, see Knox and McKinlay, 'Crime, Protest and Policing', pp. 199–206.

[129]   Knox, *Industrial Nation*, passim; and Whatley, 'The Experience of Work', pp. 234–9.

[130]   Leneman and Mitchison, *Sin in the City*. It continued, however, to have a fairly strong influence in rural areas. See Rosalind Mitchison and Leah Leneman, *Girls in Trouble: Sexuality and Social Control in Rural Scotland 1660–1780* (Edinburgh, 1998).

[131]   Brown, 'Beliefs and Religions', pp. 127–9.

[132]   Robert Heron, *Observations Made in a Journey through the Western Counties of Scotland in the Autumn of 1792* (2 vols, Perth, 1793), vol. II, p. 381. Cited in Whatley, *Scottish Society*, p. 283. See also Callum G. Brown, *The Social History of Religion in Scotland Since 1730* (London, 1987), pp. 141–2.

there were such a vast multitude concealed in the shade, who never enter the house of God, or consider that the Sabbath ought to be observed, and kept holy.[133]

By mid-century, only one in five Glaswegians of all religious denominations attended church in Glasgow.[134]

There was a complex pattern of factors behind church attendance that was by no means determined simply by class. Church membership and religious adherence transcended social boundaries and continued to be an important signifier of both working- and middle-class identity.[135] Nonetheless, poverty and social background were among the most important factors affecting the composition of the city's plethora of churches. A significant proportion of the urban masses was unable to attend church due to high pew rents and the failure of church provision to keep pace with population growth.[136] Moreover, church courts, according to MacLaren, discriminated against the urban poor and labouring/migrant population, imposing a foreign set of cultural and moral values that alienated socially disadvantaged groups from organised religion.[137] Church attendance, of course, was not the only way that churches kept watch over people: in time, they would develop social groups and leisure activities and work with police courts in the maintenance of moral standards as we explore in Chapter 5 of Volume 2. But, during the first phase of industrial expansion in the early nineteenth century, the churches' hold over the public morality and behaviour of large sections of the industrial masses in the early nineteenth century was eroding. It would leave a vacuum which the police and police courts would attempt to fill.

The remit of police court business would come to tackle not just many of the problems church courts were facing in attempting to impose discipline but also the challenges of securing convictions in higher courts. Expanding the capacity of summary justice through police courts meant that urban populations could be more effectively controlled than was possible in higher courts where formal legal procedure often had to be followed. The fact that police courts would be

---

[133]   Glasgow City Mission, *First Annual Report* (Glasgow, 1827).

[134]   Peter Hillis, 'The Barony and the Churches of Nineteenth-Century Glasgow', *Journal of Religious History*, 33/3 (2009): p. 304.

[135]   Ibid., pp. 301–27. Moreover, Callum Brown talks about the continued importance of religion for the working classes, especially the skilled working class with aspirations of social advancement. Callum G. Brown, 'Religion, Class and Church Growth', in W. Hamish Fraser and R.J. Morris (eds), *People and Society in Scotland, Volume II: 1830–1914* (Edinburgh, 1990), pp. 310–35.

[136]   Brown, *The Social History of Religion in Scotland*, pp. 141–2.

[137]   A. Allan MacLaren, *Religion and Social Class: The Disruption Years in Aberdeen* (London, 1974), passim; and A. Allan MacLaren, 'Class Formation and Class Fractions: The Aberdeen Bourgeoisie, 1836–50', in George Gordon and Brian Dicks (eds), *Scottish Urban History* (Aberdeen, 1983), pp. 112–29. For a summary of the challenge to MacLaren's contention of working-class alienation to the churches, see Brown, *The Social History of Religion*, pp. 109–11, 148–51 & 218–20.

relatively unencumbered by old rules, traditions and legal structures greatly extended magistrates' capacity to regulate the behaviour and morality of those who came before it, as Chapter 2 explores further. The absence of formal, written pleas in police court proceedings was especially attractive for magistrates when it came to dealing with vagrancy. This was arguably the biggest problem civic leaders faced in Scotland's rapidly expanding urban centres, as changing farming practices and industrial expansion combined to push and pull migrants to nearby towns and cities on an unprecedented scale. Summary justice in police courts was not only a fairly cost-effective way of dealing with the urban poor, it also allowed for 'suspicious characters' – loosely defined to cover anyone found in the street who could not give a satisfactory account for themselves – to be apprehended without any evidence that they had committed an offence. This was a major reason behind the introduction of Edinburgh's police court and, why, as the next chapter examines, the court's jurisdiction was criticised for vesting too much power in police hands.[138] The *Scots Magazine* in 1803, in discussing the motivation behind what would become the Edinburgh Police Act, listed the desire to prevent the practice of common begging, to prevent all offences against the police and good order and 'to establish an early method of bringing to trial delinquents in these particulars'.[139] Similarly, in 1818, magistrates in Calton acquired statutory police powers which included provision for a police court not long after issuing a proclamation against begging and erecting stocks 'in order to prevent Irish and other disorderly persons from going about'.[140] As Chapter 6 of Volume 2 explores further, it was an indication of the discrimination that the Irish would face from the police and the courts as the first half of the century progressed, as civic leaders sought to prevent Irish migrants becoming a burden on charities and acquiring a legal entitlement to poor relief.

Fiscal matters were also extremely important to the evolution of police courts. In many towns and counties, burgh court procurators were, until the mid-nineteenth century, paid fees on a case-by-case basis rather than an annual salary. Some of the larger burghs from the late eighteenth century paid procurators a modest allowance with further remuneration from fees,[141] the merits of which were extensively debated by law commissioners and civic and rural leaders.[142]

---

[138] ECL, *Reports of the Committee of Commissioners of Police and Minutes of General Meetings Thereto*; and *Caledonian Mercury*, 18 July 1805.

[139] *Scots Magazine*, 1803, p. 218, discussing the Edinburgh Police Bill as it was at that time.

[140] Superintendent John Ord, 'The Story of the Burgh of Calton', *East Glasgow History*, 2010, http://www.glasgowhistory.co.uk/OrdsCalton.htm.

[141] 'Eleventh Report of the Commissioners Appointed for Inquiring into the Duties, Salaries, Fees and Enrolments', p. 69.

[142] In 1840, Aberdeen Town Council debated whether the fiscal and clerk ought to be paid by the revenue of court fines or rather from a fix salaried position. *Aberdeen Journal*, 15 January 1840. For rural discussions, see 'Fourth Report by Her Majesty's Law Commissioners, Scotland, 1839', pp. 168–80.

Under the local police legislation, though, senior police officials were often charged with bringing forward prosecutions for offences and contraventions in the public interest in police courts – the expense of which was to be defrayed by a new police tax levied on all property rated above a certain level (which varied throughout the country but was low enough to include the vast majority of the urban population).[143] As Chapters 3 and 4 explore more fully, burgh procurators in some towns continued to be paid fees for leading prosecutions (mainly criminal) in the police courts well into the nineteenth century, but monies that were recovered through police-led prosecutions were generally added to public funds. The latter approach made sound financial sense for burghs, likely explaining why the police increasingly became involved in bringing forward prosecutions as the century progressed. It kept legal costs to a minimum at a time when magistrates were seeking to expand the volume of summary prosecutions.[144] It also gave men of property greater legal protection and lessened their need to subscribe to associations to bring forward prosecutions that the public purse had been hitherto incapable of financing. Moreover, magistrates also recognised that greater summary powers would help to finance the provision of new municipal services given the increased revenues that would be accrued from imposing a greater volume of fines.[145] *Observations on a Glasgow Police Bill*, published anonymously in 1807, highlighted the financial advantages of reform, noting that

> it might be advisable to appoint a special Procurator Fiscal, for the purpose of prosecuting all offences against the Police Act, and that all fines and forfeitures arising from such offences, or inflicted on persons taken up by the Servants of the Police, shall, after defraying legal expenses, compose part of police funds. In this way the City funds would be relieved of a considerable annual expense, and the Procurator fiscal of the Burgh not so much overloaded with criminal business.[146]

---

[143] There was great variation throughout the country. Some burghs, such as Edinburgh, used police officials from the outset to bring forward prosecutions. In others, such as Glasgow, police involvement in criminal prosecutions came later. For the experience of Glasgow, see 'Second Report from the Select Committee on Police', *BPP*, 1852–1853 (715), XXXVI.161, p. 111.

[144] These included town officers who aided magistrates and procurators in investigating crime and preparing prosecutions. 'Eleventh Report of the Commissioners Appointed for Inquiring into the Duties, Salaries, Fees and Enrolments', p. 72.

[145] In Kilmarnock, police commissioners instructed the local police sergeant to bring before the magistrates those who ignore police regulations as considerable sums could be raised by fining the inhabitants as occurred in Glasgow and Paisley. DI, BK/AB/1/2A/1: Kilmarnock Police Commissioners Minute Book, 1809–1828; and DI, BK/AB/1/2A/2: Kilmarnock Police Commissioners Minute Book, 1828–1849, passim.

[146] GUL, Special Collections: *Observations on the Heads of a New Police Bill for the City of Glasgow; and on the Report of the Commissioners of Police, to the Magistrates and*

Indeed, a subsequent anonymous report claimed that in 1806 that £1,272 had been raised in petty fines in the police office, which it contended was nearly equal to the annual cost of criminal prosecutions.[147] In other towns, police fines were used to fund a wide array of civic services that had implications for urban order.[148] As in the eighteenth century, financial considerations and self-interest were never too far from the thoughts of magistrates and men of property when it came to administering the law.

Although the social composition of Scotland's cities was not uniform during the eighteenth and nineteenth century, and the business classes often clashed over the management of local government, in each case, different groups within the city had both shared and distinct interests. It is interesting, and perhaps revealing, that the issue of whether to establish police courts appears to have provoked little heated debate among men of property. Unlike the discord over whether or not to vest police management in new elected commissions, discussions on the proposed police courts were recorded sporadically in the local press and municipal records. Moreover, they tended to be submerged within wider, protracted political struggles between civic leaders, legal figures, and the rising mercantile and manufacturing elites on how the new model should be financed and managed and how much powers the courts should have.[149] As Chapter 2 examines further, there was often disagreement as to what form the structure should take and who should serve in it, as both had implications for the

---

Town Council respecting the Proposed Alterations of the Present Law (Glasgow, 1807), p. 19.

[147]   GUL, *A Vindication of the Observations on the Heads of a New Police Bill for the City of Glasgow*, p. 4.

[148]   The Dundee Police minutes reveal that £130, 12s., 2d. had been recovered in fines in the police court within its first year. The funds were to be disposed of in the following manner: £40 to the kirk session; £30 to the Dundee Lunatic Asylum; £20 to the Indigent Sick Society; £15, 12s., 2d. to the Dundee Infirmary; £10 to the Dundee Female Society; £10 to the Dundee Orphan Institution; and £5 to Henderson's Mortification. DCA, TC/PBM/1: Dundee Police Board Minute Book, 1824–1832, 20 June 1825.

[149]   The issue of defining the powers and limits of police court jurisdiction was always controversial. The Faculty of Procurators criticised certain clauses in an early draft of the Glasgow Police Bill. Clause 145 imposed a penalty of 60 days on persons 'doing or omitting to do any act, the doing or omission of which is punishable by general statute, or common law'. They pointed out that the passing of such a clause 'would necessarily, and seems intended to, have the effect of bringing into the Glasgow Court a great variety of matters not properly belonging to the department of a municipal police' (p. 9). Similar concerns were raised about clause 115, which stated that the magistrate would have jurisdiction 'to try any person accused or suspected of any crime or offence within, or beyond the city, which is punishable by general statute or common law, and is triable by the magistrates of the royal burgh' (p. 10). They claimed that 'if such powers are actually obtained, it will be no easy matter to define the limits of the jurisdiction of the police courts of Glasgow' (p. 10). GCA, DTC 14.2.34, no. 16: *Report by the Committee of the Faculty of Procurators upon the Glasgow Police Bill* (Glasgow, 1862), pp. 1–13.

power, status and influence of public men, but little about the desirability of the court itself. Discussion over the possible impact that police courts would have on the liberty of citizens was fairly short-lived and exposed more the political infighting that existed between civic and legal men than any genuine concern for the rights of the broader populace.[150] This not only suggests that civic leaders and the business and legal communities were in broad agreement as to the desirability of establishing a new court structure, but also indicates their shared concerns for property and the smooth operation of commerce. Men of business and the propertied wanted a court that could prosecute suspects quickly and manage their concerns about the industrial masses, and their aspirations about the growing urban environment, at little cost to themselves. Presenting the challenges that such men faced as civic rather than private ones was a convenient way of spreading the financial burden of law and order whilst strengthening arguments for greater intervention into the lives of urban inhabitants. Tellingly, the creation of a new machinery of police in Scottish towns was accompanied by a plethora of petitions from poorer wards requesting exemption from assessment. Hardship played an important role in this, but so too did the fact that police services such as lighting, cleansing and paving were perceived to be targeted mainly at the principal streets and affluent suburbs, whilst police manpower was directed principally at controlling the behaviour of poorer communities, as subsequent chapters will show.[151] Civic and police leaders had a narrow, self-serving concept of what constituted the common good when it came to the delivery of services, but an all-embracing, communal one when it came to paying for them.

---

[150]   On 4 February 1793, a 'Petition of John MacAusland, Deacon Convenor, and James Burns, Collector, for themselves, and in behalf of the other Members of the Convener of Trades' House in the City of Glasgow', outlined opposition to the latest magistrates' police bill. Among the reasons given were 'Because many parts of the bill are repugnant to the principle of civil liberty, and the laws of Scotland.' The petition continued: 'Because the citizens will be liable to be condemned to pecuniary penalties and imprisonment by the Magistrates, without liberty or appeal; and the inhabitants, in certain cases, may be seized without a warrant from a Judge, condemned by the evidence of the witness, and their goods distrained for the penalties, in a very oppressive manner.' Opposition, however, subsided when magistrates agreed in 1800 to vest control of police affairs in the hands of a directly elected police commission rather than themselves and burgess trading privileges in the extended police district were resolved.

[151]   For protests and petitions in Dundee, see DCA, TC/PBM/1: Dundee Police Board Minute Book, 1824–1832, 31 January and 2 February 1825. Similarly, the Directors of the Glasgow University Lying-in Hospital in 1837 complained that police provisions were aimed chiefly at the main streets of the town, neglecting poorer and more obscure districts. Sheila Oliver, 'The Administration of Urban Society in Scotland, 1800–50: With Special Reference to the Growth of Civic Government in Glasgow and its Suburbs', unpub. PhD thesis (University of Glasgow, 1995), pp. 113–14.

IV. Legislative Expansion, c.1833 to 1892

The police courts which were introduced in the major Scottish towns in the first few decades of the nineteenth century were all the product of local initiative. As in England, the state would come to play a greater role in shaping the purpose and character of summary justice in Scotland from the 1830s onwards,[152] but there were important differences concerning the extent and course of central direction. In England, government legislation and directive underlay much of the expansion in summary procedure. Its rise was part of wide-ranging reforms to the English criminal justice system that sought to dismantle the infamous 'Bloody Code', strengthen the role of the inferior courts, reduce legal costs and remove certain categories of crimes and criminals from the higher courts. The 1855 English and Welsh Criminal Justice Act, for instance, allowed minor larcenies, though still classified as indictable offences, to be tried in a summary manner and immediately brought about a notable decline in indictable crimes.[153] However, there was no Scottish equivalent to the 1855 Criminal Justice Act, primarily because there was less need for it. The principles, practices and development of Scots criminal law differed greatly from that of England.[154] Scottish laws in the eighteenth and nineteenth centuries were altered gradually, in small stages, usually by administrative and judicial decisions.[155] Scots criminal law was much more flexible than its English counterpart, which meant there was less need to expand the criminal code in the eighteenth century in line with the English 'Bloody Code' – and, as a result, less need to re-classify crimes in line with the reformist zeal of the nineteenth century.[156] Moreover, sheriffs could try fairly serious acts of violence and property offences to any amount in value without having to alter the law, with the customary practice that property crimes valued at more than £10 should be tried before a jury and those under £10 in a summary manner.

The expansion of summary justice in Scottish towns that had not yet acquired statutory police powers had its origins in the municipal and police reforms of the 1830s. The 1833 Burgh Reform Act opened up town councils to election from £10 property holders.[157] This was important, as prior to then the middle ranks

---

[152]   Although, as King points out, local elites were still at the forefront in shaping the English criminal justice system. King, *Crime and the Law*, passim.

[153]   'An Act for Diminishing Expense and Delay in the Administration of Criminal Justice in Certain Areas' (18 & 19 Victoria, cap. 126).

[154]   Crowther, 'Crime, Prosecution and Mercy', p. 226.

[155]   Peter Stein, 'Law and Society in Eighteenth-Century Scottish Thought', in Nicholas T. Phillipson and Rosalind Mitchison (eds), *Scotland in the Age of Improvement*, 2nd edn (Edinburgh, 1996), pp. 148–68.

[156]   Unlike in England, which relied upon a private system of prosecution, the public prosecutor in Scotland could respond to periods of heightened tension by increasing the number of prosecutions. Consequently, there was less need to introduce new capital offences to control and order society. Crowther, 'Crime, Prosecution and Mercy', pp. 226–7.

[157]   The Royal Burghs (Scotland) Act, 1833 (3 & 4 William IV, cap. 76).

were extremely reluctant to give greater power to self-selecting and unpopular magistrates, and would tend to do so only if magistrates made some concession to the principle of representative government (which usually took the form of elected police commissions). The introduction of greater accountability in local government not only paved the way for magistrates to assume greater civic responsibilities, or, at least, somewhat reduced opposition to the idea, it also likely helped to legitimise in the mainstream press and among men of property the concept of lay justice – that is, justice administered by a certain type of propertied man. The 1833 statute was a milestone in civic government in that it opened up town councils to some degree, but the £10 property qualification ensured that the vast bulk of the Scottish urban population would continue to be excluded and power would remain concentrated in the hands of businessmen and professionals. As Maver has argued, burgh reform allowed new men to enter the system, more than they changed the system itself.[158] New men from similar social backgrounds were able to shoulder the mantle of civic power and summary justice under the old rhetoric of male civic virtue. The 1833 Burgh Police Scotland Act – the first general enabling enactment relating to burgh policing – extended this reforming zeal and allowed royal burghs to acquire statutory police powers, elect police commissioners and appoint full-time police forces. Burgh magistrates and sheriffs were vested with powers to try offences specified under the act in a summary manner at the instance of the procurator fiscal of the court. The statute made it easier to bring forward prosecutions for relatively minor offences, including breaching local bye-laws and police regulations, and ultimately a new court structure was established.[159] Police commissioners could use the sums recovered from fines and penalties for the purpose of the Act, which provided a financial incentive for procurators and commissioners to be more zealous in bringing forward prosecutions than they might otherwise have been.[160]

The 1839–1840 Law Inquiry report revealed for the first time the widespread desire that existed among the legal profession and civic representatives in small and medium-sized towns to effect reform. The inquiry was indicative of the growing interest and involvement by central government and the leading figures of the Scottish legal profession in the workings of various branches of the Scottish criminal justice system. Town clerks, burgh procurators fiscal and local justices were among those asked to respond to queries from the law commissioners,

---

[158] Maver, 'The Guardianship of the Community', p. 249.

[159] The statute built on 9 George IV, cap. 29, ss.19–20 (1828), which stated that inferior courts might try offences 'in the easiest and most expedient manner' where the libel concluded for punishment did not exceed £10 or 60 days' imprisonment. The Burgh Police (Scotland) Act, 1833 (3 & 4 William IV, cap. 46). See also Farmer, *Criminal Law, Tradition and Legal Order*, p. 78.

[160] Clause 132. Magistrates were empowered to try offences according to the summary form laid out in 9 George IV, cap. 29. It was also stated that 'prosecutions shall alone be raised and insisted in at the instance of the Procurator Fiscal of Court'.

consisting of members of government, the Lord Advocate and Scotland's chief lawyers, on the practice and efficiency of the country's national and local courts. Questions concerning burgh courts suggest that the commissioners were leading local opinion to critique existing arrangements in order to strengthen the case for reform. The local representatives were asked 14 questions in total, including whether any inconveniences were experienced in dealing with petty crimes, what improvements were needed to rectify them, and whether the burghs had acquired, or attempted to acquire, a local police act or had adopted the 1833 Burgh Police Act. Local representatives were also required to submit criminal returns for their local courts.

The statistical returns published by the Law Commission in 1840 revealed a huge disparity in the number of prosecutions between police courts in towns that had acquired statutory police powers and burgh courts that had not. Burgh courts considerably outnumbered police courts throughout the country, but the contrast in terms of the volume of cases with which they dealt could not have been more stark. The seven main police courts in the country dealt with over 37,000 crimes and offences between 1833 and 1835, compared with just over 1,000 crimes and offences dispatched in the busiest 24 burgh criminal courts (see Chapter 5 for a statistical breakdown of police court charges).[161] In the mid-1830s, Glasgow and Edinburgh's police courts disposed of more cases on a typical day than did at least three quarters of the 24 burgh criminal courts cited in the 1840 report in a typical year. Police courts in these cities prosecuted, on average, between 20 and 40 cases per day, with Edinburgh recording a peak of 98 in 1835.[162] Whereas many burgh criminal courts would meet only when required, police courts would, by contrast, sit every working day – and in the case of Greenock, twice a day.[163] Indeed, one of the defining features of the new system was the frequency with which police courts would meet. By the 1830s, police courts had, along with sheriff courts, established themselves as the main centre of summary justice and an integral wheel in the workings of the criminal justice system in Scotland's larger towns and cities (see Table 1.2 for burgh court prosecutions).

The evidence which was presented to the Commission reveals that there was a growing body of local justices and procurators who were in favour of a new, reformed system of summary justice based on the model that had been set up under local police legislation. Indeed, the creation of police courts through local initiative in the first three decades of the nineteenth century is likely to have provided not just a template for reform on a national scale

---

[161]   Please note, in Paisley and Greenock, the terms 'burgh criminal court' and 'police court' were often used interchangeably. The burgh criminal courts in these two towns were, for all intents and purposes, police courts in that their extended summary powers were constituted under statutory police legislation. For this reason, they have been included in the police rather than burgh court returns.

[162]   'Fourth Report by Her Majesty's Law Commissioners, Scotland, 1839', p. 332.

[163]   Ibid., p. 339.

Table 1.2   Burgh Court Criminal Returns, 1833 to 1835

Burgh	Offences Prosecuted in B Court	Convictions	Acquittals	Cases Remitted to Sheriff	Precognitions Reported to Crown Agent	Remitted by Crown to B. Court
Aberbrothwick	7	5	1	NS	NS	NS
Aberdeen	14	14	0	17	88	0
Ayr	118	100	18	0	0	0
Brechin	5	2	2	0	0	NS
Burntisland	17	15	2	2	3	0
Campbeltown	41	34	5	2	0	0
Dingwall	10	3	2	0	0	0
Dumbarton	44	42	2	0	1	0
Dunbar	84	82	2	1	0	0
Glasgow	236	214	22	0	157	0
Haddington	56	53	3	0	0	0
Hamilton	25	19	6	0	0	0
Inverness	4	3	0	0	1	0
Inverury	2	2	0	0	0	0
Irvine	88	71	16	6	4	4
Jedburgh	14	11	0	0	0	0
Kirkcaldy	59	59	0	0	0	0
Kirkcudbright	25	17	0	0	0	0
Linlithgow	10	3	7	0	0	0
Musselburgh	87	60	10	17	0	0
Oban	10	7	1	0	0	0
Sanquhar	21	17	3	0	0	0
St Andrews	86	47	0	0	0	0
Stranraer	4	4	0	0	0	0

Note: In the odd case where the figures for offences tried do not equate with those convicted or acquitted, it is because the accused had been admitted to, or liberated on, bail and then failed to re-appear.

but a stimulus to it by making existing court arrangements appear backward, inefficient and ineffective by comparison. The report was crammed with criticism from civic and legal figures concerning the cumbersome nature of summary process in burgh courts under the Act of Adjournal and the poor state of summary procedure in towns which had not acquired statutory police powers. The heavy expense incurred in pursuing jury trials was identified as encouraging magistrates to abandon legal action and make extra-judicial settlements.[164] According to the testimonies presented, magistrates and procurators rarely prosecuted if the offence was deemed to be disproportionate to the expense involved and the likelihood of the punishment that would follow.[165] The report reflected a consensus in favour of extending the capacity for summary procedure, prosecution and punishment in Scottish towns. Among the suggestions for reform were that magistrates should be vested with wider powers to conduct criminal trials in a summary manner provided for under burgh police legislation.[166] In doing so, the report exposed not only the perceived failings of the old system, but also the raised expectations among legal and civic men about what local courts were expected to deliver in light of the new model which had been pioneered in the major urban centres earlier in the century.

Against this background were ongoing social, industrial and political tensions and escalating concerns with crime. In 1844 an anonymous article published in *Blackwood's Magazine* noted that

---

[164] John Farish, Town Clerk of Annan, reported the case of James Richardson, accused of rioting and a violent assault on a magistrate in Annan. Despite arguing that the magistrate's representation could have been proved to the very letter, he recorded that 'the heavy expense of a jury trial induced the magistrates to make an extra-judicial settlement of the case'. Similarly, W.H. McLellan, Town Clerk of Kirkcudbright, noted that 'Crimes of a serious nature are little known in this place. When they do occur, the case is generally handed over to the sheriff, but cases of petty delinquency are of frequent occurrence, and in many instances the detection and punishment of offenders is abandoned from *the expense* of following out the machinery of the law.' 'Fourth Report by Her Majesty's Law Commissioners, Scotland, 1839', pp. 253 and 294.

[165] As the town clerk or procurator fiscal of Ayr (name not given) informed the 1839 Law Inquiry: 'In most cases, the length and expense of criminal libel, and the time consumed before sentence, is so much out of all proportion to the most of the crimes committed, that the bailies [magistrates] disapprove of the procedure, and, in many cases, instead of giving information to the fiscal, rather at once commit for 24 hours, as already stated, even when the punishment should be perhaps several days.' 'Fourth Report by Her Majesty's Law Commissioners, Scotland, 1839', p. 256.

[166] Many of the reports submitted by local clerks and procurators recommended that magistrates should be vested with powers to try offences in the summary manner as provided for in the General Police Act, and that the burgh fiscal should act as the police fiscal, without having to adopt burgh police acts with their high assessments. 'Fourth Report by Her Majesty's Law Commissioners, Scotland, 1839', pp. 252–339.

crime in England has increased 700 per cent: in Ireland about 800 per cent, and in Scotland about 3,500 per cent ... What is destined to be the ultimate fate of a country in which the progress of wickedness is so much more rapid than the increase in the number of people?[167]

Although wildly exaggerated, and failing to take sufficient account of how changing legal, prosecution and policing practices impacted on long-term trends in crime, such a claim nonetheless helped to heighten fears that crime was getting out of control. Fuelled by the publication of press reports, parliamentary statistical returns, and an ongoing middle-class fascination and concern with the urban poor, new mechanisms of law enforcement – both in the form of police forces and police courts for those towns which had yet to introduce them – were presented as being essential to a problem that was perceived in certain burghs to be ever more threatening.[168] Business leaders and communities in smaller towns, which were not eligible to acquire the 1833 Burgh Police Scotland Act, were more and more aggrieved at the difficulties they had to endure to bring offenders to justice.[169] In 1846, the proprietor of J. Fuilarpon and Co., a public works in Renfrewshire, complained to the Lord Advocate about the state of crime and disorder in his town (unnamed) and the challenges he faced in dealing with it. He had, he claimed, in the case of serious riot or misdemeanour, no resource other than to lodge an application with the prosecutor in Paisley who was four miles away. He went on: 'the interval allowed to elapse between the lodging of the information and the necessary steps taken for the apprehension of the offender has in several instances afforded an opportunity of escape, whereby the ends of justice have often been defeated.'[170] Three years later, the county of Renfrew obtained an act of parliament, known as Colonel Muir's Act, that gave justices of the peace powers of summary jurisdiction in cases of petty theft, assault, and other minor offences.[171]

---

[167]   Anonymous, 'Causes of the Increase of Crime', *Blackwood's Edinburgh Magazine*, 56/345 (1844): pp. 1–14.

[168]   See Chapter 5 for more on media reports and statistical returns.

[169]   A number of complaints are included in National Archives of Scotland (NAS), AD58/55: Correspondence of Lord Advocate's Department concerning police services: Miscellaneous Papers and Reports, 1842–1847.

[170]   NAS, AD58/55: Correspondence of Lord Advocate's Department concerning Police Services: Miscellaneous Papers and Reports, 'Letter sent from J. Fuilarpon and Co. (proprietor of public work) to the Lord Advocate', 13 August 1846.

[171]   According to a memorial, for the proprietors and manufacturers of the mining establishments in the eastern district of Renfrewshire (Pollokshields) the benefits were huge: 'The consequence was that a facility was given for the punishment of crime equal to that which exists in the police courts in large towns. Injured parties immediately obtained redress without the necessity of abandoning, sometimes for whole days, their usual occupations – travelling to Paisley and waiting at the offices connected to the sheriff courts there – a grievance more intolerable than the original injury, amounting therefore in practice to a denial of justice and an encouragement to every description of crime.' NAS, AD56/246:

The benefits for employers in the region were significant, as a memorial by proprietors and manufacturers of the mining districts pointed out a few years later, which further illustrated the importance of industrial and business concerns to the evolution of summary justice in Scotland.[172]

In 1850, parliament sought to address the problems that smaller towns throughout the country faced by introducing the 1850 Police of Towns Act.[173] The statute built on the 1833 Burgh Police Act by providing new civic and public amenity clauses, including those which made provision for the establishment of police courts.[174] Populous places – localities with more than 1,200 inhabitants – were eligible to adopt it. The act laid out the jurisdiction of magistrates, and established forms and procedure to follow. As with the local enactments that pioneered reform in the first few decades of the century, all processes before police courts were to be summary – defined under the statute as being on complaint without written proceedings.[175] The act created many new 'police offences' and the summary procedures by which these could be prosecuted.[176] It also made it lawful for juvenile male offenders, whose age in the opinion of magistrates did not exceed 14 years, to be chastised by private whipping as an alternative to imprisonment.[177] This not only helped to keep male juvenile offenders out of the higher courts and reduce the number of criminal indictments, it also meant that police court magistrates had the power to inflict corporal punishment without a jury long after it had been prohibited in sheriff courts.[178] The 1862 Burgh Police (Scotland) Act further extended the capacity for Scottish towns to acquire police powers by allowing localities with a population of just 700 or above to adopt all, or some, of its clauses, and become police burghs.[179] The Act was a milestone in civic administration, containing wide-ranging clauses relating to law and order, the built environment, pollution, public health, lighting, paving, common-lodging houses, tenements, and cleansing.[180] By this point, the police courts in

---

Lord Advocate's Department, Correspondence and Papers concerning Police Matters, 1848–1881, 'Memorial of proprietors and manufacturers of the mining establishments in the eastern district of Renfrewshire', 30 April 1856.

[172]   Ibid.

[173]   The Police of Towns (Scotland) Act, 1850 (13 & 14 Victoria, cap. 33).

[174]   R.M. Urquhart, *The Burghs of Scotland and the Police of Towns (Scotland) Act 1850 (13 & 14 Vict. c.33)* (Motherwell, 1989), pp. 7–13.

[175]   Farmer, *Criminal Law, Tradition and Legal Order*, p. 77.

[176]   Ibid., p. 72.

[177]   The Police of Towns (Scotland) Act, 1850, clause 364.

[178]   See Chapter 2 of Volume 2 for more on juveniles before police courts.

[179]   The General and Police Improvement (Scotland) Act, 1862 (25 & 26 Victoria, cap. 101).

[180]   The 1862 Act was not well defined in certain areas. It was amended by the following acts, most of which sought to clarify and define administrative and electoral matters and municipal boundaries: 1868 (31 & 32 Victoria, cap. 102); 1876 (13 & 14 Victoria, cap. 33);

Glasgow, Dundee and Aberdeen were handling upwards of 17,000, 3,500 and 1,000 cases respectively per year.[181]

Under the 1850 and 1862 Burgh Acts, police magistrates were given jurisdiction to take cognisance of all offences, misdemeanours, and breaches of police regulations, as well as crimes and offences that were punishable by public acts or common law.[182] These statutes, as Crowther has pointed out, gave police magistrates the same powers of criminal jurisdiction as sheriffs.[183] However, although police courts' judicial powers transcended statute law and were not restricted to a certain category or type of crime, they were limited by practical and material conditions, the nature of crimes, the type of punishment that procurators and magistrates deemed appropriate, and the criminal history of offenders. Such considerations came to be of increasing importance in determining where a case would be tried, with police legislation playing an important role in formalising the administration of the criminal justice system. Police magistrates, for instance, had no jurisdiction over pleas of the crown, crimes involving property valued at £10 or more and serious physical assault (often life-threatening). As with the extension of the franchise, £10 was an important signifier – in this case, of whether the accused was entitled to be judged by a sheriff, a jury of peers under solemn criminal procedure or by magistrates in a summary manner. Moreover, as police magistrates could only imprison for up to two months, more serious criminal charges deemed worthy of a longer sentence had to be remitted to a higher court for trial under solemn procedure. So, too, were those suspects who were charged with crimes who had been twice convicted of similar offences.[184] In such cases, magistrates were required to remit the case to the county procurator to decide how to proceed.[185] Sheriff courts and local procurators, therefore, continued to remain

---

1876 (39 & 40 Victoria, cap. 25); 1877 (40 & 41 Victoria, cap. 22); 1882 (45 & 46 Victoria, cap. 6); and 1887 (41 & 42 Victoria, cap. 30).

[181] ECL: *Reports as to the Watching Force of the City of Edinburgh* (Edinburgh, 1857), pp. 35–7.

[182] The 1850 Act was a little vague on this, but it was often implied in practice. The 1862 Act clarified the judicial parameters of the courts. Police courts had jurisdiction over offences punishable at common law offences (such as theft) and statutory law offences (powers acquired under police legislation, which also grew to include common law offences, such as assault and breach of the peace).

[183] According to Crowther, 'the sheriff or police magistrate was thus able to dispose of cases which in England would have required the full panoply of quarter sessions and assize courts until 1855'. Crowther, 'Crime, Prosecution and Mercy', p. 236.

[184] However, the 1892 Burgh Police (Scotland) Act noted exceptions whereby magistrates could try cases regardless of the amount specified in the charge against them or how often they had been previously convicted. Most of these related to gambling. James Campbell Irons, *The Burgh Police (Scotland) Act 1892* (Edinburgh, 1893), pp. 459 & 687–8.

[185] Usually, this would result in the cases being prosecuted before juries in sheriff courts as these could impose tougher punishments than police courts if the case was not tried summarily. Sheriff Courts could imprison offenders for two years if the case was

integral to the workings of the criminal justice system,[186] with the discretion that the latter enjoyed playing a vital role in determining whether to prosecute cases under common or statutory law and in which court they should be prosecuted (based on an estimation of the likely punishment). As Farmer has pointed out, the summary jurisdiction of sheriff courts expanded significantly in the second half of the century, increasing markedly the number of summary criminal cases sheriffs dealt with.[187] Although there was some ambiguity over sheriffs' summary powers in the first half of the century,[188] by the second half of the century these were, as with police courts, limited to a £10 fine and 60 days' imprisonment;[189] but in solemn trials, sheriffs could impose fines of up to £50 and imprison for up to two years.[190]

Nonetheless, the burgh police acts that were passed in the second half of the century were extremely important. Along with local and national legislation relating to pawnbrokers, public parks,[191] gambling and drinking, and the prevention of cruelty to children,[192] these statutes significantly increased the

---

tried before a jury. In summary trials, their powers of punishment extended to 60 days' imprisonment and a fine of up to £10 – the same as police courts. 'First Report of the Commissioners Appointed to Inquire into the Courts of Law in Scotland, together with Minutes of Evidence', 1868–1869 (4125), XXV.29, p. 7.

[186]   In 1868, Henry Glassford, the sheriff of Lanarkshire, described the criminal jurisdiction of the Glasgow Sheriff Court as 'very large and important'. In 1867, in the criminal department, there were 341 trials before the sheriff and a jury, and 113 without a jury. Glassford continued: 'Our *summary* criminal jurisdiction is not so large as in many other counties, because a great deal of it proceeds before the Justice of Peace Court of Glasgow, and I believe the Procurators-fiscal of Glasgow are very well pleased with that arrangement' (p. 2). He also claimed that sheriff courts were the most useful of all local courts and that 'they have a very strong hold on the feelings of the community' (p. 3). Although he recognised problems in constitution, he suggested that they commanded much popular support. 'First Report of the Commissioners Appointed to Inquire into the Courts of Law in Scotland', p. 3.

[187]   For more on the expansion in the summary powers of sheriff courts, see Farmer, *Criminal Law, Tradition and Legal Order*, pp. 70–71.

[188]   In the first half of the century, as Spens has pointed out, 'the powers of the Sheriff Court with reference to criminal cases at common law without the intervention of a jury … [was] probably never been accurately ascertained or defined'. Spens, *Jurisdiction and Punishments of Summary Criminal Courts*, p. 20.

[189]   According to evidence presented for the 'First Report of the Commissioners Appointed to Inquire into the Courts of Law in Scotland' by Sheriff Glassford, magistrates could, on summary conviction, impose a fine of £10 or imprisonment for 60 days. 'First Report of the Commissioners Appointed to Inquire into the Courts of Law in Scotland', p. 7.

[190]   Ibid.

[191]   Public Parks (Scotland) Act, 1878 (41 & 42 Victoria, cap. 8).

[192]   See Chapter 2 of Volume 2 for more on legislative developments relating to juveniles.

police courts' involvement in regulating facets of everyday life. As police courts matured and cemented their place in public life, their powers were extended to provide more protection for groups perceived to be vulnerable, including juveniles and victims of domestic violence.[193] This provided police courts with a particular moral remit and a justification of civic paternalism for the men who governed them. This role was further widened by the 1875 Summary Prosecutions Appeal Act,[194] which gave magistrates jurisdiction to try any offence created by statute within the same prescribed limits as governed police court jurisdiction,[195] and by the 1892 Burgh Police Scotland Act,[196] which compelled those burghs which had not yet done so to establish police courts and extended statutory police powers for matters relating to places of entertainment, popular recreations, prevention of cruelty to children,[197] public health, and the built environment.[198]

Some of the expansion in the business of police courts was the product of changing moral views and a shifting sense of civic paternalism among men who had once been motivated rather more by self-interest, which was in itself part of wider social and legislative evolution in the United Kingdom as a whole.[199] However, although the newly acquired police powers were sweeping

---

[193] See, for instance, Anna Clark, *The Struggle for the Breeches: Gender and the Making of the British Working Class* (Berkeley, 1995), p. 259.

[194] Summary Prosecutions Appeals (Scotland) Act, 1875 (38 & 39 Victoria, cap. 62).

[195] Campbell Irons, *The Burgh Police (Scotland) Act*, p. 459, 717 & 687–8. Crimes that were not to be tried in police court included those involving pleas of the crown, property crimes of more than £10, if the accused had twice been convicted of the same crime, and serious assault.

[196] The Burgh Police (Scotland) Act, 1892 (55 & 56 Victoria, cap. 55).

[197] Prevention of Cruelty to, and Protection, of, Children Act, 1889 (52 & 53 Victoria, cap. 44).

[198] See also Keedy, 'Criminal Procedure in Scotland', p. 736; and Campbell Irons, *The Burgh Police (Scotland) Act*. The act was introduced to give burghs extended statutory powers relating to obstructions, public streets, water supply, buildings, and public health. It also provided justices with additional powers for slaughter-houses, markets, hackney carriages and the licensing of theatres, music halls and places of entertainment.

[199] Shoemaker, 'Male Honour and the Decline of Popular Violence in Eighteenth-Century London', pp. 190–208; Wiener, *Men of Blood*; Margaret May, 'Innocence and Experience: The Evolution of the Concept of Juvenile Delinquency in the Mid-Nineteenth Century', *Victorian Studies*, 17/1 (1973): pp. 7–29; Deborah Gorham, 'The "Maiden Tribute of Modern Babylon" Re-Examined: Child Prostitution and the Idea of Childhood in Late-Victorian England', *Victorian Studies*, 21/3 (1978): pp. 353–79; Linda Mahood and Barbara Littlewood, 'Prostitutes, Magdalenes, and Wayward Girls: Dangerous Sexualities of Working Class Women in Victorian Scotland', *Gender and History*, 3/2 (1991): pp. 160–75; Linda Mahood, 'The Disbudding of Flowers: The Historical Construction of Female Adolescent Delinquency', in Terence Brotherstone, Deborah Simonton and Oonagh Walsh (eds), *Gendering Scottish History: An International Approach* (Glasgow, 1999), pp. 234–50; Heather Shore, *Artful Dodgers: Youth and Crime in Early Nineteenth-Century London* (Woodbridge, 1999); Linda Mahood, '"Give Him a Doing": The Birching of Young

and impacted in theory on the lives of all citizens, in practice police courts were fairly selective in terms of the types of crimes, offences and contraventions that were prosecuted and the citizens they targeted.[200] Much of the focus in terms of how the legislation was enforced was on the regulation of public space and the control of vulnerable and marginalised groups. Indeed, in practice, much of the police courts' time became preoccupied with dealing with non-criminal pursuits, pastimes and practices in favour of disciplining so-called 'deviant' behaviours – vagrancy, public drunkenness, and prostitution – the existence of which threatened a middle-class ideal of urban order.[201] As Chapter 5 examines in greater depth, the business of police courts became ever more concerned relative to their caseloads with urban order and public morality as the century progressed.[202]

The growing preoccupation with public order offences brought a larger percentage of Glasgow's population before magistrates and underlined police courts' evolving importance within the criminal justice system and municipal sphere. In 1894, Glasgow dealt with 58,173 cases.[203] By contrast, in 1898, only 2,500 criminal prosecutions throughout Scotland were dealt with under solemn procedure out of 166,000 in total. Of these, only 200 were prosecuted in the High Court, as more and more indictable crimes were tried in sheriff and police courts.[204] As in the first half of the century, some towns retained burgh criminal courts separate from police courts, with some civic leaders preferring to retain them because they had stronger powers of punishment than police magistrates enjoyed.[205] But

---

Offenders in Scotland', *Canadian Journal of History*, 37/3 (2002): pp. 439–57; Irene Maver, 'Children and the Quest for Purity in the Nineteenth-Century Scottish City', *Paedagogica Historica: International Journal of the History of Education*, 33/3 (1997): pp. 801–24.

[200] Gatrell makes a similar point in 'Crime, Authority and the Policeman–State', p. 277.

[201] For some developments in England, see ibid., p. 245.

[202] Knox and McKinlay, 'Crime, Protest and Policing', p. 205.

[203] James Bell and James Paton, *Glasgow: Its Municipal Organisation and Administration* (Glasgow, 1896), p. 109.

[204] Police courts dealt with the majority of criminal cases – albeit of a relatively minor nature – in towns that had them, with sheriff courts dealing with the bulk of criminal business in towns which did not (as well as crimes deemed too serious to be discharged summarily in police courts, but not serious enough to warrant jury trial in a justiciary court). 'Report on Judicial Statistics of Scotland, 1898', *BPP*, 1900 (cd. 28), CIII.447, p. 38. Cited in Farmer, *Criminal Law, Tradition and Legal Order*, p. 73. There was also a huge disparity between police courts and sheriff courts. Between 1866 and 1867, the Glasgow Sheriff Court conducted just 295 criminal trials, of which 81 were without a jury. GUL, Special Collections: *The Journal of Jurisprudence* (Edinburgh, 1867), vol. XI, pp. 540–41.

[205] The 'Fourth Report of the Commissioners Appointed to Inquire into the Courts of Law in Scotland, 1870' noted that in royal burghs the criminal jurisdiction of the burgh court was co-ordinated with that of the sheriff, which entitled burgh magistrates 'to investigate crimes of any magnitude, to take the declarations of prisoners, and to commit for trial; also to try cases involving punishment for two years in prison'. 'Fourth

this was the exception rather than the norm. By the late nineteenth century, police courts had well and truly surpassed the former as the main centre of urban justice throughout the country. Bell and Paton's *Glasgow: Its Municipal Organisation and Administration* (1896) recorded that the burgh criminal court had been completely absorbed by the sheriff and police courts – or rather, in the case of the latter, by eight separate police courts distributed throughout the city corresponding with different divisions and stations.[206] The foundations of the modern criminal justice system had been firmly laid.

There were some changes in the second half of the century in terms of whose influence lay behind the expansion of police court summary justice. Central government and the leading lights of Scottish legal circles – most notably, the Lord Advocate – provided a greater role in its evolution by providing legislative frameworks to adopt and follow, whilst legal commentaries and judgements helped to define the parameters of the new court structure and its judicial remit.[207] Central government and the legal profession also became more involved in framing police court procedure and practice. Much of this was drawn, in the words of Baron Henry James Moncreiff in his *Treatise on the Law of Review in Criminal cases* (1877), from a 'strong necessity for the introduction of uniformity of procedure and the suppression of such irregularities which could only be effected by statutory regulation',[208] as well as a desire to put summary proceedings before magistrates on a more solid legal footing. As Chapters 5 and 6 examine more fully, expanding the scope of summary justice was also extremely attractive to public men intent upon imposing higher levels of discipline over the urban masses, especially given the challenges involved in securing convictions in higher courts compared with the procedural and evidential advantages offered by police courts. Moreover, the summary justice administered in police courts became a convenient way of keeping down the cost of dealing with crime following the demise of transportation and the rise of imprisonment as a form of punishment from the 1840s. More and more cases were dealt with in police courts in order to ensure that sentences would not be too long and the cost of maintaining a burgeoning

---

Report of the Commissioners appointed to Inquire into the Courts of Law in Scotland', *BPP*, 1870 (C.175), XVIII.455, p. 38. However, criminal trials on indictment in burgh courts post-1850 were extremely rare and would soon become a thing of the past. The 'Fourth Report of Commissioners' in that year helped to confirm this, recommending 'that Magistrates of burghs should henceforth be relieved of the duties they at present discharge in preparation for trial of proper criminal causes, and of the jurisdiction they now exercise in their trial' and their jurisdiction confined instead to police matters. 'Fourth Report of the Commissioners appointed to Inquire into the Courts of Law in Scotland', p. 39.

[206]   Bell and Paton, *Glasgow*, pp. 105–8.

[207]   This is dealt with in greater depth in Chapter 2.

[208]   Henry James Moncreiff, *A Treatise on the Law of Review in Criminal Cases* (Edinburgh, 1877), p. 8.

volume of prisoners too expensive. As the Superintendent of the Edinburgh Police noted in the 1860 Edinburgh police returns: 'during the last three years, there has been a considerable increase in the number of cases tried summarily, so as not to involve imprisonment for a period exceeding two months.'[209] In this respect, the rise of police court summary justice was firmly embedded within wider changes to the criminal justice system that were taking place at a British level.

However, in terms of what constituted the main vehicle for shaping the expansion of police court powers, the overriding picture of the expansion of police courts was one of continuity, not change. As with the first phase, it was through police legislation that the scope of summary justice in Scottish towns was enlarged the most. Police legislation not only laid the foundations for expanding summary procedure, it was also at the forefront of its ongoing evolution and rise to prominence within the criminal justice system.[210] Over the century, police acts created a wide array of new offences, defined how minor crimes should be classified and punished, and established quicker and cheaper ways of dealing with cases.[211] Crimes and certain categories of criminal offenders, traditionally more likely to be brought before higher courts, were increasingly classified as 'police offences' rather than 'penal offences' and dealt with by police courts.[212] Provision in police legislation was also made for the building of bridewells, which provided the accommodation needed to deal with the ever-growing number of petty offenders who were brought before the courts and given short-term sentences (see Chapter 7 for more on bridewells).[213]

---

[209]   ECL, *Reports and Returns as to Crimes, Offences, and Contraventions, and to Cases of Drunkenness, within the Police Bounds of the City of Edinburgh during the last Six Years. Prepared for the Magistrates and Council, by Thomas Linton, Superintendent of Police* (Edinburgh, 1860), p. 10.

[210]   Farmer, *Criminal Law, Tradition and Legal Order*, p. 71.

[211]   Ibid., p. 84.

[212]   Crowther, 'Crime, Prosecution and Mercy', p. 236. The late nineteenth-century historians of Glasgow, Bell and Paton, succinctly summed up the huge expansion in police crimes: '"Police offences" are myriad in their number, and the catalogue gives some colour to the allegation that Glasgow is a police-ridden city. What is more, scarcely a year passes without some local enactment coming into force by which the formidable catalogue is increased; and yet the stranger may be assured that decent citizens are to be met with who have every day of their life passed through the streets of Glasgow, shared in its business and pleasures, and taken an active part in public duties, who have never had the slightest unpleasantness with the police and who have not had occasion to see the interior of a police office. The crimes and offences of which the police take cognizance are not much less varied than they are numerous, and many of the charges investigated by the bailies do not imply any personal disgrace on the part of the person called on to answer the charge.' Bell and Paton, *Glasgow*, p. 109.

[213]   For more on the development of bridewells, see Cameron, *Prisons and Punishment in Scotland*, passim.

Moreover, as in the first three decades of the century, civic men remained the principal driving force behind the rise to prominence of police courts for the rest of the century. Whereas the state took a direct approach with the expansion of summary justice in sheriff courts, the permissive rather than compulsory nature of burgh police legislation meant that it was left to civic leaders and burgh communities to decide for themselves whether or not to expand the scope of summary justice. The 1892 Burgh Police (Scotland) Act was the first obligatory burgh police act introduced by parliament (and even then Glasgow, Edinburgh, Aberdeen, Greenock and Dundee were allowed to continue with their own police acts).[214]

Throughout the century, home secretaries in London were mainly preoccupied with English matters, and were content to leave the administration of Scottish affairs to the Lord Advocate rather than take much interest themselves. This willingness to let Scots govern themselves, could, to some extent, be viewed as being the result of administrative neglect,[215] but this would not be entirely fair. The extent of parliamentary time devoted to Scottish legal affairs might have been significantly less than that afforded to English affairs, but it was still considerable.[216] Significantly, civic leaders were not looking for greater central direction in their affairs. The approach taken by government in London was very much in keeping with the Victorian conceptualisation of the state – which was always a balance between the locality and the centre[217] – and the self-governing nature of Scottish civil society. This ensured that civic men would play a major part not only in shaping the evolution of summary justice in Scottish towns, but also its delivery. As subsequent chapters explore, this was to result in strained relations between them and the legal profession, and would have profound implications for the rights of the accused in Scottish police courts.

---

[214]   See Campbell Irons, *The Burgh Police (Scotland) Act*.

[215]   Anne E. Whetstone, Graeme Morton and R.J. Morris have argued that the government was relatively content to let Scots govern themselves. See Anne E. Whetstone, *Scottish County Government*, passim; and Graeme Morton and R.J. Morris, 'Civil Society, Governance and Nation, 1832–1914', in R.A. Houston and W.W.J. Knox (eds), *The New Penguin History of Scotland: From the Earliest Times to the Present Day* (London, 2001), pp. 377–80. For a critique of the view that Parliament neglected Scottish governance, see Joanna Innes, 'Legislating for Three Kingdoms: How the Westminster Parliament Legislated for England, Scotland and Ireland, 1707–1830', in Julian Hoppit (ed.), *Parliament, Nations and Identities in Britain and Ireland, 1660–1850* (Manchester, 2003), p. 28.

[216]   See Peter Cockton, *Subject Catalogue of the House of Commons Parliamentary Papers, 1801–1900, Volume III: Law and Order, Local Government and Local Finance, Poverty and Social Administration, Education, Information and Recreation* (Cambridge, 1988).

[217]   Graeme Morton, 'Scottish Rights and "Centralisation" in the Mid-Nineteenth Century', *Nations and Nationalism*, 2/2 (1996): p. 260.

V. Conclusion

In a recent study of the Scottish justiciary courts in the period 1700 to 1830, Kilday has argued that

> both religious and legal authorities worked together to curb bad behaviour ... [which helped make the Scots] proficient at managing criminality... Along with normal criminal investigations, religious surveillance operated on the ground to maximize local cooperation in gleaning information about suspected offences and suspected offenders. Certainly, it is clear from trial papers that parishioners regularly informed on each other under examination. From this, it is difficult to see how criminals would have been able to evade capture in early modern Scotland, and as a result, the level of unrecorded crime may well be lower in a Scottish context compared to elsewhere. This suggests that far from being a barbarous nation, Scotland's system of justice was more regulated, checked, and effective than its English equivalent.[218]

The evidence from the Scottish police courts suggests that legal and religious authorities did work together in complementary ways to police urban behaviour that was deemed to be deviant by 'respectable' standards (see Chapters 5 and 6 of Volume 2, which explores the relationship between the churches and police court in more detail). However, at a local court level, the capacity of the Scottish criminal justice system to bring offenders to justice was certainly not as effective, and the likelihood of criminals being brought to justice not as great as Kilday contends for the higher courts. Indeed, the expansion in summary justice in the larger urban centres in the early nineteenth century was testament in part to the limitations of existing judicial arrangements in the lower courts. As the 1839–1840 Law Inquiry revealed, local burgh courts were failing to operate at all in many parts of the country.

Reform, though, was not simply due to problems with existing arrangements which, after all, functioned in many parts of the country without an impending sense of crisis. Neither was it simply a product of mounting concerns with crime and urban order. The old burgh court system was no longer deemed suitable in many parts of the country because it was not designed to deal with the volume of cases, administer the type of punishment, or provide the level of protection that the business classes increasingly expected in a rapidly urbanising, manufacturing and commercial society. In large urban centres, hardening attitudes towards property crime, which were often fuelled by press reports, combined with raised expectations of comfort and security to encourage a growing willingness among the propertied to prosecute. This, in turn, stretched the capacity of existing burgh courts to cope due to the financial and procedural constraints under which many functioned. In London, the development of the Bow Street Magistrates' Court, concern with the

---

[218]   Kilday, 'The Barbarous North?', p. 401.

perceived illegal practice of trading justices, and a desire to appoint stipendiary magistrates provided much of the initial thrust for the expansion in summary justice in the eighteenth century. In the larger Scottish towns, disillusionment with the self-selecting nature of local government provided an important background to reform, but summary justice's formative development had less to do with magistrates *per se* and more to do with what they and men of property expected of the inferior courts and the difficulties they faced in trying to bring offenders to justice.

Self-interest, social status and power provided important contexts to reform. In many industrial and commercial centres, the origins of reform lay in the desire of professional and businessmen to better safeguard their own property, safety and commercial transactions, as well as to provide a more accessible legal platform to defend the interests of employers. Local businessmen and property holders were seeking to re-cast the difficulties that they faced in bringing forward prosecutions as civic problems in order to ensure that they themselves would not be the only ones burdened with paying legal costs. These shared concerns manifested themselves in new summary structures that could be made at the expense of the entire urban community. The new police bureaucracy meant that manufacturers, merchants and small business owners would, in theory, no longer have to subscribe to voluntary organisations to bring suspects before the courts or employ watchmen to protect their premises. Similarly, although the desire for better ordered, urban environments was by no means the exclusive preserve of men of property, much, although by no means all, of the thirst for extended summary powers was driven by a bourgeois preoccupation with regulating and disciplining the behaviour of the lower orders. It was fitting that police courts evolved under police legislation because they were the necessary complement to the police forces which were introduced throughout the country. As in England, the evolution and expansion of police courts were very much part of the slowly emerging 'policeman state' involving greater social regulation of petty offences and a criminal justice system that was becoming increasingly preoccupied with urban order. It was a product of wider middle-class attempts to curb immorality and violent behaviour and better regulate public spaces and the built environment.

There was, of course, tremendous variation throughout the country, especially between the rapidly expanding, industrial centres and those burghs which experienced more modest, or stagnant, economic and demographic development. It would be wrong to view the rise of police courts as being simply a response to social problems or the failings of existing centres of justice.[219] Underpinning this transition was a wider societal and intellectual shift. Although, as subsequent chapters will show, magistrates and communities continued to rely upon informal sanctions for certain types of crimes and offenders, the growing volume of cases prosecuted first before burgh courts in the larger urban centres, and then before police courts, signified a

---

[219] Farmer makes a similar point for the expansion in summary process in general. Farmer, *Criminal Law, Tradition and Legal Order*, p. 97.

growing willingness to report offences, increasing confidence in the legal system, and greater desire to seek legal redress. For men of property, preventing crime in future would be best assured not by punishing it in a severe, exemplary manner or by whipping and banishing offenders indiscriminately, which had characterised eighteenth-century practices. Rather, it would be achieved by ensuring as far as possible that offenders would, in theory, be formally prosecuted and brought to justice in a fast, efficient, and cost-effective manner, even if the reality turned out to be different.[220] Indeed, the importance of efficiency and economy in shaping the expansion in summary justice cannot be overstated. As Farmer has rightly pointed out, the summary courts evolved, in part, in order to avoid the time-consuming and expensive legal technicalities and formalities involved in prosecuting crimes in the higher courts.[221] The lower costs involved in dealing with cases in a summary manner were extremely attractive to magistrates in an era when burgh finances were often in a precarious state – especially as more cases could be prosecuted and more revenue raised by imposing fines.

As with other parts of the British Isles, the rise of police courts to prominence also needs to be viewed in light of wider changes within the criminal justice system as well as a wider intellectual shift in favour of the expansion, standardisation and formalisation of summary process. However, there were also a few subtle, albeit important, distinctions in the Scottish experience. The expansion in summary criminal procedure in Scotland was much more closely linked with police development than was the case in England. Sheriff courts also played an important role in this, but it was in police courts that the vast majority of summary cases were handled. Aside from the fact that police courts and forces were often introduced under the same piece of legislation, the police's involvement in bringing forward prosecutions from early in the nineteenth century initially set them apart from their counterparts in England, where private prosecution was the norm until the police take-over of prosecutions later in the century. This ensured that the police in Scottish towns had a much more direct impact on the expansion of summary offences, over and above merely apprehending offenders, than was the case in England. It also meant that the police were able to control the number, and influence the nature, of criminal prosecutions in magistrate courts, which was to have significant implications for long-term trends in, and people's perceptions of, crime.[222] Indeed, police legislation, police forces, police prosecutions and police courts were so important to the expansion in summary justice that it would not be an overstatement to argue that the bureaucracy of police that emerged in nineteenth-century Scotland was as important, if not more

---

[220] Philips argues that growing use of summary justice reflected a change in mentality in that prosecution was to be encouraged rather than just a last resort. Philips, "'A New Engine of Power and Authority'", p. 188.

[221] Farmer, *Criminal Law, Tradition and Legal Order*, p. 97.

[222] English forces would not have the same level of influence until much later in the nineteenth century.

so, to the evolution of the modern criminal justice system than the widely lauded 1747 Heritable Jurisdiction Act.

Moreover, unlike in England, there were no major national boundary lines and watershed legislative enactments behind expansion. According to Farmer, developments in summary justice in Scotland can be divided into three periods – pre-history before 1820, then 1820–1864 which brought early developments, and post-1864 as significant reforms were made to the sheriff courts.[223] However, while the above periods might be relevant for sheriff courts on which Farmer's conclusion is mainly based, they are less so for police courts, the trajectory of which cannot be so easily demarcated. Reform was the product of series of local and national legislative enactments that stretched over a number of decades. The absence of an equivalent to England's 1855 Criminal Justice Act, combined with the permissive nature of general police acts and preference of major burghs to continue with their own, ensured that there would be great regional variation in the timing of expansion and consistent, formal, criminal procedure. The actual model of summary justice that emerged, though, was remarkably uniform throughout the country. Both the traditional civic elites and emerging men of property and business, despite their struggles for status with each other, shared similar values and faced similar challenges to their financial, personal and moral interests and, as has been shown elsewhere, they often looked at policing arrangements in other Scottish cities. But the pathway of expansion was not the same as in England. Although government influence over sheriff courts increased markedly over the course of the nineteenth century, decisions to expand summary justice in magistrate courts were more often than not taken in the localities themselves. Lords advocate played an important role in shaping local and national legislation, and in framing court processes and powers, but the government's influence on the expansion of summary justice in the police courts of Scotland was less swift and decisive than in England. The desire of both civic and legal men to respect Scottish burghal and legal history and tradition ensured that Scotland would have its own model of summary police development.

---

[223]   Farmer, *Criminal Law, Tradition and Legal Order*, p. 73.

Chapter 2
Dignity and Discretion

I. Introduction

In his influential study, 'Property, Authority and the Criminal Law' in eighteenth-century England, Douglas Hay highlighted the importance of judicial discretion for maintaining the power, position and status of local justices. Far from being an irrational mess and ineffective form of law enforcement as older, traditional histories had suggested,[1] Hay argued that the unreformed English criminal justice system was effective in preserving the social order precisely through a lack of technical rationality. Local justices, in other words, valued what seemed to be irrationalities in the criminal justice system, as it enabled them to exercise their power in a discretionary manner and reinforced paternalism, deference and terror within their communities.[2] For Hay, and a generation of scholars influenced by his writings, this informal, discretionary system of law enforcement was subsequently transformed by nineteenth-century criminal law reforms, the rise of summary justice and the move towards a more centralised and impersonal system based on greater certainty of prosecution and formalisation in legal procedure.[3]

---

[1] Leon Radzinowicz, *A History of English Criminal Law and its Administration from 1750, Volume 2: The Clash between Private Initiative and Public Interest in the Enforcement of the Law* (London, 1956); and Leon Radzinowicz and Roger G. Hood, *A History of English Criminal Law and Its Administration from 1750, Vol. V: The Emergence of Penal Policy* (London, 1986).

[2] Hay claims that inhumane rules and rituals, such as the 'Bloody Code' and public execution, gave people such a terror of the law that it served as an effective system for maintaining the hegemony of the ruling elite. Douglas Hay, 'Property, Authority and the Criminal Law', in Douglas Hay, Peter Linebaugh, John G. Rule, E.P. Thompson and Cal Winslow (eds), *Albion's Fatal Tree: Crime and Society in Eighteenth-Century England* (Harmondsworth, 1975), pp. 17–63. For studies that have critiqued this view, see John Langbein, 'Albion's Fatal Flaws', *Past and Present*, 98 (1983): pp. 96–120; and Peter King, *Crime, Justice, and Discretion in England, 1740–1820* (Oxford, 2000).

[3] E.P. Thompson, *Whigs and Hunters: The Origins of the Black Act* (London, 1980), p. 266; David Philips, '"A New Engine of Power and Authority": The Institutionalization of Law-Enforcement in England, 1780–1830', in V.A.C. Gatrell, Bruce Lenman and Geoffrey Parker (eds), *Crime and the Law: The Social History of Crime in Western Europe since 1500* (London, 1980), pp. 155–89; Michael Ignatieff, *A Just Measure of Pain: The Penitentiary in the Industrial Revolution 1750–1850* (London, 1978); and Michel Foucault, *Discipline and Punish: The Origins of the Prison* (Harmondsworth, 1978).

In recent years, the importance of discretionary justice has been widely recognised by historians as being integral to the workings of the English criminal justice system at both a summary and high court level.[4] However, whilst acknowledging the contribution and quality of Hay's penetrating analysis, other scholars have questioned aspects of his interpretation, not least the extent of change that criminal law reforms heralded. As Jennifer S. Davis has argued, 'the continuities between eighteenth- and nineteenth-century law enforcement were at least as important as the contrasts', with the nineteenth-century magistrate in London dispensing justice, handing out advice and assuming a role that was similar to his eighteenth-century counterpart.[5] Similarly, as Carolyn Conley has argued, 'the findings and actions of the [Victorian] criminal justice system were still primarily determined by the values and priorities of the local community' despite the move towards greater regularisation and bureaucratic control.[6] Moreover, rather than being simply an ideological instrument of the ruling elite, scholarship has emphasised how a range of decision-makers in the judicial process, including victims, utilised discretion to their advantage,[7] as well as the role that discretion played in shaping the gender, class and ethnicity biases evident in judicial decision-making.[8] Historians have increasingly stressed that magistrates did not simply administer the law in defence of private interests and were not preoccupied with securing convictions. The local justice's role in English summary courts, it has been claimed, extended to resolving community disputes,[9] and providing 'a poor man's system of justice'.[10]

---

[4]   King, *Crime, Justice and Discretion*, especially part 1; Garthine Walker, *Crime, Gender and Social Order in Early Modern England* (Cambridge, 2003); Robert B. Shoemaker, *Prosecution and Punishment: Petty Crime and the Law in London and Rural Middlesex, c.1660–1725* (Cambridge, 1991); John Brewer and John Styles, *An Ungovernable People: The English and their Law in the Seventeenth and Eighteenth Centuries* (New Brunswick, 1980); Norma Landau, *The Justices of the Peace, 1679–1760* (Berkeley, 1984); Drew D. Gray, *Crime, Prosecution and Social Relations: The Summary Courts of the City of London in the Late Eighteenth Century* (Basingstoke, 2009).

[5]   Jennifer S. Davis, 'A Poor Man's System of Justice? The London Police Courts in the Second Half of the Nineteenth Century', *Historical Journal*, 27/2 (1984): p. 309.

[6]   Carolyn A. Conley, *The Unwritten Law: Criminal Justice in Victorian Kent* (Oxford, 1991), preface.

[7]   See, for instance, Peter King, 'Decision-Makers and Decision-Making in the English Criminal Law, 1750–1800', *Historical Journal*, 27/1 (1984): pp. 25–58.

[8]   These themes were discussed in more depth in the Introduction.

[9]   See Peter King, 'The Summary Courts and Social Relations in Eighteenth-Century England', *Past and Present*, 183/1 (2004): pp. 125–72; Drew D. Gray, 'The People's Courts? Summary Justice and Social Relations in the City of London, c.1760–1800', *Family and Community History*, 11/1 (2008): pp. 7–15; Gwenda Morgan and Peter Rushton, 'The Magistrate, the Community and the Maintenance of an Orderly Society in Eighteenth-Century England', *Historical Research*, 76/191 (2003): pp. 54–77.

[10]   Davis, 'A Poor Man's System of Justice?', pp. 309–35; and Gray, *Crime, Prosecution and Social Relations*.

As this chapter shows, the Scottish experience would bear some similarities with that of the English, but also exhibited important differences. Growing central and legal direction would, to some extent, formalise judicial procedures; but police courts also helped to extend magisterial authority as a concept in the form of judicial process, the crimes that were brought before judges in the name of public interest, and in terms of the level of discretion afforded them as men with authority over others. Indeed, far from being undermined, the need for magistrates to dispense the law in a discretionary manner struck at the heart of much of the discourse concerning who could dispense justice in nineteenth-century Scottish police courts and would result in Scottish burgh elites resisting the introduction of stipendiary magistrates for much longer than was the case in other parts of the United Kingdom. The issue of who should sit as judges in Scottish police courts, and how they should administer the law, would raise serious questions not just about the delivery of summary justice and the authority of those who administered it, but also about the legal rights of those brought before magistrates and the governance of Scottish urban communities. Discretionary justice was, ultimately, not just integral to how magistrates saw their role in the community and a mechanism for controlling the urban masses. It also underpinned magistrates' perceived capacity to govern in an era when this was being challenged, defined and shaped by criminal returns, press reports, and the advent of local elections and greater accountability in local government.

II. Independent Men?

In the introduction to *Handbook for Magistrates on Police Court Procedure, Evidence, etc* (1951), the Right Honourable Lord Cooper, Lord Justice General, provided an illuminating insight into how the higher echelons of the police court personnel viewed themselves, the types of qualities that they perceived were required for public office, and the restrictions on those whom they deemed capable of filling either position:

> The lay magistrates and justices ... constitute the broad base of the pyramid of Scottish criminal administration. Though the offences with which they deal are minor offences and though the area of their jurisdiction is restricted, their task is not on that account any easier nor their responsibilities lighter. In some respects their responsibilities are even heavier than those of the higher courts, for it is usually the lay magistrate who has to act as arbiter of the fate of the first offender, whose initial appearance in a criminal court so often marks the parting of the ways between a career of crime and a restoration of citizenship. In every criminal court without distinction there is need for unremitting efforts to combine that wise humanity and firm discrimination which will ensure that none leaves the court embittered by a just sense of grievance, and that no proved offender departs with a diminished respect for the laws he has violated or for

those entrusted with the enforcement of these laws. This is a high ideal. Its full attainment requires a combination of qualities some of which are incapable of forced cultivation.[11]

Humility and discretion, for Cooper, lay at the heart of magisterial authority. The role of local justices was not simply to administer the law, it was also to ensure respect for law, justice and, by definition, the position and status of magistrates – a responsibility that could only be entrusted to a certain type of man whose qualifications for office rested more on his character and standing in the community than formal legal training. Such qualities were especially important in summary courts, where magistrates were responsible for deciding guilt or innocence without the aid of a jury and the level of punishment.

Magisterial authority – what it consisted of, who should wield it, and who should supervise those who enacted it – was a key focus of debates in the early years of the Scottish police courts. In early nineteenth-century Edinburgh, much of the discourse on the police court structure centred on whether judges should come from a legal background or be drawn from the wider community.[12] Debates reflected the hostile political climate that existed within civic governance between lawyers and magistrates. The latter, drawn mainly from business backgrounds and deemed to be of a lesser social standing than the lawyers who staffed the city's courts, struggled to implement civic policy without the support of the legal profession but were keen to preserve their traditional judicial rights in the new court structure. The former, who staffed the city's higher criminal and civil courts, were keen to further extend the powerful influence that the legal profession exerted over the governance of the city at the expense of the deeply unpopular, self-selecting town council.[13]

The outcome was an uneasy and, as it turned out, far from agreeable compromise. John Tait, Writer to the Signet, was appointed both Superintendent of Police (the head of the police establishment) and judge in the police court in 1805 whilst six ward police inspectors, appointed by the newly introduced police

[11]   Glasgow City Archives (GCA), PA2/21: *Handbook for Magistrates on Police Court Procedure, Evidence, etc by James Robertson, Procurator Fiscal* (Glasgow, 1951), p. 1.

[12]   See, for instance, Edinburgh Central Library (ECL): Company of Merchants, *Report of the Committees appointed by the Merchant Company, Incorporations, and Several other Public Bodies in the City of Edinburgh to consider the effects of the Act lately passed for Regulating the Police of the Said City* (Edinburgh, 1806), p. 24.

[13]   Edinburgh town councillors and magistrates were drawn from, and in many ways representatives of, the merchants and the 14 incorporated trades of the city. A 'city of lawyers', Edinburgh's business classes, and as a consequence its town council, were widely regarded as being of a lesser social standing than the city's lawyers, professors and civil servants. According to Daiches, merchants and manufacturers had less influence than lawyers in Edinburgh public life and struggled to carry through important municipal reforms without the backing of the legal profession. David Daiches, *Edinburgh* (London, 1978), p. 186.

commissioners, were given the responsibility of bringing forward police court prosecutions. In his younger years, Superintendent Tait had published poetry in *Ruddiman's Weekly Magazine* and *London Magazine* and was very much part of Edinburgh's *literati*.[14] He had also been active in public life having served in 1804 as secretary to a meeting for an application for the establishment of an office in Edinburgh for stamping papers. In his speech to open the police court, the Lord Provost remarked on both the legal and civic qualities that Tait was expected to display: 'Much legal, as well as local knowledge, just and steady principles, firmness of decision, united with moderation and mildness of manners, *ought* to characterise the person invested with such extensive powers as the act confers.'[15] Above all else, the superintendent and judge was expected to be in tune with, and represent, the feelings of the community – an important feature of public service that was to underpin the conceptualisation of the new court.[16]

The court's structure promoted a rhetoric of self-sacrifice which was very much in keeping with eighteenth-century notions of neo-classical governance and civil society, but its introduction had profound and far-reaching implications for public men. The 1805 Edinburgh Police Act saved and reserved to the Lord Provost, magistrates, sheriffs and justices, the civil and criminal jurisdiction they had always enjoyed in burgh and sheriff courts, but the powers which were concentrated in the superintendent and the ward inspectors in the new court were, in many ways, unprecedented.[17] They struck at the heart of traditional magisterial authority by empowering a new type of public servant to bring forward police prosecutions and to administer justice.[18] Commissioners argued that vesting police powers in the judge was necessary in order to bring offenders to justice quickly and inexpensively.[19] However, the rationale behind this was also indicative of tension between a politically conservative, legal elite, who sought to retain as much control over police affairs as possible, and Whig reformers intent on introducing greater accountability in council circles. Framed by the 'highest Tories' in Edinburgh, many of whom were drawn from legal circles,[20] the court's

---

[14]   'John Tait (1748–1817)', *Spenser and the Tradition: English Poetry, 1579–1830*, 2006, http://spenserians.cath.vt.edu/authorrecord.php?action=GET&recordid=33226

[15]   *Caledonian Mercury*, 18 July 1805. Italics in the original.

[16]   As Superintendent Tait remarked in the same ceremony: 'To conduct an Establishment of Police, is therefore, an important, and reflection tells us, that it must be an arduous task. But I here declare, that no considerations of personal labour, no consideration of personal safety, shall deter me from performing, so far as my abilities may reach, the duties which I conceive to be attached to the situation which I am now to hold.' *Caledonian Mercury*, 18 July 1805.

[17]   Edinburgh Police Act, 1805 (45 George III, cap. 21).

[18]   Ibid., section 76.

[19]   ECL: *Reports of the Committee of Commissioners of Police and Minutes of General Meetings Thereto, 23 February 1807* (Edinburgh, 1807), p. 11.

[20]   The Lord President, the Lord Justice Clerk, the Lord Advocate, and the Writer to the Signet were among the leading legal figures who helped to frame the 1805 Edinburgh

constitutional framework reflected the powerful influence of lawyers and advocates in Edinburgh. Its hierarchy challenged the authority of the businessmen who made up the town council and magistracy, and exerted legal influence over police affairs by making the superintendent – himself a legal man – accountable to the newly established Edinburgh Police Commission.[21] The latter, in its formative years, was dominated by leading legal figures, many of whom were named as *ex-officio* representatives, although *ex-officio* places were also reserved for magistrates and leading figures from the city's public bodies.

However, the constitutional structure of the police court soon provoked trenchant opposition both from Edinburgh's middling ranks and men in civic circles. In 1806, a letter from CIVIS to Henry Erskine, the Lord Advocate, revealed one perception of the social basis of the discontent regarding the court: 'Extreme dissatisfaction prevails throughout this metropolis ... among the intelligent, the decent, and the most respectable citizens of Edinburgh.'[22] One of a number of local correspondents who criticised the superintendent's role as both police chief and judge,[23] its author condemned the superintendent's power as 'extravagant', 'unconstitutional'[24] and tantamount to 'legal tyranny'.[25] Discontent was also voiced at the absence of appeal against decisions, 'the creation of new and arbitrary offences' and the ill-defined nature of many of them – such as vagrancy, begging and acting in suspicious circumstances. The superintendent, it was claimed, had 'the function of a legislator as well as a judge'.[26] To make matters worse for CIVIS, police officers who gave evidence in court and secured a conviction were entitled to 50 per cent of the fines that were handed down.[27] It was, in many ways, a remarkable constitutional structure, not least given Edinburgh's occupational profile and importance within the Scottish criminal justice system. The 'City of Lawyers' and widely heralded hotbed of 'jurisprudential genius'[28] had devised a new court of justice in which the separation of judicial and policing powers were,

---

Police Act and ensure its safe passage through Parliament. *Edinburgh Advertiser*, 30 April 1805.

[21]   *Caledonian Mercury*, 18 July 1805.

[22]   ECL: *CIVIS, A Letter to the Right Hon. Henry Erskine, Lord Advocate of Scotland, relative to the Act of Parliament for regulating the Police of Edinburgh* (Edinburgh, 1806), p. 2.

[23]   A Letter from M to the Editor, Entitled 'Parallel between the Edinburgh and Glasgow System of Police', in *Scots Magazine*, 1807, p. 29, criticises the absolute power with which the superintendent is vested, the obstacles thrown in the way of appeal, and the creation of new and arbitrary offences.

[24]   ECL, *Reports of the Committee of Commissioners of Police and Minutes of General Meetings Thereto*, p. 11.

[25]   ECL, *A Letter to the Right Hon. Henry Erskine*, pp. 6 & 11.

[26]   Ibid., p. 17.

[27]   Ibid.

[28]   See, for instance, James Buchan, *Crowded with Genius: The Scottish Enlightenment: Edinburgh's Moment of the Mind* (New York, 2003). For the 'genius' of Scots Law, see

at best, highly dubious, and in which police officers had a financial incentive to commit perjury![29]

In 1806, a report by the 'Merchant's Company, Incorporations and other Public Bodies in the City' condemned the court for having been 'constituted in such a manner that it cannot fail to produce great injustice' and which afforded the accused little chance of being acquitted.[30] The report reserved special criticism for the fact that a paid justice rather than a civic magistrate was at its head. The criticism reflected, to some extent, the loss of power, status and influence for the business leaders who served in the magistracy, but it was also indicative of the longstanding constitutional belief in Scottish civic circles that unpaid representatives of the community – meaning, in effect, men of a certain social standing – were better administrators of local justice than legally trained ones. Not only, it was claimed, did lay participation help legitimise the workings of the criminal justice system, it also ensured it would function more effectively.[31] As the report pointed out:

> The persons brought before him [the police judge] are the most miserable of human beings; and he is to listen to the details of their wretchedness and their vices, the latter of which it is his duty to punish. By length of time, he must gradually become accustomed to the spectacle of human degradation, and his heart must be hardened by the sight of vice and misery. He must, therefore, by degrees, become less qualified to administer the law with

Lindsay Farmer, *Criminal Law, Tradition and Legal Order: Crime and the Genius of Scots Law, 1747 to the Present* (Cambridge, 1997).

[29]   Commissioners defended the practice in principle but argued that the funds should be distributed to reflect officer performance. ECL, *Reports of the Committee of Commissioners of Police and Minutes of General Meetings Thereto*, p. 14.

[30]   As the report pointed out, in the police court 'a Police-Officer is a competent witness; while, at the same time, one half of all fines are directed to be distributed among the Police Officers. Thus the accused person has little chance of being acquitted in a Court where the witnesses against him are allowed publicly to receive a bribe, for telling such a tale as will produce his condemnation. The consequences of such an institution are very obvious. The whole Officers of Police are placed under a powerful temptation to commit the horrid crime of perjury; and if they can once habituate themselves to this crime, it will be in their power to render their office abundantly lucrative, by levying upon the public, in the form of fines, what contributions they think fit. Even in the infancy of the Establishment, when such corruption could not exist, such has been the activity produced in the hope of profit, that while in Glasgow the fines in one year have amounted only to £117, 1, 3½ including the fees paid for bail-bonds; they amounted in Edinburgh, in fifteen months, to no less than £809, exclusive of the expense of bail-bonds. But in Glasgow, as already stated, the whole fines are devoted to the use of the Public.' ECL, *Report of the Committees appointed by the Merchant Company*, pp. 25–6.

[31]   Johan Findlay, *All Manner of People: The History of the Justices of the Peace in Scotland* (Edinburgh, 2000), preface.

humanity, and to preserve that dignity of character, and sanctity of language, which ought to appear in the person guarding the morals of a people. On the other hand, temporary Magistrates have the advantage of entering a Court of Police with all the sympathies of humanity alive in their minds, and with more commiseration for the misery, than contempt for the abject condition of guilty. They are likely, therefore, to prove far more successful in the most valuable object of the Institution, that of reclaiming the vicious, and rendering virtue respectable. In the case, too, of petty nuisances and disputes, being themselves engaged in business, they are more likely to understand correctly what is, or is not a fault, and how far some inconveniences must not be submitted to by those who think fit to reside in a crowded city.[32]

Political compromise and expediency were significant reasons for the peculiar judicial arrangement, but there were other financial, political and cultural influences. Rewarding officers for securing convictions was not only intended to provide a financial incentive for good performance, it was also in keeping with the common law custom in private prosecutions known as 'moiety' which allowed half the money of a fine to be handed over to the informer. It is also possible, John McGowan points out, that the court's constitutional structure was influenced by the Dublin Police Act of 1795, where the chief magistrate was also superintendent, and by the example of the Lieutenant of Police in Paris, who served as a magistrate in his own court and commanded 3,000 police officers.[33] Although impossible to say conclusively, the latter model might have been closely examined by the framers of the 1805 Edinburgh Police Act given the close cultural and legal relationship that existed between Scotland and France in the eighteenth century. Although the function and responsibilities of the superintendents in Edinburgh and France were not the same, French influence on Scottish legal affairs was profound.[34] Moreover, the former Lord Provost of Glasgow (1782–1784), and later police reformer in London, Patrick Colquhoun, author of *A Treatise on the Police of the Metropolis* (1796), was an admirer of the French policing system and was consulted over the framing of the 1805 act

---

[32]　ECL, *Report of the Committees appointed by the Merchant Company*, p. 24.

[33]　John McGowan, *Policing the Metropolis of Scotland: A History of the Police and Systems of Police in Edinburgh and Edinburghshire, 1770–1833* (Musselburgh, 2010), pp. 329–30. For more on the police in Paris, see David Garrioch, 'The Paternal Government of Men: The Self-Image and Action of the Paris Police in the Eighteenth Century', in David G. Barrie and Susan Broomhall (eds), *A History of Police and Masculinities, 1700–2010* (London, 2012), pp. 35–54.

[34]　See, for instance, Hector L. MacQueen, 'Linguistic Communities in Medieval Scots Law', in Christopher W. Brooks and Michael Lobban (eds), *Communities and Courts in Britain, 1150–1900* (London, 1997), pp. 13–22; and T.B. Smith, 'The Influence of the "Auld Alliance" with France on the Law of Scotland', in *Studies Critical and Comparative* (Edinburgh, 1962), pp. 28 & 44.

by Edinburgh's legal and political elite.[35] Exactly how much influence he exerted over the new court structure is not known, but he did attend a meeting on the framing of the police bill in 1804 (which became the 1805 Edinburgh Police Act) and was later thanked by police commissioners for his contribution to it.[36] Police commissioners in the neighbouring burgh of Leith also acknowledged that Colquhoun's advice resulted in considerable alteration to the original bill.[37] Admittedly, the judicial and constitutional arrangements proposed by Colquhoun in his *Treatise* were not the same as those which were established in Edinburgh, with Colquhoun himself acknowledging that a city such as London required a policing system to match its unique status in the United Kingdom.[38] Nonetheless, there were enough similarities in terms of how he viewed 'police' and the purpose it should serve to suggest that his ideas might have been taken seriously in Edinburgh.[39] The Edinburgh Police Act certainly offered an improved defence for private property and made it easier to categorise, convict and punish marginal social groups and the most vulnerable in society – all of which were close to Colquhoun's heart.

The 1806 Merchant Company report condemned the structure of the police court and recommended placing at its head unpaid magistrates (men who were drawn from professions like their own which dominated the town council) rather than a paid superintendent.[40] It was an appeal to long-held notions of civil society by which urban Scotland was mainly governed,[41] but it was also indicative of the discontent that existed in civic circles about where power lay within the new court structure. In theory, the superintendent was accountable to police commissioners and could imprison offenders for two months (significantly less than the punishments in the scope of sheriffs, for example).[42] Moreover inspectors, who reported to the superintendent, could prosecute crimes and offences covered only under the 1805 Police Act. Nonetheless, there was clearly confusion surrounding the court's constitutional structure, judicial authority, and lines of supervision, with

---

[35]   For more, see David G. Barrie, 'Patrick Colquhoun, the Scottish Enlightenment and Police Reform in Glasgow in the Late Eighteenth Century', *Crime, Histoire & Sociétés/ Crime, History & Societies*, 12/2 (2008): pp. 59–79; and Patrick Colquhoun, *A Treatise on the Police of the Metropolis* (London, 1796).

[36]   McGowan, *Policing the Metropolis of Scotland*, pp. 99, 127 & 131–2.

[37]   Edinburgh City Archives (ECA), SL80/1/5: Leith Commissioners Minute Book, 30 May 1804.

[38]   Colquhoun, *A Treatise on the Police of the Metropolis*, passim.

[39]   Barrie, 'Patrick Colquhoun, the Scottish Enlightenment and Police Reform in Glasgow', pp. 59–79.

[40]   ECL, *Report of the Committees appointed by the Merchant Company*, pp. 1–36.

[41]   Graeme Morton, *Unionist Nationalism: Governing Urban Scotland, 1830–1860* (East Linton, 1999).

[42]   ECL: *A Second Letter to the Right Honourable Henry Erskine, Lord Advocate of Scotland relative to the Act of Parliament for Regulating the Police of Edinburgh* (Edinburgh, 1807).

commissioners themselves in 1807 expressing concern that 'it is very difficult to state what that check ought to be, as it appears that the general commissioners have no authority over him [the superintendent] in his judicial capacity'.[43] For many of the civic and legal elite, what was at stake was not the liberty of the populace, but rather, it seems, the threat that the new court posed to their own authority as Edinburgh's governing men.[44]

The perceived lack of adequate checks and balances over the superintendent, coupled with claims of corruption,[45] led to significant constitutional reform of the police court and the endorsement of magisterial authority under the terms of the 1812 Edinburgh Police Act.[46] The Act was framed on the recommendations of magistrates and public bodies in the city, which constituted a significant legal presence.[47] Glasgow's police court, which was conducted by magistrates alone, was rejected as a model. So, too, were the recently reformed policing and court models in London, where stipendiary magistrates had been introduced. These were not deemed suitable for Edinburgh, belying the often projected argument advanced by historians that metropolitan principles and practices served as a model for other parts of the United Kingdom.[48] Instead, the assembled parties insisted on upholding Edinburgh's distinctive structure in which 'the Sheriff should not only take a share in the performance of those judicial duties, but should be placed as much as possible at the head of the Police establishment'.[49] Under the 1812 Act, the superintendent was to be appointed by the Lord Provost, the Lord President of the Court of Session and the sheriff-depute of the county of Edinburgh, or

---

[43]   ECL, *Reports of the Committee of Commissioners of Police and Minutes of General Meetings Thereto*, p. 11.

[44]   Concern was expressed in both civic and legal circles that the superintendent was too independent of the authority of commissioners. See ibid., passim.

[45]   ECL, *A Letter to the Right Hon. Henry Erskine*, p. 29.

[46]   Edinburgh Police Act, 1812 (52 George III, cap. 172).

[47]   Although a strong legal influence was exerted in the framing of the act, it was not a determining one. Twelve of 27 men listed at the general meeting of the public bodies were from legal circles, including the Lord Advocate, the Lord President, the Lord Justice Clerk, the Solicitor General, and the Dean of the Faculty of Advocates. The others were representatives of civic life (magistrates) and the main public bodies (dean of guild, the convenor of the trades, master of the merchant company) from which the social composition of the town council was drawn. At the general meeting it was agreed to appoint a sub-committee to prepare a heads of police bill, of whom 7 of 15 representatives were drawn from the legal profession. This bill was in turn presented to the public bodies of the city for sanction. ECL, *Report of the Committee appointed at the General Meeting of the Magistrates, and the Different Public Bodies in the City, to Concert Measures for Obtaining a more Efficient System of Police* (Edinburgh, 1812), pp. 1–3.

[48]   As the 1806 *Report of the Committees appointed by Merchant Company* (p. 5) stated: 'It is evident, that a system of Police which might prove beneficial or necessary to the great City of London, would prove cumbersome and useless in Edinburgh.'

[49]   *Caledonian Mercury*, 4 April 1812.

any two of them.[50] The Act distinguished between magistrates (and the sheriff-depute or his substitutes) as judges of the police court and the superintendent as procurator fiscal, thus separating judicial and prosecutorial powers. It also prohibited officers from sharing in the proceeds of police court fines.[51] Sheriffs and magistrates were given cumulative and concurrent jurisdiction within the police district and police court in recognition of traditional judicial rights and in order to safeguard against confusion over territorial boundaries which were said to be 'ill-defined and debatable'.[52] But, interestingly, the sheriff's involvement was also an acknowledgement of the importance of a legal presence on the bench, especially for preparing cases involving aggravation that were required to be prosecuted in a higher court:[53]

> It must appear sufficiently obvious, that, for the prevention of crimes, it is not enough that offenders are detected, but that evidence must also be obtained to lead to their conviction; and that this should be accomplished with as much dispatch as possible, in order that the trial and punishment may speedily follow the offence. This laborious, important, and often difficult duty, seems much better adapted to a professional lawyer, holding the permanent situation of Sheriff, than to Magistrates who annually go out of office, and who cannot be possessed of the knowledge or habits necessary for such investigations.[54]

Justice and legal officials were now firmly placed as the authoritative supervisors of police administration, but it was Edinburgh's civic circle of manufacturers and merchants who made up the town council that would provide the court's lay magistrates.[55]

Interestingly, the appointment of magistrates and justices at the head of the police court appears to have provoked little opposition, but vesting control of the

---

[50] McGowan, *Policing the Metropolis of Scotland*, p. 163.

[51] Under the 1812 Edinburgh Police Act, the Police Court judges were the magistrates and the sheriff-depute or his substitutes. *The Edinburgh Almanack and the Scots Register for 1808* (Edinburgh, 1808), p. 197.

[52] Had sheriffs not been given jurisdiction, it was claimed that 'many difficult questions would have occurred, and serious litigation might, in many cases, have arisen'. ECL: *Case for the Commissioners of Police for the City of Edinburgh and Adjoining Districts, for the Opinion of Counsel* (Edinburgh, 1854), pp. 4 & 13.

[53] *Caledonian Mercury*, 4 April 1812. This was, in part, also to overcome any confusion that could arise over the territorial boundaries of judicial authority between the burgh and the county (with civic magistrates dealing with crimes within the town's judicial boundaries, and the sheriff dealing with those committed on the outskirts of the city).

[54] ECL, *Report of the Committee appointed at the General Meeting of the Magistrates*, pp. 6–7.

[55] For more on Edinburgh's governing elite, see Morton, *Unionist Nationalism*. For the cultural circles in which Edinburgh's elite moved, see Michael Fry, *Edinburgh: A History of the City* (London, 2009).

superintendent in the hands of just three prominent civic and legal figures rather than elected commissioners was strongly criticised in local press reports. As an anonymous letter to *The Scotsman* in 1817 noted, 'A great object, too, seems to have been, to exclude the inhabitants, as much as possible, from all control, direct or indirect, over the police system.'[56] Entrusting the superintendent with bringing forward police prosecutions was also contentious.[57] In 1821, Alexander Ponton, solicitor at law and Procurator Fiscal for the burgh court of Edinburgh, highlighted the concern that existed in legal circles over the superintendent's role as fiscal in the police court. He proposed establishing a Society for the Protection of Private Property to bring forward prosecutions against crimes such as theft, robbery, swindling, forgery and embezzlement of goods or money, which 'merit a higher punishment than the police can inflict'.[58] His sentiments were further evidence of the desire to better safeguard private property in the city, but they also belied a strong element of self-interest and loss of status on his part. This was not lost on *The Scotsman*; it not only suggested that the establishment of this society is 'unnecessary and absurd' as existing arrangements were more than adequate, but also that Mr Ponton sought to profit from an increase in the number of criminal prosecutions.[59] The proposal and the response it stimulated were indicative of the tensions between public men over the structure of the police court and the fact that its creation, for some of them, had implications for their power, position and income.

In other burghs, the new police court structure also challenged existing urban power structures, but in different ways. In Dundee, hostility from men of property towards the town council was so entrenched that mercantile and manufacturing

---

[56]   *The Scotsman*, 1 February 1817.

[57]   'Fourth Report by Her Majesty's Law Commissioners, Scotland, 1839', *British Parliamentary Papers* (*BPP*), 1840 (241), XX.115, p. 307.

[58]   *The Scotsman*, 23 June 1821.

[59]   *The Scotsman* opposed the proposal on the basis that the superintendent was best placed to investigate and prosecute crimes. It also pointed out that Edinburgh had more than enough prosecutors: 'The sheriff-depute again, has in Edinburgh, a substitute or assistant, who is a thoroughly-bred lawyer; and the *present holder of that office* has given proof of his *legal knowledge*. In the Sheriff-court, also, there is a Procurator Fiscal, equal, at least, in rank and talents to the Fiscal for the city; and the Sheriff and his functionaries, we imagine, have a more regular and familiar intercourse with the Crown Lawyers, than the City-Fiscal. Having, therefore, a Fiscal of Police, a county Procurator-Fiscal, a Sheriff Substitute, a Sheriff-Depute, various depute advocates, a Solicitor-General, and a Lord Advocate, all paid by the public for attending to the criminal business of the country, there is no city in the world, we believe, that stands so little in need of *additional prosecutors*, or an additional spur to prosecution, as Edinburgh. Were we to recommend any change, indeed, it would be to lesson, not to increase, the number of prosecutors and prosecutions.' *The Scotsman*, 23 June 1821. Italics in original. There was also opposition to the fact that the people had no control over the superintendent. As an anonymous letter to *The Scotsman*, 1 February 1817, noted: 'A great object, too, seems to have been, to exclude the inhabitants, as much as possible, from all control, direct or indirect, over the police system.'

elites insisted that magistrates in the new police court be drawn from the police commissioners who represented the 11 wards of the police district (each ward electing two commissioners).[60] The property qualification for the position of commissioner was fixed at £10, which ensured that only a certain type of man was eligible to pass judgement in the court. Nonetheless, it brought to prominence a new group of businessmen who hitherto had been excluded from the civic and judicial affairs of the city and established a new governing class based on the value of property.[61] The membership of the Dundee Police Commission in its formative years included large mill-owners, such as William Brown and James Tawse, with very few representatives who had links with the local council returned.[62]

However, while elected police commissions gave new men of wealth a voice and power base in public life which was otherwise denied them before burgh reform in 1833, in most towns the traditional civic authorities clung firmly to their privileged position as police court judges. According to the evidence presented to the 1839 Law Inquiry commissioners, judicial powers were reserved for magistrates in the overwhelming majority of police courts, including in Scotland's largest city, Glasgow.[63] Magistrates, or bailies as they were often referred to in Scots law and civic administration, were appointed from among councillors.[64] Normally, the position was reserved for more senior members of the council, who could typically serve as bailies for up to three years in most burghs.[65] Prior to burgh reform, councillors were chosen by, and from, representatives of the merchants and trades houses – in other words, affluent men of commerce, trade and industry. They were invariably Protestant. The introduction of the £10 property franchise in 1833 did little to change the social composition of councils, not least as burgess membership continued to be a pre-requisite for office.[66] Indeed, unlike

---

[60] See *Aberdeen Journal*, 4 February 1829.

[61] It also appears to have influenced similar developments in other towns. In Aberdeen, a committee of citizens, which formed to discuss the framing of the 1829 Aberdeen Police Act, opposed the original suggestion from civic leaders that four elected representatives should sit in the proposed police court. They instead wanted 'something like that of Dundee' as 'a Police Court thus numerously constituted must necessarily do away with any idea of undue influence'. Ibid.

[62] Louise Miskell, 'Civic Leadership and the Manufacturing Elite: Dundee 1820–1870', in Louise Miskell, Christopher A. Whatley and Bob Harris (eds), *Victorian Dundee: Image and Realities* (East Linton, 2000), p. 55.

[63] 'Fourth Report by Her Majesty's Law Commissioners, Scotland, 1839', pp. 319–40.

[64] In Scotland, the terms 'bailie' and 'magistrate' were often used interchangeably. In most burghs, bailies were the senior magistrates in terms of length of service.

[65] *The Dundee Courier & Argus*, 6 January 1865.

[66] Irene Maver, 'The Guardianship of the Community: Civic Authority before 1833', in T.M. Devine and Gordon Jackson (eds), *Glasgow, Volume I: Beginnings to 1830* (Manchester, 1995), pp. 239–77; and Irene Maver, 'Glasgow's Civic Government', in W. Hamish Fraser and Irene Maver (eds), *Glasgow, Volume II: 1830 to 1912* (Manchester, 2000), pp. 443–8.

Illustration 2.1   Bailie James Moir, 1872. @CSG CIC Glasgow
Museums and Libraries Collection: The Mitchell
Library, Special Collections†

Note: A former Chartist, and member of the National Reform League in the 1860s, Moir was, in his political persuasion, one of the more 'radical' magistrates who served in the Glasgow Police Court. His political leanings were by no means representative of Glasgow's civic elite which was overwhelmingly Conservative or Liberal. However, as this satirical portrait, with its exotic representation of 'the leaf of China', conveys, he was also a successful tea merchant and, like many of his civic counterparts, consumed with notions of public dignity and moral probity. According to *The Bailie*, Moir's political leanings did not prevent him from adopting a tough stance against those he convicted: 'On the bench his worship is "extra efficient". Traditions of "sixty days" imprisonment, and "the Lord have mercy on your soul" haunt his mind. He bestows "sixty days" and forgets the imprecation with a precision and regularity which could be excelled by no Stipendiary.'

† 'James Moir', *The Bailie*, no. 4, 13 November 1872, p. 3.

in Edinburgh, to come from a business background was deemed an essential requirement for public office. It was from here that a magistrate's respectability and social standing were derived.[67] Local justice in Scottish provincial centres was firmly in the grasp of mercantile and manufacturing elites, who often moved in the same social and cultural circles and had interconnected interests with civic dignitaries.[68] Magistrates were expected to be 'independent' men of wealth and 'dignity' – meaning, in effect, a certain type of propertied man of social status in their communities (see Illustration 2.1). They were unpaid amateur justices with no legal training and were expected to serve their communities as part of their civic duty – a hallmark of Scottish civil society espoused by Scottish Enlightenment rhetoric.[69] Being of independent financial means was portrayed as being essential to ensure the 'neutrality' of the law, which guaranteed that lay justice in early nineteenth-century Scotland was the domain of a small, privileged club of men from similar backgrounds and with similar values and interests.

That is not to say, though, that such men were above criticism, especially in the politically charged pre-burgh reform era. Indeed, they were often strongly criticised and portrayed as uneducated up-and-comers by those who sought to reform local government. In 1832, for instance, the Scottish poet and journalist William Motherwell wrote a comic portrayal of the made-up character, Peter Pirnie, a manufacturer and Paisley bailie.[70] Although unaware of it, Pirnie is portrayed in the text as a laughing stock in public life. Motherwell's creation was likely responding to the earlier work by John Galt, who in 1822 published the

---

[67] This extended to most aspects of public office in the early nineteenth century, not just the magistracy. See David G. Barrie, 'Epoch-Making Beginnings to Lingering Death: The Struggle for Control of the Glasgow Police Commission, 1833–46', *Scottish Historical Review*, 86(2)/222 (2007): pp. 253–77, especially p. 263; A. Allan MacLaren, 'Class Formation and Class Fractions: The Aberdeen Bourgeoisie, 1836–50', in George Gordon and Brian Dicks (eds), *Scottish Urban History* (Aberdeen, 1983), p. 112. A similar rationale governed English incorporations. See E.P. Hennock, *Fit and Proper Persons: Ideal and Reality in Nineteenth-Century Urban Government* (London, 1973), pp. 308–12.

[68] For more on the social and cultural ties among Glasgow's mercantile and manufacturing elites, see T.M. Devine, *The Tobacco Lords: A Study of the Tobacco Merchants of Glasgow and their Trading Activities, 1740–1790* (Edinburgh, 1975); Stana Nenadic (ed.), *Scots in London in the Eighteenth Century* (Lewisburg, 2010); Stana Nenadic, 'The Middle Ranks and Modernisation', in Devine and Jackson (eds), *Glasgow, Volume I*, pp. 278–311; Stana Nenadic, 'The Victorian Middle Classes', in Fraser and Maver (eds), *Glasgow, Volume II*, pp. 265–99; and Nicholas Rogers, 'Money, Land and Lineage: The Big Bourgeoisie of Hanoverian London', *Social History*, 4/3 (1979): p. 442.

[69] David G. Barrie, 'Police in Civil Society: Police, Enlightenment and Civic Virtue in Scotland, 1780–1833', *Urban History*, 37/1 (2010): pp. 45–65.

[70] Published in 1832 in *The Day, A Morning Journal of Literature, Fine Arts and Fashion &c*, 18 January 1832. See Mary Ellen Brown, *William Motherwell's Cultural Politics: 1797–1835* (Lexington, 2001), p. 138 for discussion on the text Motherwell writes, and pp. 174–229 for the text itself.

satirical novel *The Provost*, which portrays the chief magistrate, James Pawkie, as a manipulative power-wielder in the Scottish town of Irvine.[71] In both novels, the bailies in question are characterised as a lesser middling lot who, in their different ways, do not understand the rules of polite society that they are meant to uphold and police through the court. Their representations were indicative of the fractures that existed in Scottish middle-class identity between mercantile, manufacturing and legal interests and the tensions between them in the early nineteenth century.

Moreover, precisely how 'independent' the police magistrates were when it came to enforcing the law is extremely debatable.[72] As magistrates never relinquished their position as law enforcers, they would often play a role in the suppression of street riots and would help direct police officers during them.[73] More importantly, the peculiar constitutional structure of judicial, police and civic governance in Scottish burghs ensured that there would be close ties between magistrates and the police. Although the police – managed in most burghs in the first half of the nineteenth century by police commissioners, drawn overwhelmingly from affluent business backgrounds, and elected independently from town councils[74] – assumed responsibility for law and order issues from their inception, magistrates never ceded their longstanding association with law and order. Throughout the nineteenth century, magistrates served as *ex-officio* members of police commissions and appointed burgh procurators, and also, in some burghs, the chief constable (see Illustration 2.2).

---

[71]   John Galt, *The Provost* (Edinburgh, 1822).

[72]   For a study on the independence of the judiciary in England, see David Lemmings, 'Independence of the Judiciary in Eighteenth-Century England', in Peter Birks (ed.) *The Life of the Law* (London, 1993), pp. 125–49.

[73]   In November 1820, on hearing that luminous riots had occurred in London and Glasgow, the Lord Provost and magistrates of Edinburgh issued the following proclamation: 'The Lord Provost, Sheriff and Magistrates hereby intimate their determination to maintain the public peace, and to protect the inhabitants against all attempts to disturb it, by employing for that purpose the civil and military force, which the law has placed at their disposal. The Lord Provost, Sheriff and Magistrates think it right to warn the inhabitants, that any damage done to private property must be made good by assessment on the inhabitants at large. Orders have been given to the constables and others, to apprehend and bring before the Magistrates every person who may attempt to disturb the peace by forcing any illumination.' *The Scotsman*, 25 November 1820.

[74]   In most Scottish towns, eligibility for the office of police commissioner was overwhelmingly based upon property with the franchise extending to owners and occupiers of property of sufficient rateable value. Typically, commissioners would serve for three years, with one third going out of office on a rotational basis. Although the property qualifications for police and improvement commissions in Scottish towns were often lower than in England, they still ensured that commissioners, especially in the first half of the century, were overwhelmingly drawn from business backgrounds. In Glasgow, for instance, merchants and manufacturers accounted for 62 per cent of commissioners between 1800 and 1805. For more on this, see David G. Barrie, *Police in the Age of Improvement: Police Development and the Civic Tradition in Scotland, 1775–1865* (Cullompton, 2008), pp. 131–9.

Illustration 2.2 A View of the Hall of the Grand Inquisition, 1825.
By permission of University of Glasgow Library,
Special Collections†

Note: A caricature of a meeting of Glasgow police commissioners seeking to resolve what appears to have been a disputed police election in the city. Note the Lord Provost – the 'Grand Accuser' – at the centre of police affairs and the scales of justice in the background, symbolising the perceived relationship between civic leaders, the police and the courts. The image, which sought to depict public opposition to perceived mismanagement, nepotism and corruption within the police commission (made clear by the garbled extracts on the wall), highlights the relationship between police commissioners and the criminal justice system by portraying the meeting as though it was a court of law: 'The Court is perhaps the most important and powerful in the world, the members at once exercising the offices of Accusers, Judges, Jurymen, Witnesses, Executioners, &c, &c, &c.' Intriguingly, in the image are scattered pages of the *Glasgow Courier* and the *Glasgow Chronicle* (being read by one representative at the table), suggesting a preoccupation in police circles with press reporting; moreover, the accompanying commentary notes: 'In the background are two familiars or scribes [who appear to be journalists] used by and of use to the Inquisitors.'

† Glasgow University Library (GUL), Special Collections: 'A View of the Hall of the Grand Inquisition', 1825.

Although magistrates in the first half of the century were typically outnumbered by directly elected commissioners who had no immediate ties to local councils,[75] their presence on police commissions nonetheless ensured that the separation between the judicial and administrative branches of police would be highly questionable. As *ex-officio* commissioners, magistrates had a role to play in every aspect of policing and judicial decision-making: in appointing, in most burghs, superintendents and chief constables, in determining police policy, and in adjudicating charges.[76]

---

[75]   In Glasgow, the police commission in 1800 consisted of 24 elected commissioners, the Lord Provost, three bailies, the dean of guild and the deacon convenor. A similar distribution between elected and unelected commissioners was common throughout the country, although there were some burghs where the preponderance of power lay with magistrates. The 1805 Edinburgh Police Act made provision for the establishment of a two-tier system of police administration, consisting of 24 unelected (general) commissioners, comprising the most prominent political, legal, academic and commercial figures in the city (including all the magistrates) and 42 elected (residential) commissioners. Although magistrates continued to have *ex-officio* representation throughout the century, these constitutional arrangements were later reformed, as the imbalance between elected and unelected representatives swung even more in favour of the former. It is important to note, though, that police commissions were typically divided into sub-committees (each consisting of between four to six commissioners) relating to watching, lighting, sanitation, and other branches of 'police'. Magisterial capacity to direct law and order affairs was facilitated by the fact that they sought to exert as much influence and control over watching committees – regarded as being among the most important branch of police in the larger towns – as they possibly could. Quorums for exercising powers on watching committees were restricted to fairly small numbers. Moreover, the elected commissioners who staffed watching committees often had previous council or civic connections, having served as former councillors or even magistrates, or were some of the most affluent and 'respected' members of the business community. In other words, watching arrangements were generally in the hands of a small group of elite men with considerable experience in public life. For more, see Barrie, *Police in the Age of Improvement*, pp. 131–8; William Chambers, *The Book of Scotland* (Edinburgh, 1830), pp. 84–91; and Henry Cockburn, *Memorials of His Time* (Edinburgh, 1856), p. 85.

[76]   Police commissions would typically meet every week in the larger towns and every month in the smaller ones. It was not uncommon for magistrates to attempt to increase their representation on police commissions when framing subsequent police acts. In 1819, for instance, magistrates and councillors in Glasgow introduced the following bye-law to protect Glasgow Green from damage: 'The Lord Provost and Magistrates do hereby strictly prohibit and discharge every person whatever from playing golf, cricket, shinty, foot ball or any other game whatever on the Green of this city …. [Those who do] will be prosecuted with the utmost vigour of the law.' Police resources were subsequently deployed in support of council policy. GCA: Glasgow Council, Reports, Memorials, etc., 1814–24, p. 288. Indeed, magisterial directives, especially relating to begging, public drunkenness, industrial militancy and sectarian rioting were often followed by targeted police action, suggesting that magisterial and police policy was often mutually reinforcing. Barrie, *Police in the Age of Improvement*, pp. 192–213. The sheriff of Lanarkshire also drew upon Glasgow police resources, with magisterial

They also framed local police legislation,[77] while the burgh procurators they employed played an important role in gathering and passing on intelligence about criminal and subversive activities.[78] In Edinburgh, Glasgow and other towns, bailies argued that police, prosecutorial and judicial duties were so interwoven, and so integral to the civil and criminal administration of burghs, that they could not be carried out by officers over whom they had no control.[79]

As the century went on, chief constables acquired greater autonomy from police boards which somewhat moderated magisterial influence over police affairs.[80] But this was, to some extent, offset by the fact that town councils

---

approval, to deal with strikebreaking. In 1837, the Sheriff of Lanarkshire, Archibald Alison, Superintendent Miller of the Glasgow Police and local procurators fiscal spearheaded a police raid on a meeting in a local public house in Gallowgate in the east end of Glasgow where, according to Alison, plans were laid to assassinate factory owners and blackleg strike breakers. GCA, OGC I, 97; J. Ord, 'Origin and History of the Glasgow Police Force', in *Old Glasgow Club Transactions*, vol. 1, sessions 1900–1908 (Glasgow, 1908), p. 108. For more on the influence that local justices could exert over police policy in industrial disputes, and the frustration they experienced as a result of landowners' reluctance to help finance police reform, see Alan B. Campbell, *The Lanarkshire Miners: A Social History of their Trade Unions, 1775–1974* (Edinburgh, 1979), pp. 217–18; Archibald Alison, *Some Account of My Life and Writings* (2 vols, Edinburgh, 1883), vol. 1, pp. 419–24; M. Michie, *An Enlightened Tory in Victorian Scotland: The Career of Sir Archibald Alison* (East Lothian, 1997), pp. 64–91; and K. Carson and H. Idzikowska, 'The Social Production of Scottish Policing, 1795–1900', in Douglas Hay and Francis Snyder (eds), *Policing and Prosecution in Britain, 1750–1850* (Oxford, 1989), pp. 295–7.

[77] For magistrates' role in framing local police legislation, see Barrie, *Police in the Age of Improvement*, pp. 62–74. This, though, had to be done with the approval of the Lord Advocate and parliament. David G. Barrie, 'Anglicisation and Autonomy: Scottish Policing, Governance and the State, 1833 to 1885', *Law and History Review*, 30/2 (2012): p. 455.

[78] For examples of the local procurator in Glasgow passing on criminal intelligence, see Christopher A. Whatley, 'Labour in the Industrialising City', in Devine and Jackson (eds), *Glasgow, Volume I*, p. 309; National Archives of Scotland (NAS), AD 14/23/241: Lord Advocate's Papers, 'George Salmond to Crown Agent', 23 August 1823.

[79] For more on the discourse behind police reform in Glasgow, see Barrie, *Police in the Age of Improvement*, pp. 61–91. For magistrates' view on police and judicial affairs in Edinburgh, see ECL, *Report of the Committee appointed at the General Meeting of the Magistrates*, pp. 1–27.

[80] Shortly after the Glasgow Police Commission's powers transferred to the local council in 1846, the watching minutes note that the chief superintendent 'is to have charge of the whole affairs of this establishment'. GCA, E1/9/2: Minutes of Watching and Fire Engines, 10 December 1846. It was an intellectual shift that increasingly valued knowledge and expertise over public election. In giving evidence to the 1852–1853 Select Committee on Police, John List, Superintendent of the Edinburghshire Police, highlighted this: 'commissioners are not calculated to have any knowledge of matters of police; in fact, it is their interference which causes the establishment to be not so effective as it otherwise would be.' 'Second Report from the Select Committee on Police', *BPP*, 1852–1853 (715),

throughout the major Scottish cities would become solely responsible for managing police affairs as directly elected police commissions were increasingly incorporated into local government.[81] Police powers, in other words, came to be vested in the hands of civic leaders in councils and magistracies, and not police commissioners who had been independently elected from councils in most cities up until mid-century. In Glasgow, for instance, the chief superintendent (chief constable) became answerable to magistrates and the local sheriff following the transfer of police powers from the Glasgow Police Commission to the Police and Statute Labour Committee of Glasgow Town Council in 1846 after growing concerns in council circles about the social composition and political outlook of police commissions.[82] As in the first half of the century, magistrates were able to exert considerable influence over police policy. They frequently issued directives and reports to superintendents, and were responsible for disciplining officers, which raised serious issues concerning the separation of police and judicial powers.[83] They also often had shared interests with the police in terms of how civic administration should be managed – a fact that magistrates themselves pointed out concerning the regulation of music halls[84] – and often worked together over spirit licensing, unlike county justices.[85] More often than

XXXVI.161, p. 101. In practice, though, magistrates were still able to direct chief constables when the need arose, as examples in this book show.

[81] For instance, independently elected police commissions were incorporated into local government in Glasgow in 1846, Dundee in 1851, Edinburgh in 1856, Paisley in 1864 and Aberdeen in 1871. For more on the political struggle behind this transition, see Barrie, *Police in the Age of Improvement*, pp. 224–60.

[82] Barrie, 'Epoch-Making Beginnings to Lingering Death', pp. 253–77; and Irene Elizabeth Sweeney, 'The Municipal Administration of Glasgow, 1833–1912: Public Service and The Scottish Civic Identity', unpub. PhD thesis (University of Strathclyde, 1990), pp. 121–2.

[83] In Glasgow, magistrates' minutes, for instance, are crammed with references to magistrates instructing the fiscal and superintendent to enforce the law on certain issues, ranging from nuisances to illegal drinking. In 1873, for instance, after receiving petitions from ratepayers protesting about public safety in the sixth ward, magistrates in Glasgow instructed 'the fiscal and chief constable to take steps to deal with obstructions on public streets'. GCA, E1/13/3: Magistrates Committee Minute Book, 5 October 1871. See also E1/13/5.

[84] GCA, B3/1/11 (2 vols): Glasgow Newspaper Cuttings, 1910 to 1950. On 13 February 1912, it was reported in the *Glasgow Herald* that the magistrates in the Central Police Court had made the point that 'a very grave responsibility is shared between magistrates and the police' concerning the regulation of overcrowding in music halls, because if anything happened the blame would have been put on them.

[85] In his report into the state of crime in Glasgow, Superintendent Miller noted: 'The Magistrates ought also to possess the power, without appeal, of granting or withholding a license within the city; as they are the constituted guardians of the community, and must be presumed the best judges in all matters relating to the city police. It has frequently happened that worthless people who have been refused a license by the Magistrates,

not, according to contemporary reports, magistrates would side with policemen. In 1878 the Glasgow journal *The Bailie* reported,

> *The Bailie* is sorry to find usually-sensible men like Bailies Waddel and Lamberton stultifying themselves as they did last Tuesday. A policeman was found guilty of having violated his duty and brutally assaulted a woman; but the magistrates declined to inflict any punishment, on the extraordinary ground that "no malice was intended!" This is really monstrous [*sic*]. When an ordinary member of the public commits an assault, the magistrates do not pause to analyse his motives, but fine or imprison without further question; but it seems Tonalt's [the policeman's] case is different.[86]

There were even suggestions that magistrates were using police resources and police courts to promote their own political, moral and religious views. In a case involving the trial of W. Campbell Sleigh, barrister-at-law, and Thomas Russell Esq., merchant, for an alleged breach of the peace at a music hall in Edinburgh, on 8 April 1850, the Lord Provost was criticised by a broad spectrum of middle-class opinion and *The Scotsman* for using police resources to stifle opposing views on the Marriage Affinity Bill, which sought to make it legal for a man to marry his deceased wife's sister. According to contemporary reports, the provost not only ordered the police to arrest the two gentlemen cited for speaking out against his opposition to the bill, he also exerted influence on the sitting magistrate and fiscal in court. According to the author of the report into the subsequent courtroom proceedings, the provost, at the close of his evidence in the witness box, 'addressed a speech to his deputy who was sitting on the bench, the import of which was the equivalent to a declaration – "Convict! Convict! whether the law or the facts will warrant you or not"'.[87] Moreover, as members and representatives of the council, magistrates were heavily involved in promoting civic initiatives and raising public money for police services, which often influenced how local bye-laws, especially on public drunkenness, were administered.[88] As the image (Illustration 2.3), published in *The Bailie* in June 1873, of ex-Glasgow magistrate

---

have succeeded in obtaining one by an appeal to the Justices of the Peace at quarter sessions, though on such occasions the Superintendent of Police and his Officers were in attendance to support the decision of the Magistrates.' GCA, M.P.24, D-T.C.14/1/24, 23: *Papers Relative to the State of Crime in the City of Glasgow, with Observations of a Remedial Nature; and an Appendix of Tables, by H. Miller, Superintendent of Police, and City Marshal* (Glasgow, 1840), p. 9.

[86]   *The Bailie*, no. 272, 2 January 1878, p. 2.

[87]   National Library of Scotland (NLS): George Gunn, *Report of the Proceedings in the Police Court, in the Trial of W. Campbell Sleigh, esq., of London, Barrister-at-Law, and Thomas Russell, Esq., of Hunter Square, Edinburgh, Merchant, for an Alleged Breach of the Peace at the Music Hall, April 8, 1850, held with Reference to the Marriage Affinity Bill* (Edinburgh, 1850), p. 33.

[88]   See Chapter 5 for more on this.

Illustration 2.3   Bailie William Miller, 1873. @CSG CIC Glasgow
                    Museums and Libraries Collection: The Mitchell
                    Library, Special Collections[†]

Note: In an article entitled 'My Conscience', *The Bailie* exposed the various responsibilities of Glasgow magistrate William Miller. He held many positions within Glasgow Town Council, including that of City Treasurer, 1872–1875. A partner of the dyeing company Miller, Higgenbotham and Co., and a bank manager in the affluent suburb of Hillhead, *The Bailie* described Miller as 'dull, pre-eminently respectable and pliable, and yet looking clever at one and the same time'.

† 'William Miller', *The Bailie*, no. 35, 18 June 1873.

William Miller suggests, magistrates had a multi-faceted role in civic life.[89] They served on multiple committees and juggled different responsibilities, some of which had implications for how justice was administered in police courts, as is explored throughout this book.

That is not to say that civic magistrates and the police always worked together for a single purpose – a fact pointed out by Davis and Miller in their respective studies of police courts in London and New York.[90] The relationship between the police and magistrates was complex and it would be misleading to suggest that it was always harmonious. There were frequent personality, political and religious clashes in Scottish civic administration. Council leaders and senior police officials were by no means always united – indeed, up until the incorporation of elected police commissions into local government in the mid-century police commissioners were often trenchant and vociferous political opponents of town councillors. Indeed, by the 1830s, police commissions in some Scottish burghs in effect became political opponents of councils, with lower electoral rates, and a residential qualification for office, making it easier for members of the skilled, self-employed working class to get elected to police commissions than town councils.[91] Similarly, according to contemporary reports, procurators were not averse to falling out with magistrates in the heat of courtroom drama.[92] However, their relationship was much more intimate in the Scottish police courts than in the case studies examined by Davis and Miller. Magistrates, in principle, were not expected to work in tandem with the police, but in practice they often did for a range of public morality and behavioural offences in their efforts to improve urban order and reshape popular culture. Indeed, *The Bailie*, a journal sometimes critical but not overtly unsympathetic to the plight of citizen magistrates, described one of the magistrates, Bailie Walls, in 1874 as being 'a patron of the police' – except, that is, in regard to smoke offences in which he had an interest as an oil refiner (see Chapter 4 of Volume 2).[93]

---

[89]   *The Bailie*, no. 35, 18 June 1873.

[90]   Davis, 'A Poor Man's System of Justice?', p. 315; and Wilbur Miller, *Cops and Bobbies: Police Authority in New York and London, 1830 to 1870* (Chicago, 1977), p. 86. For a study of the police–magistrate relationship in Canada, see Donald Fyson, *Magistrates, Police, and People: Everyday Criminal Justice in Quebec and Lower Canada, 1764–1837* (Toronto, 2006), p. 467.

[91]   For more on the civic hostility between police commissions and local councils, see Barrie, *Police in the Age of Improvement*, pp. 234–44; and Maver, 'Glasgow's Civic Government', p. 453. Police commissions and councils themselves were often divided and by no means always spoke with one voice. In 1877, for instance, *The Bailie* published an article exposing the factions that existed within the municipal machine and the Lord Provost's 'inner-circle' of allies. *The Bailie*, no. 244, 20 June 1877, p. 1.

[92]   See, for instance, the commentary in *The Bailie* of Glasgow burgh fiscal John Lang, who according to the journal could often bully and intimidate magistrates and police officers in court. *The Bailie*, no. 9, 11 December 1872, pp. 1–2 and no. 133, 5 May 1875, pp. 1–2.

[93]   *The Bailie*, no. 91, 15 July 1874, p. 2.

While there might have been political differences between councillors and commissioners, especially prior to incorporation, for the most part they shared similar social and moral values and, at times vested interests, in terms of how the law should be administered, as the following chapters will show.

The fact that magistrates came from business backgrounds raised questions as to whether they could be relied upon to administer the law in a neutral manner, especially in cases involving property theft.[94] In eighteenth- and nineteenth-century England, there was similar concern that magistrates and justices from landed and commercial backgrounds were utilising judicial powers to safeguard and further their own interests.[95] On the surface, the situation did not appear as serious as in England – or, at least, did not provoke heated debates to the same extent – largely due to the fact that magisterial authority in Scottish towns was more limited than that enjoyed by southern county justices and often did not cover manufacturing and mining districts where industrial unrest was most common. Moreover, in 1812, the Court of Session, in keeping with the evolving free-market doctrine of the time, stripped magistrates of their powers to fix wage levels – traditionally an important mechanism for securing social stability – thereby reducing their capacity to become involved in industrial disputes.[96] For most of the first half of the century, it was sheriffs and high court justices rather than magistrates who were at the forefront of dealing with industrial militancy and political radicalism in Scotland. Indeed, the need for stronger policing powers to

---

[94] See Chapter 6 for more on this.

[95] For the ways in which the law was applied in an uncertain manner in England for the interests of propertied men, see Alexis de Tocqueville, *Journeys to England and Ireland*, ed. J.P. Mayer (London, 1958), p. 92, entry dated 1 June 1835; Douglas Hay, 'Poaching and the Game Laws on Cannock Chase', in Hay, Linebaugh, Rule, Thompson, Winslow (eds), *Albion's Fatal Tree*, pp. 189–253; P.B. Munsche, *Gentlemen and Poachers: The English Game Laws 1671–1831* (Cambridge, 1981); John Styles, 'Embezzlement, Industry and the Law in England 1500–1800', in Maxine Berg, Pat Hudson and Michael Sonenscher (eds), *Manufacture in Town and Country Before the Factory* (Cambridge, 1983), pp. 173–210; Douglas Hay, 'Master and Servant in England: Using the Law in the Eighteenth and Nineteenth Centuries', in W. Steinmetz (ed.), *Private Law and Social Inequality in the Industrial Age* (Oxford, 2000), pp. 227–64; Douglas Hay, 'Patronage, Paternalism and Welfare: Masters, Workers and Magistrates in Eighteenth-Century England', *International Labor and Working-Class History*, 53 (1998): pp. 27–48; King, *Crime, Justice and Discretion*; and David Philips, 'The Black Country Magistracy 1835–60: A Changing Elite and the Exercise of its Power', *Midland History*, 3/3 (1976): pp. 161–90. Morgan and Rushton, however, argue that the law was not administered in the interests of magistrates. Morgan and Rushton, 'The Magistrate, the Community and the Maintenance of an Orderly Society', pp. 54–77.

[96] W. Hamish Fraser, 'Patterns of Protest', in T.M. Devine and Rosalind Mitchison (eds), *People and Society in Scotland, Volume I: 1760–1830* (Edinburgh, 1988), pp. 280–81.

control trade unions and protect the safety of strikebreakers was a recurring argument of Archibald Alison, Sheriff of Lanarkshire.[97]

Nonetheless, although serious cases of industrial unrest were not brought before police courts, magistrates were actively involved in dealing with minor cases. Indeed, as Chapter 1 revealed, summary powers were acquired in many small towns from the mid-century onwards at the behest of manufacturers specifically to deal with industrial militancy. Magistrates on occasion were faced with adjudicating on cases in which they, as employers, might have had a vested interest. For the most part, they were compliant with business leaders in refusing to uphold traditional employment patterns that conflicted with free market economics, as Chapter 6 will show. Police court magistrates also often had to judge crimes involving property and were extremely useful in the business communities' attempts to clamp down upon the long-held custom of workers appropriating goods from the workplace as part of their income.[98] Indeed, for business owners, the support received from magistrates in criminalising behaviour that had been previously tolerated helped to buttress their efforts to impose workplace discipline and capitalist working practices.[99] Stipendiary magistrates, of course, would not necessarily have been more neutral in adjudicating on such matters. Nonetheless, as Philips points out in his study of summary justice in the coalfields of the Black Country, full-time, salaried and legally trained justices would certainly have offered a greater likelihood of impartiality than the industrialists, mine owners and landholders who sat in judgement on cases involving crimes which were similar to those which occurred on their own land or in their own businesses.[100]

The fact that citizen magistrates in Scottish towns came overwhelmingly from business backgrounds, however, did not mean that legal advice and direction were unavailable, or that they were all inexperienced in legal matters. Magistrates were likely to have acquired at least a basic understanding of law from their time on the bench. The number of bailies in Scottish towns was fairly small – in the early 1870s, Glasgow had only eight to serve the city's five police courts and population of approximately half a million people.[101] With police courts meeting every lawful day, bailies were required to sit in the police court on every other day, for up to four hours at a time. It was a huge commitment, and one which suggests that nineteenth-century lay justice could be almost semi-

---

[97] 'The First Report of the Commissioners appointed to Inquire as to the best means of Establishing an Efficient Constabulary Force in the Counties of England and Wales', *BPP*, 1839 (169), XIX.1, p. 84. See also M. Michie, *An Enlightened Tory*, pp. 64–91.

[98] For more on this, see Christopher A. Whatley, 'The Experience of Work', in Devine and Mitchison (eds), *People and Society in Scotland, Volume I*, pp. 234–9.

[99] Magistrates performed a similar function in London police courts. Davis, 'A Poor Man's System of Justice?', p. 318.

[100] Philips, 'The Black Country Magistracy', pp. 161–90.

[101] *Glasgow Post Office Directory, 1871–72* (Glasgow, 1872), p. 64.

professional in its workings – at least, in terms, of the level of the commitment shown by those who served. More importantly, on points of law, police court magistrates had recourse to assessors and town clerks. The former were writers to the signet (solicitors) who would provide legal direction to magistrates if called upon. They did not sit in the court unless asked.[102] Town clerks, on the other hand, did attend and would participate as clerks of the court. They helped magistrates work within a legal framework and ensured, in theory at least, that there would be no procedural or evidential errors in law (although, in practice, there often were, as Chapter 6 explores). Usually practising advocates or writers, they enjoyed wide-ranging judicial and ministerial responsibilities which included acting as judicial assessors when required. In Glasgow, their role even ranged from verbally examining those who had been committed to the police roundhouse the previous night, and helping procurators decide which complaints were worth bringing before magistrates, to imposing small fines that did not require more formal procedure.[103] Much of their time, though, was devoted to organising courtroom proceedings and providing advice to magistrates when called upon, although, ultimately, it was left to the discretion of bailies as to whether or not to take on board the advice given. As the *Glasgow Herald*, in discussions surrounding the introduction of a stipendiary magistrate for the city in 1858, claimed,

> In the case of an able and independent man he does not need, and will not take, any help from the legal gentleman who sits at his side, and he administers justice in his own way, which may differ considerably from the style of another independent amateur police judge who succeeds him next month.[104]

Lay magistrates in Scottish burghs, therefore, were not without legal support should they require it, but they certainly did not have the same legal background or training as justices in many other parts of the United Kingdom. In major cities, such as London and Dublin, legally trained stipendiary magistrates

---

[102]   'Eleventh Report of the Commissioners Appointed for Inquiring into the Duties, Salaries, Fees and Enrolments, of the Several Officers, Clerks, and Ministers of Justice, of the Courts in Scotland. Burgh Courts', *BPP*, 1822 (558), VIII.117, pp. 27–30; and 'First Report of the Law Commissioners Appointed to Inquire into the Courts of Law in Scotland, together with Minutes of Evidence', *BPP*, 1868–69 (4125), XXV.29, p. 334.

[103]   In 1822, the duties of the Glasgow Town Clerk and his deputes were described as being 'to examine verbally the persons who may have been committed to the roundhouse during the night; to discuss, and decide, verbally, such complaints and disputes as admit of determination in that mode; and to impose those smaller Police fines which do not require more formal procedure'. They also attended to the criminal business of the burgh court. 'Eleventh Report of the Commissioners Appointed for Inquiring into the Duties, Salaries, Fees and Enrolments, of the Several Officers, Clerks, and Ministers of Justice, of the Courts in Scotland', p. 56.

[104]   *Glasgow Herald*, 22 September 1858.

had been introduced to supplement lay magistrates from the late eighteenth century, whilst in the Scottish counties salaried professionals derived from legal backgrounds had been appointed by the Home Secretary and the Lord Justice Clerk to the Office of Sheriff from the mid-nineteenth century onwards.[105] For much of the nineteenth century, magistrates in Scotland were able to enforce the law with only limited legal direction. Indeed, this was something they valued and jealously clung to for much of the century. The relatively modest powers that magistrates had at their disposal, allied to the fact that more serious crimes were increasingly dealt with in a summary manner in sheriff courts from the second half of the century, certainly played an important role in civic magistrates' capacity to maintain their position in Scottish police courts. But their resilience ran far deeper than this. Not only did it reflect a desire to protect longstanding municipal traditions and burghal rights in the face of a perceived threat of greater central direction,[106] it was also, significantly, a product of how civic magistrates perceived themselves and their function in communities. As the next section examines, civic magistrates saw their role not as a narrow one confined to adhering rigidly to increasingly codified and formalised legal principles and procedure. Rather, it was a duty in which sensitivity to individual circumstances and community feelings were paramount.[107] It was a mentality less preoccupied with enshrined legal rights, and more in keeping with a view of magistrates' position as civic and moral leaders – and one, crucially, that was underpinned by and dependent upon discretionary justice and the flexible way in which legal procedural safeguards could be circumvented.

III. Procedure in the Age of Discretion

Magistrates had always enjoyed wide-ranging discretionary powers in burgh courts, but more serious criminal cases were normally tried according to formal procedure subject to common law. In police courts, however, all cases were to be tried in a summary manner – that is, before magistrates and without protracted, formal legal process and juries. Police courts were designed to remove the more formal technicalities of traditional legal procedure in order to quicken the judicial process and increase the volume of cases heard before magistrates.[108] As

---

[105] Anne E. Whetstone, *Scottish County Government in the Eighteenth and Nineteenth Centuries* (Edinburgh, 1981), pp. 14–17.

[106] In the early 1840s, for instance, civic leaders in Glasgow had successfully withstood a proposal to impose a centralised police model on the city and its surrounding environs following years of political disagreement and infighting between the different police and civic authorities in the area. See Barrie, *Police in the Age of Improvement*, pp. 227–9.

[107] For more on the idea of 'community justice' in Scottish summary courts, see Z.K. Bankowski, N.R. Hutton and J.J. McManus, *Lay Justice?* (Edinburgh, 1987).

[108] Farmer, *Criminal Law, Tradition and Legal Order*, p. 79.

such, they were governed by less formal procedural rules than higher courts.[109] Magistrates were still required to, and for the most part did, operate within formal legal parameters,[110] but procedural safeguards, especially in the first half of the century, were by no means as rigorously or uniformly applied as in higher courts. In submitting evidence to the 1839–1840 Law Inquiry, William Davie, Assessor of the Burgh and Police Courts of Glasgow, claimed that procedural inconsistencies in the administration of summary justice were not just prevalent throughout the country, but also within the same courts depending on the personnel involved.[111] This, he argued, was a 'material defect' in how the law was being enforced in Scottish towns.[112] Having said that, each police court adhered to some fairly common principles. All cases were to be tried 'in the easiest and most expedient manner'.[113] Libels were to take the form of a brief complaint and the formalities for recording evidence were simplified in order to quicken the legal process. The offenders were entitled to legal representation should they request – and be able to pay for – it. And the convicted could appeal against magisterial judgements for procedural breaches, although they could not appeal against judgements on evidential grounds (except, of course, in the Edinburgh Police Court's formative years where no appeal was allowed, although this was later amended). These basic procedural guidelines aside though, magistrates had much scope for independent action. Growth in central legislation from the mid-century onwards would establish limited legal guidelines in court procedure

---

[109]   Farmer makes the point that all the inferior courts had no formal rules of procedure in the early nineteenth century. Farmer, *Criminal Law, Tradition and Legal Order*, p. 70. Glasgow police acts in first few decades did not specify procedure. Indeed, the 1833 Burgh Police (Scotland) Act stated that police courts might use the forms of 9 George IV, cap. 29. Having said that, evidence presented to the 1839–1840 Law Commissioners reveals that certain basic guidelines concerning legal representation, rights of appeal, bail, and the organisation of trial proceedings were adhered to. 'Fourth Report by Her Majesty's Law Commissioners, Scotland, 1839', pp. 320–40.

[110]   For instance, The 1850 Police of Towns and Populous Places of Scotland Act (13 & 14 Victoria, cap. 33) laid down procedural arrangements which could be, and were, in some towns supplemented by local arrangements. See Dundee Central Library (DCL), Lamb Collection, 319 (10): *Rules and Regulations with Forms of Procedure for the Police Court of the Burgh of Dundee, Framed and Established by the Magistrates of the Burgh, and the Sheriff of the County of Forfar, Sanctioned and Approved by the Right Honourable The Lord Justice General, and the Right Honourable the Lord Justice-Clerk, in Terms of the Act of 18th and 14th Victoria, cap 33, Sect 219* (Dundee, 1851), pp. 1–5. These additional guidelines, though, were fairly limited and were framed by magistrates, albeit with the approval of senior legal figures in Edinburgh.

[111]   'Fourth Report by Her Majesty's Law Commissioners, Scotland, 1839', pp. 323–5.

[112]   Ibid., p. 325.

[113]   9 George IV, cap. 29, ss. 19–20 (1828) stated that the inferior courts might try offences 'in the easiest and most expedient manner' where the libel concluded for punishment not exceeding £10 or 60 days' imprisonment. Cited in Farmer, *Criminal Law, Tradition and Legal Order*, p. 76.

and practice,[114] but there remained scope for magistrates to run police courts in line with local laws, customs and wishes, with reduced legal rights of redress for those who experienced magisterial justice than for those brought to trial in higher courts.[115] Indeed, it is highly likely, as Doreen McBarnet found in her late twentieth-century study into summary courts, that because of their perception of the relatively trivial nature of much police court business, magistrates were more inclined not to adhere to all formal safeguards and rights.[116] The prevalence of clerks and assessors would help to ensure that justice was administered according to a legal framework, but it was a framework that bestowed upon magistrates much discretion in interpreting evidence and assessing witness testimonies and, which, on occasion, would be circumvented in order to serve what magistrates believed was a greater good.

The loose way in which many 'police offences' were defined in nineteenth-century police legislation gave magistrates tremendous scope to interpret the law as they saw fit. As the century went on, more and more people found themselves charged under local police and bye-laws with fairly vague catch-all offences such as 'disorderly conduct/breach of the peace' – the interpretation of which lay largely with police officers and magistrates.[117] While certain procedural guidelines were customary in Scottish police courts, in practice, procedural rules were often bent by magistrates in order to serve a wider purpose. Many cases were determined solely at the discretion, and by the authority, of magistrates. Magisterial discretion extended across a range of different areas, including whether a case was to be tried or not, how it should be pursued, and what the outcome and punishment should be. Police court judges would often use their

---

[114] The 1850 Police of Towns and Populous Places of Scotland Act stated that all process before police courts was to be summary.

[115] The 1850 Police of Towns Act and the 1862 Burgh Police (Scotland) Act (25 & 26 Victoria, cap. 101), for instance, noted that burghs could administer their own police court affairs, provided this was done 'with the advice and approbation' of senior judges. See sections 349 & 412 for each of these statutes. For more on the rise of summary procedure in the nineteenth century, see Farmer, *Criminal Law, Tradition and Legal Order*, p. 77; Albert V. Sheehan and David J. Dickson, *Criminal Procedure: Scottish Criminal Law and Practice Series*, 2nd edn (London, 2003), p. 41; Henry James Moncreiff, *A Treatise on the Law of Review in Criminal Cases* (Edinburgh, 1877), passim; and J.H.A. MacDonald, *A Practical Treatise on the Criminal Law of Scotland*, 3rd edn (Edinburgh, 1894), pp. 515–30. The Summary Procedure (Scotland) Act, 1864 (27 & 28 Victoria, cap. 53) provided for uniformity of process in summary criminal prosecutions and penalties in the inferior courts in Scotland.

[116] Doreen McBarnet, *Conviction: Law, The State and the Construction of Justice* (London, 1973), passim. Moody and Tombs also suggest that fiscals often did not treat district summary courts as seriously as higher ones. Susan Moody and Jacqueline Tombs, *Prosecution in the Public Interest* (Edinburgh, 1982), p. 14.

[117] Farmer, *Criminal Law, Tradition and Legal Order*, p. 116. See also Martin J. Wiener, *Reconstructing the Criminal: Culture, Law, and Policy in England, 1830–1914* (Cambridge, 1990), pp. 52–83 & 151–6.

authority to dismiss, admonish or reprimand those before them without pursuing the case, especially if the offence was trivial and the detention suffered previous to trial was deemed to be sufficient punishment for the offence.[118] They employed, with the concurrence of procurators, a range of prosecution strategies to serve what they perceived was a greater good. Children were sometimes remanded as a form of punishment, before later being released, in order to prevent them from acquiring a formal criminal record.[119] On the other hand, individuals perceived by magistrates to be of bad character and for whom the evidence was far from conclusive were sometimes remanded in order to ensure that they would serve at least some time in police custody.[120] Tremendous flexibility was also shown when it came to handing down punishments. Those women deemed to be of 'bad character' were frequently sent to bridewell for 60 days simply for being drunk and disorderly, while more 'respectable' members of the community were usually fined for the same offence.[121] Bailies also used their discretionary powers to arbitrate on disputes between neighbours and family members, although this was much less common than in the summary courts of eighteenth- and nineteenth-century England.[122] Both procurators and magistrates would sometimes use discretionary powers to exert pressure on disputing parties to achieve a settlement without resorting to formal legal action.

In applying discretion, magistrates attached great significance to character, appearance, status, gender and religious background, as Chapters 6 and 7 will explore in the context of conviction and punishment. In one case before the courts in 1831, for example, the police court periodical *The Police Intelligencer, or Life in Edinburgh* reported:

---

[118]   In Glasgow, no schedule for acquittals was kept in the returns presented to the 1839 Law Inquiry, but the records note that a considerable number of those convicted were merely admonished. 'Fourth Report by Her Majesty's Law Commissioners, Scotland, 1839', pp. 323–4.

[119]   In the Glasgow Police Court in 1829, a 12-year-old boy and another (age not given), charged with stealing lead and brass pipes, were remanded. It was reported that they were vagabonds who 'slept on a common dunghill in Glassford Street' and 'carried straw with them to answer for a bed on the top of the dungstead'. In remanding them, the magistrate noted: 'These little fellows, though heedless, and ill brought up, might yet, with care, be made capable of doing good.' *Police Reports of the Causes Tried before the Justices of the Peace, and the Glasgow, Gorbals and Calton Police Courts, from 18th July till 3rd October by John Brownlie (Police Reports)* (Glasgow, 1829), 8 August 1829, pp. 44–5.

[120]   See the testimony of William Davie, Assessor of the Glasgow Police and Burgh Courts, to the 1839 Law inquiry: 'Fourth Report by Her Majesty's Law Commissioners, Scotland, 1839', p. 327.

[121]   See the example of Nancy Campbell, charged with being drunk and disorderly and creating a crowd (and previously charged with prostitution), who was ordered to Bridewell for 60 days. *Police Reports*, 1 August 1829, p. 32.

[122]   See, for instance, Gray, 'The People's Courts?', pp. 7–15; and Morgan and Rushton, 'The Magistrate, the Community and the Maintenance of an Orderly Society', pp. 54–77.

A well dressed and respectable looking elderly woman was charged with being drunk and disorderly, on Wednesday forenoon, in the High Street. The Magistrate said that he was not a little surprised to see a person of the defender's appearance on such a charge; and as he had received satisfactory accounts of her former good conduct, he would dismiss her without entering into the particulars of the case.[123]

The magistrate's discretion about how to apply the law, how to proceed, and how to punish offenders, came down in a number of cases, it seems, to how he perceived the accused. Indeed, as the century progressed, 'character' would increasingly become a defining factor in shaping the administration of police court summary justice – a development which did much to further strengthen magisterial authority over the urban populace.[124]

Magistrates also used discretion when deciding how to deal with the convicted. Rather than imprison first-time juvenile offenders in the tolbooth or bridewell, William Davie, the Assessor of the Glasgow Police Court, asserted that magistrates often adopted

a very loose mode of administering criminal justice … [which involved] … remanding a party … and delaying sentence till another diet, at which he is brought up and discharged; the confinement which he has, in that way, intermediately undergone, being implied as punishment for the offence.[125]

This method of enforcing the law was by no means unique to lay magistrates. As Jennifer S. Davis has shown for police courts in nineteenth-century London, stipendiary magistrates also often relied upon discretionary powers. Nonetheless, in Scotland, there was a sense among contemporary commentators that such men utilised, and valued, discretion more, and were less likely to stick rigidly to the letter of the law than legally trained magistrates. Inconsistency in handing down punishments was often cited as being a characteristic of police court practice, with civic magistrates tending to take a tougher line than those with legal training. As a letter from 'An Ex-Bailie' to the editor of the *Dundee Courier* in 1869 pointed out,

There is no doubt, however, that there is a very great disparity between the sentences passed by different police Magistrates for the same offence. It is not very long since we had a Bailie who seldom gave less than the heaviest punishment he had power to inflict, even for the most trivial offence … such different measures of punishment for the same offence are an anomaly which

---

[123]   *The Police Intelligencer, or Life in Edinburgh* (*Police Intelligencer*), 23 September 1831.

[124]   See Chapter 6.

[125]   'Fourth Report by Her Majesty's Law Commissioners, Scotland, 1839', p. 327.

should not be allowed to continue: but while we have a change of Judges every week, nothing else can be expected.[126]

In deciding whether to convict or not magistrates were, in principle, bound by long-established traditions of Scots law. Local and national police acts in the first half of the nineteenth century made no specific reference to rules of evidence,[127] but many of the principles adopted seem to have been the same as those which governed higher courts, with press reports indicating that corroborating evidence from two witnesses was generally required to secure a conviction for a criminal offence.[128] For the most part, magistrates appear to have adhered to this in the first half of the nineteenth century, with many cases being abandoned due to lack of evidence or witnesses not showing up.[129] Nonetheless, in practice, magisterial discretion still played an integral role in determining the manner in which the evidence was interpreted and the rules governing how it should be administered. In 1825, the Lord Justice Clerk upheld an appeal against a judgement handed down by Edinburgh magistrates and remarked that he 'understood it was the practice, on many occasions, in the Police Court, to examine the witnesses, not on oath; – the sooner that practice was put a stop to the better'. He went on to state that 'he would not take the statement of the Superintendent of Police, nor any other officer whatever, as evidence, who was not on oath'.[130] Indeed, as the century went on, there was growing tension between legal and civic men over what constituted appropriate evidence to secure a conviction, as Chapter 6 explores.

Not surprisingly, the flexible way that civic magistrates enforced the law on occasion brought them into conflict with legally trained judges in higher courts who were responsible for hearing appeals concerning police court cases. In 1813, James Brown, Superintendent, and John Cruickshanks and Wilson Petrie, privates in the Edinburgh militia, lodged a complaint in the High Court against a sentence of 60 days' imprisonment and banishment on the basis that they were unable to defend themselves because of the informal manner in which the summary proceedings were carried out. The High Court judges upheld their appeal and resolved that

> it was necessary to follow exactly the same form of procedure established by law in criminal cases, when the accused has the benefit of being served with a regular libel, of having *inducia* to prepare his defence, of having time to bring

---

[126]   *The Dundee Courier & Argus*, 4 January 1869.

[127]   The 1866 Glasgow Police Act (29 & 30 Victoria, cap. 273) made no specific reference to rules of evidence, although for certain acts relating to publicans and weights and measures the trial had to be conducted to the provisions for such acts (c. 116).

[128]   *Police Intelligencer*, 11 April 1832.

[129]   As Chapter 6 will examine in greater depth, around one in five of those brought before magistrates and formally prosecuted was acquitted in the mid-nineteenth century.

[130]   *Caledonian Mercury*, 19 May 1825.

forward his exculpatory evidence, of having the evidence recorded, and of being assisted by legal advice in the conduct of the proceedings.

The Court was challenging the legality of summary proceeding authorised by the 1812 Edinburgh Police Act on the basis that they ran counter to long-held principles of Scots criminal law.[131] It was indicative of a clash between traditional legal procedures and the new summary ones – a clash which caused resentment in civic circles when magisterial authority was deemed to have been challenged by legally trained judges in a superior court.[132] The superintendent of police, who had led the prosecution, defended his actions by arguing that they were in keeping with what the Edinburgh Police Act allowed for summary proceedings. It was a rigorous defence of summary principles and local autonomy and would shape the course of police court procedure for the remainder of the century. All prosecutions would continue to be summary.

The matter of *how* as well as *whether* magistrates should determine the procedure of the police court, however, continued to be a pressing concern voiced in Edinburgh. *The Scotsman* reported, in February 1817, objections

> to the domination given to the Sheriff-depute, and Lord Provost and Magistrates, with the advice and approbation of the Lord President, and Lord Justice Clerk, for the time, over the forms of procedure in the Police Court. Forms in court should be unalterable by all authority, the legislature excepted. It signifies nothing that for the present, they are excellent. It is dangerous to devolve the power of remodelling, or altering, upon a few individuals. By

---

[131]   The High Court judges argued that 'It was undeniable that the summary proceeding authorised by sect. 86 of the statute was illegal in this case ... If the statute authorises any subject of this country to be imprisoned, even for the space of sixty days, without such a record of his trial as to put it in his power to have the merits of his case immediately decided by a higher tribunal, and makes the mere *ipse dixit* of the Judge, that the offence was proven, sufficient to prevent any inquiry into the merits of the case, fortunately for the liberty of the subject it goes no farther. It does not authorise any of the Bailies of Edinburgh *de plano*, and without allowing an instant to the accused to prepare himself, to sentence him not merely to a temporary imprisonment, but to perpetual banishment. Such arbitrary powers were not confined to the Police Magistrates, the summary mode of deciding having been expressly confined to those petty offences which merit a less degree of punishment. Now, though the statute authorises a summary mode of proceeding it declares that there shall at least be a written charge, and it no where declares, that the prosecutor shall be relieved from stating the charge in such explicit terms but as to time, place and circumstance, as may enable the party accused to put himself on his defence. This is essentially required by the established criminal law of this country, and it is much too valuable a privilege to be taken away, unless by express enactments.' *Caledonian Mercury*, 29 January 1814.

[132]   See *Aberdeen Journal*, 9 October 1850 for magistrates' response to a High Court judgement which challenged their judicial authority, which is discussed more fully below.

possessing a control over the forms of a court, it is possible to accomplish almost any thing in that court.[133]

Such complaints were by no means restricted to Edinburgh. They reflected common concerns about the potential abuse of magisterial power in police courts and were articulated by the accused in court and legal elites in public forums. *The Scotsman*, for example, published an anonymous letter to the editor in 1825 complaining of the lack of transparency of Aberdeen's magisterial justice:

> Bad as your Edinburgh system is, you have many privileges which we want – its proceedings are published – and any errors of the Magistrates thus laid open to comment. But here this matter is ordered differently. What may be called our Police Court, is held daily at 1 o'clock in the Court-House – but before whom? Why the Magistrate and his clerk. A person may as soon expect to get into a Mason Lodge, without being a brother, as into this Court. Here prostitutes are sent to Bridewell, roving Corinthians fined, thieves imprisoned summarily, or committed for trial, and cases of assault disposed of, of all which proceedings the public know nothing. The judgements may be Daniel-like or not, we have nothing to do with the matter. This is one way of dispensing justice certainly; a good way, for screening judicial blunders from ridicule and correction.[134]

Civic magistrates, however, refuted such criticism and questioned the power of higher legal officials to overturn their decisions. In 1850, Inverness magistrates complained about a challenge to their powers as judges. After a recruiting officer was given 60 days for drunk and disorderly conduct the Home Secretary, Sir George Grey, to whose attention the convicted man had brought the case, adjudged the sentence severe and the case was remitted to the Lord Advocate. When the recruiting officer employed a solicitor to access the police records, the commissioners of police composed a minute for the Home Office in which they supported the right to query a court decision, but asked that it should only happen rarely, or else it 'would of itself destroy the usefulness of the magistrates'. The commissioners argued that the Lord Advocate's actions had effectively made the solicitor 'the judge of the regularity and soundness of the decisions of Baillie Fraser, acting under the Inverness Police Statute', and requested instead that they be furnished with the details of the complaint against them in order to answer it, and that further enquiries be directed to the provost.[135] The case was indicative not just of the teething problems that characterised the expansion of summary justice in smaller burghs which had recently extended their summary powers, but also the tension between legal and civic men and the desire of the latter to withstand what they perceived as a challenge to their judicial and burghal rights.

---

[133]   *The Scotsman*, 1 February 1817.
[134]   *The Scotsman*, 9 November 1825.
[135]   *Aberdeen Journal*, 9 October 1850.

The uneven way in which the law was being administered in police courts brought growing criticism among legal men from the mid-century. In his work on the destitute of Edinburgh, *Day and Night in the Wynds of Edinburgh* (1849), George Bell M.D., secretary to the Original Ragged School Association of Edinburgh, expressed concern about the lack of uniformity in magisterial practice and performance.[136] Criminals, Bell suggested, were selective in their behaviour because they knew they could expect different treatment from different magistrates – a claim which played to media suggestions about criminals who were acquainted with the intricate workings of the legal system. As Bell went on:

> Four bailies – as unlike as each other, body and mind, as four bailies can be – and two sheriffs, preside in the police court. If Baillie A. tries the case, 'thirty days' will be the sentence; but if Baillie D. tries, 'sixty days,' to a certainty, will be the condemnation. He prefers Baillie A. therefore. If possible, he keeps clear of the sheriffs; they know the law – they understand the nature of their guardianship. Why should one prostitute be dismissed from the bar of the police court with a second-rate moral admonition, and another be locked up in the jail for thirty days? … Let there be, above all things, uniformity of administration.[137]

However, civic magistrates defended such lack of continuity in judicial practice as one of the chief advantages of the lay magisterial system. As Bailie Morrison argued to the Edinburgh Town Council in 1855 in the midst of debates about the permanent stipendiary appointment as judges,

> A jury came between the criminal and the Judge in serious cases of crime; and when in a Police Court one man was both Judge and jury, it was most important that, by his appointment being only temporary, his feelings should not be hardened by long habit.[138]

As this quote suggests, magistrates saw their role not simply to adhere rigidly to the law. They also viewed themselves 'as the natural guardians of the interests of the community'.[139] Theirs was a paternalistic image of justice in which the main role of magistrates was to ensure social peace from their perspective. It was a mindset rooted in neo-classical notions of civic government and in keeping with the Scottish Enlightenment rhetoric of public service.[140] But, as the next section

---

[136]   George Bell, *Day and Night in the Wynds of Edinburgh* (Edinburgh, 1849), passim.

[137]   *Aberdeen Journal*, 30 January 1850.

[138]   *Caledonian Mercury*, 31 October 1855.

[139]   Maver, 'The Guardianship of the Community', p. 240.

[140]   As Landau has put it, 'whether depicted as petty tyrant or benevolent overlord, the justice has always been credited with guiding the conduct of those fortunate enough to live in his neighbourhood'. Landau, *The Justices of the Peace*, pp. 173–4.

examines, it was also a mentality that served a much wider purpose concerning the private interests and public image of those enforcing the law.

IV. Private Interests, Public Image

Local newspapers throughout the country did not speak with one consistent voice on how magistrates administered the law. There was periodic, regional and political variation – hardly surprising in an era when newspaper ownership changed fairly frequently and when new papers and journals sprang up as rapidly as Scottish cities were expanding.[141] As Cowan, in his study of the nineteenth-century Scottish press has shown, newspaper opinion varied on a wide range of important issues and often reflected the egos, self-interests and political leanings of its proprietors and editors. Some newspapers offered little more than a news summary, others claimed to be impartial, whilst a few included detailed political comment on the important issues of the day.[142] There were also differences between newspapers and police court journals in terms of what magisterial affairs they reported. Whilst the former covered only a small number of carefully-selected police court cases, the latter reported both police court business and magistrates' wider civic activity, which had implications for the public image and role of magistrates as impartial guardians of justice, *ex-officio* police commissioners and civic leaders.

It was the radical press and satirical journals, understandably, that offered the most trenchant criticism of magisterial justice. *The Detective* – which changed its name to *Thistle or The Detective* in 1885 – was a frequent critic of both the police and civic magistrates.[143] In its weekly publications it offered a telling insight into police court proceedings rarely found in the established local newspapers and the weekly periodicals of the first half of the century. Under the heading 'Hard Lines', published in 1885, it reported the following:

> The case at Dundee lately, where a poor labourer who was starving was sent to prison for forty days for stealing three apples, is worthy of note. Bailie Hunter was the 'administrator of justice' in this case, and I think his action exhibits clearly how totally unfit those nobodies, who aspire to the dignity of an unpaid

---

[141]   For a study on Scottish newspapers in the nineteenth century, see R.M.W. Cowan, *The Newspaper in Scotland: A Study of its First Expansion, 1815–1860* (Glasgow, 1946).

[142]   Ibid., p. 16.

[143]   See, for instance, 'In Search of a Policeman', *The Detective: or, A Journal for the Exposure and Suppression of Crime* (*The Detective*), no. 7, vol. I, 23 May 1885, p. 5; 'Sauchiehall Street After Dark', *The Detective*, no. 14, vol. II (New Series), 9 July 1885, p. 2; and 'Midnight Scenes in Glasgow, by the "Tramp"', *The Detective*, no. 16, vol. II (New Series), 23 July 1885, p. 1.

Bailie, are to mete out the laws. I may ask my Dundee readers to make a mental note of the above case; it may be useful.[144]

Although by no means a politically radical journal, *The Bailie*, published in Glasgow from the 1870s onwards, also commented on the 'lottery of the law' and unjust sentences.[145] In 1874, it strongly criticised Bailie Bannerman for imprisoning a boy for 30 days for giving away a few pieces of wood from his employer to a poor woman.[146] According to *The Bailie*, the sentence was unduly harsh as the boy had been guilty of a breach of trust, not a crime.[147]

In most reports, though, such cases criticised by the media were generally portrayed as being unrepresentative of magisterial justice as a whole. Unpopular bailies, such as Bailie Bannerman, were cast as 'bad apples'. These were 'outcast' magistrates whose deviant behaviour ran contrary to a functional and just system of justice.[148] *The Bailie*, for instance, qualified its criticism of Bannerman by claiming that 'Our Bailies, as a rule, have been an able, straightforward class of men.'[149] In an earlier edition, it passionately defended the principle of lay justice, arguing that legally trained, paid magistrates could not be introduced without violating 'the first great principles of the constitution of the country, without destroying the "pallawdium" of our civil rights and liberties'. In its unusual sarcastic, tongue-in-cheek style, it went on:

> how could a Magistrate, who was a stranger to the circumstances until he heard the evidence, administer justice so well as a man who knew exactly what to do before either charge or defence was heard? His notion of official merit would lead him to rely implicitly on the testimony of 'two witnesses' in the garb of policemen, even though contradicted by half-a-dozen mere citizens, however, respectable.[150]

Criticism from the mainstream conservative and liberal newspapers was more muted and infrequent. It often reflected the political situation of the time, with the issue of law and order, and magistrates' handling of it, being an important

---

[144] 'Hard Lines', *Thistle or The Detective*, no. 24, vol. II (New Series), 17 September 1885, p. 1.

[145] See, for instance, *The Bailie*, no. 197, 26 July 1876, pp. 1–2.

[146] *The Bailie*, no. 104, 14 October 1874, pp. 1–2.

[147] Ibid.

[148] For studies in modern America which make similar claims, see Mike Owen Benediktsson, 'The Deviant Organisation and the Bad Apple CEP: Ideology and Accountability in Media Coverage of Corporate Scandals', *Social Forces*, 88/5 (2010): pp. 2189–216, esp. pp. 2189 & 2205–7; and Howard J. Ehrlich, *Hate Crimes and Ethnoviolence: The History, Current Affairs and Future Discrimination in America* (New York, 2009).

[149] *The Bailie*, no. 104, 14 October 1874.

[150] *The Bailie*, no. 2, 30 October 1872, p. 1.

issue in scrutinising civic governance, especially prior to burgh reform in 1833.[151] In the post-Napoleonic period, the *Dundee Advertiser* and *The Scotsman* were especially critical of burghal administration and its lack of accountability.[152] The latter, established in 1817, was launched by William Ritchie, lawyer, and Charles MacLaren, customs official, as a liberal newspaper specifically in response to the 'unblushing subservience' of the main local newspapers to the Edinburgh establishment.[153] Criticism of magistrates in the major local newspapers usually centred on the fact that they were not doing enough to deal with a perceived spiralling crime problem, rather than how they were administering the powers in court that they had.

Among the mainstream press, *The Scotsman* was the most likely to highlight cases in which magistrates had seemingly over-stepped the reach of their judicial powers or abused their position, although such instances were rare.[154] It was also more likely than other mainstream newspapers to publish letters from aggrieved citizens about the workings of police courts or report on appeals in the High Court of Justiciary on police court matters. Its liberal principles and self-proclaimed commitment to hold to account civic leaders played an important part in this, but so, too, was the professional profile of its readership and editors. Given the large number of lawyers who resided and worked in the city, legal issues stimulated much interest in Edinburgh and, like its east-coast rival the *Caledonian Mercury* (which claimed to be politically impartial), it took much pride in law reporting.[155] Moreover, many of *The Scotsman*'s most famous editors were drawn from legal backgrounds and had much interest in police and criminal justice matters.[156]

Where criticism of magistrates was advanced, it could have a significant impact. Newspapers could, on occasion, highlight perceived judicial abuses and act as a check on how the law was enforced. As the earlier example, in 1825, criticising Aberdeen's police court in *The Scotsman* illustrated, the publication of regular police court proceedings was viewed in certain legal circles as being

---

[151]   See David G. Barrie, 'Urban Order in Georgian Dundee, c.1770–1820', in Charles McKean, Bob Harris and Christopher A. Whatley (eds), *Dundee: Renaissance to Enlightenment* (Dundee, 2009), pp. 216–42, especially 231–2.

[152]   Ibid., and *The Scotsman*, 1 February 1817.

[153]   *The Scotsman Digital Archive*, 2013, http://archive.scotsman.com.

[154]   See, for instance, *The Scotsman*, 1 February 1817; and *The Scotsman*, 9 November 1825.

[155]   Cowan, *The Newspaper in Scotland*, p. 16.

[156]   In 1824, William Ritchie when he was the editor published *Essays on Constitutional Law and Forms of Process*. Three years later, he became an improvement commissioner and campaigned for reform of policing and prison conditions. Lionel Alexander Ritchie, 'Ritchie, William (1781–1831)', *Oxford Dictionary of National Biography* (Oxford, 2004), http://www.oxforddnb.com/view/article/23679. Similarly, John Hill Barton, who became editor in 1843, was an advocate, historian and economist. Author of *Life and Correspondence of David Hume*, he served as secretary of the Scottish Prison Board (1854–1877), and commissioner of prisons from 1877.

an important tool in preventing magistrates from abusing their powers.[157] In giving evidence for the 1868–1869 'Second Report of the Commissioners appointed to Inquire into the Courts of Law in Scotland', Charles Scott, a lawyer, concurred with this view, pointing out that press reports could reveal instances where perceived miscarriages of justice appeared to have been carried out.[158] Indeed, as the century went on, magistrates and senior police officials appear to have become increasingly aware of, and sensitive to, their representation in newspapers – hardly surprising given that in this era the press was a major source of information on crime. In 'The Secret Memoirs of Samuel Rodger', the author, a Glasgow police officer in the second half of the nineteenth century, claimed that 'the only God they [the magistrates] appeared to stand in awe of were the Newspaper Reporters'.[159] According to Rodger, the Lord Provost and senior police officers would go to great lengths to ensure damaging media portrayals were never brought to light. In describing a particular Lord Provost's attitude towards brothels, he writes:

> [I] Have heard him tell the Superintendent to do anything or everything he liked to these places, "BUT FOR HEAVEN SAKE KEEP THEM OUT OF THE COURT, for you know if you bring them there the Newspaper Reporters will get a hold of it, and then we will appear worse than the common burghs in the country."[160]

Although impossible to prove conclusively, it is likely that preoccupation with public image, as represented in the press, sometimes acted as a constraining influence on how magistrates enforced the law, or, at least, had an impact on how it was represented in the press. It certainly appears to have influenced how some magistrates performed in court, according to contemporary reports. As *The Bailie*, in describing magistrate Craig satirically as of 'the old school', reported in 1875: 'Neither is he in a state of constant anxiety, like some Bailies who might be named, to inspire the Police Court audience, and especially the Police Court reporters, with an overwhelming sense of wisdom and importance.'[161]

---

157 *The Scotsman*, 9 November 1825.

158 'Second Report of the Commissioners appointed to Inquire into the Courts of Law in Scotland', *BPP*, 1868–1869 (4188), XXV.423, pp. 549–50.

159 'The Secret Memoirs of Samuel Rodger (1846–1901) The Glasgow Teetotal Bobby', produced at the People's Palace Museum, Glasgow Green, to accompany the exhibition 'Scotland Sober and Free' marking the 150th anniversary of the temperance movement in Scotland, by kind permission of William Rodger, grandson of Samuel Rodger, p. 20.

160 Ibid. Emphasis in original.

161 *The Bailie*, no. 135, 19 May 1875, pp. 1–2.

However, for most of the first half of the nineteenth century, there was much support in the mainstream media for the lay justice that magistrates delivered. Indeed, press reports, in terms of the commentaries they offered, provide an intriguing insight into how the role of the lay magistrate was perceived, as defined by a certain type of propertied man. In its analysis in 1855 on whether Edinburgh should introduce a stipendiary magistrate, the *Caledonian Mercury* echoed the views of the majority of men in civic circles. The paper defended the role of lay magistrates by espousing the benefits that such men, as patriarchs and guardians of the community, brought to the administration of justice. They argued: 'it is not always requisite, nor would it be expedient, to abide by the strict letter of the law', especially in adjudicating on family disputes.[162] It contended that 'in the familiarities of family discourse many liberties may be taken ... in the heat of a transient passion' which if pushed to the letter of the law would be injurious to all concerned. Citing punishments to children and servants as cases where leniency was better than harsh punishment, magistrates argued that what was required was 'not so much professional accuracy as paternal sentiment, a spontaneous appreciation of the aims and motives, jealousies, and familiarities, which obtain in the intimacy of domestic life'. Tellingly, the report went on:

> What is really requisite to constitute eligibility for such an office, is parental feeling and common sense ... A power of spontaneously appreciating the merits of a case from incidental hints, the general demeanour of the accuser and accused, the harmonies or discords of circumstance and testimony, and the analogies of experience, must form substantially the media for the formation of an opinion upon the bearings of a particular case; rather than the residuary conclusion from a scrupulously careful balance of contending facts, and a cautious sifting of evidence.[163]

Sensitivity to individual circumstances and community feelings were particular qualities, and a necessary component, of discretionary justice.

Similar views were also expressed in the local press and among magistrates in Dundee. In 1877, the local sheriff questioned the magisterial practice of forfeiting bail bonds as a form of punishment for those who did not show up in court which, as in other towns, was common. Everyone charged with crimes, offences, and contraventions, he maintained, should attend court and magistrates should not seek to raise public funds at the expense of regulating the community. The *Dundee Courier* disagreed and put forward an impassioned defence of this aspect of discretionary justice:

> we think the exercise of such a power [to grant warrants for the apprehension of offenders] is pre-eminently one in which a sensible Magistrate may and ought

---

[162] *Caledonian Mercury*, 28 July 1855.
[163] Ibid.

to exercise discretion. The instances of people in respectable positions getting into small scrapes, and finding themselves almost before they are aware in the hands of the police, are not at all uncommon. We have no desire to act as the apologists of these delinquents, who, it may fairly be urged, ought to know better than take too much drink, or get into a street brawl. But at the same time it should be remembered that the public appearance of such individuals before the Police Court might not improbably lead to social ruin, and an amount of ulterior suffering out of all proportion to the nature of their offence. Where a person has been oftener than once convicted of these petty offences, there is no necessity of being over-nice with them; but we do think that, in first offences at all events, it is a wise as well as a merciful arrangement to allow the offenders to escape with the forfeiture of their bail bond.[164]

As the quote implied, not everyone was entitled to benefit from magisterial discretion. In this instance, the practice was a convenient way in which magistrates could not only uphold their own reputation as merciful protectors of public welfare, but also uphold those of individual members of the community of certain social standing, whilst discrediting others from more humble backgrounds. It was a two-tiered system of justice in which the law – or rather magisterial discretion – was applied unequally to benefit certain sections of society. As subsequent chapters in this two-volume companion will explore in greater depth, there were clear limits to those deemed vulnerable and over whom magistrates' public guardianship extended.

Newspapers and police journals would publish only a small number of police court cases. Jennifer S. Davis, among others, has argued that editors highlighted cases that involved novelty, a strong element of human interest and which reinforced popular stereotypes of criminals and migrant groups. The press, she maintained, acted as a crucial mechanism transmitting police court lessons to the general public, promoting the message that crime does not pay.[165] Similar rationales underlay publications in the Scottish press, which were often accompanied by a concern with safeguarding the reputations of certain types of men, and, in particular, the image of the magistrate and the justice he administered. The small number of cases which the press chose to report were by no means representative of police court transactions as a whole. They often involved examples where magistrates used discretion, such as to admonish and dismiss young boys for whom the alternative of prison was deemed to lead to certain ruin. In so doing, the press helped to create and support the notion of a merciful judge applying tolerant paternalism. Thus, in August 1829, one crime periodical reported that Bailie McLellan in the Glasgow Police Court had dismissed three young brush makers for public drunkenness,

---

[164]   *The Dundee Courier & Argus and Northern Warder*, 31 August 1877.

[165]   Davis, 'A Poor Man's System of Justice?', p. 317. For the dissemination of media messages on crime in Britain, see Philippe Chassaigne, 'Popular Representations of Crime: The Crime Broadside – A Subculture of Violence in Victorian Britain?', *Crime, Histoire & Sociétés / Crime, History & Societies*, 3/2 (1999): pp. 23–55.

noting that 'he would not impose a fine on the young rascals, but deliver them over to their parents, who, he hoped, would look sharply after them, and thereby prevent their utter destruction'.[166] Similarly, in September 1832, 16-year-old Ralf Mitchell was brought before Bailie George Small, at the Edinburgh Police Court, charged with theft. However, Darling, the police patrol, reported to the court that he had 'visited the family, and found the mother and four children in a state of the greatest privation. The children were crying for bread, and in a state of nudity'. When the mother and children attested to these facts after having been summonsed before the court, the magistrate 'humanely ordered them immediate relief' and 'dismissed the poor fellow, who had been forced to commit the breach of the law through dire necessity'. His was not a crime, according to the Edinburgh periodical *The Police Intelligencer*, but rather as a 'breach of the law'.[167] This representation of Mitchell's case by the media seemed to imply that those whose stricken circumstances explained their crimes might be extended the hand of charity. Perhaps Mitchell was afforded favourable coverage because his youthful action was explicitly framed by the court personnel as protecting a mother and siblings as a good householder should. The majority of thefts before the court were almost certainly the product of similar hardship but their circumstances had not been revealed in court in this way. The periodicals' coverage, which was often in conflict with most of the business of the police court, suggested police magistrates were cautious to condemn children to a life of almost certain crime by exacting heavy penalties or gaol terms for minor and first offences.

Indeed, even emotional outbursts by magistrates where they demonstrated feelings of compassion that a gentleman – literally a civilised, gentle man – ought to have towards the vulnerable, were highlighted by the press as signs of expertise to defend public sentiment and morality. In a case of attempted indecent behaviour towards a child brought before the Glasgow Police Court in August 1829, the same Bailie McLellan was reported as losing his temper while addressing John Fraser, a shoemaker, accused of attempting to 'violate the chastity' of 12-year-old Catherine Melrose.[168]

> Bailie McLellan, contrary to his usual custom, rose from his chair, and addressing the prisoner, said: 'I am at a loss, at a great loss, to find words to describe your case; a man you are not, but a brute. What you think of yourself? You wretch, have you any feeling? Look, at that child, and think where you now are!'

McLellan's publicised loss of his 'usual' decorum was no slight upon his character in the way it was presented by the press. This was instead a sign of his gentlemanly status – that he had feeling for such matters, and was in touch with community sentiment on moral order in the city.

---

[166]   *Police Reports*, 15 August 1829, p. 66.
[167]   *Police Intelligencer*, 1 September 1832.
[168]   *Police Reports*, 27 July 1829, p. 47.

The representation of magisterial justice in such a favourable light was perhaps influenced to some degree by the relationship some civic leaders enjoyed with newspaper proprietors and editors. Some editors of the *Glasgow Herald*, such as Samuel Hunter (editor from 1803 to 1837) and John Sinclair (editor 1898), even went on to serve as magistrates, whilst others, such as James Pagan (editor between 1856 and 1870), would go on to work closely with councillors and sketch the history of Glasgow in a series of publications.[169] Hunter was a staunch conservative and anti-radical. A member of the Tory Hodge Podge Club, he served as colonel of the Glasgow Corps of Gentlemen Sharpshooters which was at the forefront in suppressing radical unrest in the city.[170] *The Anecdotage of Glasgow* (1892) described him as follows:

> He was a man of wit, kindly, genial, moderate, clearsighted, and of firm integrity; qualities which he impressed upon the journal under his charge, and to which it owed its success. His jokes and smart sayings were repeated at every table in Glasgow; and even yet are not quite forgotten. … he was always popular with the people. He became a magistrate of the city, discharging his duties with shrewdness, dignity, and uprightness.[171]

He was not, however, as popular among the masses as this portrayal suggests. During the Parliamentary Reform Bill debates on the extension of franchise, his effigy was on a number of occasions burned at Glasgow Cross, and a *Stop-my-paper* crusade was commenced by those who did not share his conservative and anti-reform leanings.[172]

According to Simon Devereaux and Robert B. Shoemaker, the late eighteenth-century *Proceedings of the Old Bailey*, which reported on felonies tried in London's chief criminal court, promoted an image of justice that was favourable and supportive of the city authorities upon whose license the *Proceedings* relied.[173]

---

[169]   See, for instance, James Pagan, *Sketch of the History of Glasgow* (Glasgow, 1847). Moreover, George Outram, editor of the *Glasgow Herald* from 1837 to 1856 was an advocate.

[170]   'Samuel Hunter', *The Glasgow Story*, 2004, http://www.theglasgowstory.com/image.php?inum=TGSA03638.

[171]   'The Anecdotage of Glasgow: Samuel Hunter, Genial Editor of the "Glasgow Herald"', *Electric Scotland*, http://www.electricscotland.com/history/glasgow/anec120.htm; Robert Alison, *The Anecdotage of Glasgow; Comprising Anecdotes and Anecdotal Incidents of the City of Glasgow and Glasgow Personages* (Glasgow, 1892).

[172]   'The Anecdotage of Glasgow: Samuel Hunter, Genial Editor of the "Glasgow Herald"'. For more on radicalism in post-war Scotland, see Gordon Pentland, *Radicalism, Reform and National Identity in Scotland 1820–1833* (Woodbridge, 2008).

[173]   Simon Devereaux, 'The City and the Sessions Paper: "Public Justice" in London, 1770–1800', *Journal of British Studies*, 35/4 (1996): pp. 466–503; Simon Devereaux, 'The Fall of the Sessions Paper: The Criminal Trial and the Popular Press in Late Eighteenth-Century London', *Criminal Justice History*, 18/1 (2002): pp. 57–88; and Robert B.

In Scotland, though, there were no equivalent direct conflicts of interest between civic government and the mainstream media. The newspapers and the journals which reported on police court affairs were independent of local government. Probably of greater significance in shaping the favourable representation of lay justice were commercial imperatives, the social and moral middle-class values shared by proprietors, editors and magistrates on the purpose of the law, and the press's predominantly middle-class readership.[174] As Crone has pointed out, the success of media reporting on crime and justice was dependent upon the reports being tailored to suit the tastes and satisfy the demands of the propertied classes.[175]

Magisterial comments in cases in which bailies exercised their discretionary powers, and the way in which these were represented in the press, reflected two distinct but intertwined and potentially conflicting facets of magistrates' role as judges: one as purveyor of impartial justice on behalf of the police and good order of the city and the other as a man in touch with the community of which he was effectively a moral and social guardian. Indeed, in many ways, magistrates thought of themselves as much guardians of urban public welfare as of the law. As they made enquiries and commentary of defenders in court, and by their own conduct in court, they offered themselves as beacons and proselytisers of middle-class morality, dispensing moral as well as legal justice. Indeed, the police courtroom, in some ways, served as a civic kirk session; not perhaps so much in the offences that came before magistrates, but in the mentality with which they considered appropriate justice. This was in keeping with wider civic attempts to adapt religious life to the new urban environment as religious beliefs took on new forms and expressions in people's private and social lives in the cities.[176] Indeed, as church courts struggled to impose moral and social discipline through kirk sessions and their courts, the organisation of some key welfare and educational concerns of parishes shifted to civic structures which gave magistrates arguably an even greater role in safeguarding public morality than ever before.[177] With religion underpinning many of the progressive attempts to improve Scottish urban

---

Shoemaker, 'The Old Bailey Proceedings and the Representation of Crime and Criminal Justice in Eighteenth-Century London', *Journal of British Studies*, 47 (2008): pp. 559–80.

[174]   Shoemaker similarly argued these were the 'dominant imperatives that shaped the publishers' decisions about how to represent Old Bailey trials in the *Proceedings*', in 'The Old Bailey Proceedings and the Representation of Crime', p. 565.

[175]   Rosalind Crone, *Violent Victorians: Popular Entertainment in Nineteenth-Century London* (Manchester, 2012), pp. 210–30; and Rosalind Crone, 'Publishing Courtroom Drama for the Masses, 1820–1855', in David Lemmings (ed.), *Crime, Courtrooms and the Public Sphere in Britain, 1700–1850* (Farnham, 2012), pp. 193–216.

[176]   For the role of civic authorities in attempting to adapt religious life to large cities, see Callum G. Brown, *The Social History of Religions in Scotland since 1730* (London, 1987), p. 131. For religious belief, see Stewart J. Brown, 'Beliefs and Religions', in Trevor Griffiths and Graeme Morton (eds), *A History of Everyday Life in Scotland, 1800–1900* (Edinburgh, 2010), p. 128.

[177]   G.D. Henderson, *The Scottish Ruling Elder* (London, 1935), p. 241.

society, and councillors combining civic and religious interests to support urban improvement acts, the police magistrate's role was very much intertwined with wider civic and religious initiatives (see Chapters 5 and 6 of Volume 2).[178]

Magisterial and media representations of police court proceedings might have frequently portrayed the court as being an important mechanism for protecting public morality and the most vulnerable, but the use of the law in this way also served another, important purpose – namely, to enhance the status and authority of magistrates as governing men. The punitive options of the Scottish police courts were less dramatic than the aristocracy's flexible application of the death penalty in the eighteenth-century England, as outlined by Hay;[179] this should come as little surprise, given that the fairly moderate penalties enshrined in police legislation restricted magisterial modes of punishment to two months' imprisonment and £10 fines. Nonetheless, there was recognition in civic circles that police courts, and the discretionary justice that was often administered there, had the capacity to strengthen magisterial power and status within their communities. In giving evidence to the 1839 Law Inquiry James Clerk, Town Clerk of Irvine, highlighted this:

> were magistrates enabled more speedily, and less expensively, to try and punish minor offences in their own bounds, it would tend greatly to establish and strengthen their authority, and would be a powerful means of keeping down crime in their respective jurisdictions, and at much less trouble and expense than at present, both to parties concerned and to the public at large.[180]

Indeed, magistrates employed discretionary powers in order to reinforce magisterial authority and the deference of those brought before them. In 1832, *The Police Intelligencer* reported a number of attacks on police and Board of Health officials who were attempting to take cholera patients to the hospital. In passing sentence, Bailie Crichton made a point of noting that the contrition shown by the offenders was the key to them receiving lenient punishment:

> The Magistrate said that such conduct as the defenders had been guilty of could not be tolerated. Nothing could be more absurd and rediculous [*sic*] then [*sic*] ignorant, misled and ungrateful wretches attempting to frustrate the attempts of the humane exertions of the Managers of the Board of Health to allay that direful enemy which so deeply interests every individual. He intended to punish the defenders severely as an example to others, but as they had shewn some contrition for what they had done, he would fine them in the lowest possible sum, five shillings.[181]

---

178 Brown, *The Social History of Religions in Scotland since 1730*, p. 132.
179 Hay, 'Property, Authority and the Criminal Law', pp. 17–63.
180 'Fourth Report by Her Majesty's Law Commissioners, Scotland, 1839', p. 287.
181 *Police Intelligencer*, 11 April 1832.

What was projected both by magistrates and the major newspapers that reported on their work was an image of justice that was sensitive to communal feelings and common-sense judgement rather than one that was dictated by legal procedure. It was, in effect, an image of justice in which magistrates could be relied upon to see that justice was done – justice, that is, defined by a certain type of propertied man.

Yet behind the rhetoric and representation of discretionary justice lay wider magisterial concerns with self-image and self-interest that were linked with broader notions of urban order. Despite police forces being introduced throughout urban Scotland in the first half of the nineteenth century, law and order issues – especially spirit licensing, drinking, crime, rioting and local police acts – were matters on which magisterial performance was measured.[182] Issues surrounding licensing restrictions, which were closely intertwined with concerns about urban order and public drunkenness, were especially contentious in the 1850s and 1870s and were often accompanied by prolonged press campaigns for stronger laws and more rigorous law enforcement by both the police and the courts.[183] Significantly, sections of the press and members of the public continued to associate magistrates with law and order even after the police's introduction – hardly surprising given that police forces acted under the authority of magistrates – and even petitioned magistrates over concerns about crime.[184] Being perceived to be weak on law and order could, and sometimes did, result in magistrates and provosts losing their office, such as in Glasgow in 1848 when widespread food rioting helped contribute to the downfall of the Lord Provost.[185] In such a context, discretionary justice was an extremely

---

[182]   The framing of police acts, for instance, often featured in campaigns for local office. In 1842, William Brodie, in a campaign outline to the electors of the third municipal district, remarked: 'To a new Police Bill, founded on such principles as will ensure an economical and vigorous administration of local police, and which may tend to unite, on fair and equitable terms, the interests of all classes in the city and suburbs, I shall give my support, but to any other I will be steadily opposed.' He was one of three reformers re-elected. *Scots Reformers Gazette*, 29 October 1842 and 5 November 1842.

[183]   See Chapter 5 of Volume 2 for more on this.

[184]   See, for instance, ECL: *Address to the Inhabitants of Edinburgh, on the Necessity of Removing the Causes of the Crimes which now Disgrace the City* (Edinburgh, 1832), pp. 1–14, which called on the magistracy to instruct the police to deal with urban problems.

[185]   As magistrates never ceded their responsibility for law and order following police reform, they were still accountable, along with the police, for outbreaks of public disorder. Following the outbreak of rioting in the city by those demonstrating against unemployment and rising food prices, magistrates called in a large contingent of military personnel to aid the police in suppressing the unrest. After a lengthy inquiry, Alexander Hastier, sitting Lord Provost, was defeated in a municipal election for a ward in Glasgow's east end. As Maver notes, 'magistrates' recent mishandling of the notorious "Bread Riots" had provoked much bitterness, because of the deaths of three men during the disturbances'. It was widely believed that the incompetent way in which the authorities – magistrates, the military and the police – handled the disturbance had exacerbated the situation. As Maver continues,

important mechanism for controlling and disciplining the urban masses, and for managing public perceptions of law and order and magisterial authority. There were even claims in evidence submitted to the 1869 Law Inquiry that magisterial courtroom judgements and sentences were subject to electoral pressures.[186] The publication of criminal returns was important in this respect. In an era of growing press reports on crime and frequent publication of criminal statistics, securing convictions in court was an important means by which policing efficiency – and, to some extent, magisterial capacity for governance given their integral role in the management of police affairs – was measured (see Chapters 5 and 6 for further discussion). In 1861, the introduction of the annual Edinburgh police returns, compiled by the superintendent of police, boasted about the improved conviction rates in the previous year and claimed that the success and efficiency of the police was afforded 'by an estimate of the proportion between the number of Persons convicted for Crimes against Property, and the number of such Crimes reported to the Police'.[187] It seems likely that magistrates valued discretionary justice because it made it easier for them to secure convictions against those who might otherwise have escaped punishment had justice been administered according to the letter of the law. As contemporary reports suggested, civic magistrates were more likely than legally trained stipendiary magistrates to convict.[188] Indeed, when Glasgow councillors and magistrates finally did appoint a stipendiary magistrate in the mid-1870s the latter quickly found himself at the centre of a controversy with police officers for enforcing the law, and interrogating police evidence, in a way that hitherto civic magistrates do not appear to have done (see further analysis in Chapter 6). As Philips's research has shown for the English Midlands, the likelihood of tension and conflict between the police and magistrates was

---

'Lord Provost Hastie became the focus of particular resentment, which [James] Moir, as an erstwhile police commissioner, successfully exploited' by defeating Hastie at the municipal election. What is particularly interesting is that Moir, a police commissioner at the time of the disturbance, was not damaged politically by the unrest yet Hastie, the Lord Provost, was, illustrating that magistrates were still very much expected to maintain order as well as administer it. The chief of police, Superintendent Pearce, was also later replaced following widespread criticism of his handling of the situation. Irene Maver, *Glasgow* (Edinburgh, 2000), pp. 77–8. For more on the bread riots, see Alistair Goldsmith, '"A Local Difficulty" – The Glasgow Bread Riots of 1848', *Strathclyde Guardian: The Magazine for Strathclyde Police*, 18/2 (1994): pp. 13–15.

[186] 'First Report of the Law Commissioners Appointed to Inquire into the Courts of Law in Scotland', p. 365.

[187] ECL: *Reports and Returns as to Crimes, Offences, and Contraventions, and to Cases of Drunkenness, within the Police Bounds of the City of Edinburgh during the last Six Years. Prepared for the Magistrates and Council, by Thomas Linton, Superintendent of Police* (Edinburgh, 1860), p. 11.

[188] GUL: 'Paid v Unpaid Magistrates', *The Journal of Jurisprudence*, XI (1867): pp. 539–40.

greatest when the law was being administered by those who had studied it and for the most part applied it to the letter, and not by members of the business community who had not, and did not.[189]

Although magistrates were willing to highlight and take credit for improved statistical crime patterns in their role as members of the police board, it is important to stress that in keeping with how they saw their wider moral and civic role in the community, they were less preoccupied with statistical returns than senior police officers. What lay magistrates valued, above all else, was the ability to deal with each case on its own merits and not be restricted or dictated to by the letter of the law. What they cherished most was the flexibility to show mercy for 'deserving' recipients and to punish severely those who were not – who, crucially, might otherwise escape justice should it be applied to the letter of the law by a legally trained stipendiary (see *The Bailie's* criticism of the severity with which James Moir administered justice in the accompanying commentary for Illustration 2.1). Magistrates had to strike a balance between showing 'mercy' and 'severity' according to the merits of individual cases. It was these qualities, along with their social standing, which made magistrates, they believed, fit to govern. Discretionary powers allowed them to negotiate between serving the interests of the wider community and the individual, whilst at the same time making it easier to respond to public concerns and press reports on law and order issues. It also, crucially, often allowed them to prioritise character and morality rather than legality when administering justice and handing down punishments.

Self-image and self-interest were, therefore, integral to magisterial justice in an increasingly media-conscious age. Although mainstream liberal and conservative newspapers could, on occasion, be critical of magisterial handling of civic issues and overtly political in their reporting of police court business and the purpose that it should serve, they had much in common with magisterial opinion. In the cases upon which they chose to focus, and in the courtroom comments they chose to publish, the mainstream media helped reinforce the notion of discretionary justice and magistrates' role in the community. In portraying magistrates as paternal guardians who were sensitive to local feeling and responsive to local needs, the press helped to legitimise the law, police courts and civic magistrates' involvement in them – and, of course, the dominance of a certain class of man over another. It would take mounting criticism from another type of propertied man – a legally trained one – before such a system of justice was called into question, as the next section examines.

V. Civic Tensions and the Rise of Legal Influence

Lawyers had always played a part in framing police court procedure. All police acts had to be given statutory approval by the Lord Advocate – the government's

---

[189]   Philips, 'The Black Country Magistracy', pp. 161–90.

chief legal officer in Scotland – who oversaw, and was sometimes actively involved, in framing legislation.[190] Through High Court judgements on police court cases, and in setting legal precedents concerning laws of evidence and other facts of police court business, the supervisory influence and legal traditions of High Court justices were recognised and exerted. As the century progressed, however, the influence of lawyers on the day-to-to-day practice of police courts grew and, to some extent, began to challenge the authority of civic magistrates. Legal opinion played an increasingly important part in framing police court legislation and in defining the limits of police courts' jurisdiction, often after protracted and heated discussion with men from civic circles,[191] whilst judicial rulings and legal precedent restricted magistrates' capacity for self-direction.[192] Moreover, a growing raft of legislation and legal guidelines narrowed magistrates' discretionary powers as the operation of summary justice became more formal, structured and codified. The 1862 Burgh

---

[190]   For more on the role of lawyers in shaping Scottish policing in general, see Barrie, 'Anglicisation and Autonomy', pp. 449–94.

[191]   In 1862, the Faculty of Procurators criticised clause 145 of an early draft of the Glasgow Police Bill which proposed to impose a penalty of 60 days on persons 'doing or omitting to do any act, the doing or omission of which is punishable by general statute, or common law'. It pointed out that the passing of such a clause 'would necessarily, and seems intended to, have the effect of bringing into the Glasgow court a great variety of matters not properly belonging to the department of a municipal police'. It also opposed clause 115 which stated that 'magistrates shall have jurisdiction to try any person accused or suspected of any crime or offence within, or beyond the city, which is punishable by general statute or common law, and is triable by the magistrates of the royal burgh'. They claimed that 'if such powers are actually obtained, it will be no easy matter to define the limits of the jurisdiction of the police courts of Glasgow'. GCA, DTC, 14.2.34: *Report by the Committee of the Faculty of Procurators upon the Glasgow Police Bill* (Glasgow, 1862), pp. 9–10.

[192]   In 1859, magistrates in Glasgow resolved that after a late decision of the High Court in the case of Coyle against McKenna, it would be improper and illegal to introduce in any complaint in the police courts the charge of 'Rogue and Vagabond' as aggravations and that the words must be expunged in future practice. GCA, E1/13/1: Magistrates Committee Minute Book, 3 December 1859. Magisterial decisions concerning court powers also established clear guidelines to be followed as the punishment for certain types of crimes was increasingly prescribed. In 1856, magistrates in Glasgow resolved that all prosecutions under the acts of parliament for regulating the business of spirit dealers on Sundays were to be punished in full unless there were mitigating circumstances. For other days of the week, the penalties should be mitigated, unless second or third offences which should be punished according to the full statutory penalty. Mitigating circumstances gave magistrates some scope for discretion, although in theory not for repeat offenders or for those who sold without certification (however, in practice, these guidelines were not always rigidly adhered to). Repeat offenders or those who sold without certification were ineligible to receive mitigation of penalties. Magistrates Committee Minute Book, 11 February 1856.

Police (Scotland) Act, for instance, sought to consolidate police law into one treatise.[193] It was followed by the 1864 Summary Procedure Act [194] and the 1881 Summary Jurisdiction Act.[195] These statutes introduced a more uniform system of prosecutions for lesser crimes, regulated the mode of summary prosecution, and provided greater guidance for magistrates and justices in the formalities of legal practice.[196] Similarly, local police acts gave more and more attention to defining legal process, sometimes taking their lead from guidelines which had been laid out in national statutes.[197] From mid-century, more and more legal journals, manuals, treatises and commentaries were published.[198] These helped to clarify legal technicalities for lay magistrates and establish a greater degree of uniformity in practice.[199] In 1876, for instance, James Campbell Irons, Procurator Fiscal of Glasgow, published a *Manual of Police Law and Practice* on the 1862 Burgh Police Act specifically in response to calls from civic leaders for clearer guidelines on statutory police laws.[200] The publication of such texts revealed a growing recognition of lay magistrates' lack of legal expertise – which became more apparent as the volume of statutory laws they were acquired to interpret and enforce grew – and was a subtle way in which legal men exerted greater influence over day-to-day summary procedure and practice.

At the same time, a rising discourse of professionalism had begun to challenge the right of lay magistrates to serve in police courts. Burgh reform in 1833, the growing involvement of the state in framing national burgh and police legislation, and the expansion in police court powers helped to stimulate debates

---

[193]   Burgh Police Scotland Act, 1862 (25 & 26 Victoria. cap. 101). For more information on this, see James Campbell Irons, *The Burgh Police (Scotland) Act, 1892* (Edinburgh, 1893).

[194]   The Summary Procedure Act, 1864. The statute related mainly to summary procedure in sheriff and justice of the peace courts, but a few clauses applied to police magistrates.

[195]   The Summary Jurisdiction Act, 1881 (44 & 45 Victoria, cap. 33).

[196]   R.W. Renton, 'The Summary Jurisdiction (Scotland) Bill', *Scottish Law Review*, 24 (1908): pp. 219–22; and Thomas Trotter, *The Summary Jurisdiction (Scotland) Act 1908: With Introduction, Notes and Forms* (Edinburgh, 1909).

[197]   Glasgow Police Act, 1866. See sections VII and VIII on police courts.

[198]   See, for instance, Hugh Barclay, Sheriff-Substitute of Perthshire, *A Digest of the Law of Scotland with Special Reference to the Officers and Duties of a Justice of the Peace* (Edinburgh, 1855); James Campbell Irons, *Manual of Police Law and Practice, comprising an Analysis of the General Police and Improvement (Scotland) Act of 1862, with Notes of Decided Cases and Relative Statutes* (Edinburgh, 1876); Campbell Irons, *The Burgh Police (Scotland) Act*. For more on Scottish journals, see Reinhard Zimmermann, 'Law Journals in Nineteenth-Century Scotland', *Edinburgh Law Review*, 12/1 (2008): pp. 9–25.

[199]   It took much longer for law journals to become established in Scotland than in England, but there was growing legal reporting over the course of the nineteenth century. See ibid.

[200]   Campbell Irons, *Manual of Police Law and Practice*.

about the suitability of lay magistrates – drawn almost exclusively from business rather than legal backgrounds – sitting in police courts.[201] As a letter from 'M' pointed out in the *Caledonian Mercury* in 1835 concerning discussion of an early proposal to introduce a fully salaried police magistracy in Edinburgh: 'There is something extremely absurd in men whose modes of thinking and habits of life are altogether foreign to judicial investigations assuming the administration of a very difficult branch of the law.'[202] By the mid-nineteenth century, there was increasing concern that a £10 qualification did not constitute expertise in law. In England, some provincial towns were given extended powers in 1847 to appoint stipendiary magistrates which may also have put the issue of magisterial expertise on civic Scotland's agenda. Unease about the social composition and lack of legal expertise among burgh magistrates was voiced by George Bell, in his *Day and Night in the Wynds of Edinburgh*.

> What do baillies, *qua* baillies, know about law? Would the town employ a doctor, a minister, a writer to the signet, a merchant, a baker, a butcher, a hosier, or any other than an architect, to plan a city church? It is not enough that a man is a good, sensible, public-spirited man – that won't qualify him to be a judge. … Instead of a baker, a hosier, a merchant, and mayhap a spirit-dealer, presiding alternately in the police court, with out most admirable sheriffs, let the former be freed from their ludicrous position, and the latter from this part of their arduous and important duties; and let there be a police magistrate appointed, who is learned in the law, and skilled in its application.[203]

The matter in Edinburgh was given much publicity over a four-month period in 1850 in the dispute involving Sleigh, an English barrister, and Edinburgh magistrates, with the former questioning (as it turned out unsuccessfully) the latter's capacity to adjudicate the case.[204]

---

[201] As Maver has pointed out, burgh reform did little to alter the social composition of the town council and magistracy in Glasgow which for much of the nineteenth century continued to be dominated by men from business backgrounds. In the second half of the century, the social composition extended to include some small businessmen, as well as some well-off radicals elected to relatively impoverished east end wards. However, for the most part, municipal affairs continued to be dominated by a powerful economic elite. Maver, 'Glasgow's Civic Government', pp. 444 & 469.

[202] *Caledonian Mercury*, 3 December 1835. The financial advantages of employing a stipendiary paid for by the Crown were also recognised. *Caledonian Mercury*, 20 April 1837.

[203] Cited in *Aberdeen Journal*, 30 January 1850.

[204] Sleigh's appeal was eventually rejected by the High Court which defended the capacity of the police court to try such a case, but the controversy brought to the fore growing concerns about lay magistrates' lack of legal training. See *Caledonian Mercury*, 22 April 1850; *Caledonian Mercury*, 6 May 1850. *A Report on the Proceedings in the Police Court in the Trial of Messrs, Sleigh and Russell* was later made available for sale by

Lay magistrates and their supporters defended their expertise by espousing the benefits that they, as guardians of the community, brought to the administration of justice. In 1855, the *Caledonian Mercury* opined that

> A power of spontaneously appreciating the merits of a case from incidental hints, the general demeanour of the accuser and accused, the harmonies or discords of circumstance and testimony, and the analogies of experience, must form substantially the media for the formation of an opinion upon the bearings of a particular case.

There was a danger, Bailie Morrison argued, that an appointed and permanent salaried judge would lose contact with the people. His objection to the introduction of a stipendiary, legally trained magistrate was not that he would be a lawyer, but rather that his permanent presence in the office would 'blunt his sympathies with the class of people that came before him in that Court'.[205]

Proposals for reform were thwarted by the strength of civic opposition and the fact that legally trained sheriff-substitutes sat on a rotational basis as police judges in the Edinburgh Police Court.[206] The growing legal influence in the court, however, was increasingly deemed not to go far enough. Sheriff Jameson recommended to the 1869 Law Commission that magistrates be relieved of all judicial duties in matters of crime and should have their judicial duties restricted to cases involving contraventions of police regulations. Sheriffs, he contended, were the best judges in cases of crime and evidence, and magistrates the best judges in questions about police and sanitary regulations – a recommendation he had advanced during discussions over the most recent Edinburgh Police Act but which had been opposed by magistrates. In the police court, he contended, there were often delicate cases of evidence in regard to theft and embezzlement which required legal expertise and, unlike in Glasgow, magistrates in Edinburgh did not have the benefit of either assessor or clerk on hand should they be required.[207] Maurice Lothian, solicitor at law in Edinburgh, called for the sheriff-substitute to confine himself to the criminal affairs in the court and 'should no longer spend many of his valuable hours with the wretched and paltry cases of the

---

A. Muirhead of Edinburgh for 4d. It was advertised for sale, for example, in *Caledonian Mercury*, 17 June 1850.

[205] *Caledonian Mercury*, 31 October 1855.

[206] In giving evidence to the 1868–1869 Law Commission, Andrew Jameson, former Sheriff-Substitute in Edinburgh (1845–1865), stated that the sheriff-substitutes attended the Edinburgh Police Court for one month and magistrates the following month – an arrangement that had been introduced some time during the years he served. During his time on the bench magistrates exercised no police jurisdiction. 'First Report of the Law Commissioners Appointed to Inquire into the Courts of Law in Scotland', p. 334.

[207] Ibid., p. 334.

Police Court'.[208] It was a comment that said as much about how he, as a legal man, saw himself as about the types of cases with which police courts dealt. The evidence that was presented to the committee suggests there was not only tension between legally trained and lay justices, but also an emerging intellectual shift in parliamentary circles in favour of empowering the latter. The way questions were posed by the committee indicated that there was a body of opinion in government and legal circles in favour of extending the jurisdiction of sheriffs over police affairs in towns in general – either by giving them complete authority over criminal matters in police courts, or by giving sheriffs in their own courts greater powers to deal with crimes hitherto under the jurisdiction of police magistrates.[209] A number of leading questions were posed to identify the advantages – not least in promoting greater uniformity in practice and sentencing – in having a legally trained man sitting permanently in the police court to deal with crimes.[210] That such a man was deemed more likely than a civic one to apply the law in a uniform manner is itself interesting and acknowledges the discretionary way that lay magistrates had hitherto administered justice. Discretionary powers might have been valued by civic magistrates, but it is clear that for legal men it produced inconsistent judicial practice, even if the intentions behind their use were themselves fairly consistent. It was a practice not in keeping with the emerging discourse on criminal law in which the language of 'uniformity' was espoused as often as 'economy'.

There was even a growing body of thought that sought to divorce magistrates from the community and the influence of popular opinion. In 1869, Thomas Linton, Superintendent of Edinburgh Police, called for all bailies (senior magistrates) to hold office for three years after being appointed, as was the case with the Lord Provost. The justification for reform was to reduce the likelihood of interim bailies being dismissed from office for making unpopular judgements. He referred to an instance where a bailie was ousted from his ward mainly on account of what he had done as a judge in the police court. Apparently, a 'respectable' person who had been brought before him had not been sent to prison for committing assault, but had only been fined. Linton remarked:

> I have no doubt that where a bailie has to seek re-election soon after having been appointed a bailie, he is liable to be influenced by the consideration of what is most likely to secure his re-election to office. ... An appointment for three years would make a bailie more independent in the discharge of his duties as judge of police.[211]

---

[208]   'First Report from his Majesty's Law Commissioners, Scotland', *BPP*, 1834 (295), XXVI.179, p. 272.

[209]   'First Report of the Law Commissioners Appointed to Inquire into the Courts of Law in Scotland', pp. 334 & 340.

[210]   Ibid., p. 340.

[211]   Ibid., p. 365.

A similar desire to divorce the police from direct popular control resulted in elected police commissions in Scotland's major urban centres having their powers transferred to town councils amidst claims that police commissioners, increasingly drawn from shopkeepers and artisans, were ideologically suspect and unwilling to impose unpopular policies.[212] It was, in many ways, part of a wider intellectual shift in favour of empowering full-time professionals with 'knowledge' at the expense of elected representatives with little professional expertise in the areas they managed. But it was also indicative of the fact that in the post-burgh reform era, magistrates, in their capacity as members of the council, were subject to electoral pressures, which some believed influenced how the law was being administered.

Not everyone, however, desired reform. Robert Bruce Johnston, Procurator Fiscal for the County of the City of Edinburgh, outlined the basis of opposition: 'If you took away from the magistrates the whole criminal jurisdiction of the city, and prevented their sitting even in the police cases, you would strike at the root of municipal institutions. You would not get people in the city to take an interest in municipal affairs.'[213] It would, in other words, undermine magisterial authority and status. When asked 'Would not the best men take the civic position without the annoyance of the Police Court?,' he replied: 'My opinion is, you cannot get the dignity without the annoyance'.[214] The comment provided a clear insight into how court personnel saw the court and the types of cases with which it dealt. Even though they did not hold it in the highest regard, it was too important to their status to relinquish. Indeed, the crimes, offences and contraventions with which magistrates dealt and the types of people who were brought before them played an important part in shaping the ensuing discourse on whether criminal and non-criminal affairs should be separated. When the Law Commission asked Superintendent Linton what recommendations he would make to improve police courts, he suggested that the police court should hear criminal cases and breaches of municipal regulations separately at different times:

> There is a slight matter, but it has been made ground of complaint very often. We have to bring into the Police Court numbers of respectable citizens, and persons in their service, for trifling contraventions, and at present these persons are summoned to the ordinary Police Court; and there being only one court-room, it is complained that they are placed in the same position, as regards attendance there, as criminals, or notorious offenders.[215]

---

[212]   For the impact this had in leading to the demise of elected police commissions, see Barrie, *Police in the Age of Improvement*, pp. 227–34.

[213]   'First Report of the Law Commissioners Appointed to Inquire into the Courts of Law in Scotland', p. 341.

[214]   Ibid.

[215]   Ibid., p. 365.

Indeed, this view seems to have been widely supported in legal circles. The report noted that the law commissioners advocated a separate roll for contraventions of municipal regulation charges being made up and disposed of at a different time to criminal ones.[216] As always with criminal justice affairs, class mattered to its workings and evolution.

Calls for greater legal involvement in the Glasgow Police Court also became more common around the same time as those that were debated both in Edinburgh and by the law commissioners in parliament. In keeping with the largely positive image of justice that the conservative/liberal press portrayed, such papers focused on the burden placed upon magistrates in carrying out their duties and the need to relieve them of some of the workload under which they struggled. In 1856, the *Glasgow Herald* argued that stipendiary magistrates were required to relinquish civic magistrates of duties they had to undertake in response to a massive increase in police court business following rapid population growth and an expansion in the judicial boundary in 1846.[217] It also contended that appointing stipendiary magistrates was a natural progression: 'magistrates have gradually been relinquishing their judicial functions' in favour of sheriffs and paid justices in the city's other courts, with the Glasgow Burgh Court having not dealt with a criminal case since the introduction of the Municipal Police Act in 1846, preferring instead to remit such cases to the local sheriff court.[218] Magistrates had also recently devolved to sheriffs the time-consuming and costly responsibility for preparing preliminary precognitions and cases within their judicial bounds required to be prosecuted in the High Court. The *Glasgow Herald*'s commentary went on: 'It was a tactical admission that the relative duties are more within the provenance of a skilled professional judge, than of citizens popularly elected for their general intelligence and integrity to administer the affairs of the city, but with no special or direct view to their judicial qualifications.' Substituting civic with stipendiary magistrates in police courts would also enable the community to dispense with the services of assessors who, in Glasgow at least, now sat 'at the elbow' of police magistrates in court and advised them on matters on which they were more cognisant.[219] Similarly, it would reduce the influence of town clerks on police court business. Such men exerted considerable influence in civic circles – a feature of civic governance that was increasingly called into question by mid-century – and the relationship between them and other civic leaders was often acrimonious.[220] Moreover, with much council business being

[216]   Ibid.

[217]   *Glasgow Herald*, 3 December 1856.

[218]   *Glasgow Herald*, 24 December 1856. The 1846 Municipal Police Act extended the police boundaries of the city over a number of suburban areas not traditionally under the authority of Glasgow magistrates.

[219]   Ibid.

[220]   Maver, 'Glasgow's Civic Government', p. 447.

consumed by protracted discussions concerning civic improvement initiatives from mid-century,[221] reducing the time commitment upon magistrates in police courts was especially attractive.

Significantly, however, the *Glasgow Herald* was at pains to point out that it was not challenging magisterial authority or their capacity to administer the law: 'We did not mean – for nothing was further from our intention – that the dignity or the authority of our Civic Magistrates should be in the smallest degree impaired by this new arrangement.'[222] Far from replacing the values of the old system, the stipendiary magistrate was expected to 'combine both the virtues of the unpaid magistrate and the paid assessor'.[223] Indeed, there continued to be support among the ranks of the propertied communities for the continuation of discretionary justice. In 1858, a letter from 'A Citizen' to the editor of the *Glasgow Herald* responded to a recent report in the same paper on the need for stipendiary magistrates to avoid procedural errors that led to sentences later being quashed in higher courts:

> It is the part of the paid officials to attend to these matters, and no part of the Bailie's duties. He is there to bring common-sense and equity much more than strict law into exercise, and assuredly not to control the legal way in which the case may come into Court, or be carried out in the record.

It went on: 'In the proper disposal of Police cases, the public have the combined elements, as it were, of judge and jury, and, generally speaking, an administration of justice not exclusively consisting of stern law and precedent, but mixed up and tempered with the common-sense and merciful discernment of an intelligent civilian.'[224]

The prevalence of such an opinion among civic leaders ensured that the first calls for reform went unheeded. Also, the fact that the social composition of the town council remained unchanged following burgh reform went a long way in accounting for the lack of support for the proposal. Unlike police commissions, magistrates continued to be drawn from business (and to a lesser extent professional) backgrounds which ensured that the same questions concerning their 'independent' status – which effectively meant their economic and social background – were not raised. As Maver points out, 'If anything, the newcomers [to the council after 1833] were even more prestigiously placed than their predecessors, because of their propensity to represent lucrative growth industries like textiles and iron manufacture.'[225] Public service on the town council and magistracy continued

---

[221]   Ibid., p. 456; and W. Hamish Fraser and Irene Maver, 'The Social Problems of the City', in Fraser and Maver (eds), *Glasgow, Volume II*, pp. 394–440.

[222]   *Glasgow Herald*, 24 December 1856.

[223]   Ibid.

[224]   *Glasgow Herald*, 10 March 1858.

[225]   Maver, 'Glasgow's Civic Government', p. 444.

to be a badge of respectability in Glasgow which ensured that the wealthiest members of society remained at the forefront of it in the decades that followed burgh reform. In seeking to mock the exclusive and somewhat stuffy nature of Glasgow's public life, *The Bailie*, in its portrait of Bailie William Moir in 1873, exposed the fact that the magistracy continued to be controlled by a small cohort of wealthy, sombre men. Describing how magistrates were selected and the qualities of office they should possess, it satirically noted:

> It seems to be essential, indeed, under the present regime in the Council, that a certain proportion of the Bailies and other managing men should be entirely respectable, but not overwise. A really clever man from the outside, with strong will and strong sense, getting into the inner circle, would be apt to make sad havoc with the little projects of the sages who work the oracle. It is necessary, therefore, that the managing body should be largely recruited from that variety of human species which wears black cloth and fine linen, which looks as wise and as dull as the owl.[226]

Calls for change, however, did not go away. As time went on, a growing body within council circles themselves recognised the need for a new approach. In Glasgow in 1865, Councillor Paterson proposed that provision be made for the appointment of a stipendiary magistrate in the local police bill that was being framed in order to relieve bailies of attending to business in the Central Police Court – the busiest of the city's district police courts. The Lord Provost and magistrates opposed the proposal and it was defeated, 13 voting in favour, 28 against.[227] Two years later, a new proposal to consider whether to introduce a stipendiary magistrate was put forward by Councillor Lang, who, significantly, was a lawyer and a member of the Faculty of Procurators. The ensuing debates were published in *The Journal of Jurisprudence*, highlighting the continued legal interest in the city's policing arrangements.[228] As well as reiterating arguments concerning lay magistrates' lack of legal knowledge, Lang also offered trenchant criticism of their capacity to enforce the law in a neutral manner given that they also served as *ex-officio* representatives on police boards. Although not suggesting that magistrates acted corruptly, he pointed to a conflict of interest between their role as local justices and as police commissioners.[229] Magistrates, he contended,

---

[226] *The Bailie*, no. 35, 18 June 1873, p. 1.

[227] GCA, D-TC6. 64: The Stipendiary Magistrates of Glasgow, Minutes Relating Thereto, 1865–1876, 11 December 1865.

[228] GUL, 'Paid v Unpaid Magistrates', pp. 539–40.

[229] The *Journal* included the following dialogue that was reported to have occurred at a Police Board meeting: 'In the Police Board, a gentleman got up, and, like the Chancellor of the Exchequer, he was bringing out his budget; he told the Commissioners of Police that so much had been collected from fines during the past year – £5,000 and some hundreds – and for the next year they might safely calculate on £6,000. Was that a thing to be smiled

had been projecting future police budgets partly on fines that they would impose in administering the law.[230] Moreover, as many of those who were brought before magistrates were either too poor or had insufficient time to acquire a lawyer, Lang contended that it was essential that trained lawyers sit on the bench, especially as the business and powers of the police court were expanding.[231] Although stopping short of questioning the integrity of magistrates, he implied that they would not safeguard the interests of poor people as effectively as legally trained lawyers, arguing that 'citizen magistrates were not more but less merciful than the professional, and sometimes were too merciful'.[232] Mirroring growing criticism that was levelled against the social composition of police boards throughout the country by mid-century, he went on to question the social composition of the magistracy. In keeping with the rhetoric of self-sacrifice and public service which underpinned how governing officials presented themselves, he argued that as 'the duties of the police bench were a great burden on the mercantile community, the best qualified members ... were frequently prevented thereby from undertaking municipal duty'.[233] The social composition of the council was still made up of men from affluent backgrounds, but the implication was that its representatives were not quite of the same social status as its predecessors.

The Glasgow proposal and a further one in 1870 were defeated by councillors who voted almost two-to-one against changing existing arrangements.[234] So, too, had been proposals for a stipendiary magistrate in Dundee in the mid-1860s. In 1865, the *Dundee Courier* opposed reform by advocating the importance of character and local feeling to the administration of justice, 'counter-balancing any supposed subserviency to local influences', and a strong aversion to paid officials of the central state pushing aside unpaid public servants to the local community.[235]

---

at or laughed at? It was a matter for very serious consideration. He did not believe that the magistrate, acting as Commissioners, ever acted corruptly, but they could not prevent people from speaking about it; and they said this, that fines exacted from these people ought not to be disposed of by the parties exacting them.' Ibid., p. 540.

[230]   Ibid.

[231]   He also pointed to the fact that police courts were not handling 'cases of great civil and pecuniary interest, such as smoke and nuisance cases ... without correctory review'. Ibid., p. 539.

[232]   Ibid. On the other hand, Superintendent Linton claimed that in Edinburgh bailie judges tended to be more lenient than sheriffs. 'First Report of the Law Commissioners Appointed to Inquire into the Courts of Law in Scotland', p. 363.

[233]   GUL, 'Paid v Unpaid Magistrates', p. 539. For more on growing concern with social composition of police boards, see Barrie, *Police in the Age of Improvement*, pp. 234–43.

[234]   Twenty members of the council opposed the proposal, 12 were in favour. GUL, 'Paid v Unpaid Magistrates', p. 540; and GCA, The Stipendiary Magistrates of Glasgow, Minutes Relating Thereto, 11 July 1867 and 1 September 1870.

[235]   *The Dundee Courier & Argus*, 6 January 1865. There was also support from the public for the continuation of lay magistrates. *The Dundee Courier & Argus* published a

Indeed, the paper provided an impassioned defence of civic magistrates, who were drawn from a wider range of retail, trade and commercial backgrounds than in Glasgow, although large business owners still formed its largest occupational grouping.[236] After reporting in 1869 that the bailie of the police court and assessor had been involved in a courtroom fracas, it commented:

> we may perhaps be in danger sometimes of magnifying such dignitaries as Bailies, as well as their office, too much, and of believing too firmly in the passionless nature of legal gentlemen. ... Well, we fancy there may be an advantage in now and then reversing that order, so as to enable us to see not the Magistrate, but the man.[237]

In civic circles in Glasgow, however, opinions were beginning to change. In 1871, councillors and magistrates agreed to send a delegation to Liverpool, Manchester, Birmingham and Leeds to study the operation of stipendiary magistrates in these towns (powers for provincial towns in England to appoint a stipendiary magistrate had been further extended in 1864, although a number had appointed these through their own initiative much earlier).[238] Workload pressures, driven by population growth and the expansion in commerce, were clearly major factors in effecting the change of heart among the majority of civic men, with the minority who were not in favour arguing unsuccessfully that the increased burden should instead be alleviated by electing more lay magistrates.[239] The publication of the 'Fourth Report of the Commissioners appointed to Inquire into the Law Courts in Scotland' in 1870 might also have influenced magisterial thinking. The majority of law commissioners came out in favour of appointing a paid magistrate, although others thought 'it might tend to weaken the feeling of interest in and responsibility

---

letter to the editor from 'Malachi Malagrowther': 'I have seen more than one stipendiary in England who was nought else but a stipendiary fool; and the difference betwixt him and a stupid Bailie is just this, that the Bailie you get rid of at the end of three years, the other is rooted to the bench for life. A popularly-elected Magistrate with *a well-qualified assessor* is an infinitely preferable system to having a third-rate lawyer, who, after prowling briefless through the purlieus of higher Courts, has accepted a seat in the lowest judicatory in the land as a sort of bed of thorns from which he may vent forth the ill-natured spleen which years of fancied neglect have engendered.' *The Dundee Courier & Argus*, 1 September 1866.

[236] Louise Miskell, 'Civic Leadership and the Manufacturing Elite', pp. 51–2.

[237] *The Dundee Courier & Argus*, 14 October 1869.

[238] GCA, The Stipendiary Magistrates of Glasgow, Minutes Relating Thereto, 27 November 1871.

[239] Ibid., 16 November 1871. A few years later, a Memorandum for the Lord Advocate revealed that 'the great increase in the population and trade of Glasgow has rendered it necessary that the bailies get assistance in the discharge of their duties'. Ibid., paper entitled 'Memorandum for the Right Honourable the Lord Advocate relative to the Glasgow Stipendiary Magistrates Bill', March 1874, p. 1.

for the peace and good order of the burgh, by which the Magistrate ought to be influenced'.[240]

For those magistrates who had opposed reform, the change of heart was, to some degree, brought about by pressure from the wider community rather than representing a new way of thinking concerning the magistrate's role. As the *Glasgow Herald* reported, it was taken 'with the view of meeting the demands of the public on the subject and in order to secure uniformity of decision and practice and as conducive to economy'.[241] In the 1870s, magisterial justice was more closely scrutinised in certain media circles – especially in *The Bailie*, which, despite its general support for lay justice, regularly critiqued the uneven way the law was being administered.[242] In 1874, the journal reported on a growing wave of popular support for the introduction of a stipendiary magistrate following community revulsion after Bailie Bannerman's decision to imprison a boy for theft in the case referred to earlier.[243] The decision to send the boy to prison rather than to a reformatory or industrial school provoked widespread community anger. Indignant meetings were held against the sentence, letters of protest were published in the *Glasgow Herald* and representations were sent to the Lord Provost requesting that Bailie Bannerman be relieved in future from the business of trying people in the police court.[244] *The Bailie*, which had hitherto supported lay magistrates, claimed that the Bannerman case would rightly increase the cry for stipendiary magistrates one-hundred fold:

---

[240]   The commissioners recommended that lay magistrates should not deal with criminal affairs – not just in police courts, but burgh courts, too, where the criminal jurisdiction of the burgh court was co-ordinated with that of the sheriff – and magistrates could imprison for up to two years. 'We think that such powers should not be vested in a tribunal of fluctuating, untrained, and unpaid judges; and we recommend that Magistrates of burghs should henceforth be relieved of the duties they at present discharge in the preparation for trial of proper criminal causes, and of the jurisdiction they now exercise in their trial. At the same time, we recommend that the Burgh Magistrates should continue to exercise their jurisdiction in proper matters of police – excluding cases of theft, reset of theft, falsehood, fraud and wilful imposition, and embezzlement.' 'Fourth Report of the Commissioners Appointed to Inquire into the Courts of Law in Scotland', *BPP*, 1870 (C–175), XVIII.455, pp. 38–9.

[241]   GCA, The Stipendiary Magistrates of Glasgow, Minutes Relating Thereto, 6 July 1871.

[242]   After John Gemmell was appointed stipendiary magistrate, *The Bailie* reported: 'The punishments inflicted in the police courts must henceforth be more uniform and equitable; the line must be drawn between thoughtfulness and criminal intent; it will no longer do for three guineas to be charged by Bailie MacBean for what only costs three half-crowns at the Central; and even the delinquents, gentle and simple, must be taught to appreciate the pleasure of being chastened by a competent Judge who is paid for doing his duty.' *The Bailie*, no. 200, 16 August 1876.

[243]   *The Bailie*, no. 104, 14 October 1874, pp. 1–2.

[244]   Ibid.

So long as we have Citizen magistrates we always run the risk of having an Old Man of the Sea on our shoulders, who is as mischievous as he is uneducated. One, for instance, who will persist in spelling the common word "forfeit" "four Feet," and who will award sentences that shall irritate the minds of the entire community.[245]

In the established local newspapers, the issue of the neutrality of civic magistrates from business backgrounds sitting in judgement on crimes involving property was not discussed in ensuing debates about whether a stipendiary magistrate should be introduced. In such circles, the impartiality of the magistrate was assured by his 'independent' status. In burghs where electoral regulations, not least the residential qualification for office, had resulted in control of police commissions falling into the hands of artisans and small traders, including spirit dealers and pawnbrokers, the established press questioned whether such men could be relied upon to enforce the law in a neutral manner.[246] But in their exercise of judicial duties, men of property of a certain value were for the most part considered by the mainstream media to be above such criticism, even though there was some press comment in the 1860s and 1870s that leading Glasgow councillors, notably John Blackie and James Watson, were seeking to benefit from the city's Civic Improvement Trust slum clearance programme by buying land in slum areas.[247] Some journals, though, were more critical. As Chapter 5 of Volume 2 examines in more depth, in 1874, *The Bailie* profiled how magistrate Walls, an oil refiner and the infamous 'Smoke Bailie', had dealt with pollution cases prosecuted before him. Despite the best efforts of procurators, according to *The Bailie*, Walls would go to great lengths to ensure that large polluters would not be convicted, even taking the unprecedented stance of judging the evidence of two policemen in such cases as constituting only one competent witness. There were even reports later in the decade that magistrates were using their position on the bench to further their own temperance position.[248] It is, of course, impossible to say precisely what impact such reports had. Such criticisms of magisterial justice might well have reflected as much as shaped community attitudes as to whether a stipendiary magistrate should serve on the Glasgow bench. What is more certain is that such media criticism kept the issue on the political agenda, made existing serving arrangements appear out of date, and significantly strengthened the case for reform. In 1873, *The Bailie* published the following poem, entitled, 'The Stipendiary Magistrate: An Address to the "Great Unpaid"' in which civic magistrates were mocked:[249]

---

[245] Ibid., p. 2.
[246] See, for instance, Barrie, 'Epoch-Making Beginnings to Lingering Death', pp. 267–8.
[247] Maver, *Glasgow*, p. 172.
[248] *The Bailie*, no. 293, 29 May 1878, p. 2.
[249] *The Bailie*, no. 27, 23 April 1873, p. 2.

O Bailies, Bailies! *Ichabod's* the word!
Your glory is departing, sure as fate;
For here's a Bill that threatens Glaisca toun
Wi' a Stipendiary Magistrate.

An' if it pass, as pass it dootless will,
Greet, Bailies, greet; ye'll hae tae abdicate!
Nae longer "terrors to ill-doers," then;
Ye'll be considered judges oot o' date.

Nae mair in Court ye'll sit, on bench enthroned,
And deal sma' justice, at a sma' expense;
Nae mair condemn; nae mair acquit on laws
No' in the Statute Book o' Common Sense.

The ragged weans, the midnight roysterers,
The drunken cairters, an' the cabbies fou,
The tramway gairds, the errin' publicans,
Wife-beatin' fiends, an' a' the pilferin' crew –

They'll miss you, Bailies, sairly, when ye gang,
And sairly will they curse the meddlin' State,
That sends – in deference to J. L. Lang –
The new Stipendiary Magistrate.

But tak' ye comfort, Bailies, tho' ye fa,'
For, even should this fell Bill hap to pass,
Twa still are left to raise yer name and fame –
Your humble servant, Sirs, and eke, his Ass.

The message was clear: the citizen magistrate's fate had been sealed. It was only a matter of time before his role and status was superseded by a legally trained justice.

The delegation of magistrates who were dispatched to England reported favourably on arrangements in the towns visited and was unanimously in favour of appointing a stipendiary magistrate for Glasgow to sit in the Central Police Court.[250] Their report was approved by councillors and magistrates who resolved to frame a bill to effect this.[251] Parliament, however, beat them to it. In 1873, it drew up the Stipendiary Magistrates (Scotland) Bill which proposed that the appointment of the full-time magistrate should be vested in the Home Secretary.

---

[250]   GCA, The Stipendiary Magistrates of Glasgow, 'Report of the Delegation', 23 January 1872.

[251]   Ibid., 1 February 1872.

The appointee was to be drawn from the Faculty of Advocates and have at least five years' experience as a legal practitioner. However, the terms of the bill were not agreeable to Glasgow's civic leaders. They sought to insert clauses which reserved to civic leaders the right to appoint the stipendiary magistrate, limited his powers, and reduced the qualification for office to advocates or law agents of three years' service.[252] However, in 1874 the Home Secretary refused to place the power of appointing the stipendiary magistrate in the hands of councillors and magistrates on the basis that it was inconsistent with practice sanctioned in similar legislation applying to England.[253] Council leaders opposed the Home Secretary's plans as not only an infringement on civic autonomy, but also as inconsistent with the free constitution of Scottish municipal administration. They contended that the 'analogy of the English boroughs was not applicable to the burghs of Scotland'.[254] It was an ardent defence not only of Scottish civic institutions and civil society, but also Scottish national identity. Magistrates sent the Home Secretary's report to all the royal burghs in Scotland in an effort to mobilise opposition among Scottish councils. The Convention of the Royal Burghs in Scotland came out strongly in support of magistrates and councillors – with 62 royal burgh delegates out of the possible 66 who attended the Convention's meeting resolving to send a delegation to London in an attempt to change the Home Secretary's opinion.[255] It was successful. In May of 1874, the Lord Advocate withdrew the bill after he and the Glasgow delegation had failed to find a compromise.[256]

---

252 Ibid., 27 November 1873
253 Ibid., 16 January 1874.
254 Ibid.
255 Ibid., 7 April 1874.
256 The Home Secretary was sympathetic to civic leaders' pleas, but 'frankly held out no hope that the Government would apply to Stipendiary Police Magistrates in Scotland a different rule from that which obtained in England in regard to Stipendiary Magistrates, who are appointed by the Crown'. The Glasgow Committee in London reported that they 'are not prepared to advise the Corporation of Glasgow to accept a measure which would, for the first time in Scotland, interfere with the principal of local government by vesting in the Crown the appointment of a Police Judge, to be paid out of the local rates, for the purpose of aiding the ordinary magistrates, in the discharge of their onerous and increasing duties as judges of police. The government have been made aware of the reasons which induced the Corporation to promote the Bill; they are now informed as to the tenacity with which Scotch burghs adhere to their ancient constitutional rights and privileges, in the matter of local government by magistrates.' It went on that 'the Government should now be left the responsibility of practically withholding the measure by insisting on the appointment of Stipendiary Police magistrates being vested in the Crown, which, in Scotland, does not appoint even Sheriff Substitutes, who, exercise like Stipendiary Magistrates in England, a higher jurisdiction than that of simple Police Magistrates, are wholly paid for by the State, and hold their appointments for life'. Ibid., 23 April 1874.

Illustration 2.4   Stipendiary Magistrate John Gemmell, 1876. @CSG CIC
                    Glasgow Museums and Libraries Collection: The Mitchell
                    Library, Special Collections†

Note: As a lawyer and Procurator Fiscal of Glasgow, John Gemmell prosecuted high-profile trials,
including that of Jessie McLachlan and Dr Edward Pritchard, the last man to be publicly hanged
in the city. He was appointed stipendiary magistrate of Glasgow in 1876.

† *The Bailie*, no. 200, 16 August 1876.

A solution was finally reached the following year in the form of the 1875 Sheriff Substitute's Act.[257] The third section of the act gave the City of Glasgow all the advantages that could be served by a stipendiary magistrate, but the power of appointment and dismissal was vested in the Crown.[258] To appease civic leaders, the Home Secretary in 1876 appointed John Gemmell, former Procurator Fiscal of Glasgow, as the city's first stipendiary magistrate for the Central Police Court after liaising with civic leaders and the Lord Advocate. As Illustration 2.4 shows, Gemmell was profiled in *The Bailie*'s weekly 'portraits' of distinguished and important men in public life, which was testament to his significance in the civic and judicial arena. His selection, which was made with the approval of civic leaders, was recognition that the opinion of Scotland's municipal elite would continue to play an important, if no longer dominating, part in shaping the future form of police court justice.

The controversy over the issue of stipendiary magistrates in both Edinburgh and Glasgow was significant in revealing the varied attempts among middle-class men to assert dominance in the social and professional hierarchies of urban governance and the extent to which central government and lawyers were able to exert influence over the administration of Scottish police courts. *The Bailie* portrayed Gemmell's appointment as constituting a loss of face, status and power for citizen magistrates: 'Their days are numbered, they have been weighed, so to speak, in the balances and found wanting, and the seat of honour and of power – which so long hath known them, shall soon know them no more for ever … Unpaid justice is no longer in favour with the public.'[259]

For the most part, though, Scottish civic magistrates were remarkably resilient to challenges to their position and authority. Significantly, other burghs did not follow the lead of Glasgow, or English cities, in acquiring state-appointed stipendiary magistrates to supplement the work of lay magistrates. The 1892 Burgh Police (Scotland) Act and the 1897 Stipendiary Magistrates Jurisdiction (Scotland) Act made provision for such justices, but there was no headlong rush

---

[257]   Sheriffs Substitute (Scotland) Act, 1875 (38 & 39 Victoria, cap. 81).

[258]   By the Secretary for Scotland Act (1887), power to appoint paid magistrates switched from the Home Secretary to the Secretary for Scotland. GCA, D-TC 14-1-17: Glasgow Town Clerk's Department, Miscellaneous Papers, Paper 961.

[259]   *The Bailie*, no. 197, 26 July 1876, p. 1. The journal later also wrote that the bailies 'have this week had wrested from them – out of kindness – the crowning glory of presiding at the Central Police Court. No wonder if a big bright tear was to be seen in the eyes of some of our old magistrates, or that despair filled the bosoms of those aspiring councillors who see in the Magistracy, not forgetting the big medals, one of the main props of the constitution. But there are always some crumbs of comfort for the afflicted, and those who are not possessed of an infatuation for presiding in Police Courts will admit that the duty at the Central was irksome and unpleasant, and not always satisfactorily performed.' *The Bailie*, no. 200, 16 August 1876, p. 1.

to embrace them.[260] According to Trotter's 1936 *Summary Justice according to the Law of Scotland*, the Glasgow Central Police Court was the only urban centre of justice in Scotland to employ a stipendiary magistrate by that period.[261] Even the growth in legal texts, directives and judgements had, at best, only a modest impact on how magistrates enforced the law. Most of the relevant legal manuals were not published until the late nineteenth and early twentieth centuries and were designed to assist magistrates, not challenge their position as governing men.[262] These guides emerged significantly later than in England, where the governing principles of magistrates' courts were outlined much earlier and supported by a far wider range of legal journals, manuals and commentaries than existed in Scotland.[263] For most of the nineteenth century, Scottish law literature was preoccupied with higher courts, not police courts.[264] In addition, although the second half of the nineteenth century saw more and more national police acts being introduced, the overwhelming majority were permissive rather than compulsory and most police courts in the major leading urban centres continued

---

[260]   Under the 1892 Burgh Police Scotland Act, stipendiary magistrates were required to possess the qualification of sheriff-substitute in Scotland. Sheriff-substitutes had to be an advocate or law agent of not less than five years' standing in the profession. Stipendiary magistrates, who were to hold the same powers as burgh magistrates, were to be appointed by the secretary of state for Scotland. Campbell Irons, *The Burgh Police (Scotland) Act*, pp. 684–5.

[261]   Thomas Trotter, *Summary Criminal Jurisdiction: According to the Law of Scotland* (Edinburgh, 1936), p. 489. As late as the early twentieth century, police courts in the major burghs in Scotland continued to be governed mainly by local private police acts, with civic leaders cherry-picking the clauses of the 1892 Burgh Police Scotland Act that suited them, and ignoring those that did not. Campbell Irons, *The Burgh Police (Scotland)* Act, p. 18.

[262]   See, for instance, James Campbell Irons, *The Scottish Justices' Manual* (Edinburgh, 1900); James Campbell Irons, *Burgh Government: Being a Commentary showing the Effects of Statutes and Decisions from 1892 to 1903 upon the Law Relating to Police and Municipal Administration in Scotland* (Edinburgh, 1905); Thomas Trotter, *The Law of Summary Criminal Jurisdiction: Supplement Containing Additional Notes on the Summary Jurisdiction (Scotland) Act, 1908, also the Text, with Notes, of the Criminal Justice Administration Act, 1914, as Applicable to Scotland, and Other Statutes* (Edinburgh, 1915); Committee of Chief Constables of Scotland, *Police Manual For Scotland* (Glasgow, 1931).

[263]   Zimmermann, 'Law Journals in Nineteenth-Century Scotland', p. 10. For legal journals in England, see Stefan Vogenauer, 'Law Journals in Nineteenth-Century England', *Edinburgh Law Review*, 12/1 (2008), pp. 26–50.

[264]   See, for instance, Baron David Hume, *Commentaries on the Law of Scotland Respecting Crimes* (2 vols, Edinburgh, 1797); Archibald Alison, *Principles of the Criminal Law of Scotland* (Edinburgh, 1832); Archibald Alison, *Practice of the Criminal Law of Scotland* (Edinburgh, 1833); J. Burton, 'Practice of Criminal Law of Scotland', *Westminster Review*, 22 (1835): pp. 92–119; R. Bell, 'A Supplement to Hume's *Commentaries on the Law of Scotland Respecting Crimes'*, *The North British Review*, 4 (1844–1845): pp. 313–46; and John Inglis, *The Historical Study of the Law: An Address Delivered to the Juridicial Society, Session 1863–4* (Edinburgh, 1863).

to be governed by their own local procedures and practices.[265] Like legal texts, national guidelines relating to court procedures and practices focused mainly on sheriff courts and the judiciary courts.[266] Those provisions that were concerned with how burgh magistrates administered the law tended to be poorly defined and offered little scope for effective regulation.[267] This meant that lay magistrates often interpreted the law as they saw fit which was not always in keeping with how lawyers saw it. The power and influence of urban elites, therefore, remained remarkably stable in most parts of the country at a time when the rising discourse of professionalism – and a growing importance being attached to 'knowledge' in institutional spheres – contributed to the demise of the civic man as an assumed arbiter of justice in other parts of the United Kingdom and beyond.[268] This was testament not just to the self-governing nature of Scottish civil society and the desire among civic men to preserve Scottish institutional structures, practices and traditions, but also indicative of the continuing belief among civic men of the importance of magisterial discretion and paternal authority.

Professional differences between civic leaders and the legal profession should not, though, disguise the importance of class in shaping the delivery of magisterial justice and how it was represented in the press. In terms of occupational composition, the police court reflected the particular machinations of power between the cities' elite men, echoing the nuances of their differing political alignments and professional expertise in their positioning for status as governing men in the nineteenth-century city. But in practice it was primarily a set of shared moral and social values of men of property that were projected within the courtroom and in the judgements that magistrates made over the lives of others, even if there were differences between civic and stipendiary justices in how judgements and sentences were reached. The magistrate's display of particular emotions was a critical facet of his performance of paternal masculinity and thus his authority to judge others. His fellow middle-class counterparts interpreted this sensitivity and emotionality as a symbol of his connection to the community, in

---

[265]   Trotter, *Summary Criminal Jurisdiction*, p. 18.

[266]   These include The Summary Procedure Act (1864) and The Summary Jurisdiction Act (1881).

[267]   A number of clauses of the 1862 Burgh Police Act were amended on several occasions. For example, 31 & 32 Victoria, cap. 102 (1868).

[268]   Throughout the United Kingdom, there was a general drift towards giving greater independence to full-time, senior officers rather than elected or appointed representatives – a development that did much to impact on power structures, dynamics and relations. See Robert Reiner, *The Politics of the Police*, 3rd edn (Oxford, 2000), pp. 31–45. This diffusion of power from the centre, to local police institutions, and to full-time officers is in keeping with Foucault's notion of 'governmentality', in that it was a de-centralised model of governance that was not limited to state politics alone. See Michel Foucault, 'Governmentality', trans. Rosi Braidotti, revised Colin Gordon, in Graham Burchell, Colin Gordon and Peter Miller (eds), *The Foucault Effect: Studies in Governmentality* (Chicago, 1996), pp. 87–104.

touch with common-sense notions of right and wrong. Whether those who were required to defend their activities before him, or even those who also contributed to the functioning of the court as personnel, shared similar confidence in his ability to understand the broad sway of urban experiences and conditions was more doubtful.

VI. Conclusion

Far from the rise of nineteenth-century summary justice heralding a move towards a more formalised, procedural system which undermined the local magistrate's status and capacity for self-direction, Scottish police courts helped reinforce bailies' position, power and status within their communities. Magistrates might have conceded the establishment of rival municipal authorities to town councils in the form of police commissions in order that statutory tax-raising powers could be acquired to pay for public services, but the wide-ranging powers that police courts placed in their hands made local justices just as important as police commissioners and senior officers to law enforcement. Although there was greater central and legal direction as the century went on, magisterial discretion continued to be the hallmark of the police court structure. It was a system of justice that prioritised civic attributes over and above legal ones – a system which as James Robertson, Procurator Fiscal of Glasgow, suggested, was as dependent upon the quality and character of civic men as the law itself.[269]

Administering the law in this way helped serve the interests of the city corporation and was in keeping with how magistrates saw their position in the community. Theirs was a multi-faced role, which included not only dealing with criminals, but also safeguarding public welfare and acting as guardians of urban morality. Being able to apply the law in a flexible manner was paramount to their ability to deal sensitively with individual cases. Magistrates, in this respect, saw themselves as new Christian pastors of an urban meta-parish – as missionaries to those displaced godly masses who were deemed worthy of saving. However, it was also a practice, magistrates believed, that was essential to maintaining control over a rapidly expanding urban population and their positions within the community. As in eighteenth-century England, the uncertainty of how the law was going to be administered was an important mechanism for reinforcing the power, status and influence of local justices. Unlike in eighteenth-century England, however, this had less to do with reinforcing paternal bonds, as Hay famously argued, and more to do with magisterial capacity for governance. Discretionary justice was especially important to magistrates in an era in which their management of local affairs was being scrutinised in the press, measured by statistical returns, and dependent in principle upon them being elected into office by a predominantly middle-class electorate. It was an essential tool in safeguarding their public image as both

---

[269] GCA, *Handbook for Magistrates on Police Court Procedure*, p. 1.

paternal leaders and judges who could see that justice would be done. Whereas, for some scholars, resolving community disputes rather than securing convictions might have been the main role of magistrates in eighteenth-century England,[270] in nineteenth-century Scotland it was more complex and varied. The spread of print culture, growing concerns with urban order, and a changing ethos within the criminal justice system ensured it. Concern with the urban masses, electoral pressures and an increasingly judgemental, if usually supportive, mainstream press, determined that the civic magistrates' main role came to be concerned with dispensing, and being seen to dispense, justice towards a predominantly working-class police court clientele, as subsequent chapters show.

---

[270] Morgan and Rushton, 'The Magistrate, the Community and the Maintenance of an Orderly Society', pp. 54–77.

Chapter 3
People's Courts?

I. Introduction

In recent years a burgeoning historiography has identified summary courts in eighteenth- and nineteenth-century England as places of exchange and dialogue between different social groups.[1] Rather than viewing the criminal law as an instrument of the ruling elite, as did many left-wing analyses of the 1970s and 1980s,[2] historians have increasingly portrayed local courts as accessible public arenas in which magistrates handed out advice, negotiated disputes and settled grievances – often in an informal, discretionary manner.[3] Indeed, fulfilling this role, it has been contended, was the priority of the 'patrician guardians' who served on the bench, rather than bringing offenders to justice.[4] If not 'people's courts',[5] these were courts which empowered working-class participants and

---

[1]   See, for instance, Drew D. Gray, *Crime, Prosecution and Social Relations in London: The Summary Courts of London in the Late Eighteenth Century* (Basingstoke, 2009); Peter King, 'The Summary Courts and Social Relations in Eighteenth-Century England', *Past and Present*, 183/1 (2004): pp. 125–72; Jennifer S. Davis, 'A Poor Man's System of Justice? The London Police Courts in the Second Half of the Nineteenth Century', *Historical Journal*, 27/2 (1984): pp. 309–35; and Gwenda Morgan and Peter Rushton, 'The Magistrate, the Community and the Maintenance of an Orderly Society in Eighteenth-Century England', *Historical Research*, 76/191 (2003): pp. 54–77.

[2]   See, for example, Douglas Hay, 'Property, Authority and the Criminal Law', in Douglas Hay, Peter Linebaugh, John G. Rule, E.P. Thompson and Cal Winslow (eds), *Albion's Fatal Tree: Crime and Society in Eighteenth-Century England* (Harmondsworth, 1975), pp. 17–63; and David Philips, 'The Black Country Magistracy 1835–60: A Changing Elite and the Exercise of its Power', *Midland History*, 3/3 (1976): pp. 161–90.

[3]   Other relevant studies not cited in note 1 include Robert B. Shoemaker, *Prosecution and Punishment: Petty Crime and the Law in London and Rural Middlesex, c.1660–1725* (Cambridge, 1991); A. James Hammerton, *Cruelty and Companionship: Conflict in Nineteenth-Century Married Life* (London, 1992); David J.V. Jones, *Crime, Protest, Community and Police in Nineteenth-Century Britain* (London, 1982), pp. 23 & 111; and Carolyn A. Conley, *The Unwritten Law: Criminal Justice in Victorian Kent* (Oxford, 1991), p. 41.

[4]   Morgan and Rushton, 'The Magistrate, the Community and the Maintenance of an Orderly Society', pp. 54–77.

[5]   For a critical assessment of the extent to which summary courts could be viewed as people's courts, see Drew D. Gray, 'The People's Courts? Summary Justice and Social Relations in the City of London, c.1760–1800', *Family and Community History*, 11/1 (2008): pp. 7–15.

provided accessible justice to the urban masses.[6] According to Drew D. Gray, the fact that so many of the lower orders brought complaints before magistrates was 'testimony to the centrality and accessibility of the summary courts and to the perception that they were places where disputes could be satisfactorily aired and resolved'.[7] Similarly, Jennifer S. Davis has argued that the 'process of negotiation which took place in the police courts appears to have been essential to the effective maintenance of the social order by the nineteenth-century state'.[8] In London, she contends, police courts were not expected to work hand in hand with police forces to suppress the rougher elements of working-class culture and behaviour. Rather, they were 'to win lower-class acceptance of the law and, thus, implicitly of the social order'.[9] The criminal justice system, as Peter King has argued, was not only an arena of 'terror, exploitation, and inequality, but also one of negotiation and accommodation and every group in society helped shape it, just as their behaviour was partly shaped by it'.[10]

Any attempt to draw comparisons with this historiography must bear in mind that the Scottish legal system, court structure and prosecution practices were different to those in England. Whereas Scotland had a public prosecutor in the form of the procurator fiscal – a role that the newly introduced police forces would assume for certain offences – England relied upon a system of private prosecution for much of the nineteenth century. Moreover, the English summary courts examined in the above studies dealt with a wide range of civil matters. Scottish police courts, for the most part, did not.[11] Indeed, the capacity of magistrates in Scotland to act as conflict resolvers was somewhat diminished in the early nineteenth century following the decision in 1812 by the Court of Session – in keeping with the prevailing free-market ideology of the time – to end the power of magistrates to arbitrate on industrial disputes and fix wage levels.[12] What advice or support magistrates did continue to provide – such as

---

[6]   Davis, 'A Poor Man's System of Justice?', pp. 309–35.

[7]   Drew D. Gray, 'The People's Courts?', p. 11.

[8]   Davis, 'A Poor Man's System of Justice?', p. 310.

[9]   Ibid., p. 315.

[10]   Peter King, *Crime, Justice and Discretion in England, 1740–1820* (Oxford, 2000), p. 373. See also Peter King, *Crime and the Law in England 1750–1840: Remaking Justice from the Margins* (Cambridge, 2006), passim.

[11]   In 1831, for instance, an Edinburgh magistrate instructed a 'respectable merchant' to pursue the defender in a civil court for the recovery of money allegedly stolen by his clerk after suggesting that the clerk was guilty of a breach of trust rather than a crime. *The Police Intelligencer, or Life in Edinburgh* (*Police Intelligencer*), 19 August 1831. In another case, the sheriff sitting in the court dismissed a case which did not merit the charge of assault, only defamation which did not fall under the jurisdiction of the police court. *Police Intelligencer*, 3 October 1832.

[12]   W. Hamish Fraser, *Conflict and Class: Scottish Workers, 1700–1838* (Edinburgh, 1988), p. 102.

hearing petitions for poor relief – was usually offered in either burgh courts or at committee meetings rather than in police courts.[13] Furthermore, the time frame of this study differs from much of the scholarship on England which has, with a few notable exceptions,[14] been largely centred on the 1700s, pre-dating the development of full-time bureaucratised police forces that were introduced in English towns in the nineteenth century.[15]

---

[13]   For example, in the early 1870s, in response to a petition from the unemployed and handloom weavers in Glasgow, magistrates authorised out-of-door labouring for the destitute unemployed and instructed the chief constable to issue pay rations. The unemployed and handloom weavers in 1870 had first made an application for employment and requested that magistrates 'authorise the issue of lines for employment to such destitute applicants'. Glasgow City Archives (GCA), E1/13/3: Magistrates' Committee Minute Book, 29 February 1870. In 1873, magistrates resolved 'that out-of-door labouring work could now be procured by the unemployed in and around Glasgow in order to reduce the number at present receiving pay rations from the magistrates'. GCA, E1/13/3: Magistrates' Committee Minute Book, 11 April 1873. It is not clear whether relief was provided in the intermittent years. It was also common for petitions from the public to be dealt with in the local civil court in which magistrates presided, or before a magistrates' committee, rather than the police court. See, for instance, GCA, E1/13/4, 6: Magistrates' Committee Minute Book: an application from James McLean, Hotel Keeper, St Vincent Street, to the police magistrates' committee meeting requesting that a small space in front of his hotel should be set apart as a cab stand since not having cabs within a short distance was adversely affecting his business. Magistrates' minute books reveal petitions concerning the recovery of stolen items lost whilst assisting the police, the removal of obstructions, the reimbursement of expenses accrued for police services, and appeals against sentences handed down in police and burgh courts, to name but a few. In most cases, such issues were resolved without the petitioner having to attend to appear before magistrates, but in some instances it was required. See, for instance, GCA, E1/13/4: Magistrates' Committee Minute Book, 16 January 1879 and 21 May 1880.

[14]   The main ones include Davis, 'A Poor Man's System of Justice?', pp. 309–35; Jennifer S. Davis, 'Prosecutions and Their Context: The Use of the Criminal Law in Later Nineteenth-Century London', in Douglas Hay and Francis Snyder (eds), *Policing and Prosecution in Britain 1750–1850* (Oxford, 1989), pp. 398–426; Philips, 'The Black Country Magistracy', pp. 161–90; and Barry S. Godfrey, 'Changing Prosecution Practices and their Impact on Crime Figures, 1857–1940', *British Journal of Criminology*, 48/2 (2008): pp. 171–89.

[15]   London and Middlesex had summary courts from the eighteenth century. See J.M. Beattie, *The First English Detectives: The Bow Street Runners and the Policing of London, 1750–1840* (Oxford, 2012); and Ruth Paley, 'The Middlesex Justices Act of 1792: Its Origins and Effects', unpub. PhD thesis (University of Reading, 1983). For the rise of the policed society in England, see Clive Emsley, *The English Police: A Political and Social History*, 2nd edn (London, 2006); Clive Emsley, *The Great British Bobby: A History of British Policing from 1829 to the Present* (London, 2009); David Taylor, *The New Police in Nineteenth-Century England: Crime, Community and Control* (Manchester, 1997); and V.A.C. Gatrell, 'Crime, Authority and the Policeman–State', in F.M.L. Thompson (ed.), *Cambridge Social History of Britain, 1750–1950* (Cambridge, 1992), pp. 243–310.

Nonetheless, whilst recognising how these institutional and cultural differences will affect comparative conclusions, the lines of inquiry and conceptual frameworks advanced in the historiography surrounding English summary courts remain immensely valuable to scholars of criminal justice history in Scotland. They provide an essential historiographical context in which to locate analyses of the use of police courts by victims, the public and justices. At the same time, an understanding of the Scottish experience has the potential to further knowledge of wider developments in judicial history. This is especially relevant when considering what impact a new summary court structure characterised by police-led prosecutions – which became the dominant model across the United Kingdom in the second half of the nineteenth century – had on the accessibility, use, and purpose of local courts.[16] This chapter begins by looking at who the complainers were, their role in judicial proceedings, and why they sought legal redress, before going on to examine the role of procurators and magistrates in determining whether to pursue complaints, and the ideological barriers that restricted access to the courts for certain sections of society. It argues that while there were a number of similarities with England in terms of how Scots used police courts, the central place of procurators in the Scottish criminal justice system, allied to the new bureaucratic police machine which underpinned the courts' workings, reduced the complainer's capacity for self-direction and ultimately had a determining impact on how justice was administered. Media reports, it is contended, largely reinforced the notion that police courts were accessible centres for conflict resolution, though in practice such resolutions were often determined by a wide range of cultural, social, ethnic and gender assumptions and influences.

II. Sourcing the Complaint

Integral to the view that police courts offered a 'poor man's system of justice' was the social profile of complainers, the use that the working classes made of summary courts, and what this use suggests about the extent to which the urban masses had become reconciled to the advent of a policed society and the legitimacy of the rule of law.[17] Unfortunately, establishing the profile of complainers in Scottish police

---

[16]   For the changing relationship between policing and prosecution in Britain, see Hay and Snyder (eds), *Policing and Prosecution in Britain*; and Godfrey, 'Changing Prosecution Practices and their Impact on Crime Figures', pp. 171–89.

[17]   According to Gray, victims used summary courts to air their grievances and thus in some way involve the wider community in their disputes. Gray, 'The People's Courts?', p. 11. According to Philips, the working class increasingly abandoned informal sanctions in favour of magistrates' courts to resolve disputes in the nineteenth century. This, he claims, was an indication that more and more of the working class came to trust the legal system and believe in its legitimacy. David Philips, *Crime and Authority in Victorian England: The Black Country, 1835–1860* (London, 1977), p. 128. However, whilst recognising that 'an

courts over the course of the nineteenth century is far from easy. Neither the police court minute books, nor the annual criminal returns, consistently recorded much information on who they were. The existence of the public prosecutor ensured that the overwhelming majority of prosecutions were brought in the name of the procurator fiscal. Of the 6,234 offences listed for the Edinburgh Police Court in 1835, only 579 were listed as private complaints.[18] Even then, the vast majority, if not all, of the private prosecutions were brought with the concurrence of the fiscal, suggesting that some official approval or support was required for private complainers to undertake legal action.[19] In some towns that submitted criminal returns to the 1839–1840 Law Inquiry, all of the cases brought before magistrates were the actions of the public prosecutor.[20] The expense involved – allied to the country's longstanding tradition of public prosecutions – meant that it was highly unusual for private actions to be pursued. Indeed, in the second half of the century, private prosecutions in police courts appear to have become even less common. Many local and national police acts stated that *all* police court prosecutions were required to be at the instance of the public prosecutor – a trend which probably contributed to the police's decision not to record information on complainers or prosecutors in their criminal returns, which were published annually from 1857.[21]

---

individual's voluntary resort to the police court indicates an acceptance of the court's right to intervene in his or her affairs', Davis argues that it would be 'a mistake to conclude from this either that criminal sanctions as applied by the state were simply replacing those sanctions which had, in the past, been imposed informally in the neighbourhood; or that the urban poor were willing to accept the intervention of law enforcement authorities in all areas of their lives'. Although the working class accounted for a significant proportion of complainers in the London police magistrate courts examined by Davis, legal action was designed to achieve a specific purpose. 'If they [the working-class complainers] failed to achieve that outcome, or if the agencies of law enforcement intervened in their activities in ways they had not themselves initiated, then they were likely to perceive the law as oppressive, and even to oppose its application.' Davis, 'A Poor Man's System of Justice?', p. 330.

[18]   'Fourth Report by Her Majesty's Law Commissioners, Scotland, 1839', *British Parliamentary Papers* (*BPP*), 1840 (241), XX.115, p. 332.

[19]   Of the first 1,556 cases listed in the Edinburgh Police Court 'Abstract of Processes, 1805–1807', only 100 listed the name of a private complainer – and, often, the prosecution was brought with the concurrence of the fiscal. Edinburgh City Archives (ECA), ED006/8: Edinburgh Police Court Abstract of Processes, 1805–1807. In comparing the Scottish system of criminal investigation and prosecution with the English one in 1884, Lees claimed that, unlike in England, no common law and few statutory crimes could be prosecuted without the sanction of the procurator fiscal. J. Lees, 'The Investigation and Prosecution of Crime', *Blackwood's Edinburgh Magazine*, 136 (1884): p. 43. See also 'The Criminal Jurisprudence Scotland', *The Dublin University Magazine*, 29 (1847): pp. 391–2.

[20]   'Fourth Report by Her Majesty's Law Commissioners, Scotland, 1839', pp. 320–39.

[21]   James Campbell Irons, *The Burgh Police (Scotland) Act, 1892* (Edinburgh, 1893), section 477, entitled 'Procedure in Police Court', p. 700 noted that all prosecutions, actions and proceedings for crimes, offences and contraventions of the police laws – not exceeding £10 – were to be at the instance of the procurator fiscal.

Writing in *Blackwood's Magazine* in 1884, J. Lees claimed that, unlike in England, no common law and few statutory crimes in Scotland could be prosecuted without the sanction of the procurator.[22]

That is not to say that victims played a marginal role in deciding whether or not to instigate legal proceedings. In many instances, prosecutions followed a complaint from a member of the public about an alleged crime or offence, which the fiscal or the police would take up on a victim's behalf. Indeed, unless the accused was apprehended in the act of committing a crime or offence, the onus would be on the victim to report it to the police. How many prosecutions resulted from such public complaints is impossible to quantify throughout the century. Information on how legal proceedings were instigated, and by whom, was infrequently recorded in the few court records that exist – namely, for the Edinburgh Police Court from 1805 to 1807 and the Glasgow Police Court from 1813 to 1824.[23] Unlike the English summary courts, where victims were required to bring forward their own prosecutions, the role of procurators within the Scottish police court structure raises as many questions as it answers, not least concerning which victims used the courts for legal redress, and the precise nature of the relationship between complainer and prosecutor.

In order to supplement information in the court records themselves, the historian is forced to turn, with much caution, to trial reports published in newspapers and the unstamped periodicals: the Glasgow *Police Reports* and Edinburgh's *The Police Intelligencer*. As studies by Simon Devereaux, Robert B. Shoemaker, Rosalind Crone and others have pointed out, media representations of crime and court practice need to be handled with care as the trials which were selected for publication were not always representative of the court's day-to-day business.[24] Neither *The Police Intelligencer* nor the *Police*

---

[22]   Lees, 'The Investigation and Prosecution of Crime', pp. 391–2.

[23]   ECA, ED006/8: Edinburgh Police Court Abstract of Processes, 1805–1807; and GCA, B3/1/1/1: Glasgow Police Court Diet Books, 28 January 1813 to B3/1/1/10: Glasgow Police Court Diet Books, 8 October 1824.

[24]   Simon Devereaux, 'The Fall of the Sessions Paper: The Criminal Trial and the Popular Press in Late Eighteenth-Century London', *Criminal Justice History*, 18/1 (2002): p. 58; Simon Devereaux, 'The City and the Sessions Paper: "Public Justice" in London, 1770–1800', *Journal of British Studies*, 35/4 (1996): pp. 467–8; Simon Devereaux, 'From Sessions to Newspaper? Criminal Trial Reporting, the Nature of Crime, and the London Press, 1770–1800', *The London Journal*, 32/1 (2007): pp. 3–6; Robert B. Shoemaker, 'The Old Bailey Proceedings and the Representation of Crime and Criminal Justice in Eighteenth-Century London', *Journal of British Studies* 47/3 (2008), pp. 559–80; Rosalind Crone, *Violent Victorians: Popular Entertainment in Nineteenth-Century London* (Manchester, 2012), p. 220. For other relevant works, see also Susan Broomhall and David G. Barrie, 'Making Men: Media, Magistrates and the Representation of Masculinity in Scottish Police Courts, 1800–1833', in David G. Barrie and Susan Broomhall (eds), *A History of Police and Masculinities, 1700–2012* (Abingdon, 2012), pp. 72–101; and Clive Emsley, Tim Hitchcock and Robert B. Shoemaker, 'The Proceedings – The Value of the Proceedings as a

Reports, for instance, reported on every case brought before magistrates or on every sitting.[25] The number of cases published varied from day to day depending on the business of the court and the level of media interest in its proceedings. *The Police Intelligencer* typically reported on half a dozen cases per sitting. Coverage in the *Police Reports* (which also included some 'interesting' cases brought before the Gorbals and Calton police courts) varied according to the edition published: sometimes up to a dozen cases per day were published, but more often than not around a dozen or so cases would be published covering upwards of several court days. In the mid-1830s, the police courts in these cities each dealt with, on average, between 20 and 40 cases per day, with Edinburgh recording a peak of just under 100 in 1835.[26] These journals, in other words, reported upon probably no more than one fifth or one sixth of cases for which charges were brought at each sitting and, in the case of the Gorbals and Calton reports, usually fewer. It is difficult to be precise about how this compared with the cases that actually made it to court as many were settled before, but media reporting of actual trial proceedings is likely to have constituted, at best, no more than around one quarter of cases tried on a given day and, at worst, only one carefully selected case. Indeed, the number of trials reported varied depending not just on the caseload before the court, but also on how the editor interpreted the level of public interest. In some weeks, it was reported that there were 'no cases of interest', illustrating the moral and commercial influences that lay behind the selection of trials by the *Police Reports'* editor, John Brownlie, who used the periodical to campaign about the connection between alcohol and criminal behaviour.[27] As the previous chapter observed, such considerations influenced what editors chose to publish and what they chose to omit, so the cases that were selected for publication in these journals need to be read as much, if not more, for what they reveal about the social and political values of editors as for the actual workings of the court.[28]

Historical Source', *The Old Bailey Proceedings Online* (*OBP*), http://www.oldbaileyonline. org.

[25]   The Glasgow *Police Reports*, for instance, pointed this out: 'Notice to Subscribers: *The present size of this Publication being found too small to admit the* REPORTS *of all the* POLICE *and other* COURTS, *so copiously as the* PUBLISHERS *would wish, it is respectfully announced, that on Saturday the 10th October next, the size will be extended to* One Sheet Quarto, but without any alteration in the price.' *Police Reports of Causes tried before the Justices of Peace, and the Glasgow, Gorbals and Calton Police Courts* (*Police Reports*), XI [September/October] 1829, p. 132.

[26]   'Fourth Report by Her Majesty's Law Commissioners, Scotland, 1839', p. 325.

[27]   For instance, in 1829, the *Police Reports* noted 'On the 6th July, there were twenty-two cases before the court, generally uninteresting.' For Brownlie's views on alcohol and criminality, see p. 1 of these reports.

[28]   The *Police Reports*, for instance, frequently warned about the dangers of attending brothels: 'From what has been disclosed in this case, men ought to be on their guard against attending brothels; they are sufficiently blackened, whether married or unmarried, by going

Moreover, the level and nature of information in these journals varied from source to source and case to case. The cases covered in *The Police Intelligencer* were typically more detailed than those in the *Police Reports*, but both were often fairly short – between 250 and 750 words in length and containing only limited information. No attempt was made to record trial proceedings in full. Indeed, much more was left out than was included. It was rare, for instance, for information on the social profile of the complainer to be recorded. Those reports which did identify the provenance of police courts cases, or the occupation of the victim, were not recorded with enough regularity or on a scale large enough for meaningful statistical conclusions to be drawn over a considerable period of time. And, crucially, the small time frame for which these journals were published – 1829 to 1832 – does not correspond with the years for which police court records exist, which makes it impossible to cross-reference sources to uncover exactly how representative, or otherwise, they were of the courts' caseload.

Nonetheless, for all their limitations, if used cautiously, media reports can still be of value. They provide insights into the workings of police courts, the types of people who made use of the courts, the circumstances surrounding how cases came to court, and the social, moral and gender values that determined how they were treated when they went there. Moreover, the commentaries contained in the journals are of considerable qualitative value, especially when used in conjunction with weekly newspaper reports of trial proceedings (which, like the above journals, were also selective in their reporting, but which covered the whole of the nineteenth century). The following two sections examine the social and gender composition of complainers and why they sought legal redress. Subsequent sections will examine the role and importance of procurators and magistrates in determining the outcome of complaints, the ideological factors that are likely to have restricted the accessibility of the courts for large sections of the population, and what the nature of prosecutions suggests about whether police courts can be classified as people's courts.

III. Complainers

The large number of summary charges that were brought forward in Scottish police courts suggests that a significant proportion of the population were willing to use the legal system to seek redress for their complaints. Although covering a short period of time, the records which have been preserved for the Glasgow Police Court between 1813 and 1824 include frequent complaints from the public to the police for a range of crimes, offences and contraventions. Of the 976 cases

---

there, without running the risk of being murdered by house bullies; indeed, if they met with a misfortune there, to disable them, or otherwise incapacitate them from lawful pursuits, few would pity or have compassion on them.' *Police Reports*, 1 August 1829, p. 27.

brought before magistrates in the Glasgow Police Court in two-week periods in 1813, 1818 and 1824, 267, or 27 per cent, had a named complainer (hereafter referred to as the 1813–1824 Glasgow Police Court sample).[29] Similarly, of the 226 cases published between 6 July and 29 August 1829 in the *Police Reports*, just under one third of reports identified that proceedings had been initiated by the fiscal following an alleged offence against, or a complaint from, a member of the public. Moreover, these figures are likely to have underplayed the extent of public involvement in reporting and prosecuting crimes and offences. Police court records and reports often note only the accused and arresting officer; but it is clear that in many instances this was done with the concurrence of the victim or members of the public who observed a crime or offence but were not personally affected by it, and whose willingness to provide evidence in court was often necessary to secure a conviction.[30] Those intent on making a complaint could either lodge one at the local police office, which was common for allegations of petty theft and grievances or disputes over nuisances,[31] or with an on-duty police officer or night watchman.

Unfortunately, the occupations of complainers was rarely written in police court records (just 84 out of 976 in the 1813–1824 Glasgow sample), but where they were they show that those involved in selling and serving alcohol (publicans, spirit traders and tavern keepers) accounted for approximately 20 per cent of complainers. Small shopkeepers – shoemakers, grocers and bakers – and pawnbrokers also accounted for approximately 20 per cent (see Table 3.1). A similar picture emerges from media reports. On average, one in every six or seven cases published in the *Police Reports* listed the occupation of the victim. The majority were drawn from the self-employed, lower middle class. Shopkeepers accounted for over one third of the 39 victims/complainers whose occupations were listed in the journal between 6 July 1829 and 29 August 1829, followed by artisans who accounted for just under one third (which included tailors, fleshers and shoemakers; many of whom, might have been self-

---

[29]   GCA, B3/1/1/1: Glasgow Police Court Diet Books, 28 January 1813 to 11 February 1813, pp. 1–43; GCA, B3/1/1/5: Glasgow Police Court Diet Books, 28 January 1818 to 11 February 1818, pp. 20–101; and GCA, B3/1/1/10: Glasgow Police Court Diet Books, 25 September 1824 to 8 October 1824, pp. 1–98.

[30]   Of those that subsequently made it to trial, where information is known, complainers turned up in court to testify in the majority of them.

[31]   GCA, B3/1/1/1: Glasgow Police Court Diet Books, 28 January to 3 July 1813 record a large number of complaints to the police concerning petty theft. In giving evidence to the 1839–1840 Law Inquiry, William Davie, Assessor in the Glasgow Police and Burgh Courts, noted: 'Persons apprehended and brought before the police office, charged with an offence inferring a pecuniary penalty or fine, are informed by the duty lieutenant of his privilege to be liberated on bail on putting down a pledge. In cases inferring imprisonment or of a more serious nature the prisoner is generally detained until brought before a magistrate.' 'Fourth Report by Her Majesty's Law Commissioners, Scotland, 1839', p. 320.

Table 3.1   Occupations of Complainers in Glasgow Police Court Sample, 1813, 1818 and 1824[†]

Occupation	Percentage/Number
Publican	8% (7)
Spirit Dealer	7% (6)
Shoemaker	7% (6)
Baker	6% (5)
Grocer	5% (4)
Changekeeper	5% (4)
Pawnbroker	3.5% (3)
Slater	3.5% (3)
Writer	3.5% (3)
Tavern	3.5% (3)
Soldier	3.5% (3)
Mason	3.5% (3)
Vintner	2% (2)
Commissioner	2% (2)
Porter	2% (2)
Plasterer	2% (2)
Flesher/Butcher	2% (2)
Wright	2% (2)
Weaver	1% (1)
Servant	1% (1)
Substitute	1% (1)
Eating House Keeper	1% (1)
Gardener	1% (1)
Grave Digger	1% (1)
Landlady	1% (1)
Chimney Sweep	1% (1)
Printer	1% (1)
Labourer	1% (1)

Occupation	Percentage/Number
Waiter	1% (1)
Master	1% (1)
Sawer	1% (1)
Superintendent of Fire Engines	1% (1)
Stationer	1% (1)
Musician	1% (1)
Master of Isabella of Greenock	1% (1)
Stoneware Merchant	1% (1)
Hawker	1% (1)
Teacher of Dancing	1% (1)
Warper	1% (1)
Book Seller	1% (1)

† Data collated from GCA, B3/1/1/1: Glasgow Police Court Diet Books, 28 January 1813 to 11 February 1813, pp. 1–43; GCA, B3/1/1/5: Glasgow Police Court Diet Books, 28 January 1818 to 11 February 1818, pp. 20–101; and GCA, B3/1/1/10: Glasgow Police Court Diet Books, 25 September 1824 to 8 October 1824, pp. 1–98.

employed small business owners and shop owners themselves).[32] Merchants/ manufacturers and professionals/masters accounted for one quarter of recorded victims/complainers, and army and navy personnel the remainder. Similarly, of the 46 cases for which the occupations of the victims/complainers were recorded in Edinburgh's *The Police Intelligencer* between 18 August 1831 and 28 September 1831, shopkeepers accounted for just over one third, policemen just over one fifth, professionals/merchants/employers just under one fifth, and neighbours and tradesmen the remainder.

Although white-collar crimes did not feature much in the business of police courts, they still provided an avenue for employers to seek to safeguard business practices and promote the stability of commercial transactions within the Scottish city. The 1839–1840 Law Inquiry into Scottish courts revealed that the Edinburgh Police Court in 1833 dealt with just 169 cases of fraud. Glasgow dealt with a slightly smaller amount – approximately 40 per year – while magistrates in Paisley were handling, on average, 45 cases per year between 1833 and 1836.[33]

[32] Based on 226 cases recorded in the *Police Reports*, of which 39 included the occupations of victims.

[33] 'Fourth Report by Her Majesty's Law Commissioners, Scotland, 1839', p. 278, 304, 323, 332, 335, 336 & 338.

Significantly, such prosecutions were restricted to crimes involving property of less than £10 – with justices of the peace and sheriff courts dealing with cases that exceeded that value – and were generally directed towards the employee who breached the trust of his or her employer rather than the employer.[34] Employers pursued legal action for the illegal use of bills in commercial transactions,[35] the acquisition of money through fraudulent means,[36] fraudulent measures,[37] and breaches of trust.[38] In March 1832, for instance, John Marshall, journeyman, was charged with fraudulently obtaining £28 at different times in the name of his master, which he appropriated for his own use.[39]

Moreover, police courts, as the above examples demonstrate, also provided an avenue for employers to seek legal redress for petty theft from the workplace. In the nineteenth century, Scotland's expanding manufacturing and service economy provided tremendous opportunity for workplace appropriation and conflict between employer and employees. Indeed, studies for England in this period have suggested that in terms of the number of participants workplace theft is likely to

---

[34]   This mirrors the finding of V.A.C. Gatrell, who argued that 'The law's attention was as ever fixed on offenders who breached the trust of their employers, not on the employing class itself.' Gatrell, 'Crime, Authority and the Policeman–State', p. 271.

[35]   See, for instance, the case before the Glasgow Police Court in 1829 involving a spirit dealer who was charged with forgery and fraud for attempting to acquire wine from a fellow dealer using an illegal bill. *Police Reports*, 15 August 1829, pp. 56–7.

[36]   See, for example, the case before the Edinburgh Police Court in 1831 involving a former sheriff officer who falsely and fraudulently obtained £2 in the name of the sheriff officer and appropriated the same to his own use. *Police Intelligencer*, 27 October 1831. There were also reported cases involving fraudulent petitions. In 1829, for instance, Andrew Goodfellow and Andrew Connor were charged with forgery, fraud and wilful imposition in the Calton Police Court for presenting a forged petition under the name James Flanagan for relief for Flanagan's deceased child whose body had not been dressed or coffined. *Police Reports*, 20 July 1829, p. 16. In another case, *The Police Intelligencer* reported that a boy had been charged with obtaining several sums of money from different charitable individuals by means of a forged petition, signifying that his mother and siblings were in great distress, which was a false statement. On investigating the case, it was discovered that the boy's father was behind the attempt to extort money by means of a fabricated document, framed and drawn upon by himself. The case against the boy was continued and the father was ordered to be apprehended. *Police Intelligencer*, 27 April 1832.

[37]   In 1832, William Wilson, coal merchant in Edinburgh, was charged with fraudulently delivering 18 cwt. of coals in place of a ton, to a 'respectable' individual in Hope Street. The case was continued, although no further reference to it was made in the periodical. *Police Intelligencer*, 13 April 1832.

[38]   In 1831, a clerk to a respectable merchant, was charged with breach of trust by taking from his master's counting room the sum of £5, 8s. After evidence proved that the man did not intend to take the money for the purpose of stealing it, the magistrate instructed the employer to pursue a civil suit for recovery of the money, as such cases were not in the magistrate's purview. *Police Intelligencer*, 19 August 1831.

[39]   *Police Intelligencer*, 5 March 1832.

have constituted one of the largest categories of crime.[40] Seduced by the free-market ideology of Adam Smith, and in response to a perceived rise in industrial theft, employers in Scotland in the late eighteenth and early nineteenth centuries increasingly sought to use legal means to eradicate the long-held custom whereby workers appropriated goods from the workplace as part of their income.[41] Given Scottish police courts' limited powers, most business-related prosecutions tended to be for petty thefts from small workplaces, shops and houses, often involving employees and servants. In 1829, for instance, John Grant, shoemaker, brought charges against James Weir, shoemaker, for stealing a pair of shoes from his employer.[42] Similarly, in April 1832, a young Edinburgh man who was foreman to a Mrs Morrison, book and shoemaker, was charged with stealing a quantity of leather from his master, and also with 'a breach of trust by receiving different sums of money in name of his master, and appropriating the same to his own use'.[43] A number of other cases involved servants stealing from their masters.[44] In 1829, the Glasgow *Police Reports* published on its first page one of its longest-ever articles entitled 'Extensive Embezzlement'. It reported that Mr Tait, a spirit merchant and cork manufacturer, at the instance of the public prosecutor, had charged his foreman, three men and two boys, all in his employment, with stealing and embezzling about ten gallons of whisky, a number of bottles of port, and other items from his premises.[45] The fact the foreman was implicated in this crime is likely to have been particularly galling for Mr Tait and the business community in general as the foreman's role was to ensure workforce supervision and discipline.[46] Mr Tait said that 'he had little doubt that the nefarious practice had been carried on for a considerable time. His foreman had been in his employment for five years,

---

[40] Barry S. Godfrey and David J. Cox, *Policing the Factory. Theft, Private Policing and the Law in Modern England* (London, 2013), p. 6; and D.C. Woods, 'The Operation of the Master and Servant Act in the Black County, 1858–1875', *Midland History*, 7 (1982): pp. 93–115.

[41] For more on this, see Christopher A. Whatley, 'The Experience of Work', in T.M. Devine and Rosalind Mitchison (eds), *People and Society in Scotland, Volume I: 1760–1830* (Edinburgh, 1988), pp. 234–9.

[42] *Police Reports*, 27 July 1829, p. 44.

[43] *Police Intelligencer*, 17 April 1832.

[44] See, for instance, the case of the servant girl accused of stealing from her master. *Police Reports*, 27 July 1829, pp. 47–8.

[45] It was reported that 'One of the boys admitted that he had several times taken small quantities of spirits which he gave to the foreman and others employed in the core of his manufactory, which is situated adjacent to the spirit warehouse. He likewise acknowledged having taken several bottles of port, the necks of which were broken off to get at the liquor, and to serve the purpose of a cork screw. This destruction and audacious practice, the witness said, had continued for a number of weeks with the knowledge of the foreman and the other men who were employed at the manufactory.' *Police Reports*, 30 September 1829, pp. 102–3.

[46] Godfrey and Cox, *Policing the Factory*, p. 6.

and had full power to enter his cellars, warehouses, and other premises connected with the shop'.[47] The magistrate said that the case 'was of so serious a nature, that it would require time to look into it'.[48] The periodical's role in reporting this and similar cases is likely to have reflected not just the concern of men of property with theft from the workplace, but also the media's role more broadly in warning businessmen of its prevalence and dangers. Indeed, in 1826, the *Aberdeen Journal* published a case of fraud which came before the police court in Edinburgh, which it claimed 'was of importance to the public, as it may tend to prevent a species of swindling that appears to be easily practiced'.[49] *The Scotch Reformers' Gazette*, which typically gave less coverage to police court trials than other forms of media, was particularly concerned with reporting cases involving embezzlement and the damage it was doing to employers. In September 1842 it covered the case of a young man, formerly in the employ of a silk manufacturer, who was charged in Gorbals Police Court with stealing a quantity of shawls and handkerchiefs and embezzling articles belonging to his former employer.[50] In the following months, it published a number of similar cases,[51] including that of James Christie, recently in the employment of Mr Storer, painter, who was charged with stealing 28lbs of grain paint from his former employer.[52]

Davis, in her study of the London police courts in the second half of the nineteenth century, has argued that employer-led criminal prosecutions supplemented informal sanctions rather than replaced them.[53] Although acknowledging that employee theft was the most common offence dealt with under the Criminal Justice Act at the London police courts after 1855, larger employers in particular, she contends, were willing to overlook a great deal of workplace appropriation by their labour force, or to deal with it by dismissing those suspected of theft rather than prosecuting them.[54] Davis' investigation provides a useful corrective to studies that stress the growing willingness on the

---

[47]   *Police Reports*, 30 September 1829, pp. 102–3.

[48]   The case was continued until the following day although, frustratingly, there was no further record of it in the periodical, perhaps because it was deemed by the fiscal or the magistrate to be too serious for the jurisdiction of the police court.

[49]   *Aberdeen Journal*, 12 April 1826. Similarly, in 1858, the *Glasgow Herald* published an article under the heading 'WARNING TO MILLWORKERS' in which it was noted that 'yesterday at the Calton Police Court, a winder named Isobel Rorrieson or Bowman, was convicted of having on Friday last, stolen a quantity of yarn from Newhall Factory .... The prisoner, who was detected in the act of carrying the yarn, was sent to prison for 60 days'. *Glasgow Herald*, 22 September 1858.

[50]   *The Scotch Reformers' Gazette*, 10 September 1842, p. 4.

[51]   See the case of alleged embezzlement of a large amount of money by a young man named McColl, connected with the spirit trade, from his employer. *The Scotch Reformers' Gazette*, 22 October 1842.

[52]   *The Scotch Reformers' Gazette*, 1 October 1842.

[53]   Davis, 'Prosecutions and Their Context', pp. 398–426.

[54]   Ibid., pp. 400–413.

part of employers to utilise the judicial system to control workplace behaviour, customs and practices that had traditionally been tolerated.[55] Continuities with the past, though, should not detract from the fact that police courts provided an important avenue of legal redress for a business community who, significantly, appear to have been willing to use them when it suited. Even if employers, like other sections of society, often utilised informal forms of censure, or brought charges infrequently, the threat of prosecution, which the rise of summary justice made more likely, was in itself an important mechanism in instilling another tier of workplace discipline onto the industrial labour force. Moreover, in publishing cases of theft from the workplace, the media not only helped to disseminate the perception of what crimes mattered to be brought before the court and stamped out, but might also have encouraged the business community to seek legal redress more often.

Media and periodical reports, and the figures in Table 3.1, suggest that police courts were less a resource for those at the bottom end of the social scale than those drawn from the middle-ranking trading community. However, these sources need to be treated with caution. It is possible that the periodicals published a disproportionate number of cases involving shopkeepers and small traders to pander to their readerships and interests.[56] Moreover, police court records were more likely to note the occupation of the complainer if it was relevant to the charge, which it usually was in the case of publicans who were assaulted or had their property damaged dealing with drunks, or shopkeepers who had goods stolen from them. Although impossible to say conclusively, both sources are

---

[55] For the classic eighteenth-century studies on the ruling elite's clampdown upon customary rights and the appropriation of workplace goods, see E.P. Thompson, 'Time, Work–Discipline and Industrial Capitalism', *Past and Present*, 38 (1967): pp. 56–97; E.P. Thompson, *Whigs and Hunters: The Origins of the Black Act* (London, 1975); Eric Hobsbawm, 'Customs, Wages and Workload', in Eric Hobsbawm (ed.), *Labouring Men: Studies in the History of Labour* (London, 1968); Peter Linebaugh, 'Eighteenth-Century Crime, Popular Movements and Social Controls', *Bulletin of the Society for the Study of Labour History*, 25 (1972): pp. 11–15; Douglas Hay, 'Manufacturers and the Criminal Law in the Later Eighteenth-Century: Crime and "Police" in South Staffordshire', *Past and Present Colloquium: Police and Policing* (1983); and John Rule and Roger Wells, *Crime, Protest, and Popular Politics in Southern England, 1740–1850* (London, 1997). For an overview of writings on workplace theft in nineteenth-century factories, see Barry S. Godfrey, 'Law, Factory Discipline and "Theft": The Impact of the Factory on Workplace Appropriation in mid to late Nineteenth-Century Yorkshire', *The British Journal of Criminology*, 39/1 (1999): pp. 56–71. Godfrey's article provides a useful corrective to Davis's study by showing that 'the criminal law, administered by a private policing agency, remained a central weapon against workplace appropriation until the 1850s'. Thereafter, he contends, factories 'reinforced rather than replaced' the application of the criminal law with informal sanctions (p. 56).

[56] For factors influencing the under-recording of poor occupations, see Gray, *Crime, Prosecution and Social Relations in London*, pp. 30–31.

likely to under-represent the extent of working-class complainers who sought legal redress. Those involved in the judicial system at a summary level gave the impression that the lower orders were willing to use the courts to settle disputes and seek justice. In submitting his questionnaire to the 1839–1840 Law Inquiry, William Davie, Assessor of the Glasgow Burgh and Police Courts, claimed that 'cases of great hardship to parties are frequently brought before the magistrate in the Police Court, of persons in poor circumstances having property stolen from them which has been found in the possession of brokers and others'.[57] For the same inquiry, Archibald Alison, Sheriff of Lanarkshire, estimated that in the 1830s, three quarters of the fiscal's occupation was taken up with 'complaints made by the humblest classes of society' (although he did not differentiate between police courts and other courts).[58] Similarly, Sheriff Hugh Barclay, in his *Administration of the Law in Scotland* (1862), claimed that the working-class was not averse to utilising the services of the fiscal in order to resolve conflicts and personal disputes.[59]

The views of Davie, Alison and Barclay, of course, are statements of perception which are likely to have helped to instil the idea of police courts as supporting 'all' deserving complainers. Nonetheless, it seems likely that a not insignificant proportion of those who brought charges in Scottish police courts were drawn from fairly humble backgrounds, reflecting the research findings of scholars for the eighteenth- and nineteenth-century English summary courts.[60] Police statistical returns show that the vast majority of crimes and offences were committed in poorer, working-class areas, suggesting that those at the bottom end of the social scale were particularly vulnerable to the effects of criminality.[61] Much of police courts' caseload involved drunken assaults in poor neighbourhoods or thefts of items of extremely low monetary value. A lot of the latter cases consisted of used clothing, blankets and, in some cases, old rags, that had been stolen from washing lines, suggesting that a lot of crime was committed out of economic necessity

---

[57] 'Fourth Report by Her Majesty's Law Commissioners, Scotland, 1839', p. 329.

[58] Ibid., p. 172.

[59] Hugh Barclay, *On the Administration of the Criminal Law in Scotland* (Glasgow, 1862), pp. 8–9.

[60] This concurs with English summary courts. In his study of London's justice records in the second half of the eighteenth century, Gray found that tradesmen and artisans constituted a third of prosecutors and the labouring poor about one fifth, which is likely to have under-represented their actual proportion as they were less likely to be named in records. Gray, *Crime, Prosecution and Social Relations in London*, pp. 29–30. King, in his investigation of Essex's summary courts, found that tradesmen accounted for 31 per cent of prosecutors and those described as 'poverty vulnerable' 22 per cent. King, 'The Summary Courts and Social Relations', p. 140, Table 3.

[61] See 'Table 3C: Wards in which Thefts, &c, Occurred, with the Times at which these Thefts were Perpetrated', in Edinburgh Central Library (ECL): *Return of Crimes and Offences Reported, Persons Apprehended and Cited, and Miscellaneous Returns Connected with the Police, for the Year Ending 31st December 1880* (Edinburgh, 1881), no page numbers.

and inflicted upon those who could least afford to have such modest items stolen. In 1818, for instance, Mrs Montigham's complaint against Margaret Paterson for theft of satin was dismissed with an admonition after the complainer could not comment on the item's value, which the police records noted 'was no wonder for they appeared not worth a farthing'.[62]

The fact that fiscal-led prosecutions were funded through compulsory police and municipal taxes helped to reduce one of the main barriers to prosecution for the poorer social groups – cost. The speedy nature of summary justice certainly decreased the potential burden involved. Police courts met on a regular basis, dealt with cases quickly and were located in the municipal buildings in the centre of towns, all of which helped to reduce the inconvenience and potential loss of earnings involved in bringing a case to court. The introduction of a new bureaucratic police machine also made bringing legal action less troublesome, not least as salaried police officers were on hand to bring the accused into custody. Furthermore, it is possible that press reports of courtroom proceedings, allied to those who encountered the law as complainers, accusers and witnesses, encouraged further participation and interaction with the legal system.[63]

In the appendix to the 1837 'Report from the Select Committee on Metropolitan Police Offices' it was suggested that by investing police courts with more summary jurisdiction, redress for petty grievances could be more easily obtained and a much needed 'poor man's system of justice' established.[64] Yet, police courts were not just accessible to many male complainers, but females also. Indeed, it is possible, as was the case in England,[65] that women were much more willing to seek legal action in the summary courts than in the higher criminal courts, where legal, social and cultural barriers often restricted female access to legal redress.[66]

---

[62]   GCA, B3/1/1/5: Glasgow Police Court Diet Books, 28 January 1818, p. 21.

[63]   For the media's role in representing the message of the London police courts, consult Davis, 'A Poor Man's System of Justice?', pp. 316–18.

[64]   'Report from the Select Committee on Metropolis Police Offices', *BPP*, 1837 (451), XII.309, Appendix, p. 186.

[65]   Robert B. Shoemaker, *Gender in English Society, 1650–1850: The Emergence of Separate Spheres?* (London, 1998), pp. 295–6.

[66]   Unfortunately, a detailed study of female complainers in the Scottish higher courts is still to be carried out. For the barriers that women faced in bringing forward a prosecution in England, see Deirdre Palk, *Gender, Crime and Judicial Discretion 1780–1830* (Woodbridge, 2006); Shoemaker, *Gender in English Society*, pp. 291–304; J.M. Beattie, 'The Criminality of Women in Eighteenth-Century England', *Journal of Social History*, 8/4 (1975): passim; Lucia Zedner, *Women, Crime and Custody in Victorian England* (Oxford, 1991), p. 27; and Margaret Hunt, 'Wife-Beating, Domesticity and Women's Independence in Eighteenth-Century London', *Gender and History*, 4/1 (1992): p. 22. For studies on the relationship between gender and law breaking, and gender and judicial decisions, see Anne-Marie Kilday, *Women and Violent Crime in Enlightenment Scotland* (Woodbridge, 2007); Peter King, 'Female Offenders, Work and Life-Cycle in Late Eighteenth-Century London', *Continuity and Change*, 11/1 (1996): pp. 61–90; Joanne McEwan, 'Negotiating Support:

As Table 3.2 shows, women accounted for just under one third of all identified complainers to the fiscal sampled in the Glasgow Police Court records between 1813 and 1824.[67] Women were especially likely to bring complaints relating to offences against the peace, particularly minor assault and abuse, many of which were conducted by abusive husbands or by other women.[68] Women accounted for 46 per cent of all named complainers who brought charges for assault,[69] and 46 per cent of named complainers for abuse and molestation.[70] That they tended to bring complaints for violence-related offences is illustrated by the fact that around half of those who sought legal redress had been assaulted, abused or molested to some degree: in the above Glasgow sample, for instance, 40 per cent of female complainers brought charges specifically for assault or abuse, but others were abused or assaulted in the course of having their property damaged, or were confronted by customers who refused to pay for food, alcohol or lodgings, yet they did not cite this in the actual charge.[71] Married women, or widows, accounted for more than two thirds of all female complainers.

In cases involving theft or damage to property, the percentage of female complainers was lower than that for assault. Women accounted for just 26 per cent of named complainers for theft, men 74 per cent.[72] Theft accounted for 16

Crime and Women's Networks in London and Middlesex, c.1730–1820', unpub. PhD thesis (The University of Western Australia, 2009); J.I. Kermode and Garthine Walker, *Women, Crime and the Courts in Early-Modern England* (London, 1994); and Carolyn A. Conley, *The Unwritten Law: Criminal Justice in Victorian Kent* (Oxford, 1991).

[67]   GCA, B3/1/1/1: Glasgow Police Court Diet Books, 28 January 1813 to 11 February 1813, pp. 1–43; GCA, B3/1/1/5: Glasgow Police Court Diet Books, 28 January 1818 to 11 February 1818, pp. 20–101; and GCA, B3/1/1/10: Glasgow Police Court Diet Books, 25 September 1824 to 8 October 1824, pp. 1–98. This was considerably higher than the percentage of female prosecutors in the higher courts in England (a similar study is still to be carried out for the Scottish higher courts).

[68]   See the case of Mrs Brown, who complained against Jane Manderson for striking her on the stair. GCA, B3/1/1/10: Glasgow Police Court Diet Books, 5 October 1824, p. 66.

[69]   Based on 65 cases in which the complainer was named, with men accounting for 35 complainers and women 30. These figures are in keeping with those for England, where Shoemaker claims that women accounted for 44 per cent of prosecutions for assault. Shoemaker, *Gender in English Society*, p. 292.

[70]   Based on 26 cases in which the complainer was named, with women accounting for 12 complainers and men 14.

[71]   See the case involving Mrs Malcolm, who complained against Thomas Wilson for refusing to pay for liquor and for striking her in her home (GCA, B3/1/1/1: Glasgow Police Court Diet Books, 29 January 1813, p. 5); the case involving Mrs Grahame, who brought a complaint against William Stuart for breaking a window in her shop (GCA, B3/1/1/1: Glasgow Police Court Diet Books, 29 January 1813, p. 4); and the case involving Mrs McLean, who brought a complaint against Timothy Kerr for quarrelling in her house and breaking furniture (GCA, B3/1/1/1: Glasgow Police Court Diet Books, 3 February 1813, p. 23).

[72]   Based on 46 cases, in which 12 of the complainers were women and 34 were men.

Table 3.2   Marital Status of Female Complainers (Based on the 75 cases in the Glasgow 1813 to 1824 Sample where Female Complainers were Listed)

Marital Status	Theft	Assault	Abused	Abused & Property Damaged	Shop Windows Damaged	Refusing to Pay for Liquor*	Pledging Property	Other**
Married (including Deserted)	8	13***	6	2	3	4	3	12
Single	4	8	2	4	0	0	0	5
Widowed	0	1	0	0	0	0	0	0
% of Female Complaints	16	29	11	8	4	5	4	23

*   In some cases the complainer was also assaulted and abused.

**   Other includes: laying down a newborn female child in one of the beds in the house (probably a common lodging house); riotous behaviour in lodgings; detaining a coin on the pretence that it was base metal (2); being insulted in the street; laying down contents of a water bottle at complainer's door; being molested and abused by being hit by snow balls by boys; throwing dirty water on the complainer's daughter; seducing the complainer's daughter and keeping her for bad purposes; causing a crowd at the door; knocking a door down; disorderly and riotous conduct (2); drunk and disorderly; throwing water over windows; blocking path to house with lime; attempted burglary; and keeping a shirt made for the complainer.

***   Five of these assaults committed by husbands.

per cent of the total number of female complaints, or 21 per cent if refusing to pay for liquor is included, while cases involving damage to property accounted for 12 per cent of female complaints. As in England, it is likely that property laws, which legally defined a wife to be the property of her husband, somewhat reduced the number of prosecutions for property crimes brought in the wife's name, but wives by no means were legally prohibited from doing so. Indeed, as Table 3.2 shows, married women were more than twice as likely as unmarried women to bring property-related complaints to the police court. Unfortunately, the social status or occupations of female prosecutors was not recorded frequently enough in police minutes to give meaningful figures for individual crimes and offences – only 14 cases recorded such information, and presumably only because such information was deemed relevant to the charge. Those cases which did reveal the occupation of female complainers generally involved property-related complaints and were brought by small business women in retail or service industries, including primarily shopkeepers, landladies/publican/spirit traders (seven recorded cases), shopkeepers (four), lodging-house keepers (two), and one servant.[73] Lodging-house keepers, a significant proportion of whom were female, were reported in the press as being particularly vulnerable to theft. In 1842, the *Scotch Reformers' Gazette*, in a report not untypical of its coverage of police court cases, ran with the headline 'Another Lodging-House Thief Captured', under which it was reported that 'many poor but respectable landladies have identified the swindler and portions of recovered property stolen from their dwellings'.[74] Approximately 12 per cent of all female complaints involved quarrels or disturbances in which property was damaged, such as Mrs McLean, who in 1813, complained against three students for fighting in her house and breaking furniture.[75]

Some complainers might have been widows who inherited their husbands' businesses after they died, as appears to have been common in London.[76] But many are also likely to have been wives who were actively involved in supporting the day-to-day running of family businesses, or who ran businesses separate from their husbands.[77] In 1842, for instance, the *Scotch Reformers' Gazette* presented a police court trial report under the heading 'A Thief Captured by Female Courage – Police Court Scene', which described in great detail how the 'mistress of the shop' apprehended a young boy who had attempted to steal silver from her. The article highlighted the complainer's efforts to capture the accused, and the important part her testimony played in the defender's conviction.[78] The article's title, as with the earlier example, is particularly interesting, and is a point of difference between the coverage of the *Scotch Reformers' Gazette* and the periodicals: it directed the reader very explicitly about how to interpret the case and the important role women played in the workings of summary justice. As Elizabeth Sanderson, in her study of eighteenth-century Edinburgh, has shown, married women with burgess connections were legally entitled to trade in their own right, and, as small business owners, would have been vulnerable to property crime.[79] Similarly, Stana

---

[73]   These include Mrs Fleming, landlady, who brought a complaint against John Davis, coach driver, for assaulting her. GCA, B3/1/1/10: Glasgow Police Court Diet Books, 1 October 1824, p. 35.

[74]   *The Scotch Reformers' Gazette*, 29 October 1842, p. 4.

[75]   GCA, B3/1/1/1: Glasgow Police Court Diet Books, 3 February 1813, p. 23.

[76]   Margaret Hunt, *The Middling Sort: Commerce, Gender and the Family in England, 1680–1780* (Berkeley, 1996); and Nicola J. Phillips, *Women in Business, 1700–1850* (Woodbridge, 2006).

[77]   Elizabeth Sanderson, *Women and Work in Eighteenth-Century Edinburgh* (Basingstoke, 1996), pp. 125–31. See also Eleanor Gordon, *Women and the Labour Movement in Scotland, 1850–1914* (Oxford, 1991).

[78]   *The Scotch Reformers' Gazette*, 14 May 1842, p. 4.

[79]   Women could inherit the freedom to trade from their burgess fathers, which they retained after marriage, whilst others could apply for licenses to trade from the town council and other relevant bodies. Sanderson, *Women and Work*, pp. 130–31.

Nenadic's research into the burgeoning Victorian middle classes in Glasgow reveals that some middle-class wives held major financial assets and ran their own businesses independently of their husbands, especially in the clothing and shopkeeping trades and in lodging. These, significantly, were amongst the most susceptible businesses to theft and damaged property.[80] In such instances, it would be the female business owner who reported the complaint to the police and who would be required to attend court in order to testify. Moreover, it is possible that the urban location of police courts made them more accessible to women than other courts in rural areas. As studies of eighteenth-century prosecution in England by Beattie, Shoemaker and Landau have shown, women in urban areas were more likely to bring forward criminal prosecutions than those in rural areas as the former were more independent as business owners and, in the case of those from respectable backgrounds, had less opportunity for informal, non-judicial, conflict resolution.[81]

Women's access to police courts, though, especially those from poorer backgrounds, was not on equal terms to that of men. For certain women, access was constrained by social, cultural, financial, and in some cases, legal factors. They could not, for instance, bring charges of theft against their husbands, as legally the property was his, although husbands could bring such a prosecution against their wives. Furthermore, in Scots law, a wife was not considered a competent or credible witness to corroborate a crime against her husband until 1898, which meant that in order to secure a conviction for assault against an abusive partner two independent witnesses were required.[82] Policemen would refuse to arrest an abusive husband unless the wife's testimony could be corroborated by the testimony of witnesses, or unless they themselves had witnessed the assault.[83] The financial implications, not to the mention the shame, for the family if a violent husband was fined or sent to bridewell was a further powerful disincentive to bring legal action, or to follow through with a complaint.[84] Furthermore, as is

---

[80] Stana Nenadic, 'The Victorian Middle Classes', in W. Hamish Fraser and Irene Maver (eds), *Glasgow, Volume II: 1830 to 1912* (Manchester, 1996), pp. 269–70.

[81] J.M. Beattie, *Crime and the Courts in England, 1660–1800* (Oxford, 1986), p. 193; Shoemaker, *Prosecution and Punishment*, p. 208; Norma Landau, *The Justices of the Peace, 1679–1760* (Berkeley, 1984), p. 197.

[82] Annemarie Hughes, 'The "Non-Criminal" Class: Wifebeating in Scotland, c.1850–1949', *Crime, Histoire & Sociétés/Crime, History & Societies*, 14/ 2 (2010): p. 35.

[83] In her study of domestic violence in Glasgow, for instance, Hughes cites the example of Thomas McFarlane's wife, who sought the assistance of a policeman after reporting that her husband had fractured her jaw with an iron gate. On account of there being no witnesses, the policeman refused to arrest the husband. Ibid., p. 35.

[84] In 1813, for instance, a complainer listed only as 'wife' in the Glasgow Police Court minute books, who had brought a charge against her husband for striking and abusing her and threatening her life, failed to appear in court. GCA, B3/1/1/1/1: Glasgow Police Court Diet Books, 2 February 1813, p. 20. Even those who did appear in court often did so reluctantly. For example, in 1829, Malcolm Davidson was charged with assaulting and striking his wife

explored in Chapter 4, the testimony of 'rougher', less 'respectable' women was often not taken seriously, or as seriously as it might have been, by procurators and magistrates – men, who ultimately, determined women's access to the courts and the justice they received – which might have dissuaded other women from similar backgrounds from pursuing legal action.[85]

There were also practical and institutional factors which reduced the capacity of both men and women who wanted to complain from doing so. Few police resources were directed towards investigating and detecting crime – especially the petty crime that dominated the business of the police court. Unless the victim knew the offender or the police caught someone in the act of committing a crime, there was little likelihood of a suspect being apprehended – a fact which goes a long way to explaining why such a large percentage of victims, as is explored below, knew their offenders. Furthermore, in some instances, complainers were required to pledge a sum of money to ensure their appearance in court. Why some should have been required to do so and not others was not indicated in the court records, but it is possible that those who brought private rather than fiscal-led charges had to pledge money for security. Those who failed to appear lost their pledge. In a two-week period in 1824, for instance, five complainers in Glasgow forfeited their pledges.[86] Moreover, according to William Davie, there were instances where the complainer was detained in the Glasgow police cells on account of not being able to put forward security for their appearance in court. Although a fairly rare occurrence, it was especially significant that it was, according to Davie, complainers who were unable to give an address, had no legally recognisable means of income, and who could not rely upon the financial aid of friends or family who were most likely to be detained as a guarantee that they would appear to testify in court. Designed to prevent innocent people from being charged and detained following false allegations, the practice is likely to have erected a further

---

to the effusion of blood. She stated that 'he never struck her in his lifetime, and that she was drunk on the occasion complained of'. This, the constable said, contradicted the original testimony on which the charge was brought. The magistrate remarked that it was clear a 'paction had been made up' and sentenced the accused to pay the doctor's bill. *Police Reports*, 22 August 1829, pp. 62–3. For the barriers faced by female victims of domestic violence, see Anna Clark, 'Humanity or Justice? Wifebeating and the Law in the Eighteenth and Nineteenth Centuries', in Carol Smart (ed.), *Regulating Womanhood: Historical Essays on Marriage, Motherhood and Sexuality* (London, 1992), pp. 187–206; and Shani D'Cruze, *Crimes of Outrage: Sex, Violence and Victorian Working Women* (London, 1998).

[85]   Shoemaker and Clark also argue that women's testimony in court was less likely to be taken seriously than men's. Shoemaker, *Gender in English Society*, pp. 291–2; and Clark, 'Humanity or Justice?', p. 202.

[86]   See the complaints brought by David Finlay (GCA, B3/1/1/10: Glasgow Police Court Diet Books, 26 September 1824, p. 15); John Taylor (GCA, B3/1/1/10: Glasgow Police Court Diet Books, 2 October 1824, p. 40); Thomas Borland (GCA, B3/1/1/10: Glasgow Police Court Diet Books, 3 October 1824, p. 49); and Sarah Wilson (GCA, B3/1/1/10: Glasgow Police Court Diet Books, 5 October 1824, p. 68).

barrier to the most vulnerable seeking legal redress.[87] Those who did appear in court as complainers ran the risk themselves of being reprimanded and, in a few rare cases, fined.[88] In the Glasgow Police Court in 1818, for instance, Archibald Douglas was fined 10s. for his 'irregular and oppressive conduct' in bringing a complaint against John Stevenson then retracting it in court,[89] while in 1824 David Huggie was fined 5s. for 'concealing the truth' after bringing a complaint for fighting against James Campbell.[90]

Moreover, the possibility of having one's name appear in the media might have deterred some individuals from pursuing legal action. In 1829, a magistrate expressed his surprise that a respectable-looking man would bring a charge against a woman labelled in the press as a prostitute for the alleged theft of just 2s. before such 'a large concourse of spectators' and press gallery in the courtroom.[91] In many cases, the press would protect the reputation of middle-class male accusers and, indeed, defenders – a protection rarely afforded to working-class men, as discussed further in Chapter 7. But the implication of the magistrates' comments were still profound: namely, that the public nature of police courts could, and in many cases did, act as a barrier to legal action for those who would find an appearance in court morally or socially damaging. As Shani D'Cruze has argued, appearing in court could be particularly harrowing for women who had been sexually assaulted, as their integrity was often placed on trial as much as the defender's.[92] Police courts might have provided women with a public arena to air grievances, but it was 'one that entailed a real risk to their own reputation'.[93] An article by *The Detective*, published in 1885, entitled 'The Queen's Park: Is it a Nursery of Vice on Sunday Evenings?' alluded to this. Complaining about the sexual advances to which women were subjected in the park, the author noted that 'many women would rather submit to the indignity placed upon them than create

---

[87]   Davie stated that there was no enactment on this practice and that he would like it clarified. He also noted that complainers sometimes were required to put up money as a pledge for their appearance in court when someone was arrested on a verbal complaint or information from another person. As he stated: 'it shall be lawful for the party making the complaint to put forward security', although no information was given on how often this was put in practice. 'Fourth Report by Her Majesty's Law Commissioners, Scotland, 1839', p. 326.

[88]   See complaints brought by Mrs Dunmore (GCA, B3/1/1/5: Glasgow Police Court Diet Books, 3 February 1818, p. 60); Mrs Cunie (GCA, B3/1/1/5: Glasgow Police Court Diet Books, 7 February 1818, p. 81); and Ann Farmer (GCA, B3/1/1/5: Glasgow Police Court Diet Books, 8 February 1818, p. 88).

[89]   GCA, B3/1/1/5: Glasgow Police Court Diet Books, 8 February 1818, p. 86.

[90]   GCA, B3/1/1/10: Glasgow Police Court Diet Books, 2 October 1824, p. 39.

[91]   *Police Reports*, 5 September 1829, p. 92.

[92]   Shani D'Cruze, 'Sex, Violence and Local Courts: Working-Class Respectability in a Mid-Nineteenth-Century Lancashire Town', *The British Journal of Criminology*, 39/1 (1999): pp. 39–55.

[93]   Ibid., p. 39.

a disturbance, and have the scoundrel arrested. [It] … is a bold lady who will bear the exposure which a trial in a public court would necessarily mean'.[94] Moreover, for certain sections of the community, even reporting a crime to the police ran the risk of unwanted publicity. In 1885, the journalist for *The Detective*, reporting on stolen watches and the list of police reports which were published every day in the press, commented:

> A great many persons in preference to running the chance of being compelled to appear in Court to give evidence and have their names published in the newspapers, remain quiet and say nothing about their loss. As a result, large organised associations exist among thieves, through which, if you are willing to pay heavily, your stolen property can be recovered, and it can be shown beyond the shadow of a doubt that large numbers of people utilise the services of the association in preference to applying at the Detective Department.[95]

In many cases, bringing forward a charge also offered victims little prospect of being re-united with stolen property. An article in *The Detective* in 1885, which was entitled 'A Night Among Glasgow Thieves', claimed that organised networks of criminals moved on stolen property quickly to ensure that money, watches or valuables were never in the possession of the accused shortly after a robbery had been carried out and consequently, stolen items 'are seldom ever recovered'.[96]

Indeed, there was, in general, a reduced financial incentive to pursue a complaint through the fiscal as it was extremely rare for complainers to be compensated. Money recovered through charges laid by the fiscal would normally be applied to fund municipal services and the common good. The flipside to Scots having a public prosecutor was that judicial outcomes were designed to serve a wider sense of order. As Mr Burns, law agent, noted during a trial of unlicensed and licensed dealers who held drinking-booths on the Green at the regatta in the Glasgow Police Court in 1865: 'a prosecution by the public prosecutor, appointed by the magistrates themselves to prosecute for the public interest, [was] under the well-known arrangement that the penalties were not appropriated as by a private complainer.'[97] Those intent on acquiring financial compensation would have to initiate and fund private prosecutions in police courts, which further restricted access to those who could pay. Whereas fiscal-led prosecutions were paid for by police taxes and common funds, complainers who pursued unsuccessful private prosecutions were nearly always required to pay the legal costs of the trial (in such cases, defenders would pay the costs – and usually a small fine – should the charge be proven). Given the speedy nature of summary proceedings, the costs involved

---

[94]   *The Detective: or, A Journal for the Exposure and Suppression of Crime* (*The Detective*), vol. II (New Series), no. 19, 13 August 1885.
[95]   *The Detective*, vol. II (New Series), no. 15, July 16 1885, p. 9.
[96]   *The Detective*, vol. II (New Series), no. 23, 10 September 1885.
[97]   *Glasgow Herald*, 17 September 1865.

were not high. In Glasgow, in the early 1820s, 2s., 6d. was the minimum cost for bringing forward a charge in a local court, with additional costs often being added for witnesses.[98] By contrast, the average gross weekly wage for muslin weavers – the poorest paid sector of the city's handloom weaving industry – ranged from 13s., 1d. to 15s., 2d. Cotton weavers earned between two and three times this.[99] Private legal action, therefore, was within the reach of much of the working population, but it was unachievable for the poorest of the poor and the most vulnerable.

Although there were barriers to legal redress for those who sought it, police courts nonetheless provided an important forum for both male and female complainers from different social backgrounds to pursue grievances through judicial means. Indeed, although speculative, it is possible that the perceived accessibility of police courts might well have helped to legitimise police courts and the law among certain sections of society. However, there is no evidence to suggest, as Davis claims for England, that this was one of the intended purposes behind the expansion in police court summary justice, which was largely preoccupied with the more specific private interests of public men.[100] As the following sections examine, the Scottish police courts served multiple purposes, some of which would in all likelihood have alienated as many as it reconciled to the advent of a policed society.

IV. Complaining and Settling

Norma Landau and Drew D. Gray have suggested that in eighteenth-century England, victims were willing to use the lower courts as a form of civil action in order to obtain financial compensation.[101] However, as established above, this does not appear to have been a major reason for bringing forward complaints in the Scottish police courts. Of the 4,802 cases recorded in the Edinburgh Police Court book between 1805 and 1807, only 67 people received damages from the defender – the overwhelming majority of whose cases were the result of private complaints. A few defenders are likely to have agreed to pay damages in court before trial proceedings commenced, but these were fairly rare.[102] Similarly,

---

[98] M.A. Crowther, 'Crime, Prosecution and Mercy: English Influence and Scottish Practice in the Early Nineteenth Century', in S.J. Connolly (ed.), *Kingdoms United? Great Britain and Ireland since 1500: Integration and Diversity* (Dublin, 1999), p. 226.

[99] N. Murray, *The Scottish Handloom Weavers, 1790–1850: A Social History* (Edinburgh, 1978), pp. 43 & 92–3.

[100] Davis, 'A Poor Man's System of Justice?', pp. 314–16.

[101] Gray, 'The People's Courts?', p. 11; and Norma Landau, 'Indictment for Fun and Profit: A Prosecutor's Reward at the Eighteenth-Century Quarter Sessions', *Law and History Review*, 17/3 (1999): pp. 507–36.

[102] This is impossible to prove from the evidence that exists, but the number of cases (cited below) that were 'settled' by the complainers being awarded damages suggests that defenders might have agreed to pay compensation on being questioned by the bailie.

Glasgow magistrates awarded damages, or instructed the defender to pay for repairs to the complainer's property, in just 28 out of 976 cases sampled between 1813 and 1824. Moreover, this appeared to become less common as the century progressed, with just four complainers being awarded damages in the two-week period sampled for 1824 compared with 11 and 13 for 1813 and 1818 respectively (despite the caseload for the sampled weeks of these years being much lower than that for 1824). The sums recovered were extremely modest – varying between 1s., 6d. and 10s. depending on the extent of property damage or the level of violence used in beatings.[103] There was the odd example of fiscal-led charges resulting in magistrates awarding a proportion of the fine imposed on the convicted to be directed towards recompensing victims, but this was rare.[104] Those intent on acquiring compensation for a civil dispute would have been much more inclined to take their grievance to a small debts court, burgh court, dean of guild court or other court which offered a greater prospect of financial recompense. Nonetheless, although the numbers who used the courts for this purpose were small relative to the number of fiscal-led prosecutions, the capacity for police courts to accommodate private complaints was still significant. It provided a forum for aggrieved persons to pursue legal action that the public prosecutor was unwilling to undertake due to insufficient evidence, the relatively trivial nature of the offence, or because bringing forward a charge was not deemed to be in the public interest.

Those who did initiate private complaints were typically seeking legal redress for disputes which were alleged to have occurred in a private dwelling. This suggests reluctance on the part of the fiscal to become involved in disputes that occurred in the private sphere for which compensation was sought, especially if no specific police law was deemed to have been breached.[105] These cases often involved rowdy and disorderly behaviour that resulted in damage to property.[106]

---

[103]   For instance, ECA, ED006/8: Edinburgh Police Court Abstract of Processes, 1805–1807: Isobel Skinner received 10s. damages from James Hastie for throwing a stone that hit her on the arm; Mr Black received 10s. from David Henderson for a beating; David Cameron was ordered to pay damages of 3s. to David Bounty, porter, for beating his child; James Thomson, baker, was awarded damages of 1s., 6d. from Margaret Fraser for breaking private windows; Duncan Robertson, porter, received 5s. in damages from Magnus Elder, broker, for beating and knocking him down; and Peter Armiston was awarded damages of 9s. from three men who broke the windows of his property.

[104]   *Police Intelligencer*, 30 September 1831.

[105]   See the cases of Elizabeth Sinclair, who received 1s., 3d. damages from a soldier for being drunk and rioting in her private house, and Isabel Burgess, who was awarded 10s. from John Turnbull, sayer, for assault and breaking her property. Indeed, the Glasgow police court records show a number of cases being dismissed for not 'belonging to the police'. See the case of Jean Williamson, who brought a charge against Mrs Liddle for 'keeping a shirt she got her to make'. GCA, B3/1/1/1: Glasgow Police Court Diet Books, 2 February 1813, p. 19.

[106]   For a case in which windows were broken by stones, see ECA, ED006/8: Edinburgh Police Court Abstract of Processes, 1805–1807, pp. 38–9, no. 1,095. In another case,

This was the most common charge brought under private prosecution in the Edinburgh Police Court Book between 1805 and 1807, followed by neighbourly disputes over nuisances,[107] common assault,[108] throwing stones and breaking windows,[109] blocking passages to local works,[110] and abusing horses.[111] Victims of violence that occurred within the household also brought charges if procurators refused to do so, and these often involved female complainers. In 1805, for instance, Jean Laidlaw, spouse of a weaver, took out a private complaint in the Edinburgh Police Court against Agnes Ramage, spouse of a brass founder, for abusing and striking her in her house. The disputing parties settled their differences before proceedings commenced, although the magistrates still found the defender liable for 2s., 9d. expenses.[112] Women appear more likely than men to have been awarded damages, perhaps reflecting the fact that female complainers were more likely to initiate private complaints and/or be small, independent shopkeepers who had property damaged, or were the victims of abuse and assault. Of the 75 female complainers listed in the Glasgow sample between 1813 and 1824, five received damages (7 per cent), which was more than double the percentage of male complainers who received financial compensation. Unfortunately, the occupations of private complainers were not listed in large enough numbers to draw meaningful statistical conclusions, but as with those who initiated fiscal-led complaints, those from the middle echelons of society, including small traders, landlords and common-lodging house proprietors, were recorded the most frequently, with financial realities, no doubt, determining their capacity to pursue such action.

Newspaper coverage of police court trials and the *Police Reports* rarely gave much attention to cases in which damages were sought or awarded, which was perhaps indicative of the declining use of the Glasgow Police Court for this purpose by 1829. Interestingly, though, *The Police Intelligencer* did report on such cases in Edinburgh. Between 22 October and 1 November 1831 alone, it covered five trials where damages were awarded to the complainer.[113] On the latter date, it

---

George Cotton, tobacconist, complained against Alex Hutchison, merchant, for making a great noise in the shop above his house. Ibid., p. 28, no. 913.

[107]   For a case in which the complainer sought compensation after having filthy water thrown over the windows, see ibid., pp. 38–9, no. 1,082.

[108]   See, for instance, Robert Lowie, cabinet maker, who took out a complaint against George Pringle, drummer in the 26th Regiment of Foot, for assault. Ibid., pp. 30–31, no. 962; and Isobel Oak, who took out a complaint against John MacMillan, for assaulting and knocking her down. Ibid., pp. 39–40, no. 1,115.

[109]   Ibid., pp. 38–9, no. 1,095.

[110]   Ibid., pp. 38–9, no. 1,081.

[111]   Ibid., pp. 53–4, no. 1,389.

[112]   Ibid., pp. 44–5, no. 1,192.

[113]   These included a blind man who received a guinea in compensation from two men who assaulted him (*Police Intelligencer*, 22 October 1831); damages for broken bagpipes (*Police Intelligencer*, 24 October 1831); damages awarded to a complainer for assault

reported the case of a boy, one of three charged with breaking dishes worth 5s. in a shop. He was asked:

> Magistrate: Have you got 5s. to give him [the complainer]?
> Defender – Yes I have!
> Magistrate – Will you pay five shillings, and you will get away?

The defender's answer was not recorded, although it seems likely that he must have agreed to pay as it was noted that the two others were detained on another charge. The periodical also highlighted cases in which the magistrate instructed the complainer to take the complaint to a civil court for damages in cases where no actual crime or offence was deemed to have been committed with which the police court was competent to deal.[114] In doing so, *The Police Intelligencer* helped to provide some advice and direction to its readers on the boundaries between civil and criminal affairs, which, as scholars of criminal justice history have pointed out, were not always clear cut, especially in cases involving assault.[115] Reports also covered the odd instance where defenders, who might otherwise have been eligible for damages, chose not to seek them. In 1832, for instance, the periodical reported the case of a 'poor girl', described as having 'scarcely entered into her teens' who had been savagely beaten by her teenage husband. She disclaimed damages: 'All that she requested was that he should be kept away from her, and prevented from striking her again.'[116] It is possible that such cases were selected to raise awareness about, and interest in, police court business, and what it offered the public.

The majority of urban Scots, though, were dependent upon fiscal-led prosecutions that offered little prospect for financial compensation. Most complainers who reported crimes and offences to the police did so in the hope that the fiscal would bring charges against the accused, perhaps to punish people who had stolen from or harmed them. Some did it with the slim hope of getting their property back,[117] while others brought charges to have their day in court and let off steam, settle personal scores, negotiate personal circumstances, and

---

(*Police Intelligencer*, 27 October 1831); and damages of half a crown from a defender who tore a bonnet from a woman's head (*Police Intelligencer*, 27 October 1831).

[114]   See the case of a landlord who charged some of his tenants with disturbing and molesting him and breaking the door of his house. *Police Intelligencer*, 4 September 1832.

[115]   Peter King, 'Punishing Assault: The Transformation of Attitudes in the English Courts', *Journal of Interdisciplinary History*, 27/1 (1996): p. 48; and Landau, 'Indictment for Fun and Profit'.

[116]   *Police Intelligencer*, 15 June 1832.

[117]   In 1829 Ann Grier, classified as prostitute, was charged in the Glasgow Police Court with stealing a silver watch and appendages from a blind man in Old Wynd. She denied the charge, but called on another women who produced the items, claiming to have found them in a bed of straw. The case was dismissed when the complainer received his property back. *Police Reports*, 6 July 1829, p. 7.

seek court protection from household partners. In the Glasgow Police Court minutes from 1813 to 1824, 15 per cent of named female complainers were relatives of the accused (and this is the bare minimum as other cases might not have listed any family connection even if there was one). Media reports of police trials provide more insights into the relationship between complainer and defender and are likely to have helped create the impression among the reading public that police courts were accessible arenas of conflict resolution. A significant proportion of fiscal-led prosecutions reported in the media were the product of neighbourly, interpersonal or work-related disputes. In the trials for which a victim was recorded in the *Police Reports* between 6 July 1829 and 29 August 1829, the accused was known to the victim in approximately 40 per cent of cases.[118] Sometimes, the relationship had been a fairly fleeting one prior to the alleged incident. A large number included assaults involving men, and to a lesser extent women, who had been drinking together for a few hours, or petty thefts involving women labelled as prostitutes and their clients.[119] But often the disputes involved neighbours, relatives or friends. Of those cases in which the relationship between the complainer and the defender is known, 38 per cent were relatives, 18.5 per cent had been drinking in each other's company (and might have been friends or neighbours), 15 per cent were the outcome of encounters with women who undertook sex work, 12.5 per cent were employers, 8 per cent were friends and 8 per cent were neighbours (although a number of those who had been drinking together are likely to have fallen into this category also). The high percentage of trials in Brownlie's *Police Reports* involving women labelled as prostitutes was, no doubt, designed to serve as a moral warning to middle-class men about the dangers of looking to procure sex in common lodging houses, but, perversely, it could, on occasion, also help publicise and market the best brothels to frequent. In 1829, the journal described Mrs Robertson, charged with keeping a bawdy house, as 'the most handsome woman *of the kind*, ever before seen in the Court, and her girls appear not inferior to her'.[120] Indeed, it is not beyond the realms of possibility

---

[118] There were 226 cases recorded in this period, of which 48 listed the relationship between the complainer and the defender. Davis, in her study of the London police courts, argues that about half of the working-class prosecutions involved charges against friends and acquaintances, while a significant number were individuals who not only knew one another, but who lived in the same house. The other half of the prosecutions were made against persons unknown – usually as a result of street crime. She also argues that working-class prosecutors, although above the casual poor, still included a number of unskilled and even unemployed workers. Davis, 'A Poor Man's System of Justice?', pp. 318–19.

[119] Often the complainer and the defender had been drinking together, and sometimes even sleeping together. See, for example, the case of Walker, described as a prostitute, who was charged with 'stealing a pair of dandy boots and spurs … from a little man of the name of Hawks, in a house at the corner of Canon Street, where the parties had been drinking'. *Police Reports*, 6 July 1829, p. 6.

[120] *Police Reports*, 29 August 1829, pp. 75–6.

that the journal's fascination with the sin of prostitution could also help to serve a wider, more discreet, commercial purpose.

In many cases reported in the press, especially those involving interpersonal violence, the victim and accused resided in the same house.[121] Some women attempted to use the police court as a means of protecting themselves from the threat of physical assault from their partners. Cases of domestic violence were such a common facet of the Glasgow Police Court's daily business that the local police court journal in 1829 reported:

> how very many instances have occurred in the Police Court, of drunk men
> having cruelly and barbarously struck and abused, and inflicted severe wounds
> on the bodies of their broke-hearted wives, to the danger of their lives, and that
> of their little innocents; and exercised a tyranny over them, which the devils
> themselves, in their greatest rage, would not exercise over their brother devils.[122]

The fact that such cases were brought before magistrates, despite the many obstacles victims faced in doing this, suggests that some complainers thought that police courts could offer them protection (even if, as is explored more fully below, female victims were often overruled in what they requested). In such cases, the extent of community support that victims received played an important part in influencing the response of magistrates and the media.[123] Indeed, the fact that charges of domestic assault could be brought to court – and were deemed worthy of being reported in the media – suggests that the local community had standards of acceptable conduct and knew when these had been transgressed (even if not every victim was in a position to seek legal redress and protection).[124] In one such case, brought before the Perth magistrates in 1823, neighbours were reported in the local press to be 'shocked at the usage she had received, [and] had felt themselves called upon to bring the matter under the notice of the Police. The Sitting Magistrate declared it to be the most aggravated case of the kind that had ever come under his observation'. He sentenced the perpetrator to 60 days' imprisonment.[125] As the previous section discussed, the press could dissuade victims from coming forward by making judgements about certain behaviours as legitimate or not, but, in this instance it could, along with the Court and the local community,

---

[121]   Davis, 'A Poor Man's System of Justice?', p. 318.

[122]   'To the Public', *Police Reports*, p. 3.

[123]   *Aberdeen Journal*, 5 February 1823.

[124]   In relation to violence specifically, Nancy Tomes has argued similarly that courtroom testimonies from witnesses provide evidence of the degree of violence that could be tolerated, as well as the limits of acceptable behaviour. Nancy Tomes, 'A "Torrent of Abuse": Crimes of Violence between Working-Class Men and Women in London, 1840–1875', *Journal of Social History*, 11/3 (1978): p. 329.

[125]   *Aberdeen Journal*, 5 February 1823.

act as a form of public advocate for such complaints, which might have further induced others to report similar abuses.

Communities suffering from noisy, disorderly and troublesome neighbours were able to seek help from the police courts. Many people were successfully prosecuted following complaints from neighbours for keeping disorderly houses – which, in many cases, involved the illegal sale of alcohol – and running brothels. In 1829, for instance, Edward Walden was convicted of being drunk and disorderly on the evidence of his neighbours. When the magistrate asked if he had heard what had been said against him he replied 'Yes I have, but, sir Bailie, hearken to me, they ha'e a spite at me.'[126] These were the sort of 'neighbourly' disputes that were of particular interest to procurators and magistrates. They were deemed to be immoral, disturbed the public peace and undermined civic attempts at urban improvement. Such offences were also especially common given the crowded, high-density tenement housing stock of Glasgow, and to a lesser extent Edinburgh. What is particularly interesting about such cases is, first, that convictions were sometimes secured on the testimonies of neighbours, and second, that magistrates themselves would comment upon the detrimental impact such behaviour was having on the community.[127] This suggests not only that communities had their own perceptions of acceptable behaviour, but that they were willing to use the courts in order to improve their quality of life and shape their environment. Proprietors and tenants were, for instance, willing to complain and testify to the offences of their neighbours in both middle-class and, to a larger degree, working-class areas.[128] The periodicals provide many examples that relate to disorderly drinking dens in neighbourhoods long since abandoned by the middle class following the acceleration of residential segregation in the early nineteenth century.[129] Nor should

---

[126]   *Police Reports*, 22 August 1829, p. 64.

[127]   See, for instance, the case involving Edward Seagrave, publican, who was convicted of keeping a brothel on the testimony of three neighbours who complained about the goings-on in his house and the impact it was having on the community. *Police Reports*, 29 August 1829, p. 74.

[128]   It was especially common for complaints to be made against those who kept disorderly houses in tenements. For instance, in 1829, 'an old grey sinner' was charged with keeping a 'bawdy house ... the harbour of the dissolute and disorderly in the High Street'. It was reported that the testimony of Mr Forrest, a police commissioner who resided in the neighbourhood, 'was corroborated by the oaths of respectable neighbours'. *Police Reports*, 10 July 1829, pp. 18–19.

[129]   For background on residential segregation in Glasgow, see M. Simpson, 'Middle-Class Housing and the Growth of Suburban Communities in the West End of Glasgow, 1830–1914', unpub. B.Litt. thesis (University of Glasgow, 1970). As Checkland has pointed out, 'by the 1820s every man of substance had moved to the new areas to the west and north west of the centre, upwind from the smoke of the new engines, and in the opposite side of the town from the masses of Calton and Bridgeton, and north of Anderston'. S.G. Checkland, 'The British Industrial City as History: The Glasgow Case', *Urban Studies*, 1/1 (1964): p. 43.

this come as a surprise. Affluent districts were much less likely to be blighted by shebeens and brothels than poorer communities. For the inhabitants of working-class districts the police court therefore provided the possibility of some protection from the noise, stench, and annoyance of sharing a close with an illegal tavern or a house of ill repute.

Furthermore, there is some evidence that people attempted to employ the court to apply their own understandings of the law and of justice. In September 1831, Bailie Morton dissected a case before the bench between a complainer and her neighbours, the wife and daughter of an optician, in Edinburgh's Thistle Street. The complainer had herself been accused earlier by her neighbours. The defendants claimed 'that they had been charged by the complainer without any other cause than that they had given evidence against her some time ago, when she was convicted of keeping a disorderly house, and fined a guinea'.[130] In such ways, some police court complaints may have reflected, and been an instrument, in longer-standing neighbourly and familial feuds.

Not everyone who brought complaints to court, though, was looking for the accused to be formally dealt with by magistrates. Some used the threat of legal action as a spur to settle disputes informally. As evidence from the Glasgow and Edinburgh police courts reveals, some complainers dropped the charges or did not turn up in court to testify if the accused agreed to meet their demands. In the Glasgow Police Court in 1813, for instance, Mrs Edmonds did not turn up in court to pursue her complaint against Hugh Docherty and Andrew Stewart after they returned candlesticks to her.[131] Indeed, many cases were 'settled' if the accused returned stolen goods to the alleged victim, agreed to leave town or the accuser's employment, or gave assurances not to continue abusing or threatening the complainer.[132] Some cases in the Glasgow Police Court minute book even have the notation 'settled' inserted into the margin,[133] while others appear to have been dismissed on conditions that look as though a settlement had been reached. Some victims even specifically requested that the case be dismissed. In 1813, Mrs Hall, Mrs McArthur, Mrs Alexander and Mrs McKendrie had the complaint made against them of laying down ashes and filth in the close dismissed at the request of the complainers, John Bell and James Wright, after agreeing to settle their differences.[134] Similarly, in 1829, James Mitchell was charged in the Glasgow Police Court with being drunk and disorderly and striking his aged parents. His father testified, with 'great reluctance', that '"he had been often sore struck by the son," but says the good old man, "you may gie

---

[130]   *Police Intelligencer*, 7 September 1831.
[131]   GCA, B3/1/1/1: Glasgow Police Court Diet Books, 28 January 1813, p. 2.
[132]   See the case involving Ann Grier, charged with stealing a silver watch, at note 116.
[133]   See the complaint against John Watt, mason, for not paying for a portable lamp he had acquired some time previously. GCA, B3/1/1/1: Glasgow Police Court Diet Books, 2 February 1813, p. 18.
[134]   Ibid., p. 17.

him a trial once more and fright him weel afore ye let him awa"'.[135] The accused
was sent on his way without further court action. Likewise, in 1832, a father,
a poor old man, who had been assaulted in his house by his son 'implored the
Magistrate not to punish his son, although he was a foolish boy'. The charge was
consequently dropped.[136] In these cases, it seems as though the charges were
not being brought with support of the victims, but it is also possible that in
these cases, as in others, that family members used the threat of legal action
to improve their relationships within the household without ever intending to
pursue further action. Indeed, although many cases of domestic violence are
likely to have been dropped because the victim feared retribution or financial
hardship if the abuser was imprisoned, it is also possible that many victims made
complaints with the intention that the accused would be brought into custody as
a form of pre-trial punishment, and would then not turn up in court to prove the
charge. How widely practised this was is impossible to ascertain, but in giving
evidence to the 1839–1840 Law Inquiry, Davie, Assessor to the Glasgow Police
Court, called for all complainers to lodge a pledge as a form of security to appear
in court to prevent accusers from manipulating and abusing the system.[137]

There were similarities here with English experiences, where scholars have
noted the influence that victims could exert over judicial proceedings and the
willingness of magistrates to 'settle' cases informally. However, it is important
to stress that fiscal-led charges were brought in the public interest, not the
interest of the victim, which weakened the ability of complainers to determine
judicial outcomes and negotiate or settle cases informally, especially if the
complaint was deemed to be in the wider public interest. In 1831, for instance,
three men were charged with annoying the inhabitants in Edinburgh's West
Bow 'by calling to passengers to wonders to be seen within doors'. Despite
producing written authority from several of the complainers 'signifying that
they were not discommended by them', the magistrate stated 'that as the charge
was of a public nature, the wishes of the neighbours availed to nothing'.[138]
Indeed, there were a number of reported instances of magistrates punishing
defenders, despite the requests of complainers not to do so.[139] Where cases that
made it to court were dealt with 'informally' in the Scottish court system, it
had to be with the concurrence of either the fiscal or the magistrate. In 1831,
for instance, the brother-in-law of James Fraser brought a charge against him
for assault. After the complainer 'said that he had no objection to pass from the

---

[135]   *Police Reports*, 7 July 1829, p. 9.
[136]   *Police Intelligencer*, 17 April 1832.
[137]   'Fourth Report by Her Majesty's Law Commissioners, Scotland, 1839', p. 326.
[138]   *Police Intelligencer*, 1 November 1831.
[139]   See, for example, the case involving John Gilvray who, in 1831, was sentenced
in the Edinburgh Police Court to 30 days in bridewell for assaulting his wife despite her
testifying (in all likelihood under duress) that he had not caused her harm (discussed in
Chapter 1, Volume 2). *Police Intelligencer*, 9 September 1831.

charge if he would leave town', which Fraser agreed to, the magistrate informed the defender: 'As your brother in law has been kind enough to forgive you, and as you are going to leave town, I will forgive you; but take care to not give him a farewell kick.'[140] In this instance, the support of the complainer was integral to how the case dealt with – but the outcome was, ultimately, at the discretion of the magistrate. Complainers in Scotland could, of course, still exercise their own discretion by not turning up in court, or refusing to testify,[141] but in doing so ran the risk of being fined or reprimanded themselves, or having their pledge forfeited.[142] In 1818, for instance, John McKay, shoemaker, was fined half a crown after seizing David Liddle, weaver, for breaking a pane of glass in his shop window, then later admitting in court that 'it was all a mistake'.[143]

The capacity of complainers to determine pre-trial proceedings, manipulate criminal process, or influence the outcome of charges was, therefore, significantly reduced by the presence of the fiscal, who cast an intimidating shadow over pre-trial and courtroom proceedings, and magistrates, who saw their role as one to serve the common good. While the introduction of the new police bureaucracy made it less burdensome and expensive for many victims to seek legal redress, whether a case was formally prosecuted or dismissed was, in the first instance, at the discretion of the resident fiscal and senior police officers. Procurators had always been instrumental in determining the course of prosecutions in Scotland, especially for more serious crimes, but, as the next section examines, the police take-over of prosecutions for less serious offences went a long way in further reducing the role of the victim as an active participant in the prosecution process by constructing a new bureaucratic structure between the complainer and the criminal justice system.[144] In most cases, it was the police court personnel who made the key decisions, determined proceedings, and ultimately shaped the manner in which justice was administered in what were police, rather than people's, courts. Indeed, while certain sections of the public may have felt that the police court offered an instrument of satisfaction in such matters, there was no

---

[140]   *Police Intelligencer*, 30 September 1831.

[141]   For complainers not turning up in court, see the case of the shopkeepers in Edinburgh who complained about the practice of hawking but did not follow up their complaint (*Police Intelligencer*, 1 September 1832); or the case of a grocer 'of considerable note', residing in the New Town, who was charged with committing a breach of the peace by 'spitting in the face of a wine merchant' with whom he was doing business (*Police Intelligencer*, 22 August 1831).

[142]   See the case of William McEwan, who had his pledge of 5s. forfeited for failing to turn up in court to pursue his complaint of assault against William Baker. GCA, B3/1/1/10: Glasgow Police Court Diet Books, 26 September 1824, p. 14.

[143]   GCA, B3/1/1/5: Glasgow Police Court Diet Books, 29 February 1818, p. 27.

[144]   In his study of police magistrate courts in late Victorian and early twentieth-century England, Godfrey also found that the police's take-over of prosecutions reduced the role of the victim as an active prosecutor in the criminal justice system. Godfrey, 'Changing Prosecution Practices and their Impact on Crime Figures', pp. 171–89.

guarantee that magistrates would take seriously the public complaints that were brought before them. Far from being 'settled', it is argued below, many cases were thrown out by magistrates because they were not deemed worthy of their attention – and, significantly, not just without the concurrence of the complainer, but also for reasons that had little to do with either their interests or those of the accused.

V. Dismissing

Procurators fiscal were integral to the workings of the Scottish criminal justice system.[145] Who should fill the position of public prosecutor was a thorny and contentious issue as it struck at the heart of a power struggle between civic men. In the early nineteenth century, burgh procurators were reluctant to concede some of their responsibilities to senior police officials,[146] whilst police commissioners contended that they, not magistrates, should appoint the fiscal given the police's increasing involvement in bringing forward charges.[147] Under the new police model, men in different police and civic circles fulfilled this duty. In some burghs, responsibility for bringing forward prosecutions in police courts continued to lie with the legally trained burgh fiscal. In others, it was given to the police superintendent and his inspectors, who would initiate prosecutions in the name of the fiscal, and in a few of the larger cities, most notably Glasgow and Edinburgh, the services of both a police and burgh fiscal were utilised. In the latter instances, the police would take responsibility for prosecuting mainly minor police offences and contraventions in the police court, again in the name

---

[145] For more on the public prosecutor in Scotland, see Susan Moody and Jacqueline Tombs, *Prosecution in the Public Interest* (Edinburgh, 1982); W.G. Normand, 'The Public Prosecutor in Scotland', *Law Quarterly Review*, 54 (1938): pp. 345–57; and 'The Procurator Fiscal: Historical Evolution', *Glasgow Herald*, 18 February 1910.

[146] See the attempt in 1821 of Alexander Ponton, the Procurator Fiscal for the Burgh of Edinburgh, to establish a Society for the Protection of Private Property, discussed in Chapter 2.

[147] In Paisley, magistrates resisted for many years attempts by police commissioners to appoint the superintendent to the position of joint fiscal in the police court. Magistrates claimed it was not proper to appoint a man without legal training to this office. That they themselves had no legal training was not deemed to be significant and suggested that the issue at hand was not simply the importance of having professionally trained lawyers involved in police court proceedings, but also magistrates' desire to retain control of the appointment of police court prosecutions and the fines that were levied on offenders. Disquiet surrounded who had the right to the disposal of the whole of common law fines levied in the police court and the most appropriate means for paying the expenses of burgh fiscal and assessor. Commissioners argued that the police establishment had a right to claim the fines that went to the burgh fiscal. Magistrates, however, claimed that procurators had a right only to fines for police offences. 'Fourth Report by Her Majesty's Law Commissioners, Scotland, 1839', p. 302.

of the fiscal, with the burgh fiscal prosecuting more serious (common law) crimes in both the police and higher courts.[148] The procurator fiscal, in other words, continued to be public prosecutor, but increasingly this was a role that senior police officers would fulfil, especially to prosecute less serious crimes and offences not deemed to require the expertise of a trained lawyer.

The police's involvement in this process was heralded by those in civic circles as greatly improving judicial process, providing the institutional structure needed for the speedy dispatch of a far larger volume of cases than otherwise would have been possible. In giving evidence to the 1852–1853 Select Committee on Police, James Smart, Superintendent of the Glasgow Police, claimed that this was 'a great improvement over the English system; there is no expense in the first place involved in getting up the case'.[149] Some in parliamentary circles in London were of a similar opinion. In 1854, the Select Committee on Public Prosecutions widely praised Scottish prosecution practices and it is possible that the Scottish system might have provided a template for police-led prosecutions in England from the mid-nineteenth century.[150]

Like magistrates, procurators and senior police officers had a lot of discretion in executing their duties. Those members of the public who had been apprehended and brought to the police office for public drunkenness and disorderly conduct were often sent on their way in the morning without charge once they had sobered up, with procurators and police officers taking the view that a night in the cells was sufficient punishment, or that such cases were not serious enough to warrant a magistrate's attention. Those, on the other hand, who were charged for offences inferring pecuniary penalty or fine would usually be liberated on bail by the on-duty police lieutenant.[151] In such cases, the bail pledge was set at a sum equivalent to the fine that would be imposed on conviction, thereby acting

---

[148]   Under the terms of the 1829 Aberdeen Police Act, for instance, the procurator fiscal of the bailie or burgh court was the prosecutor or complainer against all persons accused of theft. Ibid., p. 252.

[149]   'Second Report from the Select Committee on Police; Together with the Proceedings of the Committee, Minutes of Evidence, and Appendix', *BPP*, 1852–53 (715), XXXVI.161, p. 111.

[150]   'Report from the Select Committee on Public Prosecutors; Together with the Proceedings of the Committee, Minutes of Evidence, Appendix and Index', *BPP*, 1854–55 (481), XII.1, pp. 2, 5–22 & 61–3. Lord Campbell, the Lord Chief Justice of England, informed the committee: 'In Scotland I have had an opportunity from my own observation of seeing that the system there established works most admirably, both in the Court of Justiciary, the Supreme Court at Edinburgh, and at the assizes. ... I think that if the system could be introduced into this great country of England in the same manner, it would be desirable that it should be introduced.' Ibid., p. 61. For the police's growing role in prosecuting offences in England, see Godfrey, 'Changing Prosecution Practices and their Impact on Crime Figures', pp. 171–89; and Davis, 'Prosecutions and their Context', pp. 398–426.

[151]   'Fourth Report by Her Majesty's Law Commissioners, Scotland, 1839', p. 320.

as inducement for the accused not to appear in court but rather to forfeit the sum by way of punishment.[152] Those who were unable to lodge a pledge would be detained and brought before magistrates at the next court sitting, which was usually the following morning. Trial or sentencing would immediately follow the plea of the accused unless the defendant requested that the case be deferred to a later date in order for witnesses to be cited and evidence gathered. But such occurrences were rare, especially for charges involving offences. The loss of earnings and inconvenience in having to attend another sitting resulted in many of those brought before magistrates having little opportunity to prepare an effective defence – especially if they were in the process of sobering up from the excesses of the night before. Legal authorities defended the speed at which cases were dealt with on the basis that it made it easier to secure witnesses and meant that the accused did not have to make separate appearances in court to plead and stand trial, but little regard was given to its implications for the legal rights of those concerned.[153] This policy had different implications for men and women as forfeits appear to have been used differently between them.

Those apprehended and charged with crimes inferring punishment of imprisonment would also have their cases determined at the first available court sitting unless they requested time to prepare a defence and gather witnesses.[154] Procurators had to decide quickly if there was sufficient evidence to warrant prosecution given the necessities of summary justice and the huge volume of cases that came before them.[155] The day-to-day proceedings of police courts and high turnover of cases meant that procurators, unlike the higher courts, had little opportunity to gather evidence, interrogate suspects and interview witnesses in deciding whether there was a *prima facie* case to answer. Having said that, police officers would consider the strength of the evidence and witness testimony in deciding whether or not to apprehend a suspect, even before the fiscal decided whether to bring the charge before the court. Moreover, even though the capacity to filter cases was reduced by the speedy nature of summary justice, procurators were still reluctant to bring weak cases before the courts – and it is more than likely, as Chapter 6 examines, that as the century went on the police became more effective in determining whether to proceed with a case or drop it before bringing it to court, especially given their growing preoccupation with 'clear up' rates. The

---

[152] Ibid., p. 321.

[153] Ibid., p. 326.

[154] Ibid., pp. 320–39.

[155] As the evidence that was presented to the 1839–1840 Law Inquiry revealed, the decision as to whether or not to pursue criminal actions in Scottish towns was largely dependent upon local procurators fiscal, although civic leaders could, on occasion, influence their thinking. In discussing the role of procurators, Charles Grace, Town Clerk of Stirling, noted that 'many of the actions were immediately settled, or abandoned, without being judged of by the magistrates; had they been at all of a flagrant nature, they would have been visited with more severe punishment'. Ibid., p. 307.

role of public prosecutor, as *The Bailie* in 1875 was at pains to stress in discussing the position of John Lang, Procurator Fiscal of Glasgow, was to convict.[156] Thus, even though a suspect might have been apprehended on suspicion of having committed a crime or was brought into custody in response to a complaint from a member of the public, there was no guarantee that formal legal proceedings would be commenced. Given Scotland's longstanding cultural and institutional preference for public rather than private prosecutions, victims were very much dependent on the fiscal deciding whether a case should proceed, especially as certain crimes and statutory offences could only be prosecuted with the sanction of the fiscal. The accessibility of police courts to the Scottish public was at almost every turn determined by the public prosecutor, whose very presence reduced the individual's capacity to determine whether or not they were able to have their day in court, let alone acquire legal redress, unless they could pay for it themselves.[157]

In deciding whether to charge a suspect in the local police court – and what the charge should be – procurators were not only influenced by the strength of evidence, the number of witnesses, the severity of the offence, and the caseload of the court at any given time, but also by civic directives and media reports.[158] Police- and press-led campaigns against prostitution and shebeening, for instance, produced short-term spikes in cases prosecuted. The manner in which a suspect was brought into custody was important too. Cases in which the outcomes were likely to depend on the testimony of arresting officers stood a far greater chance of being prosecuted than cases which depended solely upon the evidence of members of the public, with anecdotal evidence suggesting that procurators and magistrates were more inclined to believe the evidence of policemen than those from the wider community (see Chapter 4). The social status, character and appearance of the accused were also often instrumental in determining the outcome of apprehensions and allegations.[159] In 1870, a journalist writing in the *North British*

---

[156]   *The Bailie*, no. 133, 5 May 1875, p. 1.

[157]   Robert B. Shoemaker has questioned the accessibility of the legal system. See Robert B. Shoemaker, *The London Mob: Violence and Disorder in Eighteenth-Century England* (London, 2004), p. 288.

[158]   Procurators not only set the charges, they could also desert charges and replace them with new ones. See the case of a man named 'Dinning' and a group of women charged with robbing a packman from Paisley of a blue handkerchief containing £2, 10s. The fiscal later dropped the charge of robbery and replaced it with one of assault. No explanation was given, but it might have been because it was easier to secure a conviction. Dinning was sentenced to six weeks' confinement in bridewell. *Police Intelligencer*, 22 October 1831.

[159]   This was common not just in the police courts. When asked by the 1869 Law Committee if he thought it was an advantage to have the criminal investigation in the first instance made privately, Andrew Jameson, Sheriff of Aberdeen, said yes, because it helped to save innocent people from infamy. He explained: 'I remember of one case which made a great impression on me, of a very highly respectable gentleman in Edinburgh, who was charged with indecently assaulting some young girls at a bathing-place on the coast; and when the Fiscal came to me with the information, I said it was very extraordinary, but of course we must

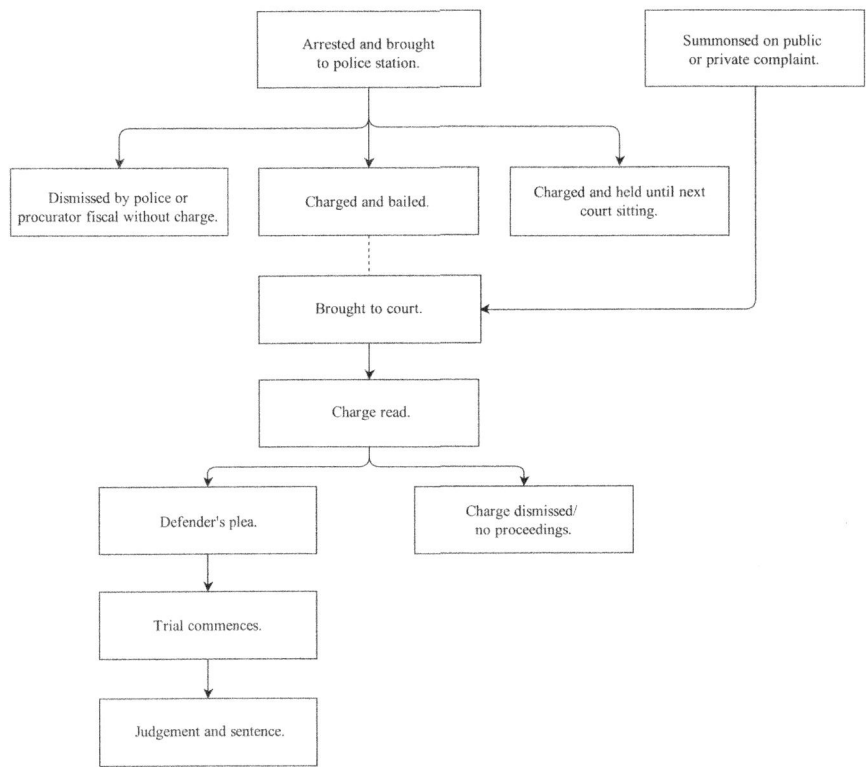

Figure 3.1   Procedural Stages Leading to Prosecution and Trial in Police Courts

Daily Mail alluded to this in a series of investigative reports titled 'The Dark Side of Glasgow'.[160] When confronted with a case involving three 'respectable'-looking servant girls of West-End families, arrested and brought before the police office for being in an illegal drinking den with their boyfriends, the reporter noticed that the police adopted a different approach from that which had been applied to a

---

do our duty, and I recommended the gentleman be summoned in a quiet manner. He came, and being warned, gave his declaration, and told all the circumstances, denying the charge entirely. The precognition went on, and in consequence of the statements that he made, Mr Lothian, the Procurator Fiscal, was enabled so to conduct the inquiry, and so to cross-examine the witnesses, that it turned out, in the course of the two days, to be an entire misapprehension, if not a gross fabrication, leaving not the slightest stain on this very honourable gentleman, who was a man moving in good society, of most unblameable character.' 'First Report of the Law Commissioners Appointed to Inquire into the Courts of Law in Scotland; Together with Minutes of Evidence', *BPP*, 1868–69 (4125), XXV.29, p. 334.

[160]   'The Dark Side of Glasgow', *North British Daily Mail*, 27 December 1870 to 30 January 1871 (five reports). These reports were located in GCA, AGN 2114: Newspaper Cuttings, pp. 1–139.

poor girl named Lizzie, wrongly accused and charged with being the keeper of a disorderly house.[161] After the girls broke down in the police office and pleaded for mercy, the reporter wrote:

> Human nature – even police human nature, the kindliness of which is often ignorantly underrated – cannot stand these appeals; and, although we do not inquire too closely how it comes about, these poor girls do not spend their night in the police cells, but are allowed to depart with a lesson they will probably not soon forget, and a judicious leniency may have saved the whole trio from going to the bad.[162]

Apparently, respectable girls who begged for mercy, and showed deference to the police's paternal role, were more likely to be sent on their way than others.

Keeping 'respectable' members of the public out of police courts for all but the more serious crimes seems to have been a concern for a number of procurators, senior police and legal figures. In 1859, Lord Ivory, a judge in the High Court and Court of Session, had observed that it was common practice that a person should not be brought summarily before the magistrate, 'when a party accused is respectable, known to the police, law-abiding, and not purposing to go abroad, and not caught in the actual commission of an offence'.[163] Samuel Rodger, a police constable for seven years, from 1876 to 1883, in the affluent district of Hillhead in Glasgow, was of little doubt as to the social bias in how the law was administered and the impact it had on the clientele of the courtroom. The introduction to his memoirs, written by an unknown source, noted that Rodger was a 'working class man of strong moral and religious conviction who had fundamental objections to the system which allowed the rich to purchase their respectability and keep themselves and their families out of the police courts'.[164] Described by the same author as being 'no respecter of social rank and privilege' and 'a champion of the poor and the

---

[161] When asked if anything could be done to save 'an attractive-looking girl of about 17' named Lizzie accused of keeping a disorderly house, who had just been released from prison and was begging for mercy not to go back to gaol, the policeman replied: 'Nothing, she is lost beyond redemption' (p. 6). Despite knowing, according to the journalist, that the two male tenants of the property were the keepers of the disorderly house, the police locked up Lizzie and her friends over the weekend and brought them before the court on Monday. One of her friends, a 16-year-old girl, thinking she was helping Lizzie, pleaded guilty – a plea that was repudiated by Lizzie and another of her friends (p. 7). It was, according to the journalist, an honourable act not mirrored in the actions of any of the men described, including the real culprits who refused to pay the fine that would have kept Lizzie out of court. 'The Dark Side of Glasgow', 2nd Report.

[162] 'The Dark Side of Glasgow', 5th Report, p. 17.

[163] Cited in Lindsay Farmer, *Criminal Law, Tradition and Legal Order: Crime and the Genius of Scots Law, 1747 to the Present* (Cambridge, 1997), p. 115.

[164] 'The Secret Memoirs of Samuel Rodger (1846–1901) The Glasgow Teetotal Bobby', produced at the People's Palace Museum, Glasgow Green, to accompany the exhibition

less fortunate', Rodger's socialist political views undoubtedly shaped his opinion of the justice that was handed out in the police court.[165] Nonetheless, his memoirs provide a fascinating insight into late Victorian law enforcement rarely found in official police and magistrate records. Rodger's memoirs describe at length not just how police resources were targeted against the poor, but also how the middle class used wealth and influence to escape the law – often, it was suggested, by exploiting bribery and corruption within the police force.[166] Describing the suburb of Hillhead he patrolled, Rodger wrote: 'I might say here that in working class districts the Police were petty public tyrants, but in this swell Burgh they were public Lick Spittles.'[167] The fiscal and magistrates would, he claimed, collude in order to keep the illegality of the middle class out of the public eye.[168] He went on:

> I knew of a young swell on one occasion while under liquor who committed one of the most immoral acts which is possible for a man to commit in the presence of Ladies and for this immoral and criminal offence he was apprehended in the very act and taken to the Police Office in the district. But instead of being locked up and brought before the court in the usual way, he was allowed to leave on depositing a pledge of two guineas. A special court was held with closed doors and the magistrate did not insist upon the young swell being present, but allowed the case to be tried by proxy, the father appearing in place of the son. He was only fined in the two guineas as left at the time of the apprehension.[169]

If the fiscal did decide to bring someone forward who had been apprehended for a crime, offence or contravention, it would then be at the discretion of the magistrate as to how the outcome was determined. In the Scottish police courts, no specific provision for pre-trial courtroom interviews was enshrined in any local police laws. In so far as such examinations were permitted, it was to determine whether the seriousness of the offence was within the limited jurisdiction of the police court – a role which sometimes brought magistrates into conflict with the fiscal. In practice, though, a huge volume of cases in the Scottish police courts, especially in the early nineteenth century, were dismissed by magistrates before, it seems, formal trial proceedings had commenced. Indeed, the fact that the majority

---

'Scotland Sober and Free' marking the 150th anniversary of the temperance movement in Scotland, by kind permission of William Rodger, grandson of Samuel Rodger, p. 1.

[165] Ibid., p. iii.

[166] As the introduction to his memoirs claimed, 'Unlike his fellow policemen, he could not turn a blind eye and his silence was not for sale.' Ibid., p. i.

[167] Ibid., p. 8.

[168] The introduction to his memoirs claims that 'the sophisticated misdemeanours of the rich citizens evidently shocked him to the core, and his inability to ignore them earned him the displeasure of the Provost, the Police Inspector and the Police Sergeants'. Ibid., p. ii.

[169] Ibid., pp. 1–2.

of charges in the Scottish police courts were brought by the fiscal might have given Scottish magistrates more scope to dismiss cases pre-trial than in England where, according to Cox and Godfrey, the criminal justice system did not afford magistrates very much power over victims who were determined to initiate private prosecutions.[170] Within the courtroom itself, and in front of the defender, the complainer, the press and the gallery, magistrates would determine whether a case was worthy of proceeding or whether it should be dismissed. The number of cases which fell into the latter category was huge. Of the 1,148 people who appeared or were summonsed before magistrates in the 1813–1824 Glasgow Police Court sample, 569 (50 per cent) were dismissed.[171]

The high number was partly explained by the way in which judgements were recorded. Dismissals sometimes included cases of persons who had been tried and found not guilty, or admonished and reprimanded, which should caution against attaching too much significance to bland figures.[172] Indeed, just under half of the dismissals in the Glasgow Police Court between 1813 and 1824 were accompanied by a reprimand or admonition, sometimes on condition that the accused fix the source of the complaint or leave the city. Occasionally, notes were recorded in the police minute books stating that the magistrate had heard from the defenders and examined policemen before dismissing a charge,[173] so it would be wrong to conclude that dismissal in every case implied that magistrates had not gone to the trouble of investigating the charge to make an informed judgement.

Many cases, though, do appear to have been dismissed much more informally and with much less consideration on the part of the magistrate. A large number of people charged with vagrancy and petty offences who were apprehended by the police without a complaint from the public were dismissed, sometimes with admonition, because they were not in a position to pay a fine and magistrates did not want the burgh burdened with their prison maintenance costs.[174] Moreover, as argued in the previous section, magistrates appear to have been willing in some cases to act as conflict arbitrators. Indeed, in 1840, Captain Miller of the

---

[170]   David J. Cox and Barry S. Godfrey (eds), *Cinderellas and Packhorses: A History of the Shropshire Magistracy* (Almeley, 2005), passim.

[171]   GCA, B3/1/1/1: Glasgow Police Court Diet Books, 28 January 1813 to 11 February 1813, pp. 1–43; GCA, B3/1/1/5: Glasgow Police Court Diet Books, 28 January 1818 to 11 February 1818, pp. 20–101; and GCA, B3/1/1/10: Glasgow Police Court Diet Books, 25 September 1824 to 8 October 1824, pp. 1–98.

[172]   It was not uncommon for dismissals to be accompanied with a 'not proved' commentary thereby suggesting that magistrates had taken the time to consider the case. See, for example, the case of Messr McLivie, charged with having a foul vent. GCA, B3/1/1/1: Glasgow Police Court Diet Books, 28 January 1813, p. 1.

[173]   See the case of James Melville, charged with fighting, calling out murder and annoying neighbours. GCA, B3/1/1/5: Glasgow Police Court Diet Books, 30 January 1818, p. 37.

[174]   For a number of those charged with vagrancy dismissed with certification for begging, see *Police Intelligencer*, 31 August 1831.

Glasgow Police claimed in his report into the state of crime in the city that 'few, if any of them [charges] were dismissed for want of evidence',[175] which suggests that magistrates were not averse to resolving disputes pre-trial. In the Glasgow Police Court in 1813, for instance, Nicole McKenzie was dismissed 'on return of coat and vest which she did',[176] the case against Francis Ransum was dismissed when Mrs Smith received a shawl back,[177] Lizay Sharp was dismissed on the condition that she leave town,[178] and Mary Paterson was dismissed 'on taking away the child' she had tried to leave behind in the complainer's house.[179] As these examples suggest, it was especially common for women to have their cases dismissed or settled informally, which was the product of a range of social, cultural and economic factors that will be explored throughout this study, as well as how magistrates saw their paternal role. Some dismissals involved assault cases if the incident in question was perceived to be a private dispute that had not threatened public security. This, as Chapter 1 of Volume 2 explores more fully, was a judicial judgement call that spoke to magisterial perceptions about who was injured and who mattered to be protected from violence.[180] Discretion was a critical facet of summary justice, and magistrates sometimes used their discretion to adjudicate their own forms of compensation for those they considered worthy.

Repeat offenders, and those charged with property crimes, were nearly always formally tried, but magistrates were more flexible and willing to deal with those brought before them for a range of offences in a less formal manner. Disputes between certain working-class neighbours, for instance, did not always rank highly in the male court officials' assessment of what the police courts' priorities should be.[181] Often, such cases were dismissed quickly with the accused, and sometimes

---

[175] GCA, M.P.24, D-T.C.14/1/24, 23: *Papers Relative to the State of Crime in the City of Glasgow, with Observations of a Remedial Nature; and an Appendix of Tables, by H. Miller, Superintendent of Police, and City Marshal* (Glasgow, 1840), p. 6.

[176] GCA, B3/1/1/1: Glasgow Police Court Diet Books, 31 January 1813, p. 11.

[177] Ibid., 4 February 1813, p. 25.

[178] Ibid., 4 February 1813, p. 27.

[179] Ibid., 3 February 1813, p. 23.

[180] Magistrates adopted a similar approach in summary courts in England. See, for instance, Drew D. Gray, 'Settling their Differences: The Nature of Assault and its Prosecution in the City of London in the Late Eighteenth and Early Nineteenth Centuries', in Katherine Watson (ed.), *Assaulting the Past: Violence and Civilization in Historical Context* (Cambridge, 2007), pp. 124–40. Similarly, John Weaver's study of crime in Ontario, Canada, found that magistrates often settled cases of assault informally before judicial action was taken. John C. Weaver, *Crimes, Constables and Courts: Order and Transgression in a Canadian City, 1816–1970* (Montreal, 1995).

[181] Laura Gowing, for example, has argued for the early modern period that litigation over slander 'offered women a rare, institutional weapon in the daily and occasional conflicts of their local lives'. Laura Gowing, 'Language, Power and the Law: Women's Slander Litigation in Early Modern London', in Kermode and Walker (eds), *Women, Crime and the Courts*, p. 42. But, although similar cases were brought forward exposing disagreements

the complainer, being given a short, sharp reprimand and little evidence of careful consideration from the judicial bench. Magistrates, for instance, had a dismissive attitude towards violence they deemed to be fairly minor if both the accused and the defender were deemed to be guilty, or if it was a regular occurrence.[182] Cases involving working-class women or Irishmen who had engaged in slander and low-level violence against one another were often dismissed with a reprimand from the magistrate that they not bother the court again with such a trivial offence.[183] Interpersonal neighbourhood disputes of this kind were of less interest to magistrates than those which threatened a perceived wider public interest. In 1831, for instance, the magistrate dismissed a charge of assault brought by a labourer's wife against an Irishman and his wife and ordered each party to pay the expense of the private complaint. Both, he maintained, were to blame and should pay accordingly.[184] The fact that the case was the product of a private complaint was significant in itself in highlighting that the fiscal did not deem it worthy of public prosecution as it was, apparently, not in the public interest.[185] The implication was that such offences were beneath the dignity of the court.

Magistrates were recorded in the local press expressing their surprise that some men who fought among themselves should have made recourse to the courts to settle their differences. Assaults committed between men of different social and ethnic groups were precisely the types of cases that police courts were designed to deal with; but disputes among themselves that did not significantly threaten public order, involve members of a wider public, or involve an 'unacceptable' level of violence were of less concern to the court – or, put another way, were amongst the ones most likely to be dismissed without formal proceedings.[186] In such cases, magistrates, and indeed the police, were often happy to let the warring parties sort out their own problems. As one magistrate in Glasgow in 1829, in convicting bakers whose fight got out of hand, commented: 'men might quarrel among themselves, but their guilt was highly aggravated by abusing and wounding

---

between women, the nineteenth-century police courts do not appear to have operated as successfully to resolve such disputes.

[182]   Godfrey, Farrall and Karstedt make a similar point. Barry S. Godfrey, Stephen Farrall and Susanne Karstedt, 'Explaining Gendered Sentencing Patterns for Violent Men and Women in the Late Victorian and Edwardian Period', *British Journal of Criminology*, 45/5 (2005): pp. 696–720.

[183]   See, for instance, the case involving two women, described as 'craws' by the magistrate, fiscal and press, charged with rioting and fighting with each other. The case was dismissed. *Police Intelligencer*, 19 August 1831. See Chapter 1 of Volume 2 for further discussion.

[184]   *Police Intelligencer*, 24 October 1831.

[185]   This mirrors the finding by Bankowski, Hutton and McManus, who argued that procurators in the Scottish district summary courts as recently as the 1980s often took the view that family and neighbourly disputes were unsuitable for prosecution in court. Z.K. Bankowski, N.R. Hutton and J.J. McManus, *Lay Justice?* (Edinburgh, 1987), p. 142.

[186]   *Police Intelligencer*, 22 August 1831.

innocent men appointed to keep public tranquillity.'[187] Moreover, as Chapter 1 of Volume 2 explores in more depth, magistrates were often dismissive of complaints of domestic violence unless they infringed upon social and gender norms and involved a level of violence that they determined to be unacceptable. In 1832, for instance, a married woman had the charge of assaulting her husband dismissed by the magistrate who claimed there was 'fault on both sides'. The husband claimed his wife pawned every article they owned, and the wife claimed her husband 'drank every farthing he earned'.[188] Whether the man had been assaulted or not seemed of little importance to the magistrate compared with the character of the clients before him – people, it seemed, who were less worthy of the court's time and attention than others. Indeed, the experience of the Scottish police courts bears a number of similarities with the conclusions of D'Cruze and Zedner who argued that while women in England in the nineteenth century increasingly sought legal protection from violent abusers, the treatment they received was determined by middle-class male values and perceptions concerning who was worthy and unworthy of the court's support.[189] Magistrates were also reluctant to get involved in property disputes within families. In 1824, for instance, Mrs MacDonald had her complaint against her daughter, Sally Russell, for stealing a pair of blankets, dismissed with admonition to *both* parties because it was, the court records state, 'a family affair'.[190]

As a result, many complainers who had their cases dismissed are likely to have left the court feeling aggrieved. Although impossible to quantify from the limited evidence that exists, what information has been preserved suggests that many cases which were dismissed had not been 'settled'.[191] As police courts could cope with only a limited volume of business, a significant proportion of cases which

---

[187]   *Police Reports*, 25 July 1829, p. 21.

[188]   *Police Intelligencer*, 27 April 1832.

[189]   D'Cruze, 'Sex, Violence and Local Courts', p. 64; and Zedner, *Women Crime and Custody*.

[190]   GCA, B3/1/1/10: Glasgow Police Court Diet Books, 25 September 1824, p. 2.

[191]   There were many examples in the police court minutes and media reports of magistrates appearing to adopt a fairly dismissive attitude towards certain complainers and complaints (exemplified throughout this study). Interestingly, in cases in which no reference was made either to evidence or the complainer not turning up in court, dismissals were much more common for offences than crimes, especially simple assaults, thereby suggesting that these charges were of lesser concern to magistrates in the early nineteenth century than those regarding property (although presumably not to the person who brought the complaint). Indeed, sometimes cases were 'dismissed with a reprimand to both parties' if the magistrate thought both the complainer and accused deserved it. See the case of Tess Farm, charged in the Glasgow Police Court with striking and abusing Margaret Flurr 'in the close leading to her house'. Ibid., 4 February 1813, p. 24. Interestingly, for the two-week period studied in the first Glasgow Police Court diet book there was only one case which had 'settled' in the 'outcome' column. See the charge brought against John Watt for not paying for a portable lamp he had in George Street. Ibid., 2 February 1813, p. 18.

were dealt with informally by procurators and magistrates are likely to have been so without the concurrence of the complainer. The approach adopted by the courts' officials was often less about acting as paternal protectors and conflict settlers, and more about managing and prioritising the pragmatic realities of a burgeoning caseload – much of which was conditioned by the social and moral values of magistrates themselves. In many such instances, the police court was not a people's court where community disputes were primarily to be resolved, or a place where working-class grievances were heard and addressed by magistrates; rather it was a centre of justice where the police, procurators and magistrates determined which people and which cases should be dealt with, and which grievances were worthy of court time and attention. It was a place where large numbers of people came looking for formal legal redress to their problems, only to have their complaints dismissed swiftly.[192]

An intriguing example of public sentiment towards magisterial justice was provided by William Smith, Edinburgh author and printers' joiner, who was an active publisher of penny chapbooks and at least two illegal periodicals during the 1830s. Both periodicals were concerned with issues of law and order combined with 'amusing and instructive' songs, stories and images: the *Bawbee Bagpipe* of 1833, lasting 12 numbers, and the *Advocate* of 1834, consisting of six numbers.[193] The *Bawbee Bagpipe* seems to have been influenced in part by a personal vendetta on the part of Smith, its author, over his failure to achieve what he believed to be justice in the Edinburgh Police Court. Costing only half a penny, the journal offered satirical material on the police and Edinburgh's civic institutions.[194] His *Advocate* ran with mottos such as 'whether this ends in a laugh or a frown, I'll make it known thro' out the town'[195] and claimed its intent was 'to let the public know that there is no justice got at law'.[196] Smith himself was something of a lone crusader, many of whose complaints before the police court, typically claiming he was a victim of abusive language, broken windowpanes, or malicious theft, had been dismissed by magistrates as frivolous. Smith had even verbally attacked one magistrate whilst the latter was officiating as an elder in the Greyfriars' Church, and used print as a way to pursue his criticisms of the police courts. He may have

---

[192]   See the case of a flesher who brought a charge against an old woman for stealing a leg of lamb from his market stand, then had his case dismissed because he could not identify the meat. *Police Intelligencer*, 1 November 1831.

[193]   John Bulloch (ed.), *Scottish Notes and Queries*, II (1906): p. 5.

[194]   Joel H. Wiener, *The War of the Unstamped: The Movement to Repeal the British Newspaper Tax, 1830–1836* (Ithaca, 1969), p. 175. See also *The Advocate*, no. 1–6 (1834), cited in John S. North (ed.), *The Waterloo Directory of Scottish Newspapers and Periodicals, 1800–1900* (2 vols, Waterloo, 1989), vol. 1, p. 121.

[195]   North (ed.), *The Waterloo Directory of Scottish Newspapers and Periodicals*, vol. 1, p. 121.

[196]   'Address to the Medico-Chirurgical Society by D. Yellowlees M.D, Assistant-Physician at the Royal Edinburgh Asylum, 4 June 1862', published in *Edinburgh Medical and Surgical Journal*, 97 (1863): p. 109.

been mentally unbalanced. Indeed, a lengthy account of his activities and 20-year stay at the Royal Edinburgh Asylum (having first been confined as a result of his attack on the police court magistrate) was later published in the *Edinburgh Medical and Surgical Journal* of 1863.[197] On his ninth appearance as a complainer before the Edinburgh Police Court, Smith wrote a letter to the Lord Advocate observing:

> I knew perfectly well that [Bailie] Tait would not give me justice in this case, no more than in my former ones. I wrote my mind on a large sheet of paper and as soon as the offender was acquitted [Smith accused him of attempting to set fire to his shop], I said loudly, in the hearing of all that were in the Court, My Lord, I knew perfectly well that you would not give me justice in this case no more than in my former ones. I have written my mind on this large sheet of paper and intend to shut up my shop as soon as I go home, and paste the said grievance on the front of my shop.

Smith duly posted a copy of the notice on his shop front for a month which stated that it was shut 'in consequence of the injustice of the Police Court. … Was I, the complainer, not in the right, and could prove it, or durst I have read my grievances in the Court or pasted them on the front of my shop to be read publicly'. Smith placed this letter and notice in his last publication, the 1840 *The Police Retort*, along with a series of alarming threats:

> If I do not get justice in this said case, serious will the consequences be; and I humbly hope my fellow-citizens will assist me in battle, if one takes place, and raise a riot, as I have broken the ice for them, and have justice given them in future at Court.[198]

Although his personal vendetta against Edinburgh's bailies is likely to have coloured his opinion, his campaign illustrated that for some individuals bringing complaints, the police courts were ineffectual in providing satisfaction.

Even those seeking assistance from magistrates in carrying out their day-to-day business could receive short shrift. In 1889, in an example that exposed the social and cultural values of justices, the *Glasgow Herald* reported that at the close of the police court in Greenock a woman had presented herself before the bailie with a request that he should in the usual way sign her affidavit under the Pawnbrokers Act. The woman was reported as being 'exceedingly dirty in appearance':

> 'Are you Mrs Gallocher,' asked Bailie Maconie?
> 'Yes.'
> 'Why don't you wash your face?'

---

[197] Ibid., pp. 105–24.
[198] *The Police Retort*, pp. 25–6. Cited in Yellowlees, pp. 108 & 110.

Response – a laugh.

'I say, why don't you wash your face when you come before a gentleman? Go away, you dirty woman, and when you have cleaned yourself come back, and I will sign your affidavit.'[199]

Clearly, the pastoral care of the magistrate in question did not extend to those who failed to uphold his standards of cleanliness.

While the capacity of those who sought magisterial intervention to acquire justice and support in police courts might have been restricted and determined by what magistrates allowed, and what courtroom etiquette they insisted upon, for others, especially the urban poor who bore the brunt of police attention, suspicion of the police is likely to have deterred them from looking to the courts for assistance. As the following section examines, the police's relationship with the populace – and the extent to which police courts were regarded as a tool for policing certain sections of the populace – is likely to have gone a long way in reducing the willingness of many to seek legal redress in police courts.

VI. Police and the Populace

In his last speech as a judge in the Edinburgh Police Court in 1812, Superintendent Tait stressed the importance of public support towards the police for the success of law enforcement in the city. Repeating a remark that had been earlier made by the Lord Provost and which, Tait stated, 'cannot be too strongly enforced', he claimed that 'no institution of police can be effectual without the cordial support of the community'.[200] Indeed, some contemporaries contended that Tait's unpopularity in civic and legal circles led to his removal in 1812. As John Kay, in *A Series of Original Portraits and Caricature Etchings* (1838), wrote:

> Whether from a too exalted idea entertained of the trust reposed to him, or from a dislike on the part of the public to the new system of Police – or probably from a combination of both – certain it is "Judge Tait" was not among the most popular of the civic rulers.[201]

He went on: 'However inflexible or abstractly just in his conceptions of equity, the administration of Justice by Judge Tait was far from satisfactory. His conduct was viewed as too severe and unbending; and there were not a few to accuse him of occasionally overstepping the limits of his commission.'[202]

---

[199]   *Glasgow Herald*, 28 August 1889.
[200]   John Kay, *A Series of Original Portraits and Caricature Etchings* (2 vols, Edinburgh, 1838), vol. II, part I, p. 147.
[201]   Ibid., vol. II, p. 146.
[202]   Ibid.

Although impossible to say definitively, it is likely that those who turned to the courts to settle disputes and acquire justice constituted a small percentage of the actual number of crimes and offences to which the working class fell victim. Large sections of the urban poor, especially its rougher sections, preferred to settle disputes themselves rather than lodge formal complaints. Indeed, some ended up in court after being arrested by the police precisely because they preferred to use violence rather than the law. In 1829, the *Police Reports* recorded one such incident involving a blacksmith's apprentice and two others, who were charged with brutally assaulting a free mason. According to the report, the 'feelings of the crowd were so much exasperated' at their violent actions that they proceeded 'to inflict instant punishment upon the individual apprehended' before the police intervened.[203] In other cases, members of the public may have been reluctant to give evidence. When a Glasgow magistrate, in 1829, asked 'what do the neighbours say about this house?' (which was reputed to be a common brothel), the watchmen replied: 'what can they say, they are all as bad as Dustan [the accused] himself; they all follow the same line; they would be the last to complain.'[204] Even those who themselves were the alleged victims of offences were recorded in some media reports as siding with their offenders rather than the authorities. In 1823, for instance, *The Scotsman* reported that the police arrived at a disturbance to arrest a man who 'after severely beating a wretched woman with whom he cohabits … forced an entry into the house of a cobbler, whose few articles of furniture he threw out of the window, and the cobbler himself after them'. It went on: 'Detachments of policemen now arrived from all quarters, who overpowered the fellow after a desperate resistance, to which he was encouraged by the very woman who had just suffered so much from his brutality.'[205] The women's response, of course, is likely to have been shaped to some extent by fear of violent reprisal from her partner, but it also serves to highlight that for certain sections of the community there was an unwillingness to seek judicial redress.

Although working-class complainers were listed among newspaper reports and court records, this by no means suggests a groundswell of popular support for the new form of summary justice or the legitimacy of the newly emerging policed society. The willingness of the working class to use what legal means of redress were available to them was indicative of the fact that they had a pressing problem to resolve, not necessarily that they fully supported the moral values of civic leaders or fully accepted the rule of law and how it was enforced.[206] Given the central role the police played in determining whether suspects were apprehended and charged, the public's attitudes towards the police is likely to have been important in determining whether they would report crimes in the hope that the fiscal would initiate a charge. Tellingly, there is evidence of endemic suspicion and

[203] *Police Reports*, 22 August, 1829, p. 62.
[204] *Police Reports*, 5 September, 1829, p. 93.
[205] *The Scotsman*, 13 December 1823.
[206] Davis, 'A Poor Man's System of Justice?', p. 310.

hostility towards the police among the 'rougher' sections of the working class.[207] In 1829, in a case brought before the Glasgow Police Court involving a major disturbance and fighting between policemen and Irishmen, it was reported that during the alleged incident an old Irish lady shouted: '*houly* Father, and *houly Jasus*, the watchmen, the barbarous dogs that they are; was there ever a man among you could do anything?'[208] In another case, John McAra, a mason from Perthshire, was charged with being drunk and disorderly in the house of Andrew Stark, Gallowgate, and attempting to cut people with a knife. 'He said he did not care a d___ n for all the policemen in Glasgow, and that if he had a pistol, he would blow Mr Stark's servant's brains out.'[209] Although impossible to prove, such media portrayals which revealed the contempt for authority that existed among the rougher sections of society are likely to have helped legitimise the actions taken by the courts and the police in punishing them.

Police records themselves highlighted how fraught the relations between the police and certain communities were. In Glasgow, 'obstructing, striking and molesting watchmen' were common offences listed in the 'Fiscal's Accounts for Prosecutions, 1807–1819'.[210] Moreover, as the authors of the *Report of the Special Committee appointed by the Board of Police, to Inquire into the Moral and Physical Character of the Watching Force, July 1846*, pointed out, they

> cannot refrain from expressing their strong conviction as to the necessity of a cordial co-operation with, and understanding between, the Public and the Police, which, a reference to the records of the Police Court proves, do not at present exist. The Police Records abound with complaints against our citizens for alleged interference with the Police in the execution of their duty.[211]

The report went on to highlight how the physical and moral conduct of officers, as well as policing practices designed to secure convictions in the police court, produced great resentment among certain sections of the community:

> The committee also strongly recommends the discontinuance of the practice of two constables, or of one constable and sergeant *patrolling together by day* for the purpose of *proving cases.* Such a mode of procuring evidence may suit some

---

[207]   For the key study on working-class attitudes towards the police, see Robert D. Storch, '"The Plague of Blue Locusts": Police Reform and Popular Resistance in Northern England, 1840–57', *International Review of Social History*, 20/1 (1975): pp. 61–90.

[208]   *Police Reports*, 6 July 1829, p. 7.

[209]   *Police Reports*, 8 August 1829, pp. 55–6.

[210]   GCA, B3/1/5: Fiscal's Accounts for Prosecutions, 1807–1819. There are also regular reports in the media of watchmen being assaulted. See *Police Reports*, 6 July 1829, p. 7.

[211]   ECL, *Report of the Special Committee appointed by the Board of Police, to Inquire into the Moral and Physical Character of the Watching Force, July 1846* (Edinburgh, 1846), p. 6.

peculiar localities in London or Dublin, but is singularly inappropriate to this city; and is, moreover, injurious, by reducing the strength of the day force, and by tending to foment a jealous feeling of interference on the part of the police against the public, from whom they should be taught to *look* for support, and on whom they should always feel disposed to rely for assistance when required. The maintenance of the *"esprit de corps"* is valueless, if it puts the force beyond the pale of public sympathy.[212]

If the public had to be 'taught' to look to the police for support, then the implication was that hitherto large sections of them were more inclined to resolve disputes themselves within their own communities rather than seek legal redress.

As the century progressed, it is possible that sections of the working class became more reconciled to the advent of a policed society and more willing to report crimes and offences and pursue legal action, as scholars for England have suggested.[213] Unfortunately, police criminal returns, published annually from 1857 onwards, do not give any information on the complainers, and no detailed court records have been preserved for the second half of the century to assess changing attitudes towards the legal system. However, it is clear that opposition to the law was fairly entrenched among large sections of society as late as the late Victorian period. In their *Municipal History of Glasgow* (1896), Bell and Paton not only emphasised this, but felt compelled to try to change what they believed was a popular misconception of the police that prioritised their coercive role over their welfare one:

> To many good citizens the term Glasgow police means little more than the embodiment of law and order, the constable, as he walks the streets clothed in the official blue symbol of authority. To these citizens there comes once a year a disagreeable reminder of the Glasgow police in the form of a demand for the remainder of police rates, and that claim being satisfied that ratepayer imagines that there his relations with the police of Glasgow begin and end. Viewed from these two points alone the police of Glasgow cannot be expected to evoke much popular enthusiasm or to be the object of ungrudging support. And the lower we descend in the social scale the greater will be found the popular antagonism to the police, till the shady circles verging towards the regions of filth, vice, and crime the very name "police" is hated as much as it is feared.[214]

Even senior police officers concurred. When asked at the 1908 Royal Commission on Police about community relations, the Chief Constable of Glasgow remarked:

---

[212]   Ibid., pp. 20–21.

[213]   For an overview on working-class attitudes towards the police, see Taylor, *The New Police in Nineteenth-Century England*, pp. 102–27.

[214]   James Bell and James Paton, *Glasgow: Its Municipal Organisation and Administration* (Glasgow, 1896).

'The feeling towards the police is decidedly good in the better class localities, and amongst the shopkeeping class. In the rougher localities the feeling is hostile and always in favour of the arrested person.'[215] If police courts were designed not just to punish petty crimes, offences and misdemeanours, but also to ensure working-class acceptance of the law and the social structure,[216] then clearly they had only a limited impact.

It is possible that the police's involvement in bringing forward charges alienated them from certain sections of society, as it had the potential to call into question their neutrality as both prosecutor and witness. This point was succinctly outlined by Henry Turner Waddy in his investigation of police magistrates in early twentieth-century London:

> The fact that a police officer has apprehended a prisoner, or is the informant named on the summons, ought not to lead to the officer being allowed to assume the position of prosecutor upon the hearing of the charge. His proper function is that of witness and no more ... There are two unfortunate impressions as to police courts which exist in the minds of the working classes. One is that the policeman is both witness and prosecutor, and the other is that the magistrate is the creature of the police.[217]

Although not stated in such explicit class terms as here, the controversy surrounding the police's involvement in the Edinburgh Police Court in the early nineteenth century suggests that such a view was not restricted to London. As Chapter 2 discussed, the practice of awarding policemen extra payments on conviction was strongly criticised by many in legal circles as 'it is a temptation to perjury on the part of the officers, as upon their evidence many of the decisions depend, and of course a reward is held out to find the prisoners guilty'.[218] As the Committee of Magistrates and Public Bodies in Edinburgh, concerned with establishing a more effective police, itself acknowledged in 1812: 'It gave the officers an interest in the conviction of offenders, and thereby tended to disqualify them as witnesses, and to render the public doubtful of the real motive of their proceedings on all occasions.'[219]

Whether certain sections of the community perceived the police and the courts to be one and the same is difficult to say, but, as the next chapter will show, there

---

[215] 'Royal Commission on the Duties of the Metropolitan Police, Volume III', *BPP*, 1908 (cd. 4261), LI.1, p. 917 (q. 40246). Cited in Robert D. Storch, 'The Policeman as Domestic Missionary: Urban Discipline and Popular Culture in Northern England, 1850–1880', *Journal of Social History*, 9/4 (1976): p. 494.

[216] Davis, 'A Poor Man's System of Justice?', p. 315.

[217] H.T. Waddy, *The Police Court and its Work* (London, 1925), p. 58.

[218] ECL, *Reports of the Committee of Commissioners of Police and Minutes of General Meetings Thereto* (Edinburgh, 1807), p. 14.

[219] *Caledonian Mercury*, 4 April 1812.

is evidence from courtroom discourse to suggest that many believed that they could not get a fair trial in the police court and that magistrates' close relationship with the police called into question magisterial neutrality. Interestingly, Davis, in her study of London's police courts, argued that magistrates' growing association with the police as the century progressed contributed to police courts' decline as a working-class resource and centre of conflict resolution.[220]

However, attitudes towards the police and the courts are likely to have been shaped not just by their perceived relationship, but also by their perceived roles as levers of urban discipline. Police courts did what their name suggested – police behaviour. Significantly, a large volume of the business of police courts had not been instigated in response to a complaint from the public, but by a police arrest.[221] In early nineteenth-century Glasgow, a sizeable proportion of defenders listed in the Police Court diet books were 'apprehended by a watchman' without a complaint from a member of the public.[222] Indeed, the most frequent complainer in the city's police courts was the police itself. As was demonstrated above, approximately one quarter of the charges brought in the Glasgow Police Court between 1813 and 1824 had a named complainer. That is not to say, though, that such prosecutions did not have some community backing: many of those apprehended by the police and convicted for being drunk and disorderly were causing annoyance to members of the public prior to their arrest.[223]

Nonetheless, a large proportion of the business that Scottish police courts dealt with was 'victimless' in the sense that it was not the product of a victim's complaint and, in many instances, did not have a victim at all. In other words, as Volume 2 shows, a sizeable proportion of the court's business reflected more the police's attempts to regulate public space, control urban order, and clamp down

---

[220]   Davis, 'A Poor Man's System of Justice?', p. 333.

[221]   There were a number of ways that a defender could be brought before the court that did not first involve a complaint from a member of the public. These included when apprehended in the act of committing a crime and detained by police, by summons from the fiscal, and on a complaint from the court granting a warrant to apprehend the accused. A fiscal's summons (a charge) or court petition on complaint were normally issued for offences involving breaches of local bye-laws relating to the built environment. Those who were caught in the act of committing a crime, or being drunk and disorderly, would be brought to the local police office and detained until the next magistrates' sitting. In most towns, trial would occur the following day.

[222]   GCA, B3/1/1/1: Glasgow Police Court Diet Books, 28 January to 3 July 1813. This supports the conclusion of Davis who found that in 1869 the police in the London police courts were involved as arresting officers, and as prosecutors as well, in 72,951 of the 83,582 offences proceeded against. Davis, 'Prosecutions and Their Context', p. 419.

[223]   Even in cases – often involving breach of the peace – in which there were no victims giving evidence or listed as complainers, the persons apprehended had often been causing annoyance to the public. 'Molesting' and 'annoying' passengers were common phrases used in reports and when witnesses gave evidence. *Police Reports*, 6 July 1829, p. 5.

on public immorality and anti-social behaviour than a groundswell of popular support for the use of legal sanctions for minor offences. Although speculative, this is likely to have had implications for police–community relations and the willingness of certain sections of society to report crimes to the police and press charges in courtrooms where many had themselves been fined, reprimanded or sent to bridewell.

VII. Conclusion

According to Davis, crucial to the popularity of police courts in London was magistrates' willingness to satisfy working-class expectations of what they thought was the just application of legal power 'even if by doing so they might find themselves, at times, endorsing behaviour and values at odds with those acceptable to the propertied classes or representatives of the state'.[224] Magistrates, she contends, were acutely aware of their 'mission to help resolve those problems and disputes that arose from the social relations of ... [the working] class', often on terms laid out by the working class themselves, even though it often brought them into conflict with police and other civic institutions. This matched the practice of eighteenth-century English summary courts, where, according to Gray, the public perception that these were places 'where disputes could be satisfactorily aired and resolved' placed them 'at the forefront of understanding of social relations'.[225] As he continues:

> It may be overstating the case to argue that the summary courts were 'the people's courts'. But they were courts that all of the people could use; they may have been of less benefit to the poor and more useful to the propertied but we cannot dismiss them as simply a disciplinary tool of the ruling elite.[226]

Similarly, while recognising that 'the law courts [in England] were not entirely consensual', Godfrey and Lawrence claim that neither can they be viewed entirely as 'a mechanism of social control, but rather an admixture of both fairness and support for the existing social order'.[227]

It is certainly the case that the introduction of police courts in Scotland gave the working class greater opportunity for legal redress than they had been afforded under the old burgh court structure. Despite the ideological and moral values that underpinned them, these courts were more accessible than burgh courts – and, significantly, a sizeable percentage of the Scottish urban population, often involving families, friends and neighbours, were willing to utilise them in order to

---

[224] Davis, 'A Poor Man's System of Justice?', p. 331.
[225] Gray, 'The People's Courts?', p. 11.
[226] Gray, *Crime, Prosecution and Social Relations in London*, p. 174.
[227] *Police Reports*, 22 August 1829, p. 61.

resolve grievances. In reporting grievances to the police, complainers applied their own standards of socially acceptable conduct and believed that the police courts could uphold them. This should caution against portraying the new bureaucratic police machine that was introduced in Scottish towns as being simply a one-dimensional class tool. Although, according to press reports anyway, many of the complainers for theft were drawn from the ranks of the small business class, there were sufficient numbers from the working class to counter the notion that these courts were solely an instrument of the business class. Indeed, as in England, the members of the public who interacted with the court helped to shape the system's workings, just as the courts were helping to shape the behaviour of the urban masses.[228] The fact that the overwhelming majority of charges laid were financed out of police municipal taxation meant it was easier for the urban poor to resolve their differences in a court of law than it had been under the old burgh court system. Although the presence of the courtroom journalist might have deterred some from publicising their grievances, it also, for the most part, is likely to have encouraged more members of the public to consider the courts as a place for legal redress.

The accessibility of police courts, and their capacity and willingness to negotiate disputes, however, should not be overstated. Access by all classes and both sexes was far from equal due to practical and cultural reasons. Whether complaints were proceeded against was often dependent upon not just the crime or offence, but also the middle-class sensibilities of procurators and magistrates. Just as in the nineteenth-century English courts, the legal protection that the judicial system afforded women reflected what middle-class men felt was appropriate,[229] with the courts' response to female criminality and crimes in which women were victims often being assessed 'according to displays of deference, modesty, and silence in the courtroom'.[230] Moreover, as Godfrey and Lawrence point out, 'there is a limit to how "consensual" a system [was] which excluded approximately half the population from direct participation' as magistrates, procurators and police officers.[231] Not only did the presence of the fiscal reduce the complainer's ability to use the courts to settle disputes informally, the limited nature of police court jurisdiction reduced the victim's capacity to seek legal redress for civil disputes – an important point, given that the dividing lines between police, criminal and civil actions were often blurred. As a result, the general public in Scotland was likely to have been much less willing, or able, to resort to police courts as a forum for advice and informal mediation than their English counterparts.

This might also have reflected the differing ways that the public perceived and used the courts, and, crucially, how procurators and magistrates perceived their role. The fact that complainers in Scotland did not have to pay at the point

---

[228]   King, *Crime, Justice, and Discretion in England*, p. 373.
[229]   D'Cruze, 'Sex, Violence and Local Courts', p. 64.
[230]   Zedner, *Women, Crime and Custody*, p. 28.
[231]   Barry S. Godfrey and Paul Lawrence, *Crime and Justice, 1750–1950* (Cullompton, 2005), p. 64.

of delivery for bringing forward a charge might have encouraged procurators and magistrates to be more willing to dismiss cases without commencing formal proceedings, or more reluctant to act as arbiters and negotiators, than in England where victims had to take the lead themselves. As Chapter 5 explores in greater depth, the number of cases per head of population brought before Scottish police courts was often lower than that in the English police courts. Senior police officers in Scottish burghs held this up as evidence of their effectiveness in dealing with crime, but it is also likely to have reflected the differing prosecution practices between the two countries and the central role of the fiscal – and the role of the police in acting as the public prosecutor in particular – in the Scottish criminal justice system. Not only did procurators, as the century went on, suppress the recorded crime rate by filtering out and not proceeding with weak cases, in doing so they are also likely to have produced a system in which there was less scope for police courts to become centres of advice and conciliation, and less opportunity for the masses to manipulate what constituted a close network of civic, elite, male power.

Magistrates' role was complex and multi-faceted. They had to reconcile the need to show understanding and mercy with a desire to clamp down on the immorality and petty criminality of the urban poor. Like their eighteenth-century southern counterparts, they were willing, on occasion, to settle disputes informally, but they were also part of a wider bureaucratic police machine intent upon imposing a greater level of discipline onto the urban masses which somewhat reduced their capacity to act as informal conflict arbiters. Indeed, the whole purpose of the new police model that was introduced in early nineteenth-century Scottish towns was to bring to justice huge numbers of people who otherwise would have escaped it. It was, in other words, to use the courts to better control and discipline the urban masses. That so many cases were dismissed was, among other things, indicative of the fact that magistrates never lost their sense of being guardians of public welfare, and should caution against overstating the extent to which the emergence of policed society resulted in the abandonment of informal means of administering justice; but, equally, this should not disguise the wider trend towards control and discipline that the police courts served. Nor should it hide how this fitted in with the changing ethos of the criminal justice system, the move towards prosecuting and punishing more and more people, and the use of the law to regulate behaviour. Indeed, in an era when specialist boards of propertied men were emerging to manage Scottish civil society, and rival other aspects of public life, magistrates' role in the administration of the police assumed particular importance to their status and authority.[232] Ultimately, police courts helped individuals to settle disputes, but as a judicial resource they

---

[232]   This is illustrated by the great efforts magistrates went to in wresting control of police affairs from elected police commissions in mid-century. See David G. Barrie, *Police in the Age of Improvement: Police Development and the Civic Tradition in Scotland, 1775–1865* (Cullompton, 2008), pp. 224–60.

were as, if not more, important in helping magistrates control their communities and safeguard the status quo. Far from satisfying, and winning, the working class's acceptance of the law even if it brought them into conflict with other civic institutions, as has been claimed for London,[233] the Scottish courts were much more likely to uphold and endorse the values of the state and its middle-class personnel and suppress dissenting or subversive views, as the following chapter examines.

The media's role in conveying the accessibility of police courts and the extent to which they were centres where legal redress was achievable and conflicts were resolved was complex. There were variations between, and within, newspapers and periodicals. Some periodicals, such as the *Bawbee Bagpipe*, were openly critical of the justice delivered in police courts, while others sent out mixed messages from report to report. Indeed, the media's desire to entertain, send out moral messages, inform, and pander to the interests of middle-class readers ensured that there was no single discourse that was being conveyed. Having said that, the media did put forward a dominant one. There was an implied assumption that police courts were effective vehicles for dealing with the range of urban social problems and interpersonal disputes. Periodicals like *The Bailie* and *The Detective* had a more cynical eye to court workings than the mainstream media, but they did not really overturn this notion even if they sometimes reported complaints that magistrates were ineffective in delivering justice to complainers. For the most part, the media created the impression that the magistrate knew best – he was someone who could intervene in the management of less fortunate and less capable people who needed his help and guidance. In its coverage of interpersonal disputes, in particular, the media helped to portray police courts as arenas in which conflicts could be aired, negotiated and settled, even if the outcome was not always what the complainer wanted. In doing so, it helped to create the impression that these courts were, indeed, more people's courts than police courts, though the reality was somewhat different.

---

[233] Davis, 'A Poor Man's System of Justice?', p. 331.

Chapter 4
Public Theatres?

I. Introduction

The importance of ritual, symbolism and theatre within the English criminal justice system has been widely recognised.[1] Until fairly recently, it was common to portray courtrooms as solemn, dignified and sombre environments that were designed to control certain emotions. The structural and spatial design of eighteenth- and nineteenth-century courtrooms, the formal and ritualistic nature of trial proceedings, and the costumes and apparel worn by courtroom personnel have all been acknowledged as showcasing and legitimising the majesty of the law, symbolising state authority and buttressing the status quo.[2] Justices would sit on a raised platform to reinforce the law's supremacy and their own status, wigs and robes would be adorned to convey authority, and courtrooms would be spatially and socially demarcated to be 'physically and psychologically imposing'.[3] Trials were awe-inspiring spectacles akin to public theatre designed as much to convey wider social messages as to administer justice. Lawyers and justice officials were central actors in the court and in shaping the production of the criminal trial,[4] reflecting a criminal justice system that was very much weighted in the interests of men of property.

---

[1]   David Lemmings, 'Ritual and the Law in Early Modern England', in S. Corcoran (ed.), *Law and History in Australia* (Adelaide, 1991), pp. 3–19. For the nineteenth-century courts, Ginger Frost draws direct analogies between the theatre of the courtroom in civil cases and other kinds of theatrical performance. Ginger Frost, *Promises Broken: Courtship, Class and Gender in Victorian England* (Charlottesville, 1995). In their study of the Scottish summary courts, though, Bankowski, Hutton and McManus argue that there is a 'tension between the ritual symbolic function of the court and the lowly ordinaries of its daily practices'. Z.K. Bankowski, N.R. Hutton and J.J. McManus, *Lay Justice?* (Edinburgh, 1987), p. 52.

[2]   Clare Graham, *Ordering the Law: The Architectural and Social History of the English Court to 1914* (Aldershot, 2004); and Peter Goodrich, *Languages of Law* (London, 1990), p. 193.

[3]   Quote from Michael T. Davis, 'Prosecution and Radical Discourse during the 1790s: The Case of the Scottish Sedition Trials', *International Journal of the Sociology of Law*, 33/3 (2005): p. 150. See also Goodrich, *Languages of Law*, p. 193.

[4]   For the growing importance of lawyers in the eighteenth-century English criminal court, see David Lemmings, *Professors of the Law: Barristers and the Culture of English Law in the Eighteenth Century* (Oxford, 2000).

Although these aspects created certain theatrical elements and inspired particular emotions, a growing historiography has questioned the impact of courtroom rituals in reinforcing judicial authority and the extent to which courtroom proceedings were one-sided manifestations of repression.[5] As John Beattie has argued,

> we have perhaps been in some danger of exaggerating the dignity and order of eighteenth century courts and perhaps overemphasising their success as theatre – taking the robes, full bottom wigs and black caps as guarantee ... that the solemnity and hushed seriousness the judges would have wanted was in fact always achieved.[6]

It has become more common to view the courtroom as a contested space in which different social groups interacted and negotiated – one in which a range of participants from diverse social backgrounds shaped the workings of the criminal trial.[7] As Barry S. Godfrey has pointed out, courtrooms not only communicated moral messages to the accused and the wider public, they also provided an opportunity for the participants to challenge magisterial authority and project their own messages.[8] Similarly, as Michael Davis, in his study of the Scottish sedition trials of the 1790s, argued, the courtroom was a powerful forum for political expression in that it provided an arena for counter-discourse and counter-theatre:

> [The courtroom was] a site of an insurgent counter-culture, where radical discourse and performance was used to articulate, legitimate and sustain the cause of political reform. [This could be] ...a crucial forum for radical expression, contest, negotiation and self-assertion. ...They [the radicals] realized that trials publicized and vindicated the cause they were intended to suppress, in a synergy E.P. Thompson identifies as 'a two-edged weapon'.[9]

As Peter King has observed, the 'openness' of the criminal trial provided a means through which dissent was conveyed.[10] An essential component of the

---

[5] See, for instance, Peter King, *Crime, Justice and Discretion in England, 1740–1820* (Oxford, 2000), passim. Similarly, the extent to which eighteenth- and nineteenth-century legal proceedings in England may be understood as theatre and counter-theatre, and the role and impact of print media in relation to trials, is explored in David Lemmings (ed.), *Crime, Courtrooms and the Public Sphere in Britain, 1700–1850* (Basingstoke, 2012).

[6] J.M. Beattie, *Crime and the Courts in England, 1660–1800* (Oxford, 1986), p. 399.

[7] King, *Crime, Justice and Discretion*, p. 258.

[8] Barry S. Godfrey, 'Sentencing, Theatre, Audience and Communication: The Victorian and Edwardian Magistrates' Courts and their Message', in Benoît Garnot (ed.), *Les tésmoins devant la justice. Une histoire des status et des comportements* (Rennes, 2003), pp. 161–71.

[9] Davis, 'Prosecution and Radical Discourse during the 1790s', pp. 148–50. See also E.P. Thompson, *The Making of the English Working Class* (Harmondsworth, 1968), p. 141.

[10] King, *Crime, Justice and Discretion*, pp. 252–5.

law's legitimacy, the public gallery not only allowed for public scrutiny of trial proceedings, it also enabled 'the crowd' to exert influence over judgements and sentencing patterns. Far from being orderly, the gallery's gasps, protests, hisses, applause and even laughter could, as a number of scholars have pointed out, alter the dynamics of judicial interactions and were thus a volatile component of trial proceedings.[11] Pressure from the public gallery, and sometimes the baiting of crowds outside the courtroom, ensured that courtroom decisions in English courts were not always representative of elite opinion or at odds with popular sentiment, but were instead the product of negotiation, accommodation and compromise.[12] Composed of a largely, but by no means only, plebeian audience, the gallery allowed for 'theatre and counter-theatre' to be played out in an interactive, reciprocal manner, which E.P. Thompson has claimed characterised eighteenth-century social relations more generally.[13] As King goes on, many trials may perhaps be more accurately regarded as 'participatory theatre', with the performance of judicial authority being balanced, as Peter Linebaugh points out, by the 'counter-theatre' of the crowd.[14]

More recently, scholars have also acknowledged the importance of the press within the courtroom as a vehicle for conveying moral messages on the workings of the criminal justice system.[15] While some have argued that the media's reporting

---

[11]   King notes that crowds often expressed anger at decisions, for example by hissing when verdicts were handed down. King, *Crime, Justice and Discretion*, pp. 253–7. See also Peter Linebaugh, *The London Hanged: Crime and Civil Society in the Eighteenth Century* (Cambridge, 1992), p. 87; Beattie, *Crime and the Courts*, p. 399; and V.A.C. Gatrell, *The Hanging Tree: Execution and the English People, 1770–1868* (Oxford, 1994), p. 95.

[12]   King, *Crime, Justice and Discretion*, pp. 252–7.

[13]   E.P. Thompson, 'Patrician Society, Plebeian Culture', *Journal of Social History*, 7/4 (1974): p. 396; and E.P. Thompson, *Customs in Common* (New York, 1991), pp. 56–96. See also King, *Crime, Justice and Discretion*, p. 255.

[14]   King, *Crime, Justice and Discretion*, p. 255; and Linebaugh, *The London Hanged*, pp. 87–8.

[15]   Until fairly recently the bulk of work that was produced by scholars of criminal justice history on newspaper reporting had focused mainly on crime. See, for instance, David Lemmings and Claire Walker (eds), *Moral Panics, the Media and the Law in Early Modern England* (Basingstoke, 2009); Robert B. Shoemaker, 'Print Culture and the Creation of Public Knowledge about Crime in Eighteenth-Century London', in Paul Knepper, Jonathan Doak and Joanna Shapland (eds), *Urban Crime Prevention, Surveillance and Restorative Justice: Effects of Social Technologies* (Boca Raton, 2009); Peter King, 'Newspaper Reporting and Attitudes to Crime and Justice in Late Eighteenth and Early Nineteenth Century London', *Continuity and Change*, 22/1 (2007): pp. 73–112; and Peter King, 'Newspaper Reporting, Prosecution Practice and Perceptions of Urban Crime: The Colchester Crime Wave of 1765', *Continuity and Change*, 2/3 (1987): pp. 423–54. More recent work, however, has looked at the media's representation of the criminal justice system and the social and moral messages it conveyed. See, for instance, Donna T. Andrew, 'The Press and Public Apologies in Eighteenth-Century London', in Norma Landau (ed.), *Law, Crime and English Society, 1660–1830* (Cambridge, 2002); and Judith Resnik and

of criminal trials offered the possibility for dissent to be recorded and disseminated to a wider audience,[16] some have viewed the press as an essentially conservative force that rarely recorded the public gallery's opposition to judicial judgements.[17] Shani D'Cruze, for instance, has argued that there was 'a symbiotic relationship between the press and the gallery' in the way that 'gendered components of respectability among working men and women' were constructed, judged and represented in courtroom narratives.[18] Others have questioned the media's impartiality. As studies by Ian Bell, Simon Devereaux and Robert B. Shoemaker have shown, the trial accounts of London's central criminal court, which were recorded in the *Proceedings of the Old Bailey*, were selectively reported in order to construct a particular image of justice that served wider social, moral, commercial and civic purposes.[19] While acknowledging that the *Proceedings* reports could be interpreted in different ways, Shoemaker, for instance, contends that the messages that were sent out helped to legitimise the workings of the court and to portray it as being an accessible and impartial source of justice.[20] On the other hand, Crone, in her study of nineteenth-century newspapers, has questioned the extent to which the press advanced a dominant or consistent discourse on police court trials – reflecting a similar conclusion to that found by King in his study of eighteenth-century newspaper crime reports and the effectiveness of the authorities in dealing with lawlessness.[21]

It has been widely recognised, therefore, that eighteenth- and nineteenth-century courtrooms had many participants – each of whom could exert influence

---

Dennis Curtis, *Representing Justice: Invention, Controversy, and Rights in City-States and Democratic Courtrooms* (New Haven, 2011).

[16]   Davis, 'Prosecution and Radical Discourse during the 1790s', p. 155.

[17]   King, *Crime, Justice and Discretion*, p. 253.

[18]   Shani D'Cruze, *Crimes of Outrage: Sex, Violence and Victorian Working Women* (London, 1998), p. 138.

[19]   Robert B. Shoemaker, 'The Old Bailey Proceedings and the Representation of Crime and Criminal Justice in Eighteenth-Century London', *Journal of British Studies*, 47/3 (2008): pp. 559–80; Simon Devereaux, 'The Fall of the Sessions Paper: The Criminal Trial and the Popular Press in Late Eighteenth- Century London', *Criminal Justice History*, 18/1 (2002): p. 58; Simon Devereaux, 'The City and the Sessions Paper: "Public Justice" in London, 1770–1800', *Journal of British Studies*, 35/4 (1996): pp. 467–8; and Ian Bell, *Literature and Crime in Augustan England* (London, 1991), p. 73. For histories which accept the *Proceedings of the Old Bailey*'s accuracy and impartiality in reporting on criminal trial proceedings, see John H. Langbein, *The Origins of Adversary Criminal Trial* (Oxford, 2003), p. 185; and John H. Langbein, 'Shaping the Eighteenth-Century Criminal Trial: A View from the Ryder Sources', *The University of Chicago Law Review*, 50/1 (1983): p. 25.

[20]   Shoemaker, 'The Old Bailey Proceedings and the Representation of Crime and Criminal Justice', pp. 559–80.

[21]   Rosalind Crone, *Violent Victorians: Popular Entertainment in Nineteenth-Century London* (Manchester, 2012), pp. 185–209; and King, 'Newspaper Reporting and Attitudes to Crime and Justice', pp. 73–112.

on judicial proceedings in subtle and, in some cases, not so subtle ways. However, this line of inquiry is still fairly under-researched, with scholars devoting more attention to how people used the courts to settle grievances than to their experiences within the courtroom itself.[22] Moreover, what work has been done has, with a few notable exceptions focused primarily on criminal trials in higher courts involving juries and indictable offences.[23] The paucity of sources which exist for eighteenth-century summary courts has largely determined this, but fortunately the information that exists for nineteenth-century police courts is richer. Newspaper reports on nineteenth-century police court cases, for all their limitations, offer intriguing insights into courtroom discussions. Moreover, looking at courtroom interactions promises to shed light on the relationship between the public men in court – magistrates, procurators and clerks – and the police, whilst offering further information about debates on the accessibility and nature of justice offered by police courts.

This chapter examines the experiences and discussions of the courtroom by exploring who the participants were, how they experienced the summary trial, and the dynamics of crowd, court and media interaction. In doing so, it builds upon the previous chapter by assessing the wider implications of courtroom discourse for police–community relations as expressed through a judicial forum. As magistrates were the main focus of Chapter 2, particular attention will be given to other courtroom participants such as the fiscal, the police, the accused, the gallery, witnesses and journalists, as well as the significance of the architecture and the media representation of the auditory of the courtroom. This chapter recognises that the space of the police court was interactive, and the process and practice of the law negotiated between participants from a wide array of backgrounds, albeit with differing capacities to impose their own ideas, values and viewpoints. However, as in the process of bringing forward a charge, it argues that the central place of procurators in the Scottish criminal justice system reduced complainers' capacity for self-direction within the courtroom and during the trial itself. The fiscal's role also, along with interference from town clerks and magistrates, restricted and, on occasion, stifled, the accused's capacity to advance a thorough legal defence. The courtroom might, in theory, have provided a legal forum in which the voices of defenders could be heard, but, in practice, the court's officials (magistrates, procurators, clerks and police officers) ensured that this would be limited to no more than a few sentences. Far from being centres of empowerment, the chapter contends that for large cohorts among the working classes police courts were places of humiliation – places where their accents and appearances were mocked and where courtroom officials and journalists reinforced their own middle-class social and cultural rules and expectations. These were places where language was

---

[22]   See, for instance, Drew D. Gray, *Crime, Prosecution and Social Relations in London: The Summary Courts of London in the Late Eighteenth Century* (Basingstoke, 2009).

[23]   See, for example, Pat Carlen, *Magistrates' Justice* (London, 1976).

a mechanism of power that determined how people were treated and how seriously they were listened to. Police courts were judicial arenas where communicative actions established and determined courtroom relations to the benefit of the educated, according to middle-class assumptions of knowledge, and to the detriment of those who were not.[24] For the most part, the police court environment reflected and developed the views of its middle-class personnel, including those of police officers, who, though of lower status, were expected to enforce the values of their superiors, even if their own moral conduct sometimes fell below what was expected of those in positions of authority and power.

The mainstream media – both the police periodicals and the established newspapers that reported on courtroom trials – and the public gallery were important interlocutors in the courtroom. As Chapter 3 concluded, while the press and the periodicals did not offer a single discourse in their coverage of the Scottish police courts, they certainly presented a dominant view. Thus, this chapter goes on to explore how journalists derived their view and delivered their message. It shows that they were able to present magisterial justice in a generally favourable light by reporting cases in which the reactions of the gallery were represented as being largely supportive of the judgements and punishments that were handed down from the bench. Indeed, rather than directly influencing courtroom proceedings, this chapter argues that the mainstream media was of particular significance in representing public opinion on courtroom justice as being just, fair and even-handed. As public attendance at police courts declined as the century went on, the printed media is likely to have become even more important in shaping readers' perceptions of crime and magisterial justice – and, significantly, in sending out social, moral and ideological messages about not just the workings of police courts, but also crime and criminals.

II. Procurators and Police

In an article entitled 'A Monday Morning at the Central Police Court', published in *The Detective* in 1885, the journalist captured the sombre and intimidating scene that confronted the accused as they entered the courtroom:

> Passing up a narrow stair through an iron gate at the top we found ourselves in
> a not very spacious building, lined round on every side by policemen. At the

---

[24] For more on language and discourse in the courtroom, see Anne Wagner and Le Cheng (eds), *Exploring Courtroom Discourse: The Language of Power and Control* (Farnham, 2011); and John Conley and William O'Barr, *Just Words: Law, Language and Power*, 2nd edn (Chicago, 1998). For more on the power of language in general, see Pierre Bourdieu, *Language and Symbolic Power*, ed. John Thompson (Cambridge, 1991); and Jürgen Habermas, *On the Pragmatics of Communication*, ed. Meave Cook (Cambridge, 1998).

back, on a raised platform, sits the magistrate. Below are grim, stately-looking gentlemen with black gowns thrown over their shoulders – limbs of the law, we presume – neatly-smoothed hair, and the inevitable glass eye.[25]

The 'limbs of the law', as *The Detective* put it, included the public prosecutor, the procurator fiscal. As Chapter 3 discussed, the police superintendent and his lieutenants often filled the role of fiscal for offences and contraventions and, in some cases, less serious crimes. Indeed, the police were so heavily involved in leading such prosecutions that in 1860, in his annual report, Colonel Kinloch, Her Majesty's Inspector of Constabulary for Scotland, claimed that the practice was a substantial drain on police resources. He lamented the fact that in Edinburgh

> the chief superintendent and his staff of officers, [and] the lieutenants … [were] so much engaged in the business of the Police Court, in which, during the last year, there have been some cases, protracted day after day, involving very nice points of law; and thus the usual and proper duties of a police 'office' are made second to those of the police 'court'.[26]

More serious criminal cases were generally prosecuted by the burgh fiscal – who, unlike police prosecutors, was legally trained.

In addition to being responsible for whether a person should be brought before magistrates, the fiscal – whether it be the superintendent of police or the burgh fiscal – played an important role in the courtroom itself. Whereas in early nineteenth-century England the victim would often lead the prosecution in court, in the Scottish police court the fiscal cast a long shadow over judicial proceedings and was significant in marginalising the victim's role within them. He examined and cross-examined witnesses, contextualised cases for magistrates and encouraged particular responses from them.[27] He was also integral to the terror and theatre of the court. Describing the role of the burgh fiscal, John Lang, in the Glasgow Central Police Court in 1875, *The Bailie* reported:

---

[25]   'A Monday Morning at the Central Police Court', *The Detective: or, A Journal for the Exposure and Suppression of Crime* (*The Detective*), no. 7, vol. I, 23 May 1885, pp. 1–2.

[26]   *Caledonian Mercury*, 5 July 1860.

[27]   For example, the *Aberdeen Weekly Journal* reported in July 1880 the case of 73-year-old Helen Bruce who appeared in the Aberdeen Police Court charged with breach of the peace. The case had already been twice adjourned because of Bruce's violent conduct in court, but the fiscal said that as the woman had been in custody since Sunday (it now being Wednesday) 'He fancied she was possessed with a temper which she really had no control over for the time, and he did not think it was dignified for them to waste time over her, or to be over-severe.' He recommended that they liberate her as she had been so long in prison, 'but it would be with this remark, that if she came up again and misbehaved in the same way, he would not adjourn the case from day to day, but from one week to another, till she should learn to control her temper a little better. That was what was done in certain Police Courts'.

Drop in of a forenoon, and watch the white-haired individual who acts as public prosecutor. Observe his stern, almost menacing cast of features. Note the keenness of his aspect – how he turns everybody, prisoners, witnesses, nay, even Assessors and Bailies, inside and out – how he flouts and jeers, and generally sits upon all who are opposed to him. The BAILIE, much as he dislikes illdoers, can hardly help pitying them when they come into the grasp of Mr LANG. His look, when he puts on his prosecuting face, sends a thrill through you in spite of yourself. His business is to convict; and convict he will.[28]

Even magistrates, according to the report, stood in awe of Lang: 'Many a time and often has the Magistrate trembled beneath the piercing glance and strident tongue of the fiscal.'[29]

As this quote highlights, it would be wrong to suggest that procurators always worked in harmony with magistrates. In the courtroom itself there were a number of occasions on which they clashed, usually centring on the unwillingness of magistrates to adhere to legal technicalities. Newspaper reports sometimes revealed tensions between the fiscal (both the burgh fiscal and the superintendent in his capacity as fiscal) and magistrate, particularly in terms of the degree of leniency to be applied. In a case that came before the Paisley Police Court in September 1835, Bailie Patison gave a young boy caught stealing fruit from a gentleman's backyard, his first offence, ten days' imprisonment. When Patison discovered that his sentence had not been carried out, he demanded in court that the fiscal, Mr Barr, Jnr, explain. Barr noted that he had explained the reasons privately, but that, if the magistrate insisted, he believed that to put the boy in prison would break his character and his spirit, wound the feelings of his parents and that it was a most irregular punishment for a first offence. In addition, there had been no written complaint from which the prosecution proceeded, so, he suggested, the matter could have been handled lightly to no one's complaint. The magistrate thanked him for his 'fine speech' but insisted that the punishment stood.

Significantly, Bailie Patison went on to note that he knew that it made a difference to the fiscal because if a prisoner went to gaol, it cost the prisoner 5s., but if only fined, Fiscal Barr would receive the money.[30] He continued: '"mind I do not say that this is your motive, mind I do not say that is the case with you, Mr Barr"; which, to the astonishment of the Court, was repeated three times over by the Magistrate.' Fiscal Barr indicated that he had consulted the Assessor to

---

[28]   *The Bailie*, no. 133, 5 May 1875, p. 1.
[29]   Ibid.
[30]   Lang later criticised the practice of allowing the fiscal to share in proceeds of fines. In 1860 he 'declared his view that the division of the fines should be changed, particularly insisting that it was not right that the Public Prosecutor be entitled to a share of the penalties'. 'Report by Her Majesty's Commissioners for Inquiring into the Licensing System and Sale and Consumption of Excisable Liquors in Scotland, with Minutes of Evidence', *British Parliamentary Papers* (*BPP*), 1860 (2684), XXXII.1, p. 334.

the Court, who shared his view that the sentence should not be carried out. The assessor, a different Mr Lang from the one referred to above, was duly sent for by the magistrate, and asked why he would not carry out the sentence. Mr Lang 'expressed his astonishment at such a question; it was not his duty to carry out the sentences of that Court into execution'. He continued that 'he would not submit to be spoken to in that manner' and then, when asked his opinion directly, said that he thought the sentence too severe for a first offence of that nature. Bailie Patison asked it to be recorded in the Police Court book that the assessor had refused to carry out his sentence, and Lang responded that 'there was no use in his coming there, when the present Magistrate was on the Bench, because he would neither hearken to his opinions nor the law as regarded the causes'. With this, Patison himself wrote it into the book and Lang asked him to add the reason – that he was not the executioner of sentences.

> The first Police case on the roll was then called, when Mr Lang remarked, that he did not think the Court in a fit state at present to proceed with the business. On this, Bailie Patison closed the book with a slap, seized his hat and left the Bench, saying, he supposed Bailie Hendry would dispose of all the cases on Monday.[31]

Such a case encapsulated the myriad tensions among the senior official personnel of the police court over their power to insist on their authority, the expertise on which their judgement was drawn, as well as the traits of masculinity which it called into question – between mercy, pride, authority and reasoned judgement.

In his memoirs, Samuel Rodger, former police officer in the Hillhead District of Glasgow in the late nineteenth century, alluded to these tensions. Referring to a case in which he was criticised by the Lord Provost for apprehending a German street musician for begging, he explained that he did so because 'the Provost often passes judgement on honest men who resort to begging because they are unable to find work'. The comment provoked the Provost's fury. He shouted to the Inspector, who had brought forward the prosecution, 'Is it possible Sir that you keep men in this force who dare to criticise anything I may think fit to say or do while presiding on the bench as a Magistrate?' After Rodger burst out laughing and pointed out the inconsistency with which begging laws were enforced by the police, the Provost, as recorded in Rodger's memoirs, stormed off, swearing to the Inspector that Rodger would 'be hanged yet as a murdering Socialist'.[32] The case highlighted not just how the law was often administered in a discretionary manner to the detriment of the poorest social groups and the protection of more

---

[31] *Caledonian Mercury*, 5 and 12 September 1835.

[32] 'The Secret Memoirs of Samuel Rodger (1846–1901) The Glasgow Teetotal Bobby', produced at the People's Palace Museum, Glasgow Green, to accompany the exhibition 'Scotland Sober and Free' marking the 150th anniversary of the temperance movement in Scotland, by kind permission of William Rodger, grandson of Samuel Rodger, p. 8.

affluent, but also the intimate, if at times, volatile relationship between magistrates, prosecutors and police officers.

For the most part, though, it appears that prosecutors and magistrates shared social and moral values, which often manifested themselves in derision of those in the dock. Press reports recorded the superintendent, who as chief of police brought prosecutions for offences and contraventions in the name of the fiscal, making throwaway jibes constituting public commentary on cases before magistrates. These applied primarily to the poorer Irish or female defenders in court, who could be, it seems, a source of amusement amongst senior court officials, with the fiscal and magistrate sometimes assuming the role of a patronising and condescending comedy double-act. In September 1831, *The Police Intelligencer* recorded a case before Bailie Morton of a poor woman accused of begging in the New Town of Edinburgh:

> Magistrate to the defender – 'Do you reside in Edinburgh?'
> Defender – 'I go to the country during the summer, and stay in the town in the winter.'
> Superintendant[33] – 'O, that's quite fashionable.'[34]

Despite the superintendent's flippant interjection, the accused was dismissed. In some instances, cynical comments about the accused's responses helped to frame the magistrate's view. In March 1832, John St George came before Bailie Anderson, charged with stealing a bottle basket:

> Superintendant (to St George) – 'You have a pension, have you not?'
> St George – 'I have only 9d a day.'
> Superintendant (ironically [*sic*]) – 'Only 9d that's not much. I suppose when you get your quarter's payment it will not last you long?'
> St George – 'I have a failing about me, when I sit down it will not last me many days; but I have seen it last me the quarter out!'
> Superintendant – 'That's a very rare occurrence.'
> Magistrate – 'You make the pension which is given you with a good intention a curse rather than a blessing. I am glad to learn that pensioners are going to be done away with altogether. I am sure it will put an end to many a drunken brawl.'[35]

---

[33]   Contemporary sources, especially up to the mid-nineteenth century, often used the term 'superintendant' not 'superintendent', reflecting the word's French origins. We have retained the original spelling of the term (superintendant) where it was recorded in quotes, but have used the modern spelling (superintendent) when we have referred to it ourselves.

[34]   *The Police Intelligencer, or Life in Edinburgh* (*Police Intelligencer*), 12 September 1831.

[35]   Ibid.

He was likewise dismissed.

In other cases, press reports suggest not only a form of physical or mental abuse within the Police Office, but also the capacity of the superintendent to provide information for the judge about the accused's previous behaviour that was not relevant or exhibited in the case at hand. In April 1832, before Bailie Crichton in Edinburgh, the Superintendent introduced the case of a woman charged with begging in the following manner:

> Superintendant (to the Magistrate) – 'This woman here takes at pleasure a fit of dumbness, the last time she was here, she could not speak a word!'
> Defender – 'I dinna denied, Sir!'
> Superintendant – 'I believe a few hours down stairs brought you to your senses, and made you to hear?'
> Defender – 'it did indeed, Sir!'
> Superintendant – 'Police Officers have a powerful effect upon dumb people.'[36]

In such reports, the superintendent often appeared harsh towards those he prosecuted, while the magistrate was represented as performing a moderating role that tempered the prosecutor's assessments of the court's accused.

Most frequently, however, reports of the Superintendent's jibes and social commentary suggested that they were directed towards a certain type of accused woman – women who, it seems, were considered beneath the protection of the court's personnel. Mary Martin and Margaret Campbell, for example, came before Bailie Anderson in Edinburgh on charges of rioting and fighting in the streets in August 1831. When Martin exclaimed, 'She ca'd me a black B__! and I cried craw, craw!' the superintendent responded, 'You are much more like a craw than her.'[37] Through his commentary, the superintendent implied that the dispute, whatever its origins, was not to be taken seriously and both were later dismissed by the magistrate. In November 1831, Bailie Aitchison heard the case of Rachel Stewart, charged with stealing. The court officials mocked her supposed vanity in what they imagined might be a persuasive argument to prevent further offences:

> Magistrate – 'If you do not take care of yourself you will lose your beautiful curls!'
> Superintendant – 'O sir, these curls are false; she has been in Bridewell!'
> Stewart – 'They are not false, it's my own hair.'

Both the judge and the superintendent openly made fun of Stewart's appearance, and implied a hidden reality of her guilt that, despite her appearance, they could detect. When her accuser failed to appear Stewart was dismissed, but what claims she had to a good reputation had been destroyed – in court and through the media

---

[36] *Police Intelligencer*, 17 April 1832.
[37] *Police Intelligencer*, 19 August 1831.

– nonetheless.[38] The shared social and moral values between prosecutors and magistrates were, therefore, often exhibited in different ways, with superintendents offering a more explicit reference to 'respectable' values than 'impartial' magistrates who determined the guilt of the accused.

Procurators might have been at the forefront in deciding whether or not to prosecute cases, but it was police officers who were responsible for bringing the accused before them in most instances. Officers exercised all the powers of the office of constable and were responsible for enforcing local police rules and taking cognisance of all acts of parliament in which duties were imposed upon the police. This involved not only enforcing the law on the streets, but also giving evidence in court. Their interactions with both the courtroom personnel (magistrate, fiscal and clerk) and its clients (complainer, accused and witnesses) responded to their position in the court's hierarchy of authority, subordinate to the magistrate and superintendent, but superior to the majority of defenders. Like procurators, they formed an intimidating presence. *The Detective*'s illustration of 'A Monday Morning at the Glasgow Police Court' portrayed officers as being as numerous as the accused standing in line waiting to be called to the dock, collectively forming a visible and less than welcoming presence of authority (see Illustration 4.1).[39] The policemen stood in direct opposition to the accused both in terms of their role in court and their sheer physical presence and demeanour. The policemen were tall, confident, arrogant, and well-turned out, everything the accused were not. Indeed, in many ways, the illustration was a powerful metaphor for courtroom dynamics, the imbalance in power that these dynamics produced, and the experience of the law of most of those accused.

In the early nineteenth century, there was a vigorous debate in Edinburgh as to whether proof of good police work was borne out by conviction rates. In 1823, for instance, the commissioners of police in Edinburgh discussed whether officers ought to be more clearly aware that they were rewarded on the basis of diligent work, not the success of the case in court.[40] Commissioner Ritchie argued:

> that the officers of the Establishment had no controul [*sic*] over cases after they were transmitted to other courts, nor were they responsible for any judgements pronounced even in the Police Court. If they did their duty in apprehending and watching offenders, and preparing evidence so far as was within their power, they were not to be blamed, whether prosecutions were instituted, or were successful or not.[41]

As the following chapter explores, the publication of criminal statistics from the mid-nineteenth century, however, helped to bring crime even more readily

---

[38] *Police Intelligencer*, 1 November 1831.
[39] 'A Monday Morning at the Central Police Court', pp. 1–2.
[40] *The Scotsman*, 18 January 1823.
[41] Ibid.

THE

Detective:

OR,

A JOURNAL FOR THE EXPOSURE AND SUPPRESSION OF CRIME.

No. 7, Vol. I.　　　　LONDON and GLASGOW, MAY 23, 1885.　　　　One Penny.

A MONDAY MORNING AT THE CENTRAL POLICE COURT.

Saturday night is the time for relaxation and enjoyment with most of the multitude, Sunday for repentance, and Monday morning for punishment. The majority of them are free after dinner-time to spend the evening as they choose, and it is cause for regret that the hundreds who are not over-particular as to their amusement (?) find themselves in the Police Court on Monday mornings.

In addition to these, there is always the usual complement of rogues and vagabonds who have been "run in;" some caught in the act of "nabbing," others simply because they were considered dangerous. The visitor to the "Central" on a Monday morning is always sure of having a varied programme set before him.

Passing up a narrow stair and through an iron gate at the top we found ourselves in a not very spacious building, lined round on every side by policemen. At the back, on a raised platform,

"Strange fish found in low-life deeps."

Sketches of a Bar in Saltmarket (Saturday Night), and the "Bar" at the Police Office (Monday Morning), with Portraits of Officers and the Chief Magistrate, The Lord Provost.

Illustration 4.1　　A Monday Morning at the Central Police Court, 1885.
By permission of University of Glasgow Library,
Special Collections†

Note: Notice the strong police presence, the magistrate on a raised platform on the right-hand side of the courtroom to convey his judicial authority, the somewhat dishevelled appearance of the accused, and the play on words and imagery symbolising the connection between the 'bar' of the police court and the 'bar' of the public house.

† 'A Monday Morning at the Central Police Court', *The Detective: or, A Journal for the Exposure and Suppression of Crime* (*The Detective*), no. 7, vol. I, 23 May 1885, pp. 1–2.

into the public eye, especially as they were recorded in the press. It made senior police officers more conscious of their officers' performance in court and the need to secure compelling evidence, as was made clear by the fact that police officers in Edinburgh patrolled in pairs as two witnesses were needed to secure a conviction.[42] Increasingly, securing convictions was a means by which policing efficiency and the masculinity of the police officer giving evidence were measured.[43] For superintendents, high conviction rates were proof that the police were winning the war on crime (see Chapter 6). For the rank and file, 'nailing an offender' in court was, along with physical prowess and stature, an important way in which a police officer's authority to control and govern the beats he patrolled was assessed.[44]

As Chapter 2 observed, in Edinburgh there were concerns from some in civic and judicial circles about the reliability of police officers' evidence and the neutrality of the law in the early nineteenth century.[45] The 1812 report of the committee in Edinburgh which reviewed the policing of the city reiterated concerns that allocating half of the fines levied in the police court 'gave the officers an interest in the conviction of offenders, and thereby tended to disqualify them as witnesses, and to render the public doubtful of the real motive of their proceedings

---

[42]   In 1846, a police report recommended that this be discontinued as it is 'injurious, by reducing the strength of the day force, and by tending to foment a jealous feeling of interference on the part of the police against the public, from whom they should be taught to *look* for support, and on whom they should always feel disposed to rely for assistance when required'. Edinburgh Central Library (ECL): *Report of the Special Committee appointed by the Board of Police, to Inquire into the Moral and Physical Character of the Watching Force, July 1846* (Edinburgh, 1846), pp. 20–21.

[43]   For more on the relationship between police and masculinity in Scotland, see David G. Barrie and Susan Broomhall, 'Policing Bodies in Urban Scotland, 1780–1850', in Susan Broomhall and Jacqueline Van Gent (eds), *Governing Masculinities: Regulating Selves and Others in the Early Modern Period* (Farnham, 2011), pp. 263–82; Susan Broomhall and David G. Barrie, 'Changing of the Guard: Policing, Masculinity and Class in the Porteous Affair and Walter Scott's *Heart of Midlothian*,' *Parergon: Journal of the Australian and New Zealand Association for Medieval and Early Modern Studies*, 28/1 (2011): pp. 65–90; and Susan Broomhall and David G. Barrie, 'Making Men: Media, Magistrates and the Representation of Masculinity in Scottish Police Courts, 1800–1835', in David G. Barrie and Susan Broomhall (eds), *A History of Police and Masculinities, 1700–2010* (London, 2012), pp. 72–101.

[44]   Clive Emsley, *The English and Violence since 1750* (London, 2005), p. 135.

[45]   ECL: *CIVIS, A Letter to the Right Hon. Henry Erskine, Lord Advocate of Scotland, relative to the Act of Parliament for regulating the Police of Edinburgh* (Edinburgh, 1806), p. 17. This practice was strongly criticised by many in legal circles as 'it is a temptation to perjury on the part of the officers, as upon their evidence many of the decisions depend, and of course a reward is held out to find the prisoners guilty'. Commissioners defended this in principle but said that the funds should be distributed to reflect officer performance. See also ECL: *Reports of the Committee of Commissioners of Police and Minutes of General Meetings Thereto* (Edinburgh, 1807), p. 14.

on all occasions'.[46] Indeed, the concern expressed by justices in the High Court in 1825 that the police in Edinburgh were in the habit of giving evidence in the local police court when not under oath implied that the evidence might not have been impartial.[47] The accused were equally alert to the possibility of collusion between the official personnel of the court against their own interests. In August 1831, one woman accused of assaulting police officer Francis McGarrgal had no compunction in offering the Edinburgh Police Court's Bailie Anderson her view of his reliability: 'Oh, dear, don't believe him – sure, now, you would not believe any thing that a Policeman says.' Such commentary, especially from a migrant woman, was met unsympathetically by the magistrate who replied 'Hold your tongue: I want none of your advice, I am inclined to think by your conduct that you are a very bad character.' The Irishwoman was confined for 20 days after a second witness confirmed the officer's testimony.[48]

As the century progressed, magistrates appear to have attached greater weight to the witness testimonies of policemen rather than those of members of the public.[49] Writing in 1811, John Burnett, in *A Treatise on Various Branches of the Criminal Law of Scotland*, claimed that in criminal trials greater significance was given to the evidence of neighbours concerning the character of defenders than the evidence of police officers.[50] This was, in all likelihood, linked to the fact that the concept of employing full-time, salaried police officers was fairly new and the men who performed this work had little social standing.[51] However, by the 1830s, it was more widely recognised that policemen were an integral component of the criminal justice system. In 1838, Lord Meadowbank resolved that to prove an aggravation on which he was passing judgement it was enough that 'two officers depone that the prisoner is a habitual and reputed thief, even if they themselves do not think the repute well-founded'.[52] In 1869, a letter signed 'One of the Public' to the editor of *The Dundee Courier & Argus* complained that the odds were stacked against the accused because of the police's involvement in bringing forward prosecutions:

> The Police Court is an anomaly in many respects. There is a general feeling that as the trials are managed at present, to be accused is only another name for being condemned. A policeman apprehends a man on the ground that he is committing an offence or breach of the peace, or of being drunk. A complaint is written out

---

[46] *Caledonian Mercury*, 4 April 1812.

[47] *Caledonian Mercury*, 19 May 1825.

[48] *Police Intelligencer*, 22 August 1831.

[49] Lindsay Farmer, *Criminal Law, Tradition and Legal Order: Crime and the Genius of Scots Law, 1747 to the Present* (Cambridge, 1997), p. 119.

[50] John Burnett, *A Treatise on Various Branches of the Criminal Law of Scotland* (Edinburgh, 1811), p. 131.

[51] Barrie and Broomhall, 'Policing Bodies in Urban Scotland, 1780–1850,' pp. 263–82.

[52] Cited in Farmer, *Criminal Law, Tradition and Legal Order*, p. 119.

in mere form by the superior police officers in name of the Superintendant, and the man is tried next morning before the Police Court, and the witnesses against him are the police officers who report the case. The policemen will, of course, support their own actings. To be accused in this Court is therefore in most cases to be condemned. There ought to be some impartial hand as Fiscal or prosecutor to consider policemen's reports, and to distinguish as to the propriety of raising the prosecutions.[53]

This is not to say that magistrates accepted at face value police evidence on every occasion and could be guaranteed to convict on the basis of it. As the century progressed, the police were likely to have become more skilled at giving evidence in court given the determination of commissioners to employ more literate officers, and those who were deemed to have presented unsatisfactory evidence were given short shrift by the media and the magistrate. In 1873, *The Bailie*, in an article entitled 'Scene in a Police Court', reported the following exchange between 'Policeman X 45' in the witness box and the magistrate:

> BAILIE – What is the next case?
> ASSESSOR – Betty Forger – uttering base coin, as also previous conviction.
> *Policeman X 45 –* Ay, and worse than that – uttering base language.
> *Court Officer –* Wheesht, Tugal; you'r no to spoke yet.
> (The witness having been sworn, the case was proceeded with.)
> BAILIE – What is your name?
> *Witness –* Tugal M'Tonalt, son of Shon M'Tonalt, Mull.
> BAILIE – Well, Dugald, let the Court hear what you know about this case.
> *Witness –* Well, you know, Tonalt M'Tugal is on the next wi' me; and we was both cried in to the whisky shop, where she was 'kicking up a row.'
> BAILIE – Was she inebriated?
> *Witness –* No; she was drunk, I think.
> BAILIE – What was the cause of the disturbance?
> *Witness –* She was only for pay a sixpence for a big gill, and she no take a wee one, and the sixpence was a bad one.
> BAILIE – What did you say to her, then?
> *Witness –* I said she was a bad sixpence, and wouldna be taken for a big gill.
> BAILIE – Did you tell her it was counterfeit?
> *Witness – No; I just said it was a bad sixpence.*
> BAILIE – You said this to the prisoner at the Bar?
> *Witness – No; I said it to her at the counter.*
> BAILIE – Then what did she say or do?
> *Witness –* She swear and kick and curse us all, and break a bit of the counter.
> BAILIE – Then, I suppose you took her into custody?
> *Witness –* No; we took her to the Central [police office].

---

[53]   *The Dundee Courier & Argus*, 4 January 1869.

BAILIE – I suppose you can swear to the identity of the panel [defender] at the bar?

Witness – Yes, yes; for she broke it all to pieces.

BAILIE – Broke what to pieces?

Witness – The 'panel,' to be sure –

BAILIE – I have just one other question to ask you, and that is this – Do you think the panel is *compos mentis?*

Witness – No; I sink its mahogany.

BAILIE – You may go. Call the next witness.[54]

Indeed, highlighting the 'ignorance' of the highlanders who made up a significant proportion of the rank and file of the Glasgow Police Force was a common theme of *The Bailie* in the late Victorian period.[55] Similarly, in an article published in *The Detective* in 1885, it was reported that a man charged with drunk and disorderly conduct was found not proven on account of conflicting evidence presented by a policeman making his first appearance in court. The journalist wrote: 'Of course, he is a new hand, and beyond a few hints nothing is said of his stupidness.'[56] His error in presenting evidence, in terms of how it was reported, indicates that this was a rare occurrence and one he was unlikely to repeat.

The police court also provided a place in which the qualities and status of police officers were publicly tested. It offered an opportunity for them to assert their moral and social claim to be superior to many of the accused who came from similar working-class backgrounds, but the visibility of their work in and out of the court left it open to examination by the very system from which they derived their authority among the ranks of governing men. That authority could be undermined both by the claims of those accused, but also by the senior officials who measured their own status by distance from the behaviour of the subordinate personnel. In August 1831, for example, one defender refuted the evidence of the police officer, saying to him 'I don't care what you say, a glass of whisky will turn your noddle at any time!' The superintendent replied jokingly, 'You were wrong in not giving him a glass last night; it would have saved you considerably!' and the defender responded 'Aye! That would have made all right!'[57] Although the defender was fined, damage was also done to the reputation of the police officer by the accusations of the defender and the implied acceptance of the claim by his senior officer. The latter's actions undercut the authority that police officers could achieve through their contribution as official participants, supportive of middle-class values and status, in the police court.

---

[54] *The Bailie*, no. 30, 14 May 1873, p. 2.

[55] See, for example, *The Bailie*, no. 9, 11 December 1872, pp. 1–2 and no. 19, 26 February 1873, pp. 1–2.

[56] 'A Monday Morning at the Central Police Court', p. 2.

[57] *Police Intelligencer*, 20 August 1831.

Magistrates were especially critical of officer misconduct in the courtroom itself. Police officers had a physical role to play in court, acting as ushers by accompanying and sometimes restraining those who came before the bench. However, they were still expected to behave in a manner in keeping with a man of authority. In the 1835 courtroom argument between Bailie Patison, on the one hand, and Fiscal Barr and Assessor Lang on the other, the sergeant of police was chastised by Lang for his rough manhandling of a bystander who had attempted to enter the judicial arena. Lang remarked in a rather unsubtle rebuke of Patison's ability to keep order in the court, that 'such proceedings surpassed any thing he had ever witnessed. There was open violence committed in a Court of Justice, without ever being noticed by the Magistrate on the Bench'. The sergeant insisted that his action had been intended to protect Lang, but the latter suggested that he could have done so in another manner. 'Here Sergeant Russell justified his conduct with great warmth, and, striking the table with his fist, said, if he was to be interfered with in the discharge of his duty, he would certainly resign his office.'[58] In this interaction, Lang had commented on the weak masculine behaviour of both the magistrate (who could not keep order in his house) and of the sergeant (who could not contain his physical force). Indeed, the sergeant's impassioned and physical response only served to demarcate him as being unlike those senior court officials whose superior quality of calm rationality and mercy were implicitly favoured by the press. The case suggests that within the courtroom the police officer's *potential* physicality placed him as implicitly inferior in authority to the theoretically sober and restrained magistrate, assessor and fiscal.

Although magistrates, procurators and police officers did not always work together, their relationship was much more intimate than has been suggested in other studies of major English and American cities.[59] Where civic magistrates and police clashed, it was often over issues concerning each other's status and authority or the level of punishment or fine to be imposed rather than concern about the role of magistrates in the courtroom or the rights of those before them.[60] The actual workings of the courtroom suggest that magistrates and procurators enjoyed, with the exception of a few isolated cases, a complementary relationship. As Chapter 6 shows, conviction rates for a wide range of offences and contraventions that made it to trial were at over 90 per cent for much of the century – with magistrates and procurators often offering little opportunity to the accused for an effective defence. Magistrates and superintendents relied on officers not only to protect them physically, but also to support their authority as models of middle-class masculine ideals in

---

[58]   *Caledonian Mercury*, 5 September 1835.

[59]   Jennifer S. Davis, 'A Poor Man's System of Justice? The London Police Courts in the Second Half of the Nineteenth Century', *Historical Journal*, 27/2 (1984): pp. 328–9; and Wilbur Miller, *Cops and Bobbies: Police Authority in New York and London, 1830–1870* (Chicago, 1977), pp. 74–103.

[60]   This is explored at various stages throughout both volumes.

word and deed. These men of inferior status served to buttress the position of more senior personnel as moral, social and legal experts worthy of respect. It was in many ways a mutually beneficial relationship for, in return, the social status of police officers was improved by the accreditation of their voices and actions by more senior officials.

III. The Accused and Legal Representation

In 1829, the Glasgow *Police Reports* began with the following reflection on the daily diet of accused dealt with by the city's central police court:

> On Thursday, among others of all ages, classes and conditions, from the merchants' clerk down to the parochial pauper, brought before the Magistrates, on the casual charges of being drunk and disorderly, was a naughty young fellow, evidently either a waiter's supernumerary, a barber's substitute, or a tailor's deputy, (at least if we might judge from the cut of his costume,) charged with the same joint offences in the Gallowgate on Wednesday evening.[61]

As this extract suggests, men and women from a wide spectrum of society were charged in police courts. Indeed, police officers were not the only 'civic guardians' to find themselves charged with an offence; magistrates and senior justice officials were too. In 1805, Fraser McKay, vintner, and several other proprietors of houses on Grassmarket took out a private complaint against the Lord Provost, magistrates and treasurer of Edinburgh for erecting sheep bughts (enclosures) on the nearby streets to the annoyance of proprietors.[62] The case was dismissed. In the same year, magistrates in the Edinburgh Police Court fined the Rt. Hon. Henry Erskine (then Lord Advocate of Scotland) 5s. and 2s., 5d. in expenses for allowing his home chimney vent to go on fire.[63] The following year his son, also named Henry Erskine, and two others were fined £2 and required to pay 2s., 6d. in expenses for breach of the peace and kicking Sergeant Robertson.[64] Moreover, local court records for the early nineteenth century show that it was not uncommon for property holders, especially small shopkeepers, to be prosecuted for contravening local police laws relating to paving, nuisances and obstructions.[65] In early nineteenth-century Scottish towns, keeping the streets clear was not simply about 'moving on' and 'breaking up' popular pastimes,

---

[61] *Police Reports of Causes tried before the Justices of Peace, and the Glasgow, Gorbals and Calton Police Courts* (*Police Reports*), 12 September 1829, p. 101.

[62] Edinburgh City Archives (ECA) ED006/8: Edinburgh Police Court Abstract of Processes, 1805–1807, no. 1,025, pp. 34–5.

[63] Ibid., 6 December 1805, no. 1,088.

[64] Ibid., 1 February 1806, no. 1,559.

[65] Ibid., passim.

culture and congregations; it was also about ensuring that the cityscape was constructed in a manner that was conducive to trade and commerce, as Chapter 3 of Volume 2 explores further.

Such cases should caution against viewing police courts as being simply a one-sided class instrument, but, equally, they should not detract from the bigger picture. These were unrepresentative of the bulk of police court business. When the middle classes were summonsed to the courtroom it tended to be for contraventions of local bye-laws – a fact illustrated in 1870 by the recommendation of senior police and legal officials to the 'Fourth Report of Law Commissioners' to have separate police courts rolls for crimes, offences and contraventions to ensure that 'respectable' people accused of breaches of local bye-laws would not have to spend time in the same courtroom as those charged with criminal or drunken offences, prostitution and vagrancy.[66] McGowan, in surveying the Edinburgh Police Court records between 1805 and 1807, concluded that the working classes were vastly overrepresented as defenders relative to population, especially for minor common law crimes.[67] Unfortunately, the annual returns of crimes, offences and contraventions published by the police from the mid-nineteenth century did not include the occupations of those brought before magistrates. But the 1880 Edinburgh returns – which were as typical as any other year sampled – reveal that more than half of those arrested for crimes were unemployed.[68] Almost half of the apprehensions (for both crimes and offences) were made in the poor ward of St Giles – just one of 13 police wards in the city – which was far in excess of its population relative to the city as a whole. The fewest arrests were in the affluent ward of St Stephen's, indicating how the police's resources were clearly directed primarily at one section of the community.[69] The Edinburgh police returns for that year note that 'of the 10,135 Arrests only 225 persons could be said to have had the advantage of a good education. 1,267 could neither read nor write, while 8,643 could read only, or read and write imperfectly'.[70] Goldsmith's research for

---

[66]   'Fourth Report of the Commissioners Appointed to Inquire into the Courts of Law in Scotland', *BPP*, 1870 (C–175), XVIII.455, p. 39.

[67]   John McGowan, *Policing the Metropolis of Scotland: A History of the Police and Systems of Police in Edinburgh and Edinburghshire, 1770–1833* (Musselburgh, 2010), p. 140.

[68]   Out of those convicted, 725 were employed (194 female and 531 male) and 734 were unemployed (521 male and 214 female). ECL: *Return of Crimes and Offences Reported, Persons Apprehended and Cited, and Miscellaneous Returns Connected with the Police, for the Year Ending 31st December 1880* (Edinburgh, 1881), Table 4.

[69]   Ibid., Table 7.

[70]   Ibid., p. 1. Similarly, of the 168 boys and girls under 16 who were convicted of crime in 1859, only four could read and write well, while 112 could not write, and 44 could neither read nor write. Of the 782 criminals above 16 years of age, only 85 could read and write well, while 303 could not write, and 104 could neither read nor write. ECL: *Reports and Returns as to Crimes, Offences, and Contraventions, and to Cases of Drunkenness, within the Police Bounds of the City of Edinburgh during the last Six Years. Prepared*

Glasgow suggests that 75 per cent of those in custody in the first half of the century had some degree of literacy,[71] but the level is likely to have been extremely basic. Of the 3,155 of those charged with more aggravated offences in Glasgow in 1871, 877 could neither read nor write and 833 could read only.[72] As in Edinburgh, the overwhelming majority of those brought before magistrates in Glasgow for crimes and offences were drawn from the unemployed, the socially disadvantaged, the unskilled and, to a lesser extent, skilled working classes.[73] Indeed, many of those charged with theft were likely to have owed their appearance in court directly to poverty, such as Mary Gray, who appeared before the Edinburgh Police Court in 1832 and 'who had in her arms a half starved and naked infant'.[74] Many others owed it to the excesses of alcohol and abusive behaviour. *The Bailie*, in 1873, described the type of person charged in the following sombre and miserable terms: 'The raggit weans, the midnicht roysterers, /The drunken cairters, an' the cabbies fou,/ The tramway gairds, the errin' publicans, Wife-beatin' fiends, an' a' the pilferin' crew-'.[75]

For the accused, police courts could be an extremely intimidating environment – especially for young, first offenders. In 1829, the Glasgow *Police Reports* published a case involving a father named Drummond, a city porter, who had his daughter charged with being drunk and disorderly. According to the periodical, 'she became so nervous and anxious before the magistrate, that she had to be taken away'. The case was a good example not just of how harrowing appearing in court could be, but also how families used the courts to discipline relatives, and how magistrates were often reluctant to interfere in domestic affairs.[76] The experience could be equally traumatic for young men. In 1885, *The Detective* reported a case involving a young man who had been held in a police cell from Saturday night until Monday morning, charged with 'assaulting a policeman', 'breaking a lamp' and generally 'enjoying himself' – which, in itself, was almost tantamount to an 'offence' in the eyes of some dour, tee-totalling justices who sat on the Glasgow bench in the late nineteenth century.[77] *The Detective* lamented: 'It is not a pleasant

---

for the Magistrates and Council, by Thomas Linton, Superintendent of Police (Edinburgh, 1860), p. 11.

[71] Alastair Goldsmith, 'The Development of the City of Glasgow Police 1800–1939', unpub. PhD thesis (University of Strathclyde, 2002), p. 195.

[72] Mitchell Library (ML): *City of Glasgow Police Criminal Returns for the Year Ending 31st December 1871* (Glasgow, 1872), p. 23.

[73] According to Sheriff Alison, 'It is from the lowest class that nine tenths of the crime and nearly all professional crime, which is felt so great an evil, flows.' Quoted in W.W.J. Knox and A. McKinlay, 'Crime, Protest and Policing in Nineteenth-Century Scotland', in Trevor Griffiths and Graeme Morton (eds), *A History of Everyday Life in Scotland, 1800 to 1900* (Edinburgh, 2010), p. 203.

[74] *Police Intelligencer*, 13 April 1832.

[75] 'The Stipendiary Magistrate', *The Bailie*, no. 27, 23 April 1873, p. 2.

[76] *Police Reports*, 25 July 1829, p. 20.

[77] 'A Monday Morning at the Central Police Court', p. 2.

sight, those young fellows, trembling and confused, standing at the bar in charge of a policeman.' On pleading guilty, the young man received 'the frightful[ly] too-strong for the occasion sentence' of 10s., 6d. fine, or seven days' imprisonment, before being 'hustled out of the court by the aforesaid policeman'.[78]

A substantial proportion of the court's accused were recidivists. Of the 1,470 persons convicted of crimes in Edinburgh in 1880, only slightly more than one third (546) were categorised in the annual police returns as being of 'previously good' character. The remainder were listed as 'known thieves' (394), 'suspected persons' (306), 'prostitutes' (66), 'habitual drunkards' (50), 'vagrants' (5), and 'unknown' (103).[79] The overwhelming majority were accused of minor property crimes. Those charged with offences – mainly drunk and disorderly, assault and breach of the peace – were more likely to be first offenders than those charged with crimes. Of the 8,605 persons charged with offences in the same year, just under half were categorised as being of 'previously good' character (4,179) and 1,002 were 'unknown'. The remainder were known to the police in some form.[80]

Some defenders were thus experienced, if not with the legal specificities of summary justice, at least with the dynamics of the courtroom. Indeed, the mainstream media gave the impression that recidivists manipulated the law for their own ends, in the process helping the reader to form judgements about their character. There were a number of well-publicised cases of offenders answering back to magistrates, which gave an impression that the accused were equal interlocutors with capacity to speak and defend their actions. For example, in the case of Higgins and Murphy, two previously convicted thieves brought before the Dundee Police Court in 1886, *The Dundee Courier & Argus* described the defenders as making 'no secret of their intimate acquaintances with Police Court procedure and, indeed, one of them wished to dictate to the Bailie the course that he must take in dealing with them'. Although this resulted in the bailie giving them the maximum punishment, the journalist concluded mockingly: 'Clearly the body of gentlemen known as "the Great Unpaid" have in Dundee men of great dignity and force of character among them.'[81] Moreover, the press sometimes reported cases of court personnel alluding to the knowledge they assumed that offenders possessed of the law, thereby making punishments appear just and fair. In 1871, the *Glasgow Herald* reported the case of James Fisher, charged in Glasgow's Central Police Court with harbouring thieves and prostitutes under the newly enforced Glasgow Police Act in 1870, which cracked down on prostitutes and brothel-keepers. He denied knowledge of the new act's provisions. The assessor retorted, however: 'you are supposed to know it, and I have always found that

---

[78]   Ibid.

[79]   ECL, *Return of Crimes and Offences Reported, Persons Apprehended and Cited, and Miscellaneous Returns Connected with the Police, for the Year Ending 31st December 1880*, Table 4.

[80]   Ibid.

[81]   *The Dundee Courier & Argus*, 15 June 1886.

people of your profession are pretty well up in the law affecting yourselves; you are careful of that.'[82] Fisher's case being found proven, Bailie Walls fined him £10 or 2 months' imprisonment.

Such a view of the 'cunning criminal', operating deftly within the court in order to achieve the best outcome, justified propositions for harsher punitive regimes (see Chapter 7). However, although it was in the interests of the accused, particularly those frequently charged, to become familiar with a system that was so significant in determining their fate, it seems unlikely that the majority of defenders had a sufficient degree of expertise to argue a sophisticated defence. Indeed, it is clear also from some media reports that some of those who brought forward cases, or were brought forward themselves, were unaware of the remit of the police court and its powers of justice. For example, in September 1831, the young wife of a lace weaver sought the assistance of the Edinburgh Police Court to obtain a separation from her husband due to his allegedly abusive conduct.[83] *The Police Intelligencer*, in reporting the case, portrayed Bailie Morton as sympathetic, but informed her 'that the Police Court was not competent to give her redress by separation; but should the charge be proved, he would be bound under a heavy penalty to keep the peace towards her'. When the case had been heard, Morton indeed insisted that the husband provide a substantial £10 caution.

Critical as well as common to the experience of the court for most of the accused was a lack of legal knowledge or representation. Whereas defenders in the Scottish high courts had access to free legal representation, those in the summary courts did not. Indeed, publicly-funded access to defence lawyers in Scottish burgh summary courts was not introduced until the late twentieth century.[84] Financial constraints played an important role in this, but it is also possible that civic men viewed the introduction of legal defence aid as a threat to their ability to administer justice based on their interpretation of common-sense judgement, community sentiment and local knowledge. As studies for eighteenth-century England have shown, the introduction of defence lawyers helped to formalise judicial proceedings to the detriment of informal customs and practices that had hitherto characterised the

---

[82]   *Glasgow Herald*, 13 November 1871.

[83]   *Police Intelligencer*, 23 September 1831.

[84]   In Scotland, the accused had the right to legal representation from 1587 although he or she had to pay for it themselves. In 1672, the Faculty of Advocates agreed to provide free representation in the High Court for accused individuals in indigent circumstances. In 1825, a system known as a poor's roll was established which gave such persons the right to be represented free of charge by a solicitor in the sheriff court, although no time was given for detailed investigation and preparation of the defence case prior to the trial. This was addressed in 1964 with the introduction of free legal aid. Albert V. Sheehan and David J. Dickson, *Criminal Procedure: Scottish Criminal Law and Practice Series*, 2nd edn (London, 2003), p. 35. However, according to Bankowski, Hutton and McManus, it was not until the introduction of the duty solicitor and the expansion in legal aid in 1975 that it became common for the accused to acquire legal representation. Bankowski, Hutton and McManus, *Lay Justice?*, p. 154.

criminal trial.[85] Moreover, as with the early modern trial in England, courtroom proceedings were structured to force defenders to speak and exculpate themselves,[86] and few defenders in the nineteenth century had the financial means to pay for legal support themselves. The evidence presented to the 1839–1840 Law Inquiry reveals that only a very small number of those charged had the services of a lawyer.[87] As Gabriel Miller, Clerk of the Police Court of Dundee, stated 'It seldom happens that persons accused avail themselves of professional assistance. This does not occur above three or four times in a year.'[88] Even those who could afford to pay for legal representation rarely did. As William Davie, Assessor of the Burgh Police Courts of Glasgow, observed: 'In very few cases the prisoners avail themselves of professional assistance, even when they can afford to pay for it – perhaps not in more than one case in a week.'[89] Perhaps many calculated that the costs of a fine were still less than a lawyer's fees. In the overwhelming majority of cases the accused either did not cross-examine prosecuting witnesses or were compelled to do so on their own without any real understanding of the law or appreciation of legal process.[90] Given their likely lack of legal knowledge of how the court system operated, it is also possible that some did not understand what benefits the assistance of a lawyer could provide. Others may have chosen to represent themselves. For some, it is possible that they understood the court as similar to a kirk session, in which they answered for their moral misdemeanours individually and personally with promises of redemption. Certainly, some offered little defence for their offence other than weakness of character. In August 1831, for instance, a husband and wife appeared in Edinburgh Police Court before Bailie Anderson, charged with drunk and disorderly conduct in the Cowgate. As *The Police Intelligencer* indulgently reported, the wife proceeded to explain her view on her husband's weakness to the magistrate: 'Me deer honey, you have no deception what a puir silly idiot this man of mine is when he gets a drop o' the crater.' Bailie Anderson ordered the man to give caution and his wife was dismissed.[91]

The absence of defence counsel had significant implications for the legal rights of the accused and the manner in which magistrates administered justice.

---

[85]   David Lemmings, 'Criminal Trial Procedure in Eighteenth-Century England: The Impact of Lawyers', *Journal of Legal History*, 26/1 (2005): pp. 73–82; and Malcolm Gaskill, *Crime and Mentalities in Early Modern England* (Cambridge, 2000), ch. 7, esp. pp. 269–70, 273–5 & 279.

[86]   Langbein, *The Origins of Adversary Criminal Trial*, pp. 20–21, 35–6, & 48–61.

[87]   The accused could request that trials be suspended so that legal representation could be sought, but most could not afford the lawyer or the loss of another day's pay. Thomas Trotter, *Summary Criminal Jurisdiction: According to the Law of Scotland* (Edinburgh, 1936), p. 221.

[88]   'Fourth Report by Her Majesty's Law Commissioners, Scotland, 1839', *BPP*, 1840 (241), XX.115, p. 334.

[89]   Ibid., p. 321.

[90]   Ibid., p. 334.

[91]   *Police Intelligencer*, 20 August 1831.

In the late eighteenth century the increasing use of defence lawyers in high court criminal trials in England allowed the accused to test and challenge more effectively the case for the prosecution and improved their chances of acquittal.[92] Indeed, it has been argued that the success of defence counsels in procuring acquittals in such trials was one reason behind the rise of summary justice.[93] In 1844, the *Caledonian Mercury* published a letter to the editor, concerning the case of William McLean and Alexander Dempster, servants in a baker's shop, which alluded to the impact that no legal representation had on the case (the accused were convicted of fraud and imposition, after a complaint from a customer who claimed that they charged the same price for both bread and coarse loaf). It noted:

> so little were they apprehensive of the accusation, and conscious of their own innocence, that they employed no agent, and took no means of vindicating their characters in the Police Court, which their confusion and inexperience rendered them unable to do for themselves, and on the evidence above-mentioned they were subjected to punishment, and their families plunged into the deepest distress.[94]

As this extract suggests, the absence of defence counsel is likely to have made it easier for procurators to secure convictions. The media acknowledged, too, the disadvantages the accused faced in police courts – a point that was also made by Bankowski, Hutton and McManus in their investigation into lay justices in the Scottish district courts in the 1980s.[95] In 1872, *The Bailie* outlined the invaluable role that legal representation could play in the police court and the importance of theatrical performance and media representation within it. Describing John Lang's role in court as a defence lawyer prior to working in the town clerk/fiscal's office, it reported:

> He could bully the Magistrate, overawe X24, and treat with contempt even the tremendous functionary – a police superintendent. In five minutes he would reduce a Highland constable, in the witness-box to such a state of mental bewilderment, that the luckless Argyllshireman could not tell "her richt han'

---

[92]   Langbein, *The Origins of Adversary Criminal Trial*, esp. pp. 113–27; Beattie, *Crime and the Courts*, pp. 356–7; J.M. Beattie, 'Scales of Justice: Defense Counsel and the English Criminal Trial in the Eighteenth and Nineteenth Centuries', *Law and History Review*, 9/2 (1991): pp. 226–8; John H. Langbein, 'The Criminal Trial before the Lawyers', *The University of Chicago Law Review*, 45/2 (1978): pp. 311–14; and Lemmings, 'Criminal Trial Procedure in Eighteenth-Century England', pp. 73–82.

[93]   Bruce P. Smith, 'The Presumption of Guilt and the English Law of Theft, 1750–1850', *Law and History Review*, 23/1 (2005): pp. 133–72.

[94]   *Caledonian Mercury*, 25 January 1844.

[95]   Bankowski, Hutton and McManus, *Lay Justice?*, p. 52.

frae her left." This tormentor of the Courts was a favourite with the reporters –
perhaps he rather cultivated the acquaintance of these useful scribes – for he was
invariably obliging, and his cases were generally so conducted as to be really
amusing.[96]

Without legal representation, the accused had to choose between questioning
and cross-examining witnesses themselves, or leaving this to magistrates, the
clerk or the assessor to carry out on their behalf.[97] Many of those reported in
the press adopted the latter position, which, in many ways, was understandable
given their lack of basic legal skills and anxiety about speaking out in a public
arena under the preying gaze of the media and the public gallery. But this had
significant implications for the quality of the defence that the accused received,
because magistrates, clerks and assessors were not versed with the intricacies
of their case, and were not in court to act as defence lawyers. The chances of
acquittal were weakened further by the fact that the accused were often up against
a legally trained prosecutor in the burgh fiscal, or a senior police official who had
the support of the fiscal's office behind him.

Those who chose to carry out their own defence faced other difficulties. The
accused had no right to compel witnesses to offer testimonies in court – only
magistrates could do this – and there were, as the next section discusses, often
difficulties in getting witnesses to appear in court. Having spent the night in police
custody, many were tired, hung-over and hungry when brought before the bench
and not in a fit condition to represent themselves effectively. The fact that many
reeked of alcohol from the excesses of the night before would have done much
to alienate those magistrates who were tee-totaller – and further re-affirmed the
latter's belief of the link between the alcohol, crime and immorality.[98] Moreover,
the capacity of defenders to advance an effective defence to a large extent rested
on how well they could articulate an argument. Not only were the overwhelming
majority insufficiently skilled in either the rules of evidence and procedure or
the technique of cross-examination to produce an effective defence, they were
often not given sufficient opportunity to do so by magistrates and procurators.
Proceedings might have been structured to force the accused to defend themselves,
but in practice they were often given only a limited opportunity to do so. The
fiscal, in particular, helped to stifle and mute the views of those before the
bench – reflecting developments in eighteenth-century criminal trials following
the introduction of lawyers in the courtroom.[99] Police court cases were often
extremely short – typically not longer than 15 or 20 minutes for the more serious
criminal charges; considerably less for offences and contraventions. It was not

---

[96]   *The Bailie*, no. 9, 11 December 1872, pp. 1–2.

[97]   'Fourth Report by Her Majesty's Law Commissioners, Scotland, 1839', pp. 321
& 327.

[98]   See Chapter 5 for more.

[99]   Lemmings, 'Criminal Trial Procedure in Eighteenth-Century England'.

uncommon, at least in media coverage, for magistrates and procurators to ask the accused just a handful of questions, and sometimes just one or two.[100] In 1885, for instance, a young man – described by *The Detective* as 'a full blown specimen of the Glasgow rough' – was charged with being in possession of stolen goods. The magistrate asked where he got them and for how long he had been out of gaol. On being told that he bought the goods from a man in the street and that he had been out of gaol for just three days, the magistrate found him guilty, deeming the evidence 'sufficient'.[101] The accused was imprisoned for another 60 days. Police courts would typically meet at 10am each working day and would sit for three to four hours. With busy caseloads to get through, magistrates simply did not have the time to carefully consider every case. As has been pointed out by Beattie, this had significant implications for the legal rights of the accused, as quick trials offered considerable advantages to prosecutors.[102]

In publishing courtroom dialogue, the media might have helped to create the impression that courts were places where the urban masses could air grievances and let off steam – places where they had the opportunity to argue their position and engage in dialogue with justice officials. In 1873, for instance, *The Bailie* described the case of a female offender locked in verbal combat with the police court personnel: 'The Fiscal having evidently the best of this clash of intellects, Bailie Moir turned to sharpen his wits upon the prisoner; but here, likewise, he failed, as the female had far the better of the Bench in the delightful and instructive colloquy which took place.' But *The Bailie* was wise to the real power dynamics within the courtroom. Any loss of the authority of the court and its personnel was reinstated by the sentences that magistrates could deliver to its interlocutors: 'Having tempered justice with mercy so far, the Judge suddenly bethought himself of his personal dignity, and with a frowning look he sentenced the miserable-looking culprit to "sixty days imprisonment."'[103] This female defender's courtroom eloquence was shown in the press to have earned her the maximum sentence.

The majority of media reports, though, were more likely to reflect the case for the prosecution and justification for conviction, not the defence. The early century periodicals introduced many of the accused with a quick description that conveyed their social and cultural status in shorthand for readers, with scant

---

[100]   In discussing the extraordinary length of court time devoted to the case involving Sleigh and Russell, the magistrate revealed that he usually dealt with more serious cases in 15 or 20 minutes. National Library of Scotland (NLS): *Report of the Proceedings in the Police Court, in the Trial of W. Campbell Sleigh, Esq., of London, Barrister-at-Law, and Thomas Russell, Esq., of Hunter Square, Edinburgh, Merchant, for an Alleged Breach of the Peace at the Music Hall, April 8, 1850, held with Reference to the Marriage Affinity Bill, by George Gunn, Reporter* (Edinburgh, 1850), p. 23.

[101]   'A Monday Morning at the Central Police Court', p. 2.

[102]   J.M. Beattie, *Policing and Punishment in London, 1660–1750: Urban Crime and the Limits of Terror* (Oxford, 2001), pp. 108–13.

[103]   *The Bailie*, no. 43, 23 August 1873, p. 2.

regard for the reputations of defenders and perpetuating social and criminal stereotypes that could damage them in court. For example, in April 1832, *The Police Intelligencer* described Catherine Sutherland, in the court for theft, as 'a randy Highland woman'.[104] In August 1822, an Irish woman accused of attempting to stab a police officer was referred to by the same periodical as 'the female Hibernian' rather than by her name.[105] An 1885 case described in *The Detective* highlighted how the voices of the urban poor were often stifled by the magistrate, the fiscal and the police: 'A batch of dirty women, with unkempt hair and tattered clothing, some of them sporting "black" eyes, besides sundry bruises and scratches, are ushered in. There has been a stairhead battle; their faces bear testimony to the fact':

> 'Please sir, will yez allow me to spake?' roars one of the group – a tall, ruddy-faced woman – to the Magistrate. Without waiting permission, she commences: 'Yez [You] must know that on Saturday night my man went out and got drunk with Biddy Maloney's man, and she, the murthering villyan [murdering villan].' – [indicating an interruption]
>
> 'Order!' shouts the Magistrate.
>
> 'Silence!' cries the usher, as a titter runs through the court.
>
> 'When he took her baste [beast] of a man home' –
>
> 'Policeman, keep that woman quiet.'
>
> 'Will he begob! that dirty blue-bottle [no he won't, that dirty policeman]', and she shook her fist under the policeman's nose.
>
> 'What are the facts?' asks the Magistrate and the Fiscal.
>
> 'Biddy Maloney let my husband slape [sleep] on her dirty flare [floor]', continued the virago.
>
> 'There seems to have been a serious quarrel', says the magistrate. With little deliberation or attempt to uncover the facts, 'The fine is fifteen shillings or fourteen days'.[106]

In cases such as this, police courts were places where the voices of the accused, and sometimes the complainers, were shouted down by the courtroom personnel – places where the primacy of the judicial 'voice' was paramount. These were sites where, as Carlen has pointed out, 'alternative' voices were silenced and where court procedure was structured in a way that restricted, and in some cases, excluded meaningful participation by the defender.[107]

---

[104]   *Police Intelligencer*, 5 April 1832.
[105]   *Police Intelligencer*, 22 August 1831.
[106]   'A Monday Morning at the Central Police Court', p. 2.
[107]   Carlen, *Magistrates' Justice*, pp. 21–2.

Gender clearly affected courtroom experiences. Women were frequent offenders before police courts. The figures fluctuated at periodic intervals according to police policy, the state of the economy and changes in behaviour, but they were always substantial. In Glasgow, women accounted for approximately one third of those charged in 1860 and 1871, rising to just under a half by the late Victorian period as the police clamped down upon public order offences for which women were most likely to be prosecuted (see Table 4.1). In

Table 4.1   Gender Profile of People Brought before Magistrates in Glasgow, 1860 to 1890[†]

	1860	1871	1880	1890
Crimes	17,481* Male: 12,805 Female: 4,676	5,162 Male: 3,043 Female: 2,119	6,393 Male: 4,281 Female: 2,112	5,050 Male: 3,572 Female: 1,478
Offences	17,481*: Male: 12,805 Female: 4,676	26,492 Male: 19,117 Female: 7,375	40,772 Male: 25,869 Female: 14,903	50,084 Male: 32,542 Female: 17,542
Contraventions	5,690 Male: 4,994 Female: 696	12,739 Male: 8,992 Female: 3,747	6,984 Male: 5,380 Female: 1,604	4,718 Male: 3,694 Female: 1,024
Total	23,171: Male: 17,799 Female: 5,372	44,393 Male: 31,152 Female: 13,241	54,149 Male: 35,530 Female: 18,619	59,852 Male: 39,808 Female: 20,044

* Recorded together

† ML: *The Number of Persons taken into Custody by the City of Glasgow Police and the Results for the Year Ending 29th September 1860* (Glasgow, 1861), pp. 6–11; ML, *City of Glasgow Police Criminal Returns for the Year Ending 31st December, 1871*, pp. 14–19; ML: *City of Glasgow Police Criminal Returns for the Year Ending 31st December, 1880* (Glasgow, 1881), pp. 12–17; ML: *City of Glasgow Police Criminal Returns for the Year Ending 31st December, 1890* (Glasgow, 1891), pp. 12–17.

Edinburgh, women rarely accounted for less than 40 per cent of the total number of defenders (see Table 4.2). In general, they were much more likely to be brought before a police court than any other criminal court. Whereas crime in the Scottish High Court in the nineteenth century was, according to Donnachie, 'overwhelmingly male' – with male criminals outnumbering female ones by at least three to one – in the police courts the gender differential was significantly

Table 4.2   Gender Profile of People Brought before Magistrates in
             Edinburgh, 1859 to 1880†

	1859	1868	1880
Crimes	619 Male: 357 Female: 262	649 Male: 427 Female: 222	1,470 Male: 1,062 Female: 408
Offences	9,471* Male: 4,922 Female: 4,459	11,166* Male: 6,256 Female: 4,910	8,665 Male: 4,785 Female: 3,880
Contraventions	9,471* Male: 4,922 Female: 4,459	11,166* Male: 6,256 Female: 4,910	Not Recorded
Total	10,090 Male: 5,279 Female: 4,721	11,815 Male: 6,683 Female: 5,132	10,135** Male: 5,847 Female: 4,288

*   Recorded together

**   This does not include contraventions (which were not recorded) or the 1,032 people who were
     summonsed before the court (as it was not stated whether this was for a crime or an offence).

† ECL, *Reports and Returns as to Crimes, Offences, and Contraventions, and to Cases of
Drunkenness, within the Police Bounds of the City of Edinburgh, during the Last Six Years, Prepared
for the Magistrates and Council, by Thomas Linton, Superintendent of Police, 1860*, p. 17; ECL:
*Report and Returns as to Crimes, Offences, and Contraventions, within the Limits of the Police of
the City of Edinburgh. Prepared for the magistrates and Council, by Thomas Linton, Superintendent
of Police, 1869* (Edinburgh, 1869), p. 19 & 32; and ECL: *Return of Crimes and Offences Reported,
Persons Apprehended and Cited, and Miscellaneous Returns Connected with the Police, for the Year
Ending 31st December 1880* (Edinburgh, 1881), p. 2.

lower.[108] Men were still more likely than women to be tried for crimes, but the
ratio was often less than two to one. Moreover, for offences, the ratio was often
even lower, not least due to prostitution, which as far as the official records were
concerned, was a female offence.

Women's defence of their behaviour in court was commonly reported in the
popular media as a source of particular ridicule for officials. Thus, a press report
on Catherine Sutherland, accused of stealing in April 1832, who appeared before

---

[108]   Ian Donnachie, '"The Darker Side": A Speculative Survey of Scottish Crime
during the First Half of the Nineteenth Century', *Scottish Economic and Social History*,
15/1 (1995): pp. 5–24.

Bailie Crichton in Edinburgh, correlated her speech in court with a previous appearance, noting that she was 'endowed with such volocity [*sic*] of tongue, that on a former occasion while before the Court for disorderly conduct, her tongue went with such rapidity, that the Magistrate observed he never till now believed the possibility of perpetual movement'.[109] The voices of poor female defenders may have offended elite male ears, but with even less access to the finances and community networks to gather respectable witnesses than men of equivalent status, their own speech was also one of the few mechanisms at their disposal to mount a defence of their actions.[110] The limited opportunity that many working-class women were given to articulate fully their defence, therefore, had significant implications for their chances of being acquitted. In general, the evidence reported in the press appears to suggest that women much more readily and openly argued back to magistrates than did male defenders. Yet it was precisely because their words were taken much less seriously that they could do so. In 1829, for instance, a woman appeared in the Glasgow Police Court on charges of abandoning her illegitimate child. The Magistrate insisted that she care for the child:

'Well,' says she [the prisoner], 'keep it who will, I will not.'

Magistrate: 'Take away the child, and take care of it, it is a fine little boy.'

Prisoner: 'I will not.'

Magistrate: 'The child must be kept, and you are an unfeeling wretch to desert the little innocent.'

Prisoner: 'Feeling here, or feeling there, I will not keep it.'

When the magistrate threatened to send her to bridewell, she took the child and the case was dismissed.[111] While the magistrate achieved the outcome of having the child 'cared' for, he did not fine the woman for her act of abandonment or her conduct in court.

Women's innocence or guilt was often assessed according to displays of deference, modesty and silence in the courtroom, as Lucia Zedner's study of female criminality in Victorian England has shown.[112] Even the attitude and appearance of women could impact on their experience in court and restrict their capacity to articulate their point of view. These aspects were often commented upon in newspaper and periodical reports, which, as Chapter 6 explores in more depth, helped readers to form judgements about the defenders' characters and indeed,

---

[109]   *Police Intelligencer*, 5 April 1832.

[110]   See, for example, evidence of gender as a factor in imprisonment in sixteenth-century Paris: Susan Broomhall, 'Poverty, Gender and Incarceration in Sixteenth-Century Paris', *French History*, 18/1 (2004): pp. 1–24.

[111]   *Police Reports*, 1 August 1829, p. 31.

[112]   Lucia Zedner, *Women, Crime and Custody in Victorian England* (Oxford, 1991), p. 28.

their guilt and thus their conviction. In 1831, for instance, *The Police Intelligencer* reported the brazen entrance of Bess McAlpin to the Edinburgh Police Court:

> Bess McAlpin, the Chieftainess of the Edinburgh Thieves, made her entrance, but in a far different manner than her illustrious predecessor. Instead of endeavouring to hide her face, Bess entered the Court with a smiling countenance, turned round and surveyed the audience, and finally faced right about to the Sheriff.[113]

Clearly, the journalist believed, the accused should have been shame-faced and deferential to magisterial authority, harking back to the style of the kirk session. Moreover, *The Police Intelligencer* described a case in August 1831 where a crockery merchant and his wife, noted as a 'thin scranky Irishwoman', were presented in court for being drunk and disorderly. Her attitude and, in particular, her 'gift of the gab or velocity of togue [*sic*] so annoyed the Court, that it was with the greatest difficulty they could get her to be silent for a single moment'. This caused Bailie Anderson to remark: 'Your tongue goes like the pendulum of a clock! Will you not hold your tongue?'[114]

The Irish featured prominently in the business of the police court and in press coverage of trial reports. They were the largest national grouping represented in court after Scots. On average, the Irish accounted for between one quarter and one fifth of those accused of crimes and offences in Edinburgh and in Glasgow – proportionately higher than their population within each city.[115] The frequency

---

[113]   *Police Intelligencer*, 28 September 1831.

[114]   *Police Intelligencer*, 20 August 1831.

[115]   In Edinburgh in 1880, 342 out of 1,470 persons arrested for crimes were Irish and 1,865 out of 8,605 persons arrested for offences. In Glasgow, 755 out of the 3,853 persons charged with aggravated offences were Irish. ECL, *Return of Crimes and Offences Reported, Persons Apprehended and Cited, and Miscellaneous Returns Connected with the Police, for the Year Ending 31st December 1880*, Table 4. For Glasgow's figures, see ML, *City of Glasgow Police Criminal Returns for the Year Ending 31st December, 1880*, pp. 20–21. A study of the Scottish prison population in 1881 estimated that one third of prisoners were of Irish origin. C.N. Johnston, 'The Punishment of Crime', *Judicial Review*, XX (1908–1909): p. 328. The police figures did not identify Irish offenders by religion, but there was also a sectarian bias to patterns of criminal prosecution in general. In 1880, 66 of the 270 boys (24 per cent) admitted to reformatory schools were Roman Catholic, and 29 of the 58 girls (50 per cent). 'Twenty-Fourth Report of the Inspector Appointed, Under the Provisions of the Act 5 & 6 Will. IV. C. 38, to Visit the Certified Reformatory and Industrial Schools of Great Britain', *BPP*, 1881 (c.3004), LIII.1, p. 24. See also Knox and McKinlay, 'Crime, Protest and Policing in Nineteenth-Century Scotland', p. 205. Although the percentage of Glaswegians of Irish descent was considerably larger, the Irish-born population of Glasgow in 1881 stood at 13 per cent. Charles Withers, 'The Demographic History of the City, 1831–1911', in W. Hamish Fraser and Irene Maver (eds), *Glasgow, Volume II: 1830 to 1912* (Manchester, 1996), p. 149. The Edinburgh figure was much lower. For more on the nature of Irish migration to Scotland, see Ben Braber, 'The

with which the Irish were brought before the bench was, in all likelihood, a legacy of the poverty and explicit discrimination based on their ethnicity that many faced from the police.[116] The widespread contemporary belief that the Irish were more criminally prone than other nationalities shaped how they were treated in court and represented in the press. Irish women were particularly reputed by the press with unruly speech that gained them only the scorn of court personnel. Although it was much less common for the press to report men defending their actions, the gift of the gab among the Irish seems a commonplace trope of court reporting. It seems highly probable that cases involving the Irish were more likely to be selected for publication than other cases in order to reinforce ethnic and national stereotypes and to amuse the native population. Whether or not these people committed the offences of which they were accused, it is noticeable that they were not afforded the protection of gentlemanly conduct by magistrates or the media in their public interactions. These particular women and men were not perceived as vulnerable, they were rarely depicted as silent, and their speech seemed to equate in the court and the press with an ability for self-protection. In 1825, the *Caledonian Mercury* reported a case of several young Irishmen who had been charged with rioting on St Patrick's Day. When they appeared in court, two were fined small amounts, 'for which lenient punishment they were indebted chiefly to the homespun eloquence of one of the party'.[117] Although this defence had successfully seen the men paying reduced fines, the paper critiqued the men's attempt to explain themselves. Using words, rather than 'taking the punishment on the chin' and paying the original fine, seemed to be cast as an emasculating form of conduct for certain accused men.

Distinct from the words offered in defence, the actions and comportment of the accused were sometimes critical in shaping the outcome of their case. Some of those brought to court were prepared to voice their opinions volubly. William Grant, banished for stealing and appearing in Edinburgh Police Court for breaking his banishment, was sent to bridewell. 'In place of shewing any sorrow

---

Influence of Immigration on the Growth, Urban Concentration and Composition of the Scottish Population, 1841–1911', *Journal of Scottish Historical Studies*, 32/2 (2012): pp. 190–212. For the perceived challenges posed by Irish migration to Edinburgh and the public's response, see Graeme Morton, *Unionist Nationalism: Governing Urban Scotland, 1830–1860* (East Linton, 1999), especially pp. 83–4 & 123–4.

[116] Knox and McKinlay make a similar point in 'Crime, Protest and Policing in Nineteenth-Century Scotland', p. 205. While recognising the bias and police attention to which the Irish were subject, Roger Swift also claims that Irish migrants were overrepresented in criminal statistics relating to violence, in part, because it was often perceived as a suitable form of conflict resolution. Roger Swift, 'Heroes or Villains? The Irish, Crime and Disorder in Victorian England', *Albion: A Quarterly Journal Concerned with British Studies*, 29/3 (1997): pp. 403–19. For more on the Irish in Scotland, see Martin J. Mitchell (ed.), *New Perspectives on the Irish in Scotland* (Edinburgh, 2008); and Terence McBride, *The Experience of Irish Migrants to Glasgow, Scotland, 1863–1891: A New Way of Being Irish* (Lewiston, 2008).

[117] *Caledonian Mercury*, 24 March 1825.

or contrition', reported the *Caledonian Mercury*, 'he tole [*sic*] the Magistrate it was hard, and a d–d shame to punish him'.[118] Such 'outbursts' of despair, anger and frustration were unlikely to be met with sympathy from the court officials, especially when they were voiced by working-class men. As Chapter 7 explores, what might have been momentarily empowering for accused men, to critique the magistrate and court openly, almost inevitably ended in increased punishment.

Magistrates judged outbursts from defenders by the social origins of those who voiced them. In a case before the Aberdeen Police Court in 1890, the father of a boy charged, along with his four friends, with playing football in the street, shouted at the fiscal who sought to instruct him on how to cross-examine a witness. The 'gentleman' replied:

> 'Don't you dictate to me.'
> Mr Lamb – 'Oh, but you must only ask questions.'
> The Parent – 'Hold your tongue.'

In this case, the boy was released with an admonition, while his father, 'the gentleman who had addressed Mr Lamb so sharply while questioning a witness, apologised to the Fiscal for having spoken in the heat of the moment'.[119] Significantly, this man was not reprimanded or fined for his impassioned outburst at the court officials who were trying to protect the witness, as were men of lesser status than that of 'gentleman'. Neither did his actions apparently jeopardise the severity of punishment meted on his son. Instead his behaviour was interpreted by the press at least as the conduct of a loving father towards his son in trouble, and his apology *after* the case was settled a measure of his gentlemanly ability to recognise error in his behaviour. Such interpretations were not available to all the court's clientele, however.

The accused, through their words and actions, were vital participants in the process and outcomes of police court justice: positively where women displayed modest, silent or contrite behaviour, and negatively in the case of outbursts of anger. However, rather than police courts settling cases and administering justice in terms defined by its working-class clientele, as has been claimed for Metropolitan London,[120] in most cases it required compliance to middle-class assumptions and values for the behaviour and voice of others to be taken seriously by procurators and magistrates. Participation in the courtroom's politics of power and authority rarely equated to an ability for the accused to assert their own values and notions of justice, especially if they were female, poorly educated or Irish. Although these people were by no means silent about what police court justice should involve, their chances of achieving it were remarkably slim. The social and cultural origins of the majority of defenders

---

[118]   *Caledonian Mercury*, 25 October 1817.
[119]   *Aberdeen Weekly Journal*, 12 July 1890.
[120]   Davis, 'A Poor Man's System of Justice?', pp. 309–35.

served to demarcate the court officials as, if not a homogenous cohort, at least proponents of a shared, middle-class set of moral values and legal principles which were not always interpreted or understood in the same way by the accused. The opportunity to speak out in court was a vital part of courtroom dynamics and may have offered a form of power to a severely disenfranchised portion of the urban population, but it came at a steep price for the individuals who seized it. Momentarily empowering, it almost inevitably saw defenders chastised, ridiculed and/or sentenced in the long term, especially if they spoke 'out of turn' or failed to show deference to the magistrate in a way that a defence lawyer might have done. Indeed, the accused were critical participants in as much, if not more, for what they contributed to the processes and hierarchies of power enacted in the courtroom than for their capacity to lodge a serious legal defence. Their presence enabled elite and aspiring men to gain social meaning and status over those brought before them, which ensured the primacy of one voice of authority over another in the judicial sphere.

IV. Witnesses

The role of the fiscal in leading prosecutions somewhat reduced the role of the complainer in court, as was argued earlier. Nonetheless, victims were anything but passive actors in court. Their willingness to testify was crucial to the success of prosecutions. Indeed, a number of cases were abandoned throughout the century because complainers failed to give evidence.[121] However, prosecutors required more than the testimony of victims in order to secure convictions. They also required, in theory, two independent witnesses to confirm guilt. In the early years of the police courts, the procedures for examining witnesses were not explicitly defined in police legislation. Sometimes it was clear that complainers and defenders were unaware of how many witnesses they should produce. In April 1832, Bailie Crichton asked a complainer seeking to prosecute a case of assault

> if he had any witnesses, [he] replied that he had three, viz: a brother flesher, himself, and a black eye. The Magistrate said as his eye was not a competent witness, there was only one besides the complainer, it would therefore be necessary to try the case upon a public charge, otherwise it would not prove.[122]

In some rare cases magistrates handed down convictions on the basis of only one witness testimony, so long as it was accompanied by proven corroborative

---

[121]   See, for instance, the charge against Hugh Docherty and Andrew Stewart, charged with stealing a candlestick from Mrs Edmond. Glasgow City Archives (GCA), B3/1/1/1: Glasgow Police Court Diet Books, 28 January 1813, p. 2.

[122]   *Police Intelligencer*, 11 April 1832.

facts or documentary evidence.[123] In 1817, for instance, a man charged in the Edinburgh Police Court with obtaining ale, spirits and the loan of 3s. under false pretences – which were found in his possession – was convicted on the evidence of the victim testifying under oath and just one other witness (a boy).[124]

In order to encourage participation, independent witnesses in Glasgow in 1861 (the first year for which information is known) received 3s., 6d. per day (from police funds) for a maximum of six days.[125] It is not clear when this practice started or whether expenses were given to both witnesses for the defence and the prosecution. There was, however, no reference to witnesses having their expenses reimbursed from public funds in the 1839–1840 Law Inquiry which looked at police court practice, although there were instances of private complaints recorded in the Edinburgh Police Court books from 1805 to 1807, in which the losing party was ordered to pay court costs that might have covered witness expenses.[126]

In most cases, the fiscal would call only the minimum number of witnesses needed to secure a conviction. Often, these were police officers. The defenders had the right to cross-examine, but the court personnel often restricted the manner in which they could do this. For instance, the five middle-class boys charged for playing football in the streets were defended by their fathers in 1890, one of whom was cautioned by the fiscal that he could not put words into the witness's mouth, but could only ask questions. This led to the courtroom fracas between the fiscal and father described above.[127] Given their lack of legal expertise, it is not surprising that defenders may have poorly worded their examination. The number of defence witnesses was usually fairly low and it was common for none to be called. As argued previously, the speedy nature

---

[123]   Thomas Trotter noted that in regard to the question of the sufficiency of the proof or evidence in any particular case to convict, it should be kept in view that, as the Lord Justice Clerk stated in *Lockwood v. Walker*, 1909, 6 Adam, 124, and at p. 128: 'No doubt our law does not require that every fact in a case shall be proved by two witnesses, but it most certainly does require that every crucial fact shall be so proved, or proved where there is only one witness by corroborative facts and circumstances proved, or by corroborative documentary evidence.' *Scott v. Jameson*, 1914, 7 Adam, 529. 'Where the crucial point depends on the uncorroborated evidence of one witness, no conviction can follow.' Trotter, *Summary Criminal Jurisdiction*, p. 222.

[124]   *Caledonian Mercury*, 25 September 1817.

[125]   Although in 1861, it was decided that in future expenses should not be paid from police funds. GCA, E1/13/1: Magistrates Committee Minute Book, 18 January 1861.

[126]   Robert Lowie, cabinet maker, took out a complaint against George Pringle, drummer in the 26th Regiment of Foot, for assault. He was found guilty and ordered to pay a fine and expenses. ECA, ED006/8: Edinburgh Police Court Abstract of Processes, 1805–1807, no. 962, pp. 30–31.

[127]   *Aberdeen Weekly Journal*, 12 July 1890.

of summary justice made it difficult for the accused to organise witnesses for their defence, especially if the accused had spent the previous night in police custody.

What constituted 'competent' evidence was largely open to the interpretation of magistrates.[128] In July 1823, *The Scotsman* explicitly emphasised the social origins of a witness, implicitly linking it to the outcome of the case. In an altercation between carters and police officers brought to Edinburgh's court, 'a respectable gentleman, a witness for one of the defendants, fully justified the conduct of the officers'.[129] As with other aspects of the courts' practice, social and moral judgements shaped the value accorded by court officials to people as witnesses before the court, thus to defenders' abilities to locate witnesses whose testimony would be deemed reliable, and consequently to the processes of justice the police courts performed.

Witness testimony could be problematic in ways that were influenced by expectations of appropriate male and female conduct too. A woman brought to the Aberdeen Police Court as a witness to testify to the annoyance of a fellow tenant, potato farmer George Mennie, residing in Mounthooly, stated 'that the language used by Howie was of such a character that she would be ashamed to utter it'. Upon which statement Howie's lawyer, a Mr Shivas, pressed her to specify precisely what language was used. At this, 'the Procurator-Fiscal interfered, remarking that when the expressions used were of such a character that a respectable female was ashamed to utter them, the civilized way was to write them upon a piece of paper. Mr Shivas did not, however, press the matter so far as this'.[130] Nonetheless, it is clear that women as witnesses could not provide the full support to a defender (similarly if they were themselves the defender) if their evidence would in turn expose them to moral judgements – and thus undermine the perceived quality of their testimony.[131]

On occasion, a witness could cause the magistrate to acknowledge a lack of all-encompassing expertise in the court when they spoke in terms he did not understand. The *Aberdeen Journal* reported on the 'considerable mirth' caused when a witness described a case of men swindling men as 'a Greenland move'; and on being asked to explain what that was, replied '*to ticket mutton*'.

---

[128] In his study into Scots law in the twentieth century, Trotter noted that 'A judge is entitled to convict upon the uncorroborated evidence of *socii criminis* if he believes their evidence (*Brown v. Macpherson*, 1918, J.C. 3), but not upon the uncorroborated testimony of one *socius criminis* (*Townsend v. Strathern*, 1923, J.C. 66).' Trotter, *Summary Criminal Jurisdiction*, p. 223.

[129] *The Scotsman*, 2 July 1823.

[130] *Aberdeen Weekly Journal*, 10 April 1880.

[131] Such arguments have been advanced in historians' analysis of women's ability to describe sexual violence in early modern courts by Miranda Chaytor, 'Husband(ry): Narratives of Rape in the Seventeenth Century', *Gender and History*, 7/3 (1995): pp. 378–407; Garthine Walker, 'Rereading Rape and Sexual Violence in Early Modern England', *Gender and History*, 10/1 (1998): pp. 1–25.

The magistrate's sentence was severe, and the paper continued: 'The panels have by this time learned, however, that Greenland moves sometimes finish in an Aberdeen Bridewell.'[132] Similarly, sometimes expert witnesses had to explain to judges who did not understand the nature of the specific evidence in question. In 1865, a veterinary surgeon from Dalkeith, Mr J. Horsburgh, in a letter to the *Caledonian Mercury*, voiced his dissatisfaction with the Leith Police Court and its magistrate, who did not accept his professional witness testimony regarding the quality of a butcher's beef. He reported:

> I was asked by the judge why it was soft – softer than beef was [that] he had seen or got. In reply I said that beef fed for a prize was mostly tallow, which kept a great deal longer firm than lean beef, especially in such close, damp weather as we had had for a month and that that was not very soft yet, though kept in such a close, damp place as it had been for eight days [in the cellar of the police office].

For his part Horsburgh insisted that the beef was fit for sale, as did two other witnesses but the judge persisted in the charge of unwholesome and unmarketable meat. Horsburgh asked for what purpose he had come to court if his evidence was to be ignored by a magistrate without his professional expertise.[133]

Indeed, magistrates sometimes struggled to have the court taken seriously by middle-class witnesses. Getting them to treat the process of summary justice with sufficient respect to turn up in court could be a challenge. The same Horsburgh complained in his letter that he 'had to be in Court at nine o'clock AM, certainly a very untimeous hour for bringing witnesses from a distance' and noted that 'several from Edinburgh were not forward, having mistaken the hour of their summons'.[134] Similarly, Bailie Forbes in Aberdeen moaned publicly about one witness, Alexander Gray, whose refusal to appear had caused a case to be continually prolonged. When he finally appeared,

> Baillie Forbes pointed out to him the serious inconvenience he had created … and that Gray's refusal was the first he had ever got; that he could not easily believe that any one would refuse a few minutes' time to assist in forwarding the ends of justice, while he and the other magistrates devoted several hours daily for that purposes … Gray stated 'in future he would not attend the Court, either for the baillie's message or warrant.' The Baillie remarked, 'You are an impertinent fellow,' and requested him to leave the Court. 'On which Gray, as he went out, mumbled, 'I thank you, Baillie; I beg to return you the compliment.' Baillie Forbes remarking, 'Don't be impertinent.'[135]

---

132   *Aberdeen Journal*, 31 July 1833.
133   *Caledonian Mercury*, 7 January 1865.
134   Ibid.
135   *Aberdeen Journal*, 11 September 1844.

Such exchanges and the lack of witness attendance that provoked them highlighted both a perception of the court as one that operated to administer justice against predominantly those of lower social status, as well as a magistrate's struggle to stake his authority among his fellow middle-class citizenry.

Witnesses were by no means a homogenous group, and the quality of their evidence was accordingly filtered by a variety of social and moral lenses. This created a clear challenge for complainers and even more so defenders to produce witnesses whose testimony would be deemed competent by magistrates. For those accused, their ability to challenge the evidence of witnesses was severely limited by a lack of technical, legal expertise as well as expectations about the manner in which they could comport themselves in court when, for most, passivity was expected and aggression pointedly condemned. Importantly, the participation of particularly middle-class witnesses in the courtroom served to validate the court as an appropriate place for the resolution of justice, a point made most visibly when they refused to attend, symbolically threatening the validity of the court's practice and its authority over the entire urban population. How people experienced the courtroom was not just by appearance as victims, accused or as witnesses, however, but often as it was represented in the press. The following section explores how the press sought to portray the emotions of the courtroom for its own entertainment and moral purposes.

V. Architecture, Auditory and Audience

Scholars of criminal justice history have recognised the symbolic significance and power of courtroom architecture.[136] In the early 1820s, Dr John Aitken, Commissioner of the Glasgow Police, made a similar point. Commenting on the need for a new police office to serve the rapidly expanding urban population,[137] he resolved 'to build a structure for ourselves, which would be a terror to evildoers, and at the same time, the pride of the whole kingdom'.[138] Like many Scottish burghs, the new police office which was subsequently constructed in the city in 1824 not only served as a station house for officers and a detaining centre for prisoners, it was also home to the main court house – the central court, as it would come to be known. Located in Albion Street, in a location known as 'Police Lane', the physical structure of the new police building and its accompanying court served as a symbol of the close ties that existed between the

---

[136] Bankowski, Hutton and McManus, *Lay Justice?*, p. 36.

[137] Crimes deemed to be of a fairly serious nature were initially dealt with in the City Chambers building which served the burgh court; less serious offences and contraventions in the local police office. John Ord, 'Origin and History of Glasgow Police Force', *Old Glasgow Club Transactions*, vol. I, sessions 1900–1908 (Glasgow, 1908), pp. 97–112.

[138] Ibid., p. 100.

police and the courts and is likely to have helped to cement in popular perception that there was no tangible separation between the enforcers and administrators of law and justice.

As in English courts, the public gallery, the press and the physical and structural design of the Scottish police courtroom were important vehicles for sending out judicial messages. The courtroom was designed to transmit judicial and civic authority, to put fear into the hearts of the accused and to project warnings to the wider public. The image of Glasgow's Central Courtroom that was published in *The Bailie* in 1885 sought to portray its strong theatrical and religious symbolism (Illustration 4.1).[139] The comparison between the 'Bar' of the public house on a Saturday night and the 'Bar' of the Police Court on a Monday morning was designed to send out a strong moral lesson of the link between excessive alcohol consumption and criminal and disorderly behaviour. The magistrate, in this case the Lord Provost, was represented as a solemn, almost stately, quasi-religious, figure.[140] His stool was raised above the others to convey his authority and to distinguish him in the room in a manner akin to a kirk session. The public gallery, 'fashioned after the style of church pews', provided the opportunity for community participation in a manner suggestive of eighteenth-century church courts.

Having said that, for most of the century and in most towns, the structural design of police courts was less intimidating and symbolically significant than appears to have been the case for higher courts, despite Commissioner Aitken's bold claim. Police courts were often unimpressive, cramped and noisy environments, lacking the pomp and ceremony of justiciary courts.[141] Even in Glasgow, home to the country's busiest police court, magistrates in the first two and a half decades of the century would deal with police business in a small 'office' near the main station house. The new police office which opened at Albion Street in 1824 was able to accommodate a larger number of people, but it was, according to *The Detective*'s description of it, still 'not very spacious'.[142] Far from being theatres of high drama, police court business was often characterised by the drudgery of day-to-day mundane business – a fact which went a long way in explaining the low status in which it was held in middle-class circles. Tellingly, in 1875, *The Bailie* alluded to the dangers of overstating the symbolic impact of what were modest, unassuming buildings. In describing the role of

---

[139]   'A Monday Morning at the Central Police Court', p. 1.

[140]   Some law courts were described in quasi-religious terms as 'cathedrals' of secular power. See J.M. Schramm, *Testimony and Advocacy in Victorian Law, Literature and Theology* (Cambridge, 2000), p. 163.

[141]   Indeed as Miller has pointed out for London, contemporaries were worried that in a crowded and noisy chamber the law would lose its 'impressiveness' and 'moral power'. Miller, *Cops and Bobbies*, pp. 82–3.

[142]   'A Monday Morning at the Central Police Court', p. 1.

the fiscal, John Lang, in the Glasgow Central Police Court, it claimed: 'A Court of Justice, even "the Central," is, or ought to be, an imposing spectacle. ... The Court of itself is of course nothing; it is the people who sit in the Court who adorn it, who give it dignity, and terror, and air of majesty.'[143]

Although not referred to in *The Bailie*, 'the people' included the gallery. Its size varied from town to town. The new police court in Glasgow's Albion Street was described in police reports in 1829 as being large enough to accommodate 'a large concourse of spectators'.[144] In 1873, *The Bailie* published a portrait of a local police court reporter which showed the public gallery in the background, three or four rows deep and probably capable of holding up between 50 and 100 hundred people (see below). But it was a different situation in Aberdeen. When civic leaders in Aberdeen in 1870 redesigned the local police court, just three places were made available for the public.[145] Attendance is likely to have been determined by the business of the police court on a given day, the performance of the economy, the weather and the availability of recreational facilities. In 1829, the Glasgow *Police Reports* published the case of an Irishman named William Bell, charged with 'having violated the sepulchres of the dead, and with having in his possession the bodies of an old man and woman suspected to have been exhumated'. The case was described as having taken place among an 'unusual concourse of spectators', which suggests the public knew when certain crimes were being tried and that attendance often targeted certain cases.[146] Prosecutions that had implications for local businesses, and which might serve as test cases for municipal policy, drew especially large numbers of spectators. In 1889, for instance, the trial of Charles Moore, charged with displaying diseased meat in contravention of the 1866 Glasgow Police Act, had to be moved from the police courtroom to the justiciary buildings to accommodate public interest.[147] Cases involving sporting events and political protest also stimulated particular interest.[148] In 1912, 'a large crowd' was reported in the *Glasgow News* as having gathered to hear the case of suffragette Rhoda Walker, charged with smashing the window of a car which she believed contained Winston Churchill, then First Lord of the Admiralty, on his visit to Glasgow (he was, in fact, in another car).[149] In this instance, the police court served not simply as a warning to others, but also as a means for those in court to advance a political message, despite repeated

---

[143]   *The Bailie*, no. 133, 5 May 1875.

[144]   *Police Reports*, 1 August 1829, p. 29.

[145]   *Aberdeen Journal*, 13 July 1870.

[146]   *Police Reports*, 5 September 1829, p. 101.

[147]   *Glasgow Herald*, 25 May 1889.

[148]   In 1912, for instance, the *Glasgow Herald* reported that 'there was a large attendance of the public at the Southern Police Court this morning to hear a case of an alleged break-in of a crowd of spectators at Shawfield Park during a football match'. GCA, B3/1/11, 2 vols: Newspaper Cuttings, 1910 to 1950, 13 February 1912.

[149]   *Glasgow News*, 23 February 1912.

interjections from the magistrate that they confine their evidence to the facts of the case being examined.

In describing the scene at the gallery on a Monday morning in 1885, *The Detective* claimed that:

> All descriptions, from the middle to the lowest class inclusive, are represented. Here and there among them you can see a decent married woman with her husband, who have come through curiosity to hear the result of a case in which they have more than an ordinary interest. There is a pale-faced woman, with a chubby baby clasped in her arms, her eyes red and swollen with weeping. Her young husband she trusted so implicitly lies in a drunkard's cell, and she is waiting till he is dragged forth to receive a penalty which will probably be for her the cause of more grief and agony than it is to him. …Slatternly, frowsy women, smelling strongly of vile whisky; men with hang-dog countenances and blood-shot eyes that only too plainly indicate their avocation; youths just entering on manhood, but with faces that already tell tales of vice, – all waiting with more or less patience for the Magistrate who is to dispose of their more unfortunate brethren.[150]

It is likely, however, that the public gallery regularly attracted a mainly working-class clientele. While some well-to-do regulars might have attended for popular amusement, to satisfy a voyeuristic moral purpose, or to see that justice was served for a petty crime or offence from which they had suffered, it appears that the largest proportion of the gallery's social composition – as the above quote suggests – mirrored the social composition of those accused. Many who sat in the gallery may have attended simply to support a relative or friend.[151] Others are likely to have been there to escape the cold or to give them something to do during periods of unemployment. Moreover, growing middle-class disdain towards the police court in the second half of the nineteenth century and the fact that knowledge of the police court could be obtained from channels other than attendance itself would have reduced the willingness of the middle classes to sit in galleries on a regular basis. When they did, it was more than likely because they had a vested interest in a particular case. In the trial in the Edinburgh Police Court alluded to earlier involving W. Campbell Sleigh, barrister-at-law, and Thomas Russell Esq., merchant, for an alleged breach of the peace at the music hall, it was reported that 'the courtroom was exceedingly crowded, and the audience included many respectable inhabitants'.[152] The fact that the reporter

---

[150]   'A Monday Morning at the Central Police Court', p. 2.

[151]   In their study of the district summary courts in Scotland in the 1980s, Bankowski, Hutton and McManus also found that friends and relatives tended to fill the public galleries. Bankowski, Hutton and McManus, *Lay Justice?*, pp. 38–9.

[152]   ECL, *Report of the Proceedings in the Police Court, in the Trial of W. Campbell Sleigh, Esq., of London, Barrister-at-Law, and Thomas Russell, Esq., of Hunter Square, Edinburgh, Merchant*, p. 3.

felt the need to report the audience's particular social composition suggests this was not the norm. In this case, the large attendance is likely to have reflected both the political and morally contentious nature of the case, as well as the fact that the Lord Provost and Edinburgh's civic elite were required to give evidence as witnesses.

The gallery helped to legitimise the workings of police court justice. It enabled the public to see that justice was being done, made legal redress appear more accessible and could serve as a warning to others. Indeed, in this respect, the public gallery performed a role not dissimilar to that of a high court jury. E.P. Thompson argued of the jury:

> The English common law rests upon a bargain between the law and the people. The jury box is where the people come into the court: the judge watches over them and the jury watches back. A jury is the place where the bargain is struck. The jury attends in judgement not only upon the accused, but also upon the justice and humanity of the Law.[153]

The public gallery allowed, in theory at least, people to scrutinise the administration of summary justice over which they had no direct control.

Moreover, it provided a forum for public expression, hence making it appear more legitimate. For instance, in the case involving William Bell referred to above, 'on leaving the court, the audience expressed their abhorrence of the alleged crime by a general hiss'.[154] The public gallery also added to the nature of punishment. As with church courts, the shame of being publicly rebuked before one's own community in the police court was potentially an important mechanism for imposing discipline and control and for attempting to legitimise magisterial justice. Although impossible to prove conclusively, it is also likely that the absence of a jury might, to some degree, have increased the capacity of the gallery to influence judicial sentences, as it had only one magistrate, not a whole jury, to sway. Certainly, magistrates appear to have been acutely aware of the gallery, and, indeed, were recorded in the press as playing to it. In 1829, the Glasgow *Police Reports* published the following report of a man, charged with being drunk and disorderly (singing) on the Burgh Kirk roof:

> On being brought before the magistrate, the case was clearly proved, to the amusement of the audience; and the tailor was fined 10s. 6d. – Bailie McLellan remarked, that the tailor had surely not been in the inside of the church through the day, or he would not have had such a passionate love for the outside at night. – *A Laugh*.[155]

---

153 E.P. Thompson, *Writing by Candlelight* (London, 1980), p. 108.
154 *Police Reports*, 5 September 1829, p. 101.
155 *Police Reports*, 25 July 1829, p. 19.

However, although the gallery had an important political and legal role to play in the court, there is a danger of overstating its significance and influence on trial proceedings. Public galleries could restrict the victim's access to justice. As the previous chapter showed, the prospect of appearing before an audience and publicising the intimate details surrounding a case acted as a deterrent to middle-class men whose sexual indiscretions resulted in petty theft. Magistrates' surprise when such cases involving petty sums were brought to court illustrated how unusual it was – and, more importantly, how the public gaze of the gallery and the media kept men, especially those of a certain social standing, from seeking legal redress for crimes that befell them whilst engaged in sexual encounters.[156] Moreover, although it is difficult to draw too strong a conclusion given the selective nature of newspaper reporting, it is significant that instances of magistrates being directly swayed by the sentiment of the courtroom were recorded very rarely. Not only were most galleries small, with public officials and policemen outnumbering, in all likelihood, the number of people in attendance, but the drudgery of the dull, monotonous day-to-day petty crimes, offences and contraventions with which the courts dealt is likely to have stifled the possibility for the carnivalesque atmosphere that was apparently so popular in eighteenth-century English higher courts. Furthermore, given the class of person who sat in the gallery, the chances of magistrates' bowing to crowd pressure were slim, as magistrates were much more likely to respond favourably to the opinions of the middle class who shared similar moral values and who could vote them out of office – something most working-class ratepayers were unable to do until the extension of the local franchise in the late nineteenth century.[157] Indeed, far from influencing magistrates, dissent from the gallery could also be counter-productive if magistrates viewed it as a threat to their authority. From what can be gathered from newspaper reports, magistrates were much more likely to chastise and order silence from noisy or rowdy galleries rather than be swayed by them.

Arguably, the public gallery's real significance was in how it was represented in the press and the impression of justice that was created as a consequence. Approximately one in every dozen or so cases would make reference to the public's gasps, laughter, applause and jeers. These outbursts were placed in square brackets or italicised to distinguish them from the dialogue of those involved in the trial. Recording the auditory of the gallery, as Crone has alluded to, is likely to have been driven by commercial pressures.[158] It helped to spice up cases, made them appear more interesting, and added to the perceived theatre of the courtroom

---

[156]   *Police Reports*, 5 September 1829, p. 92.

[157]   The impact of the extension of municipal franchise in 1868 in Glasgow is explored in Irene Maver, 'Glasgow's Civic Government', in Fraser and Maver (eds), *Glasgow, Volume II*, p. 460. For Aberdeen, see Clive Lee, 'Local Government', in W. Hamish Fraser and Clive H. Lee (eds), *Aberdeen. 1800–2000: A New History* (Edinburgh, 2000), p. 245.

[158]   Crone, *Violent Victorians*, p. 235.

proceedings. It is likely, in other words, to have been inserted mainly to help boost sales, but it might also have served a wider moral purpose and have been intended to offer commentary on magisterial justice. The response of the gallery as it was recorded in the media provided a commentary on the courts and how the law was being administered, as well as immediate feedback of citizens' perceptions of the court's practices and justice.

There was the odd report in which the accused too showed an awareness of the role the media could play in publicising what defenders perceived were injustices. The case of Christian Dowel or Anderson, charged with assault in the Edinburgh Police Court in 1832 and who had by her own admission been about 60 times in bridewell and ten times in the lock-up house, provides a good case in point. On her last appearance she had promised to leave the town but did not as, according to her, 'the vessel had not sailed yet'.

> Superintendant (ironically) – 'O sir, the vessel will be going to sail next Tuesday!'
> Magistrate – 'We must make her sail over to Calton Hill [home to Edinburgh Bridewell]!'
> Defender – 'Ye winna be sae cruel!'
> Magistrate – 'there is no cruelty in that, it is rather conferring a favour on you, it will keep you out of harms way!'
> Clerk of the Court –' For how long sir?'
> Magistrate – 'thirty day.'
> Defender – 'Reporter mark down that!'[159]

Media reports on the gallery also revealed the public's displeasure at how civic affairs were being governed. In the trial of Sleigh and Russell at the Edinburgh Police Court in 1850 for an alleged breach of the peace in protesting at the Lord Provost's opposition to the Marriage Affinity Bill, *The Scotsman* – which was the most likely of the mainstream press to criticise magistrates in the city – reported that 'the proceedings were frequently interrupted by applause and marks of disapprobation'.[160] In this case, such outbursts were usually directed in support of witness testimonies that challenged the evidence of the Lord Provost and magistrates and supported those of the defenders. Much of the auditory that was recorded related to claims that the Lord Provost – in instructing the police to arrest the two accused for speaking out of turn at the meeting – was attempting to thwart free speech and public expression and advance his own religious and moral views. As Dr Renton, Commissioner of Police, testified:

---

[159]   *Police Intelligencer*, 2 October 1832.
[160]   *The Scotsman*, 17 April 1850, under the title of 'Soiree in Honour of Messrs Sleigh and Russell'; and NLS, *Report of the Proceedings in the Police Court, in the Trial of W. Campbell Sleigh, Esq., of London, Barrister-at-Law, and Thomas Russell, Esq., of Hunter Square, Edinburgh, Merchant*, p. 24.

> This city has been allowed for too long to be the tool and dupe of a sectarian
> faction, which, arrogating to itself all that is true in doctrine or correct in
> discipline, would banish religious toleration from its walls, and establish a
> spiritual despotism in its crusades against alleged railway and post-office
> desecration, worthy of the dark ages – [applause].[161]

The interaction of witnesses with the auditory even provided illuminating
insights into public perceptions that magistrates were convicting people on
less than compelling evidence. In alluding to how loosely 'breach of the peace'
was classified in the Edinburgh Police Court, another witness, Melville Bell,
thanked his stars he was not at the music hall 'for he feared he must have
been constrained to become to some extent a "disturber of the peace" – at
least in the Police Court acceptation of the term, which he trusted was not a
legal one, although according to *Law*. [Laughter and applause.]'[162] Moreover,
his evidence, and the reaction it provoked among the gallery, alluded to the
intimate relationship that existed between magistrates and the influence the
Lord Provost exerted over police affairs:

> It was unworthy of the president [the Lord Provost] of a meeting to order out
> a gentleman in an ungentlemanly way; it was most unworthy of a magistrate,
> being president, to have his police minions in attendance, and to set them with
> rude hands upon gentlemen as upon drunken brawlers, who were incapable of
> attending to the usages of society [cheers].

That members of the Edinburgh Police Commission were so outspoken in
criticising aspects of the police court's workings was testament to how fractious
and bitter Edinburgh's civic administration and political life was.[163] As in other
Scottish cities, the relationship between magistrates and certain factions of the
police commission was particularly fraught at this time, leading to the Edinburgh
Police Commission's incorporation into local government in 1856.[164] The fact
that *The Scotsman* published a detailed commentary on such proceedings, with
frequent references to the auditory of the gallery, highlighted that the media's
coverage was by no means always fully supportive of magistrates. Indeed in
the case of *The Scotsman*, a liberal newspaper which supported the Marriage

---

[161]   Ibid., p. 26.

[162]   Ibid.

[163]   On 4 May 1850, the Edinburgh Police Commission held an emergency
meeting to consider a bill of suspension against the Edinburgh Police Court's
decision to convict Sleigh and Russell, during which a number of commissioners
criticised how the Lord Provost and magistrates had handled the case. *The Scotsman*,
4 May 1850.

[164]   David G. Barrie, *Police in the Age of Improvement: Police Development and the
Civic Tradition in Scotland, 1775–1865* (Cullompton, 2008), pp. 231–4.

Affinity Bill, the press could exploit the courtroom auditory to echo their own political views and agendas.

Significantly, however, even when disquiet such as that above was reported in the mainstream media, it tended to reflect a wider political agenda rather than questioning whether justice was being administered even-handedly. Rarely was criticism directed towards the interests of the accused unless, of course, it involved, as in the above case, men of a certain social standing. Media recording of dissenting voices from the public gallery, however, was rare, which is likely to have reflected the intimidating nature of the police court environment with its large police presence – which would have helped to muffle dissenting grumblings – as much as any intentional selective reporting on the part of journalists. For the most part, the journals and newspapers that reported the auditory of the gallery selected cases which were likely to be of interest to readers for public amusement, to reinforce ethnic, gender and national stereotypes, and to reflect fairly favourably on how magistrates administered justice.

Rarely did the mainstream media record the public galleries' response to run-of-the-mill cases in which magistrates took a tough line against petty theft out of economic necessity, or where magistrates were supportive of the evidence of policemen charged with assault – cases where the wrath of the gallery was more likely to have been vented against judicial judgements. Whether this was designed to serve a specific purpose is impossible to say, but for the most part it reflected only one side of public opinion on how the law was being administered – that crime did not pay, and that magistrates, as guardians of the community, could be relied upon to protect its most vulnerable members. This was, without question, the dominant message being projected. Not only did the reporting of positive feedback from the gallery help to legitimise the criminal justice system by showing that members of the public were participating in it, the majority of such reports created the impression that this was a just system of law enforcement which attracted the support of the community. It was especially common for galleries to be reported as reacting to courtroom discourse with a singular, shared, sympathetic voice on specific cases in which the magistrate had showed leniency. For example, in 1831 *The Police Intelligencer* reported on the trial of a country girl accused of stealing cheese from a shop in Edinburgh. The fact that the girl had been overcharged by the female shopkeeper won her the sympathy of the gallery and the magistrate, with the *Intelligencer* reporting that 'The auditory seemed to feel, as if by electricity, a sensation of delight when the Magistrate ordered that the poor girl should receive the cheese imputed to have been stolen, also the payment of the part which had been sold.'[165] Such description implied the auditory's innate sense of 'commonsense justice' and most frequently provided approval of the court's practice and the magistrate's decisions. The moral message that was conveyed was that magistrates could be relied upon to administer justice in keeping with public sentiment.

---

[165]   *Police Intelligencer*, 23 September 1831.

Indeed, magistrates were also reported as having felt compelled to instruct the auditory in what they believed was the appropriate response in cases involving child welfare. When six-year-old Edward Devon appeared in the Glasgow Police Court in July 1829, charged with stealing from a shop, it was reported that 'the little urchin had to be placed on the Court table that he might be seen'. When Edward explained to the magistrate that he had indeed attempted to steal but had not been strong enough to open the shop drawer which contained the money, 'The audience laughed at the child's confession, but were sharply reprimanded by the Magistrate, who said "he did not see what they could laugh at, it was a distressing case to see such a young child bringing itself to the gallows".'[166] It is interesting, as the above examples illustrate, that newspaper reports in which the reaction of the public gallery was recorded often concerned cases involving vulnerable young women or children, and often represented magistrates as having the welfare of the accused at heart. In using the gallery's comments to show concurrence with their own views, the mainstream media provided an implicit assurance that their reading of court trials was right. More commonly though, there was no third-party validation on the court by the public gallery other than the journalist himself, and no check on the correct assessment made by the journalist of the court personnel's judgements. This was to have a major impact on the dynamics of the courtroom because the press confirmed the moral assessments of court officials and likely also influenced how the accused understood courtroom dynamics.

Whether the press was subject to civic restrictions in terms of what they could and what they could not report is difficult to determine, but for the first half of the nineteenth century there was not the same level of publicised concern about formal checks and controls on journalists as existed in London with the *Proceedings of the Old Bailey*.[167] There were suggestions, though, that civic leaders were able to exert influence over the content of police court trial reports. In discussing the public meeting concerning the Marital Bill, Melville Bell went so far as to imply that the press in Edinburgh did not always accurately cover police proceedings, under influence from the Lord Provost. He claimed:

> And what a mockery was it, although an unintentional one, arising from the thoughtless adherence to customary technicalities, for the reporters of the press to record this seeming unanimity in support for the response of magistrates, when they knew and saw, that it was at the peril of the purse and person that one dared to differ from the sagacious heads of the community.[168]

---

[166]   *Police Reports*, 13 July 1829, p. 11.

[167]   Devereaux, 'The Fall of the Sessions Paper', p. 58; Devereaux, 'The City and the Sessions Paper', pp. 467–8.

[168]   NLS, *Report of the Proceedings in the Police Court, in the Trial of W. Campbell Sleigh, Esq., of London, Barrister-at-Law, and Thomas Russell, Esq., of Hunter Square, Edinburgh, Merchant*, p. 27.

Moreover, the fact that George Gunn, reporter, felt compelled to publish the trial proceedings in full with a local printer suggests there was a concern with how proceedings were being represented in certain media circles.[169] The implication was that some mainstream media was in the habit of suppressing opposition to unpopular police court practices.

As the century progressed, however, some journalists alienated those in civic circles with their coverage of trial proceedings and the methods by which they gathered their information. In 1858, a controversy between Alexander Munro, recently appointed Town Clerk and Assessor in the Glasgow Police Court, and certain journalists of the Glasgow press provided an intriguing insight into the practice of courtroom reporting adopted by certain newspapers and their staff. Journalists who covered police court proceedings, it was reported, had since the court's inception in 1800 been in the habit of not personally attending court on a regular basis.[170] As Munro pointed out, 'It is a matter of notoriety that the reporters did not in general attend the Police Courts while cases were going on, and equally notorious that daily reports were published by them as if they did so.'[171] The *Glasgow Herald* explained that 'the reason is this, that there are six Police Courts held in Glasgow every day, and, generally speaking, there is not a staff attached to any newspaper sufficient to attend them all, and at the same time to perform the other reporting duties requisite in a community like Glasgow'.[172] Reporters, the *Glasgow Herald* claimed, had been allowed to inspect the police court books [which contained the *'res gestae'* of the court] to find matters of interest that occurred in their absence, 'but, whenever, they became aware that important cases were likely to take place, they invariably attended in person'.[173] Exactly how journalists knew when 'important' cases were scheduled suggests pre-trial contact and transferral of information with either police or court officials. Representatives of the press had been permitted access to the books, the *Glasgow Herald* explained, because 'the Court is often managed in such a confused, hurried, and occasionally slovenly manner, that it is not easy to obtain a correct version of the proceedings without some reference to the written data on which they are founded'.[174]

However, shortly after his appointment, Munro denied journalists access to the court books and called for a new form of record-keeping. Unhappy about the

---

[169]   Ibid., p. 23.

[170]   'The Glasgow Press and Mr Munro, the Police Assessor', *Glasgow Herald*, 13 September 1858.

[171]   'Mr Munro and the Glasgow Reporters' to the Editor of the Glasgow Herald, by Alexander Munro, Town Clerk, 23 September 1858', quoted in *Glasgow Herald*, 24 September 1858.

[172]   It went on: 'Next, even when attendance has been regularly given, it was found that the reporters might sit six times six days without meeting with any matter of sufficient interest to put in print. Constant attendance, therefore, would have been time thrown away.' Ibid.

[173]   Ibid.

[174]   *Glasgow Herald*, 22 September 1858.

alleged accuracy of published trial accounts, and the journalistic approach that lay behind them, Munro claimed 'that such reports could not fairly represent the proceedings in Court, and certainly, in point of fact, did not do so'.[175] He continued:

> The nature of the book on which they had been relying ... was not the record of the proceedings – that it contained charges against individuals which should never have been seen, because they were abandoned, and the parties charged admittedly innocent, and that the book had been used by the reporters for other purposes than reporting.[176]

He ordered a new mode of keeping police books and instructed journalists that he would supply the press with all the necessary information they required. His decision was approved by a majority of magistrates who stated that the 'method of reporting police cases formerly adopted was wrong, and resulted in erroneous and defective reports'.[177]

Munro's actions seem to have divided the Glasgow press. He claimed he was supported by several newspapers that strongly condemned, according to newspaper quotes that Munro himself provided but did not cite, 'an idle and careless system of reporting, in which imagination plays a much greater part than fact' and that which 'under an implied pretence of being a narrative ... is nothing short of gross imposture'.[178] However, in response, unnamed 'Representatives of the Glasgow Press' submitted a memorial to magistrates complaining at the attempt to 'invade their privileges'.[179] Exactly which newspapers were involved in the controversy was never revealed, but it seems likely that Munro's criticism was directed mainly at the new popular press which flourished in Scotland following the repeal of the

---

[175] 'Mr Munro and the Glasgow Reporters' to the Editor of the Glasgow Herald, by Alexander Munro, Town Clerk, 23 September 1858', Quoted in *Glasgow Herald*, 24 September 1858.

[176] Ibid.

[177] The resolution prohibiting press access to the police court books was unanimously approved by those bailies in attendance at a magistrates' meeting, although two later indicated their opposition to it. At a subsequent meeting, however, Bailie Couper declared that 'he had not given his support to the resolution of the Magistrates sanctioning Mr Munro's order for the exclusion of the press from the Court book', and Bailie Clouston declared that 'he had no objection to the exhibition of the Court-book as formerly, and would willingly place at the service of the Press his own book'. 'Town Council Proceedings', *Glasgow Herald*, 24 September 1858; and 'The Glasgow Press and Mr Munro, the Police Assessor', *Glasgow Herald*, 13 September 1858.

[178] 'Mr Munro and the Glasgow Reporters' to the Editor of the Glasgow Herald, by Alexander Munro, Town Clerk, 23 September 1858'. See also Munro's views in 'Mr Munro and the Press. To the Editor of the Glasgow Herald, 28 September 1858'. Quoted in *Glasgow Herald*, 29 September 1858.

[179] 'Memorial of the Representatives of the Press, 10 September, 1858'. *Glasgow Herald*, 13 September 1858.

Stamp Act in 1855 rather than the mainstream press that had hitherto covered police court trials.[180] As Rosalind Crone has recently shown, the second half of the nineteenth century witnessed the rise of crime reporting in weekly and Sunday newspapers and other new forms of popular print culture.[181] By the late Victorian period, there were over two hundred 'weeklies' in Scotland.[182] Aided by the improvements in functional literacy, these newspapers were aimed mainly at entertainment for the masses and tended to sensationalise and exaggerate selected trial reports – a practice consistent with criticisms Munro levelled.[183] Significantly, the *Glasgow Herald* claimed that the criticism did not apply to its journalists and that not every newspaper was guilty of misrepresenting courtroom proceedings. Acknowledging Munro's allegation of inaccurate reporting in some newspapers, it pointed out:

> This statement may be correct as regards isolated cases which are served in an exaggerated and probably a malignant style in certain newspapers; but surely it does not apply to all; and if so, why restrict the privileges of the whole for the errors of the few? If the Magistrates mean that all deal in 'erroneous and defective reports,' then we simply take leave to deny the verity of their statement.

Despite giving it considerable coverage, the *Glasgow Herald* attempted to play down the dispute. In a comment that should caution against attaching too much significance to media representations, it noted: 'We cannot say that we feel much interest in this matter, for we have not been accustomed to look upon the Police Court books as furnishing material in which the public was greatly interested either in the way of amusement or instruction.'[184] The controversy died down after two weeks of heated claim and counter-claim. In a letter to the Editor of the *Glasgow Herald*, Munro made it clear it was never his intention to deny the press the right to access the court books, only to modify the mode of recording information. Indeed, he made a point of stressing that the press would be allowed to consult the books and that he was 'still willing to assist the press in the discharge of their duties in every way consistent with the interests of the public'.[185]

> My experience in these Courts has deepened my previous convictions as to the vast importance to the due administration of justice, of a vigilant and correct system of reporting; and I am happy to observe, since the measure in question

---

[180]   William Donaldson, *Popular Literature in Victorian Scotland: Language, Fiction and the Press* (Aberdeen, 1986), p. ix.

[181]   Crone, *Violent Victorians*, p. 209.

[182]   Donaldson, *Popular Literature in Victorian Scotland*, p. x.

[183]   Crone, *Violent Victorians*, pp. 209–56.

[184]   *Glasgow Herald*, 22 September 1858.

[185]   'Mr Munro and the Press. To the Editor of the Glasgow Herald, 28 September 1858'.

was adopted, that a good commencement has been made of such reporting; and I trust that we shall see no more of the old system, which has been so strongly condemned by several of the Glasgow newspapers, and which has found some apologists, but no defenders.[186]

Nonetheless, although fairly short lived, the controversy was significant in revealing not just how seriously civic men took newspaper representations, and, indeed, the power of the printed word, but also the relationship that had existed between the mainstream media and magistrates up until that point. The *Glasgow Herald* claimed the relationship had until fairly recently been harmonious and that the practice of allowing journalists to inspect police court books – which significantly, had to be signed by magistrates in order to be authenticated – had been done 'to the satisfaction of a long succession of Magistrates and public officials'.[187] It continued: 'the members of the Press never were adversaries of his until he [Munro] made them so. He will not, and cannot deny, that everything was peaceful, and everything was going on as it had been going on for years, when he suddenly came in and made himself an adversary of theirs.'[188] Intriguingly, the *Glasgow Herald* opposed denying journalists access to the books on the basis of how it would look to the public:

> it will be erroneously set down by many as an attempt to conceal matters in the Police Office which will not brook the light; and the unpopularity of a resolution pompously issued, may innocently attach to the Police Force itself, which, from recent events, cannot afford to lose any portion of that public fervour and confidence which it still possess.[189]

Here was a mainstream newspaper alluding to the public's perceived association between the courts and the police. It was a comment that spoke volumes about how in certain circles the police institution and the police court were viewed as one and the same.

More tellingly, the *Glasgow Herald*'s response suggested that courtroom officials were sometimes in dialogue with reporters about police court trials on which journalists had not sat:

> Mr Munro tells us that if the reporters had waited upon him (that is after he had closed the book) he would have been prepared to have made some comforting explanations to them. Why they did not go to him, we know not, unless that they looked to the Magistrates and not to him as the 'head of the house;' and to the Magistrates they did go.[190]

---

[186]   Ibid.
[187]   *Glasgow Herald*, 24 September 1858.
[188]   Ibid.
[189]   *Glasgow Herald*, 22 September 1858.
[190]   *Glasgow Herald*, 24 September 1858.

There was an implied assumption in the above remark that the court personnel had, in such instances, been able to influence how courtroom proceedings were portrayed.

As the century progressed, controversies about the accuracy of newspaper reporting were also recorded in other towns. In 1880, for instance, John Coghill, the Senior Police Magistrate in Caithness, went so far as to charge William Docherty, proprietor and editor of the *Caithness Courier*, with misrepresenting almost every case in that court. Mr Coghill said that 'he was inclined to commit Docherty for contempt of Court, and that if he did not give correct reports of their proceeding there was no alternative but handing him over to the burgh Fiscal'.[191] There were similar concerns in police circles, with Glasgow magistrates in 1856 resolving that the superintendent of police should admonish journalists who did not report the meetings of police commissioners accurately.[192] Such instances highlight that the police and civic leaders were having to contend with a new type of journalism that was potentially more critical and less flattering than the mainstream media had hitherto been.[193] More importantly, they also suggest that courtroom public officials were not only becoming even more media aware and concerned with how trial proceedings and, to some degree, they themselves were being portrayed as the century progressed, but also that they were attempting to police the content of reports too.

Greater accountability in local government and the annual publication of police criminal returns are likely to have played an important part in determining media sensitivity, but so, also, was the changing importance of the public and press galleries. As in England, it appears as though the latter became less important in sending out moral messages and serving as a warning to the masses as the century progressed,[194] while the former became ever more pervasive in shaping popular perceptions of, and discourse on, law and order. The three seats which were made available to the public in the Aberdeen Police Court following its redesign in 1870 illustrated this. The gallery's capacity was smaller and its location less to the fore than the new press box, which was given a status and position in the court second only to that of the magisterial bench.[195] As the *Aberdeen Journal* noted: 'the space is better apportioned for

---

[191] *Aberdeen Weekly Journal*, 3 February 1880.

[192] GCA, E1/13/1: Magistrates Committee Minute Book, 11 February 1856: The Glasgow Magistrates 'resolve that newspaper reporters should be admonished by the Superintendent of Police to be careful that Police cases be correctly reported by them'.

[193] For more on the development of the new popular press from the mid-nineteenth century, see Donaldson, *Popular Literature in Victorian Scotland*, p. ix.

[194] There was growing criticism of public galleries in late nineteenth century – which was probably part of a wider criticism of the criminal justice system being a vehicle for entertainment – with those who attended summary trials often described as being the dregs of society. Godfrey, 'Sentencing, Theatre, Audience and Communication', p. 165.

[195] *Aberdeen Journal*, 13 July 1870.

the convenience of those who have first claim to consideration, viz Officials, Procurators, and Reporters. Three seats only are provided for the public.'[196]

The importance of journalists within the courtroom by this point was highlighted by two articles published in *The Bailie*. In 1873, in an article entitled 'The Court Jester', it reported how magistrates and procurators tried to play to journalists and outperform each other in court, often at the expense of the accused and other participants:

> When he [the reporter] entered [the Courtroom press box], a poor woman was being tried for some delinquency or other; but perfectly unmindful of the prisoner at the bar, Bailie Moir and Captain Robb were busy making sundry and ineffectual attempts at 'wut;' which although the poorest jokes ever heard by our Ass [reporter], were received by those in the Court with loud laughter, while the pencils of reporters were flying over the paper as if Mr Gladstone were unfolding his programme for the next session of Parliament. ... Our Ass [reporter] shortly afterwards left the Court, firmly impressed of the truth of the adage, that 'a living donkey is better than a dead lion'.[197]

The following year, *The Bailie* selected for its weekly 'portrait' of distinguished and important men in public life none other than William Gardner, the Central Police Court reporter, and provided the following commentary: 'There is no better-known figure in the Central Police Court, where his grey head and ruddy countenance are looked for as regularly as the appearance of a magistrate on the bench' (see Illustration 4.2).[198] That the court reporter was deemed worthy of being profiled alongside civic dignitaries was testament to the significance of the press in representing Glasgow's municipal and judicial administration.

As middle-class interest in police court affairs waned in the second half of the nineteenth century, public access to the court was assumed to be reached not by attending in person, but by reading its work in the media. It was a development which implied that reporters' narratives were a reliable account of the courts' actions. But with such access being restricted to those who could afford to buy and read the newspapers in which the reporters' narratives were to be found, it was, in essence, suggestive of a middle-class perspective – and a perspective in which magistrates, the police and journalists had, as men of a particular social standing, a vested interest in projecting.

The press, therefore, had a crucial role to play in shaping the dynamics of the courtroom. For the most part, the mainstream press acted as a form of respondent and point of commentary on cases and their meanings, and as an interpreter of middle-class ideals and expectations of the behaviour and experiences of others. Sometimes acting as a constraining influence on magistrates, and sometimes

---

[196]   Ibid.
[197]   *The Bailie*, no. 43, 13 August 1873, p. 2.
[198]   *The Bailie*, no. 82, 13 May 1874, p. 2.

Illustration 4.2   William Gardner, Glasgow Police Court Journalist, 1874.
@CSG CIC Glasgow Museums and Libraries Collection:
The Mitchell Library, Special Collections†

Note: What is particularly interesting about this image is not just that *The Bailie* chose to profile the Glasgow Police Court reporter, William Gardner, but also that his portrait was put to the forefront of the court. In the background can be seen the magistrate on a raised platform, the clerk by his side, the accused, the gallery, a policemen and other indistinguishable participants.

† 'William Gardner', *The Bailie*, no. 82, 13 May 1874, p. 1.

affecting how bailies performed and handed down sentences, journalists were an important vehicle for disseminating moral messages about the court and magisterial capacity for governance to a wider audience. Variations in press coverage of the auditory should not disguise the fact that the overwhelming majority of mainstream media reports represented the courts in a favourable light. When dissent was recorded, it tended to be the dissent of a certain type of man – the propertied man, expressing discontent with civic government, not the dissent of the working class expressing displeasure with their experience of police court summary justice. For the most part, the media representation of the public gallery, and the audience it reached, not only entertained the public and satisfied voyeuristic interest in court proceedings, but also helped make police court justice appear transparent and, through selective media reporting, reflective of public opinion, just and legitimate. There were shared motivational forces at work – moral, social and entertainment – which, far from being contradictory, typically contributed to the same end.

VI. Conclusion

In 1885, the journalist for *The Detective* rounded off his portrayal of summary justice as it was experienced in Glasgow's Central Police Court in the following manner:

> Thus the wheels of justice roll on their dismal course. Day after day the same miserable scene, the same sodden and besotted players, the same grave and dignified Magistrate. It is little wonder that officials become hardened and policemen cruel, for in the whole performance there is not a redeeming feature.[199]

These 'performances' were not scripted by the working classes. Indeed, the role of the urban masses within what was often a sad, sorry and depressing narrative was usually marginal and second to that of the courtroom officials. While magistrates, procurators and senior policemen could, on occasion, clash over evidential and procedural issues, for the most part they shared and upheld similar social and gendered ideals and ideologies on the expected behaviour of those brought before them. Conflicts and posturing over courtroom authority should not hide the fact that the civic men who staffed police courts were working to a similar agenda in that much of what they were doing was protecting private property, upholding attempts to reshape working habits and popular culture, and disciplining and controlling the masses. However, although police courts punished those who failed to meet middle-class standards of behaviour that was deemed to constitute a breach of police or common law, the way in which cases were examined and commented upon in the court suggested distinct

---

[199]   'A Monday Morning at the Central Police Court', p. 2.

expectations of different kinds of defenders. The representations offered by the press suggested that women of lower status who appeared in court were, for example, forceful interlocutors in their defence but this did not render them more successful in achieving their ends. Behaviour at odds with middle-class expectations was generally punished or ridiculed by court officials. If the record of courtroom dialogue is to be believed, superintendents, police officers and witnesses could play an important role in contextualising cases for magistrates, and did not hesitate to add their own moralising, pejorative or other asides. The role of the auditory was also important, since the press demonstrated how the gallery's laughter or compassion might affect judgements (as well as what influenced their own reactions to cases). Thus, through their actions and commentary, the magistracy, superintendents, police officers, witnesses, the auditory and the authors of the press imposed their own values upon the police court.

In his study of police courts in late Victorian and early twentieth-century London, Godfrey has suggested that 'the theatrical organization of the courts, and archaic distancing practices, served to depress excitement and emotional outbursts, so that evidence could be presented dispassionately'.[200] It is certainly true that the structure, organisation and design of Scottish police courts aimed to serve this purpose too, although the small, cramped format of many of them somewhat restricted the symbolic impact that public men desired. Having said that, emotional dynamics mattered in the courtroom, especially in demonstrating its personnel's capacity for governance. As Chapter 2 showed, magistrates were expected to keep their emotions in check in order to uphold the dignity of the bench and the image of justice. Thus *The Bailie*, commenting on Bailie James Hamilton's performance in court in 1875, reported: 'His temper is said to be a short one, but ... the Bailie succeeds very admirably in keeping it under in public, no "scene," either in the Council Chamber or the Police Court, having ever been recorded against him by those terrible fellows the "liners" for the daily press.'[201] Defenders' outbursts of feeling rarely served their better interests; their expression of strong emotions was usually interpreted by the courts and press as evidence of their inability to attain middle-class standards of rational composure for men or modest comportment for women.

Above all else, though, the symbolism of the court, and more importantly its personnel, were designed to impose onto the accused a different type of emotion – intimidation. Indeed, the public men who staffed the courts, and the camaraderie they often enjoyed, stood in sharp contrast to the nervous, worried bewilderment of those testifying before them.[202] As Duff has pointed out for the modern-day summary courts, the trial process was, in itself, a form of 'moral criticism' and 'communicative enterprise' that enabled the courtroom personnel

---

[200] Godfrey, 'Sentencing, Theatre, Audience and Communication', p. 167.
[201] *The Bailie*, no. 154, 29 September 1875, pp. 1–2.
[202] Carlen makes a similar point: Carlen, *Magistrates' Justice*.

to 'inform the sensibilities of the poor from a position of rhetorical power'.[203] The body language, demeanour and actions of magistrates, allied with the gaze of the public gallery and presence of journalists, helped to impose judicial discipline and public censorship in an atmosphere that was anything but welcoming, and often threatening. All worked to uphold a power hierarchy within the court and shape how people experienced the law. If police courts were public theatres, then the victim and the accused were, at least in terms of their media representation, often afforded only modest and restricted speaking parts – with the presence of the fiscal and the power of the legal discourse, it seems, reducing their agency and capacity to articulate their roles. It was the public men who were often portrayed as being centre stage: the fiscal as the producer and casting agent, the magistrate as the director and critic, policemen as the supporting cast, the journalist as the performance reviewer and publicist, and the accused, all too frequently it seemed from press reports, the pantomime villain to be mocked and booed.

---

[203] Antony Duff and David Garland (eds), *A Reader on Punishment* (Oxford, 1994), p. 223.

Chapter 5
Practices, Patterns and Perceptions

I. Introduction

Nineteenth-century Scottish towns were centres of contrasts. The splendour of commercial success and the flourishing middle-class suburbs which sprang up in the west ends of the larger cities differed markedly from the rapidly-expanding, squalid, inner-city dens, lanes and lodging houses which were home to the poorest of the poor. Glasgow's contrasting fortunes, in particular, stood out. The city that boasted about its contribution to Enlightenment thought, commercial expansion, and trade and industry had by the early nineteenth century acquired the unenviable reputation for being home to some of the most crime-ridden communities in Western Europe.[1] In *Midnight Scenes and Social Photographs* (1858), the social investigator 'Shadow' – a pseudonym for Alexander Brown, a letterpress printer in Glasgow – depicted a wretched image of social segregation, urban squalor, criminality and moral destitution.[2] Describing the inhabitants of alleyways in Argyle Street and the Gallowgate and Trongate districts he noted: 'riot, drunkenness, theft and profligacy of every kind – it may be murder itself – are pastimes in which they are engaged.'[3]

Brown was just one of a plethora of social investigators to portray Glasgow and other Scottish cities in such a light. His comments were mirrored in a series of parliamentary inquiries and investigations into urban Scotland's social problems, reflecting burgeoning middle-class fascination with the dark side of life and growing governmental interest in the challenges brought by rapid urban expansion.[4] Such contemporary reflections, as scholars have pointed out, did

---

[1]   'Reports on the Sanitary Condition of the Labouring Population in Scotland: in Consequence of an Inquiry directed to be made by Poor Law Commissioners', *British Parliamentary Papers* (*BPP*), 1842 (008 House of Lords), XXVIII.I, p. 71.

[2]   Shadow, *Midnight Scenes and Social Photographs being Sketches of Life in the Streets, Wynds and Dens of the City: Glasgow, 1858*, intro. John F. McCaffrey (Glasgow, 1976), p. 12.

[3]   Ibid., p. 94.

[4]   'Report from the Select Committee on Hand-Loom Weavers' Petitions', *BPP*, 1834 (556), X.1; 'Hand-loom Weavers. Return to an Address of the Honourable the House of Commons, dated 15 February 1839; Copies of certain Reports of the Assistant Hand-Loom Weavers' Commissioners', *BPP*, 1839 (159), XLII.511; 'Reports on the Sanitary Condition of the Labouring Population in Scotland'; George Bell, *Day and Night in the Wynds of Edinburgh* (Edinburgh, 1849); and George Bell, *Blackfriars' Wynd Analysed* (Edinburgh, 1850).

much to forge the reputations of Scottish cities – not least Glasgow – as being cities that were home to unparalleled urban misery, crime and drunkenness.[5] Yet, rarely have the criminal histories of these cities, and how they were informed and shaped by police, statistical and media representations, been subject to detailed attention. Indeed, it is somewhat surprising that the nineteenth-century fascination with crime, immorality and drunkenness in Scottish burghs has not been matched by detailed academic scrutiny. Scholars of Scottish criminal justice history, in assessing the national impact of industrialisation on crime, have, with the odd exception,[6] focused more on recorded indictable returns[7] and Scottish Crown Office precognition papers[8] – both of which show a steady increase in recorded crime to the mid-nineteenth century followed by a fairly consistent decline thereafter – than on the non-indictable crimes and offences which constituted the bulk of urban lawlessness. Serious scrutiny of trends in summary cases in industrial centres tend to be submerged within wider studies on urban social crises, confined to fairly short periods of time, and often neglect the cultural context which influenced contemporary perceptions of crime and the production of criminal records. This chapter seeks to address this by situating the practice of the courts within wider social and cultural perceptions of crime and summary justice in the era. It examines the changing business of the court and the statistical pattern of recorded crime, the factors that influenced quantitative trends through the production of police data, and how criminal statistics were used by contemporaries and came to help shape perceptions of police courts' caseload and, indeed, Scottish cities themselves.

---

[5]   T.M. Devine, 'The Urban Crisis', in T.M. Devine and Gordon Jackson (eds), *Glasgow, Volume I: Beginnings to 1830* (Manchester, 1995), pp. 402–16; and W. Hamish Fraser and Irene Maver, 'The Social Problems of the City', in W. Hamish Fraser and Irene Maver (eds), *Glasgow, Volume II: 1830 to 1912* (Manchester, 1996), pp. 352–94.

[6]   W.W.J. Knox and A. McKinlay, 'Crime, Protest and Policing in Nineteenth-Century Scotland', in Trevor Griffiths and Graeme Morton (eds), *A History of Everyday Life in Scotland, 1800 to 1900* (Edinburgh, 2010), pp. 196–203; and Fraser and Maver, 'The Social Problems of the City', pp. 352–94.

[7]   See, for instance, Anne-Marie Kilday, *Women and Violent Crime in Enlightenment Scotland* (Woodbridge, 2007); Carolyn A. Conley, *Certain Other Countries: Homicide, Gender, and National Identity in Late Nineteenth-Century England, Ireland, Scotland and Wales* (Columbus, 2007); Carolyn A. Conley, 'Homicide in Late-Victorian Ireland and Scotland', *New Hibernia Review*, 5/3 (2001): pp. 66–86; and V.A.C. Gatrell and T.B. Hadden, 'Criminal Statistics and their Interpretation', in E.A. Wrigley (ed.), *Nineteenth-Century Society: Essays in the Use of Quantitative Methods for the Study of Social Data* (Cambridge, 1972), pp. 336–96.

[8]   Ian Donnachie, '"The Darker Side": A Speculative Survey of Scottish Crime during the First Half of the Nineteenth Century', *Scottish Economic and Social History*, 15/1 (1995): pp. 5–24; Ian Donnachie, 'Profiling Criminal Offences: The Evidence of the Lord Advocate's Papers during the First Half of the Nineteenth Century in Scotland', *Scottish Archives: Journal of the Scottish Records Association*, 1 (1995): pp. 85–92.

In doing this, particular attention will be given to examining the relationship between criminal returns and the media. This is important, as the reliability and usefulness of criminal statistics,[9] and the role of sensationalist media-reporting, moral panics, and criminal broadsides in generating fears about crime and control and in shaping statistical patterns and structures of law and governance, has become a fertile area of historical investigation in recent years.[10] The chapter highlights the important role of the media, the police, and the data the police themselves produced in reflecting the business of police courts and how it evolved over the course of the century. In an era when senior police officers became increasingly aware of their own media representation, police court periodicals and newspapers, it is contended, played a critical role in reporting courtroom proceedings and statistical data. They served as an extension of the discursive nature of police courts and, in all likelihood, influenced contemporary perceptions of crime and, on occasion, statistical prosecution patterns for certain moral and public order offences. Media reports and police court returns, it is argued, had a dialogic relationship that often reaffirmed contemporary perceptions of certain facets of Scottish urban life in the way they were interpreted, accepted, and used by those in authority to serve their own purposes.[11] Indeed, as police-produced statistical data was represented uncritically in newspapers, social reports and other contemporary forms, the assumptions that were embedded in them came to offer an analysis of the business of police courts and the character of Scottish cities as the century progressed.

II. The Business of Police Courts in their Formative Years

As Chapter 1 has argued, civic men presented the police courts' function as being concerned with the common good, but behind the rhetoric were implied social distinctions and assumptions that anticipated what police courts would do.[12]

---

[9] The literature on this is too detailed to cite in full. A good overview is provided by Clive Emsley, *Crime and Society in England, 1750–1900*, 3rd edn (Harlow, 2005), Chapter 1.

[10] Among the most recent additions that examine the media are Judith Rowbotham and Kim Stevenson (eds), *Behaving Badly: Social Panic and Moral Outrage – Victorian and Modern Parallels* (Aldershot, 2003); Judith Rowbotham and Kim Stevenson (eds), *Criminal Conversations: Victorian Crimes, Social Panic, and Moral Outrage* (Columbus, 2005); and David Lemmings and Claire Walker (eds), *Moral Panics, the Media and the Law in Early Modern England* (Basingstoke, 2009).

[11] Jeff Ferrell and Neil Websdale have argued that interrelations between media, crime and crime-fighting are such that 'policing can in fact hardly be understood apart from its interpenetration with media at all levels'. Jeff Ferrell and Neil Websdale (eds), *Making Trouble: Cultural Constructions of Crime, Deviance and Control* (New York, 1999), p. 15.

[12] See *Caledonian Mercury*, 18 July 1805.

Superintendent Tait, in his speech to mark the opening of the Edinburgh Police establishment, highlighted this:

> I shall be sorry indeed to be obliged to sink those in the inferior ranks of life still lower, by inflicting punishments of a degrading nature. And I shall regret still more to be obliged to apply the punishments which naturally belong to the inferior ranks, to those in a higher class. But I am bound by the sacred oath which I have take, to discharge my duty as my conscience dictates, and that my conscience tells me that I am to look not to *persons*, but to *crimes*.[13]

Although limited, the powers of the Edinburgh Police Court were, according to the Lord Provost, 'sufficient to give an essential protection to virtue, in every situation, and to give check to vice and profligacy, in whatever rank of life they may be found'.[14] Indeed, although police courts had charge of different kinds of offences to the church courts, they in many ways filled the vacuum that had been created by kirk sessions' weakening influence over the behaviour of parishioners, especially in the rapidly expanding industrial centres where church provision failed to keep pace with population growth. Tait, in the same opening speech, alluded to the importance of the police in regulating public morality:

> Much of the virtue of a nation depends upon the exertions of Police, in preventing crimes, in suppressing them in their advanced progress, especially in the Metropolis, which must always greatly influence, and may I say, even regulate the morals of the country, to which it belongs.[15]

Although he stopped short of actually saying it, there was even an implied assumption from the Lord Provost in his opening address that the police magistrates should uphold religious values that were assumed to be shared among the community:

> Our ardent and united wish being to see this Metropolis, (long since deservedly in the highest estimation for its Seminaries of Learning, and its Courts of Law) equally distinguished by purity of manners, propriety of conduct, and an uniform veneration for, and undeviating obedience to the laws, both civil and religious, in every class, and individual member of the community.[16]

---

[13]   Ibid.
[14]   Ibid.
[15]   Ibid.
[16]   Ibid.

Similarly, police commissioners in Dundee in the first few weeks of being appointed in 1824 deliberated a memorial from the local kirk session concerning the profanation of the Sabbath.[17] It was resolved that public houses be closed on Sunday during the hours of divine service, except for the reception of travellers, and policemen were instructed to ensure that licensing laws were rigorously enforced.[18] The police, in other words, assumed responsibility for upholding morality in a manner similar to that which had been carried out by kirk session elders in the eighteenth century.

The statistical evidence that exists for this period reveals that clamping down on public order and public morality offences were high on the list of priorities for police commissioners, procurators and magistrates. The earliest records did not classify police court cases into 'crimes', 'offences' and 'contraventions' in the way later ones would, but instead listed them individually. John McGowan's research has shown that the most common cases prosecuted in the Edinburgh Police Court involved minor assault, breach of the peace, petty theft and blocking the streets with articles for sale (see Table 5.1).[19] Assault and breach of the peace accounted for approximately one third of cases in the court's formative years. In many instances, the offence occurred after the closure of a public house with the offender being drunk at the time of arrest. On average, theft made up one quarter to one fifth of cases. The vast majority of these, as Chapter 3 demonstrated, were for relatively small sums (although even modest financial penalties could, of course, hit the pockets of the poorest social groups hard). Although difficult to be precise given that cases were not classified in the records in this period as 'crimes' and 'offences', it appears as though crimes against the person involving violence were as numerous as crimes against property without violence (even when the generally referred-to 'offence' of disorderly conduct is excluded). Traffic and welfare offences each accounted for about one sixth of cases, and public health and cleansing contraventions, on average, made up just under one tenth.

McGowan's figures suggest that the number of people who were brought before magistrates was far higher than had been possible in the burgh courts. This was indicative of the desire of men of property to use the legal system to promote higher levels of urban order. In the Edinburgh Police Court's first month alone, over 300 cases as diverse as trespassing, keeping mischievous dogs, running improper shows and riding dangerously in the streets, were resolved.[20] In total, magistrates examined 2,496 cases in the first 12 months

---

[17] Dundee City Archives (DCA), TC/PBM/1: Dundee Police Board Minute Book, 1824–1832, 3 November 1824.

[18] Ibid., 10 November 1824.

[19] John McGowan, *Policing the Metropolis of Scotland: A History of the Police and Systems of Police in Edinburgh and Edinburghshire, 1770–1833* (Musselburgh, 2010), p. 139.

[20] *Edinburgh Advertiser*, 27 August 1805.

Table 5.1   Number and Nature of Edinburgh Police Court Cases,
1805 to 1807[†]

Crime, Offence & Contravention	17/07/05 to 14/07/06	01/01/06 to 31/12/06	15/07/06 to 30/07/07
Assault	314	365	279
Wife Assault	33	31	23
Police Assault	30	31	19
% of Court Cases	15	18.5	18
Rioting and Disorderly Behaviour	440	362	255
% of Court Cases	17.5	15.5	14.5
Theft	305	349	284
Dishonesty	116	119	171
Vagrancy	85	74	62
% of Court Cases	20.5	23	29
Sexual Offences	36	29	6
% of Court Cases	1.5	1	0.5
Malicious Damage	18	13	25
% of Court Cases	0.5	1	1.5
Welfare Obstructions	446	399	278
% of Court Cases	18	17	16
Cleansing	194	222	150
% of Court Cases	8	9.5	8.5
Traffic Cases	479	336	211
% of Court Cases	19	14.5	12
Total Cases Examinable	2,496 out of 2,651	2,335 out of 2,475	1,763 out of 1,827

Note: The above classification was put together by McGowan. Breach of the peace often included assault but it has been distinguished because no complainer was identified. The dishonest category includes 'wilful imposition'. This usually fell short of fraud, and often involved deficient measurements and goods. Sexual offences include street prostitution and attempting to procure young girls for prostitution. Cleaning offences usually involve throwing filth onto the streets. Welfare offences include allowing poultry to stray onto the streets and allowing chimney vents to catch fire. The most common traffic offence was riding a cart on the pavements or in a dangerous manner on the streets.

[†] John McGowan, *Policing the Metropolis of Scotland: A History of the Police and Systems of Police in Edinburgh and Edinburghshire, 1770–1833* (Musselburgh, 2010), p. 139.

(although, as police reports later in the century were keen to point out, these often involved repeat offenders, so the actual percentage prosecuted relative to population would have been lower and impossible to pinpoint precisely).[21] It was not uncommon for cases – especially those involving disorderly conduct – to have two defenders, so the ratio of people charged to population was even greater than these figures suggest. Although Scotland had been served by a public prosecutor since the fifteenth century, the growing involvement of the police in the prosecution process initially resulted in a considerable increase in the number of cases involving crimes, offences and contraventions brought before the courts. This was especially the case for offences and contraventions for which police prosecutors were most likely to take cognisance. Mainstream newspapers tried to allay concerns about the financial burden imposed on ratepayers by emphasising the preventive role of the police and the police court. After noting that more than three hundred cases had been determined (brought before magistrates) in the first month of the Edinburgh Police Court, the *Aberdeen Journal* stressed:

> We hope that a vigorous Police will soon diminish the number of cases. In many instances, the punishment in the Court of Police has taken place within 12 hours, and in most cases within 24 hours, of the time of committing the crime, which ought certainly to have a considerable effect in preventing future offences.[22]

Indeed, the large volume of cases that police courts processed in their first few years was recorded in the press as a sign of the efficiency of summary justice.[23]

The Glasgow Police Court minute books for 1813 to 1824 were also crammed with minor offences relating to petty theft, disorderly conduct and the built environment. Much of the court's time was concerned with public order, keeping the streets clear of obstructions and structuring property. The fiscal prosecuted obstructions and nuisances, deliverymen who blocked public and commercial thoroughfares, and illegal market traders. People were charged with a wide range of contraventions, including dirty pavements, leaving horses and carts unattended in the street, property not being properly railed, smashing public lamps, not closing cellar doors, failing to secure shop windows, and drunk and disorderly conduct.[24] Such prosecutions were symbolic of the business communities'

---

[21]   This covered the period 17 July 1805 to 14 July 1806. McGowan, *Policing the Metropolis of Scotland*, p. 139. The population of Edinburgh in 1801 stood at 122,954. By 1811 it had risen to 148,607. 'Population. Comparative Accounts of the Population of Great Britain in the Years 1801, 1811, 1821, and 1831', *BPP*, 1831 (348), XVIII.1, p. 380. The population for 1805 on which the ratio has been calculated has been estimated at 128,000.

[22]   *Aberdeen Journal*, 4 September 1805.

[23]   Ibid.

[24]   Glasgow City Archives (GCA), B3/1/1: Glasgow Police Court Diet Books, 28 January to 3 July 1813.

growing preoccupation with regulating public space in order to remove obstacles to commerce and suppress illegal street trading.[25] This developed the courts' role in shaping the nineteenth-century cityscape, as Volume 2 will explore further. The fiscal's accounts for prosecutions from 1807 to 1819 also included a large number of offenders fined for obstructing, striking and molesting watchmen, indicating that the transition to a policed society was far from smooth.[26]

The problems involved in using statistical returns to gauge trends of criminality have been well documented.[27] Court returns reveal as much about changing prosecution and policing practices as the extent of law breaking. They record only crimes, offences and contraventions that were reported and prosecuted, not the extent of crime and disorder within the society *per se*. Moreover, there are major gaps in the minute books, and the flexible, and on occasion loose, manner in which the law was applied makes it difficult to be too precise in drawing conclusions about prosecution patterns. McGowan's research, however, shows that after an initial surge, prosecutions in the Edinburgh Police Court were not sustained at the same rate for the first ten or so years of the court.[28] Whereas magistrates had dealt with approximately 2,500 cases in the first year of the court's operation, by mid-1810 to mid-1811 it dealt with just 1,213.[29] However, from 1813 to 1819, the business of the court grew dramatically amidst escalating anxieties about the level of crime (see Table 5.2). These returns, which unlike those listed in Table 5.1 record persons and not cases, show the court's ability to handle a larger volume of cases. By 1830, the clerk of police was recording up to 7,000 cases per year – the overwhelming majority of which were prosecuted in police courts.[30]

Maurice Golden's research for Dundee – whose economy, like that of Glasgow, suffered in the immediate post-war years – also identified an upward trend in prosecutions, both in the burgh court up to 1824, and then in the newly established police court. Assault and public order offences accounted for approximately two thirds to three quarters of the court's business and were

---

[25]   Drew D. Gray, 'The People's Courts? Summary Justice and Social Relations in the City of London, c.1760–1800', *Family and Community History*, 11/1 (2008): p. 12.

[26]   GCA, B3/1/5: Fiscal's Accounts for Prosecutions, 1807–1819.

[27]   The most trenchant critics of the usefulness of criminal statistics in gauging levels of criminality include R.S. Sindall, 'The Criminal Statistics of Nineteenth-Century Cities: A New Approach', *Urban History*, 13 (1986): pp. 28–36. Those who recognise the limitations but use them as a starting point for understanding trends in crime, and changing attitudes towards it, include V.A.C. Gatrell, 'The Decline of Theft and Violence in Victorian and Edwardian England', in V.A.C. Gatrell, Bruce Lenman and Geoffrey Parker (eds), *Crime and the Law: The Social History of Crime in Western Europe since 1500* (London, 1980), passim; and Emsley, *Crime and Society*, p. 30.

[28]   McGowan, *Policing the Metropolis of Scotland*, p. 142.

[29]   McGowan notes an inconsistency in the recording of the number of cases. His own research uncovered 2,496 cases examined; however, he notes that the *Edinburgh Advertiser* on 19 July 1811 claimed that the number of cases dealt with in the first year was 2,857. Ibid.

[30]   Ibid., p. 271.

Table 5.2   Number of People Prosecuted in Edinburgh Police Court,
              1812 to 1819†

Period	Number of Persons
August 1812 to December 1812	854
1813	2,857
1814	3,453
1815	4,727
1816	4,283
1817	4,577
1818	5,056
1819	5,409

† McGowan, *Policing the Metropolis of Scotland*, p. 210.

prosecuted more frequently in the post-war years. The highest increase was in crimes relating to property, which rose significantly between 1825 and 1830. Theft, for instance, rose by 130 per cent between 1825 and 1830 followed by vagrancy, which rose by 40 per cent.[31] Charges concerning breach of police regulations relating to the built environment, on the other hand, fell by 20 per cent between 1816 and 1833. These were mainly for contraventions of paving and nuisance laws. According to Golden, the decline suggests that people were becoming compliant with environmental regulation.[32]

A similar post-war upward trend in recorded and prosecuted crime and offences was evident in Glasgow. In his *Enumeration of the Inhabitants of the City of Glasgow* (1820), James Cleland noted that in 1819, 7,945 cases were heard by magistrates in the police office.[33] He estimated that 'as police cases averaged nearly two persons, it is supposed that, including the witnesses, 20,000 appeared before the magistrates' in the Glasgow Police Court in

---

[31]   Maurice C. Golden, 'Criminality and the Development of Policing in Dundee 1816–1833', unpub. MPhil thesis (University of Dundee, 2003), pp. 25–6.

[32]   Ibid., p. 26.

[33]   James Cleland, *Enumeration of the Inhabitants of the City of Glasgow and its Connected Suburbs; together with Population and Statistical Tables, relative to Scotland and England* (Glasgow, 1820), p. 29.

1819.[34] In 1822 he submitted the following opinion for the 'Eleventh Report of Commissioners into Legal Practices in Scotland': 'Of the great number of cases in this Court, it is only necessary to state, that it is very great, and has increased with the increase of the population, and the improvement of the Police of this city.'[35] The following year, in the third edition of his *Statistical Tables relative to the City of Glasgow, with other Matters therewith connected*, he noted that 13,564 persons in 1822 had been brought before the police court in Glasgow.[36] Table 5.3 shows the business of the court in the month of January in that year.

The surge in recorded apprehensions was mirrored in the Glasgow burgh court, where the number of criminal cases prosecuted by the fiscal rose from 464 in 1812 to 1,028 in 1820.[37] That court's capacity to deal with the burgeoning volume of cases was facilitated by the appointment in 1804 of advocate James Reddie to the position of Town Clerk. Unlike clerks in other towns, he was to devote his energies full-time to municipal affairs, which was, again, symbolic of the strengthening resolve of the civic elite to improve the capacity of the local burgh machine to deal with criminal affairs.[38] He also gave magistrates advice in the police court. Joseph John Gurney, penal reformer, claimed in 1818 that the Glasgow gaol was crowded to the point of suffocation: 'There are seldom less than 200 prisoners in the jail ... The number of criminals committed during the last three years amounting to 3,068.'[39] This compared to 27 in gaol and 90 in bridewell in 1802.[40] He added that 'crimes have of late been rapidly increasing in Glasgow. The fact may be

---

[34]   Ibid.

[35]   'Eleventh Report of the Commissioners Appointed for Inquiring into the Duties, Salaries, Fees and Enrolments, of the Several Officers, Clerks, and Ministers of Justice, of the Courts in Scotland. Burgh Courts', *BPP*, 1822 (558), VIII.117, p. 56.

[36]   James Cleland, *Statistical Tables relative to the City of Glasgow, with other Matters therewith connected*, 3rd edition (Glasgow, 1823), p. 91.

[37]   'Eleventh Report of the Commissioners Appointed for Inquiring into the Duties, Salaries, Fees and Enrolments', p. 56.

[38]   The business of the burgh court also soared, especially in the post-Napoleonic period amidst growing concerns with crime and disorder. The number of criminal cases prosecuted by the fiscal rose from 464 in 1812 to 1,028 in 1820, with a further 90 cases being remitted for trial in the High Court of Justiciary. 'Eleventh Report of the Commissioners Appointed for Inquiring into the Duties, Salaries, Fees and Enrolments', p. 56. However, the burgh court's role in handling criminal cases diminished considerably in the 1820s as the powers of the police court were extended under the 1821 Glasgow Police Act and a resident sheriff was acquired to serve the city. Irene Maver, 'The Guardianship of the Community: Civic Authority before 1833', in Devine and Jackson (eds), *Glasgow, Volume 1*, pp. 254–5.

[39]   Joseph John Gurney, *Notes on a Visit made to some of the Prisons in Scotland and the North of England, in Company with Elizabeth Fry; with some general Observations on the Subject of Prison Discipline* (London, 1819), pp. 52–3.

[40]   James Neild, *State of Prisons in England, Scotland and Wales* (London, 1812), pp. 187, 200, 238, & 241–2. Cited in Joy Cameron, *Prisons and Punishment in Scotland from the Middle Ages to the Present Day* (Edinburgh, 1983), pp. 57–8.

Table 5.3   People Accused and Brought before Magistrates in the Glasgow
Police Court in the Month of January 1822[†]

Disorderly in Houses: 185	Molesting Watchmen: 18
Disorderly on the Streets: 166	Having Chimney on Fire: 17
Fighting on the Streets: 77	Breach of Spirit License: 15
Found Drunk on the Streets: 69	Offering to Sell Stolen Goods: 15
Encumbering the Streets with Sale Articles: 61	Found Lying on Stairs at Night: 11
Petty Thefts: 46	Indecent Conduct: 13
Acting Suspiciously: 44	Obstructing Footpaths: 10
Being Concerned in Pick Pockets: 42	Not Keeping Lamps Next to Building Mats: 9
Not Cleaning Foot Pavements: 40	Leaving Horses and Carts Unattended: 7
Encumbering the Streets with Barrows: 27	Throwing Nuisance Out of Windows: 6
Keeping Dirty Closes: 23	Other*: 60

Other*: Includes boys lying on the top of bakers' ovens through the night (6), selling fish by improper weights (6), overloading carts with dung (6), carrying bundles through the night (5), breaking lamps wilfully (5), being disorderly in houses of bad fame (5), change-keepers for harbouring persons in their houses during Divine Service (5), keeping houses of bad fame (4), riding on carts without reins (3), stealing lead from houses (3), housebreaking and theft (2), acting as porters without badges (2), keeping a biting dog (2), swine going at large on streets (2), bad pavement (2), watchmen insolent on duty (1) and fighting dogs (1).

Total: 961, of whom 686 were men and 275 were women.

† James Cleland, *Statistical Tables relative to the City of Glasgow, with other Matters therewith connected*, 3rd edn (Glasgow, 1823), p. 91.

accounted for, partly by the vast increase of manufacturing establishments, partly by the large accession of uneducated Irish, but, perhaps, chiefly by the powerful machinery of corruption'.[41]

Gurney's views were typical of the prejudice that Irish migrants faced from those working in the criminal justice system. Although impossible to quantify, it is likely that actual property crime, rather than merely recorded apprehensions, did rise over the short term in the post-war years. However, this was due to a downturn in Glasgow's post-war economy rather than Irish migration. The city's reliance on the textile industry made it susceptible to periodic outbreaks of cyclical trade depression and economic downturn. The post-war years were scarred by high unemployment as wartime demands for industrial goods dried up. At the same time, thousands of migrants poured into the city following agricultural change in the Scottish rural lowlands and highlands. With the Scottish Poor Law offering no legal right to relief to the able-bodied or to those who did not have a legal settlement in their resident parish, the consequences for the urban poor were dire. Denied the safety blanket of poor law provision or the possibility of regular employment, the harsh realities of the evolving free-market economy are likely to have induced some on the margins of society to steal out of economic necessity.

Poverty, and the changing perceptions of the urban poor that accompanied economic downturn, are, therefore, likely to have greatly affected the recorded patterns of crime, offences and contraventions in Scottish cities, but so too were changing police practices. The influence that the police could exert over prosecution rates was considerable. This was recognised by police commissioners in Edinburgh in 1846 in reflecting upon, and criticising, the early nineteenth-century practice of rewarding officers for bringing cases as it could lead to corruption: 'Under the first Police Act for Edinburgh (1805), *when* one half of the Court *fines* were *divided* among the *Police* ... it was soon found that *cases so rapidly increased* as to leave no doubt as to the *real cause* of their multiplication.'[42] It went on:

> When a constable owes his promotion in the service to the number of cases he reports, there is a strong temptation offered – the strongest that can be offered, viz. *self-interest, to get cases;* and in connection with the demoralizing effects of a detective system on the minds of those engaged in it, it is impossible to overlook the fearful amount of moral delinquents among the Watching Force here, as shown by the Returns of Dismissals, since the *introduction of the new system.*[43]

---

[41]   Gurney, *Notes on a Visit*, p. 75. Cited in Cameron, *Prisons and Punishment in Scotland*, p. 65.

[42]   Edinburgh Central Library (ECL), *Report of the Special Committee appointed by the Board of Police, to Inquire into the Moral and Physical Character of the Watching Force, July 1846* (Edinburgh, 1846), p. 10. Italics in the original.

[43]   Ibid., pp. 9–10. Italics in the original.

In 1823, at a meeting of the general police commissioners in Edinburgh, one commissioner, Mr Ritchie 'observed, that the officers of the Establishment had no controul [*sic*] over cases after they were transmitted to other courts, nor were they responsible for any judgements pronounced even in the Police Court'.[44] Although, as he pointed out, police officers could not guarantee that procurators would proceed with cases or that magistrates would convict, the actions they took, and the evidence they presented often had a determining influence in shaping the outcome of apprehensions.

In Glasgow, trends in police court cases in the early nineteenth century were also influenced by the acquisition of wider judicial powers. Following the passing of the 1800 Glasgow Police Act, minor offences – usually those in which relatively small fines of 1s. to 5s. or short prison sentences were likely to be imposed – were dispensed with in a summary manner in the 'police office'.[45] More serious criminal cases were tried in the town clerk's office (the burgh court) according to formal criminal procedure or remitted to a higher court. The summary powers of the 'police office' – which increasingly was referred to as the 'police court' as the century progressed – were clarified and extended under subsequent local police legislation. The 1807 Glasgow Police Act stated that all prosecutions against police offences were to be carried out in a summary manner, so long as punishment did not exceed 30 days' confinement in bridewell and or a fine of more than £2.[46] The 1821 Glasgow Police Act extended summary powers to cover fines up to £5 and imprisonment to 60 days. This ensured that a greater range of offences were covered by the police court's jurisdiction.[47] The act also made provision for a resident sheriff to serve the city.[48] His appointment contributed to the police court's increasing significance, as it weakened the importance of the burgh court in the administration of criminal affairs.

Moreover, the upward trend in the city's police court business to the early 1820s was also indicative of the growing willingness on the part of the police to prosecute crime and to clamp down on perceived acts of immoral and illegal sociability. The political and industrial tension of the post-war period – culminating in 1820 in the infamous attempt at armed insurrection

---

[44]   *The Scotsman*, 18 January 1823.

[45]   The 1800 Glasgow Police Act had stated that magistrates' existing judicial rights were to be safeguarded, but made no specific reference to summary justice. Glasgow University Library (GUL), Special Collections: *A Vindication of the Observations on the Heads of a New Police Bill for the City of Glasgow and on the Report of the Commissioners of Police, to the Magistrates and Town Council, Respecting the Proposed Alterations to the Present Law* (Glasgow, 1807).

[46]   The Glasgow Police Act, 1807 (47 George III, cap. 29), clause 56.

[47]   GUL, Special Collections: John Scott, *Abstract of the Police Acts of Glasgow* (Glasgow, 1821).

[48]   Maver, 'The Guardianship of the Community', pp. 254–5.

by handloom weavers known as the 'Radical War' – produced growing calls in civic circles for tougher policing action against illegal drinking dens, vice and profligacy.[49] Increasingly, middle-class opinion, fuelled by sensationalist newspaper reporting surrounding the threat posed by political radicalism and crime, started to look to the police and the courts for solutions.[50] The Lord Advocate highlighted this after the Radical War in 1820, arguing that

> in maintaining the peace of the country ... [the Government] ... must look, in the first place, for aid from the Police of the city and county, and ... less on the zealous Magistracy now in court. ... I hope and trust that every description of Magistrates in this country and city ... will exert themselves in the exercise of a vigorous police; or if they find the present not sufficient, they will give their cordial consent and cooperation to the establishment of a better; that they will set themselves as a wholesome example of morality and religion in their private families.[51]

This revealed how integral magistrates were to policing and the administration of justice – and, tellingly, how they utilised their powers to impose discipline over their communities. Chapter 7 analyses punishments in greater depth, but the heightened anxiety brought by the economic, social and political tension appears to have resulted in magistrates adopting a tougher stance in administering justice. Whereas 64 per cent of the 274 individuals brought before the Glasgow Police Court between 28 January and 11 February 1813 had their cases dismissed – with more than half of those who were dismissed being reprimanded – by 1818 the figure had fallen to just 36 per cent (based on 388 individuals dealt with by magistrates in the same two-week period). More than two thirds of defenders were fined and one in ten had their case remitted to the burgh court, which had stronger powers of punishment.[52]

T.M. Devine, in his study of Glasgow's social problems, has argued that police resources in the post-Napoleonic War years were increasingly directed at sanitising the moral rather than the urban environment: 'it was not so much the physical health of the community which was seen to be in danger (except

---

[49]   In the face of falling earnings, unstable employment, appalling social conditions, and a general deterioration in living standards, a small group of weavers attempted armed revolt against the government in 1820. After a violent clash with a troop of cavalry, the radical participants were arrested and radical workers excluded from employment. For a colourful account of this, see P. Berresford Ellis and S. Mac A'Ghobhainn, *The Scottish Insurrection of 1820* (London, 1970).

[50]   Stanley H. Palmer, *Police and Protest in England and Ireland, 1780–1850* (Cambridge, 1988) provides a good account of this for England. See pp. 8–11.

[51]   *Glasgow Herald*, 28 July 1820.

[52]   GCA, B3/1/1/1: Glasgow Police Court Diet Book, 28 January 1813 to 11 February 1813, pp. 1–43; and GCA, B3/1/1/5: Glasgow Police Court Diet Book, 28 January 1818 to 11 February 1818, pp. 20–101.

during serious epidemics) but rather its social order, hierarchy, morality and religion.'[53] Whereas environmental misdemeanours had featured prominently in police court books in both Glasgow and Edinburgh in the early nineteenth century, by 1822 only 3.2 per cent of police summonses in Glasgow concerned issues such as dirty closes and streets.[54] The remainder of police court business dealt with assaults, begging, larceny, prostitution and the profanation of the Sabbath. Police commissioners were particularly keen to keep the streets clear of drunks. In 1829, 80 per cent of arrests were for drunkenness and disorderly behaviour.[55] Although the police's commitment to public health was never superseded by law and order issues in this period, health regulations tended to be rigorously enforced during outbreaks of disease only.[56] Between April 1818 and July 1818, in response to the directions from police commissioners, 261 persons were summonsed before magistrates for failing to keep closes and lanes clean.[57] The clampdown, however, was short-lived and subsided along with the typhus threat. Indeed, in 1830, fewer people (13) were brought before the court for keeping dirty closes than had been summonsed in one month in 1822 (23). The 13 people in question who were charged accounted for just 0.25 per cent of police court business in that year (see Table 5.4). It would take an outbreak of cholera the following year for greater police resources to be directed towards the public health branch of police, as Chapter 4 of Volume 2 explores.[58]

The press offered its own opinions of urban criminality and the work of the courts. Coverage largely took the form of recounting the transactions of just two or three cases of special interest rather than recording all police court business.[59] The 'rogues' who appeared in the Edinburgh Police Court in March 1824 set *The Scotsman*'s journalist to thinking that

> Their histories, as related to the Magistrate by the higher officers of the establishment, would have made a proper supplement to the Newgate Calendar. Some were footpads, some shop-lifters, some pickpockets, (for roguery has its distinct professions) and among the latter was one youth, who lately signalized

[53]   T.M. Devine, 'Urbanisation and the Civic Response: Glasgow, 1800–30', in A.J.G. Cummings and T.M. Devine (eds), *Industry, Business and Society in Scotland since 1700: Essays Presented to Professor John Butt* (Edinburgh, 1994), p. 192.

[54]   Ibid., p. 194.

[55]   Mitchell Library (ML): Strathclyde Regional Council, Department of Education Glasgow Division, *'The Polis': Material relating to the Glasgow Police Force in the First Half of the Nineteenth Century* (Glasgow, 1978), p. 6.

[56]   Sheila Oliver, 'The Administration of Urban Society in Scotland, 1800–50: With Special Reference to the Growth of Civic Government in Glasgow and its Suburbs', unpub. PhD thesis (University of Glasgow, 1995), p. 14.

[57]   Devine, 'Urbanisation and the Civic Response', p. 190.

[58]   See also Oliver, 'The Administration of Urban Society in Scotland', p. 158.

[59]   McGowan, *Policing the Metropolis of Scotland*, p. 155.

Table 5.4   Number of Sentences Passed in the Glasgow Police Court during the Year 1830[†]

Theft: 166	Exposing for Sale Unwholesome Butcher Meat: 5
Embezzlement: 10	Drunk and Disorderly: 2,398
Pocket-Picking: 42	Entertaining Watchmen on Duty: 1
Contravention of Banishment: 13	Driving Cattle through Streets on Sundays: 9
Rogues and Vagabonds: 49	Cattle going at Large: 5
Swindling: 7	Barbers Shaving in Shops on Sundays: 5
Imposition: 4	Riding Furiously on the Streets: 11
Assault: 478	Plying as Porters without Badges: 2
Pubs open during Divine Service: 22	Running Horses Improperly at Market: 2
Disorderly Houses: 148	Carrying Goods on Pavement: 10
Molesting Watchmen on Duty: 199	Having Dirty Pavements: 79
Street Prostitution: 443	Showing Horses for Sale on Streets: 70
Coals Deficient in Weight: 34	Contravention of Carters Act: 701
Using False Weights: 47	Incumbering Streets with Articles for Sale: 332
Issuing Base Money: 3	Having Chimneys on Fire: 120
Porters Overcharging: 2	Portable Lamps not Burning: 40
Having Dirty Closes: 13	Throwing Water over Windows: 4
Overloading Dung Carts: 8	Incumbering Streets with Building Materials: 13
Burning Shavings in a Street: 1	Lifting Dung at Unauthorised Hours: 3
Beating Carpets on Streets: 2	Exposing Articles for Sale outside Shops: 7

Note: Total Number of Sentences: 5,508 (exclusive of persons summonsed before the Police Court and assoilzied), of which 4,426 were fined, 955 were committed to bridewell, 11 committed to gaol, 83 cautioned to find the peace, and 33 coals were confiscated.

[†] James Cleland, *Enumeration of the Inhabitants of the City of Glasgow and County of Lanark for the Government Census of 1831 with Population and Statistical Tables relative to England and Scotland* (Glasgow, 1832), p. 112.

himself by picking the Sheriff's pocket upon the streets. Many of them were from Glasgow and other places, and some under sentence of banishment.[60]

The reports tended to be succinct with little coverage given to courtroom dialogue. Where such dialogue was reported it was usually that of the magistrate or senior court personnel, therefore ensuring that only one side of courtroom proceedings would be represented and typically reinforcing the work and authority of the police court.[61] The typical early nineteenth-century trial report consisted of one or two short paragraphs, usually listing the features and outcomes of a few select cases.[62] Those selected for publication were often specifically referred to as being 'entertaining', 'extraordinary', or 'of some importance'; others were published because they afforded the press the opportunity to provide brief moral commentary, usually in support of the judgement of, or penalty handed down by, magistrates.[63] Indeed, although the mainstream press, as another study has

[60] *The Scotsman*, 20 March 1824.

[61] See, for example, *Glasgow Herald*, 21 April 1826: 'On Monday, in the Police Court [Glasgow], Mr. Davie [Assessor of the Court] took occasion to pay a most deserved compliment to the peaceable and exemplary conduct of the weavers belonging to this city and neighbourhood, notwithstanding the deep distress with which that body were at present struggling. He called the attention of the Sitting Magistrate to the fact (and it was not at all an uncommon circumstance), that, in the multiplicity of cases which were that day to come before them, there were only one or two persons connected with the profession alluded to who stood charged with disturbing the peace. – Baillie Mirrlees fully concurred in the sentiments expressed by Mr. Davie, and likewise paid a tribute of applause to the praise-worthy behaviour of the weavers, who were, with the greatest philosophy, suffering privations and hardships of no ordinary description. Their demeanour might well be a pattern to all other tradesmen similarly circumstanced; and he sincerely trusted they would yet reap those blessings to which their claim and studied forebearance so justly entitled them.'

[62] The following was typical of the type of police court coverage in the *Caledonian Mercury*: 'On Friday, Mary Thomson was committed to Bridewell, for stealing several articles from the area of a house in Elder Street; and being the third of her commitments by the Court of Police, she was ordered to be fed on bread and water.' *Caledonian Mercury*, 4 October 1806.

[63] See, for example, *Caledonian Mercury*, 4 October 1806: 'the chairmen belonging to two chairs were fined 2s., 6d. each, for an overcharge of threepence in each chair, besides forfeiting the hire, and paying costs. We hope this example will prevent similar attempts in future.' Also, *Glasgow Herald*, 24 April 1820: 'A circumstance occurred in the Police Court yesterday, which completely proves the assertion which has been often made, that the depravity of the boys in this city [Edinburgh], and the number of crimes committed by them, are more to be attributed to the negligence of their parents than to any other cause.' Furthermore, the *Glasgow Herald*, 10 February 1826 covered a case of theft in the following way: 'In the Police Court [Glasgow], on Monday, an old hag of the name of Wilson, was found guilty, on the clearest evidence, of stealing a shawl and a silk handkerchief from the persons of two little girls in Stockwell Street. – It appeared that she had recourse to the old trick of enticing the children to give her the articles to hold, until they went up a stair to

pointed out, was an important instrument for critiquing civic policy on law and order issues and for informing the context in which police courts evolved,[64] its coverage of police court business appeared, at times, to reinforce the work and messages of the police and the courts, often giving a wider public platform to magistrates' warnings about the consequences of crime.[65] As the *Caledonian Mercury* noted when reporting on a conviction for overcharging handed down in the Edinburgh Police Court: 'We hope this example will prevent similar attempts in future.'[66] It is, of course, extremely difficult to measure the impact of press reporting on public opinion and prosecution practices. Nonetheless, although the coverage was far from comprehensive, it could be extremely important in shaping popular perceptions. The distribution and reproduction of early newspaper content meant that their opinions could reach a wide audience and provide a means by which readers throughout Scotland could assess the courts' performance. For example, prior to the establishment of Aberdeen's own local court in 1829,[67] the *Aberdeen Journal* reported regularly on both statistics and cases before the capital's court, with local coverage appearing unassumingly on the third or last pages.[68] Indeed, the regular media exposure of the business of Edinburgh's police court and the workings of a new model of law enforcement might well have provided an added impetus for a reformed system of summary justice in Aberdeen itself. As has been explored elsewhere by David G. Barrie, police reform in Scottish urban centres was often influenced by developments in neighbouring or rival towns, as what had once been acceptable came to be viewed as unacceptable in light of raised expectations and new models.[69]

Some contemporaries were convinced that the media could have a direct impact on criminality. In an article entitled 'Murder Mania', published in *Chambers' Edinburgh Journal* in 1841, the author attributed blame for a spate of brutal murders to detailed media coverage of the cases. Gruesome images, he argued, tended to excite the mentally weak: 'the vulgar drink in the details with a hideous delight and soon a new murder proclaims that these have come

---

enquire for a person whom she named. – The thief was sentenced to 60 days confinement in Bridewell.' It is likely that the *Herald* published this case to shock readers as the accused's behaviour went against how an old lady was expected to treat children.

[64]   David G. Barrie, 'Urban Order in Georgian Dundee, c.1770–1820', in Charles McKean, Bob Harris and Christopher A. Whatley (eds), *Dundee: Renaissance to Enlightenment* (Dundee, 2009), pp. 232–4.

[65]   Jennifer S. Davis makes a similar point. Jennifer S. Davis, 'A Poor Man's System of Justice? The London Police Courts in the Second Half of the Nineteenth Century', *Historical Journal*, 27/2 (1984): p. 317.

[66]   *Caledonian Mercury*, 4 October 1806.

[67]   *Aberdeen Journal*, 9 December 1829.

[68]   R.W. Cowan, *The Newspaper in Scotland: A Study of its First Expansion, 1815–1860* (Glasgow, 1946), pp. 18–19.

[69]   David G. Barrie, *Police in the Age of Improvement: Police Development and the Civic Tradition in Scotland, 1775–1865* (Cullompton, 2008), pp. 107–8.

into contact with some predisposed mind.'[70] However, while the weekly reports of police court business might well have shaped public perceptions that police courts were places to prosecute crimes and offences, especially given what appears to have been editorial preference for reporting theft and assault over more mundane cases and contraventions (see further discussion below), their capacity for generating moral panics and influencing statistical patterns in prosecutions is likely to have been fairly low. Not only were the relatively few trials published fairly ordinary compared with the more gruesome cases brought before higher courts, the nature and extent of coverage does not appear to have significantly altered in line with increases in prosecutions and heightened concern with crime and public order in the post-Napoleonic period. Although such reports sometimes contained moral messages, there was little attempt to use particularly emotive language. Moreover, the fact that reports were short and were selected with 'public interest' in mind, or at least with an eye to entertaining the reader, is likely to have somewhat dampened their capacity to generate hysteria. Probably of much greater significance in shaping contemporary perceptions of law and order were press reports and commentaries on the state of public safety and levels of crime, which usually increased during periods in which crime was perceived to be on the rise. The *Dundee Advertiser*, for instance, ran a sustained post-war campaign calling for a tougher stance on law and order which is likely to have influenced post-war crime trends in the burgh court and strengthened the case for the introduction of a local police court in 1824.[71] Similarly, the *Glasgow Herald* was at the forefront of the Conservative campaign in Scotland, warning readers of the dangers that radicalism and Scottish nationalism posed to private property and stability.[72] In a number of editions during the height of political and industrial unrest it published articles rallying support behind the British constitution and the status quo and called on the civic and judicial authorities, as well as 'loyal' citizens, to suppress the radical threat.[73] As Philippe Chassaigne has argued, the profound socio-economic changes to British cities began to be reflected in media representations of urban insecurity

---

[70]   'Murder Mania', *Chambers' Edinburgh Journal*, N.S. 12 (6 October 1849): pp. 209–11.

[71]   Barrie, 'Urban Order in Georgian Dundee', pp. 232–4.

[72]   See, for instance, the front-page article of *Glasgow Herald*, 10 April 1820, entitled 'Scotland's Rise and Progress of the City of Glasgow'. This article espoused the benefits of the Act of Union with England and the reports in the same edition on the following pages on radical events in Scotland. The timing of the paper's emphatic support for the Act of Union, and the prominence it gave it, suggests that the paper might have been concerned that there was an element of nationalism to the radical unrest in Scotland. For more on the 'Radical war', and its links or otherwise with Scottish nationalism, see Gordon Pentland, *Radicalism, Reform and National Identity in Scotland, 1820–1833* (Woodbridge, 2008); Gordon Pentland, 'Betrayed by Infamous Famous? The Commemoration of Scotland's "Radical War" of 1820', *Past and Present*, 201/1 (2008): pp. 141–73; and Berresford Ellis and Mac A'Ghobhainn, *The Scottish Insurrection of 1820*.

[73]   *Glasgow Herald*, 3 April 1820.

and the 'dangerous city'.[74] *The Scotsman*, for instance, publicised the dramatic surge in court business by reporting in October 1821 that at the last Police Statutory Meeting: 'It had been said that the complaints before the Police Court had increased from 800 in one year to upwards of 5000.'[75]

The production and press publication of such data was particularly significant. It enabled comparisons to be made between cities in ways which would have implications not only for their policing and legislation (see Section IV) but also for developing perceptions of their specific urban characters. In 1824, for instance, *The Scotsman* made a comparative analysis between the available data for Glasgow and Edinburgh:

> It seems to be worthy of remark, that the cases of assault in the Police Court of Glasgow are, for one month, 143, while in Edinburgh they are only 285 for three months. This is in the proportion of 2 to 3; while the Glasgow cases for being drunk and disorderly are 409 in one month, in Edinburgh 535 for three months, or in the proportion of 5 in Edinburgh for 12 in Glasgow. The cases of begging, however, are nearly in the same proportion in both places, which rather surprises us; and what is still more curious, Edinburgh, had 70 cases of pocket-picking in the course of the last three months, while the Glasgow report does not exhibit one. But Glasgow has, in one month, 120 cases of 'loose characters'.[76]

The press even used police court returns to make judgement on the character of Scots as well as reaffirm Irish stereotypes.[77]

As the first few decades of the century progressed, the press become an increasingly important vehicle for disseminating wider messages about the state of urban crime and law and order, often drawing uncritically upon court data produced by the police themselves. They reported when crime was perceived to be on the increase and accepted police assurances when they claimed it was falling. In 1823, for instance, *The Scotsman* reassured its readers that based on the level of business in the police court, the 'Superintendant stated his belief that crime was diminishing'.[78] Indeed, the police appear to have become more

---

[74]   Philippe Chassaigne, *Ville et Violence: Tensions et Conflits dans la Grande-Bretagne victorienne (1840–1914)* (Paris, 2005), p. 39.

[75]   *The Scotsman*, 6 October 1821.

[76]   *The Scotsman*, 20 March 1824.

[77]   In 1823, London's *The Morning Chronicle* reprinted a report it had received from the *Glasgow Chronicle* on the city's police report: 'Though we have a very high idea of the sobriety and good order of our northern neighbours, of which we hear a great deal from witnesses best acquainted with the facts (their own country-men), the following Police Report ... will show that even Scotsmen are not exempt from all the frailties of our common nature. The population of the city in which these 1,303 cases occur in a month is about 150,000; every Scotsman, however, will remark that there are many Irishmen in Glasgow.' *The Morning Chronicle*, 12 March 1823.

[78]   *The Scotsman*, 28 May 1823.

aware of the power and influence of the media, which R.W. Cowan has argued was growing in the post-war period in Scotland.[79] In his *Statistical Returns of Glasgow* (1832), local civic administrator and statistician John Cleland reported that 'the commissioners of police, for time beyond, directed a monthly list of sentences passed in the police court, to be made known to the public, through the medium of the newspapers'.[80] This followed the decision in the late 1820s to allow journalists to attend police commissioners' meetings and was indicative of a growing recognition in civic circles of the influence that the press could exert on public opinion. Such developments were symbolic of a wider concern with public image that would come to play an increasing role in the production, dissemination and attempted suppression of criminal statistics in later years, as the following sections examine.

III. The Qualitative to Quantitative Turn, c.1829 to 1857

The second quarter of the nineteenth century brought with it new sources that provided contemporary insights into the business of police courts and the level of urban order in Scotland's major cities. In giving evidence to the 1851 Select Committee on Newspaper Stamps, Michael James Whitty, editor of the *Liverpool Journal*, described police court media reports as 'the most instructive and most desirable reading in the world … Many individuals involve themselves in difficulties from an ignorance of the facts, which they might have learnt had they read the previous police reports'.[81] The *Police Reports of Causes Tried before the Glasgow, Gorbals and Calton Police Courts* (1829) and *The Police Intelligencer, or Life in Edinburgh* (1831–1832) provided amusing and sometimes disturbing portrayals of select police court cases in greater detail and for more cases than newspapers had previously. The inconsistent manner in which trial reports were classified, recorded and presented in and between periodicals, allied to the fact that criminal statistics were not consistently recorded for the years in which the periodicals were published, makes it difficult to ascertain with pinpoint accuracy just how representative these reports of police court business actually were (especially as there is no way of ascertaining what percentage of police court business made it to court, and what percentage was settled by the accused forfeiting a pledge). However, as Tables 5.5 and 5.6 show, media reports of cases involving property

---

[79] Cowan, *The Newspaper in Scotland*, passim.

[80] Cleland, *Enumeration of the Inhabitants of the City of Glasgow and County of Lanark for the Government Census of 1831*, p. 112.

[81] 'Report from the Select Committee on Newspaper Stamps; Together with the Proceedings of the Committee, Minutes of Evidence, Appendix, and Index', BPP, 1851 (558), XVII.1, pp. 106–9, evidence of Michael James Whitty, editor of the *Liverpool Journal*. Cited in Rosalind Crone, *Violent Victorians: Popular Entertainment in Nineteenth-Century London* (Manchester, 2012), p. 229.

Table 5.5   Police Court Cases Reported in the Glasgow *Police Reports*, between 15 August and 17 September 1829

Crime/Offence/Contravention	Number of Cases Covered	Percentage of Total Reports
Drunk and Disorderly	86	26
Theft	67	20.5
Assault	57	17
Other*	20	6
Riotous Conduct	16	5
Disorderly Conduct	11	3
Bawdy/Disorderly House	10	3
Fighting	8	2.5
Drunk and Incapable	6	2
Robbery and Housebreaking	5	1.5
Contravening Banishment	5	1.5
Keeping a Brothel	4	1
Rogue and Vagabond	4	1
Carrying Out Business on Sunday	4	1
Annoying Neighbours	3	1
Vagrancy	3	1
Breach of the Peace	3	1
Fraud	3	1
Assault and Theft	3	1
Fighting Dogs	2	0.5
Cruelty to Animals	2	0.5
Interfering with Watchmen	2	0.5
Breaking and Entering	2	0.5
Total	326	

* Other includes single cases of the following: license breach; Orange Row; uttering a base sovereign; assault and battery; stripping clothes from a boy; selling drink on the Sabbath; exposing and deserting a child; answering a summons; loitering in a suspicious manner; profanation of the Sabbath; child murder; secreted on premises; killing a diseased cow with intent to sell; attempting to violate the chastity of a girl; lounging with a prostitute; lounging; forgery; keeping a vicious dog; riding dangerously; and violating the sepulchres of the dead.

Note: it is difficult to be precise about the above charges as a number of cases involved more than one charge. For example, it was not uncommon for those charged with being drunk and disorderly to also be accused of assaulting or molesting a watchmen, or annoying neighbours. But, in general, these figures provide a fairly accurate picture of the cases that were reported in the periodical.

Table 5.6   Police Court Cases Reported in the Edinburgh *Police Intelligencer*,
8 October 1831 to 11 October 1832

Crime/Offence/Contravention	Number of Cases Covered	Percentage of Total Reports
Theft	74	30
Assault	53	21
Drunk and Disorderly	21	8.5
Other*	19	8
Forgery/Fraud	9	3.5
Riotous Conduct	8	3
Disorderly Conduct	8	3
Obstructing Passers by	7	3
Abusive and Offensive Epithets	5	2
Breach of Trust	5	2
Vagrancy	5	2
Publicans Profaning Sabbath	4	2
Robbery	4	2
Annoying Neighbours	4	2
Fighting	3	1
Breaking Glass in Shop Windows	3	1
Cruelty to Animals	3	1
Entering a House to Steal	3	1
Indecent Exposure	3	1
Threatening and Intimidating	2	1
Attempting to Rescue a Prisoner	2	1
Bawdy/Disorderly House**	2	1
Total	247	

* Other includes: carrying a board on foot pavement; throwing a quantity of vitriol; breach of the peace; boxing the female turnkey; exposing fruit to the annoyance of passers-by; attempting to stab; imposition; interfering with police officers; destroying a batch of bread; vandalism; keeping a dining school; driving a cart carelessly; breaking dishes; breaking a lamp; laying down nuisance on the street; calling out murder; drunk and unable to manage a cart house; uttering base money; taking possession of someone's house.

** *The Police Intelligencer* was not overly concerned with reporting on disorderly houses, but on 4 October 1832 it took the unusual step of publishing 22 cases of allowing men and women of bad character to drink in their houses on Sunday. The journal reported that there were over 50 cases that day, but covered only cases on this issue in an attempt to highlight the impact new police laws were having and to serve as a warning to publicans. It was a good indication of how the media could reinforce the work of the police and the courts. As these cases appeared in one report, it was recorded only once in the above table.

theft and assault were overrepresented relative to the volume of prosecutions. In the 1832 Edinburgh *Police Intelligencer*, theft accounted for under one third (30 per cent) of reports, but just one fifth (18 per cent) of police courts returns for the year 1835 (the nearest year for which detailed statistical information on the court can be uncovered). The number of property offences published in the Glasgow's *Police Reports* was also higher relative to the caseload of the court, although these were recorded more infrequently than in *The Police Intelligencer*. These accounted for a fifth (20.5 per cent) of reports, considerably higher than the number of similar cases recorded by Cleland in his 1830 statistical survey of police court business (see Table 5.4).[82] Moreover, in both cities, coverage of trials involving assault was proportionately slightly higher than the actual number dealt with by the courts, although the loose way in which different periodicals used the terms 'breach of the peace' and 'disorderly conduct' makes it impossible to be too precise.

The *Police Reports* also included reports of a small number of cases from the Gorbals and Calton police courts (which have been included in the above returns) and the justice of the peace courts (which have not). As Tables 5.5 and 5.6 show, police contraventions were rarely reported in either periodical.[83]

In her study into nineteenth-century 'offences against the institution of marriage', Joanne Bailey has recently argued that English print culture 'played a part in the policing of domestic conduct, since by reporting middle- and working-class cruelty cases it constructed a "community in which marital conduct was never private"'.[84] It helped, in other words, to keep domestic violence in the public eye and to politicise such behaviour. In Glasgow and Edinburgh, though, police court trial reports were not overly concerned with reporting wife assault among the working classes. Such trials were underrepresented in media coverage, featuring much less frequently than their actual representation in the 1813–1824 Glasgow Police Court sample discussed in Chapter 3. *The Police Intelligencer* reported just a handful of cases of wife assault in 1832. This was despite the fact that in June 1832, the same periodical reported one magistrate as saying: 'There is scarcely any case so common that comes before the court as that of men for

---

[82] In Cleland's survey, property crimes accounted for approximately 5 per cent of police court business. However, Cleland's survey recorded only convictions, not actual cases, so the proportion of property crimes actually dealt with by the court is likely to have been slightly higher than 5 per cent (as it was more difficult to secure a conviction for property crimes than offences and contraventions; see Chapter 6), although still lower than the media representation suggests. Cleland, *Enumeration of the Inhabitants of the City of Glasgow and County of Lanark for the Government Census of 1831*, p. 112.

[83] Cleland's 1830 returns for Glasgow shows 701 convictions for contraventions of the Carter's Act and 332 convictions for 'incumbering' the streets with articles for sale, but these rarely featured in the press reports. Ibid.

[84] Joanne Bailey, 'Cruelty and Adultery: Offences against the Institution of Marriage', in Anne-Marie Kilday and David Nash (eds), *Histories of Crime: Britain, 1600–2000* (Basingstoke, 2010), p. 43. Quote within quote: Lisa Surridge, *Bleak Houses: Marital Violence in Victorian Fiction* (Athens, 2005), pp. 8–9.

assaulting their wives.'[85] Yet, despite him also noting 'nor any so uncommon as women for striking their husbands', the periodical published almost as many cases of wives assaulting their husbands.[86] The Glasgow *Police Reports* also acknowledged the frequency with which domestic violence was brought before the court,[87] yet reported on such trials very infrequently. The fact that both periodicals published some cases of wife assault, and sometimes provided moral condemnation of the behaviour, should caution against overstating the extent to which the media failed to advance discursive criticism;[88] but in most instances wife assault appears to have been too common to be worthy of the periodicals' attention, except for a small number which were deemed to be particularly unusual or exceptional.

The Edinburgh *Police Intelligencer* appeared generally disinterested in reporting on cases of drunk and disorderedly conduct, but Glasgow's *Police Reports* gave the latter much more attention. Indeed, it was the periodical's most published offence – reflecting the fact that its editor, John Brownlie, was an avowed campaigner of the link between alcohol, crime and immorality.[89] But even this was considerably lower than the volume of such cases processed by the court, and, significantly, the length of coverage of such cases tended to be shorter than that of other cases, especially those involving property and assault. On 6 July 1829, the *Police Reports*, in covering the proceedings of the Calton Police Court, gave an indication of what cases it found interesting, and more likely to report on, and those which were uninteresting and worthy, at best, of fleeting comment. It reported:

> there were twenty-two cases before the court, generally uninteresting. Several shop-keepers were charged for not shutting up their shops, by twelve o'clock on Saturday night; and others for selling drink at unseasonable hours on Sunday. On the 11th July, there were twenty-five cases, and on the 20th July, there were twenty-three cases, the greater part of which embraced weavers charged with being drunk and disorderly, who were, on conviction, fined in different sums.[90]

---

[85] *The Police Intelligencer, or Life in Edinburgh* (*Police Intelligencer*), 15 June 1832.

[86] Ibid. On that day, it reported the case of Jean Millar, charged with being drunk and disorderly and assaulting and striking her husband. Despite the fact that her husband did not turn up in court, the accused was sentenced to ten days' confinement. Cases of domestic violence in which the husband was charged included that of James Fraser, who was sentenced to 30 days' confinement in bridewell for assaulting his wife (*Police Intelligencer*, 12 April 1832) and Mr McIver, who was ordered to find security or be confined in the police office for three days for maltreating his wife (*Police Intelligencer*, 1 September 1832).

[87] 'To the Public', *Police Reports of Causes tried before the Justices of Peace, and the Glasgow, Gorbals and Calton Police Courts* (*Police Reports*), p. 3.

[88] Annemarie Hughes, 'The "Non-Criminal" Class: Wifebeating in Scotland, c.1850–1949', *Crime, Histoire & Sociétés/Crime, History & Societies*, 14/2 (2010): pp. 31–54.

[89] See the introduction to *Police Reports* for more on this.

[90] *Police Reports*, 6 July 1829, pp. 15–16.

It continued: 'The only case of importance was that of Andrew Goodfellow, and Andrew Connor, weavers from Duke Street, Glasgow. They were apprehended by Sergeant Major Leckie and Sergeant Glasgow in Calton, charged with forgery, fraud and wilful imposition.'[91] That this case was the only one out of 70 that was deemed to be of interest spoke volumes as to where the periodical's priorities lay. Indeed, as Table 5.6 shows, the cases of fraud and forgery were also the fifth most commonly reported cases in *The Police Intelligencer*, accounting (along with breach of trust) for 6.5 per cent of reports, which was higher than the proportion of such cases recorded in the 1835 Law Commission returns (see below).

The Glasgow and Edinburgh media reports, therefore, were selective in their coverage, although it would be inaccurate to suggest that they provided a grossly unrepresentative picture of police court business.[92] The three most common charges dealt with in the police courts – drunk and disorderly conduct, assault and theft – were also the three most common offences reported in the periodicals' reports (accounting for just under two thirds of the periodicals' coverage). Nonetheless, by prioritising property crime and public assault, it is likely that these reports skewed the impression of the courts' everyday business towards cases which interested middle-class readers and which 'revealed' the lives of the criminal and working classes, ignoring the many run-of-the-mill traffic, footpath or cleansing contraventions. Although, as Shoemaker has pointed out, it is extremely difficult to assess the impact of media court reports on public opinion,[93] there was a fascination with reporting on the darker and immoral side of urban life, which is likely to have helped to shape not just portrayals of the business of police courts but also city life and the nature of urban crime.[94] Indeed, the periodicals' preference for listing the occupations of the convicted from working-class (often Irish) backgrounds, and protecting the reputation of those from middle-class backgrounds, is likely to have cemented a notion of the poorer inhabitants as being the 'other' and in need

---

[91]   Ibid.

[92]   Crone, in her study of the representation of Metropolitan police court trials in the *London Weekly News* and *The Times*, suggests that 'it would be difficult to argue that certain categories of crime were consistently over-represented'. Crone, *Violent Victorians*, p. 230.

[93]   Shoemaker argues that trial reports could be read in many ways. Robert B. Shoemaker, 'The Old Bailey Proceedings and the Representation of Crime and Criminal Justice in Eighteenth-Century London', *Journal of British Studies*, 47/3 (2008): p. 578.

[94]   They also painted a character not just of towns but also of communities, employment and social conditions and the misery faced by certain occupational groups in industrial society. On 5 September 1829, for instance, the *Police Reports* gave a depressing insight into life in the burgh of Calton: 'This little burgh of Barony, according to last reports, was in a wretched state of misery, want and despair, and according to the latest information, affairs are looking no better, but complaints above complaints, *of want*, are daily increasing. Hitherto the great number of cases have arisen from drunken weavers; occasioned by their meeting friends, and getting drunk in their passion for *cheap whisky*. Government must sooner or later interfere to relieve the present existing distress.' *Police Reports*, 5 September 1829, p. 108.

of greater control and regulation. Moreover, the periodicals' preferred reporting on public thefts and assaults relative to contraventions emphasised the problem of crime and public disorder in Scottish cities.[95] It also, by understating the number of police-led initiatives of drunk and disorderly conduct that dominated the caseload of magistrates, helped to portray police courts as accessible public arenas for conflict resolution and justice. This form of reporting gave a sense of the victim's plight, and in some cases voice, rather than merely the witness testimonies of the arresting officers in drunk and disorderly cases.

Significantly, Brownlie's *Police Reports* also included quantitative data, concluding each week's summary of proceedings with the number of commitments and those sent to gaol or bridewell, each divided by sex. Prison reform was a topic of considerable debate in this period, as Chapter 7 examines. This had the effect of presenting Brownlie, already noted as a writer on the front cover, as a pseudo-official compiler of police statistics. It reinforced his self-proclaimed authority to reflect on the moral aspects of the cases he presented for public consumption. His quantitative analysis echoed the emerging interest in numerical data as a measure of the value of police court work. Rounding off each week's cases with such a numerical summary placed these data as the final 'say' in the effectiveness of the police court in committing criminals to appropriate confinement. It was a trend that was repeated in the wider press. In 1840, the *Aberdeen Journal* published a report from the Banff Police Board meeting which quantified the number of offences that had come before the court since it had been created.[96] The journalist concluded: 'The public will thus see that the Commissioners and their officers have not been quite so *idle* since their appointment as those who are not conversant with the details of the business may have been apt to imagine.'[97]

The tendency towards using quantitative data to measure the business of the police courts was reflected also at a national level. In 1840, parliament published the first national police court returns in its Inquiry into the Law Courts of Scotland. The evidence was derived from numerical information presented by town clerks in the six major burghs in which police courts had been established – Glasgow, Edinburgh, Aberdeen, Dundee, Paisley and Greenock – in response to a request from the commissioners. There were some similarities in the production of statistical data: returns were, for instance, classified into 'crimes', 'offences' and 'contraventions against police regulations'. 'Crimes' were dominated by theft and serious assault, 'offences' by simple assault, disorderly conduct and drunkenness,

[95] Shoemaker makes a similar point in relation to the Proceedings of the Old Bailey in London. Shoemaker, 'The Old Bailey Proceedings and the Representation of Crime and Criminal Justice', p. 567.

[96] It reported that 33 offences had come before the court since it had been created (13 of which were for breach of the peace and 11 for leaving dung on streets after the prescribed hours). Twenty-four of the cases had resulted in fines. Moreover, 60 vagrant and intoxicated people had been taken off the streets. *Aberdeen Journal*, 30 December 1840.

[97] Ibid.

and 'contraventions' by a range of infringements of police laws relating to the built environment. Beyond that, however, there was considerable variation. Glasgow's returns gave category breakdowns for crimes only, not offences and contraventions. Edinburgh's returns, on the other hand, were much more detailed: a wide range of offences were categorised individually and listed under the broad headings of 'crimes', 'petty offences' and 'breaches of police regulations'. William Davie, Assessor of Glasgow Police and Burgh Courts, explained the reason for the variation:

> the difference of form in the several courts arises from the absence of any enactment or authoritative order or regulation on the subject, for the general police act does not universally apply. And the non-observance of the same form, in every case, in the same court, results further from the nature and variety of the cases – all cases thus not appearing to require the same minuteness of specification and technical phraseology.[98]

Although there were variations in terms of how returns were listed, they all indicate a growing preoccupation with clamping down on urban order, public morality and petty theft (see Table 5.7). They also highlight the central place occupied by police courts in both municipal governance and the Scottish legal system. The bulk of court time was concerned with offences, most notably breach of the peace, drunk and disorderly conduct and assault. In 1835, offences accounted for 62 per cent of all cases, crimes (mainly petty theft) for 20 per cent and contraventions (mostly obstructions and nuisances) for 18 per cent. The 1833 Glasgow returns list 6,343 crimes, offences and contraventions. By contrast, the burgh court dealt with just 68 criminal cases in the same year.[99] The number of individuals involved in these police court cases amounted to approximately 3 per cent of the city's population. As with the Edinburgh returns, these included repeat offenders. Nonetheless, this is a conservative estimate of prosecutions to population, as not all of those who were admonished were included in the returns, whilst the number of people living within the official police district was smaller than the population returns listed in the census.[100] In Edinburgh, just over

---

[98] 'Fourth Report by Her Majesty's Law Commissioners, Scotland, 1839', *BPP*, 1840 (241), XX.115, p. 325.

[99] Ibid., pp. 323–4.

[100] It is difficult to be too precise about the ratio of people brought before magistrates relative to population because of the inconsistent way in which data was recorded by police court clerks and the fact that police boundary lines did not correspond with the boundary lines used to record census data. For instance, some of the poorer districts of Glasgow's parliamentary constituency were not subject to police jurisdiction, whilst the affluent suburb of Blythswood was incorporated into the city in 1830 for policing purposes only. The population of Glasgow in 1831 was 202,426, but the number of people living within the actual police district was much smaller. This, and subsequent references to population in Glasgow over the course of the nineteenth century, are taken from Charles Withers, 'The Demographic History of the City', in Fraser and Maver (eds), *Glasgow, Volume II*, p. 142.

Table 5.7   Police Court Offences, 1833 to 1835†

Burgh	B of P.	Assault	Theft	Fraud	Police Reg.	Vagr.	Rape	Exposing Children	Other	Total
Glas.^	1,689^	247^	1,566	116	N.L.	165	N.L.	N.L.	N.L.	3,783
Edinb.*	1,855	1,114**	1,141	169	1,096	273	5	1	574	6,228
Pais.	464	1,156	601	135	3,175	253	2	2	4	5,792
Dundee	N.L.	2,018	481	N.L.	715	462	N.L.	N.L.	5	3,681
Grnck	1,049	711	416	40	402	N.L.	N.L.	2	176	2,796
Perth	1,009	259	187	***	355	N.L.	N.L.	N.L.	N.L.	1,810
Aberd.	168	334	249	11	15	N.L.	N.L.	N.L.	22	799

N.L. Not Listed

* All of the above returns for Edinburgh relate only to 1835

** The assault returns for Edinburgh were broken down thus: assault and wounding to the danger of life (15), breaches of the peace accompanied with assault (520) and complaints, at the instance of private parties, for assaults (579)

*** Theft and Frauds listed together

^ Only those cases deemed to be crimes were categorised under a specific offence and recorded in the Glasgow returns (totalling 3,783 out of the 16,109 offences before the court). The majority of cases which were brought before the Glasgow Police Court in the 1839 Report were not categorised.

† The information in Table 2 has been collated from the returns which were presented by local procurators and clerks to the 'Fourth Report by Her Majesty's Law Commissioners, Scotland, 1839', pp. 278, 304, 323, 332, 335, 336 & 338.

6,000 individuals were brought before magistrates in the police court in 1835, which was approximately 4.5 per cent of the city's population.[101] Significantly, these returns refer to cases, not people accused (with cases often having more than one defender), repeat offenders or people who were brought into the police court either as defenders or witnesses.

Significantly, the publication of these returns helped to make crimes and offences – and the handling by police and magistrates of them – more visible and further heightened the police's concern with their own public image. This was evident in the quantitative data that the police subsequently produced and the commentary they provided on them. In the same year that parliament published its 1840 Law Inquiry, the Glasgow Police published their own statistical returns. Superintendent Miller's *Papers Relative to the State of Crime in Glasgow* boasted that law breaking had been in decline for many years:

> No materials exist for forming an accurate comparison between the period embraced in the table [below] and former years ... it had been ascertained that the number of cases per month, including those for contravention of the Police Act, during the years from 1825 to 1830, averaged 650 to 700, while in late years, the number has averaged only from 350 to 400 a month, the cases generally being now also of a much less aggravated nature than formerly.[102]

As Table 5.8 shows, the number of people brought before the Glasgow Police Court for crimes and offences had fallen – albeit with the odd periodic interruption – from the mid-1820s to the late 1830s following the traumatic events of the post-war years. The number of cases declined from 7,587 in 1829 to 5,126 (involving 7,687 offenders, of which 5,770 were male and 1,917 female) in 1839 in an era when the city's population rose at an unprecedented rate.[103] Miller attributed the decline to effective policing and the influence of temperance societies,[104] but the returns also highlighted the fact that large numbers of persons apprehended for crimes and offences – 1,031 – were discharged without being formally prosecuted, even when there were sufficient grounds for pursuing a prosecution. As Miller pointed out:

---

[101]   These returns, though, included a small number of cases that were remitted to higher courts. The population of Edinburgh in 1831 was approximately 125,000. 'Fourth Report by Her Majesty's Law Commissioners, Scotland, 1839', p. 332.

[102]   GCA, M.P.24, D-T.C.14/1/24: *Papers Relative to the State of Crime in the City of Glasgow, with Observations of a Remedial Nature; and an Appendix of Tables, by H. Miller, Superintendent of Police, and City Marshal* (Glasgow, 1840), p. 6.

[103]   Ibid., p. 26.

[104]   His view was testament to the ongoing Victorian perception of the link between drunkenness and illegal behaviour which was reiterated in every police report published in the period, Ibid., p. 6.

Table 5.8   Number of Cases Brought before the Glasgow Police Court and
the Amount of Fines Recovered each Year, 1826 to 1839†

Year	Number of Cases	Amount of Fines: Pounds
1826	6,971	828
1827	6,495	1,417
1828	7,123	1,544
1829	7,587	1,606
1830	7,376	1,376
1831	7,591	1,108
1832	7,631	1,037
1833	6,118	813
1834	5,126	851
1835	4,627	804
1836	4,247	576
1837	3,689	367
1838	5,010	559
1839	5,047	762

† GCA, M.P.24, D-T.C.14/1/24: *Papers Relative to the State of Crime in the City of Glasgow, with Observations of a Remedial Nature; and an Appendix of Tables, by H. Miller, Superintendent of Police, and City Marshal* (Glasgow, 1840), p. 26.

Of the 1.301 persons discharged, many were charged with being drunk and for abusing their families, and who were released at the pressing solicitation of their wives and friends: others of them were charged with petty thefts and minor offences, with regard to whom the confinement undergone in the office was deemed a sufficient punishment; and few, if any of them were dismissed for want of evidence.[105]

His comments suggested the way in which the law might be administered in a flexible manner in order to limit the number of cases before police magistrates and therefore reduce the overall level of prosecuted crime. The police, it seemed, could be as selective in prosecuting crimes and offences as newspapers were in reporting them.

---

[105]   Ibid.

Table 5.9   Comparative View of the Number of People Charged with Crimes
and Offences in London, Dublin, Liverpool and Glasgow, 1839†

Cities	Year	Population	Persons charged with Crimes and Offences	Offenders in Proportion to Population	Extent of Police Force	Inhabitants to Each Police Officer
London	1839	1,600,000	65,965	1 in 24 ¼	4,500	355
Dublin	1839	300,000	45,682	1 in 7	1,170	256
Liverpool and Suburbs	1839	265,000	16,689	1 in 16	600	442
Glasgow (Police District)	1839	175,000*	7,687	1 in 22 ¾	223	784

* The population figures for Glasgow related only to the number of people within police jurisdiction (175,000). Another 97,000 persons, according to the report, lived beyond the police district. It is possible that the populations given for the other British and Irish cities extended beyond the respective police jurisdictions (it was unusual for early nineteenth-century police jurisdictions to mirror census boundaries) which would have lowered the ratio of offenders to population. The fact that the above report chose to cite the population for the police district in Glasgow only – and thereby reduce the number of offences to population – illustrates the desire in police circles to present the returns in as positive a light as possible.

† GCA, M.P.24, D-T.C.14/1/24: *Papers Relative to the State of Crime in the City of Glasgow, with Observations of a Remedial Nature; and an Appendix of Tables, by H. Miller, Superintendent of Police, and City Marshal* (Glasgow, 1840), p. 29.

Significantly, Miller's report was at pains to point out that many thefts were committed in circumstances 'outwith the control of the police' where 'they could not act in a preventative capacity'.[106] Despite pointing out that the structural design of Glasgow's housing made the commission of crime easier than in other major British and Irish cities, where police numbers relative to population were also greater than in Glasgow, the report went to great lengths to highlight that the number of Glaswegians relative to population charged with crimes and offences (most of whom were brought before magistrates) was lower than in most

---

[106]   Ibid., p. 4.

other metropolitan areas (see Table 5.9).[107] Miller also stressed that in a large number of cases the property stolen was of a 'very trifling' value – a statement presumably addressed to middle-class readers for whom the sums involved might have been insignificant, but perhaps not to the victims who reported the crimes or the accused who in many cases might have stolen out of economic necessity. Indeed, he commented that many of the people convicted were not habitual thieves, but rather wives deserted by husbands and children by parents. This was a rare admission on the part of police officers of the link between poverty, economic necessity and criminality, although one which appeared to have been motivated less by sympathy for the plight of the offenders in question and more to highlight the apparent petty nature of crime and the police's role in keeping in check indictable crime and hardened criminals.[108]

Edinburgh police returns – published half-yearly from 1847 – were also keen to highlight declines in recorded crime (see Table 5.10) and to use them for their own purposes.[109] There was a rise in recorded levels of apprehensions for crimes and offences in the early 1840s, followed by a fairly steady fall until mid-century. In 1843, offences accounted for just under two thirds of all prosecutions and crimes slightly more than one third. Contraventions were listed in separate returns – itself indicative of the growing preoccupation with crimes and offences, especially the former which dominated the accompanying commentary by police superintendents and chief constables. Of those classified as crimes, rather than offences, the overwhelming majority were simple thefts – which accounted for between one quarter and one third of all apprehensions. This mirrored a wider trend within the criminal justice system towards more prosecutions for property crimes rather than crimes against the person.[110]

Sensitivity to public image was compounded by the fact that the publication of returns by city police officials enabled comparative analysis between Scottish cities (and between Scottish cities and those of England). In 1853, a report in the *Glasgow Herald* went to some length to defend the city's moral character, which had been impugned by the comparative statistics between cities, by elaborating upon the precise system by which police data was recorded:

> At first sight the return is not very creditable to the morality of Glasgow. … it must
> be remembered that much depends upon the practice of one city as compared

---

[107] Ibid., p. 7.

[108] Ibid., p. 4.

[109] ECL: *Half-Yearly Report and Return, by Superintendent, of Crimes and Offences, reported at the Edinburgh Police Office, since the Year 1841* (Edinburgh, 1847), pp. 1–6. This pattern mirrored a wider trend within the criminal justice system towards more prosecutions for property crimes rather than crimes against the person.

[110] Knox and McKinlay, 'Crime, Protest and Policing', p. 203; Donnachie,'"The Darker Side"', p. 10; and Emsley, *Crime and Society*, p. 27.

Table 5.10   Apprehensions for Crimes and Offences by the Edinburgh Police, 1842 to 1854[†]

Year	Apprehensions
1842	10,410
1843	12,113
1844	11,288
1845	8,839
1846	7,750
1852	9,285
1853	9,250
1854	7,852

† Information tabulated from ECL, *Half-Yearly Report and Return, by Superintendent, of Crimes and Offences, 1841*, pp. 1–6; and ECL: *Return of Crimes, Offences and Contraventions and Cases of Drunkenness within the Bounds of the Edinburgh Police. Prepared by the Superintendent for the Commissioners of Police, 1855* (Edinburgh, 1855), pp. 1–7.

with another, and also upon the mode in which the data from which the returns are furnished, is kept. In Glasgow it is the custom to carry every drunken person found on the streets in an incapable state to the Police Office. In the metropolis – and we state this on the authority of a gentleman long connected with the London Police – it is the custom, to a large extent, to carry drunken patients to their own homes, when these are known and in the vicinity. In Glasgow, the name of every drunkard is entered by the lieutenant on duty in a permanent bound record. In Edinburgh, complaints in cases of drunkenness are entered upon separate sheets or slips, and it is not unlikely that many of them may be lost. The total cases of drunkenness in Glasgow are thus at once apparent, while it is not unlikely that many of those in Edinburgh pass out of sight. In the Parliamentary return before us we find that the total cases of drunkenness in Edinburgh in 1843 were 5372, while in 1845, in the face of an advancing population, the total cases of drunkenness, according to the same return, had decreased to 1826. This disparity is explained simply by a different mode of disposing of the cases in one year as compared with the other.[111]

---

[111]   *Glasgow Herald*, 28 February 1853. Under the heading 'Statistics of drunkenness', the *Herald* wrote: 'The returns for London and Edinburgh extend from 1831 to 1851 inclusive; that for Glasgow from 1847 till 1851 inclusive – the former being the year

Moreover, the commentary argued that the more developed system of police courts in Glasgow enabled more antisocial drinking to come before the courts:

> In Glasgow, we have six stations and five daily Police Courts, which makes the disposal of drunken cases regular and easy. In Edinburgh there are four or five stations, and only one Police Court; and we have reason to know that a great many of these drunkards are turned out of the station houses when sober, and no record kept.[112]

By the 1840s, Glasgow had the highest number of public houses per head of population in Britain. Sheriff Archibald Alison – never one to underplay a case – estimated that the proportion of public houses to dwelling houses was one to ten for Glasgow, compared to one to 56 for London.[113] He also claimed 'that the proportion of whiskey drunk in Glasgow is twice or thrice as much as in any similar population upon the face of the globe'.[114] Although both of these claims were probably exaggerated,[115] by this period there were more licensed premises than food sellers in the city,[116] which suggests that the city's notorious reputation for excessive alcohol consumption is unlikely to have been without foundation. Nonetheless, given that early Victorian social commentators often linked together crime, drunkenness and immorality,[117] the manner in which

---

subsequent to the passing of the Municipal Extension Act, by which five different police establishments in Glasgow and suburbs were placed under one system of management.'

[112]   Furthermore, the paper reported that magisterial practices varied within police courts: 'Much also depends on the practice of the police magistrate at one period as compared with another. In Glasgow in 1847, 14,041 persons were apprehended on drunken and disorderly charges, of whom 5,847 were convicted, and 8,554 were discharged. In 1851, the number apprehended was 14,870; but by a more stringent application of magisterial functions, 9,095 were convicted, and only 5,775 discharged.' It further pointed out: 'this grand total of 14,870 refers to cases, not separate persons. It includes 1,200 female street pests, and other disorderly characters, who may be in the various police offices twice or thrice a week under different names. One drunken wretch may therefore figure as a great variety of separate drunkards; and it is a fact well known to the police that this grand total of drunkenness is perpetrated by a comparatively limited number of persons.' 'The Statistics of Drunkenness', *Glasgow Herald*, 28 February 1853.

[113]   'Reports on the Sanitary Condition of the Labouring Population in Scotland', p. 191.

[114]   Cited in ibid.

[115]   C.R. Baird, in his investigation of the sanitary condition of the lower classes in Glasgow, estimated that within the ten parishes of the city there were 1,393 licensed spirit retailers and 19,467 families, or one licensed person or public house for every 14 families. Ibid., p. 191.

[116]   D. Paton, 'Drink and the Temperance Movement in Scotland in the Nineteenth Century', unpub. PhD thesis (The University of Edinburgh, 1976), pp. 133–5.

[117]   As Sheriff Alison noted: 'In Scotland it may safely be affirmed that four fifths, probably seven eighths, of the crimes committed originate in the effects of, or the desire

Glasgow policed drunkenness, and the statistics this produced, might have gone some way to shaping the city's reputation for drinking.

Increasingly, the courts, the media and social campaigners drew upon the emerging statistics to understand the role and practices of police courts in regulating drinking habits and behaviours; in particular what was drunk, how much was drunk and where.[118] In 1848, for example, the *Scottish Temperance Review* published Dundee Police Court's data on drunk and disorderly offences from 1847 in 1848, as well as figures for Dunfermline where the police records had isolated committals from 1836 to 1839 that were perceived to have had their origins in drinking, and calculated the extent of the courts' time that was occupied by drunk and disorderly offences.[119] Magistrates also drew upon quantitative data when considering spirit licensing applications,[120] to make persuasive public speeches,[121] and to make assessments about long-term trajectories of police court business.[122]

Newspapers continued to perform a vital role as key conduits for knowledge about the police courts and assessment of their efficiency and 'success' in

---

for, whisky.' Cited in S. Meikle, *The Church and Scottish Social Development, 1780–1870* (London, 1960), p. 85.

[118] The social concerns of these societies were wide and varied, although certainly not all of their Scottish reports applied statistical analysis to demonstrate perceived problems or to argue for their solution. The transactions of the Social Science Association Congress – held in Edinburgh in October 1863, the second of five meetings held in Scotland over the next 30 years – offered discussion that ranged from James Valentine's 'Report on the Statistics of Aberdeen, in Its Educational, Criminal, Sanitary, and Economical Aspects, in 1863' using the same local quantitative data published annually in the *Aberdeen Journal*, to a paper offered by Provost Lindsay of Leith at the request of the Social Science Association's Public Health Committee on the working of the General Police and Improvement (Scotland) Act, 1862, which used none at all. James Valentine, 'Report on the Statistics of Aberdeen, in Its Educational, Criminal, Sanitary, and Economical Aspects, in 1863', p. l–liii; and Provost Lindsay, 'The General Police and Improvement, Scotland, Act, 1862', pp. 525–32. Both in John W. Parker, *Transactions of the National Association for the Promotion of Social Science* (London, 1864).

[119] *The Scottish Temperance Review: The Organ of the Scottish Temperance League* (Edinburgh, 1848), pp. 279–80.

[120] See *Aberdeen Journal*, 8 May 1850.

[121] Bailie David Smith of Glasgow presided over a 3,000 strong public meeting and music for visiting reformers for the Scottish Temperance League under the patronage of the Lord Provost and the magistrates of the city, Sheriff Alison and Sheriff Bell. Smith concluded the evening with his own reflections in which 'the worthy magistrate referred to his experience in connection with the police courts, and stated that on that morning, 71 cases had been brought before him, implicating at least 140 individuals, and that four fifths of the offences were directly traceable to intemperance'. *The Scottish Temperance Review* (Edinburgh, 1848), pp. 231–2.

[122] *Aberdeen Journal*, 24 January 1855.

controlling urban order and crime.[123] As in the first quarter of the century, the mainstream press continued to publish selective accounts of police court trials of commercial and moral value, and, on occasion, provide short commentary on police court work.[124] As with other sources, though, newspapers placed growing emphasis upon the statistics produced by the court and were all too ready to accept, at face value, police data and the police's claims about improved efficiency, thereby cementing the notion that the police and police courts were effective vehicles for public order. In 1825, for instance, the *Glasgow Courier* attributed the decrease in crime to 'a greater diffusion of moral and religious instruction among the lower orders; improvement in trade, and a constant demand for all kinds of manual labour'. It continued: 'a general improvement has also taken place in the police establishment; in most cases there is now almost a certainty of conviction following crime, and consequently a prompt removal of criminals from society.'[125] The police, though, hesitated over the public release of quantitative data that seemingly impugned the reputation of urban communities and could be critical when it was published. Thus, when the *Aberdeen Journal* reported on the city's Police Meeting of 1840, at which the Superintendent's Report had revealed that some 2,445 men and 4,566 women (of which a sizeable proportion – 891 men, 3733 women – were apprehended for being drunk and disorderly) had been brought into the watch-house, the Provost stated that 'it was a pity to let a statement of this kind go out to the public'. He suggested that, 'for the credit of the town', a note should be added to the report to indicate how often the same women were brought in, as a distinct number of cases concerned a particular group of female re-offenders.[126] His proposal was agreed to. Clearly, the volume of police court cases in this area was widely perceived to be a measure of public morality.

As the business of police courts in the second quarter of the century was increasingly reported and measured in qualitative, then quantitative, terms, the statistics that the police and the media would publish, and the comments they attached to them, would come to take on increasing significance. These are likely to have reinforced in the public mind (and then, in the minds of police court personnel) that quantitative data was the means by which courts and the police were to be judged. Partly by dint of the volume of cases, what other form of

---

[123]   See, for example, the quote reproduced in the Introduction of Edward Bulwer-Lytton who claimed the newspaper as 'the chronicle of civilisation' and its coverage of law and order a critical part of civic society. *Aberdeen Journal*, 9 October 1850.

[124]   For instance, *Glasgow Herald*, 13 October 1848: 'On Wednesday, at the Central Police Court, before Baillie D. Smith, a great number of publicans were examined, charged with keeping open houses at unseasonable hours. In the majority of cases, the charge was clearly proved, and the parties fined in sums varying with the magnitude of the offence. We observe that the authorities are exercising their powers in a very summary manner against parties who contravene the provisions of the act.'

[125]   *Glasgow Courier*, 21 April 1825.

[126]   *Aberdeen Journal*, 30 December 1840.

overview or snapshot could the commissions and public be provided about court activities? Thus, numerical data became a shorthand measure for police court efficiency and effectiveness. Yet how was the public to interpret such data? Did fewer cases mean an ineffective police force and court system or an effective and well-integrated system of summary justice? Newspapers offered evidence of both views at this period, often operating simultaneously, as did the police themselves. Whereas the courts' capacity to process large numbers of cases in the first quarter of the century was perceived as being the hallmark of efficiency, by the second quarter of the century a decline in police court business was deemed in the eyes of senior police officers to be testament to police effectiveness. Whether the declining trend in recorded crime was indicative of a real change in behaviour is, of course, impossible to say.

By the 1850s, the use of quantitative analyses to emphasise and track social, especially urban, concerns was firmly established. The growing importance that was attached to police court criminal statistics would prove significant for, as Goldman and Hilts have argued, statisticians who were learning how to use the data they were creating, and the kinds of relationships it could and should hold to contemporary social issues.[127] As the following sections examine, police-produced court statistics would come to take on even greater significance in the second half of the century beyond what they revealed about prosecution patterns in the city. They would not only help to shape perceptions of the city, but also further underpin civic authorities' initiatives to govern it.

IV. The Demand for Order in Civil Society, 1857 to 1892[128]

From 1857 onwards, police forces in Scotland published annual statistics of all crimes, offences and contraventions committed within respective police bounds. As these were presented to magistrates, the media and, more importantly, senior government officials, they were meticulously put together and represent important social surveys and commentaries on nineteenth-century urban experiences, criminality and social challenges. The returns provided statistical breakdowns of offences known to the police, arrests, cases prosecuted,

---

[127]   For the growing importance of statistics, see L. Goldman, 'Statistics and the Science of Society in Early Victorian Britain: An Intellectual Context for the General Register Office', *Social History of Medicine*, 4/3 (1991): pp. 420 & 423–4; V.L. Hilts, 'Aliis Exterendum, or, the Origins of the Statistical Society of London', *Isis*, 69/1 (1978): pp. 21–43; and Theodore M. Porter, *The Rise of Statistical Thinking, 1820–1900* (Princeton, 1986). See also L. Goldman 'The Origins of British "Social Science": Political Economy, Natural Science and Statistics, 1830–1835', *The Historical Journal*, 26/3 (1983): pp. 587–616.

[128]   This was a phrase first coined by Allan Silver, 'The Demand for Order in Civil Society: A Review of some Themes in the History of Urban Crime, Police and Riot', in David Bordua (ed.), *The Police: Six Sociological Essays* (New York, 1967), pp. 1–24.

conviction rates and sentencing and are extremely wide-ranging and beguiling in their detail. The result of direction from London, they were compiled by police superintendents and chief constables and had to be submitted to both central and local government. Along with the introduction of national police acts in 1856 and 1857, which compelled county authorities in England, Wales and Scotland to establish police forces and appoint inspectors of constabularies to assess police efficiency, the returns were indicative of greater central involvement in police affairs. They were also a product of the rise of the governmental bureaucratic machine and the raft of statistics that it produced. As Sindall has argued, nineteenth-century criminal statistics – which police forces in England were also to publish – became a phenomenon in themselves in that they shaped contemporary perceptions of criminality[129] and police efficiency. Victorian perceptions of both came to be increasingly dependent upon the returns that the police themselves produced, with declining crime rates being held up as evidence that the police were winning the 'war' on crime.[130] From 1860, a year after the first 'Inspector of Constabulary Report' into Scottish police efficiency was published, the annual police reports were accompanied by introductory commentaries, which did much to reveal the police's growing preoccupation with public image. Moreover, as a number of scholars have pointed out, criminal statistics from this point onwards helped to account for the development of a new construction of criminality between a 'respectable' and honest working class, and an 'underclass' that was perceived to be responsible for the bulk of crime.[131] The returns were in many ways self-reinforcing: local and central government used them to shape police and criminal laws relating to behaviour deemed to be immoral or socially disruptive, such as public drunkenness or begging; and the police used them to construct criminal profiles and to target certain social groups.[132] It was, as Foucault has argued, indicative of a society

---

[129] Sindall, 'The Criminal Statistics of Nineteenth-Century Cities', pp. 28–36.

[130] Chris A. Williams, 'Labelling and Tracking the Criminal in Mid-Nineteenth Century England and Wales: The Relationship between Governmental and Creating Official Numbers', in Ann Rudinow Sætnan, Heidi Mork Lomell, and Svein Hammer (eds), *The Mutual Construction of Statistics and Society* (Abingdon, 2011), pp. 157–71; Chris A. Williams, 'Police and the Law', in S. Berger (ed.), *A Companion to Nineteenth-Century Europe, 1789–1914* (Oxford, 2006), pp. 345–54; and Chris A. Williams, 'Counting Crimes or Counting People: Some Implications of Mid-Nineteenth Century British Police Returns', in *Crime, Histoire & Sociétés/Crime, History & Societies*, 4/2 (2000): pp. 77–93.

[131] Jennifer S. Davis, 'The London Garrotting Panic of 1862: A Moral Panic and the Creation of a Criminal Class in Mid-Victorian England', in Gatrell, Lenman and Parker (eds), *Crime and the Law*, pp. 190–213; J. Davis, 'Jennings' Buildings and the Royal Borough: The Construction of the Underclass in Mid-Victorian England', in David Feldman and Gareth Stedman Jones (eds), *Metropolis, London: Histories and Representations since 1800* (London, 1989), pp. 11–39; and Martin J. Wiener, *Reconstructing the Criminal: Culture, Law and Policy in England, 1830–1914* (Cambridge, 1990), pp. 149–56.

[132] Wiener, *Reconstructing the Criminal*, pp. 149–56.

that was increasingly concerned with categorising and measuring in an attempt to better control and regulate its populace.[133]

Like all criminal statistics, the returns provide a measurement only of those crimes, offences and contraventions that were either reported or brought before the courts, not the actual level of illegal activity or infringements of local bye-laws. Until 1860, the data recorded suspects/offenders apprehended by the police. Thereafter, it also recorded crimes known to the police. As the returns recorded all crimes dealt with by the police, they included those which were remitted to higher courts. These consisted of between just 10 per cent and 15 per cent of crimes in a typical year for much of the 1860s and 1870s – although there was a slight upward trend as the century went on in line with the expansion in sheriff court summary justice from mid-century.[134] Of those criminal charges that were brought before magistrates, approximately one quarter to one third in a given year would have no proceedings taken against them, which meant that sheriff (and other higher) courts would typically deal with approximately one quarter to one third of criminal cases that made it to trial and magistrates between two thirds and three quarters.[135] Moreover, the overwhelming majority, if not all, of cases dealt with in Glasgow's Sheriff Court were brought, in the first instance, before magistrates who along with procurators, and in some cases senior police officers, would decide whether to proceed with the case in the police court, remit it to a higher court, or take no further proceedings. Police courts also dealt with the vast bulk of cases of simple theft which constituted the majority of the criminal cases recorded in the returns. Furthermore, they adjudicated on all of the recorded offences and contraventions. For all their limitations, the criminal statistics provide an illuminating insight into the day-to-day business of police courts, and how this was perceived to change and be recorded over time.

---

[133]   Michel Foucault, *Discipline and Punish: The Origins of the Prison* (Harmondsworth, 1978).

[134]   In 1871, for instance, of the 5,162 persons taken into custody by the Glasgow police for criminal offences, only 699 (10 per cent) had their cases remitted to the sheriff court. ML: *City of Glasgow Police Criminal Returns for the Year Ending 31st December 1871* (Glasgow, 1872), pp. 14–15. In 1880, of the 6,393 people taken into custody by the Glasgow police, 1,039 (16 per cent) had their cases remitted to the sheriff. ML: *City of Glasgow Police Criminal Returns for the Year Ending 31st December 1880* (Glasgow, 1881), pp. 12–13. In 1890, of the 5,050 people taken into custody for crimes, 1,336 (26 per cent) had their cases remitted to the sheriff which was higher than earlier in the century. ML: *City of Glasgow Police Criminal Returns for the Year Ending 31st December 1890* (Glasgow, 1891), pp. 12–13. Only a small number of people in a typical year had their cases remitted to a justiciary court.

[135]   In 1880, for instance, of the 6,393 people apprehended by the Glasgow police, no proceedings were taken against 2,040 and 1,013 had their cases remitted to the sheriff court. ML, *City of Glasgow Police Criminal Returns for the Year Ending 31st December 1880*, pp. 12–13.

The statistics for Glasgow and Edinburgh paint a different picture in terms of the number of people brought before police courts relative to population. As Table 5.11 shows, the ratio of people to population apprehended for crimes and offences in Edinburgh declined from a peak of 5.4 per cent in 1864 to 3.3 per cent in 1880 (although these figures do not include contraventions, which at most would have added 0.5 per cent to totals). The 1881 Edinburgh police returns included trends in crimes and offences from mid-century, which did much to highlight the importance that the force attached to publicising its capacity to control urban order. As the following section will demonstrate, the number of crimes prosecuted relative to population in the Glasgow Police Court also declined in the second half of the century, but the total percentage of the population that was brought, or at least bailed to appear, before magistrates rose significantly due to a rise in the number of offences prosecuted. By the 1890s, this amounted to more than one tenth of the city's population. In 1860, the number of people relative to population charged with crimes, offences and contraventions had stood at approximately half of this (see Table 5.12). As mentioned earlier, the image-conscious superintendents who compiled the returns were at pains to point out that the statistics included a large number of repeat offenders, so the actual percentage of Glaswegians who experienced magisterial justice was lower than this figure suggests.[136] Nonetheless, the overall total was still considerable and underlined the police courts' growing importance within the criminal justice system and municipal sphere.

The changing business of the Glasgow Police Court reflected a small decline in the number of crimes and contraventions that were prosecuted relative to population. As a percentage of police court practice, contraventions declined, for instance, from 17 per cent in 1860 to just 7 per cent in 1890. There were, as in the first half of the century, fluctuations in line with concerns about an increase in disease and urban improvement initiatives – with such prosecutions accounting for 26 per cent of police court business in 1871 – but the overall trend in prosecuting contraventions was downward. Above all, though, the returns suggest that the business of the Glasgow court became ever more consumed with public order and public morality offences such as drunkenness and disorderly conduct as the century progressed – a fact which probably did much to account for the court's loss of status among the middle ranks.[137] As Tables 5.12 and 5.13 show, just over half of those apprehended, summonsed and brought before magistrates in Glasgow in 1860 were charged with 'offences'. By 1890, this figure had risen to over three quarters. The 1888 Glasgow police returns described these statistics as 'more an index to the vices and follies of a portion of the people than to any criminal propensity of the

---

[136] This was emphasised throughout all of the police returns cited in this chapter from 1860 onwards.

[137] Knox and McKinlay, 'Crime, Protest and Policing', p. 205.

Table 5.11   Number of People Apprehended for Crimes and Offences by the
              Edinburgh Police, 1835 to 1880†

Year	Population	Apprehended for Crimes and Offences	Percentage of Population Apprehended
1835		5,132	
1842		10,410	
1843		12,113	
1844		11,288	
1845		8,839	
1846		7,750	
1854	162,648	7,968	4.9
1855	163,430	7,159	4.38
1856	164,212	6,959	4.23
1857	164,994	6,706	4.06
1858	165,776	6,908	4.17
1859	166,558	8,431	5.06
1860	167,340	7,238	4.32
1861	168,121	8,075	4.8
1862	171,006	8,613	5.03
1863	173,891	9,096	5.23
1864	176,777	9,576	5.42
1865	179,663	9,240	5.14
1866	182,549	9,345	5.12
1867	185,435	8,792	4.74
1868	188,321	9,317	4.94
1869	183,207	8,436	4.64
1870	184,093	8,445	4.58
1871	196,979	8,388	4.26
1872	199,864	8,276	4.16
1873	202,749	7,627	3.76
1874	205,635	7,922	3.85
1875	208,526	8,620	4.13
1876	211,411	8,903	4.2
1877	214,296	8,920	4.1
1878	217,181	9,960	4.5
1879	220,066	9,620	4.3
1880	222,095	7,406	3.3

†   The years 1854 to 1880 are recorded in the following source: ECL: *Return of Crimes and Offences
Reported, Persons Apprehended and Cited, and Miscellaneous Returns Connected with the Police, for
the Year Ending 31st December 1880* (Edinburgh, 1881), Table 8.

Table 5.12   Number of People Apprehended or Summonsed for Crimes, Offences and Contraventions in Glasgow, 1860 to 1890[†]

	1860	1867	1870	1876	1880	1886	1890
Offences	13,664*	19,078	27,326	39,873	40,772	36,024	50,073
Contraventions	5,690	11,425	15,170	8,593	6,984	4,695	4,718
Crimes	3,817*	5,042	5,077	5,509	6,207	5,276	4,938
Total	23,171	Unknown	47,573	53,975	53,963	45,995	59,729
Population	395,503	Unknown	477,732	Unknown	511,415	Unknown	565,839
Percentage of Population brought before Magistrates	5.9	Unknown	9.9	Unknown	10.5	Unknown	10.5

Note: The crime returns include those prosecuted in all courts, not solely police courts (with more serious crimes being remitted to higher courts by either the fiscal or magistrates). In some cases, proceedings were dropped without trial, so the actual number brought to court was slightly lower than the above figures suggest.

* In this year, 45,436 persons were brought to police offices in the city, charged with crimes and offences, and discharged by the superintendent without being brought before the court. They were therefore not formally listed in the returns presented. These included: drunk and incapable (18,872), prowling or prostitution (12,018), criminal charges (1,608), drunk and disorderly (1,024) and disorderly (594). The 1871 returns also state that in addition to the number of persons listed in the official police statistics, 3,534 were charged with disorderly conduct, 23,724 for being drunk and incapable.

† The data have been collated from information presented in ML: *The Number of Persons taken into Custody by the City of Glasgow Police and the Results for the Year Ending 29th September 1860* (Glasgow, 1861), pp. 6–9; ML, *City of Glasgow Police Criminal Returns for the Year Ending 31st December, 1871*, pp. 14–19; ML, *City of Glasgow Police Criminal Returns for the Year Ending 31st December, 1880*, pp. 12–17; and ML, *City of Glasgow Police Criminal Returns for the Year Ending 31st December, 1890*, pp. 12–17.

Table 5.13   Number of People Brought before Glasgow Police Court
Magistrates Relative to Population, 1860 to 1890[†]

	1860	1871	1880	1890
Offences	13,890*	26,253	40,650	49,314
Contraventions	2,978	11,747	6,944	4,273
Crimes	13,890*	2,786	3,128	2,462
Total Formally Dealt with	16,868	40,786	50,722	56,049
Other**	613	3,645	3,497	3,859
Total before Magistrates	17,481	44,431	54,219	59,908
Population	395,503	477,732	511,415	565,839
Percentage of Population brought before Magistrates	4.4%	9.3%	10.6%	10.5%

*   Offences and crimes recorded together for this year – the figure represents the combined total.

**   Other includes those who were brought before magistrates and had their cases dropped, remitted to a higher court, were awaiting trial, or dealt with other than being formally charged.

† Data gathered from: *The Number of Persons taken into Custody by the City of Glasgow Police and the Results for the Year Ending 29th September 1860* (Glasgow, 1861), pp. 6–9; ML, *City of Glasgow Police Criminal Returns for the Year Ending 31st December, 1871*, pp. 14–19; ML, *City of Glasgow Police Criminal Returns for the Year Ending 31st December, 1880*, pp. 12–17; and ML, *City of Glasgow Police Criminal Returns for the Year Ending 31st December, 1890*, pp. 12–17.

population'.[138] The comment was indicative of the delicate balancing act on the part of the police in bringing more offenders before the courts and raising more revenue (see Chapter 7) without overly damaging the public image of the city – and, just as important, the police's perceived capacity for maintaining law and order. Assault and disorderly conduct – sometimes used interchangeably with the offence of 'breach of the peace' – accounted for the overwhelming majority of offences as an ever-increasing volume of such cases was brought before police courts (see Table 5.14). In the Glasgow Police Court, in 1871, one in every 27 individuals in the city was charged with this offence; in 1880 and 1890 the corresponding figure was one in every 22.

---

[138]   Cited in A. Goldsmith, 'The Development of the City of Glasgow Police, 1800–1939', unpub. PhD thesis (University of Strathclyde, 2002), p. 106.

Table 5.14   Most Common Types of Offences for which People were
Apprehended and Brought before Glasgow Police Court
Magistrates, 1860 to 1890†

Offence	1860	1871	1880	1890
Assault (Simple)	2,137	17,439	22,735	25,223
Drunk and Incapable	4,706	4,999	13,458	20,904
Disorderly Conduct	2,336	Listed under either 'Assaults' or 'Drunk and Incapable'	Listed under either 'Assaults' or 'Drunk and Incapable'	Listed under either 'Assaults' or 'Drunk and Incapable'
Drunk and Disorderly	2,986	Listed under either 'Assaults' or 'Drunk and Incapable'	Listed under either 'Assaults' or 'Drunk and Incapable'	Listed under either 'Assaults' or 'Drunk and Incapable'
Drinking in Shebeens	N.S.	489	66	317
Begging and Destitute	329	272	949	239
Rogues/ Vagrants	Listed with begging	499	605	202
Cruelty to Animals	132	137	98	33
Prostitution	N.S.	1,639	1,986	2,171
Population	395,503	477,732	511,415	565,839

† Data gathered from: *The Number of Persons taken into Custody by the City of Glasgow Police and the Results for the Year Ending 29th September 1860* (Glasgow, 1861), pp. 6–9; ML, *City of Glasgow Police Criminal Returns for the Year Ending 31st December, 1871*, pp. 14–19; ML, *City of Glasgow Police Criminal Returns for the Year Ending 31st December, 1880*, pp. 12–17; and ML, *City of Glasgow Police Criminal Returns for the Year Ending 31st December, 1890*, pp. 12–17.

Although historians, as the following section will show, have argued that crime in the nineteenth century was overwhelmingly male – with men outnumbering women three to one – the gender disparity was less significant for offences. Women were heavily involved as defenders in the new police court structure. In Glasgow, fewer women than men were charged with offences, but the total number was still extremely large, and significantly, increased relative to men and population as the second half of the century went on. The number of women prosecuted rose from 2,502 in 1862 (representing 23 per cent of charges for offences), to 7,375 (28 per cent), to 14,903 (37 per cent) in 1880 to 17,542 (35 per cent) in 1890. Disorderly conduct and simple assault were the most common offences for which women were prosecuted (accounting for just over half of all women taken into custody in 1862), followed by drunk and disorderly (approximately one quarter), and drunk and incapable (just over one tenth).[139] A toughening resolve on the part of police authorities to clamp down upon drunkenness and assault mainly accounted for the increase in women before the courts, with both offences collectively accounting for 13,973 of the 16,173 female convictions in 1890.[140]

As Chapters 6 and 7 will explore more fully, much scholarly attention has focused on the extent to which the police and courts in mid-Victorian England were at the forefront of the 'civilising process' – a hypothesis developed by Norbert Elias to explain how modern western societies came to reject pre-modern forms of violent behaviour in favour of self-restraint and control.[141] A burgeoning body of scholarship has, for instance, argued that it was male, working-class violence, in particular, that the police and the legal system targeted, with men being two to three times more likely to be prosecuted for assault than women.[142] Violent men came to be viewed as being in need of greater control, while women who conformed to the feminine ideals of passivity and domesticity were increasingly perceived as less threatening and worthy of support.[143] As Martin Wiener has contended, the

---

[139]   ML: *City of Glasgow Police Criminal Returns for the Year Ending 29th September 1862* (Glasgow, 1862), pp. 8–9.

[140]   Data gathered from sources listed below Table 5.12 (†).

[141]   Norbert Elias, *The Civilizing Process* (Oxford, 1994, first published in 1939). Elias's stimulating and controversial theory has provoked much debate and criticism. See, for instance, the collection of essays in Stuart Carroll (ed.), *Cultures of Violence: Interpersonal Violence in Historical Perspective* (Basingstoke, 2007); Katherine Watson (ed.), *Assaulting the Past: Interpersonal Violence in Historical Perspective* (Cambridge, 2007); and David Lemmings and Ann Brooks (eds), *Emotions and Social Change: Historical and Sociological Perspectives* (New York, 2014).

[142]   For studies that have explored the extent to which the police and courts were able to civilise modern society, see J. Pratt, *Punishment and Civilization: Penal Tolerance and Intolerance in Modern Society* (London, 2002); Pieter Spierenburg, 'Violence and the Civilizing Process: Does It Work?', *Crime, Histoire & Sociétés/Crime, History & Societies*, 5/2 (2001): pp. 87–105; Martin J. Wiener, ' The March of Penal Progress?', *The Journal of British Studies*, 26/1 (1987), pp. 83–96; John Carter Wood, ' Self-Policing and the Policing of the Self: Violence, Protection and the Civilising Bargain in Britain', *Crime, Histoire & Sociétés/Crime, History & Societies*, 7/1 (2003): pp. 109–23; and Barry S. Godfrey, 'Counting and Accounting for the Decline in Non-Lethal Violence in England, Australia and New Zealand, 1880–1920', *British Journal of Criminology*, 43/2 (2003): pp. 340–53.

[143]   Martin J. Wiener, 'Alice Arden to Bill Sikes: Changing Nightmares of Intimate Violence in England, 1558–1869', *Journal of British Studies*, 40/2 (2001): pp. 184–212.

Victorian era, in response to emerging sensibilities and concerns with the future well-being of British society, witnessed attempts to reconstruct working-class manhood through judicial means; a phenomenon which, it has been suggested, although not without challenge, resulted in the 'criminalisation of men'.[144]

As in England, men in Scotland were more likely to be charged with assault than women, but there were important differences. Significantly, in Glasgow, the increase in the number charged with assault relative to population in the late nineteenth century was greater for women than for men. While population growth rose by slightly less than one fifth between 1871 and 1890, the numerical increase in male prosecutions for assault was just 25 per cent, compared to 43 per cent for women.[145] Moreover, whereas women had accounted for approximately one quarter of those charged with simple assault in 1860, in 1890 the corresponding figure was just under half.[146] Over the same period, an increasing number of men relative both to population and female offenders had charges of serious assault remitted from police courts to higher (mainly sheriff) courts following the expansion in sheriff court summary jurisdiction in the second half of the century.[147] This might suggest that in so far as the late Victorian legal system in Scotland had become particularly concerned with male violence, at a local level it was the sheriff courts, which had greater powers of punishment than police courts, that were at the forefront in tackling it (as sheriff courts could imprison for up to two years if a case was tried before a jury).[148] Even so, the number of criminal assault charges that were remitted to these courts was too small relative to police court simple assault charges, and the extent of increase too modest relative to population growth, to conclude with any degree of certainty that the

---

[144] Martin J. Wiener, 'The Victorian Criminalization of Men', in Pieter Spierenburg (ed.), *Men and Violence: Gender, Honor and Rituals in Modern Europe and America* (Columbus, 1998), p. 197.

[145] The figures for men apprehended and brought to court for simple assault were 12,571 in 1871, 14,622 in 1880 and 16,721 in 1890. For women, the corresponding figures were 4,868, 8,113 and 8,502. ML, *City of Glasgow Police Criminal Returns for the Year Ending 31st December 1871*, p. 16; ML, *City of Glasgow Police Criminal Returns for the Year Ending 31st December 1880*, p. 14; ML, *City of Glasgow Police Criminal Returns for the Year Ending 31st December 1890*, p. 14. The population figures can be discerned in Table 5.14.

[146] In 1860, for instance, 1,606 men and 533 women were taken into custody for simple assault. ML, *The Number of Persons taken into Custody by the City of Glasgow Police and the Results for the Year Ending 29th September 1860*, pp. 6–7.

[147] See Lindsay Farmer, *Criminal Law, Tradition and Legal Order: Crime and the Genius of Scots Law, 1747 to the Present* (Cambridge, 1997), pp. 70–71 for the expansion in sheriff court jurisdiction under summary procedure.

[148] As Chapter 1 mentioned, the expansion in the summary jurisdiction of sheriff courts in the second half of the century facilitated a larger criminal caseload as the century progressed – and, significantly, men were more likely to have their charges of assault remitted to these courts than women.

Table 5.15   Number of Serious Assault Charges Remitted by Glasgow Police
Magistrates to a Higher Court, 1860 to 1890[†]

	1860	1871	1880	1890
Population	395,303	477,732	511,415	565,839
Male	68	86	168	201
Female	25	18	34	26

Please note, assault was increasingly broken into different classifications in police statistical reports as the century went on, including, for the 1890 returns, assault with intent to ravish, assault by stabbing, assault with intent to rob, and assault on police officers. The figures in the above table represent the total number of assaults deemed serious enough to be classified as a crime.

[†] ML, *The Number of Persons taken into Custody by the City of Glasgow Police and the Results for the Year Ending 29th September 1860*, pp. 6–7; ML, *City of Glasgow Police Criminal Returns for the Year Ending 31st December 1871*, pp. 14–15; ML, *City of Glasgow Police Criminal Returns for the Year Ending 31st December 1880*, pp. 12–13; ML, *City of Glasgow Police Criminal Returns for the Year Ending 31st December 1890*, pp. 12–13.

legal system had become preoccupied with clamping down on male violence compared with female violence in this period (see Table 5.15). As the police returns show, women were more than capable of being violent, with much of it directed at other women or members of their family, and often of behaving in a manner far removed from the Victorian ideal of womanhood. This mirrors Anne-Marie Kilday's findings for the Scottish Justiciary Court, which identified a determination on the part of the Scottish authorities to bring violent female offenders to justice, a subject explored further in Chapter 1 of Volume 2.[149]

There were also a number of offences for which women were more likely to be prosecuted than men. In the Edinburgh police returns for 1852–1854, for instance, women accounted for 100 per cent of those prosecuted for offences relating to prostitution, 96 per cent for being drunk and incapable of taking care of children under their charge, 94 per cent for using profane or obscene language, 80 per cent for harbouring thieves and prostitutes, 69 per cent for contravening cleaning regulations, 65 per cent for obstructing thoroughfares and hurlies and 63 per cent for begging or suffering children to beg.[150] The number of women charged with

---

[149]   Anne-Marie Kilday, 'The Barbarous North? Criminality in Early Modern Scotland', in T.M. Devine and Jenny Wormald (eds), *The Oxford Handbook of Modern Scottish History* (Oxford, 2012), p. 393.

[150]   ECL, *Return of Crimes, Offences and Contraventions and Cases of Drunkenness within the Bounds of the Edinburgh Police, 1855*, p. 3.

contraventions – which was typically two to three times lower than that for men in the second half of the century – also outstripped population growth over this period, increasing from 5,180 in 1866 to 14,683 in 1875.[151]

The expansion of police court summary justice, therefore, had profound implications for women. The majority of those with whom the court interacted were, as Chapter 4 showed, drawn from working-class backgrounds. Indeed, the regularity with which women appeared in court for mundane offences did not escape the media's notice. In April 1887, a journalist for the *Motherwell Times* wrote at length about female offending:

> Artemus Ward once exclaimed, when his feelings were worked up to a high poetic pitch, 'O, woman, woman! You air [*sic*] a angle [*sic*] when you behave yourself.' This may be true of women, but those we are accustomed seeing at the Court are – well, they aren't on their good behaviour. ... Here are a few members of 'one of the greatest institooshuns of which the land can boste,' with the value his honour [Bailie Grieve] placed on them: – Mrs McDonald, no fixed place of abode, drunk, 5s. or 24 hours; Mrs Connor, no fixed place of abode, drunk, 5s. or 24 hours; Mrs White, Windmillhill, breach of the peace, 7s. 6d. or five days; Bridget Rafferty, Old Logan's Rows, breach of the peace, 7s. 6d. or five days; Mrs O'Niel, Old Logan's Rows; Mrs Buchan; and Christina Cameron, Kirk Square – cases continued; Mrs Richardson Russell and her 'lesser half' – warrant granted for their apprehension. Might we suggest that they be photoed in a group and hung up to the wondering gaze of the populace?[152]

As this quote suggests, women in the court were a subject of media interest when their actions subverted contemporary assumptions about femininity. Although closely embedded in class assumptions, police and judicial policy were also steeped in Victorian values concerning the role women should fulfil in society.

Men, like women, were also much more likely to be prosecuted for being drunk and incapable in the late nineteenth century as senior police officials, procurators and magistrates sought to clamp down on such behaviour. Until the mid-1870s, huge numbers of people who had been apprehended for this offence were later discharged with no further proceedings taken. The 1860 Glasgow police returns, for instance, show that 45,436 persons apprehended for crimes and offences (two thirds of all apprehensions for that year) were released the following morning by the duty lieutenant without troubling the magistrates, including 18,872 for being drunk and incapable. Just 13,664 persons were formally charged for public order offences. It was not untypical for up to 30,000 people per year to be discharged. The majority of these had been apprehended for being drunk and incapable, but large numbers were also arrested for assault and

---

[151] ML: *City of Glasgow Criminal Returns for the Year Ending 31st December 1875*, p. 5.
[152] *Motherwell Times*, 23 April 1887.

later sent on their way with no further legal proceedings – a fact that did much to reduce the recorded level of violence prosecuted in Scottish courts. Both sexes were discharged in large numbers, although women were much more likely to be dismissed than men relative to the numbers apprehended. The Glasgow police courts and gaols simply did not have the capacity for much of the century to formally process the large numbers of individuals picked up by the police. In 1874, the Police Magistrates' Committee minutes alluded to the difficulties that the police and the courts faced in dealing with a burgeoning workload when they considered a proposal from Bailie Morrison, of the Civic Improvement Trust, to extend the Central Police Station 'which is now inadequate in accommodation and defective in many essential points' by securing 'adequate space'.[153] Aside from the implied structural difficulties in dealing with more and more people, the proposal revealed how the judicial business could become interwoven with wider civic initiatives and the role that magistrates played in this. The records do not reveal any official policy on the filtering of cases, but it is possible that up to the mid-1870s the senior police officers and magistrates were working to rough targets in terms of the number of cases that the police courts could process. The beat constable could apprehend as many people as he saw fit – but the burgh and police fiscal had to determine how they should be dealt with. Indeed, for those who were apprehended for offences, there was a considerable element of chance as to whether they would be let on their way after spending the night in a local police cell or brought before magistrates. There does not appear to have been a coherent pattern as to how senior police officers, in their capacity as fiscal, decided on whether to pursue a prosecution for an offence or not, as similar offences were often treated differently. Character, previous convictions, and ability to pay a fine are likely to have been at the forefront of the fiscal's thoughts, but so, too, was the sheer number of people he had to process, the capacity of the court to deal with them and the available resources at the court's disposal. For the petty offender, the outcome of misdemeanours and petty offences was often based as much on luck as due legal process. It was a system of law enforcement in which the police not only produced the recorded data, but, along with magistrates, were also instrumental in shaping the actual cases that made it to court.

From the mid-1870s, however, individuals apprehended for offences were more likely to be formally charged than had previously been the case.[154] As the 1875 Glasgow police returns noted, in discussing a rise in the number of offences for simple assault and drunkenness, the increase was 'due to the action of the magistrates in dealing with all such offenders by trial in the police courts, instead of the officers on duty discharging a large number of them after being sober, as

---

153 GCA, E1/13/3: Police Magistrates' Committee Minutes, 26 November 1874.

154 'Fourth Report of the Royal Commission on Liquor Licensing Laws', *BPP*, 1898 (c.8821), XXXVIII.1, p. 21 (Evidence of John Boyd, Chief Constable of Glasgow, q. 43,736); and Fraser and Maver, 'The Social Problems of the City', p. 383.

was the practice previously'.[155] From that point on, all of those listed in the police returns as having been apprehended and charged with offences were brought before magistrates. It is, of course, possible that the returns stopped recording the number of people dismissed as it is highly unlikely that everyone apprehended on suspicion of having committed an offence was actually prosecuted. Nonetheless, there was clearly a change in policy as the number of persons prosecuted for offences soared after 1875 – almost doubling from what it had been five years earlier.[156] By 1890, the figure of those charged had risen to 50,073. No evidence was uncovered to show whether magistrates or senior police officers were responsible for this, but it seems likely that they were both significant. Armed with stronger licensing and policing powers acquired under the 1853 Forbes MacKenzie Act, illicit drinking dens were subject to greater police attention as the century progressed.[157] That drunkenness underpinned much of the business of the police court as the century went on was pointed out by Bell and Paton in their municipal history of Glasgow, published in the late nineteenth century: '[it] formed about one third of the whole cases dealt with by the magistrates, and it is safe to say that were the drink element eliminated from the City at least three fourths of the duty of the magistrates would disappear.'[158] *The Detective* concurred. In an article, published in 1885, entitled 'A Monday Morning at the Central Police Court: Sketches of a Bar in Saltmarket (Saturday Night), and the "Bar" at the Police Office (Monday Morning)', it highlighted the association between alcohol consumption and the police court, lamenting the fact that it was a short step from the public bar on a Saturday night to the police bar on a Monday morning (See Illustration 4.1).[159] The situation in Edinburgh was similar. According to the 1860 police returns, 40 to 50 out of every 100 individuals were drunk when apprehended for crimes and offences.[160]

Some contemporaries attributed the rise in the number of drink-related offences to an increase in living standards. Although employment opportunities for many

---

[155] ML, *City of Glasgow Police Criminal Returns for the Year Ending 31st December 1875*, p. 8.

[156] Ibid., p. 9.

[157] The act prohibited Sunday opening, regulated opening hours and the issuing of licenses, and increased police powers on infringements. Ibid., p. 383.

[158] James Bell and James Paton, *Glasgow: Its Municipal Organisation and Administration* (Glasgow, 1896), p. 110.

[159] As the author noted in his report of proceedings: 'Another drunk! Judging from the number here, one would fancy that the step from the public-house to the police bar is an easy, and as our artist has it, a comparatively short one.' 'A Monday Morning at the Central Police Court', *The Detective: or, A Journal for the Exposure and Suppression of Crime* (*The Detective*), no. 7, vol. I, 23 May 1885, p. 2.

[160] ECL: *Reports and Returns as to Crimes, Offences, and Contraventions, and to Cases of Drunkenness, within the Police Bounds of the City of Edinburgh during the last Six Years. Prepared for the Magistrates and Council, by Thomas Linton, Superintendent of Police, 1860* (Edinburgh, 1860), p. 13.

women contracted between 1841 and 1891 due to the decline in the textile industry in Glasgow,[161] this period saw a modest, albeit periodically interrupted, rise in living standards and alcohol consumption for many male workers.[162] Most social commentators were convinced there was a relationship between the performance of the economy and the extent of drunkenness. In a remark that revealed the social bias of the police court, John Gemmell, Stipendiary Magistrate for Glasgow, claimed in 1886 that

> Police offences are much more numerous when the working classes are well employed than when trade is dull; and it is a matter of deep regret that despite all efforts to raise the moral standard of the masses, a large number of our working classes, when earning good wages, spend so much on strong drink, and as a necessary sequence swell the registers of the police court, making little, if any, provision for times of distress.[163]

Other commentators, though, recognised a different economic dimension – namely, the economic incentive to prosecute drunken behaviour. In 1851, the 'medical gentleman' who wrote *Low Life in Edinburgh* pointed out:

> The police, again, though perfectly acquainted with the nature of the trade carried on, only interfered in a case of any fighting or quarrelling on the premises; when a fine next morning at the Police Court, for a breach of the peace, which was usually at once paid, settled the affair.[164]

As Chapter 6 explores in more depth, the police's willingness to prosecute a larger volume of those apprehended for public order offences helped to raise a huge amount of revenue for the public purse – much of it from the working class. As Gemmell stated in 1886: 'The fines imposed in the 166,874 cases [in the last few years of Glasgow police court business amounted to] £72,051, of which there was paid no less than £37,479, and it may safely be assumed that at least four fifths of that

---

[161]   Richard Rodger, 'The Labour Force', in Fraser and Maver (eds), *Glasgow, Volume II*, pp. 168–72.

[162]   Of course, there continued to be many, especially those who faced regular periods of unemployment, who lived below the breadline. See Trevor Griffiths, 'Work, Leisure and Time in the Nineteenth Century', in Trevor Griffiths and Graeme Morton (eds), *A History of Everyday Life in Scotland, 1800 to 1900* (Edinburgh, 2010), pp. 170–95; and W.W.J. Knox, *Industrial Nation: Work, Culture and Society in Scotland, 1800–Present* (Edinburgh, 1999), pp. 94–103.

[163]   GCA, D-TC-14.1.17: 'The Condition of Glasgow Streets: The Stipendiary Magistrate on His Defence', papers extracted from the *North British Daily Mail*, 2 August 1886.

[164]   *An Inquiry into Destitution, Prostitution and Crime in Edinburgh* (Edinburgh, 1851). Published as *Low Life in Victorian Edinburgh, By a Medical Gentleman* (Edinburgh, 1980), p. 80.

amount came from the pockets of the lower classes.'[165] That Gemmell should have pointed this out was ironic, for the increasing tendency on the part of magistrates to fine those convicted of public drunkenness was, in part, designed to pay for his salary.[166] The tough line on drunkenness also reflected the growing strength of the 'tea-total' party in Glasgow's civic life in the mid-1870s.[167] Moreover, with the civic fathers continuing improvement and slum clearance programmes that had begun in the mid-nineteenth century,[168] targeting the immorality and drunkenness of the lower orders was a convenient way of reducing the tax burden on 'respectable' members of the community and of helping to ensure that the poorer inhabitants would pay a disproportionate cost to tackle the city's spiralling social problems. Indeed, such was the importance to civic administration of the revenue raised by police court fines that it continued to form an integral component of budget projections.[169] As in the first half of the century, the desire of men of property for greater levels of urban order was usually intertwined with their own fiscal and moral objectives. The changing business of the police court – and the statistics it produced – reflected wider attempts to curb the city's spiralling problem with alcohol. As Hamish Fraser and Irene Maver argue, excessive drinking became for reformers a convenient scapegoat for the cause of poverty.[170] An army of social reformers, temperance societies, and trade union leaders lamented the huge sums of money that the working class spent on alcohol. Increasingly, working-class leaders rallying against the perceived evils caused by excessive alcohol consumption exerted considerable influence on the temperance movement.[171]

As in the first half of the century, contemporary sources are likely to have helped to shape public perceptions and statistical patterns. In their annual returns, the chief constables presented statistical information in a way that reflected prevailing views and justified police policies. Police statistics, for instance, became critical to the investigation, analysis, and campaign to curb working-class drinking in the nineteenth-century Scottish city. Assumptions about who was drinking, what was drunk and the locations in which it was consumed were all embedded in police information offered to the public, further justifying how police resources were targeted. Police returns were presented in such a way as to confirm the opinions of police and magistrates that the drunkenness and criminality of certain citizens were linked. Indeed some of the earliest public returns encouraged a conflation of these behaviours in readers' minds, as the *Return of Crimes, Offences and Contraventions and Cases of Drunkenness within the Bounds of the Edinburgh Police*, prepared

[165] GCA, D-TC-14.1.17: 'The Condition of Glasgow Streets'.

[166] See *The Bailie*, no. 158, 27 October 1875, pp. 1–2.

[167] See ibid.

[168] Hamish W. Fraser and Irene Maver, 'Tackling the Problems of the City', in Fraser and Maver (eds), *Glasgow, Volume II*, pp. 421–5.

[169] See Chapter 7 for more on this.

[170] Fraser and Maver, 'The Social Problems of the City', p. 383.

[171] Knox, *Industrial Nation*, p. 95.

by the Superintendent in 1855.[172] Table 13 in the *Returns* explicitly laid out data
as to how many people were drunk when they were apprehended (between 36
per cent and 46 per cent for both men and women over the three years listed).[173]
Glasgow, on the other hand, was by 1860 separating 'drunk and disorderly' and
'drunk and incapable' as two separate categories; for which 2,212 men and 674
women, and 4,476 men and 230 women were apprehended accordingly.[174] The
1862 Public Houses Amendment (Scotland) Act[175] made incapable drunkenness
a police offence in its own right, whereas previously it had only been so where it
caused a public disturbance.

Press reports of police court case data also conducted and reflected on various
forms of comparative analysis, over time, across gender and age, and by isolating
particular behaviours for attention (typically, thefts, drunkenness, and prostitution).
They also emphasised the financial income to be gained from fines and forfeitures. By
1855, the *Aberdeen Journal* was using locally compiled statistics of the city's police
court to make assessments about long-term trajectories of police court business. In
January of that year, it included details of the total police court cases over the past
four years, revealing that charges had first dropped slightly before rising to their
highest level in 1854.[176] These figures were included in a summary of local statistics
that also provided data on baptisms, marriages and burials, public health, pauperism,
banking, trade, emigration and customs. The identification of these as the key points
of interest from court data was itself a commentary on what was important to
measure. A decade later, the *Journal* reported the police court case data for 1864 as
a long-term comparison with the previous seven years. Offences involving alcohol
were signalled as particularly noteworthy for detailed specification.[177] The following
month, when the formal presentation of the 1864 data on crimes and offences in the
city was presented by Police Inspector Duthie, the paper highlighted his analysis that
the number of those apprehended for drunkenness (1,573 males, 986 females) was
'a decrease of 169 males and 478 females, as compared to 1863'.[178] In relation to
the business of the police courts, Duthie also noted the numbers of those who were
under 15 years of age, the nature of police court punishments, fines and forfeitures,
the decreasing quantity of thefts and house-breakings, licence certificates held, cases
of breach of the public house act and of shebeen keepers and finally, of prostitutions.
These topics reflected the interests of the journal and their perceived readers.

---

[172]   Data drawn from ECL, *Return of Crimes, Offences and Contraventions and Cases
of Drunkenness within the Bounds of the Edinburgh Police, 1855*, p. 7.

[173]   Ibid., p. 6, Table XIII.

[174]   ML, *The Number of Persons taken into Custody by the City of Glasgow Police and
the Results for the Year Ending 29th September 1860.*

[175]   (25 & 26 Victoria, cap. 35).

[176]   The returns for crimes for the following years were 1851: 608; 1852: 582; 1853:
592; 1854: 702. *Aberdeen Journal*, 24 January 1855.

[177]   *Aberdeen Journal*, 1 February 1865.

[178]   *Aberdeen Journal*, 1 March 1865.

Focused attention on these matters also encouraged community members and police to become concerned about them in the belief that others already were.

It is possible that the police's presentation – and accompanying introductory commentaries – of statistical data were orchestrated with media portrayals in mind, which makes it essential to locate the production of statistical returns in the context of media representations such as that of the *Aberdeen Journal* discussed above. Certainly, the interpretation of police return data became an annual fixture in most major cities' newspapers and came to be seen, not just as a matter of practices and choices in policing, but as a reflection of the city's behaviour. As the *Glasgow Herald* commented in 1874, 'The Chief Constable has issued his annual criminal statistics, telling us how we have behaved ourselves in the past year.'[179] Significantly, newspapers and police worked hand in hand to present and confirm the validity of police return quantitative data as evidence of the character of Scottish cities. When the *Herald* presented for its readers the previous year's returns in March 1875, it lamented:

> We are afraid we are a quarrelsome people, especially in our cups. Not less than 14,414 men and 6,089 women – or a total of 20,503 persons – were apprehended for what are called simple assaults; and of these, 18,430 were convicted, showing that the apprehensions were not made without sufficient warrant. Of course, the great bulk of these assaults were committed under the influence of liquor. The Glasgow man sober is a harmless and inoffensive being, but rouse him with his native fiery drink, and he will quarrel with his own shadow if there is no friend, foe or neighbour at hand.[180]

Numbers were becoming an increasingly significant barometer for measuring police and judicial efficiency, but media reporting of them was especially important. There was a dialogic relationship between police court statistics and the mainstream media that was, for the most part, mutually re-affirming.

The press could also, on occasion, play an important role in shaping the changing nature, character and workings of police court summary justice, both in terms of providing moral commentaries on a range of urban social issues and criminal returns, and by projecting the public image of increasingly media-aware magistrates. Newspapers frequently reproduced quotations from the introductory statements that chief constables attached to the publicly-released statistics. When the Aberdeen Police Inspector, Duthie, released the 1864 data on crimes and offences in the city, the *Aberdeen Journal* ratified its information and importance: 'evidently prepared with much care, and containing valuable statistics'.[181] Of course, others also interacted with the court through the press in letters to editors. Newspaper reporters themselves were developing their own public profile and took on certain

[179] *Glasgow Herald*, 11 March 1874.
[180] *Glasgow Herald*, 1 March 1875.
[181] *Aberdeen Journal*, 1 March 1865.

issues as flagships of their paper's identity.[182] Charles Cameron, physician and editor of the *North British Daily Mail* from 1864 to 1874, was a strong social campaigner concerned with alcoholism (see Illustration 5.1). He was elected as a Radical MP for Glasgow in 1874, a role in which he was influential in introducing the Publicans' Certificates (Scotland) Act, 1876.[183] As *The Bailie* reported on Cameron in 1873:

> His conception of his mission aims a little higher than the mere catering of news and echoing of public opinion in leading articles – finding acceptance and approval because they are echoes placing before men neatly and clearly what they think, but lack power to express. He has aimed, and not without success, at leading and forming public opinion; at giving public opinion fresh and original material on which to form itself; and at making his journal a formidable weapon for the assailing and destruction of abuses wherever they can be shown to exist. ... The Special Commissions he has issued from time to time did yeoman's service in letting light into dark places, and showing people where reform was required.[184]

The crackdown on public drunkenness in the 1870s occurred not long after the *North British Daily Mail* conducted and published a series of reports entitled 'The Dark Side of Glasgow' in 1870 and 1871, in which blame for the city's appalling social problems was largely attributed to unlicensed drinking dens known as 'shebeens'. After the first of the five reports was published, the police launched a campaign involving ongoing raids on shebeens in the first few months of 1871, which led the paper to report, somewhat optimistically, that the shebeens had been 'now weeded out'.[185] Indeed, what is particularly interesting is not just that the press reports appear to have had a direct impact on police policy, but also that the paper was fully aware that it could have. In launching its investigation, the paper stated its intention to arouse 'public interest in the great cause of social reform' and to illuminate public opinion in a way that statistical returns produced by the police court could not.[186]

---

[182]   See, for instance, Joel H. Wiener (ed.), *Innovators and Preachers: The Role of the Editor in Victorian England* (London, 1988).

[183]   39 & 40 Victoria, cap. 26.

[184]   *The Bailie*, no. 51, 8 October 1873, pp. 1–2.

[185]   GCA, D-TC-14.1.17: 'The Condition of Glasgow Streets', pp. 32–41 for police policies, and p. 42 for quote.

[186]   It went on: 'Beyond the bald narrative conveyed in the daily list of Police Court convictions, very little is known by the public generally respecting the life-habits and condition of the criminal and unfortunate classes in this city. To the great mass of readers the recital of these convictions is a mere statistical return, the details of which excite no more special interest than do the figures which make up the sum-total in a general account. To them the "dark side of Glasgow" is a sealed book, and they have neither the inclination nor the power to realise for themselves the vast amount of individual misery and degradation which is summed up in the brief record of the Police Court.' GCA, AGN 2114: 'The Dark Side of Glasgow', First Report, *North British Daily Mail*, 27 December 1870, p. 1.

Illustration 5.1   Dr Cameron, Editor of the *North British Daily Mail*, 1873.
@CSG CIC Glasgow Museums and Libraries Collection:
The Mitchell Library, Special Collections†

† 'Dr Cameron, Editor of the *North British Daily Mail*', *The Bailie*, no. 51, 8 October 1873, p. 3.

Over the course of the century, police court practices changed markedly in relation to alcohol-related apprehensions. By its end, more offenders were charged and fined, far fewer were released without punishment when sober, and the court held greater powers to control licensing across the city. Procurators' concerns and a growing intolerance towards public drunkenness played a part in this, but changes in the legislative powers of the police court had also occurred because police officials had chosen to reflect press and civic concerns about drinking behaviours in quantitative terms that purported to measure, track and interpret social behaviours. In doing so, they implicitly and then explicitly correlated drinking alcohol of certain kinds, quantities and in particular venues, to criminal acts. These assumptions which were embedded in statistical presentations were then reflected and reinforced as that data was represented and interpreted to readers of newspapers and social reports. It came to offer an analysis of the character of Scotland's cities, as higher volumes of quantitative data were made to stand for inhabitants' social practices, a reading that has been pervasive and largely seen as persuasive to the present day. What do we really know of Glasgow's alcoholism, when so much of the century's reporting churned quantitative data that was by no means innocent of moral and media-minded messages?

In summary, greater police efforts aimed at punishing drunken behaviour were part of a wider civic attempt to control more effectively public space and safeguard urban order. Police courts acted as 'a new lever of urban discipline' in that they facilitated the explosion of prosecutions for offences which traditionally were rarely dealt with formally in such large numbers.[187] The 'demand for order in civil society' was not aimed primarily at the male population, as has been suggested elsewhere. Indeed, women were charged in police courts on a scale hitherto unseen in the judicial sphere. As such, police courts were not only a new mechanism for controlling the behaviour of urban populations; they are also an important arena for unearthing women's experiences and interactions with the law and the legal system. The police, as both agents of law and order and prosecutors of a significant proportion of police court business, were at the vanguard in attempting to reshape popular culture – and, through the publication of the statistical returns they produced, shape perceptions of public safety. Indeed, as the century went on, the declining number of crimes relative to offences prosecuted was indicative of a wider trend towards police-led prosecutions that were, in all likelihood, the direct result of police action rather than a complaint from a member of the public. Both statistical patterns of lawlessness and perceptions of public safety had become inseparable from the police and the courts themselves.

---

[187] For the police as a 'new lever of urban discipline', see Robert D. Storch, 'The Policeman as Domestic Missionary: Urban Discipline and Popular Culture in Northern England, 1850–80', *Journal of Social History*, 9/4 (1976): pp. 481–509.

V. The Prosecution and Filtering of Crime, 1857 to 1892

While statistical returns for offences could be viewed as a means of measuring how effectively the police were maintaining public safety and controlling public space, it was crime figures that superintendents focused upon most in the commentaries that accompanied the statistical breakdown of police business. The publication of criminal returns helped to make crime, and the handling of it by police and magistrates, appear more transparent. As such, crime statistics were extremely important in measuring police efficiency – and, more importantly, how the police wanted others to see them. Declining crime rates, improved conviction rates, and favourable comparisons with forces in other areas were always highlighted in the introduction to the statistical returns;[188] conversely, rising crime rates were excused or used to justify calls for more resources.[189] That senior officers felt the need to illuminate and qualify statistical patterns was indicative not just of the importance the police and the media attached to crime statistics, but also the capacity of the statistical turn to shape public perceptions of crime and the capacity of the police and the courts to deal with it.

In Glasgow, the trend in the first half of the century towards prosecuting more property crimes relative to other crimes continued in the second half. Property crimes accounted for 92 per cent of crimes recorded in the 1890 Glasgow police statistical returns, the overwhelming majority of which were committed without violence. Just 338 individuals were apprehended for crimes against the person involving violence (representing 8 per cent of total crimes recorded) and this was an unusually high figure. In the previous year, only 193 persons had been apprehended for such crimes.[190] Whether these were prosecuted in the police courts was determined by the severity of the offence (which usually involved the value of the property involved and/or the level of violence used) and the level of punishment deemed appropriate by procurators and magistrates, but the overwhelming majority – 85 per cent on average – were dealt with in a summary manner before magistrates.

The Glasgow police returns show a modest fall in both reported crime and those charged with crime relative to population in the second half of the nineteenth century (see Table 5.16). Those apprehended and charged with crimes between

---

[188] The introduction to Glasgow's 1871 police returns boasts that there has been a diminution of crime in the last year. ML, *City of Glasgow Police Criminal Returns for the Year Ending 31st December 1871*, p. 3.

[189] For instance, in his opening remarks on the 1880 criminal returns the superintendent was keen to stress that in Glasgow there was a considerable number (3,069) of petty thefts 'in which the property stolen was under 5s. value, few, if any of which would appear in English statistics'. He went on: 'in this way the Returns of Crime for Glasgow present an unfavourable appearance when compared with those of large cities in England.' ML, *City of Glasgow Police Criminal Returns for the Year Ending 31st December 1880*, p. 1.

[190] ML, *City of Glasgow Police Criminal Returns for the Year Ending 31st December 1890*, p. 7.

Table 5.16   Reports, Apprehensions and Convictions for Crimes in Glasgow
               Police Annual Statistical Returns, 1860 to 1890[†]

	1860	1870	1876	1880	1886	1890
Reported	5,958	8,702	8,569	9,581	9,243	6,858
Apprehended	3,817	5,077	5,509	6,207	5,276	4,938
Convicted*	1,437	3,000	3,138	3,394	3,004	3,128
Population	395,503	477,732		511,415		565,839

* Not all were dealt with in police courts and a number were remitted to higher courts. See Chapter 6 for more on trends in convictions.

† The data have been collated from information presented in ML: *The Number of Persons taken into Custody by the City of Glasgow Police and the Results for the Year Ending 29th September 1860* (Glasgow, 1861), pp. 6–9; ML, *City of Glasgow Police Criminal Returns for the Year Ending 31st December, 1871*, pp. 14–19; ML, *City of Glasgow Police Criminal Returns for the Year Ending 31st December, 1880*, pp. 12–17; and ML, *City of Glasgow Police Criminal Returns for the Year Ending 31st December, 1890*, pp. 12–17.

1860 and 1890 increased by just 30 per cent, from 3,817 to 4,938, at a time when the population rose by 43 per cent (from 395,503 to 565,839). Over the same period, reported crime rose by only 15 per cent. This was particularly significant, as crimes known to the police provide a far better barometer for measuring crime than crimes prosecuted. Although, as Howard Taylor has pointed out, the police could themselves consciously manipulate these figures,[191] crimes reported to the police were less likely to be subject to the same legal and procedural influences that shaped the statistical patterns of cases that made it to court. Within this general trend, property crimes not involving violence saw the biggest decline (see Table 5.17). The number of reports of property crimes committed with violence relative to population was higher in 1890 than in 1860, but this might indicate a growing willingness on the part of victims to report cases to the police. The actual number apprehended relative to population was lower in 1890 than in 1860, although the numbers involved and the extent of change were fairly modest. Crimes against the person relative to population saw a slight rise both in reports and charges, but again the numbers involved were fairly small and the extent of change unremarkable for such a large and expanding city. Unlike offences involving violence (such as simple assault), the majority of crimes that involved violence were more likely to be dealt with by sheriff or high courts, although the way in which the evidence was recorded in the returns makes it impossible to quantify this accurately.

---

[191]   Howard Taylor, 'The Politics of the Rising Crime Statistics of England and Wales, 1914–1960', *Crime, Histoire & Sociétés/Crime, History & Societies*, 2/1 (1998): pp. 5–28.

Table 5.17   Most Common Types of Crimes Reported and for which People
were Apprehended in Glasgow, 1860 to 1890

Crime	1860	1871	1880	1890
Offences against the Person*	Apprehended 119	Apprehended 120	Apprehended 251	Apprehended 338
	Reported 78	Reported 105	Reported 211	Reported 300
Offences against Property committed with Violence**	Apprehended 241	Apprehended 176	Apprehended 273	Apprehended 272
	Reported 487	Reported 390	Reported 1,037	Reported 1,142
Offences against Property committed without Violence***	Apprehended 3,346	Apprehended 4,309	Apprehended 5,120	Apprehended 3,711
	Reported 5,316	Reported 6,793	Reported 8,011	Reported 5,070

*   Includes murder, culpable homicide, assault with intent to ravage, assault (serious), bigamy, exposing children and carelessly administering drugs.

**   Includes assault and robbery, theft by housebreaking, by opening lockfast places, and housebreaking with intent to steal.

***   Includes theft, reset of theft, fraud and imposition, breach of trust and embezzlement, horse, sheep and cattle stealing, and attempts to steal.

Within this modest long-term downward trend, there was considerable periodic variation (see Table 5.18). The 1860 returns, for instance, warned that serious assaults had risen alarmingly in the previous 12 months.[192] The years 1864 to 1870 saw sharp rises in property offences (which peaked in 1867) due to downturns in the economy and boundary changes in Glasgow.[193] This was followed by a decline from the early 1870s, and a short-term rise in the late 1870s, with housebreaking and robbery rising in the city in the economically depressed years of 1877–1878.[194] The 1881 chief constable's reports noted that although recorded

---

[192]   Ibid.

[193]   The 1871 returns stated that crimes reported to police in 1867 reached a high point, 10,905, since records were produced in 1858. The lowest point was 1863. ML, *City of Glasgow Police Criminal Returns for the Year Ending 31st December 1871*, p. 3.

[194]   Goldsmith, 'The Development of the City of Glasgow Police 1800–1939', pp. 201–5. According to Chief Constable John Boyd, total crime in the city reached a maximum in 1867 and then declined to a minimum in 1889 before rising again. Offences

Table 5.18   Average Annual Number of Reported Violent and Non-Violent Crimes in Glasgow, 1860 to 1894[†]

Years	Against the Person	Against Property Involving Violence	Against Property without Violence
1860–1864	76	489	6,564
1865–1869	81	487	8,768
1870–1874	115	655	6,837
1875–1879	149	1,018	7,881
1880–1884	232	1,184	7,825
1885–1889	209	1,351	6,646
1890–1894	266	1,375	5,879

† Fraser and Maver, 'The Social Problems of the City', p. 386.

crime had fluctuated in the city since the publication of the annual returns, the overall trend, when population change is accounted for, had been slightly upward.[195] Thereafter, there was a fairly sustained fall until 1889. Short-term rises in petty theft were, in many ways, an inevitable consequence of unemployment given the harsh nature of the Glasgow economy. Although the second half of the nineteenth century saw a modest rise in living standards for many male workers – which is likely to have played an important part in explaining the decline in recorded crime – the numbers living on the breadline were still substantial. In the late Victorian period, an estimated one quarter to one third of households in Glasgow lived in what Seebohm Rowntree would later describe as primary poverty, defined as when families lacked earnings sufficient to obtain minimum necessities.[196] The association between property crime and poverty was further highlighted by a statistical survey of the Scottish prison population in 1898 which revealed that 1,944 male prisoners were classified as unskilled labourers compared with the next highest category of 103 iron trade workers.[197]

---

against property not involving violence did not reach the 1867 figure of 9,477 until 1904. Fraser and Maver, 'The Social Problems of the City', pp. 385–6.

[195]   ML, *City of Glasgow Police Criminal Returns for the Year Ending 31st December, 1881*, p. 1.

[196]   Fraser and Maver, 'The Social Problems of the City', p. 380.

[197]   Information sourced in Knox and McKinlay, 'Crime, Protest and Policing', p. 206.

There was also considerable variation between the sexes. In 1861, women accounted for 45 per cent of the 4,278 persons taken into custody for crimes and brought before magistrates during the year ending September 1861, and 42 per cent of the 2,295 persons tried either in the police court or a higher court.[198] However, by 1890, women were much less likely than men to be both taken into custody for crime and brought to trial. By that date, women accounted for 29 per cent of the 5,050 persons taken into custody for crimes during the year ending 31 December 1890, and 25 per cent of the 3,916 who were formally proceeded against (see Table 5.19).[199] Approximately one in every three women taken into custody for crime in 1890 had their charges dismissed compared with approximately one in every five or six men (see Tables 5.20 and 5.21). In 1885, *The Detective* alluded to a possible reason for such gender variation – namely, shame, and the reluctance of men who had fallen victim to female criminality to come forward. On 6 June 1885, in an article entitled 'The Shebeen and the Thieving Dens of the Old Wynd. Extraordinary Revelations', the journalist described the criminality contained within the Trongate district of Glasgow and the difficulties in getting victims to give evidence in court if the defender was a women or if the complainer had been engaged in a sexual encounter with a suspected prostitute that might bring humiliation on themselves or their families. After reporting that a man who had allegedly been attacked and robbed by a gang of women in a house of ill-repute had failed to turn up in court to give evidence, *The Detective* claimed: 'Very often this happens when the police have good cases against thieves. The complainers fail to put in an appearance ... to give their statement, not wishing to get their name exposed. The consequence is, the thieves are liberated, and return to their old occupation.'[200]

Whether the fall in the number of women charged with crimes relative to men reflected a real change in behaviour on the part of the former is difficult to say. Malcolm Feeley and Deborah Little have argued that a similar downward statistical pattern in England (albeit over a much longer period) was indicative of an actual decline in the level of crime committed by women. This, they contend, was the product of the shifting role of women in society and the growth of new, private forms of social control,[201] including increased patriarchal control and greater surveillance

---

[198]   ML, *City of Glasgow Police Criminal Returns for the Year Ending 20th September 1861* (Glasgow, 1861), pp. 6–7.

[199]   ML, *City of Glasgow Police Criminal Returns for the Year Ending 31st December 1890*, pp. 12–13.

[200]   *The Detective*, no. 9, vol. 1, 6 June 1885, p. 7.

[201]   Malcolm Feeley and Deborah Little, 'The Vanishing Female: The Decline of Women in the Criminal Process, 1687–1912', *Law and Society Review*, 25/4 (1991), pp. 719–57. This long-term decline, though, has been challenged. Peter King has questioned whether there was a significant decline in female criminality at all over the long eighteenth century, pointing to the fact that Feeley and Little's analysis began in the late seventeenth and early eighteenth centuries when England was at war and when there was a high proportion of female offenders relative to male, many of whom were engaged in conflict

Table 5.19   Percentage of Women Taken into Police Custody in Glasgow
and Charged with Crimes, 1861 to 1894[†]

1861	1865	1871	1875	1880	1885	1890	1894
45	46	41	34	33	29	29	25

Table 5.20   Gender Profile of No Proceedings for Criminal Cases in
Glasgow, 1871 to 1890[††]

	1871	1880	1890
Male	777 out of 3,043 (23%)	1,170 out of 4,281 (27%)	646 out of 3,572 (18%)
Female	811 out of 2,119 (38%)	870 out of 2,112 (41%)	488 out of 1,478 (33%)

† ML, *City of Glasgow Police Criminal Returns for the Year Ending 31st December 1861*, pp. 6–7;
ML: *City of Glasgow Police Criminal Returns for the Year Ending 31st December 1865*, pp. 6–7; ML,
City of Glasgow Police Criminal Returns for the Year Ending 31st December 1871, pp. 14–15; ML,
City of Glasgow Police Criminal Returns for the Year Ending 31st December 1875, pp. 12–13; ML,
City of Glasgow Police Criminal Returns for the Year Ending 31st December 1880, pp. 12–13; ML:
City of Glasgow Police Criminal Returns for the Year Ending 31st December 1885, pp. 12–13; ML,
City of Glasgow Police Criminal Returns for the Year Ending 31st December 1890, pp. 12–13; ML:
City of Glasgow Police Criminal Returns for the Year Ending 31st December 1894, pp. 12–13.

†† Tabulated from statistics provided in ibid.

in the workplace.[202] Other scholars, though, point to an increasing reluctance on the
part of victims to prosecute female offenders, either because they were regarded
as less threatening or less criminal than men[203] or because they came to be seen as
victims of wider social forces beyond their control.[204] Some historians have also

overseas. Peter King, 'Female Offenders, Work and Life-Cycle Change in Late Eighteenth-
Century London', *Continuity and Change*, 11/1 (1996): pp. 61–90; and Peter King, *Crime
and the Law in England 1750–1840: Remaking Justice from the Margins* (Cambridge,
2006), chapter 6.

[202]   Barry S. Godfrey, 'Workplace Appropriation and the Gendering of Factory "Law":
West Yorkshire, 1840–80', in M. Arnot and C. Usborne (eds), *Gender and Crime in Modern
Europe* (London, 1999), pp. 137–50.

[203]   Lucia Zedner, *Women, Crime and Custody in Victorian England* (Oxford, 1991), p. 27.

[204]   Robert B. Shoemaker, *Gender in English Society, 1650–1850: The Emergence of
Separate Spheres?* (London, 1998), p. 298.

argued that female indictment rates were further depressed by the move towards confining 'deviant' women in medical institutions,[205] and by the increasing tendency for female defenders to be prosecuted in the summary rather than the higher courts.[206] Employment opportunities and real wages declined for women in late Victorian Glasgow,[207] so the statistical downward trend in female criminality – which like male crime overwhelmingly concerned theft – is unlikely to have been linked to wider economic improvements. What can be concluded with greater certainty is that the fall in female criminal prosecutions in Glasgow cannot be simply attributed to cases being prosecuted in a different court structure. The vast majority of female criminal charges in the second half of the nineteenth century were brought before the police court with very few cases being remitted to the sheriff court, as was outlined above. The fact that proceedings were less likely to be taken against women than men suggests that male crime, as Wiener has argued, might have been of greater concern to the police, procurators and magistrates in the late nineteenth century, but even this should not disguise the fact that the number of women apprehended for crime declined at a far faster rate than for men in this period.[208] In the first half of the century, media reports suggested that women classified as prostitutes were often charged with the crime of theft – and, significantly, were often dismissed without trial due to the reluctance of male victims to give evidence. However, as Chapter 6 of Volume 2 shows, the number of women charged with the offence of 'importuning passengers for the purpose of prostitution' increased significantly in the second half of the century following the acquisition of stronger statutory police powers. Whether this had a bearing on crime returns is impossible to determine, but it is possible that procurators in the second half of the century saw greater value in prosecuting women under the offence of soliciting rather than bringing them before a court on a criminal charge only for the case to be dropped pre-trial. Convictions for 'importuning passengers for the purpose of prostitution' could be secured on police evidence alone. But, even if the police were able to, and did, manipulate the nature of charges in such a way, it seems likely that it was just one of a myriad of social, institutional and cultural factors that accounted for the decline in recorded female crime. The second half of the century saw more female offenders with a history of re-offending being institutionalised in a variety of punitive and reformative regimes, which might also have shaped the changing pattern of female criminality.

---

[205] R. Smith, *Trial by Medicine* (Edinburgh, 1981); and Emsley, *Crime and Society*.

[206] For a survey of relevant studies, see Emsley, *Crime and Society*, pp. 92–113.

[207] Women's participation in the Glasgow labour force fell in the late nineteenth century due to a decline of textile-based employment brought about by Glasgow's changing industrial base and growing foreign competition. Whereas women accounted for 38 per cent of the Glasgow labour force in the mid-nineteenth century, by 1891 it was 32 per cent. Wages for women, like men, remained extremely low. See Rodger, 'The Labour Force', pp. 165 & 169. For a wider study, see Eleanor Gordon, *Women and the Labour Movement in Scotland, 1850–1914* (Oxford, 1991).

[208] Wiener, 'The Victorian Criminalization of Men', pp. 197–212.

Police returns paid little attention to gender variations. In highlighting the long-term – and periodically variable – downward trend in crime, police reports provided their own commentary on the changing statistical pattern. Slum clearance programmes, the introduction of industrial schools and reformatories,[209] and increased protection through criminal legislation (most notably, the Prevention of Crimes Act, 1871) were cited as influencing the statistical pattern.[210] Tougher policing laws and policies aimed at street prostitution and vagrancy, as well as greater surveillance of the 'criminal classes', helped to reduce the threat posed by those who committed the majority of crimes, the reports suggested.[211] Perhaps more intriguingly, police superintendents also alluded to the important role that police courts – in conjunction with police efficiency – played in effecting the long-term decline.[212] Indeed, they were especially keen to highlight the integral role of the police and magistrates. In seeking to account for the general decline in crime, the 1871 report pointed to better police organisation, higher discipline, 'and greater repressive powers with which they have been recently armed' which ensured that crime will 'be followed inevitably by conviction and punishment'.[213] It was, in other words, becoming more likely that those charged with crimes would be convicted, and more difficult for the accused to prove their innocence. The 1871 report continued:

> Sentences have been imposed with regulated severity, and rigidly enforced with unbending discipline. The sentimental treatment pursued in the Convict Prisons at one period, has been replaced by a rationally punitive hard labour and deterrent discipline, and a codified dietary by wholesome regimen. And, as a consequence, many of those who have returned to the City upon license,

---

[209] The first industrial school was established in Glasgow in 1847. By the 1860s, there were four reformatories and four industrial schools following government legislation relating to juvenile delinquency in 1854 and 1866. See Goldsmith, 'The Development of the City of Glasgow Police 1800–1939', p. 222. According to the 1871 Glasgow police returns, reformatory and industrial schools helped to save young offenders from becoming hardened offenders. ML, *City of Glasgow Police Criminal Returns for the Year Ending 31st December 1871*, p. 4.

[210] ML, *City of Glasgow Police Criminal Returns for the Year Ending 31st December 1871*, p. 4.

[211] Ibid., pp. 5–6.

[212] This was usually done by alluding to improved conviction rates, discussed below. For the impact that legal and police reforms had on recorded crime in England, see Gatrell and Hadden, 'Criminal Statistics and their Interpretation', pp. 339–40 & 361; and Gatrell, 'The Decline of Theft and Violence', pp. 240–48.

[213] ML, *City of Glasgow Police Criminal Returns for the Year Ending 31st December 1871*, p. 4.

and with whom I have conversed, revert to their incarceration with dread, and contemplate the possibility of its recurrence with salutary apprehension.[214]

Indeed, the police and the courts – and the resource and supply pressures to which they were subject – were potentially as important in shaping the pattern of criminal returns as the changing behaviour of Scots. Although impossible to quantify, the police's growing preoccupation with policing urban order might have depressed recorded crime rates, as appears to have occurred in Victorian England, as more and more police resources and time were directed towards policing drunkenness and rowdy behaviour.[215]

According to Taylor, the police in England set targets and capped criminal prosecutions due to their limited human and financial resources, therefore lowering the overall crime rate from the mid-nineteenth century.[216] He suggests that criminal prosecutions were kept artificially low by the prohibitive costs of prosecutions, the use of summary justice such as the police courts as cheaper alternatives, and the desire of police officials to demonstrate the value of their intervention on the state of crime.[217] Thus Taylor argues, by mid-century, criminal justice administration had become 'an impersonal machine' with 'little to do with "justice", and far more to do with bureaucracy and social policy'.[218] In fact, Taylor's view had been foreshadowed by Scottish legal professionals as early as the 1860s. Advocate J.F. McLennan began his paper on 'Scottish Criminal Statistics' by stating that his

---

[214]   Ibid., p. 4. Gatrell also argues that improvements in police efficiency – which saw the ratio of convictions to crimes known, arrests and trials narrow over the course of the second half of the century – played a part in the decline in crime. Gatrell, 'The Decline of Theft and Violence in Victorian and Edwardian England', p. 307.

[215]   As Taylor has pointed out, in England the police's concern with non-indictable crime reduced indictable crime rates from the mid-nineteenth century as more and more resources were directed towards policing vagrants, drunks, and the labouring classes. Howard Taylor, 'Forging the Job: A Crisis of "Modernization" or Redundancy for the Police in England and Wales, 1900–39', *British Journal of Criminology*, 39/1 (1999): pp. 113–36.

[216]   Howard Taylor, 'Rationing Crime: The Political Economy of Criminal Statistics since the 1850s', *Economic History Review*, 51/3 (1998): pp. 569–90; and Taylor, 'The Politics of Rising Crime Statistics of England and Wales', pp. 5–28. For a critique, see Robert M. Morris, 'Lies, Damned Lies and Criminal Statistics: Reinterpreting the Criminal Statistics in England and Wales', *Crime, Histoire & Sociétés/Crime, History & Societies*, 5/1 (2001): pp. 111–12; and Barry S. Godfrey, 'Changing Prosecution Practices and their Impact on Crime Figures, 1857–1940', *British Journal of Criminology*, 48/2 (2008): p. 179. For a summary of the debate, and the value in assessing police arrests rather than crimes, see Chris A. Williams 'Counting Crimes and Counting People: Some Implications of mid-Nineteenth-Century British Police Returns', *Crime, Histoire & Sociétés/Crime, History & Societies*, 4/2 (2000): pp. 77–93.

[217]   Taylor, 'Rationing Crime: The Political Economy of Criminal Statistics since the 1850s', pp. 573, 575 & 580.

[218]   Ibid., p. 589.

object was 'to test the value of our criminal statistics as indications of the progress of crime'.[219] He argued that:

> the returns in their present shape do not afford reliable guidance in an inquiry into the movements of crime. ... But even could we modify the figures in the tables, and make allowances for changes in the repressing forces from time to time, it would yet be nice work to infer from them whether crime was advancing or retrograding. ... the true conclusion as to the progress of crime may be the opposite of that which even the corrected statistics are, on a first view, calculated to suggest.[220]

McLennan deduced that 'the excess (of number of serious crimes per year compared to commitments) exists, and is enormous, is beyond dispute'.[221] Like modern scholars, he concluded that because the police and the fiscal system did not remain invariable over the period under study, 'the tables before us affords measures not of crime but of the mutual pressure of crime, and the State machinery for keeping it under'.[222]

More recently Barry S. Godfrey, in his survey of the police take-over of prosecutions in England post-1850, has argued that the removal of the victim from the prosecution process might have reduced violent crime rates as the police prosecuted only cases they believed would result in conviction.[223] Indeed, he contends that the police's role as prosecutors, and their propensity for statistically conscious and fiscally aware chief constables, might, in part, explain the decline in recorded violence and the widely-heralded, but somewhat contentious, 'civilising process' that occurred from the mid-Victorian period onwards.[224] The impact of police-led public prosecutions in post-1850 Scotland is likely to have been less dramatic than in England given that the former had been involved in prosecuting offences in many towns from their inception in the early nineteenth century. Moreover, the more serious criminal offences – including those brought before the police court – were usually undertaken by the burgh fiscal, not the police fiscal (who continued to prosecute petty offences, misdemeanours and contraventions). It seems likely, however, that the burgh prosecutor helped to keep criminal prosecutions rates lower and

---

[219]   John Ferguson McLennan, 'Scottish Criminal Statistics', *Transactions of the National Association for the Promotion of Social Science* (London, 1864), p. 384.

[220]   Ibid., p. 390.

[221]   Ibid., p. 386.

[222]   Ibid.

[223]   Godfrey, 'Changing Prosecution Practices and their Impact on Crime Figures, 1857–1940', pp. 171–89.

[224]   Ibid. For budgetary pressures and the extent to which chief constables and home office officials were able to depress the overall crime pattern, see Taylor, 'The Politics of Rising Crime Statistics of England and Wales', pp. 5–28.

more stable in the city than they might otherwise have been (see below).[225] The pattern of cases in which no proceedings were taken, for instance, suggests that magistrates, the police and procurators (including criminal charges brought by the burgh procurator who was appointed by magistrates) worked together to filter the number of criminal cases that were brought to court and to put a ceiling on the number formally prosecuted. Until Glasgow acquired a stipendiary magistrate and a new court in the 1870s, the actual number of people who were brought to trial for crimes was fairly stable – usually between 3,000 and 3,600 persons per year at a time when the numbers apprehended fluctuated between 4,500 and 6,500 (see Table 5.21). During peak years for arrests, the ratio of individuals who were discharged with no further proceedings taken relative to apprehensions would rise, and then would fall in low years. The degree of change was not huge, but was significant enough to suggest that the police, procurators and magistrates were able to exert influence over the statistical pattern. Although impossible to prove conclusively, it is possible that the number prosecuted in a typical year was informally capped due to the financial, and probably practical, constraints of limited judicial resources. As Chapter 1 has illustrated, the number of criminal prosecutions in Scotland had always been determined by the capacity of burgh courts to deal with them and the capacity of the public purse to pay for them, so it should come as no great surprise that fiscal, building and workload pressures might have impacted upon the practice of the courts in the second half of the nineteenth century. The introduction of police courts and the expansion of summary procedure in sheriff courts helped to narrow the gap between those who were arrested and those who were charged over the course of the century, but the number who escaped prosecution continued to be considerable – even in the newly emerging 'policeman-state'.

As in England there is evidence to suggest that the police and fiscal became increasingly wary about taking on court cases for which they did not think they could secure a conviction. As Chapter 6 explores more fully, the conviction-to-acquittal ratio improved over the second half of the century. Moreover, the number of cases that were abandoned, or which magistrates took no proceedings against, fell over the same period. In 1898, for instance, the number of persons in Glasgow against whom no proceedings were taken was 300 per cent lower than in 1861. Whereas in the early part of the century,

---

[225] In Glasgow, the fiscal received an annual salary for his criminal prosecutions in the police court. He was not remunerated on a case-by-case basis – the propriety of which was discussed by magistrates in the early 1870s. GCA, E1/13/3: Magistrates' Committee Minute Book, 23 April 1868 and 6 August 1872. As numerous law reports published in the nineteenth century pointed out, the absence of fees reduced the incentive on the part of procurators to prosecute more criminal cases, whilst annual remuneration helped ensure a greater level of workload consistency.

Table 5.21   Number of People Apprehended and Charged with Crimes
for which No Proceedings in Court were taken by Police or
Magistrates in Glasgow, 1861 to 1898[†]

Year	No Proceedings/Discharged by Magistrates	Total Number of Persons Taken into Custody
1861	2,003 Male: 1,014 / Female: 989	4,278
1862	1,869 Male: 963 / Female: 906	4,504
1863	1,877 Male: 887 / Female: 990	4,914
1864	2,061 Male: 1,031 / Female: 1,030	5,340
1865	1,968 Male: 911 / Female: 1,057	5,216
1866	1,531 Male: 730 / Female: 801	4,639
1867	1,539 Male: 843 / Female: 696	5,134
1868	1,336 Male: 693 / Female: 643	4,831
1869	2,041 Male: 1,154 / Female: 887	6,552
1870	1,681 Male: 878 / Female: 803	5,205
1871	1,588 Male: 777 / Female: 811	5,162
1872	1,518 Male: 837 / Female: 681	5,383
1873	1,585 Male: 853 / Female: 732	5,900
1874	1,565 Male: 902 / Female: 663	5,824
1875	1,825 Male: 1,087 / Female: 738	5,576
1876	1,871 Male: 1,099 / Female: 772	5,617
1877	2,367 Male: 1,444 / Female: 932	6,735
1878	2,630 Male: 1,523 / Female: 1,107	7,245
1879	2,475 Male: 1,516 / Female: 959	6,750

Year	No Proceedings/Discharged by Magistrates	Total Number of Persons Taken into Custody
1880	2,040 Male: 1,170 / Female: 870	6,393
1881	2,067 Male: 1,171 / Female: 896	6,161
1882	2,762 Male: 1,508 / Female: 1,254	7,104
1883	2,407 Male: 1,330 / Female: 1,077	6,720
1884	1,980 Male: 1,134 / Female: 846	6,323
1887	1,635 Male: 928 / Female: 707	5,462
1888	1,700 Male: 995 / Female: 705	5,679
1895	845 Male: 582 / Female: 263	4,520
1896	810 Male: 547 / Female: 263	4,677
1897	784 Male: 567 / Female: 217	4,736
1898	649 Male: 465 / Female: 184	4,968

† ML, *City of Glasgow Police Criminal Returns for the Year Ending 31st December 1865*, pp. 6–7;
ML, *City of Glasgow Police Criminal Returns for the Year Ending 31st December 1871*, pp. 14–15;
ML, *City of Glasgow Police Criminal Returns for the Year Ending 31st December 1875*, pp. 12–13;
ML, *City of Glasgow Police Criminal Returns for the Year Ending 31st December 1880*, pp. 12–13;
ML, *City of Glasgow Police Criminal Returns for the Year Ending 31st December 1895*, pp. 12–13.

between one half and one third of those arrested would have no further proceedings taken against them, by the late nineteenth century the number of people against whom no proceedings were taken had dropped to about one sixth of those arrested.[226] The appointment of the stipendiary, the opening of a new police court in St Rollex in 1878,[227] and the expansion in sheriff court summary justice is likely to have narrowed the gap between charge and trial

---

[226] This appears to have been a common trend across the United Kingdom. See David J. V. Jones, *Crime, Protest, Community and Police in Nineteenth-Century Britain* (London, 1982), pp. 134–6.

[227] GCA, E1/13/4: Magistrates' Committee Minute Book, 20 June 1878. The city's police courts by this date were called central, northern, eastern, southern and western.

rates in Glasgow.[228] But the improved conviction ratios in line with a fall in the number of cases which were abandoned before trial proceedings had commenced suggests that the police might also have become more cautious in charging suspects on less than compelling evidence, and that procurators became more effective in weeding out weak cases before they made it to court. As V.A.C. Gatrell has argued, keeping the rates of detection and conviction close together became a measure of police efficiency in the second half of the nineteenth century – and one that senior police officers were keen to ensure. As a result, the statistical pattern of crime is likely to have been shaped not just by public behaviour, but also the public image and the priorities of public men.

Social investigations and portrayals of urban life which appeared with growing regularity from the mid-century onwards often did not report on criminal statistics, but their commentaries on public safety and urban order were, nonetheless, also important in painting an image of crime in Scotland's largest cities.[229] In *Midnight Scenes* (1858), for instance, Shadow's harrowing and disturbing picture of urban misery in Glasgow's slums exposed a sub-culture that existed beneath 'respectable' society – an underbelly which, in many ways, would form the focal point of criminal statistical profiling and police policy described above.[230] As McCaffrey has pointed out, Shadow conveyed the image of an alien race that came alive under

---

[228]   As the century went on, procurators and magistrates remitted a higher percentage of crimes to sheriff courts and justice of the peace courts than they had done in the earlier part of the century. In 1880, 6,207 persons charged with crimes came before Glasgow's magistrates, of which 1,039 were remitted to the sheriff, 32 to the Justice of the Peace Court. ML, *City of Glasgow Police Criminal Returns for the Year Ending 31st December 1880*, p. 13. As summary procedure in sheriff courts was reformed in the second half of the century, the courts' capacity for administering a large volume of cases grew markedly – a development which helped further reduce the criminal business of burgh courts. Sheriff courts' capacity and attractiveness for handling criminal prosecutions also increased following the introduction of lawyers onto the county bench, but pragmatic concerns are also likely to have been behind this. Remitting cases to higher courts meant that county procurators, and the county purse, became responsible for undertaking and paying for the preliminary stage of criminal investigation – a fact which is likely to have been attractive to senior police officials given the manpower and fiscal constraints under which they operated. The existence of a nearby justice of the peace court (which dealt with minor offences committed outwith the jurisdiction of magistrates but within the local county) also provided another forum to which cases could be remitted. As Henry Glassford, the Sheriff of Lanarkshire, pointed out in 1869: 'Our *summary* criminal jurisdiction is not so large as in many other counties, because a great deal of it proceeds before the Justice of Peace Court of Glasgow, and I believe the Procurators-fiscal of Glasgow are very well pleased with that arrangement.' See 'First Report of the Law Commissioners Appointed to Inquire into the Courts of Law in Scotland; Together with Minutes of Evidence', *BPP*, 1868–69 (4125), XXV.29, p. 2.

[229]   See for instance, George Bell, *Blackfriars' Wynd Analysed* (Edinburgh, 1850).

[230]   Shadow, *Midnight Scenes*, passim.

the cover of darkness, a world of illegal drinking dens, brothels and petty thieves.[231] The public streets were a hive of immorality, entertainment and danger.

Periodicals published in the late nineteenth century carried on this theme and appropriated danger, violence and crime in visual representations. In the mid-1880s, *The Detective*, for instance, ran a series of articles on Glasgow's underbelly alluding to just how well organised criminals were, how difficult it was to bring them to justice and how unsafe the streets were at night (see Illustrations 5.2, 5.3, 5.4 and 5.5).[232] As Illustration 5.2 shows, the article entitled 'The Same Old Game', depicted pickpockets in 1685 and 1885 in order to highlight how skilled criminals had become and what the periodical claimed was a rise in street robberies.[233] Likewise, in article entitled 'Midnight Scenes in Glasgow' *The Detective* reported that 'The policemen, prowlers, and young thieves have taken undisputed possession of the Trongate.'[234] There was, as with the *Police Reports* and *The Police Intelligencer*, a desire to send out moral messages about the dangers of excessive drinking and attending brothels and shebeens. In doing so, such images sought to inform and entertain; but in illuminating Glasgow's dark side, they also helped to shape contemporary views about the city's character.

What is particularly interesting about the series *The Detective* ran on Glasgow's darker side was that it was published in the middle of a decade that saw reported and prosecuted crime in the city decline. While mainstream newspapers, as the previous section discussed, continued for the most part to accept police data uncritically, other qualitative sources came to offer their commentaries on the state of public safety and order in Scotland's towns and cities. The police, in their capacity as public prosecutor, could filter cases and produce statistical returns that reflected their own values and priorities, but they had little capacity to police the representation of the state of law and order in periodicals that were published in the late nineteenth century. Nonetheless, in portraying the streets and parks of Glasgow as being disorderly, crime-ridden and dangerous, *The Detective* re-affirmed the police's ongoing calls for a strong, vigorous system of law enforcement. And, in doing so, it, like other media forms, served as an extension of the discursive nature of law enforcement in reinforcing stereotypes of the Scottish city that had been forged in the first phase of industrial expansion.

---

[231]   Ibid., p. 8.

[232]   See, for instance, these articles in the following editions of *The Detective*: 'A Monday Morning at the Central Police Court', no. 7, vol. I, 23 May 1885, pp. 1–2; 'Detective Sketches of Dangerous Characters', no. 9, vol. I, 6 June 1885, pp. 1–16; 'Sunday on Glasgow Green', no. 10, vol. I, 13 June 1885, pp. 1–3; 'Sauchiehall Street after Dark', no. 14, vol. II (New Series), 9 July 1885, pp. 1–2; 'Midnight Scenes in Glasgow', no. 16, vol. II (New Series), 23 July 1885, pp. 1–2; and 'The Shadow of Crime', no. 25, vol. II (New Series), 24 September, p. 4.

[233]   'The Same Old Game', *The Detective*, no. 11, vol. 1, 20 June 1885, p. 1.

[234]   'The Tramp', *The Detective*, no. 16, vol. II (New Series), 23 July 1885.

THE

Detective.

No. 11, Vol. I.   LONDON AND GLASGOW, JUNE 20, 1885.   ONE PENNY.

THE SAME OLD GAME.

SINCE the time of Adam, human nature has been singularly perverse, and given to devious ways. The "rogue" family is a very large one, and the majority of its members attempt to tread the narrow path that separates the mean and paltry from the wholesale and gigantic swindling of their more accomplished brethren. Personally we have the most profound contempt for the man who, unknown to the owner, "sneaks" a watch or steals a purse. Of course it is possible that the "fishermen" who fish for purses might excuse themselves on the ground "that he who steals a purse steals trash." But, unfortunately for them, we live in a totally different age from that which William Shakespeare adorned with his genius. Gold is to-day the god of the world. Everyone bows down before its shrine, and while some affect to despise it, yet the mainspring of life is carried in our purse. We do not intend to trace the origin and development of the "art." It is sufficient to know that in the march of progress it has not lagged, and to-day, so well are the fraternity organised, that one man may empty your pocket while another of the gang engages you in conversation, and professes great sympathy with you when the robbery has been discovered. Judging from the very heavy calendar which comes up for disposal at the next Circuit Court, it is evident that pocket-picking and street robberies are on the increase. In our sketches below we endeavour to convey an idea of how the art has progressed during a couple of centuries.

1685.   1885.

POCKET-PICKING IN THE TRONGATE.

Illustration 5.2   The Same Old Game: Pocket-Picking in the Trongate, 1885. By permission of University of Glasgow Library, Special Collections[†]

† 'The Same Old Game', *The Detective*, no. 11, vol. I, 20 June 1885, p. 1.

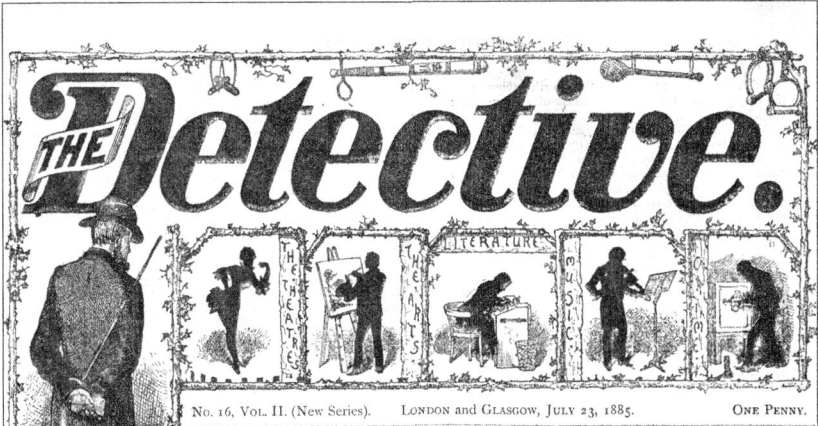

No. 16, Vol. II. (New Series).   London and Glasgow, July 23, 1885.   One Penny.

MIDNIGHT SCENES IN GLASGOW.

By THE "TRAMP."

IT is midnight—so the clanging tongue of the Tron Steeple tells me—as I stand at the Cross of Glasgow. I am deep in thought; a law, which is seldom broken in the journalistic world, compels me to find subject matter to-night for my weekly contribution to the *Detective*, clearly I can't go home for some hours. Legions of ideas chase each other through my weary brain, but I am not prepared to adopt any of them. What am I to do? The silence of the night is beginning to fall around. Respectable wayfarers have gone home, and those who are not respectable increase with alarming rapidity. The policemen, prowlers, and young theives have taken undisputed possession of the Trongate. Now a potato engine drives along and the prowlers make a fierce attack upon it, occasionally a beggar, heavily laden, waddles past on his way home, and yet, I a respectable citizen, stand at the corner of the High Street. But am I not a Tramp? Most assuredly. Thousands knows me as the Tramp who never heard of me as a respectable citizen. Why then should I go home? The dirty streets about the centre of the city with their tatter-demalion crew are good enough for me. A red-bearded policeman eyes me cunningly as he passes. I believe he mutters to himself, "he's a new hand," I can see it in his face as he turns and looks back at me. Somehow I begin to be afraid of policemen, the clatter of their boots unnerves me. I never transgressed the laws, yet I momentarily expect to be "run in." Goodness only knows why I am so frightened, but to avoid suspicion I sneak round the corner and walk up the High Street. Things are very quiet here, and I am pursuing my way northwards, when a fearful sound of voices, cursing, screeching, and bawling attracts my attention. The noise proceeds from a "cook shop" situated at the corner of a lane and buttoning my coat tightly around me I venture to step across the threshold. It is not a pleasant smell that greets the olfactory organs, nor is the language that strikes upon the ear of the *most* refined character, but I am in search of *life*, life as it is seen in our back streets and alleys at midnight.

It is not a very lofty or spacious building that I am in. The counter runs down one side, while, on the other, there are a number of rooms, so that the space between is somewhat narrow. There are large crowds of customers, hot and hungry; drunken and dirty, clamouring for the edibles that are piled anywhere behind the counter. In a corner, I can see a stock of salt fish which is being rapidly reduced by the demand.

Illustration 5.3   Midnight Scenes in Glasgow, 1885. By permission of University of Glasgow Library, Special Collections[†]

† 'Midnight Scenes in Glasgow', *The Detective*, no. 16, vol. II (New Series), 23 July 1885, pp. 1–2.

No. 14, Vol. II. (New Series).   London and Glasgow, July 9, 1885.   One Penny.

SAUCHIEHALL STREET AFTER DARK.

By THE "TRAMP."

HALF-PAST ten o'clock on a fine summer's evening, and here I am in Sauchiehall Street. What a crowd of mashers and neatly attired young ladies, hurrying from the concert halls and places of amusement, block the pavement. I am in the thick of it, elbowing and push-ing my way through a mass of collars and eye-glasses. A feeling strong, however inde-finable, prompts me to spend an hour or so in the study of what has been termed the "Strand of Glasgow."

Probably the knowledge that the *Detective* will recompense me for my time, urges me to carry out my fancy. At any rate I select a quiet door-way, opposite that charming (?) resort called "Eden," and having planted myself where the eye of the policeman won't reach me; I watch with a species of lazy curiosity the life that throbs in the macadamized arteries of Sauchiehall Street. What a busy scene. Cabs rattle along; seedy clerks, who love a promenade, when the inky seams of their coats cannot be seen, stroll past me while elderly folks, for whom cosy beds wait, hurry home. The crush is over soon. The public houses are beginning to put up their shutters and those who have spent their evening—and their money there—are being very unceremoniously thrust out. Then the crowd melts away, and the street is left to solitary wanderers, to darkness, and to me. Flitting shadows of women pass me at intervals, and occasionally a drunken swell staggers along the pathway, but with these exceptions time hangs heavily. Now there is a little episode in the shape of an excited policeman rushing down the street after a pickpocket who dodges round lamp-posts, up this entry and down that, until ultimately he is lost in the gloom.

I stand in the doorway and watch the midnight haunt of our gilded youth on the opposite side. There is a row in the lobby leading to the garden. A group of staggering roysterers are quarrelling over their rights to the company of a female, who, with auriferous locks and powdered and painted face, stands

Illustration 5.4   Sauchiehall Street After Dark, 1885. By permission of University of Glasgow Library, Special Collections†

† 'Sauchiehall Street After Dark', *The Detective*, no. 14, vol. II (New Series), 9 July 1885, pp. 1–2.

No. 19, Vol. II. (New Series).   LONDON and GLASGOW, AUGUST 13, 1885.   ONE PENNY.

THE QUEEN'S PARK:
Is it a Nursery of Vice on Sunday Evenings?
BY THE "TRAMP."

WHEN I first proposed to write this article, it was my intention to deal with the subject in a purely descriptive manner. To present to my readers a pen sketch, replete with the most amusing characteristics of the great crowd that flocks to the Park on Sunday evenings. For this purpose I paid a visit to the resort of youth and beauty last Sunday, but the state of matters which presented itself to my observation as I walked along seemed to me to demand more serious consideration than I had intended giving it. And here I hasten to state that a prettier place, or one more carefully arranged than the South Side Park, could not easily be found. The flower-beds, the walks, the broad patches of grass, are all as nice as possible, and exactly the place to which a working man would take his family, by way of a rural retreat, or a young man his sweetheart. It was early in the evening when I arrived, yet there was a vast number of young people strolling round the plots, or lounging on the seats. Their appearance said much either for the prosperity of the trades they worked at, or for the self-denial in setting aside for dress so large a proportion of what at best can only be a moderate wage. The young men were decked out in one fashion—the latest, with their "masher" collars, their "crutch" walking sticks, and just a little bit of a drawl in their voice. If you are a regular visitor to the Park, and your only motive there be flirting, then among the *habitues* you will have a nick-name. Ask any girl who is a flirt, and frequents the Park. She knows plenty of captains (Captain So and So being quite a favourite title) who have to work hard at a desk for their miserable eighteen shillings a week, and then on Sunday impersonate for a few brief hours a young military swell. I only ask the reader to walk out to the Park, and for a moment survey the groups of young men who hang about the top of the grand staircase. There you will see captains by the score—brainless insipid creatures, who have a vague idea that the title makes a deep impression on the little flirt they wish to captivate.

Look at them as they stand ogling and winking at every girl who passes them. Gaze with fear and trembling upon their dignity, which is so strongly supported by the laundry-maid. Pity them as you think on the fact that the twopenny cigar which they indulge in on this especial day means a biscuit and a glass of milk only, for dinner to-morrow. Poor,

Illustration 5.5   The Queen's Park: Is It a Nursery of Vice on Sunday Evenings? 1885. By permission of University of Glasgow Library, Special Collections†

† 'The Queen's Park: Is it a Nursery of Vice on Sunday Evenings?', *The Detective*, no. 19, vol. II (New Series), 13 August 1885, pp. 1–2.

VI. Conclusion

The value of criminal returns has, in recent years, rightfully come under question as a meaningful barometer for measuring crime. What these statistics can reveal, though, is how various branches of the criminal justice system shaped the official pattern of recorded crime. The records of police courts, which constituted the bulk of the police returns, are especially important in this respect. As police courts were the first point of judicial interaction within the criminal justice system, their returns illuminate the impact that institutional procedures, policies and practices had on statistical trends. As such, police court data, in conjunction with the accompanying information produced by the police on reported crimes and apprehensions, are valuable crime records in revealing the (often intimate) relationship between the police, the courts, and justices, as well as how these interact with the aims of, and constraints on, civic administration. Prosecutions could be, and sometimes were, driven by financial considerations, as has been claimed for England. But these financial considerations were not always about cost cutting. Indeed, in regards to offences, it was often the opposite.

The media, too, was able to exert considerable influence on short-term police returns, especially relating to urban order offences such as drunkenness. Criminal behaviour was always a popular topic of newspaper reporting and its perceived reader-interest value alone should give the historian pause to consider how this might have influenced the presentation of crime on its pages. For the police courts, this was reflected in an uneven reporting of its business, highlighting the sensational, unusual and topical, as well as cases from which authors, journalists, letter-writers, and editors could draw social commentary of their own. More specifically, while the early periodicals opened up a broader amount of the day-to-day business of the police courts to wider public scrutiny than had previously been the case, this too was pursued with specific economic and moral motivations of its publishers at the forefront. The shift from qualitative reports and investigation to a preoccupation with the persuasive power of numbers may have seemed more 'accurate' but was clearly governed by similar motivations and should be read with similar circumspection. The power of the press to exert influence over the manner of quantitative presentations, on police policy, and therefore upon statistical peaks and troughs reflected the growing preoccupation of police and courts with public image as the century progressed. Alcohol-related behaviours were just one area of their concern, but the control of violence and the fate of children in police courts were two others emphasised by construction of returns and by media reporting of them that will be explored further in chapters of their own. The police courts' relationships went well beyond legal colleagues and clients in the courtroom. As print commentary expanded, so too did the reading public by whom their business and practices were judged.

For all their limitations, the sources that were produced by the police court, and which reported on police court proceedings, reveal a great deal about the role, purpose and significance of summary justice in Scottish towns. As the business of police courts became increasingly concerned with enforcing municipal regulations and 'victimless offences', the capacity for the local state to intervene in the lives of the urban masses grew considerably. Although the returns and press reports shows that magistrates were often unable and unwilling to intervene directly into the day-to-day affairs of everyone brought before them, police courts were, nonetheless, the necessary accompaniment to the emerging 'policeman-state' and a vehicle for imposing a new level of urban order. Gatrell charts the emergence of this phenomenon in England from the 1860s,[235] but in Scotland's largest cities the police were an integral tool of the local state much earlier. From soon after their inception, police courts became processing centres for dealing with drunks, vagrants, petty thieves, misdemeanours and indiscretions; in the process filling the vacuum that had been created by the difficulties burgh and church courts had faced in dealing with such challenges.

---

[235] V.A.C. Gatrell, 'Crime, Authority and the Policeman–State', in F.M.L. Thompson (ed.), *Cambridge Social History of Britain, 1750–1950* (Cambridge, 1992), pp. 243–310.

Chapter 6
Legal, Social and Cultural Convictions

I. Introduction

> It is a fundamental maxim of our criminal law that an accused person is presumed to be innocent until his guilt has been proved by the Prosecutor beyond all reasonable doubt. The accused therefore is entitled to the benefit of a reasonable doubt. ... The meaning of the presumption is simply this, that a person accused of a crime or an offence is not bound to make any statement or to offer any explanation of circumstances which throw suspicion upon him. His presumed innocence is a complete answer to mere suspicion. ... Keeping in mind the presumption of innocence, it follows that in a criminal trial the strictest regard to the rules of evidence must be paid.[1]

Despite the presumption of innocence being a central tenet of modern Scots criminal law, it has been widely acknowledged both by contemporaries and historical scholars that the chances of being acquitted in the nineteenth-century Scottish higher criminal courts were slim.[2] In giving evidence to the 1854–1855 Select Committee on Public Prosecutions, Lord Broughton pointed out that in England between one fifth and one sixth of defendants went free, compared to less than half that number in Scotland.[3] In the Scottish justiciary courts, conviction rates rarely fell below 80 to 85 per cent.[4] The central role of the

---

[1]   Glasgow City Archives (GCA), PA2/21: James Robertson, Procurator Fiscal of Glasgow, *Handbook for Magistrates on Police Court Procedure, Evidence, etc* (Glasgow, 1951), p. 22.

[2]   S.J. Connolly, 'Albion's Fatal Twigs: Justice and Law in the Eighteenth Century', in Rosalind Mitchison and Peter Roebuck (eds), *Economy and Society in Scotland and Ireland* (Edinburgh, 1980), p. 121; and E.P. Thompson, *Whigs and Hunters: The Origins of the Black Act* (London, 1975), pp. 2 & 59–65.

[3]   'Report from the Select Committee on Public Prosecutors; together with the Proceedings of the Committee, Minutes of Evidence, Appendix and Evidence', *British Parliamentary Papers* (*BPP*), 1854–55 (481), XII.1, p. 7.

[4]   Lindsay Farmer, *Criminal Law, Tradition and Legal Order: Crime and the Genius of Scots Law 1747 to the Present* (Cambridge, 1997), p. 108. See also 'Scotland. A Return of Persons Male and Female, Committed, in the years 1805, 1806, 1807, 1808, 1809, & 1810, to the several Gaols in Scotland, till Liberated in due course of Law, and afterwards detained in Prison for Trial before the High Court of Justiciary at Edinburgh, or the Circuit Court of Justiciary, or reported by Sheriffs of Counties as tried by a Jury in the Sheriff Courts: and the Numbers Convicted; and Acquitted or Discharged on

public prosecutor in both filtering out weak cases and in conducting criminal trials meant that the odds were stacked against the accused should a case make it to trial. Moreover, although Scots criminal law was more lenient than its English counterpart in terms of the number of capital crimes on the statute books and public executions that were carried out, Scottish legal elites were by no means squeamish when it came to administering the law.[5] The public prosecutor and the higher courts showed themselves more than willing to adopt a tough, repressive stance against the accused, especially during periods of political unrest that posed a threat to the security of the state.[6] Whereas the English judiciary would increase the number of executions during periods of heightened concern with law and order,[7] in Scotland the procurator fiscal, it has been claimed, would respond by increasing the number of criminal prosecutions before a largely supportive justiciary.[8]

Other evidence, though, brings a different perspective on the Scottish criminal justice system's treatment of the accused. As Lindsay Farmer has pointed out, procedural safeguards were rigorously adhered to and up to 20 per cent of high court criminal prosecutions in the early nineteenth century were dropped by the public prosecutor for lack of sufficient evidence or for breach of legal process.[9] This, he maintains, was less about protecting the rights of the accused than preserving the dignity of the judicial process, but it nonetheless serves to highlight the dangers of overstating the extent to which the Scottish courts of justiciary could be relied upon to convict.[10] However, the summary courts, he contends, offered the accused less protection. In these courts, 'procedural safeguards were not modelled on the criminal trial, but on a calculus that weighed the cost to the individual against the cost to the system. The imperative to this system was

---

Account of the Prosecution: against them being Abandoned; or Dismissed by Sentence of Court: – and the Sentences of such as were Convicted; and the Number of such as were Convicted who have received Unconditional Pardons: and under each head of Offence, the Numbers of those Capitally Convicted, who have been Executed', *BPP*, 1812 (45), X.217.

[5]   M.A. Crowther, 'Crime, Prosecution and Mercy: English Influence and Scottish Practice in the Early Nineteenth Century', in S.J. Connolly (ed.), *Kingdoms United? Great Britain and Ireland since 1500: Integration and Diversity* (Dublin, 1999), p. 233.

[6]   See, for instance, Michael T. Davis, 'Prosecution and Radical Discourse during the 1790s: The Case of the Scottish Sedition Trials', *International Journal of the Sociology of Law*, 33/3 (2005): pp. 148–58.

[7]   Douglas Hay, 'Property, Authority and the Criminal Law', in Douglas Hay, Peter Linebaugh, John G. Rule, E.P. Thompson and Cal Winslow (eds), *Albion's Fatal Tree: Crime and Society in Eighteenth-Century England* (London, 1976), pp. 17–63.

[8]   Crowther, 'Crime, Prosecution and Mercy', p. 233.

[9]   Farmer, *Criminal Law, Tradition and Legal Order*, p. 108; and 'Scotland. A Return of Persons Male and Female, Committed, in the years 1805, 1806, 1807, 1808, 1809, & 1810, to the several Gaols in Scotland'.

[10]   Farmer, *Criminal Law, Tradition and Legal Order*, pp. 107–8.

not the presumption of innocence but the demand for an internal order based on efficiency and speed'.[11]

This chapter examines the factors that affected conviction in Scottish police courts and how these played out in practice over the course of the century. In doing so, it also explores how assumptions about character circulated within the court and were projected through the media, and how gender, ethnicity and class all contributed to what kind of offenders would most likely be convicted. It argues that there were similarities between the police courts and higher courts in prosecution and conviction patterns which should not be overlooked. However, the institutional workings of police courts were not determined purely by concern for economy and the dignity of procedural safeguards. While both were extremely important in shaping how a burgeoning caseload was dealt with, so, too, were the public faces of both the police and magistrates. As the century progressed, securing convictions became particularly important, especially for the police, in an era when police efficiency was increasingly defined by apprehension and prosecution to conviction ratios; but for magistrates, this was balanced by how they saw their wider role in the community. Decisions about conviction were administered with a set of social and cultural assumptions held by court personnel – assumptions which were also reflected in police data. Protecting the rights, reputations and career paths of recipients who were considered to be 'deserving', such as children or men and women of certain social standing, was another imperative for a system in which magistrates served as paternal moral leaders within a Christian framework. In such cases, procedural rules were often circumvented in order to protect the individuals concerned, and not, as was the case in many other instances, in order to make it easier to secure guilty verdicts.

For the majority of those brought before magistrates though, police court summary justice gave rise to a two-tiered criminal justice system in which stringent procedural and evidential legal safeguards in higher courts coexisted with a system of lesser protection for those tried before magistrates.[12] The summary justice that was administered in police courts not only made it possible for procurators to bring more people before justices, secure convictions and determine potentially life-changing consequences than would have been possible for higher courts, they also helped magistrates to manage their own position, effectiveness and reputation as civic and moral leaders at a time when their

---

[11] Ibid., p. 81. For a debate on this for the eighteenth-century summary courts in England, see Bruce P. Smith, 'The Presumption of Guilt and the English Law of Theft, 1750–1850', *Law and History Review*, 23/1 (2005): pp. 133–72; Norma Landau, 'Summary Conviction and the Development of the Penal Law', *Law and History Review*, 23/1 (2005): pp. 173–89; and Bruce P. Smith, 'Did the Presumption of Innocence Exist in Summary Proceedings?', *Law and History Review*, 23/1 (2005): pp. 191–9.

[12] For more on this concept, see Farmer, *Criminal Law, Tradition and Legal Order*, p. 78; and Smith, 'The Presumption of Guilt and the English Law of Theft, 1750–1850', pp. 133–72.

work was being increasingly scrutinised in the media and measured by annual budgetary civic balance sheets and statistical returns. Safeguarding the sanctity of procedure, saving or punishing those before the court, and protecting the community from crime all played in the mix along with managing the perception of magistrates in the wider community.

II. Implementing the Legal Framework and Its Representation, c.1800 to 1857

Any attempt to compare conviction to acquittal ratios is fraught with difficulty. Such statistics were not recorded consistently over the course of the century, or from burgh to burgh. Moreover, some of the earlier crime returns used the term 'discharged' and 'acquitted' interchangeably.[13] For the former, in particular, it is not always clear whether an actual trial took place, or whether accused individuals were sent on their way prior to formal proceedings being undertaken. Furthermore, crime statistics often reveal little about the nature of criminal prosecution and trial. They do not, for instance, indicate which cases were contested with a not guilty plea. Rarely do they make clear whether cases that were discharged or had no further proceedings taken were dropped by procurators or thrown out of court by magistrates.

As Chapters 3 and 5 have demonstrated, the flexible manner in which the law was administered resulted in huge numbers of individuals being dismissed and discharged.[14] The fact that no proceedings were taken against up to one third of those picked up for crimes in a typical year in Glasgow should caution against assuming that procurators and magistrates rode rough-shod over legal rights in order to secure convictions. Even though fiscal and judicial constraints are likely to have influenced to some extent the large number of cases which were dropped, the frequency with which this occurred suggests that the public men who staffed police courts were in most cases capable of acting judiciously – or, at least, believed that they were acting judiciously in so far as their understanding of the law and the discretion they enjoyed in interpreting it permitted. Dismissals were especially common in the first few decades of the century. Approximately half of the individuals charged in the formative years of the Glasgow Police Court had their cases dismissed – albeit often with a reprimand from the magistrate. In Edinburgh, approximately one third of cases brought before magistrates between 1805 and 1807 were either dismissed or assoilzied (that is, acquitted or freed from

---

[13]   See, for instance, the evidence presented to the 'Fourth Report by Her Majesty's Law Commissioners, Scotland, 1839', *BPP*, 1840 (241), XX.115, pp. 278, 304, 323, 332, 335, 336 & 338.

[14]   In Glasgow's submission to the 1839 Law Inquiry, for instance, no schedule for acquittals was kept, but the records note that a considerable number of those convicted were merely admonished. Ibid., p. 323.

prosecution and censor).[15] In 1824, the figure was even higher. *The Scotsman* reported that between April and October of that year, 2,097 of the 3,930 cases dealt with had been dismissed by magistrates.[16] These included 576 cases of drunk and disorderly conduct (15 per cent of total dismissals), 567 cases of assault (14 per cent of total dismissals), 453 cases of theft (12 per cent), and 146 cases of pick-pocketing (4 per cent). The article offered no commentary on the reasons for such a high dismissal rate, but it is likely that in some cases the magistrate adopted the view that the short period of confinement to which the accused had been subject prior to the commencement of court proceedings was sufficient penalty for the offence charged – especially drunk and disorderly.[17] The figures, though, were enough to concern *The Scotsman* which warned that 'Nuisances of an indecent and offensive nature on the streets have certainly become more general and the list of these will increase if the police do not become more vigilant, and the Magistrates more resolute in fining or punishing.'[18] Others were dismissed on evidential grounds. The 1847 Edinburgh returns for theft, for instance, show that 494 people were discharged in court 'for want of proof', compared with 882 people who were convicted.[19]

Magistrates, police commissioners and, especially policemen, sometimes bemoaned the large number of people who were not convicted. As was pointed out in Chapter 2, justices in mid-nineteenth-century Edinburgh complained about the number of cases abandoned due to lack of evidence. Lamenting the loss of fine income that such a result produced, in 1851, Bailie Fyfe complained in relation to prostitutes and those running houses of ill repute that:

> The great proportion of the cases which were abandoned, are so chiefly because of the difficulty of finding a sufficient amount of legal evidence – namely, that of having at least two parties as witnesses to the robbery. … a relaxation of the law of evidence would be beneficial in this matter, and thought that if the deposition of one person was made sufficient to convict such offenders, it would tend to convict a larger number, and would go far to root out the evil.[20]

---

[15]   Out of the first 427 cases for which the outcome was recorded in the Edinburgh Court book, 1805–1807, just under two thirds were found to be, or pleaded, guilty (64 per cent discerned against), and approximately one third were either dismissed (23 per cent) or assoilzied (11 per cent). Edinburgh City Archives (ECA), ED006/8: Edinburgh Police Court Abstract of Processes, 1805–1807.

[16]   *The Scotsman*, 18 December 1824. See also John McGowan, *Policing the Metropolis of Scotland: A History of the Police and Systems of Police in Edinburgh and Edinburghshire, 1770–1833* (Musselburgh, 2010), p. 271.

[17]   Ibid., p. 271.

[18]   Cited in ibid.

[19]   Whether 'discharged' and 'acquitted' were used interchangeably in this instance is impossible to say, although this seems likely as no acquittals were recorded.

[20]   *An Inquiry into Destitution, Prostitution and Crime in Edinburgh* (Edinburgh, 1851), published as *Low Life in Victorian Edinburgh, By a Medical Gentleman* (Edinburgh, 1980), p. 117. Aggregate returns show that there had been 1,332 robberies in brothels,

He claimed from his experience as a public and police magistrate that thefts committed by prostitutes in brothels and on the streets were increasing and highlighted the huge disparity between crimes reported and convictions. A return for Edinburgh, which had been produced by the superintendent of police, showed that during the years 1848, 1849, and 1850, 1,046 robberies committed in brothels had been reported to the police. Of these 36 were convicted in the police court, 40 were remitted to a higher court, and 970 were abandoned.[21] Fyfe claimed that he had obtained similar results for Glasgow, Aberdeen, Dundee, and Perth. There was an aggregate of 3,455 robberies committed in these houses and on the streets for all five cities, of which only 354, or 10 per cent, were convicted, 141, or four per cent, were remitted to a higher court, and 2,960, or 86 per cent, were dropped.[22] These figures, admittedly, included reported crimes, not just those who were charged.[23] Nonetheless, they highlight the evidential difficulties the police and magistrates faced in bringing offenders to justice.

However, the high dismissal rate was not always due to insufficient evidence.[24] In his comparative study of police in London and New York, Wilbur Miller has argued that the high acquittal rate in the London police courts in the early nineteenth century was a product of discord between local magistrates and the centralised new police model that was created under the 1829 Metropolitan Police Act.[25] Justices, he contends, were resentful of how the Metropolitan police structure impacted on their own position, power and status and were suspicious and, at times, unsupportive of the police and the evidence they presented in court. In Scotland, relations between magistrates and police commissions were also tense in the early nineteenth century. Magistrates in the large Scottish towns had attempted, unsuccessfully in most cases, to establish new police models under their own control. Middle-rank unwillingness to give more power to unpopular and unaccountable local authorities before burgh reform in 1833 meant that civic leaders, after years of resistance, had little alternative but to concede to demands for elected commissions to manage police affairs in order to secure statutory powers to levy taxes and fund much-needed public services. Municipal and police administration became particularly adversarial

---

of which 113 resulted in convictions, 11 were remitted to higher courts, and 1,208 were abandoned. There was no return of the number of thefts committed on the streets, but the total amount of property stolen on the streets and in brothels was, £509, 13s., 8d. Similar results were obtained from Aberdeen, Dundee, and Perth. Combining these five cities, the total sum of money stolen amounted to £14,840, 19s., 9d.

[21]   Ibid.

[22]   Ibid., pp. 117–18.

[23]   Ibid.

[24]   Indeed, Captain Miller of the Glasgow claimed that very few were abandoned on evidential grounds. GCA, M.P.24, D-T.C.14/1/24, 23: *Papers Relative to the State of Crime in the City of Glasgow, with Observations of a Remedial Nature; and an Appendix of Tables, by H. Miller, Superintendent of Police, and City Marshal* (Glasgow, 1840), p. 6.

[25]   Wilbur Miller, *Cops and Bobbies: Police Authority in New York and London, 1830–1870* (Chicago, 1977), pp. 76–85.

in the 1830s and 1840s as demographic change, residential qualifications and the growing unwillingness of 'respectable' members of the community to serve as police commissioners resulted in men of a 'lesser' social standing to that of councillors, and some with Chartist leanings, being elected to police commissions.[26]

The question of whether magisterial resentment about the management of police affairs in the first half of the nineteenth century influenced courtroom acquittals is difficult to say with any degree of certainty. According to contemporary reports, magistrates became more willing to accept police evidence uncritically in court as the century progressed. This is probably reflective of the fact that the police became more skilled in testifying in court over time, but it also might suggest that relations had been far from harmonious in the early nineteenth century. In so far as magisterial treatment of those who abused police officers is an indication of police-judicial relations, bailies were not as supportive of police officers as they were to become later in the century. In the early 1800s, magistrates often dismissed or treated leniently those who had molested watchmen.[27] In 1818, for instance, John McArthur, weaver, was dismissed with a reprimand and admonition for assaulting a watchman and members of the public in a drunken state.[28] Indeed, there was almost an expectation in civic circles in the police's formative years that ill-treatment was part of a policeman's job, with abusive behaviour against watchmen often being recorded as a notation in police court records rather than forming part of the charge.[29] However, it is unlikely that the nature of police governance would have adversely affected conviction rates in Scottish police courts in the same way that Miller suggested for London. Significantly, while senior police officers in Scotland did, on occasion, bemoan the difficulties of securing convictions, there was not the same degree of concern about an unsupportive judicial bench as existed in London in the early nineteenth century. Indeed, in Edinburgh it was the public complaint about the strength of convictions and the lack of separation between the police and the judiciary that was more common. Moreover, the fact that magistrates in other

---

[26] David G. Barrie, *Police in the Age of Improvement: Police Development and the Civic Tradition in Scotland, 1775–1865* (Cullompton, 2008), pp. 224–60.

[27] Peter McPherson, labourer, had his charge of being riotous in the city and abusing a watchman dismissed with a reprimand. GCA, B3/1/1/1: Glasgow Police Court Diet Books, 4 February 1813, p. 26. Bernard Hughes, who was convicted of being drunk and molesting a watchman received the modest fine of just 5s. GCA, B3/1/1/1: Glasgow Police Court Diet Books, 7 February 1813, p. 34.

[28] GCA, B3/1/1/5: Glasgow Police Court Diet Books, 28 January 1818, p. 23.

[29] See, for instance, the charge of abusing the complainer and watchman brought against John Craig, weaver, by Mrs Robertson, vintner, when he refused to pay for liquor. He had his case dismissed with a reprimand on the condition that he paid the complainer 5s. in damages. No action was taken against him for abusing the watchman. GCA, B3/1/1/1: Glasgow Police Court Diet Books, 29 January 1813, p. 6. Even potentially serious incidents were treated fairly leniently. In 1842, one man convicted of kicking up a disturbance in a tavern, and attempting to stab the watchman by whom he was arrested with a sheath knife, was fined one guinea. *Scotch Reformers' Gazette*, 10 September 1842, p. 4.

Scottish towns still served as *ex-officio* police commissioners – albeit significantly outnumbered by directly elected ones – is likely to have reduced to some degree the potential for conflict in police–judicial relations within the courtroom (as would the fact that criminal prosecutions in Scotland in the police's formative years were led in the majority of cases by burgh fiscals, who were appointed by magistrates).

The high dismissal rate in the Scottish police courts in the early nineteenth century was much more a product of how magistrates saw their role in the community than simmering tension between magistrates and elected police commissioners. In keeping with their self-perception as guardians of public welfare, magistrates sometimes dismissed cases in order to protect 'respectable' or 'vulnerable' offenders from the consequences of legal action. Some children, as well as a small number of those accused of begging and prostitution as the century progressed, were perceived as capable of redemption and thus, it was thought, would benefit from magisterial discretion (the changing treatment of those accused of begging and prostitution is examined in more detail in Chapter 6 of Volume 2). In an 1829 case before the Glasgow Police Court, for example, the magistrate dismissed two young boys who had been drunk in the street with an eye to their future potential, remarking: 'I shall let you go for this time, on your promising never to get drunk again, and to conduct yourself properly in future.'[30] Those who were deemed respectable by court officials could also on occasion receive sympathy for their deviant behaviour. In March 1832, Bailie Anderson heard a case in the Edinburgh Police Court of a man charged with vagrancy. According to *The Police Intelligencer*, the accused explained that 'he was at one time a respectable merchant in the city of Glasgow' and 'at one time worth a number of thousand pounds, – that he was now greatly reduced, and had a wife and six children under five years of age'. This moved Anderson to bestow charity upon the unfortunate offender (who offered no defence against the actual charge) and thus 'the poor fellow was dismissed with certification'.[31]

Such instances spoke volumes about how magistrates employed their own social and cultural ideas in deciding whether to convict or dismiss defenders. However, if a magistrate deemed that there was sufficient evidence to proceed to trial, the acquittal-to-conviction rate indicates that the chances of acquittal in the first half of the century were fairly low. Much depended on the type of crime or offence and the particular sitting magistrate, but as in higher courts, those who had a judgement pronounced upon them in the police courts were generally much more likely to be convicted than acquitted. The 1839 Law Inquiry – the first national police court returns to list convictions – showed that of the 37,238 offences that the Scottish police courts dealt with between 1833 and 1835, 23,479 (just under two thirds) resulted in a conviction (see

---

[30] *Police Reports of Causes tried before the Justices of Peace, and the Glasgow, Gorbals and Calton Police Courts* (*Police Reports*), 22 August 1829, p. 68.

[31] *The Police Intelligencer, or Life in Edinburgh* (*Police Intelligencer*), 31 March 1832.

Table 6.1   Police Court Cases, 1833 to 1835[†]

Burgh	No. of Crimes/ Offences	Convictions	Acquittals	Imprisonment	Fined	Remitted to Sheriff	Highest Daily No.
Glasgow	16,109	10,629	Not Std.**	3,783	6,847	0	40
Edinburgh	6,234*	3,190	2,742**	1,091****	1,178*****	143	98
Paisley	5,792	2,285	3,128	170	1,705	187	Not Std.
Dundee	3,681	3,191	See Below***	1,139	2,052	103	29
Greenock	2,813	2,278	518	807	1,613	17	Not Std.
Perth	1,810	1,188	582**	342	846	40	20
Aberdeen	799	718	81	578	455	0	7

*   All of the above returns for Edinburgh relate only to 1835.

**   A considerable number of those convicted were merely admonished and were not recorded in the list of convictions or punishments given above. Please note, the slight disparity between the number of convictions and the number of acquittals/sentences cited for some burghs is explained by the inconsistent manner in which acquittals/admonitions were recorded.

***   The figures for the years 1834/35 for Dundee are ineligible, but of the 1,489 cases in 1835, 1,281 resulted in convictions, 161 in acquittals and 47 were remitted to the sheriff.

****   905 offenders were also cautioned in Edinburgh.

† 'Fourth Report by Her Majesty's Law Commissioners. Scotland. 1839', pp. 278, 304, 323, 332, 335, 336 & 338.

Table 6.1). The actual number deemed by magistrates to be guilty, however, was probably nearer three quarters, given that those who were admonished for having committed petty offences were included in the acquittal returns in this survey. In 1840, a report into the state of crime in Glasgow provided a more detailed picture of how magistrates had dealt with the 7,687 people charged with crimes and offences for the preceding year. Of these, 5,410 were summarily convicted, 1,178 were admonished, 468 discharged and just 179 acquitted. The remainder were transferred to other courts or counties or were ordered to find bail.[32] Conviction rates for contraventions and offences were especially high, with convictions for property crimes slightly lower. In 1846 in Edinburgh, two thirds of those prosecuted for property crimes were convicted – a rate higher than in the Metropolitan police courts in the mid-nineteenth century.[33] This was in keeping with conviction rates for the justiciary courts, which were consistently higher in Scotland in the nineteenth century than in England.[34]

The above parliamentary returns did not distinguish between convictions of women and men, but by the early 1850s the records produced by the Edinburgh Police did break down returns according to sex. There was no discernible difference in the conviction rate between men and women for offences and contraventions that were determined by a guilty or not guilty verdict, with both standing at 96 per cent for the years 1854 to 1857 inclusive.[35] This was partly influenced by the fact that a significant proportion of those convicted were

---

[32]   GCA, M.P.24, D-T.C.14/1/24, 23: *Papers Relative to the State of Crime in the City of Glasgow*, p. 25.

[33]   The returns for 1846 show that of the 1,909 persons apprehended for theft, 882 were convicted in the police court, 533 were remitted to higher courts, and 494 were discharged in the police court for want of proof. Edinburgh Central Library (ECL): 'Edinburgh Police Office, Half Yearly Report showing State of Crime during the Last Five Years' (1847), p. 4. Wilbur Miller's research on the Metropolitan police courts found that between 1831 and 1841 magistrates convicted, held to bail, or committed for jury trial, an average of about 49 per cent of the arrestees brought before them. From 1856 to 1870, they convicted or committed 65 per cent of felony and misdemeanour cases. Miller, *Cops and Bobbies*, p. 87.

[34]   Archibald Alison, in *Practice of the Criminal Law of Scotland* (Edinburgh, 1833) stated that the average convictions to acquittals ratio in Scotland was six to one, and in England as low as two to one. Cited in 'Report from the Select Committee on Public Prosecutors', p. 7, evidence of Lord Broughton. Broughton's comparative figures, though, were a little more conservative, noting that acquittals in England were twice as high as in Scotland. This is discussed more fully below.

[35]   Of the 16,262 men charged with offences and contraventions, 15,691 were convicted compared with 15,450 of the 16,008 women charged. ECL: *Reports and Returns as to Crimes, Offences, and Contraventions, and to Cases of Drunkenness, within the Police Bounds of the City of Edinburgh, during the Last Six Years, prepared for the Magistrates and Council, by Thomas Linton, Superintendent of Police* (Edinburgh, 1860), p. 17.

likely to have forfeited their pledge rather than turn up in court. However, men charged with crimes were much more likely than women to be found guilty. Of the 1,814 men who had their criminal cases disposed of in the Edinburgh Police Court between these years, 89 per cent were convicted (1,610 convictions and 204 desertions or not proven verdicts). By contrast, of the 1,741 women who were brought before magistrates in the same period, just 68 per cent were convicted (1,187 convictions and 554 desertions or not proven verdicts).[36] This was, as is explored more fully below, because women were much more likely than men to have their criminal charges dropped before trial proceedings commenced.[37]

The fast, cost-effective nature of summary justice gave prosecutors procedural and evidential advantages over the accused. Defenders had little time and opportunity to gather supporting evidence and were denied access to publicly funded legal representation. The latter was particularly significant given that the accused were often unable to express their position in legal terms and, in criminal cases, were usually up against prosecutors who were trained lawyers. Indeed, in giving evidence to the 1854–1855 Select Committee on Public Prosecutors, Lord Broughton argued that the higher ratio of convictions to prosecutions in Scotland relative to England was due to the fact that Scotland had a public prosecutor and England did not. Proceedings in Scotland, he maintained, were conducted by experienced professional public men rather than private individuals, which significantly improved the strength of prosecution and the chances of conviction.[38] Moreover, it was suggested that having civic rather than stipendiary magistrates worked against the accused. Aside from the fact that civic magistrates were, according to contemporary portrayals, more likely to convict than stipendiary magistrates,[39] they did not have the legal expertise to defend effectively the interests of the accused against legally trained prosecutors. According to the *Caledonian Mercury* in 1855, many people brought before the police court in Edinburgh suffered from 'blunders which a trained lawyer [acting as judge] would avoid'.[40] The limited powers of punishment which magistrates had at their disposal, allied to the fact that courtroom proceedings and evidence were not formally recorded and

---

[36]   Ibid., p. 18.

[37]   As the records did not distinguish desertions from acquittals it is not possible to determine the rate of convictions for charges which made it to trial.

[38]   'Report from the Select Committee on Public Prosecutors', p. 7.

[39]   *Caledonian Mercury*, 28 July 1855; and Glasgow University Library (GUL), Special Collections: 'Paid v Unpaid Magistrates', *The Journal of Jurisprudence*, XI (1867): p. 539.

[40]   *Caledonian Mercury*, 28 July 1855. The application of the law was constantly evolving according to judicial judgements. For more, see Thomas Trotter, *The Summary Jurisdiction (Scotland) Act 1908: with Introduction, Notes and Forms* (Edinburgh, 1909), p. 223.

written down, ensured that in practice legal safeguards were not as stringent as those in higher courts or always as rigorously enforced.[41]

It seems likely that procurators were more inclined to prosecute cases in police courts that would not have been deemed strong enough to be successfully prosecuted in a higher court. Given the comparable advantages of securing a conviction before magistrates, procurators appear to have used police courts to prosecute certain criminal cases – usually involving property crimes – that deserved to be brought before a sheriff or burgh court. There is evidence, for instance, that procurators undervalued stolen items, underplayed the severity of crimes, and ignored the criminal histories of the accused in order to keep the alleged crime within the jurisdiction of police court magistrates, even if it meant that those convicted would receive a lesser punishment.[42] In 1825, for instance, a judge in the High Court of Justiciary questioned why a woman who had been convicted by an Edinburgh magistrate of robbery – an offence which should have been prosecuted in a sheriff or justiciary court – had been convicted on 15 previous occasions by the same police court (the case only came before the Lord Justice because the defender appealed against the magistrate's sentence). Under the local police act, those who had been convicted on three occasions of the same offence were required to be remitted to a higher court. The Lord Advocate stated that:

> he could only explain this conduct of the Magistracy, in permitting such a course of depredation to be followed, by stating that they [magistrates] were annually renewed, and therefore the Magistrates of one year may not be aware of what convictions had taken place in former years; but he certainly did consider it the duty of the Fiscal and clerks of Police, where this was the case, to inform the Magistrates how many times an offender had already been convicted of the same offence, and that it was the duty of the Magistrates to refer all aggravated cases to this Court, and not to allow a system of crime like this to be carried on, subject only to the trivial penalties which the Police were competent to impose.[43]

Despite the Lord Advocate's attempts to pass off the above example as an oversight, it was far from exceptional. Edinburgh police returns for 1880 cite the example of P. Martin, who was charged and convicted for crimes and offences – mainly relating to breach of the peace, assault and being drunk and incapable – on 138

---

[41]   Leon Radzinowicz and Roger G. Hood, *A History of English Criminal Law and its Administration from 1750, Vol. V: The Emergence of Penal Policy* (London, 1986), ch. 19.

[42]   In the Aberdeen Police Court in 1880, the fiscal and bailie interacted to temper the charge and punishment meted out to a woman accused of keeping hold of a watch that did not belong to her by undervaluing the property. *Aberdeen Weekly Journal*, 8 March 1880. See further discussion of this case in Chapter 7.

[43]   *Caledonian Mercury*, 1 December 1825. The High Court judge retorted that in future all complaints and judgements were to be kept and remitted to a higher authority, and that only a higher court try crimes of this nature. *Caledonian Mercury*, 15 December 1825.

occasions between 1861 and 1879.[44] Tellingly, the statistics also reveal that a small number of people who were arrested and initially charged with housebreaking, shopbreaking, robbery and theft from locked premises – crimes outwith the judicial reach of police courts given the level of expected punishment – had, after judicial investigation, their charges reduced to simple theft and to simple assault.[45] All were convicted by magistrates.

There was a strong sense that procurators and magistrates saw procedural advantages in prosecuting cases that might not have been strong enough to be remitted to a higher court. The number of cases that magistrates referred to higher courts was extremely low in the first half of the nineteenth century. Returns to the 1839 Law Inquiry show that only 490 cases were remitted in all seven police courts in Scotland between 1833 and 1835 – approximately 3 per cent of all police court cases.[46] There were numerous examples where judicial discretion was used to reprimand and convict the accused. In 1825, the Lord Justice Clerk – after an appeal had been lodged with him – suspended the contempt of court judgement an Edinburgh magistrate had handed down to a young woman on the basis of insufficient evidence. The *Caledonian Mercury* reported that the Lord Justice 'made some forcible observations as to the duty of the Police Magistrate, who was as strictly bound to administer justice according to his oath of office as his Lordship was in the Court of Justiciary'.[47] If the Lord Justice had to follow legal procedures, then magistrates were expected to do the same.

Appeals to the High Court of Justiciary against magisterial decisions were not common in the first few decades of the nineteenth century, due in no small part to the time and expense involved in pursuing such action.[48] In many burghs, judgements could be contested only if magistrates or procurators had not adhered to legal principles and formalities; the judgement itself could not be contested.[49]

---

[44]   ECL: *Return of Crimes and Offences Reported, Persons Apprehended and Cited, and Miscellaneous Returns Connected with the Police, for the Year Ending 31st December 1880* (Edinburgh, 1881), Table 5.

[45]   Ibid., Table 3B.

[46]   'Fourth Report by Her Majesty's Law Commissioners, Scotland, 1839', pp. 278, 304, 323, 332, 335, 336 & 338.

[47]   *Caledonian Mercury*, 15 December 1825.

[48]   The returns for the Aberdeen and Glasgow police courts between 1833 and 1835 show no appeals lodged. Indeed, A. Cadenhead, Procurator Fiscal of Aberdeen, informed the inquiry that 'from the time the Police Court of Aberdeen was instituted, there has not been a single case brought under the review of the Supreme Court by Bill of Suspension, appeal, or otherwise'. Similar evidence was presented to the 1839 Law Inquiry. 'Fourth Report by Her Majesty's Law Commissioners, Scotland, 1839', pp. 320 (Glasgow) & 333 (Aberdeen).

[49]   For an overview of rules and petitions concerning appeals in the Glasgow and surrounding police courts in the second half of the nineteenth century, see James Campbell Irons, *The Burgh Police (Scotland) Act, 1892* (Edinburgh, 1893), clause 495, pp. 717–23. Campbell Irons, in reporting on an appeal against a conviction of theft in

In Edinburgh, no appeals were allowed under the first police act (although this was subsequently amended),[50] and there were sufficient grumblings in various sources to suggest that members of the community believed they could not get a fair trial in police courts.[51] As Chapter 2 has discussed, the first few years of the Edinburgh Police Court saw a number of petitions from 'respectable' members of the public complaining about the 'despotic' and 'unaccountable' powers of the police judge. Over time, the number of appeals increased, although they continued to be fairly infrequent and, in all likelihood, just a fraction of the overall total of those who believed they had been convicted unjustly.[52] The complaints that were lodged in the early nineteenth century were sometimes successful and centred on the fact that magistrates had not adhered to legal principles and formalities and had abused their power.[53]

Scholars of criminal justice history in England have identified summary courts as places where the law was often enforced in a less than neutral manner by justices who had a vested business interest in securing convictions in certain cases.[54] In

---

1787, published the following observation from the Justiciary Court: 'that the Court has for long treated the judgement in cases brought before a Police Magistrate under the Act 9 Geo. IV. c.29 as final, unless upon a statement of the occurrence of some substantial error of justice' (p. 718).

    [50]   ECL: *CIVIS, A Letter to the Right Hon. Henry Erskine, Lord Advocate of Scotland, relative to the Act of Parliament for regulating the Police of Edinburgh* (Edinburgh, 1806), p. 17.

    [51]   This comes out strongly in the appeal made to the High Court of Justiciary by seven boys in the burgh of Dumbarton who had their conviction for theft of strawberries in the local court suspended on the basis 'that the proceedings were oppressive'. They complained that they were not made aware that a complaint was made against them until they were brought before the court which hindered their defence. The defenders were described as 'sons of respectable parents', which might have played a part in the High Court's decision. Campbell Irons, *The Burgh Police (Scotland) Act, 1892*, pp. 719–20. See also evidence (discussed more fully later in the chapter) presented by Charles Shand, lawyer, in 'First Report of the Law Commissioners Appointed to Inquire into the Courts of Law in Scotland; Together with Minutes of Evidence', *BPP*, 1868–69 (4125), XXV.29, p. 549.

    [52]   Campbell Irons, *The Burgh Police (Scotland) Act, 1892*, clause 495, pp. 717–23.

    [53]   Ibid.

    [54]   For the nineteenth century, see, for instance, David Philips, 'The Black Country Magistracy 1835–60: A Changing Elite and the Exercise of its Power', *Midland History*, 3/3 (1976): pp. 161–90; and Jennifer S. Davis, 'A Poor Man's System of Justice? The London Police Courts in the Second Half of the Nineteenth Century', *Historical Journal*, 27/2 (1984): p. 318. For the eighteenth century, see Douglas Hay, 'Patronage, Paternalism and Welfare: Masters, Workers and Magistrates in Eighteenth-Century England', *International Labor and Working-Class History*, 53 (1998): p. 32; Douglas Hay, 'Poaching and the Game Laws on Cannock Chase', in Hay, Linebaugh, Rule, Thompson, Winslow (eds), *Albion's Fatal Tree*, pp. 189–253; and John Styles, 'Embezzlement, Industry and the Law in England 1500–1800', in Maxine Berg, Pat

Scotland, as Alan Campbell and Christopher A. Whatley have pointed out, the police, magistrates and county justice figures were at the forefront in suppressing industrial and political radicalism and in promoting business interests – even if, in many instances, the fiscal or the magistrate would remit the case for trial in a court higher than the police one.[55] Indeed, the support justices afforded business interests was recognised in the late eighteenth century by the Scottish economist and moral philosopher, Adam Smith, who argued in *The Wealth of Nations* (1776) that:

> We rarely hear, it has been said, of the combination of masters, though frequently of those of workmen. But whoever imagines, upon this account, that masters rarely combine, is as ignorant of the world as of the subject. Masters are always and everywhere in a sort of tacit, but constant and uniform combination, not to raise the wages of labor above their actual rate[.] When workers combine, masters … never cease to call aloud for the assistance of the civil magistrate, and the rigorous execution of those laws which have been enacted with so much severity against the combination of servants, labourers, and journeymen.[56]

Although the number of cases involving workplace unrest that was prosecuted in police courts was not large,[57] procurators and magistrates were typically recorded as siding with employers to defend commercial interests. In prosecuting three men in the Aberdeen Police Court in 1840 for obstructing operatives of local machinery during an industrial dispute, the fiscal remarked: 'it was not to be endured that operatives were to interfereir [*sic*] and dictate to their employers what wages were proper to be given, and to hinder those who were inclined to work at the offered wages from going to their work.'[58] The sitting magistrate spoke sympathetically of the workers' plight, but insisted upon 'the necessity [that] existed for a general reduction of wages'. He subsequently fined them

---

Hudson and Michael Sonenscher (eds), *Manufacture in Town and Country Before the Factory* (Cambridge, 1983), pp. 173–210. Morgan and Rushton, though, contend that the law was not administered purely in magistrates' interests. Gwenda Morgan and Peter Rushton, 'The Magistrate, the Community and the Maintenance of an Orderly Society in Eighteenth-Century England', *Historical Research*, 76/191 (2003): pp. 54–77.

[55] Alan B. Campbell, *The Lanarkshire Miners: A Social History of their Trade Unions, 1775–1974* (Edinburgh, 1979), p. 218; Christopher A. Whatley, 'Labour in the Industrialising City', in T.M. Devine and Gordon Jackson (eds), *Glasgow, Volume 1: Beginnings to 1830* (Manchester, 1995), p. 309.

[56] Adam Smith, *An Inquiry into the Nature and Causes of the Wealth of Nations* (2 vols, London, 1776), vol. 1, ch. 8: 'Of the Wages of Labour'.

[57] Prosecutions that centred around industrial tension were usually remitted to higher courts.

[58] *Aberdeen Journal*, 2 September 1840.

– money, which in all likelihood, would have been hard for the men to find.[59] Significantly, he 'could assure the working-classes that, so soon as the depression in trade wore off, the employers would restore the wages to the old footing'. In giving this baseless assurance, the magistrate might have perceived himself as a paternalistic conflict arbitrator akin to the pre-1812 era when magistrates in certain Scottish cities were able to intervene in workplace disputes and set wage levels,[60] but on this occasion he was effectively acting as a spokesperson for the industrialists in seeking to dampen down workplace tensions.

The absence of detailed information in police court minute books for much of the first few decades of the nineteenth century makes it impossible to say whether magistrates worked hand in hand with employers in seeking to eradicate theft from the workplace, but qualitative evidence from media reports in the above examples suggests that police courts helped to criminalise behaviour that employers traditionally might have been more inclined to turn a blind eye to, and, in doing so, played a part in imposing workplace discipline and capitalist working practices. In 1829, for instance, James Weir, shoemaker in Glasgow, was convicted and sent to bridewell for 60 days for stealing a pair of shoes from his employer. This was the most severe punishment the court could administer.[61] Similarly, in April 1832, a young Edinburgh man, the foreman to a Mrs Morrison, book and shoemaker, was convicted of stealing a quantity of leather from his master and of 'a breach of trust by receiving different sums of money in the name of his master, and appropriating the same to his own use'. He was sentenced to ten days' confinement in the lock-up house.[62] There were also a number of reports of servants being convicted of stealing from masters, which, although by no means a new phenomenon, was much more common than had been possible before the expansion in police court summary powers.[63]

---

[59]   Ibid.

[60]   In the late eighteenth century, local magistrates and national judges had statutory powers in some parts of the country to fix wages at times of rising prices to alleviate the possibility of social disorder. However, influenced by the eighteenth-century writings of Adam Smith, justices in Lanarkshire in 1812 refused to intervene and fix wage levels in a dispute between weavers and employers. The justices' decision was supported by the Court of Session following an appeal by weavers. The court's ruling effectively ended wage regulation and heralded a bitter dispute between employers and employees. This marked a watershed in industrial and paternal relations. The concept of the moral economy, which related wages to living costs, had been firmly rejected in favour of the market economy. For more on this, see W. Hamish Fraser, 'Patterns of Protest', in T.M. Devine and Rosalind Mitchison (eds), *People and Society in Scotland, Volume 1: 1760–1830* (Edinburgh, 1988), pp. 280–81; and W. Hamish Fraser, *Conflict and Class: Scottish Workers, 1700–1838* (Edinburgh, 1988), p. 102.

[61]   *Police Reports*, 27 July 1829, p. 44.

[62]   *Police Intelligencer*, 17 April 1832.

[63]   See, for the instance, the case of a servant girl accused of stealing £15 from her master. After the accused had admitted to stealing money from time to time – but only to

Such judicial action among local justices was not confined to magistrates. On 25 July 1829, the Glasgow *Police Reports* published what was by the periodical's standards a detailed account of James Mitchell, weaver, who was charged in the Glasgow Justice of the Peace Court 'with making an effigy of old clothes shavings of William Laird, weaver, suspending and burning the same before his door, and creating a crowd in breach of the peace'. The incident happened in the Bridgeton district of Glasgow, which was outwith the jurisdiction of Glasgow magistrates. It was reported that Laird had rendered himself unpopular with weavers by employing webs (those who wove fabric) below the October prices. In passing sentence, the local justice gave an indication as to where his priorities lay – with the free market. He remarked: 'it was altogether out of the question, in this free country, to adopt compulsory measures to cause a man to take out work, at whatever prices a body of infatuated idiots might fix on.'[64] Mitchell was sentenced to 21 days in bridewell. What was particularly interesting about the case is not only the magistrate's view on workers' combination,[65] but also the type of coverage the *Police Reports* gave it – which was much more detailed than most other reports. It went to great lengths to show how intimidating the mob outside Laird's door was, shouting 'is Laird dead yet', and suggests that he was almost 'frightened to death'.[66] In reporting the magistrate's opinion, the unruly actions of the mob, and the tough stance taken by the court, the periodical was championing capitalist working practices, the physical dangers posed by workers organising themselves for improved pay and conditions, and the fact that the court could be relied upon to defend business interests.

Mainstream media also played a powerful role in conveying views about offenders, their guilt, and their prospects to a wider audience as well as reinforcing the views of court officials. Newspapers and periodicals regularly highlighted and mocked ethnic differences, reported accented speech, and commented upon the standards of clothing and cleanliness of those brought to the courts. Just as importantly, concerns about the strength of evidence or the legality on which convictions were based rarely featured in media reporting on police court proceedings. This was even the case in those periodicals, published in the late 1820s and early 1830s, which were focused entirely on the operations of the police courts. The *Police Reports* covered only one occasion when such disquiet within the court was recorded. In 1829, it reported on a case involving a lawyer who challenged a police summons against him for having house tickets (business boards) in front of his premises, in contravention of the local police act. He argued, unsuccessfully, that the police act conferred no legal right for the fiscal to charge

---

a total of £1, 15s. – the magistrate remitted the case to the burgh court, which had stronger powers of punishment. *Police Reports*, 27 July 1829, pp. 47–8.

[64]   *Police Reports*, 25 July 1829, p. 14.

[65]   The Combination of Workmen Act, 1825 (6 George IV, cap. 129) prohibited trade unions from attempting to bargain collectively for improved employment terms and conditions. It imposed criminal sanctions for picketing and forcing others not to work.

[66]   *Police Reports*, 25 July 1829, p. 14.

him for not taking down the tickets. The trial was likely selected for publication because it involved a lawyer, was entertaining, and was of interest to the journal's middle-class readership. Indeed, the report gave an unusual amount of coverage to the lawyer's 'long narration' which was delivered to 'the amusement of the court'.[67] Significantly, the *Police Reports* never questioned the strength of evidence on which convictions were secured in the other cases it reported on.

Robert B. Shoemaker, in his investigation of the *Proceedings of the Old Bailey*, has pointed out that it was important for the coverage to include both acquittals and convictions in order to help make the courts appear accessible and impartial.[68] Glasgow's *Police Reports* also did this: of the first 100 cases published, one quarter were dismissed.[69] Some had been dropped on the basis of insufficient evidence, but these were fairly rare. Many more dismissed cases were reported, although the dialogue of the court personnel also included in the media report suggested guilt on the part of the defender. Often, in such cases, the accused would be admonished with accompanying moral chastisement and guidance from magistrates, helping to reinforce their image as paternal community leaders. In 1829, the *Police Reports* published a case involving a servant charged with being drunk and disorderly in the house of her employer, a spirit dealer. The magistrate, after being informed that the woman had been disorderly in his house four times, remarked: 'you ought to have dismissed her ere now.' On being informed by the employer that she would not leave, the magistrate replied: 'if you had taken proper means, she would not have stopt.'[70] Dismissals were also common for cases in which magistrates did not deem it proper to get involved. In 1829, George Brown, tailor, was charged with abusing and striking his wife. The journal reported that 'the one accused the other in the end'. The magistrate dismissed the case and 'the parties went off laughing, and well pleased'.[71] The fact that the journal chose to highlight the response of the married couple was an attempt to ridicule them, not the fiscal or the magistrate who seemed all too willing to dismiss a case of violence in the home. Such cases, which were not unrepresentative of those dismissed by magistrates, were not published by Brownlie to represent justice in a bad light, but rather to suggest that some people were not worthy of the court's protection.

Of greater significance, though, were the ways in which Brownlie's periodical suppressed the accused's evidence or testimony. In cases where it was included,

---

[67]   *Police Reports*, 1 August 1829, p. 33.

[68]   Robert B. Shoemaker, 'The Old Bailey Proceedings and the Representation of Crime and Criminal Justice in Eighteenth-Century London', *Journal of British Studies*, 47/3 (2008): p. 567.

[69]   Convictions were often the product of guilty pleas or of the accused not turning up in court and forfeiting their bail money, so there is no way of ascertaining how many cases made it to court for trial for journalists to report on. *Police Reports*, 6 July 1829 to 8 August 1829, pp. 5–38.

[70]   *Police Reports*, 1 August 1829, p. 30.

[71]   Ibid.

the defender's input was usually restricted to just one or two sentences. In 1829, for instance, Brownlie reported that the charge of drunk and disorderly against Benjamin Dalrymple ('alias Royal Ben') 'was clearly proved', despite Dalrymple protesting his innocence.[72] His defence, as it was recorded in the journal, consisted only of the fact that Dalrymple claimed 'that he had not tasted drink "that day"'. The emphasis placed on 'that day' highlighted that Brownlie was, in keeping with the magistrate, passing judgement on his character. The defence of the accused was more likely to be recorded in greater depth, ironically, if it was the subject of ridicule by magistrates and procurators. The more implausible the accused's defence appeared to be or the more they struggled to convey their side of the story, the more likely that their voices would be recorded for the entertainment value they offered – a fact which likely helped to make the convictions handed down by magistrates seem all the more just to the middle-class readership. It was also extremely rare for witness statements in support of the defence to be published in the journal's reporting of courtroom proceedings. In only two of the first 100 cases reported between 6 July 1829 and 7 August 1829 was the evidence of defence witnesses recorded. Even then, coverage was restricted to a short comment on the character of the accused and the fact that they had gainful employment, not anything the witness had said about the case itself. Of course, the rarity with which defence witnesses' testimonies were recorded in the journal, to some degree, reflected the fact that the accused often had little opportunity to call witnesses on their behalf.[73] Nonetheless, it also served a wider purpose: it helped to strengthen the case for the prosecution among the reading public and made convictions seem clear cut.[74] This style of reporting may have reflected Brownlie's desire to present a compelling and entertaining narrative rather than his deliberate attempt to portray magisterial justice in a favourable light; but, regardless of its intent, it helped to create the impression that the judgements of the court were legitimate.

Of particular importance in this respect was the tendency for Brownlie to report upon the character of the accused. This was often given more prominence in the reports than actual evidence, which served to highlight the importance that middle-class opinion attached to it when it came to how justice should be

---

[72]   *Police Reports*, 6 July 1829, p. 5.

[73]   In England defence witnesses in higher court trials were often character witnesses until quite late in the nineteenth century, because if they had anything of relevance to say regarding the case they were bound over as a prosecution witness. This would inevitably have affected the reporting commentary on the case. It is not clear whether a similar situation existed in police courts in Scotland, which were often governed by local rules, regulations and statutes in the first half of the century, but evidence presented to the 1839–1840 Law inquiry states that the accused were allowed time to call their own witnesses separate from the witnesses for the prosecution, although time and fiscal constraints often worked against them. 'Fourth Report by Her Majesty's Law Commissioners, Scotland, 1839', p. 321.

[74]   This mirrors the conclusion of Shoemaker for the Old Bailey Proceedings. Shoemaker, 'The Old Bailey Proceedings and the Representation of Crime and Criminal Justice', pp. 567–8.

administered.[75] Around one in every four or so reports which detailed cases in any depth (that is, at least a developed paragraph) would indirectly allude to the fact that the accused was known to the police and had a criminal history. It was common for commentaries to begin by describing the accused as 'an old offender', 'an old police customer', 'a common thief', a 'dangerous character', 'a very conceited dandy', or a 'bad character'.[76] Crucially, in the overwhelming majority of cases, the accused was convicted. Indeed, in cases where reference to character was recorded, the conviction rates were disproportionately higher than others in which the reference to character had not been made. This style of reporting helped to portray the accused as guilty even before information on the actual charge was provided and was a powerful way in which the media could legitimise the decisions of police court magistrates. As Shani D'Cruze has argued in her study of the Victorian courts in England, judicial decisions were legitimised in media reports by marrying established legal principles with specific circumstances centring around character, reputation and appearance.[77]

It was especially common for the Irish, brothel keepers and prostitutes to have their reputations questioned by the media, which helped to demarcate these groups as particularly prone to criminality and to isolate other members of the community as less inclined to illegal behaviours.[78] Brownlie's reporting suggested that some of the accused had been lucky to escape conviction. In 1829, Isobel Smith was dismissed for want of proof after being charged with stealing a handkerchief. Brownlie, however, described her as 'a young lady whose character is formed, and whose education was finished at the boarding house at Duke Street' (a well-known brothel).[79] In a similar case, a woman described as a prostitute, who was charged with stealing boots from a married man identified only as Hawks, was also dismissed for want of evidence. This time it was the magistrate who left readers in little doubt as to the woman's character: 'It was

---

[75] By contrast, periodicals often expressed surprise when a 'respectable' person of good appearance was brought before the court (see Chapter 7).

[76] See the reports involving Daniel McDonald, 'an old offender' charged and convicted of fighting, and John Gourley, 'an old police customer' charged with being drunk and disorderly, and with throwing stones and brandishing a knife. *Police Reports*, 6 July 1829, p. 8; and *Police Reports*, 10 July 1829, p. 18.

[77] Shani D'Cruze, *Crimes of Outrage: Sex, Violence and Victorian Working Women* (London, 1998), p. 169.

[78] Similar findings have also been identified by researchers in modern studies. See, for example, Mike Owen Benediktsson, 'The Deviant Organisation and the Bad Apple CEP: Ideology and Accountability in Media Coverage of Corporate Scandals', *Social Forces*, 88/5 (2010): pp. 2189 & 2205–7. Interestingly, Howard Ehrlich has noted a similar reporting phenomenon in coverage of contemporary hate crime perpetrators, who are also portrayed as outcasts exercising individual agency in an otherwise functional, invisible 'white culture'. Howard J. Ehrlich, *Hate Crimes and Ethnoviolence: The History, Current Affairs and Future Discrimination in America* (Boulder, 2009), passim.

[79] *Police Reports*, 22 August 1829, p. 67.

a shame for him, a married man, and the father of no less than ten children, to be drinking with a common prostitute' – a comment which was then conveyed to a wider public through Brownlie's *Police Reports*.[80] Typically, Brownlie's periodical, one of only a few across the century which focused specifically on reporting of police court proceedings, legitimised the judgements that magistrates handed down. By omitting the case for the defence and alluding to the accused's criminal history, poverty or immorality, published accounts of court proceedings not only presented one side of the case, they also helped to create the impression that police court convictions were valid. This was reaffirmed by the language, style and tone of the reports that were published, with character and ethnicity often being placed at the fore.

In summary, magisterial judgements about conviction in the first half of the century were administered in line with bailies' own social and cultural assumptions about what forms of behaviour were worthy of police courts' time, who needed to be brought to justice and disciplined, and who should be protected. They also, in many ways, reflected the business backgrounds from which magistrates, as lay justices, were drawn, with judicial judgements often defending workplace property laws and the economic imperatives of the free market. Police courts not only gave procurators procedural and evidential advantages, they also provided civic magistrates with tremendous scope to administer justice in a fairly loose, informal manner – a manner that attached much significance to character, that was in keeping with the 'common-sense' justice that epitomised lay justice, and that was largely supported in the mainstream media. As the next section explores, the importance of character to the workings of the police courts would, in the second half of the century, become enshrined in legislative developments which further reduced the legal rights of the accused and would, in some cases, even threaten the presumption of innocence in Scottish police courts.

III. Profiling Convictions, c.1857 to 1892

Drawing statistical comparisons with conviction returns for the earlier part of the century is of limited worth given the fairly loose and inconsistent way in which the statistics were recorded, and the often informal manner in which magistrates administered justice. For instance, whereas some of the 1839 Law Inquiry returns included those who had been admonished in the list of acquittals, in the post-1857 police figures they were listed separately from other trial outcomes. From this point onwards, however, the returns were recorded more consistently and in greater detail, listing convictions for crimes, offences and contraventions separately, and dividing them by sex. They do not state whether the accused pleaded guilty or not guilty, but a brief snapshot into this

---

[80]   *Police Reports*, 6 July 1829, p. 6.

is provided in the 'Records of the Criminal Proceedings of the Pollokshields Police Court', which cover the period from 12 April 1888 to 30 April 1891. Of the 91 cases which were recorded, 58 pleaded guilty, 31 pleaded not guilty and ten did not appear in court.[81] In other words, no formal trial proceedings were commenced in two thirds of cases, which needs to be borne in mind when assessing what conviction data reveals about how likely or not magistrates were to find guilt on the part of the accused. These figures also suggest that one third of those brought before magistrates believed that they stood a chance of being acquitted – which was perhaps influenced by the fact that, in this court, a guilty plea did not appear to have significantly reduced the level of punishment administered.[82]

As in the first half of the nineteenth century, a considerable percentage of people taken into custody and charged with a crime or offence in the late nineteenth century continued to have no proceedings taken against them, but, significantly, the trend was downwards. Between 1861 and 1865, 9,733 of the 24,252 individuals (or 40 per cent) who were taken into custody had their proceedings dropped without trial.[83] Between 1891 and 1895, the corresponding figure was 4,776 of 24,266 (or 20 per cent).[84] Moreover, not only were more people being brought to trial relative to apprehensions, proportionately more were being convicted. In 1860, the percentage of those apprehended for crimes who were subsequently convicted in the Glasgow Police Court was 38 per cent. In 1870 it was 59 per cent, in 1880 it was 55 per cent, and in 1890 it was 63 per cent. There were, as can be seen from Table 6.2, slight fluctuations in the overall upward trend, perhaps influenced by the scale of business the courts had to deal with, the number of cases which were remitted to higher courts, and the introduction of the paid magistrate in the mid-1870s, but in general the fiscal and the police became more adept at securing convictions as the century progressed.

---

[81]   GCA, H-SH1/14 and 15: Pollokshields Police Court.

[82]   In deciding whether or not the accused's plea should influence the sentence, much seems to have depended on the magistrate and how he perceived the case. In most instances where the accused pleaded guilty and others not guilty for the same charge – although there were only a few where records have been kept – there was no difference in terms of the fine or length of sentence imposed. For example, John Easton and John Clerk both pleaded guilty, and Thomas Reid not guilty, of theft in the Pollokshields Police Court in the late 1880s. They all received a punishment of 2s., 6d. or 2 days' imprisonment. There was the odd example of those who pleaded guilty, such as Edward Morley, who received 2s. or 6 days for theft, being fined less than his co-accused who pleaded not guilty and was fined 5s. or 2 days. Ibid.

[83]   Mitchell Library (ML): *City of Glasgow Police Criminal Returns for the Year Ending 31st December 1865* (Glasgow, 1866), pp. 6–7.

[84]   ML: *City of Glasgow Police Criminal Returns for the Year Ending 31st December 1895* (Glasgow, 1896), pp. 12–13.

Table 6.2   Reports, Apprehensions and Convictions for Crimes in Glasgow Police Annual Statistical Returns, 1860 to 1890[+]

	1860	1866	1870	1876	1880	1886	1890
Reported	5,958	9,517	8,702	8,569	9,581	9,243	6,858
Apprehended	3,817	4,639	5,077	5,509	6,207	5,276	4,938
Convicted*	1,437	2,102	3,000	3,138	3,394	3,004	3,128
Population	395,503		477,732		511,415		565,839

* Not all dealt with in police courts and a number remitted to higher courts (although all of the above conviction rates were determined in the police court). This slightly skews police courts conviction rates although the above figures are still useful in providing insight into how pattern of convictions changed over the century.

[+] The data have been collated from information presented in the ML. *The Number of Persons taken into Custody by the City of Glasgow Police and the Results for the Year Ending 29th September 1860* (Glasgow, 1861), pp. 6–7; ML: *City of Glasgow Police Criminal Returns for the Year Ending 31st December 1871* (Glasgow, 1871), pp. 14–15; ML: *City of Glasgow Police Criminal Returns for the Year Ending 31st December 1880* (Glasgow, 1881), pp. 12–13; and ML: *City of Glasgow Police Criminal Returns for the Year Ending 31st December 1890* (Glasgow, 1891), pp. 12–13.

As Table 6.3 shows, on average, around 85 per cent of all criminal cases that were proceeded with in the Glasgow Police Court resulted in a guilty plea or verdict. For offences and contraventions, 90 per cent of such cases resulted in conviction (see Tables 6.4 and 6.5), with a significant proportion being determined by people not turning up in court and forfeiting their bail money by way of penalty. Police prosecutors had slightly higher conviction rates than burgh prosecutors given that the latter dealt with the more serious criminal cases and the former minor ones for which it was easier to secure a conviction, but there was little difference between them and both were extremely adept at securing convictions by the late nineteenth century. Convictions for crimes that made it to trial were slightly lower in the 1890s than they had been in the 1870s, perhaps reflecting the introduction of the stipendiary magistrate in 1876 who, as is explored more fully below, was reported as being more likely to acquit than civic magistrates on matters of evidence. But overall, conviction rates for all categories of police court business were higher in the second half of the century than they had been for the first, which mirrored a wider trend in the criminal justice system.[85] In some of the smaller burghs, the conviction-to-acquittal rate averaged just over 90 per cent for all cases tried in burgh and police courts in Aberdeen, Dundee, Perth and Paisley (see Table 6.6). In 1880, just 129 out of 8,322 individuals tried in the Edinburgh Police Court for offences were acquitted – a conviction rate of 98 per cent. For crimes, the figure was 80 out of 552 – a conviction rate of 87 per cent, far higher than in the first half of the century. These were also higher than in England, where conviction had also risen from the middle of the century.[86] Within this broad pattern, there were variations according to crime. Acquiring evidence to secure a conviction for attempting to steal was, for instance, more difficult than for other property offences. Typically, between one in four or five such cases resulted in acquittal which was much higher than for other property offences that made up the bulk of crimes magistrates handled.

As Table 6.3 shows, there was little discernible difference in the percentages of male and female convictions for crimes that were determined by a guilty or

---

[85]   In 1868, 119,623 people were arrested in Scotland, resulting in 87,156 trials and 81,901 convictions. Of these, 3,000 were tried before juries in the justiciary and sheriff courts, with the remainder being disposed of in a summary manner. 'First report on Judicial Statistics of Scotland rendered to the Right Honourable the Secretary of State for the Home Department, in terms of the Judicial Statistics (Scotland) Act, 1868, and of the Instructions of the Secretary of State, being for the year 1868', *BPP*, 1871 (C.233), LXIV.477, p. 37.

[86]   In 1858, 40 per cent of those brought before metropolitan magistrates were discharged, reflecting the lack of police thoroughness in collecting evidence. By 1861, this number had fallen to 33 per cent and by 1865 it was just 30 per cent. R.S. Sindall, 'Statistics of Nineteenth-Century Cities: A New Approach', *Urban History*, 13 (1986): p. 31.

Table 6.3   Glasgow Police Annual Statistical Returns: Crimes, Acquittals and Convictions, 1871 to 1890[†]

Category	1871	1880	1890
Crimes Reported to the Police	7,521	9,581	6,858
Number taken into Custody	5,162 Male: 3,043 Female: 2,119	6,393 Male: 4,281 Female: 2,112	5,050 Male: 3,572 Female: 1,478
Proceedings Dropped without Trial	1,588 Male: 777 Female: 811	2,040 Male: 1,170 Female: 870	1,134 Male: 646 Female: 488
Acquitted (Of Those Proceeded Against in Police Court)	366 (13%) Male: 241 (14%) Female: 125 (12%)	537 (17%) Male: 370 (17%) Female: 167 (18%)	385 (16%) Male: 288 (16%) Female: 97 (15%)
Convicted (Of Those Proceeded Against in Police Court)	2,420 (87%) Male: 1,469 (86%) Female: 951 (88%)	2,591 (83%) Male: 1,843 (83%) Female: 748 (82%)	2,077 (84%) Male: 1,527 (84%) Female: 550 (85%)
Remitted to other Courts	788 Male: 556 Female: 232	1,225 Male: 898 Female: 327	1,454 Male: 1,111 Female: 343
Sent to Ind. Schools or Reformatories	94 Male: 71 Female: 23	92 Male: 71 Female: 21	41 Male: 38 Female: 3

† The data have been collated from information presented in ML, *City of Glasgow Police Criminal Returns for the Year Ending 31st December 1871*, pp. 14–15; ML, *City of Glasgow Police Criminal Returns for the Year Ending 31st December 1880*, pp. 12–13; and ML, *City of Glasgow Police Criminal Returns for the Year Ending 31st December 1890*, pp. 12–13.

not guilty verdict, but women, as in the first half of the century, were much more likely than men to have their cases dropped without trial. In 1871, 25 per cent of men who were taken into custody and charged with crimes in Glasgow had no proceedings taken against them, compared with 38 per cent of women. In 1880, the corresponding figures were 27 per cent for men and 41 per cent for women. In 1890, they were 18 per cent and 33 per cent respectively. The fall in the percentage of cases for which no proceedings were taken against both women and men in the 1880s is likely to have reflected improvements in policing and the greater capacity of the courts to handle a larger caseload; but this should not disguise the fact that within a broader picture, the gap in the proceedings/no proceedings ratio between men and women increased in the second half of the century, with the likelihood of charges against women for criminal offences actually going to trial in police courts

Table 6.4   Glasgow Police Annual Statistical Returns: Offences, Acquittals and Convictions, 1871 to 1890[†]

Category	1871	1880	1890
Persons Taken into Custody	26,492 Male: 19,117 Female: 7,375	40,772 Male: 25,869 Female: 14,903	50,084 Male: 32,542 Female: 17,542
Acquitted (Of Those Proceeded Against in Police Court)	2,519 (10%) Male: 1,665 (9%) Female: 854 (12%)	3,637 (9%) Male: 2,271 (9%) Female: 1,366 (9%)	3,421 (7%) Male: 2,104 (7%) Female: 1,317 (8%)
Convicted (Of Those Proceeded Against in Police Court)	23,734 (90%) Male: 17,276 (91%) Female: 6,458 (88%)	37,013 (91%) Male: 23,508 (91%) Female: 13,505 (91%)	46,314 (93%) Male: 30,141 (93%) Female: 16,173 (92%)

† The data have been collated from information presented in ML, *City of Glasgow Police Criminal Returns for the Year Ending 31st December 1871*, pp. 16–17; ML, *City of Glasgow Police Criminal Returns for the Year Ending 31st December 1880*, pp. 14–15; and ML, *City of Glasgow Police Criminal Returns for the Year Ending 31st December 1890*, pp. 14–15.

Table 6.5   Glasgow Police Annual Statistical Returns: Contraventions of Police and Bye-Laws, Acquittals and Convictions, 1871 to 1890[†]

Category	1871	1880	1890
Persons Summonsed	12,739 Male: 8,992 (71%) Female: 3,747 (29%)	6,984 Male: 5,380 (77%) Female: 1,604 (23%)	4,718 Male: 3,694 (78%) Female: 1,024 (22%)
Acquitted (Of Those Proceeded Against in Police Court)	1,070 (9%) Male: 761 (10%) Female: 309 (8%)	719 (11%) Male: 560 (11%) Female: 159 (10%)	445 (9%) Male: 349 (9%) Female: 96 (9%)
Convicted (Of Those Proceeded Against in Police Court)	10,677 (91%) Male: 7,239* (90%) Female: 3,438 (92%)	6,225 (89%) Male: 4,785 (89%) Female: 1,440 (90%)	4,273 (91%) Male: 3,345 (91%) Female: 928 (91%)

† The data have been collated from information presented in ML, *City of Glasgow Police Criminal Returns for the Year Ending 31st December 1871*, pp. 18–19; ML, *City of Glasgow Police Criminal Returns for the Year Ending 31st December 1880*, pp. 16–17; and ML, *City of Glasgow Police Criminal Returns for the Year Ending 31st December 1890*, pp. 16–17.

For Tables 6.3, 6.4 and 6.5, please note:

• 992 men had no proceedings taken against them for smoke pollution. These were not recorded in either the convicted or acquittal returns.

• Gender percentages concerning acquittals and convictions are based on the number of cases specific to that gender rather than total number.

• The acquitted/convicted percentages are based on the total number of cases in which an acquittal or conviction was reached, not the total number taken into custody or crimes, many of which never made it before the court (as not everyone who was taken into custody had their cases determined before magistrates). The fact that there are some small discrepancies in the total number of persons taken into custody and the number who had their cases determined by magistrates for Table 6.4 is also explained by the fact that not all cases that were determined were done so before magistrates in the police court. A small number were determined before other courts.

falling relative to that for men. When it came to pursuing criminal charges, the judicial system appears to have become increasingly concerned with male rather than female criminality as the second half of the century progressed, although, as Chapter 7 explores, this was by no means always reflected in the punishments that were handed down.

For offences, the highest conviction-to-acquittal rates were for those accused of being drunk and incapable.[87] Charges for many such cases were uncontested by the accused who simply forfeited bail money. Indeed, according to Farmer, convictions for drunk and incapable in the Glasgow Police Court up until 1875 were not sought where bail pledges had been made as the forfeiture was deemed sufficient punishment.[88] Those importuning passengers for the purpose of prostitution or charged with breach of the peace were also highly unlikely to be acquitted. These were offences where the accused was more likely to have been apprehended by the police in the act of committing an alleged offence, which underlines the importance of police evidence to successful convictions. For simple assault, the conviction-to-acquittal rate averaged 90 per cent, although there were variations within this. As Chapter 3 showed, the courts were often reluctant to get involved in domestic disputes, with many being 'settled' or dismissed informally. But on the occasions where trial followed, convictions often did likewise. The 1880 Edinburgh police returns record 75 apprehensions and charges for 'criminal' assault on wives and 112 for 'simple'

---

[87]   Unless otherwise stated, the information in this paragraph is based on ML: *City of Glasgow Police Criminal Returns for the Year Ending 31st December 1872* (Glasgow, 1873).

[88]   Farmer, *Criminal Law, Tradition and Legal Order*, p. 117. See 'Departmental Committee on Habitual Offenders, Inebriates, &c. (Scotland). Report from the Departmental Committee on Habitual Offenders, Vagrants, Beggars, Inebriates, and Juvenile Delinquents', *BPP*, 1895 (C.7753), XXXVII.1, pp. vii–viii.

Table 6.6   Burgh and Police Courts: Return as to Criminal and Police Business, 1868[†]

Burgh	Pros.	Conv.	Acqu.	Person	Property	Police	Other	Imprison.	Fined
Aberd.	1,716	1,641	75	218	156	1,059	501	162	1,413
Dundee	2,886	2,821	65	337	376	1,179	216	321	1,198
Edinburgh	1,205	1,184	67	171	58	312	664	132	929
Glasgow	3,497	3,382	165	1,537	259	1,117	584	379	2,704
Paisley	1,136	1,013	93	207	217	692	18	142	710
Perth	660	607	53	83	74	252	251	74	533

Note: In the above returns, no attempt was made to distinguish police courts from burgh courts and it is not clear which court these returns refer to. However, given that the returns for Glasgow and Edinburgh were considerably lower than those recorded in the police returns, it seems likely that their respective figures relate to burgh courts. Similarly, in Dundee, it was noted that magistrates held a burgh court separate from the police court. For some of the smaller burghs, the burgh and the police court were one and the same. In Dundee, Kilmarnock, Stirling and Dunfermline, the procurator fiscal was also the superintendent of police.

† 'Fourth Report of the Commissioners appointed to Inquire into the Courts of Law in Scotland', *BPP*, 1870 (C.175–1), XVIII.511, Appendix II, no. 16.

assault on wives.[89] Of the 112 charged with simple assault, 108 were convicted and four acquitted (the conviction figures were not recorded for those charged with criminal assault).[90] Indeed, this category of crime/offence had, along with breach of the peace and prostitution, the highest rate of conviction for that year. Eighty-six of the 112 convicted were drunk at the time of arrest.[91] All of those convicted resided in the poorer districts of Edinburgh, illustrating that for procurators and magistrates domestic violence was largely a crime committed by working-class males,[92] although the reality is likely to have been somewhat different.[93] In terms of acquittals, those accused of being rogues and vagabonds and drinking in shebeens were most likely to be found not guilty. Securing evidence for the latter was, as was discussed above, often difficult, whilst the prospect of conviction for the former offered little financial reward for the public purse.

As with crimes, there was, at best, negligible difference between male and female convictions for offences that made it to trial. As Table 6.4 shows, women were slightly more likely than men to be acquitted, but typically by no more than a few per cent. A large proportion of these were for simple assault – an offence which has taken on particular significance in recent years in debates on Norbert Elias's theory of the 'civilising process' and the extent to which the courts were at the forefront of this.[94] It has been argued, for instance, that in the English courts in the second half of the nineteenth century men were more likely to be convicted for violence than women relative to prosecutions, as the criminal justice system increasingly targeted male violence as the century progressed.[95] However, there is little evidence to suggest that police

---

[89]   ECL, *Return of Crimes and Offences Reported, Persons Apprehended and Cited, and Miscellaneous Returns Connected with the Police, for the Year Ending 31st December 1880*, Table 7.

[90]   Ibid., Table 2.

[91]   Ibid., Table 7.

[92]   Of the 75 husbands who were arrested and charged with a 'crime' for assaulting their wives in Edinburgh in 1880, 38 of them occurred in St Giles – a poor district of Edinburgh – ten in Canongate, eight in St Leonard's, six in Calton, four in St George Square, three in Newington, two in St Cuthbert's, and one each in Broughton, St Bernard's, St George's and St Andrew's. There were no such assaults recorded for the affluent wards of St Stephen's and St Luke's. Ibid.

[93]   As is explored in Chapter 1 of Volume 2, media reports sometimes reported on cases of domestic assault among the middle class.

[94]   Norbert Elias, *The Civilizing Process* (Oxford, 1994, first published in 1939). For scholarly engagement with Elias's theory, see Stuart Carroll (ed.), *Cultures of Violence: Interpersonal Violence in Historical Perspective* (Basingstoke, 2007); and Katherine Watson (ed.), *Assaulting the Past: Interpersonal Violence in Historical Perspective* (Cambridge, 2007).

[95]   Studies that have examined the role of the courts in civilising modern society include J. Pratt, *Punishment and Civilization: Penal Tolerance and Intolerance in Modern*

courts in Scotland were inclined to do likewise.[96] In the years 1871, 1880 and 1890, male convictions for simple assault were remarkably similar to those of women: for men, they were 89 per cent, 88 per cent and 89 per cent for the respective years, compared with 85 per cent, 88 per cent and 88 per cent for women (see Table 6.7).[97] In Edinburgh, conviction rates between women and men for assault were also comparable (see Table 6.8). In 1880, 95 per cent of both men and women proceeded against for simple assault were convicted.[98] Unfortunately, unlike crimes, neither the Glasgow or the Edinburgh police records recorded 'no proceedings' under the category 'offences', so it is not possible to determine whether women apprehended for assault were more likely than men to have their cases dropped without trial. Nonetheless, when it came to actual cases which made it to trial, it seems as though the capacity of the fiscal to filter out weak cases overrode any blatant gender bias in conviction rates for simple assault. As the century went on, conviction rates for assault rose slightly, but, significantly, this was the case for both men and women. Whether this reflected a toughening resolve on the part of the courts to clamp down on violence *per se* is impossible to say, but it is likely to have reflected to a large extent wider trends in conviction rates and the fiscal's capacity to prepare and filter cases better.

Society (London, 2002); Pieter Spierenburg, 'Violence and the Civilizing Process: Does It Work?', *Crime, Histoire & Sociétés/Crime, History & Societies*, 5/2 (2001): pp. 87–105; Martin J. Wiener, 'The March of Penal Progress?', *The Journal of British Studies*, 26/1 (1987), pp. 83–96; John Carter Wood, 'Self-Policing and the Policing of the Self: Violence, Protection and the Civilising Bargain in Britain', *Crime, Histoire & Sociétés/Crime, History & Societies*, 7/1 (2003): pp. 109–23; and Barry S. Godfrey, 'Counting and Accounting for the Decline in Non-Lethal Violence in England, Australia and New Zealand, 1880–1920', *British Journal of Criminology*, 43/2 (2003): pp. 340–53.

[96] Studies for England which have shown that the courts were more likely to convict men charged with assault than women in the eighteenth century (where much of the historical scholarly attention has focused) include: J.M. Beattie, 'The Criminality of Women in Eighteenth-Century England', *Journal of Social History*, 8/4 (1975): pp. 80–116; J.M. Beattie, *Crime and the Courts in England, 1660–1800* (Oxford, 1986); and Peter King, 'Female Offenders, Work and Life-Cycle Change in Late-Eighteenth-Century London', *Continuity and Change*, 11/1 (1996): pp. 61–90.

[97] ML, *City of Glasgow Police Criminal Returns for the Year Ending 31st December 1871*, pp. 16–17; ML, *City of Glasgow Police Criminal Returns for the Year Ending 31st December 1880*, pp. 14–15; and ML, *City of Glasgow Police Criminal Returns for the Year Ending 31st December 1890*, pp. 14–15. The 1880 and 1890 returns might be skewed to some extent as the simple assault figures were included alongside disorderly conduct, but this was not the case for the 1871 returns which recorded simple assault separately from other offences.

[98] ECL, *Return of Crimes and Offences Reported, and Persons Apprehended and Cited, and Miscellaneous Returns with the Police, for the Year Ending 31st December 1880*, Table 2.

Table 6.7   Percentage Convicted of Simple Assault relative to Number of
People Charged in Glasgow Police Court, 1860 to 1890[†]

	1860	1871	1880	1890
M	1,331 out of 1,604 (83%)	11,175 out of 12,571 (89%)	12,899 out of 14,622 (88%)	14,959 out of 16,721 (89%)
F	423 out of 533 (79%)	4,212 out of 4,868 (87%)	7,127 out of 8,113 (88%)	7,512 out of 8,502 (88%)

Note: The negligible difference in male and female conviction rates for assault was, to some degree, influenced by the willingness of the police courts to accept bail pledges in lieu of court appearance. As Chapter 7 explores more fully, typically between one third and one quarter of men forfeited bail; for women, it tended to be one in every six or seven. As a result, it seems likely that men were less likely to turn up in court to contest charges (it is impossible to say this definitely as the records do not record the plea of those who attended court).

[†]   ML, *The Number of Persons taken into Custody by the City of Glasgow Police and the Results for the Year Ending 29th September 1860*, pp. 6–7; ML, *City of Glasgow Police Criminal Returns for the Year Ending 31st December 1871*, pp. 16–17; ML, *City of Glasgow Police Criminal Returns for the Year Ending 31st December 1880*, pp. 14–15; ML, *City of Glasgow Police Criminal Returns for the Year Ending 31st December 1890*, pp. 14–15.

Table 6.8   Convictions for Simple Assault in Edinburgh, 1880[††]

	Men	Women
Assault on Wives	108 out of 112	0
Police	148 out of 152	25 out of 25
Others	446 out of 471	150 out of 160
Total	702 out of 735 (95%)	175 out of 185 (95%)

[††]   ECL, *Return of Crimes and Offences Reported, Persons Apprehended and Cited, and Miscellaneous Persons Connected with the Police, for the Year Ending 31st December 1880*, p. 5.

Men and women summonsed for contraventions, like offences, were nearly always convicted (with figures averaging around 90 per cent), but the returns reveal interesting insights into how the courts supported civic priorities. In the Glasgow 1872 returns, the highest conviction rates recorded were for contraventions relating to lodging houses and pawnbrokers, both of which had been subject to increased regulation and control from magistrates from mid-century.[99] Indeed, in this respect magistrates used police courts to buttress their own civic initiatives. Prosecution practices reflected gender biases, and these were reflected, to some extent, in conviction patterns for specific contraventions. The most common contraventions for which women were convicted were those related to questions of morality or the household, including harbouring prostitutes and managing brothels, keeping disorderly houses, and general nuisance. For magistrates, women charged with such offences displayed characteristics deemed undesirable for their sex and were more likely to be convicted as a consequence.

On the other hand, men were much more likely to be discharged than women for the contravention of smoke pollution and the numbers were often significant. In 1872, 1,193 men in Glasgow had no proceedings taken against them in court for this contravention. No women, by contrast, were summonsed or dismissed for the same charge. Indeed, years in which the police clamped down on smoke pollution would often produce a greater gender disparity in the total ratio of convictions to summonses. Also in 1872, 5,889 of the 7,910 (76 per cent) men summonsed for contraventions in Glasgow were convicted, compared with 2,278 of the 2,417 women who were summonsed (94 per cent).[100] The absence of women in the smoke pollution returns for that year suggests that these were not ordinary householders who were being summonsed, but the business classes. Guilty verdicts for this contravention fluctuated wildly, reflecting, in part, the complexities involved in establishing negligence.[101] In 1872, one third of those for whom proceedings were determined were convicted (22 people), and two thirds acquitted (33). The following year judgements were reversed with 111 convicted and 66 acquitted. But for each year the numbers for whom no proceedings were taken vastly outnumbered – by up to 20 to one – those for whom they were. Indeed, press reports questioned whether procurators and magistrates had the same resolve to prosecute and convict those men with whom they had shared business interests. Tougher action, it seemed, was mostly reserved in practice for the most vulnerable social groups in Scottish cities, and not the industrialists.

Overall, the police criminal returns that were published from 1857 onwards not only showed high – and largely improving – conviction rates relative to apprehensions and trials for crimes, offences and contraventions, they also

---

[99]   ML, *City of Glasgow Police Criminal Returns for the Year Ending 31st December 1872*, pp. 18–19.

[100]   Ibid.

[101]   Ibid.

shaped ideas about criminality in important ways. These documents presented social profiling which informed expectations about guilt and which was seemingly confirmed in data they presented about conviction patterns.[102] The 1880 Edinburgh returns, for example, implicitly linked class and criminality by identifying offenders' degree of instruction. Those convicted were ranked into categories of literacy, recording which individuals could 'neither read nor write'; 'read only, or read and write imperfectly'; 'read and write well'; or possessed 'superior instruction'. The relationship between education and crime was reflected in the summary of the superintendent: 'of the 10,135 arrests only 225 persons could be said to have had the advantage of a good education. 1,267 could neither read nor write, while 8,643 could read only, or read and write imperfectly.'[103] From 1860, police returns had developed to a seemingly sophisticated level of criminal demarcation. Glasgow returns even included a breakdown of the profile of those charged with the more aggravated offences that had been remitted to the sheriff and justices, which included their 'character'. This was classified by categories such as 'known thieves', 'suspicious', 'unknown' or 'previously good'. 'Nativity' divided the criminal population into those from Glasgow, other parts of Scotland, Ireland, England and foreign.[104] By 1880 Edinburgh defined character as 'thieves', 'suspected persons', 'prostitutes', 'habitual drunkards', 'vagrants', 'unknown' and 'previously good'.[105] Indeed, the effect of the police court data's social profiling was foregrounded in the superintendent's preface to the tables:

> The figures in this Return strongly point to the great necessity that exists for a complete change in the mode in which habitual offenders should be dealt with ... shewing the trouble which is caused by this class and the non-deterrent effects of the sentences inflicted on them ... If some plan could be devised to deal in a comprehensive manner with this class there is no doubt that a vast

---

[102] This had already occurred in related documentation as early as the 1830s, when the returns on those imprisoned in Scotland had noted prisoners' level of literacy and educational attainment. 'Criminal Offenders (Scotland). Tables of Criminal Offences for the year 1836', *BPP*, 1837 (109), XLVI.147. A version of this mentality was evident in the 1860 Returns of Edinburgh where Table 4 listed the Degree of Instruction for persons convicted of crimes or remitted to higher court. ECL, *Report and Returns as to Crimes, Offences, and Contraventions, and to Cases of Drunkenness, within the Police Bounds of the City of Edinburgh, during the last Six Years*, Table 4, p. 23.

[103] ECL, *Returns of Crimes and Offences Reported, Persons Apprehended and Cited, and Miscellaneous Returns Connected with the Police, for the Year Ending 31st December 1880*, p. 1.

[104] ML, *The Number of Persons taken into Custody by the City of Glasgow Police and the Results for the Year Ending 29th September 1860*, Table 3, pp. 12–13.

[105] ECL, *Return of Crimes and Offences Reported, Persons Apprehended and Cited, and Miscellaneous Returns Connected with the Police, for the Year Ending 31st December 1880*, Table 5.

improvement would be effected in the lower parts of the City where crime and disorder are most prevalent.[106]

There was no recognition that the tabularised figures suggested this conclusion because these were things that the police had chosen to measure and put into focus through their returns report.

As the next section explores, such social and cultural profiling was part of a wider trend in the criminal justice system that would further diminish the chances of acquittal for the accused. It not only informed expectations of guilt for magistrates, it was also embedded within legal and administrative changes that worked to the defender's disadvantage. Criminal profiling would, when accompanied by the changing role of the courts, more targeted prosecutions, and developments in policing, go a long way to account for the upward trend in convictions.

IV. Classifying Character and Police Profiling

As the century progressed, a raft of legislation sought to provide more guidelines that upheld the procedural principles of summary justice and weakened the legal rights of those charged with certain crimes and offences. As with crimes prosecuted in higher courts, the onus was on the prosecutor to prove guilt for most cases, but legislation relating to pawnbroking laid out new rules for proof and guilt, and required pawnbrokers to account for goods in their possession.[107] Unless dealers could provide proper documentation showing where they gained items, the police could demand that pawnbrokers deliver to the police station items they believed were stolen and the onus was on the broker to prove they were not.[108] In such cases, the presumption of innocence did not exist. In addition, the oath of one credible witness, instead of two as for other crimes and offences, was stated in such cases as being sufficient to establish guilt.[109] Further statutes and legal rulings extended this to other crimes.[110] Following the

---

[106] Ibid., p. 1.

[107] Under the terms of the Glasgow Police Act, 1866 (29 & 30 Victoria, cap. 273), section entitled 'Special Provisions – Pawnbrokers and Brokers', different rules for both proof and guilt were laid out which significantly increased police powers (clause 204).

[108] Ibid., clause 206.

[109] Ibid.

[110] Henry Hilton Brown noted that under the Summary Procedure Act (1864), section 14, 'the law demands that, except in certain cases, there shall be at least two persons to establish guilt against the respondent, [but] it is not essential that every fact shall be spoken by a couple of witnesses'. He points out that any fact in a case may be proved by one credible witness although it is preferable to have two persons to speak to the more important points. Henry Hilton Brown, Procurator-Fiscal of Elginshire, *The Principles of Summary Criminal Jurisdiction According to the Law of Scotland* (Edinburgh, 1895), p. 149.

introduction of the Forbes MacKenzie Act, magistrates, according to the 1862 Glasgow police returns, 'convicted on circumstantial evidence, instead of, as formerly, making it imperative on the prosecutor to prove a sale in each case'.[111] Moreover, the 1862 Burgh Police Act put the onus on those accused of begging and vagrancy to prove that they earned an honest living.[112] Increasingly, it was up to 'suspicious persons' – a catch-all title that gave the police wide-ranging discretionary powers – to show that they were providing for themselves legally. This was part of a growing emphasis by those who enforced the law on the importance of 'character' as being a determining element in terms of how the law was administered.[113] This had always played an important part in shaping the workings of the criminal justice system, but it became even more significant in the late nineteenth century in that it was affecting legislation, the classification of offenders, and policing policy. The commentary from the chief constable in the 1880 Edinburgh police returns linked law-breaking to 'the lower parts of the City where crime and disorder are most prevalent'.[114] Police acts also gave the police and the courts tremendous powers for suppressing prostitution, which was defined widely as 'loitering and importuning'. As the 'Report of the Departmental Committee on Habitual Offenders' pointed out in 1895, this definition made it virtually impossible for a woman who was perceived by procurators and magistrates to be immoral to escape conviction.[115]

Moreover, procurators increasingly charged defenders under the category 'breach of the peace' for crimes and offences which were worthy of a more serious charge but which would have been more difficult to prove.[116] In Edinburgh, of the 9,725 offences for which people were apprehended in 1880, breach of the peace accounted for 3,377.[117] Indeed, so important was

---

[111]   ML: *The Number of Persons taken into Custody by the City of Glasgow Police and the Results for the Year Ending 29th September 1862* (Glasgow, 1863), p. 3.

[112]   The General and Police Improvement (Scotland) Act, 1862 (25 & 26 Victoria, cap. 101), sections 331–4. Similar developments took place in England. See Martin J. Wiener, *Reconstructing the Criminal: Culture, Law and Policy in England 1830–1914* (Cambridge, 1990), pp. 148–51.

[113]   Farmer, *Criminal Law, Tradition and Legal Order*, p. 116. See also Wiener, *Reconstructing the Criminal*, pp. 52–83 & 151–6.

[114]   ECL, *Return of Crimes and Offences Reported, Persons Apprehended and Cited, and Miscellaneous Returns Connected with the Police, for the Year Ending 31st December 1880*, p. 1.

[115]   'Report from the Departmental Committee on Habitual Offenders, Vagrants, Beggars, Inebriates, and Juvenile Delinquents', pp. 12–14.

[116]   Unless otherwise stated, the remainder of this paragraph is based on Farmer, *Criminal Law, Tradition and Legal Order*, pp. 114–15.

[117]   ECL, *Return of Crimes and Offences Reported, Persons Apprehended and Cited, and Miscellaneous Returns Connected with the Police, for the Year Ending 31st December 1880*, Table 2.

the category of 'breach of the peace' to the administration of the Scottish criminal law that by the early twentieth century it accounted for more than one third of all Scottish criminal statistics and more than half of the Scottish prison population.[118] This had significant implications for the presumption of innocence as the scope of 'breach of the peace' was wide and relatively easy to prove – so long as the alleged offence was committed in public. In the 1880 Edinburgh police returns, offenders were more likely to be convicted for breach of the peace and prostitution than any other offence. Of the 3,377 persons apprehended for breach of the peace, only 33 (less than 1 per cent) were acquitted.[119] This category of offence gave the police and magistrates wide-ranging discretionary powers.[120] As with a number of the new statutory police offences that were introduced in the nineteenth century, it was not considered necessary with this charge to prove intent.[121] To secure a conviction, procurators simply had to prove that the behaviour of the accused might have produced alarm to the general public. This was not too difficult as policemen's corroborating evidence in the second half of the century was reported as being usually sufficient to ensure that magistrates found the defender guilty. As Farmer has pointed out, 'the crime of breach of the peace was ... sufficiently elastic to catch actions on the edge of illegality, where it might otherwise have been difficult to obtain a conviction'.[122] Local police laws were being moulded by law makers – that is, magistrates in compliance with the Lord Advocate – in a way that made them easier to enforce. This gave magistrates the power to define as well as enforce moral standards in an attempt to exert greater control and discipline over urban communities.

---

[118]   W. Hamish Fraser and Irene Maver, 'The Social Problems of the City', in W. Hamish Fraser and Irene Maver (eds), *Glasgow, Volume II: 1830 to 1912* (Manchester, 1996), p. 383; D.M. Ross, *A Plea for Temperance Legislation: Lord Peel's Proposals for Scotland* (Glasgow, 1906); and A.B. McHardy, 'The Economics of Crime', *Juridical Review*, XIV (1902): p. 48.

[119]   ECL, *Return of Crimes and Offences Reported, Persons Apprehended and Cited, and Miscellaneous Returns Connected with the Police, for the Year Ending 31st December 1880*, Table 2.

[120]   V.A.C. Gatrell, 'Crime, Authority and the Policeman-State', in F.M.L. Thompson (ed.), *Cambridge Social History of Britain, 1750–1950* (Cambridge, 1992), p. 262.

[121]   For further information on this technicality, see Farmer, *Criminal Law, Tradition and Legal Order*, p. 123.

[122]   Farmer refers to the case of *Jackson v. Linton* in 1860 in which the High Court of Justiciary upheld a conviction against a man convicted of attempting to pickpocket despite the High Court having recently ruled that an attempt to steal was not a criminal offence. In rejecting the High Court's earlier argument, Lord Justice Inglis noted: 'As to its criminality, I have never had any doubt. It is a breach of the peace, and a breach of the peace with felonious intent.' Ibid., pp. 114–15.

New legal practices also reduced the chances of the accused being acquitted. As the century went on it became common practice in police courts for the relevant previous convictions of defenders to be read out as part of the charge before the trial had begun. Only convictions for the same offence on which the accused was currently being tried were permitted to be revealed, but the 1887 Criminal Procedure Act extended this so that the offence need only fall within a broad class of crimes.[123] Referred to as aggravation for 'habit and refute', this practice presumed guilt before the trial had even started and put character at the centre of summary justice.[124] The criminal law – and the police courts which were at the forefront in enforcing it – was increasingly being geared by its framers and practitioners towards making it easier to secure convictions, thereby encouraging guilty pleas and minimising the time and cost involved in facilitating a rising volume of prosecutions. It was, as Farmer points out, indicative of a legal system that was becoming increasingly preoccupied with efficiency and effectiveness to the detriment of legal rights.

Significantly, improved conviction rates were always highlighted by police superintendents in their annual reports.[125] These statistics became essential to the public presentation of police efficiency. As the introduction to the 1860 Edinburgh police returns claimed, police efficiency was afforded 'by an estimate of the proportion between the number of Persons convicted for Crimes against Property, and the number of such Crimes reported to the Police'.[126] Being perceived to be effectively controlling law and order in the local community was an important part of this, but so too was inter-city rivalry with superintendents measuring their own performance by comparing conviction returns with forces in other towns and cities. The 1860 report, for instance, not only boasted about the improved number of convictions,[127] it also devoted much attention to the fact that 'the proportion of Convictions for Crimes against Property to cases reported, is considerably higher in Edinburgh than in the Metropolitan District of London – the average percentage for the 5 years ending in 1858 being 14.94 in London and 22.3 in Edinburgh'.[128] It even went on to claim that the margin between the conviction rates in Edinburgh and London was even greater than the returns suggested, as the London returns included all the convictions secured, but not all the crimes committed, which would significantly lower London's

---

123   Ibid., p. 120.

124   Ibid.

125   For example, ECL, *Reports and Returns as to Crimes, Offences, and Contraventions, and to Cases of Drunkenness, within the Police Bounds of the City of Edinburgh, during the last Six Years*, p. 9.

126   Ibid., p. 11.

127   The introduction boasts 'that while only 978 of the 1,359 persons apprehended in 1854 were convicted, convictions were obtained against 670 of the 777 persons apprehended during the last year'. Ibid., p. 9.

128   Ibid., p. 11.

ratio of convictions to cases reported.[129] That superintendents felt the need to make such claims is more important than the returns themselves in underlining just how important public image was to the police – and how senior police officers deemed performance in court, demonstrated through conviction returns, to be essential to good police work. With the police filling the role of fiscal for a large percentage of police court business, it was, in many ways, inevitable that their capacity to pursue a successful prosecution would form an important part of their own public image.

How far this preoccupation with public image shaped the statistical pattern of convictions is impossible to quantify. As the century progressed, police commissioners, superintendents (in their roles as public prosecutors) and procurators fiscal certainly, though, devoted more and more attention to securing convictions in court. The speedy nature of summary justice meant that they had less time than for indictable crimes in higher courts to conduct preliminary inquiries or interview witnesses prior to making their decision on whether or not to prosecute, but some degree of filtering was still evident even for the lesser crimes and offences with which police magistrates dealt. In 1856 the *Glasgow Herald*, in an opinion piece in favour of stipendiary magistrates, observed: 'The relative Procurator-Fiscal may be said to act at his own risk, because, unless he clearly sees his way to a conviction, and is dealing with a subject that can *fine*, and not simply *pine*, he declines to prosecute.'[130]

Moreover, improvements in the strength, professionalism and efficiency of police forces after 1857 following the introduction of annual police inspections by Her Majesty's Inspectorate of Constabulary are also likely to have increased the number of convictions.[131] Whereas in Glasgow just 24 per cent of crimes known to the police in 1860 resulted in a guilty verdict, by 1870 it was 34 per cent, by 1880 35 per cent and by 1890 46 per cent. Although it is impossible to establish a direct link between changing policing practices and conviction rates, the police themselves argued that these developments underpinned the improved figures.[132] The 1871 annual police returns for Glasgow pointed to

---

[129]   Ibid., p. 12.

[130]   *Glasgow Herald*, 24 December 1856. Italics in original.

[131]   Forces deemed to be efficient had one quarter of police expenses paid by central government. The Glasgow police was singled out as being among the best in the country. 'Police (Scotland). Report of the Inspector of Constabulary for the year ended 15th March 1859, made to Her Majesty's Principal Secretary of State, under the provisions of the statute 20 & 21 Vict. c. 72', *BPP*, 1859 Session 2 (40), XIX.687, p. 46.

[132]   Gatrell also argues that improvements in police efficiency – which saw the ratio of convictions to crimes known, arrests and trials improve over the second half of the century – played a part in the decline in recorded crime. V.A.C. Gatrell, 'The Decline of Theft and Violence in Victorian and Edwardian England', in V.A.C. Gatrell, Bruce Lenman and Geoffrey Parker (eds), *Crime and the Law: The Social History of Crime in Western Europe since 1500* (London, 1980), p. 307.

better police organisation, higher discipline, 'and greater repressive powers with which they have been recently armed', which ensured that crime would 'be followed inevitably by conviction and punishment'.[133] The boast of certainty of conviction was inaccurate, but the connection between police policy and performance and successful prosecutions is likely to have been real. Not only did police commissioners in Edinburgh deploy officers in pairs to secure convictions in court, they also sought to recruit and retain a higher calibre of officer whose intelligence and experience would serve them well in court.[134] Ill-discipline and high turnover rates continued to pose a problem for Scottish forces in the second half of the century, but the average length of service increased significantly.[135] The typical officer post-1857 was much more experienced and, in all likelihood, skilled in giving evidence in court than he had been in the first half of the century.

Magistrates' role in accounting for the upward trend in convictions was complex and by no means as clear-cut or as one-dimensional as the police in prioritising convictions. On occasions justices were exceptionally lenient and willing to deviate from judicial procedures. In 1888, for instance, *The Bailie* highlighted how a whole raft of offenders had been let off at the Greenock Police Court 'on account of the Queen's visit'.[136] Likewise, some tee-totaller magistrates in Glasgow dismissed offenders for alcohol-related behaviours if they promised to 'take the pledge'. This was roundly criticised by *The Bailie* in 1878: 'What would be thought of the magistrate who should release the unruly on condition of their promising to turn Freemasons, or Baptists, or members of the Anti-Tobacco Society, or Mormons, or Shakers, or disciples of Darwin?'[137] The practice, the paper argued, showed the legal responsibilities of the position of magistrate to be of lesser priority for some justices than their personal moral stances. Furthermore, magistrates never lost their desire to protect those whom they perceived to be deserving, vulnerable, recipients, especially middle-class children and victims of violence, although this could, in some instances, add an incentive to convict. For example, as Chapter 2 of Volume 2 explores, by the 1860s, reformatory and industrial schools offered magistrates a way to assuage their fears about the consequences of convicting juveniles. Whereas in the first half of the century concern that convicting young offenders would lead to them being imprisoned sometimes resulted in magistrates dealing with cases informally, the emergence

---

[133] ML, *City of Glasgow Police Criminal Returns for the Year Ending 31st December 1871*, p. 4.

[134] ECL, *Report of the Special Committee appointed by the Board of Police, to Inquire into the Moral and Physical Character of the Watching Force, July 1846* (Edinburgh, 1846), pp. 20–21.

[135] 'Report of the Inspector of Constabulary for the year ended 15th March 1859', passim.

[136] *The Bailie*, no. 828, 29 August 1888, p. 2.

[137] *The Bailie*, no. 293, 29 May 1878, p. 2.

of new 'reforming' and 'improving' alternatives in the second half of the century meant that some children were more likely to be convicted because magistrates felt that the consequences of the conviction would be in their best interests. Thus, changing punitive provisions, in some cases, went hand in hand with decisions about conviction.

However, despite fulfilling what they perceived as their paternal role, the higher conviction rates, allied with a reduction in the number of cases that were dismissed and/or settled informally, suggests that magistrates' role in police courts as the century went on became less about negotiating disputes and more about administering justice to discipline the urban masses. Such a development reflected wider institutional developments in the second half of the nineteenth century aimed at controlling the working classes, but it might also have been influenced in a small way by changes in police management. Miller has shown that improved relations between the police and the magistrates' courts in London resulted in higher conviction rates as the century progressed.[138] Relations between magistrates and the police in the major urban centres of Scotland also improved (or at least were not characterised by the political and personal squabbling that typified the early 1800s), following the demise of elected police commissions and the transfer of their powers to watch committees appointed from among town councillors and bailies. Although in some instances claiming to be administratively separate from other branches of local government, town councillors and magistrates effectively assumed responsibility for police management in Glasgow in 1846, Dundee in 1851, Edinburgh in 1856, Paisley in 1864 and Aberdeen in 1871.[139]

The conflict of interest they faced as justices, police commissioners and civic leaders had serious implications for the legal rights of those before them. It made it extremely difficult for magistrates, as members of police boards, to openly challenge the evidence of police officers. To do so would, to some extent, be to question their own authority and would have threatened to undermine the whole system.[140] According to *The Bailie*, civic magistrates were all too willing to accept the evidence of policemen in the second half of the century. In praising the reforms that the new chief constable, McCall, had introduced to improve policing in the city, in 1873 the journal alluded to the bias that hitherto had existed in the city:

> The oath of one policeman is no longer accepted as equal to that of three citizens, nor is a constable thought to resemble the king in his quality of doing no wrong ... We may even remonstrate with a policeman, and yet

---

[138]   Miller, *Cops and Bobbies*, pp. 80–83.

[139]   Barrie, *Police in the Age of Improvement*, pp. 224–60.

[140]   In their study into the Scottish district courts, Bankowski, Hutton and McManus quote a court clerk who made a similar point. On the reliability of police evidence, he claimed: 'I think they often tell lies, but it is difficult to catch them at it. If you don't believe the police the whole system breaks down.' Z.K. Bankowski, N.R. Hutton and J.J. McManus, *Lay Justice?* (Edinburgh, 1987), p. 136.

not apprehend being 'taken up.' If we are 'took,' we may reckon with some degree of confidence on our complaints being heard, and if they are well founded, receiving due effect.[141]

Reporting on another case in which a Greenock policeman professed to have had his feelings and reputation injured to the extent of £50 by the insinuation that his evidence was not in strict accordance with truth, *The Bailie* sarcastically noted: 'Your Sugarpolitan bobby seems to be made of more sensitive stuff than his Glasgow brother. Our guardians bear such insinuations with the utmost equanimity – possibly because they are so accustomed to them.'[142]

As the head of the police establishment, chief constables were not divorced, nor indeed, immune, from the pressures that the police faced in being perceived to be tough on crime and effective on law and order. Magisterial capacity to govern continued to be linked, in part, with their ability to maintain urban order. Indeed, civic debates in some smaller burghs in the second half of the nineteenth century on whether to become 'police burghs' often centred specifically on law and order issues.[143] Magistrates were certainly not averse to applying justice loosely in order to secure convictions that served a wider civic purpose, as the case trial of Sleigh and Russell at the Edinburgh Police Court in 1850 illustrated.[144] As this case highlighted, the legality of the flexible way in which the term 'breach of the peace' was defined and applied by magistrates was, in itself, satirised by members of the community and by *The Scotsman*.[145] Moreover, that magistrates in Aberdeen in mid-century considered lowering their evidentiary requirements in order to secure more convictions and raise more funds in fines illustrated the growing importance of the police court as an economic resource and vehicle for civic improvement and municipal governance. Convicting those deemed to be guilty of certain types of public order offences became especially important following press reports and campaigns, such as that against shebeens in the 1870s.

Indeed, the mainstream press frequently highlighted evidential barriers to successful prosecutions, which was indicative of the interest they took in law and order issues. In its series of reports on 'The Dark Side of Glasgow' in 1870, the *North British Daily Mail* provided intimate details of the problems the police faced in securing convictions, especially against the illegal drinking dens known as shebeens:

---

[141] *The Bailie*, no. 19, 26 February 1873, p. 1.

[142] *The Bailie*, no. 335, 19 March 1879, p. 2.

[143]   Barrie, *Police in the Age of Improvement*, pp. 170–87.

[144]   ECL: *W. Campbell Sleigh, Esq., of London, Barrister-at-Law, and Thomas Russell, Esq., of Hunter Square, Edinburgh, Merchant, for an Alleged Breach of the Peace at the Music Hall, April 8, 1850, held with Reference to the Marriage Affinity Bill, by George Gunn, Reporter* (Edinburgh, 1850), p. 26.

[145]   Ibid.

The difficulties in the way of detection and conviction are very great, there being many cases with which the police find it utterly impossible to reach ... Shebeens, and keepers of houses of ill fame, although known to every moral evidence to be such, cannot be punished unless discovered in some overt act in contravention of the law; but this they guard against by such a vigilant system of scouts that detection is almost impracticable, and long before the police can obtain admission into the premises every evidence that could convict is removed.[146]

The reports painted a picture of a highly organised criminal network and underworld culture that relied upon intimidation and entrenched distrust of the police to keep lawbreakers out of court, as well as statute laws relating to illegal drinking that favoured the offender over the police.[147] A similar claim was made in 1907 by J.V. Stevenson, the Chief Constable of Glasgow, in a speech read before the Royal Philosophical Society of Glasgow:[148]

The police are often blamed for their failure to bring criminals to justice, especially in cases of house-breaking, or thieving, where the security of property is violated; but the fact is that the advantage is largely on the side of the criminal. In a great many cases, the police could, with moral certainty, put their hands on the criminals, but the law presumes innocence until a perfect chain of evidence has been established, and this must be traced out, link by link, with patience, skill, and perseverance. The police have to keep within the rules of the game while the criminal has a free hand.[149]

The presumption of innocence, he maintained, should be reserved only for first offenders, not convicted criminals.[150] Underpinning Stevenson's remarks was a concern with public image and the damaging impact that less than favourable press reports might have on the police's reputation – a fact he alluded to by claiming it would be for the public good if the press would cease to publish reports that glamourised criminals.[151] But his remarks, and the press reports mentioned above, indicate that the legal system was not completely one-sided,

---

[146] GCA, AGN 2114, 1–139: 'The Dark Side of Glasgow', First Report, *North British Daily Mail*, 27 December 1870, pp. 2 & 4–5.

[147] Ibid., p. 5.

[148] GCA, T-PAR1/8: J.V. Stevenson, Chief Constable of the City of Glasgow, *The Punishment and Prevention of Crime* (Glasgow, 1907), pp. 1–14.

[149] Ibid., p. 6.

[150] He argued that 'Against the presumption of the innocence of an accused person, there can be no ground for complaint; but there is ground for complaint in the treatment of the convicted criminal.' He criticised a system in which a convicted offender who was charged on indictment 'still appears before the court with the presumption of innocence in his favour, as at his first offence'. Ibid., pp. 6–7.

[151] Ibid., p. 10.

and that procurators, magistrates and policemen did not always act in unison and with scant regard for legal rules and procedures in order to secure convictions.

Nonetheless, there was a growing body of opinion in the second half of the nineteenth century that criticised how police courts disadvantaged the accused. According to lawyer Charles Shand, the absence of written proceedings in police court cases weakened legal rights as it reduced the possibility of a successful appeal. In giving evidence for the 'Second Report of the Commissioners appointed to Inquire into the Courts of Law in Scotland' in 1868–1869, Shand argued that having a written record of proceedings would offer the accused greater protection from unsound convictions and that a shorthand writer should be allowed for cases of theft. When asked 'if a great deal of care is generally taken by the magistrates in such cases, not to convict if it can be possibly avoided', he replied: 'The magistrate acts to the best of his ability, but the proceedings are not always satisfactory, nor the result safe.'[152] He went on: 'I have no doubt that injustice is very often done there [in the police court], especially to young persons alleged to be criminal, and which ends in their destruction.'[153] Indeed, Shand suggested that the press offered better protection to the reputations and liberties of the accused than the police courts in that the media acted as the only official record and, on occasion, reported on cases in which the evidence appeared, to a trained lawyer anyway, far from satisfactory.[154] His testimony was indicative not just of the growing legal commentary on police court proceedings, but also of the unease among lawyers about the strength of summary convictions and the lack of checks and balances on magistrates.

Similarly, periodicals expressed concern about the workings of police courts and the overbearing nature of urban policing. In 1874 *The Bailie*, in a satirical article entitled 'Additional Powers', criticised the attempt on the part of magistrates to acquire more police powers in a local police bill on account of the fact that it would further infringe upon the rights and liberties of the general community:

> The Glasgow Police Act of 1866 having been found not comprehensive or overbearing enough, a bill is said to be in preparation requesting Parliament to confer fresh powers on municipal 'masters and pastors.' Among its clauses are the following ...

> Any person who fails to return the most courteous reply to any impertinent and ungentlemanly question put to him by a member of the 'Force,' will be liable to immediate apprehension.

---

[152] 'First Report of the Law Commissioners Appointed to Inquire into the Courts of Law in Scotland', p. 549.

[153] Ibid.

[154] Ibid.

Any person who resists being dragged to the 'Office,' will be liable to have the handcuffs placed on his wrists and carried thither head downwards, or otherwise, as the police may determine.

Any person who has been 'done' to within an inch of his life by policemen and prefers a complaint, will be liable to be laughed and sneered at by the officer on duty.

…Any person who is displeased at the decisions of the Citizen Magistracy can appeal to the Court of Session.[155]

[Note by the Animile – 'We all know what he'll make of his appeal when he goes there.'][156]

Although stopping short of openly criticising magistrates, there was an implication in the article – and a number of others that were published – that the courts were failing to offer fair and equitable justice, especially for those who were brought before magistrates on the evidence of policemen. The chances of acquittal, in other words, appeared to be getting slimmer and slimmer with the rise of a more closely policed society and the growing importance attached to character and criminal profiling.

As the next section shows, however, the appointment of the stipendiary magistrate in Glasgow in 1876 – who was, unlike other magistrates, not a member of the police board or town council and did not have to submit himself for popular election – would prove significant. It would highlight the different way that a legally trained magistrate administered the law and the implications this had for securing convictions in the city's police courts.

V. The Stipendiary, the Police and the Propertied in Glasgow in the 1870s and 1880s

According to contemporary reports in Glasgow, the employment of a stipendiary magistrate – who knew the intricacies of the law better than civic magistrates – had made it more difficult for the fiscal to secure convictions. In 1886, a memorial was sent to the civic magistrates from shopkeepers, warehousemen and tradesmen in the Trongate district of the city expressing their annoyance at the loss and interruption of business caused by 'disreputable persons loitering and misbehaving in a disorderly

---

[155]   Appeals were typically sent to the High Court of Justiciary.
[156]   *The Bailie*, no. 110, 25 November 1874, p. 2.

manner in the streets'.[157] A similar complaint had been sent to magistrates three years earlier, which suggests that it was an ongoing concern.[158] The memorial was published in the *North British Daily Mail* under the heading 'The Condition of Glasgow's Streets'. Criticism was expressed not at police officers, but instead at the stipendiary magistrate, John Gemmell, on the basis that the petitioners 'were not supported by the Bench as far as they might be'.[159] The memorial, as represented in the *North British Daily Mail*, stated that the blame for the rowdyism and crime which took place in Trongate and adjoining streets was the stipendiary magistrate's fault, because he gave 'little support to the police in their endeavours to clear the streets of criminal men and women'.[160] Gemmell, it was claimed, not only refused to convict criminal men and women, but 'administered reprimands from the judicial bench to officers who seek faithfully to perform their duty'.[161]

Unfortunately, police returns do not record separate conviction rates for the central and district courts in the city, which makes it impossible to assess whether Gemmell's Central Police Court had a higher acquittal rate than the courts in which civic magistrates presided. However, it is likely that this was the case. As Table 6.9 shows, conviction rates for crimes in the city as a whole declined following his appointment in the last few months of 1876. From standing at 90 per cent on his introduction, conviction rates fell to percentages in the low-to mid-80s: a significant decline given that a sizeable proportion of cases was likely to have been determined by a guilty plea.

Table 6.9   Percentage of Criminal Convictions Relative to Acquittals in Glasgow, 1864 to 1887[†]

1864	1865	1866	1867	1868	1869	1870	1871	1872	1873	1874
86	84	88	92	94	93	?	87	86	86	87

1875	1876	1877	1878	1879	1880	1881	1882	1883	1884	1887
90	90	86	85	81	83	82	82	86		85

† These figures have been collated from the Glasgow police annual returns, for the years cited, passim.

Why Gemmell's acquittal rates should have been lower could have reflected the fact that as a trained lawyer he was much more skilled in spotting evidentiary defects than civic magistrates. But it is also likely that his legal background and

---

[157] See GCA, D-TC-14.1.17: 'The Condition of Glasgow Streets: The Stipendiary Magistrate on His Defence', papers extracted from the *North British Daily Mail*; and GCA, E1.6A.12: Glasgow Magistrates and Council Minutes, 1886.

[158] GCA, D-TC-14.1.17: 'The Condition of Glasgow Streets'.

[159] GCA, E1.6A.12: Glasgow Magistrates and Council Minutes, 1 September 1886.

[160] GCA, D-TC-14.1.17: 'The Condition of Glasgow Streets'.

[161] Ibid.

independence from the police commission meant that he sought to apply the law to the letter of the law, and not to reflect civic interests or 'common-sense judgement' in a way that characterised other magistrates. The events surrounding the Trongate dispute suggest that this was the case. In an unusual turn of events, Gemmell opened the court sitting following the publication of the *North British Daily Mail*'s article by defending his position – a defence he obviously felt was necessary given that, in his words, he carried out his judicial duty 'under the censorship of the press'.[162] In it, he stated that the law and legal principles and procedure determined his judgements:

> Of course, before sentencing, I must convict, and it is my duty, as I consider it is my privilege, in trying an habitual offender on a new charge, to follow the same course as is done in the case of an accused person with an unstained character, by satisfying myself that the charge is a relevant one, and that the prosecutor establishes his complaint by full and complete legal evidence, and giving the accused every opportunity of establishing his innocence by rebutting evidence.[163]

The reference to 'character' was especially significant. It suggests that, for Gemmell, evidence rather than personal circumstances should determine the outcome of cases. In many ways, it was the perception that Gemmell was reluctant to convict known offenders upon police evidence alone that lay at the heart of the dispute.[164] For the memorialists, legal rights did not appear to apply equally to everyone. They argued that in cases where the accused had been previously convicted, social standing, and by implication character, and magisterial discretion should play as large a role in determining the validity of evidence as the evidence itself. Indeed, this was a view shared by senior police officers, as the published lecture of J.V. Stevenson, Chief Constable of Glasgow, also indicated.[165]

Significantly, the criticism of the stipendiary magistrate suggests that civic magistrates were less preoccupied with legal guidelines in their approach to administering the law. No similar criticisms were levelled against them in the memorial – although *The Bailie* suggested that this was not uncommon.[166] An anonymous article in the *North British Daily Mail* made it clear that a large section of the public – or, probably more accurately, men of property – were looking for a more informal approach to law enforcement: 'Common-sense people who look to the broad principles of justice, and not to small legal quibbles, will consider the case a scandalous protection of the criminal, and just the sort of thing to encourage crime.'[167] There was also a sizeable body within the police who shared

---

[162]   Ibid., paper 977.

[163]   Ibid.

[164]   Ibid., paper 978.

[165]   GCA, T-PAR1/8: Stevenson, *The Punishment and Prevention of Crime*, pp. 6–7.

[166]   *The Bailie*'s criticism of magisterial judgements is referenced throughout both volumes.

[167]   GCA, D-TC-14.1.17: 'The Condition of Glasgow Streets', paper 979.

the same view as the memorialists and the author of the article. Indeed, there were even suggestions that police officers had helped to draft the memorial.[168] In the investigation which followed the controversy, civic magistrates found no evidence to support this,[169] but reports in the press alleging widespread disillusionment among police officers towards Gemmell suggest that they might have had an input, at least providing information on the matter. A number of officers had even submitted a petition to the civic magistrates against the stipendiary magistrate.[170] Gemmell, it seemed, was in the habit of regularly and rigorously challenging police evidence and testimonies and reprimanding officers in court – a practice that seems to have been fairly novel in the city's police courts up until that point.[171]

Although stressing that the vast majority of officers in his experience were honest and reliable, Gemmell claimed that there were some who were untrustworthy and who falsified evidence in order to secure convictions and settle personal scores.[172] He argued it would be a dereliction of duty not to interrogate the evidence presented by police officers the same way as he did evidence from other sources.[173] Referring to a death threat he received on a previous occasion when about to adjudicate on the trial of a police officer accused of committing assault on a young women, the stipendiary magistrate remarked:

> It will be a dark day for the citizens of Glasgow if countenance be given to the present attempt to put the Bench under censorship of any member of the police force, and when those charged with police offences have to be judged by a Magistrate who is expected to see with the eyes of every policeman.[174]

The officer was convicted. As he suggested, much of the unease between Gemmell and others in public life stemmed from the fact that he attached more significance to evidence than character when administering the law. While stressing his support for officers who were indeed assaulted in the course of their duty, Gemmell noted

---

[168]   See evidence provided to the magistrates' committee appointed to discuss the memorial. GCA, E1.6A.12: Glasgow Magistrates and Council Minutes, 1 September 1886.

[169]   Ibid.

[170]   GCA, E1/13/7, Police Magistrates' Committee Minutes, 19 August 1886. The Police Magistrates' Committee minute book reveals that there was a petition submitted by police officers to magistrates in response to the stipendiary magistrate's comments.

[171]   Gemmell claimed that he had reprimanded constables, although not so often as he might, 'for failing in the performance of their duty'. GCA, D-TC-14.1.17: 'The Condition of the Streets', paper 977.

[172]   For instance, the papers reveal that two officers had accused a young lady, with whom one of the officers had fallen out over a quarrel in a pub, of prostitution. However, the police evidence, according to Gemmell, was shown to be lies. He continued by stating that he 'would be lacking in my duty did I not thus notice glaring instances of abuse of power and untruthfulness displayed in the evidence given before me'. Ibid.

[173]   Ibid., paper 977 & 978.

[174]   Ibid., paper 978.

that where the 'alleged assault upon the police turn out on investigation the very opposite of that presented by the force', then 'the accused are acquitted, even though criminal men or women'.[175] That he felt the need to mention that *even* those who had criminal records would be acquitted if the evidence did not support a conviction gives a telling insight into how the law had often been administered by civic magistrates up to that point.[176]

After being at the forefront in stimulating public interest in the case, an editorial in the *North British Daily Mail* sought to diffuse the dispute, perhaps with an eye to recognising the detrimental impact it was having on the public image of law enforcement in the city or their voice as one authority in the matter. It published a letter from an anonymous law agent who pointed out that the public were not aware of the legal evidence on which it was necessary to secure a conviction.[177] The letter revealed the tension between what men of property believed the purpose of the police court should be, and legal opinion on how the law should be administered:

> It is not the function – it is not in the power – of a Magistrate to punish a man or a woman for being 'suspicious'. The most notorious criminal has rights as well as the most immaculate citizen, and one of these rights is a share of street room. The fact of a thief being found in a crowded thoroughfare does not prove that he was thieving, and the police, in their doubtless honest efforts to clear the streets, may bring dozens of persons before the Magistrate daily whom the Magistrate can do nothing but discharge. It is not his business to judge character and to interpret intentions. He is there to administer the law, and the law holds everyone innocent until proved to be guilty. It is impossible for any Magistrate – Stipendiary or otherwise – to refuse to convict on the evidence of the police if that evidence be clear and sufficient. It is equally impossible for him to convict without such evidence.

Significantly, the author of the letter went on to highlight the dangers of relying too much on police evidence:

> Experience, too, has shown that the evidence of the police has a natural professional bias which requires counter-balancing, and no citizen would like to feel his character and liberty were at the mercy of a single illiterate constable. Loafing, again, is not an offence punishable at law, but it is a practice which the police have authority to prevent. If they bring loafers before the Court without evidence to prove an indictable offence against them, they are exceeding their duty and expose themselves to reprimand.[178]

---

[175]   Ibid.
[176]   Ibid.
[177]   Ibid., paper 979.
[178]   Ibid.

After carrying out an extensive investigation, civic magistrates found that there was no evidence to substantiate the memorialists' claim that Gemmell had not been supporting police officers in their efforts to deal with lawless and disorderly behaviour in the Trongate.[179] But it was notable that the civic magistrates and the chief constable were more vociferous in their defence of police officers than they were of Gemmell. The former group found 'no cause for complaint' against officers in the district, despite Gemmell's assertions that some of them were far from honest and spent much of their time fraternising with prostitutes.[180] Indeed, the silence from civic magistrates and the chief constable when it came to defending Gemmell was striking.[181] It is clear that civic magistrates shared in the discontent directed towards Gemmell. Aside from the fact that Gemmell was a challenge to their own authority and status, the stipendiary magistrate seems to have been more willing to punish those convicted of crimes according to the letter of the law than civic magistrates. He claimed that he handed down a far higher percentage of imprisonments than fines compared with his colleagues.[182] This was a system of administering justice that was likely to alienate civic magistrates who were more inclined to impose fines as a means of raising public funds than the stipendiary magistrate,[183] who did not have to submit himself to qualified householders for election. There was also a clash of personalities between the justices and a sense that the old was slowly being undermined by the new. Just over a year after the conflict, the *Glasgow Evening News* reported 'How the Magistrates must love him' [Gemmell] after he ordered three civic magistrates to leave his courtroom so that

---

[179]   GCA, E1.6A.12: Glasgow Magistrates and Council Minutes, 1 September 1886.

[180]   On this point, Gemmell was reiterating information which had been presented to him from Superintendent Boyd, after learning that several of the night constables 'were during the day in the habit of sitting in a room of the public-house referred to in company with prostitutes, and were in use to be admitted along with the same woman to Henger's Circus at midnight, where they remained for two and three hours when supposed to be on duty'. The conduct of the officers surprised Superintendent Boyd 'because some of the constables, so acting in violation of their duty, had shortly before been selected as exemplary members of the force to be sent out to Hong Kong'. GCA, D-TC-14.1.17: 'The Condition of the Streets', paper 978.

[181]   The civic magistrates made no direct reference to Mr Gemmell and did not state support for him, in contrast to the backing they gave police officers. The chief constable made specific reference to the fact that he did not support Mr Gemmell's claim that some of his officers were in the habit of spending their nights in the company of prostitutes whilst on duty. GCA, E1.6A.12: Glasgow Magistrates and Council Minutes, 1 September 1886.

[182]   'I desire not to earn the reputation of being a severe judge, but in dealing with habitual offenders I invariably on conviction treat them in a very different fashion from the way they are generally dealt with by the city magistrates. In their case I very seldom give the alternative of a pecuniary penalty, but pronounce what most people would call a smart sentence of imprisonment.' GCA, D-TC-14.1.17: 'The Condition of the Streets', paper 977.

[183]   The importance of police court fines to civic administration is examined in Chapter 7.

he could judge a sensitive case in private.[184] To the amusement of the journalist, the three magistrates were heard cursing among themselves as they left the room. Indeed, it was not just his fellow magistrates who often showed Gemmell a lack of respect, but often the press too. A letter, from 'An Old Reporter', to the *Glasgow Herald* in 1876 alluded to this:

> In the reports of the proceedings at the Central Police Court I note that the reporters seem to find a difficulty in designating the presiding magistrate. 'The Stipendiary Magistrate' or 'the Stipendiary,' are evidently felt to be dreadfully stiff and somewhat invidious, for why should the fact of the Police Magistrate being a paid official be constantly harped upon, seeing that in that respect he stands on the same footing as our Sheriffs and Lords of the Court of Session? Then, 'Mr Gemmel' wants in distinctiveness, and fails to give that gentleman what is surely his due – a decent title. Allow me to suggest that in Scotland stipendiary police magistrates should be designated Judges. This would interfere with no one's honours, as though all magistrates are judges, it has not been in this part of the world customary to give that term to any of them as a courtesy title.[185]

The controversy surrounding Gemmell was significant in a number of ways – not least in terms of what it meant for the future direction of police court summary justice, and what it suggests about how magistrates had administered it up until then. The fact that men of property no longer believed that the Central Police Court was serving their interests gives a telling insight into what purpose they thought it should serve – and, furthermore, about what purpose it, and the district police courts in the city that were overseen by civic magistrates, had served up until then. It highlighted the importance of character in determining how the accused were dealt with, and how legal rights had sometimes been sacrificed in order to secure what civic men perceived was a greater good. What was at stake in the controversy surrounding Gemmell was the changing face of police court justice and the role of magistrates within it. Gemmell was advocating a new role for magistrates – a role in which personal judgement and common sense, as defined by civic men, would play a less significant part than legal procedure and principles in determining judgements. It was a role in which justices would rigidly interpret the law according to legal and procedural guidelines and not as they themselves saw fit – a requirement that would reduce their capacity to determine the outcome of cases on the basis of how they defined the character of those before them. Legality, in other words, was to be given even greater

---

[184] GCA, D-TC-14.1.17: 'The Condition of the Streets', paper 983; *Glasgow Evening News*, 17 January 1888; GCA, D-TC 14-1-17, Glasgow Town Clerk's Department: Miscellaneous Papers, 2 February 1888. After being asked to explain this, the paid magistrate said he did not mean to cause offence and would allow access in future.

[185] *Glasgow Herald*, 26 October 1876.

preference over moral assessments. Given this, it should come as no great surprise that Scottish burghs did not follow Glasgow's example in appointing a stipendiary magistrate in 1876.

VI. Conclusion

Magisterial justice in Scottish police courts was always a balancing act between defending those deemed worthy of protection and those who needed to be disciplined, controlled and punished. But it was a balancing act that swung against the accused until at least the third quarter of the century. As nineteenth-century legal reforms placed more and more emphasis on character, and bureaucratic police machines became ever more important to the administration of Scottish municipal life, the legal rights of the accused for certain offences were diminished. Police courts gave civic magistrates tremendous scope to secure convictions on the basis of probability rather than beyond reasonable doubt – something which became more and more important to them in light of civic affairs and media interest. Indeed, the police magistrate's capacity to establish guilt based on character and what he deemed to be 'suspicious circumstances' was as fundamental to the emergence of the 'policeman-state' as the policeman's truncheon. Although procedural safeguards were never abandoned, they were not as consistently adhered to as in the higher courts and often offered little check on how magistrates interpreted evidence and the credibility of witnesses. This is likely to have been influenced to some degree by the 'trivial' nature of offences, as Doreen McBarnet concluded in her study into Scottish district courts in the 1970s.[186] But it was also because it made it easier for magistrates to administer justice as they saw fit, and, ultimately, better control urban communities.

Convictions could not be divorced from the consequences they produced, and it is clear that magistrates never lost sight of this, or their desire to protect vulnerable groups, when deciding whether to convict. However, the beneficiaries of such protection were increasingly restricted to a small group of offenders, or became instead the anonymous populace that magistrates protected from morally dangerous offenders, as subsequent chapter will show. In the face of increased media scrutiny into urban administration, the publication of criminal returns, and the desire to utilise police court fines to increase public expenditure, the administration of justice in police courts in Scottish towns came to be more about saving a few and convicting the many, from whom magistrates protected the wider community.

---

[186] Doreen McBarnet, *Conviction: Law, The State and the Construction of Justice* (London, 1973); and Susan Moody and Jacqueline Tombs, *Prosecution in the Public Interest* (Edinburgh, 1982).

Chapter 7
Punishment and Protection

I. Introduction

The nineteenth century was a watershed in British penal history. Prisons replaced the death penalty as the cornerstone of the criminal justice system,[1] transportation to the colonies ended,[2] and most forms of public corporal punishment were outlawed.[3] Rehabilitation, rather than the retributive and exemplary punishment that had characterised pre-modern judicial censure, became the growing principle of a penal system capable of punishing a far larger number of offenders than had been hitherto possible. Community-sanctioned visible shaming rituals became less common as the relationship between humiliation and punishment became increasingly embedded within state-controlled institutions and media cultures.[4]

---

[1]   For overviews of changes to punishment in the eighteenth and nineteenth centuries, see Clive Emsley, *Crime and Society in England, 1750–1900*, 3rd edn (Harlow, 2005), pp. 253–96; David Taylor, *Hooligan, Harlots, and Hangmen: Crime and Punishment in Victorian Britain* (Santa Barbara, 2010), pp. 145–210; and Barry S. Godfrey and Paul Lawrence, *Crime and Justice, 1750–1950* (Cullompton, 2005), pp. 68–88. In Scotland, the death penalty was never as widely used as in England, but it still played an important role in the Scottish legal system. See, for instance, M.A. Crowther, 'Crime, Prosecution and Mercy: English Influence and Scottish Practice in the Early Nineteenth Century', in S.J. Connolly (ed.), *Kingdoms United? Great Britain and Ireland since 1500: Integration and Diversity* (Dublin, 1999), pp. 225–38.

[2]   Simon Devereaux, *Convicts and the State: The Administration of Criminal Justice During the Reign of George III* (Toronto, 1997); and Robert Hughes, *The Fatal Shore: A History of the Transportation of Convicts to Australia, 1787–1868* (London, 1987). For transportation in Scotland, see Ian Donnachie, 'The Convicts of 1830: Scottish Criminals Transported to New South Wales', *Scottish Historical Review*, 65(1)/179 (1986): pp. 34–47; and Malcolm D. Prentis, 'What Do We Know about Scottish Convicts?', *Journal of the Royal Australian Historical Society*, 90/1 (2004): pp. 36–52.

[3]   For more on eighteenth-century corporal punishment, see Randall McGowen, 'The Body and Punishment in Eighteenth-Century England', *Journal of Social History*, 59/4 (1987): pp. 651–79.

[4]   See, for instance, Robert B. Shoemaker, 'Streets of Shame? The Crowd and Public Punishments in London, 1700–1820', in Simon Devereaux and Paul Griffiths (eds), *Penal Practice and Culture, 1500–1900: Punishing the English* (Basingstoke, 2004), pp. 232–57. For the ways in which cultures of shame survived as a form of punishment in modern society, see David Nash and Anne-Marie Kilday, *Cultures of Shame: Exploring Crime and Morality in Britain 1600–1900* (Basingstoke, 2010); and Carolyn A. Conley, *The Unwritten Law: Criminal Justice in Victorian Kent* (Oxford, 1991), pp. 23–7.

Whereas in the eighteenth century many punishments took place in public to serve as a warning to others,[5] those of the nineteenth century were increasingly hidden behind institutional walls and prison gates. Changing perceptions of criminals and the causes of crime brought with them new specialist forms of reformative punishment in industrial schools and correction houses for 'vulnerable' juvenile offenders. Punishment, which at the start of the nineteenth century had often been designed to humiliate, deter, and inflict pain on the body was, by the end of the century, increasingly characterised by 'modern penal welfare' that moderately punished offenders and sought to protect, care and reform them.[6]

The huge body of scholarship that has charted this transformation has focused mainly on the demise of public executions and the birth of the prison – in other words, high court punishment for more serious crimes – and less so on the expansion in nineteenth-century summary punishments.[7] Indeed, historians have been much more inclined to examine the wide array of eighteenth-century summary punishments or godly discipline administered in religious courts than the more limited and formulaic penalties handed out by magistrates in the nineteenth century.[8] What work has been carried out on the latter has looked

---

[5]   For theories on the role of punishment in bringing about social cohesion, see David Garland, *Punishment and Modern Society: A Study in Social Theory* (Oxford, 1990); and Émile Durkheim, *L'Education Morale* (Paris, 1925).

[6]   David Garland, *Punishment and Welfare: A History of Penal Strategies* (Aldershot, 1985). For more on the extent to which growing revulsion towards violent forms of punishment influenced penal reform, see Randall McGowen, 'A Powerful Sympathy: Terror, the Prison and Humanitarian Reform in Early Nineteenth-Century Britain', *Journal of British Studies*, 25/3 (1986): pp. 312–34; Randall McGowen, 'Civilising Punishment: The End of Public Execution in England', *Journal of British Studies*, 33/3 (1994): pp. 257–82; and Greg T. Smith, 'Civilised People Don't Want to See That Kind of Thing: The Decline of Physical Punishment in London, 1760–1840', in Carolyn Strange (ed.), *Qualities of Mercy: Justice, Punishment and Discretion* (Vancouver, 1996), pp. 21–51.

[7]   Landmark studies include Leon Radzinowicz and Roger G. Hood, *A History of English Criminal Law and Its Administration from 1750, Vol. V: The Emergence of Penal Policy* (Oxford, 1990); David D. Cooper, *The Lesson of the Scaffold* (London, 1974); Michael Ignatieff, *A Just Measure of Pain: The Penitentiary in the Industrial Revolution, 1750–1850* (New York, 1978); Michel Foucault, *Discipline and Punish: The Origins of the Prison* (Harmondsworth, 1978); and V.A.C. Gatrell, *The Hanging Tree: Execution and the English People, 1770–1868* (Oxford, 1994).

[8]   See, for instance, the collection of essays in Devereaux and Griffiths (eds), *Penal Practice and Culture*; Simon Devereaux, 'The Abolition of the Burning of Women in England Reconsidered', *Crime, Histoire & Sociétés/Crime, History & Societies*, 9/2 (2005): pp. 73–98; and Robert B. Shoemaker, 'The Decline of Public Insult in London, 1660–1800', *Past and Present*, 169/1 (2000): pp. 97–131. Pre-modern punishment in Scotland has tended to focus on kirk session censure rather than that imposed in burgh or sheriff courts. See, for instance, Leah Leneman and Rosalind Mitchison, *Girls in Trouble: Sexuality and Social Control in Rural Scotland, 1660–1780* (Edinburgh, 1998); and Leah Leneman and Rosalind Mitchison, *Sin in the City: Sexuality and Social*

at the emergence of new sensibilities which made pre-industrial punishment appear inhumane,[9] statistical patterns and the gendered nature of sentencing,[10] the treatment of offenders convicted of isolated offences such as domestic violence or assault,[11] or specific social groups such as convicted juveniles.[12] More often than not, though, the concentration has been on the offender, or offence committed, rather than the wider economic, social, political and cultural significance of magisterial justice and how it was represented in the media.[13]

On first reflection, historians' intrigue with eighteenth-century punishment rather than nineteenth-century summary justice might appear unsurprising. The former, it is claimed, often took place in an emotionally charged, carnival-like atmosphere, was often gory, bloody, and brutal, and helped to reinforce paternal and deferential

---

Control in Urban Scotland 1660–1780 (Edinburgh, 1998). As previous chapters have noted, studies which have taken the administration of nineteenth-century magistrate courts as their specific subject matter have tended to be concerned with whether the law was administered to protect the vested interests of local justices, or the role of the courts in settling disputes.

[9] For an examination of the abolition of public flogging of women in England, see Gwenda Morgan and Peter Rushton, *Rogues, Thieves, and the Rule of Law: The Problem of Law Enforcement in North-East England, 1718–1800* (London, 2004), pp. 132–8.

[10] This has been referenced extensively throughout the book, especially in the Introduction. Useful studies for the nineteenth century, although not always looking specifically at magistrate courts, include Deirdre Palk, *Gender, Crime and Judicial Discretion 1780–1830* (Woodbridge, 2006); Barry S. Godfrey, Stephen Farrall and Susanne Karstedt, 'Explaining Gendered Sentencing Patterns for Violent Men and Women in the Late Victorian and Edwardian Period', *British Journal of Criminology*, 45/5 (2005): pp. 696–720; Angus McLaren, *The Trials of Masculinity: Policing Sexual Boundaries, 1870–1930* (Chicago, 1997); and Martin J. Wiener, *Men of Blood: Violence, Manliness and Criminal Justice in Victorian England* (Cambridge, 2004).

[11] See, for instance, Annemarie Hughes, 'The "Non-Criminal" Class: Wifebeating in Scotland, c.1850–1949', *Crime, Histoire & Sociétés/Crime, History & Societies*, 14/2 (2010): pp. 31–54.

[12] Margaret May, 'Innocence and Experience: The Evolution of the Concept of Juvenile Delinquency in the Mid-Nineteenth Century,' *Victorian Studies*, 18/1 (1973): pp. 7–29; Heather Shore, *Artful Dodgers: Youth and Crime in Early Nineteenth Century London* (Woodbridge, 1999); Deborah Gorham, 'The "Maiden Tribute of Modern Babylon" Re-Examined: Child Prostitution and the Idea of Childhood in Late-Victorian England', *Victorian Studies*, 21/3 (1978): pp. 353–79; and Peter King, 'The Rise of Juvenile Delinquency in England, 1780–1840: Changing Patterns of Perceptions and Prosecutions.' *Past and Present*, 160/1 (1998): pp. 116–66.

[13] A number of studies, though, have looked at newspaper reporting of magistrate courts without focusing specifically on punishment. See, for instance, Joanne Jones, '"She Resisted with all Her Might": Sexual Violence against Women in Late Nineteenth Century Manchester and the Local Press', in Shani D'Cruze (ed.), *Everyday Violence in Britain, 1850–1950: Gender and Class* (London, 2000), pp. 104–18.

bonds.[14] It was as much about the spectacle of theatre, and letting the community see that justice was being done, as about disciplining the individual.[15] The censure administered in nineteenth-century magistrates' courts, by contrast, could easily appear sombre, dull and relatively unimportant, not least, as David Taylor has pointed out, as trials in English provincial towns frequently took place in locations that were anything but grand.[16]

However, the significance of the punishing potential of police courts should not be understated. As Jennifer S. Davis has argued, magistrates in these courts wielded more unsupervised judicial power than any other legal representative in the criminal justice system – a role which takes on even greater importance in Scottish police courts given the absence of stipendiary bailies for much of the century.[17] Despite, in the overwhelming majority of cases, having no legal training or expertise, magistrates could dismiss at pre-trial hearings charges worthy of being remitted to a higher court, imprison for up to two months, and hand out fines of up to £10 – the equivalent of several weeks' work for a handloom weaver in early nineteenth-century Scotland (although in the early part of the century the maximum fine was often much lower prior to national police legislation establishing a uniform system of practice).[18] The most common trial experience in the Scottish criminal justice system took place in police courts, and the fines, admonitions and short periods of confinement magistrates handed out were the most common forms of punishment the legal system administered in the nineteenth century. Moreover, the number of

---

[14] Douglas Hay, 'Property, Authority and the Criminal Law', in Douglas Hay, Peter Linebaugh, John G. Rule, E.P. Thompson and Cal Winslow (eds), *Albion's Fatal Tree: Crime and Society in Eighteenth-Century England* (London, 1976), pp. 17–63.

[15] J.M. Beattie, *Policing and Punishment in London, 1660–1750: Urban Crime and the Limits of Terror* (Oxford, 2001), passim; Peter King, *Crime, Justice and Discretion in England, 1740–1820* (Oxford, 2000), passim; and Peter Linebaugh, *The London Hanged: Crime and Civil Society in the Eighteenth Century* (Cambridge, 1992), passim.

[16] Taylor, *Hooligan, Harlots, and Hangmen*, p. 108.

[17] Jennifer S. Davis, 'A Poor Man's System of Justice? The London Police Courts in the Second Half of the Nineteenth Century', *Historical Journal*, 27/2 (1984): p. 311.

[18] As Chapter 3 noted, the average gross weekly wage for muslin weavers in Scottish industrial towns in the first half of the nineteenth century ranged from 13s. to 15s. N. Murray, *The Scottish Handloom Weavers, 1790 to 1850: A Social History* (Edinburgh, 1978), pp. 43 & 92–3. In 1891, an inquiry by the Presbytery of Glasgow accepted the evidence of Bruce Glasier, former secretary of the Glasgow branch of the Socialist League, that more than one quarter of the male workforce in the city in that year were paid less than 20s., and 'an undoubtedly larger number of female workers whose wages are much under 20s'. Presbytery of Glasgow, *Report of Commission on the Housing of the Poor in Relation to their Social Conditions* (Glasgow, 1891), p. 22. In giving evidence to the 1839 Law Inquiry, William Davie, Assessor in the Glasgow Police and Burgh Courts, noted that the maximum fine the police court could impose was £5. 'Fourth Report by Her Majesty's Law Commissioners, Scotland, 1839', *British Parliamentary Papers* (*BPP*), 1840 (241), XX.115, p. 320.

people subjected to them vastly exceeded those executed, transported, whipped and shamed in the eighteenth century.[19] The sentences passed by magistrates in police courts, therefore, reveal a great deal about the implementation of the law in an era when it was being moulded and reformed by a plethora of local and national statutes. As bailies were also responsible for administering civic affairs, how they used the powers they had at their disposal has significance beyond the confines of criminal justice history. It was also extremely important to the governance of urban communities and the operation and distribution of power in society. As this chapter shows, magistrates, in their self-perceived role as not only administrators of justice but also custodians of social welfare and guardians of the community, took into account a multitude of social, moral, economic, practical and cultural factors when passing sentence. And, as always, their own image and how it was represented in the media was never far from their thoughts.

Perhaps most intriguing of all, the growth in newspaper coverage of police courts in the nineteenth century provides the historian with an opportunity to address a notable gap in criminal justice history by investigating the media representation of magisterial decisions post-conviction. A burgeoning literature has focused on portrayals in eighteenth-century broadsides, ballads and criminal biographies of the experience, process and significance of public hangings and secondary punishments,[20] and on how representations of punishment could be used as a form of moral chastisement and to convey the message that crime did not pay.[21] But less attention has been given to examining newspaper coverage of the actual sentencing that followed courtroom trials.[22] While it has been argued that media coverage could help to legitimise the workings of the criminal justice

---

[19] In fact, fining had always been a feature of judicial punishment. As James Sharpe has suggested: 'it seems likely that, if the records of all courts with a "criminal" jurisdiction were to be consulted, it would be revealed that the most common form of punishment inflicted on criminals … would be fining: whatever the early modern criminal justice system was doing to the body or the soul of offenders, it was certainly damaging their purse.' James A. Sharpe, 'Civility, Civilizing Processes, and the End of Public Punishment in Eighteenth-Century England', in Peter Burke, Brian Harrison and Paul Slack (eds), *Civil Histories: Essay Presented to Sir Keith Thomas* (Oxford, 2000), p. 223; and James A. Sharpe, *Judicial Punishment in England* (London, 1990), p. 49.

[20] See, for instance, Andrea McKenzie, *Tyburn's Martyrs: Execution in England, 1675–1775* (London, 2007); Andrea McKenzie, 'From True Confessions to True Reporting? The Decline and Fall of the Ordinary's Account', *London Journal*, 30/1 (2005): pp. 55–70. For newspaper reporting on the experience and emotion of public executions, Gatrell's *The Hanging Tree* is still the most detailed and impressive study published.

[21] See, for instance, Robert B. Shoemaker, 'The Old Bailey Proceedings and the Representation of Crime and Criminal Justice in Eighteenth-Century London', *Journal of British Studies*, 47/3 (2008): pp. 578–9.

[22] Zoe Dyndor's investigation of the portrayal of capital punishment in the Northamptonshire press is one of the few studies to focus specifically on newspapers, but it deals primarily with the representation of the execution reports and process, not newspaper

system, scrutiny has largely centred on how the selective coverage of courtroom trial proceedings could make convictions appear just and less on how subsequent judicial decisions on punishment were represented.[23] As Shani D'Cruze has pointed out, uncovering information on magisterial sentencing patterns can be difficult as sources – both court and media – often made no explicit comment on what factors determined judicial decisions.[24] Nonetheless, the relative paucity of work in this area remains somewhat surprising, especially given the importance of discretionary powers of punishment to the position, status and authority of local elites. Examining media portrayals of courtroom sentencing and punishment practices in police courts promises to reveal a great deal about how magistrates governed their communities and the image they sought to cultivate in the press.

Significantly, this chapter also develops the theme that the press could serve as an important discursive participant in summary justice, not just in legitimising, or otherwise, judicial punishments, but also in continuing the process of shaming that had been such a feature of the eighteenth-century penal code. As David Nash and Anne-Marie Kilday have recently observed, shame as a form of punishment was incorporated within the print culture of modern society and functioned to support judicial judgements and practices.[25] It could also serve to punish victims. D'Cruze, for instance, has alluded to the ways in which police courtroom reporters could stigmatise and damage the reputations of female victims of physical and sexual violence by attributing judgements about their character, respectability and morals.[26] However, precisely how shaming in the nineteenth-century media played out generally in the public sphere of the nineteenth-century magistrate court remains under-researched, as does the press's coverage of secondary punishment in this period in general.[27] As this chapter argues, the media, in the coverage it gave to police court trials, was in many ways an extension of pre-modern forms of shaming and an important part

---

coverage of trial sentences. Zoe Dyndor, 'Death Recorded: Capital Punishment and the Press in Northampton, 1780–1834', *Midland History*, 33/2 (2008): pp. 179–95.

[23]   Shoemaker, 'The Old Bailey Proceedings and the Representation of Crime and Criminal Justice', pp. 559–80; Simon Devereaux, 'The Fall of the Sessions Paper: The Criminal Trial and the Popular Press in Late Eighteenth-Century London,' *Criminal Justice History*, 18/1 (2002): pp. 57–88; Simon Devereaux, 'The City and the Sessions Paper: "Public Justice" in London, 1770–1800,' *Journal of British Studies*, 35/4 (1996): pp. 467–8; and Simon Devereaux, 'From Sessions to Newspaper? Criminal Trial Reporting, the Nature of Crime, and the London Press, 1770–1800', *London Journal*, 32/1 (2007): pp. 3–6.

[24]   Shani D'Cruze, *Crimes of Outrage: Sex, Violence and Victorian Working Women* (London, 1998), p. 167.

[25]   Nash and Kilday, *Cultures of Shame*, passism, although especially pp. 11, 19, 135 & 153.

[26]   D'Cruze, *Crimes of Outrage*, pp. 70, 140 & 178.

[27]   See David G. Barrie, 'Naming and Shaming: Trial by Media in Nineteenth-Century Scotland', *Journal of British Studies*, forthcoming at time of publication, 54/1 (2015).

of the disciplinary culture of police court trials. Periodical and press reporting of courtroom discourse meant that shaming had the potential to become, and in some cases was, an intrinsic part of police court punishment, even if it was not always intended. The media served, in some ways, as a judicial and religious resource, often operating with magisterial approval and under magisterial direction in exposing the identities of some and protecting others.

II. Sentencing and Civilising

Having convicted an offender, magistrates had a range of punitive options available to them. They could admonish, fine, find security against and imprison; and, by mid-century (and in some cases earlier) refer 'vulnerable' offenders to houses of refuge, lock hospitals, magdalene asylums or reform and industrial schools. Although police court magistrates' powers of punishment were mandated by law to two months' imprisonment or a £10 fine, they were not, in most cases that involved adults, prescribed by fixed penalties for specific crimes, offences and contraventions.[28] As long as they did not exceed the parameters of their judicial powers, magistrates were afforded tremendous discretion when handing out punishments. This discretion often resulted in different punishments being administered for similar offences – a point which was noted and criticised by contemporaries and which was used by reformers to justify the case for a stipendiary magistrate. In determining judicial outcomes, magistrates took into account a number of factors over and above the crime and the character of the offender. The condition of the economy, the extent of bridewell accommodation, the state of poor law provision, the circumstances of offenders and, significantly, how the punishment handed down reflected upon magistrates as governing men, were key practical, social and cultural factors that influenced sentences.[29]

As Table 7.1 shows, fining was the most common form of punishment administered by magistrates in the Glasgow Police Court in the early nineteenth century (accounting for 46 per cent of punishments dispensed). Superintendent John Ord, in *The Story of the Burgh of Calton* (published some time in the early twentieth century when he was active in the force), put the percentage of fines

---

[28]   They could also restrict food to bread and water for a particularly severe offence. See the case involving Andrew Neilson, a master tailor, on the fourth charge of maltreating his wife. *The Police Intelligencer, or Life in Edinburgh* (*Police Intelligencer*), 23 August 1831.

[29]   In giving evidence to the 1839 Law Inquiry, Gabriel Miller, Clerk of the Dundee Police Court noted: 'The mode of punishment has certainly been very objectionable hitherto, owing to the inadequate size of the gaol, and the want of the means of classification of offenders.' He went on to state that the mode of punishment had 'greatly injured the efficiency of the Court'. 'Fourth Report by Her Majesty's Law Commissioners, Scotland, 1839', p. 334.

Table 7.1   Sample of Glasgow Police Court Sentences, 1813 to 1824*†

	Number	Percentage
Admonished/Reprimanded	309	43
Fined	326	46
Imprisoned	57	8
Cautioned/Coals Confiscated	20	3

* As outlined in Chapter 3, the sample covers two-week periods for the years 1813, 1818 and 1824.

Note: It is not clear whether the early records used admonished or reprimanded interchangeably or whether there was an implied degree of difference in the level of censure. Although both were recorded in early court records and involved a verbal warning, it is possible that admonition was a milder form of disapproval, involving an implied element of learning and correction, than was a reprimand. The latter was generally regarded as a formal form of discipline and indicated magisterial displeasure at what he deemed to be unacceptable behaviour. However, by the second half of the century, police statistical returns recorded only admonitions, thereby suggesting that this had become the official classification for verbal censure.

† Glasgow City Archives (GCA), B3/1/1/1: Glasgow Police Court Diet Books, 28 January 1813 to 11 February 1813, pp. 1–43; GCA, B3/1/1/5: Glasgow Police Court Diet Books, 28 January 1818 to 11 February 1818, pp. 20–101; and GCA, B3/1/1/10: Glasgow Police Court Diet Books, 25 September 1824 to 8 October 1824, pp. 1–98.

for that burgh much higher.[30] Fines were used to punish a wide array of crimes, offences and contraventions. The 1839–1840 Law Inquiry noted that it was common practice in some Scottish police courts for bail pledges to be forfeited, and accepted by magistrates as a form of punishment.[31] As long as the pledge was deemed to be of equivalent value to the fine that would have followed on conviction, magistrates were willing to let those accused of some offences not appear before them as it reduced pressure on their burgeoning workloads. Unless the crime or offence was deemed to be particularly serious, those who turned up

---

[30]   He notes that the Calton Police Court book from 1 September 1821 to 26 October 1822 (which, unfortunately, appears to have since been lost) contained 1,769 cases involving 2,694 persons. Of these, he claims, only 27 people were committed to bridewell, 'all the others convicted having managed to pay their fines'. It is likely, though, that Ord did not record admonishments with convictions, which was common in this period, so the overall percentage of those convicted who were fined is likely to have been a lot lower than Ord's numbers imply. Superintendent John Ord, 'The Story of the Burgh of Calton', *East Glasgow History*, 2010, http://www.glasgowhistory.co.uk/OrdsCalton.htm.

[31]   'Fourth Report by Her Majesty's Law Commissioners, Scotland, 1839', pp. 320–21.

in court and were convicted were usually given the option of either paying a fine or being committed to bridewell. This ensured that bridewells and gaols were generally comprised of not just those deemed to be the most hardened offenders, but also the poorest and most financially vulnerable. In the burgh of Calton, on the outskirts of Glasgow, the police and magistrates accepted almost any article of value in pledge until the offenders paid their fines – a practice that spoke volumes about the poverty of the burgh as the handloom weaving industry went into decline following the introduction of the powerloom.[32] Articles accepted in pledge included a barber's hone (whetstone), a handkerchief, a pair of trousers, a pair of blankets, a gown, a bed-tick (cloth bag for enclosing bed materials), and a straw hat. On 29 May 1822, for instance, Mrs Fraser from New Street, who had been fined half-a-crown, left a watering-can. A week later, Mrs M'Farlan, a pedlar, left a pack containing beads, earrings, and tapes until she could pay a fine of 1s., 6d. If pledged items were not redeemed within 14 days the police would sell them. Sometimes the courts recouped more than the original fine, sometimes less.[33] It was a flexible, pragmatic system of administering justice that reflected not only the mores of public men in making judgements about how serious they perceived certain types of behaviour to be, but also the local circumstances of the populace brought before them.

As the above Table shows, fining was closely followed by admonition/ reprimand as the most common form of judicial censure (43 per cent). This punishment tended to be reserved for those offences which the magistrate deemed too trivial to warrant more formal discipline, or because there was little serious prospect of a fine being recovered. Magistrates also sometimes deemed that a public reprimand, or the detention suffered prior to trial, was sufficient compensation for the offence of which the accused had been convicted. Others determined that the damage to third parties in the offender's environment would be too great for other punishments. Significantly, such incidents were often chosen for selection in the press, with the latter reaffirming the notion of magistrates' paternal role within the community. For example, in the Glasgow court in 1829, an old man charged with cruelly striking and ill-using his orphan grandchild aged 11 was dismissed with an admonition. This struck the periodical's author John Brownlie as lenient for such an unsavoury offence, but he rationalised the magistrate's decision thus: 'Probably if the magistrate had

---

[32]   Jones, in his study of crime in Wales, also found that those who were fined could pledge clothing. As in the Scottish courts, the practice was common because those convicted were allowed to pay their fines by instalments. In England and Wales this provision was not enshrined in national law until the Summary Justice Act of 1879, although it might have been practised locally. David J.V. Jones, *Crime in Nineteenth-Century Wales* (Cardiff, 1992), p. 234.

[33]   In July, 1822, for instance, John Gillan pledged a watch and coat in security for a fine of 21s. It was subsequently sold for 25s. The following month, though, a watch left in security for a fine of 15s. received 10s. Ord, 'The Story of the Burgh of Calton'.

inflicted a fine, he would have vented out his spleen on the poor child.'[34] Such reports highlighted the typically supportive role of the media when representing magisterial justice.

As Table 7.1 shows, in the early nineteenth century it was quite rare for offenders convicted in Scottish police courts to be imprisoned or cautioned. Just 8 per cent of those sentenced in the 1813–1824 Glasgow Police Court sample were sent to either bridewell or the local gaol. In Calton, a mere 27 out of 2,694 people proceeded against in the local police court between 1 September 1821 and 26 October 1822 were imprisoned. These low figures reflected in part the less serious nature of crimes and offences with which police courts dealt and the lack of available accommodation for prisoners. The Glasgow and Edinburgh bridewells in the early nineteenth century could only accommodate between 150 and 250 prisoners and conditions were often cramped and overcrowded.[35] In smaller burghs, accommodation rarely ran into double figures. Gaolhouse accommodation was often smaller.[36] The vast majority of imprisoned offenders were sent to bridewells, which, in theory, were designed to house the unemployed and vagrants and provide meaningful correction, unlike gaols which were primarily for holding offenders. However, as Cameron points out, the dividing line between gaols and bridewells had become blurred by the early nineteenth century, with the latter holding a wide array of petty criminals and offenders.[37] Indeed, bridewells had, by this point, become the main form of imprisonment for those convicted and police courts were at the forefront in producing Scotland's bridewell population. A summary of the period from 1811 to 1826 showed that 16,897 of the 19,426 commitments to Edinburgh bridewell, or 87 per cent, stemmed from the police court.[38] As Tables 7.2 and 7.3 show, the vast majority of offenders were imprisoned for property offences, drunk and disorderly conduct or vagrancy, and their length of stay tended to be relatively short. Many of the inmates, as the following section will explore, were women and juvenile offenders. Indeed, there were widespread concerns in civic and penal circles about the ineffectiveness and dangers of imprisonment for

---

[34]   *Police Reports of Causes tried before the Justices of Peace, and the Glasgow, Gorbals and Calton Police Courts* (*Police Reports*), 7 July 1829, p. 10.

[35]   Evidence presented to the 'Report from the Select Committees on the State of Prisons in Scotland' in 1826, for instance, reveals that when the new Glasgow bridewell was opened it could accommodate 275 prisoners, which was considerably more than the old one. The penal reformer Joseph Gurney claimed that the Edinburgh bridewell was meant for 144, but the persons committed were far more numerous, resulting in improper overcrowding. J.J. Gurney, *Notes on a Visit Made to Some Prisons in Scotland and Northern England* (London, 1819), pp. 41–9. The average number of prisoners in Edinburgh's bridewell in 1816 was 207. 'Report from the Select Committees on the State of Prisons in Scotland', *BPP*, 1826 (381), V.1, pp. 14 & 90.

[36]   Joy Cameron, *Prisons and Punishment in Scotland* (Edinburgh, 1983), pp. 65–6.

[37]   Ibid., pp. 46–7.

[38]   'Edinburgh Bridewell. Returns of Commitments to the Bridewell of the City and County of Edinburgh: 1810–1827', *BPP*, 1828 (233), XX.851, pp. 6–14.

Table 7.2   Returns of Commitments to Bridewell in Edinburgh: 1811 to 1826[+]

	1811 Total commitments; Number from Police Court	1816 Total commitments; Number from Police Court	1821 Total commitments; Number from Police Court	1826 Total commitments; Number from Police Court
House or shop-breaking and theft, or with intent to steal	10, 10 (100%)	9, 9 (100%)	13, 9 (69%)	6, 0 (0%)
Theft, pocket-picking &c., including accessaries [sic] and attempts to steal	143, 109 (76%)	358, 312 (87%)	465, 392 (84%)	452, 325 (72%)
Reset of theft	3, 2 (67%)	27, 21 (78%)	24, 17 (71%)	12, 5 (42%)
Swindling, falsehood, fraud and wilful imposition	10, 9 (90%)	46, 42 (91%)	27, 22 (82%)	26, 14 (54%)
Making base money	3, 3 (100%)	2, 2 (100%)	4, 4 (100%)	
Having in possession base money	1, 1 (100%)	5, 5 (100%)	4, 4 (100%)	
Vending base money	1, 1 (100%)	24, 22 (92%)	25, 25 (100%)	16, 15 (94%)
Garden breaking	1, 1 (100%)			

Table 7.2　*Continued*

	1811 Total commitments; Number from Police Court	1816 Total commitments; Number from Police Court	1821 Total commitments; Number from Police Court	1826 Total commitments; Number from Police Court
Assault	14, 10 (71%)	30, 28 (93%)	44, 38 (86%)	62, 53 (86%)
Stabbing and wounding (1811, 16) / Wounding and maiming (1821,26)	1, 1 (100%)		3, 3 (100%)	2, 0 (0%)
Begging	5, 5 (100%)	29, 27 (93%)	130, 130 (100%)	63, 63 (100%)
Vagrancy, drunkenness, rioting and disorderly conduct, and other breaches of the peace	88, 78 (89%)	820, 780 (95%)	649, 637 (98%)	250, 227 (91%)
Robbery		3, 3 (100%)	18, 17 (94%)	
Embezzlement and breach of trust		13, 13 (100%)		3, 2 (67%)
Keeping disorderly house, and harbouring vagrants and disorderly persons		5, 5 (100%)	2, 2 (100%)	1, 1 (100%)

Table 7.2   *Continued*

Rescuing and attempting to rescue prisoners		4, 4 (100%)	1, 1 (100%)	5, 5 (100%)
Hindering the due execution of the Bridewell Act, by holding communication with the prisoners from the windows of their cells		7, 7 (100%)		
Returning from banishment under former convictions		19, 0 (100%)	140, 71 (51%)	36, 19 (53%)
Issuing forged bank notes			2, 2 (100%)	
Contempt of court			4, 4 (100%)	
Exposing and abandoning children				2, 1 (50%)
Escaping from Bridewell and retaken				2, 1 (50%)
Total annual commitments	283, 230 (81%)	1436, 1280 (86%)	1554, 1374 (88%)	857, 731 (85%)

Note: The commitments from courts other than the police court which make up the remainder of the above totals are from magistrates of the City, Leith and Musselburgh, Sheriff of County, Justice of County, Courts Martial, and High Court of Justiciary.

† 'Returns of Commitments to the Bridewell of the City and County of Edinburgh: 1810–1827', pp. 6–14.

Table 7.3   Police Court Imprisonment Sentences, 1833 to 1835[†]

Burgh	1 Day	2–8 Days	9–14 Days	15 Days to 1 Month	1–2 Months	2–3 Months	Total
Glasgow	0	0	24	573	3,186	0	3,783
Edinburgh*	2	78	230	512	269	0	1,091
Paisley**	0	1	2	119	40	8	170
Dundee	94	356	266	234	161	28	1,139
Greenock**	48	322	153	284	0	0	807
Perth	97	95	64	54	32	0	342
Aberdeen	0	39	145	239	155	0	578

*   All of the above returns for Edinburgh relate only to 1835.

** In these burghs, the summary powers of the burgh criminal court were extended under local police legislation (and the terms burgh criminal court and police court were often used interchangeably). As these courts were responsible for dealing with offences against the local police acts, as well as criminal business, they were often referred to as police courts.

† 'Fourth Report by Her Majesty's Law Commissioners, Scotland, 1839', pp. 278, 304, 323, 332, 335, 336 & 338.

convicted juveniles, or, as the *Aberdeen Journal* put it in 1821: 'the total failure of the utility of Bridewell.'[39] In 1821, *The Scotsman* reported on an Edinburgh police meeting where it had been argued that the

> appalling fact, that within the year from May 1820 to May 1821, there were one hundred and thirty-six persons under 14 years of age committed to Bridewell from the Police Court, and some of them above ten times, is thought to demonstrate not the inefficacy only, but the mischievous tendency of indiscriminately adopting this mode of punishment.[40]

As Chapter 2 of Volume 2 explores, by the 1860s reformatory and industrial schools offered magistrates a way to assuage their fears about the consequences of convicting juveniles.

---

[39]   *Aberdeen Journal,* 15 August 1821.
[40]   *The Scotsman,* 3 November 1821.

After touring Scotland's bridewells in the early nineteenth century, a number of penal reformers claimed that conditions there were of a comfortable standard.[41] This, though, was almost certainly overstated. In July 1822, for instance, the Calton Police Court sentenced Thomas Miller, a weaver, to 28 days' solitary confinement, during which he was to be fed on bread and water, for stealing a black silk cloth from the house of Miss Parrat.[42] Some newspaper reports recorded the sarcasm of the convicted, alluding to the harshness of the punishments administered. In 1829, the *Police Reports* noted the response of Nancy Campbell, described as a prostitute, who was ordered by a Glasgow police magistrate to bridewell for 60 days for being drunk and disorderly and creating a crowd: 'Hech sirs', she says, is that all!'[43] Court mockery of bridewell, though, ignored offenders' very real fears about the effect of their imprisonment. In 1829, for instance, Betty Wardrop, 'an old offender', was convicted of stealing a gown from a neighbour and sentenced to 60 days' confinement in bridewell – a severe punishment illustrating the court's preoccupation with safeguarding private property. On hearing her sentence, it was reported that she became quite distracted and cried out, 'O what will I do! What has come owre me now!' Fiscal Graham replied 'O, you need not be alarmed, you have been often there before.'[44] This report highlighted how procurators and the media could seek to legitimise the punishment handed out by referring to, and recording, past indiscretions and the criminal history of the accused – and also how cruel the court's officers could be in their attempts to make light of what were traumatic circumstances for the person convicted. Indeed, the periodicals had a particular fascination with highlighting the anguished response of those being sent to bridewell. In 1829, the *Police Reports* covered the case

---

[41] Joseph Gurney, for instance, claimed that prisoners in the Aberdeen, Glasgow and Edinburgh bridewells were well paid for their labour, received religious instruction and lived in comfortable surroundings. Gurney, *Notes on a Visit Made to Some Prisons*, pp. 46. See also James Neild, *State of the Prisons in England, Scotland and Wales* (London, 1812), passim. These descriptions stood in stark contrast to the view of Edinburgh's old tolbooth expressed by Advocate and Edinburgh Police Commissioner, Henry Cockburn, who described it as: 'A most atrocious gaol it was, the very breadth of which almost struck down any stranger who entered its dismal door; and as ill placed as possible, without one inch of ground beyond in black and horrid walls. And these walls were very small; the entire hole being filled with little dark cells; heavy manacles of security; airless, waterless, drainless; a living grave. One week of that dirty, fetid, cruel torture-house was a severer punishment than a year of our worst modern prison – more dreadful in it sufferings, more certain in its corruption, overwhelming the innocent with a more tremendous sense of despair, provoking the guilty to more audacious defiance.' Henry Cockburn, *Memorials of His Time* (Edinburgh, 1909), p. 229.

[42] Ord, 'The Story of the Burgh of Calton'.

[43] *Police Reports*, 27 July 1829, p. 32.

[44] *Police Reports*, 10 July 1829, p. 21.

of John Simpson and Betsy Taylor, 'charged with being infamous characters, common thieves and being drunk and disorderly on public streets'. On being sentenced to 60 days' confinement, Betsy was reported to have 'screamed wildly when sentence was given'.[45] In recording the pained response of the convicted, such reports served a judicial and civic function: they in all likelihood functioned as a warning to readers about the consequences of conviction, while reassuring the 'respectable' members of the community that magistrates could be relied upon to see that justice would be done. Moreover, they also provide an insight into why bailies so valued the discretionary powers they had at their disposal: they allowed them to hand out stiff punishments for fairly minor public order offences against people whom they believed to be morally suspect.

Whipping rarely featured as a form of punishment in the early nineteenth century. Police court powers in this area varied from burgh to burgh and were largely governed by local police acts, but most did not make any specific provision for this form of chastisement. Whereas corporal punishment had been a popular form of discipline in eighteenth-century Scotland, changing sensibilities brought with them a growing revulsion towards public displays of violent punishment. It is also likely, as Robert B. Shoemaker has argued for eighteenth-century London, that changing concepts of public space contributed to growing opposition to displays of visible, exemplary punishment that involved the participation of large crowds at market places.[46] Police legislation was designed to impose order and regulate public streets, ensuring that trade could flourish – the very priorities that civic-sanctioned exemplary punishment would have threatened. Indeed, as Volume 2 shows, magistrates clamped down on public behaviour that threatened not just urban order but the smooth running of commercial transactions. Therefore, on the few occasions when magistrates ordered young male offenders to be whipped in the first half of the century, chastisement was to take place in the police office, not in public (the power of the court to whip women, either publicly or privately, was abolished in Scotland in 1820).[47] Such instances, though, were extremely rare and seem to have fallen out of fashion by mid-century. Indeed, in 1850 Bailie Smith of Glasgow Central Police Court observed that 'he regretted that the Court had not the power of whipping, a species of punishment which was essential for their reformation'. He went on:

---

[45]   *Police Reports*, 1 August 1829, pp. 29–30.

[46]   Shoemaker, 'Streets of Shame?', p. 284. See also Robert B. Shoemaker, *The London Mob: Violence and Disorder in Eighteenth-Century London* (London, 2004), pp. 290–98.

[47]   (1 George IV, cap. 57). In 1829, for instance, the *Police Reports* published the case of Richard Trenor and John McMillan, two 'old offenders' who were convicted of stealing butcher meat. McMillan's parents were ordered to flog him. Trenor was sentenced to 60 days in bridewell with the periodical noting that he had been previously let off on the promise of amendment by the court. *Police Reports*, 27 July 1829, p. 31. The same edition of the journal recorded that two boys, also named McMillan, were ordered to be chastised by their parents in the police office after being found guilty of stealing glasses.

The Police Court of Edinburgh had that power, – it was the law of England, – and while the juveniles took imprisonment lightly, they were terrified at the idea of corporal punishment; and if their parents did not flog them for their offences, the magistrates should have the power to do so.[48]

In the second half of the century, national legislation sought to clarify the punitive role of police courts and establish greater uniformity in practice by giving magistrates greater statutory powers and guidelines for corporal punishment. The 1851 Prisons (Scotland) Act allowed magistrates to punish by private whipping boys under the age of 14 who were convicted of a crime or offence punishable by imprisonment or fine. The 1862 Whipping Act, meanwhile, made it clear that whipping was a suitable punishment only for boys, not men: no person over 16 years of age could be whipped for crimes committed against the person or property, only for treason.[49] The use of this form of corporal punishment signified that those in governing and judicial circles were becoming uneasy with locking up those who were deemed to be worthy of protection with hardened adult offenders, but the numbers flogged remained small. As David J.V. Jones has pointed out, whipping tended to fall in and out of favour in judicial circles, being used most often during heightened concern with youth crime in the 1860s and the late nineteenth century.[50] In 1890, the Glasgow police records show that corporal punishment was administered to just 22 boys.[51] Early concerns with juvenile imprisonment were primarily tackled not by whipping, but by the development of reformatory organisations which were seen to offer opportunities for educational improvement that bridewells could not.

Such new initiatives did little to alter the hierarchy in police court sentencing. Imprisonment continued to be an unpopular form of punishment among magistrates, accounting for just 3.5 per cent of punishments handed down in the Glasgow Police Court in 1890 (see Table 7.4). Indeed, the chances of an offender convicted in the police courts being imprisoned declined significantly following the ruling that offenders convicted on three occasions were to be remitted for trial in a higher court (where the chances of imprisonment were much higher).[52] Admonition, on the other hand, remained a common form of judicial

---

[48]   *Glasgow Herald*, 4 January 1850.

[49]   'The Cadogan Report, 1938 (Report of the Departmental Committee on Corporal Punishment, HMSO, Cmd. 5684)', *World Corporal Punishment Research*, 2009, http://www.corpun.com/ukjur4.htm.

[50]   Jones, *Crime in Nineteenth-Century Wales*, p. 234.

[51]   Mitchell Library (ML): *City of Glasgow Police Criminal Returns for the Year Ending 31st December 1890* (Glasgow, 1891), p. 13.

[52]   In giving evidence to the 1826 Inquiry into Scotland's prisons, Adam Duff, Sheriff-Depute of the County of Midlothian, alluded to the fact that this provision, which had recently been introduced in a local police bill, would help to keep separate hardened offenders from less serious ones, as the former were more likely to be sent to gaol than bridewell if convicted in a higher court. 'Report from the Select Committees on the State of Prisons in Scotland', p. 14.

Table 7.4   Glasgow Police Court Sentences, 1890[†]

	Crimes	Offences	Contraventions	Total No.	Total % of Sentences	Total % of Sentences Exc Admonitions
Admonished	654	6,441	13,733	20,828	32	Not Applicable
Fined	249	26,488	1,815	28,332	44	65
Whipped	22	0	0	22	0.5	0.5
Prison	949	1,178	10	2,137	3.5	5
Bail Forfeited	44	12,207	715	12,966	20	29.5

† ML, *City of Glasgow Police Criminal Returns for the Year Ending 31st December 1890*, pp. 12–17.

censure, although as a percentage of the overall total of punishments it fell to just under one third in that year. Fining remained the most frequently used penalty. While 44 per cent of offenders convicted in the Glasgow Police Court were fined, a further 20 per cent had their bail forfeited for failing to turn up in court. By 1890, just under two thirds of those convicted in the Glasgow Police Court had their case determined by financial penalty, which represented 95 per cent of convictions for crimes, offences or contraventions deemed serious enough to warrant more than admonition.

As Table 7.5 shows, the sums levied in Glasgow's police court in fines and forfeited pledges rose by 300 per cent between 1860 and 1890 at a time when the city's population increased by 43 per cent. This was, to some extent, indicative of the changing business of the court and magistrates' desire to clampdown on public

Table 7.5   Fines Levied, and Forfeited Pledges, in Glasgow Police Court for Crimes, Offences and Contraventions, 1860 to 1890[†]

Year	Convicted	Fined	Forfeited	Percentage of those Convicted who were Fined or who Forfeited Pledges	Total Raised* Pounds
1860	12,453 Male: 10,093 Female: 2,360	4,721 Male: 3,249 Female: 1,472	6,717 Male: 6,206 Female: 511	91.8	4,325
1871	23,734 Male: 17,276 Female: 6,458	11,073 Male: 6,717 Female: 4,356	9,716 Male: 8,799 Female: 917	87.5	10,507
1880	37,013 Male: 23,508 Female: 13,505	21,635 Male: 12,969 Female: 8,666	8,486 Male: 7,325 Female: 1,161	81	10,160
1890	46,314 Male: 30,141 Female: 16,173	26,488 Male: 15,885 Female: 10,603	12,207 Male: 10,292 Female: 1,915	83.5	12,537

[†] ML: *The Number of Persons taken into Custody by the City of Glasgow Police and the Results for the Year Ending 29th September 1860* (Glasgow, 1861), pp. 6–7 & 18; ML: *City of Glasgow Police Criminal Returns for the Year Ending 31st December 1871* (Glasgow, 1872), pp. 16–17 & 29; ML: *City of Glasgow Police Criminal Returns for the Year Ending 31st December 1880* (Glasgow, 1881), pp. 14–15; and ML, *City of Glasgow Police: Criminal Returns for the Year Ending 31st December 1890*, pp. 14–15 & 26.

Table 7.6   Number of Fines for Crimes, Offences and Contraventions, Edinburgh and Glasgow, 1852 to 1890[†]

Fined	Edinburgh: 1852	Edinburgh: 1859	Glasgow: 1860	Edinburgh: 1868	Glasgow: 1871	Edinburgh: 1880	Glasgow: 1880	Glasgow: 1890
Crimes	629 Men Convicted (0 Fined)	292 Men Convicted (0 Fined)	708 Men Convicted (24 Fined or 3%)	421 Men Convicted (0 Fined)	1469 Men Convicted (155 Fined or 11%)	381 Men Convicted (0 Fined)	1843 Men Convicted (210 Fined or 11%)	1527 Men Convicted (213 Fined or 14%)
	400 Wmn Convicted (0 Fined)	185 Wmn Convicted (0 Fined)	728 Wmn Convicted (1 Fined or 1%)	218 Wmn Convicted (0 Fined)	951 Wmn Convicted (22 Fined or 2%)	171 Wmn Convicted (0 Fined)	748 Wmn Convicted (32 Fined or 4%)	550 Wmn Convicted (36 Fined or 6%)
Offences and Contraventions	5133 Men Convicted (2655 Fined or 52%)	4808 Men Convicted (2514 Fined or 52%)	15744 Men Convicted (5787 Fined or 37%)	6146 Men Convicted (4260 Fined or 69%)	24515 Men Convicted (10604 Fined or 43%)	4573 Men Convicted* (3802 Fined or 83%)	28293 Men Convicted (15198 Fined or 54%)	33486 Men Convicted (17244 Fined or 51%)
	4518 Wmn Convicted (1709 Fined or 38%)	4381 Wmn Convicted (1761 Fined or 40%)	3276 Wmn Convicted (2102 Fined or 64%)	4767 Wmn Convicted (2543 Fined or 53%)	9896 Wmn Convicted (6535 Fined or 66%)	3759 Wmn Convicted* (2242 Fined or 60%)	14945 Wmn Convicted (9283 Fined or 62%)	17101 Wmn Convicted (11059 Fined or 67%)

* Offences only. Contraventions not listed

Please note, a number of convicted offenders had their sentences delayed or forfeited their bail pledges which explains the disparity between convictions and punishments recorded in Tables in 7.6, 7.13 and 7.14.

[†] ML: *The Number of Persons taken into Custody by the City of Glasgow Police and the Results for the Year Ending 29th September 1860* (Glasgow, 1861), pp. 6–7 & 18; ML: *City of Glasgow Police Criminal Returns for the Year Ending 31st December 1871* (Glasgow, 1872), pp. 16–17 & 29; ML: *City of Glasgow Police Criminal Returns for the Year Ending 31st December 1880* (Glasgow, 1881), pp. 14–15; and ML, *City of Glasgow Police: Criminal Returns for the Year Ending 31st December 1890*, pp. 14–15 & 26; Edinburgh Central Library (ECL): *Return of Crimes, Offences and Contraventions, and of Drunkenness, within the Bounds of Edinburgh Police, Prepared by the Superintendent for the Commissioners of Police* (Edinburgh 1855), passim; ECL: *Report and Returns as to Crimes, Offences, and Contraventions, and to Cases of Drunkenness, within the Police Bounds of the City of Edinburgh, during the Last Six Years, Prepared for the Magistrates and Council, by Thomas Linton, Superintendent of Police* (Edinburgh, 1860), pp. 18 & 27; ECL: *Report and Returns as to Crimes, Offences, and Contraventions within the Limits of the Police of the City of Edinburgh, Prepared for the Magistrates and Council by Thomas Linton, Superintendent of Police, 1868* (Edinburgh, 1869), pp. 18 & 33; ECL: *Return of Crimes and Offences Reported, Persons Apprehended and Cited, and Miscellaneous Returns Connected with the Police, for the Year Ending 31st December 1880* (Edinburgh, 1881), Tables 2 & 3.

drunkenness, which constituted a significant proportion of revenue raised by fines. As Table 7.6 indicates, fines were much more likely to be imposed for public order offences than for crimes. Whereas prior to the 1870s, police desk sergeants set free those who had been apprehended for public drunkenness without bringing them before the court, in the late nineteenth century such people were being fined or were being asked to pledge bail money that would, in all likelihood, be forfeited.

In exacting fines from those convicted, it seems that raising revenue was as, if not more, important to magistrates as moral chastisement. The financial implications of bad behaviour did not go unnoticed by the convicted. In 1829, Benjamin Dalrymple, baker, was fined £2, 2s. for disorderly conduct in the Glasgow court. As he was led away from the bar, Dalrymple sarcastically said that he thought he would be pardoned this time 'as the office had already got upwards of £50 of his money'. Indeed, Brownlie reported that Dalrymple 'was a character long known by various Police Courts'.[53] When the Clerk of the Edinburgh Police Court, Mr James Morham, asked to have his salary raised from £200 to £300 in 1865, he added that his proposition was that £50 was to be charged against police revenues and the other from fines imposed under the Forbes Mackenzie Act. This was approved.[54] Magistrates' willingness to use police courts as a means of raising revenue to pay for court personnel and 'services' built upon practices that had been pioneered earlier in the church courts. The kirk sessions' system of levying fines as well as public punishment from those deemed guilty of moral misdemeanours to support the poor had been banned by the General Assembly of 1837, with many fearing that it edged close to Catholic practice.[55]

While civic leaders and penal reformers bemoaned the cost of maintaining prisoners in gaols,[56] the labour from inmates in bridewell helped to raise much-needed funds for prison costs and meet the needs of local economies.[57] In giving evidence to the 1826 Prison Inquiry, Sheriff Duff claimed that the commissioners of the bridewell in Glasgow – who included magistrates – were able to take advantage of the fact that the city had a strong manufacturing base and workforce. Indeed, he even claimed that 'almost all of those in prison [bridewell] have some knowledge of the work before they are imprisoned' – which, as is explored below, needs to be borne in mind when considering

---

[53] *Police Reports*, 6 July 1829, p. 5.

[54] *Caledonian Mercury*, 16 August 1865.

[55] G.D. Henderson, *The Scottish Ruling Elder* (London, 1935), p. 243.

[56] This was a common gripe in the first half of the nineteenth century. 'The Report of the Select Committee appointed to Inquire into the State of Prisons in Scotland', concluded that many burghs had insufficient funds to pay for suitable prisoner accommodation or aliment.

[57] For the relationship between punishment and the economy, see G. Rusche and O. Kirchheimer, *Punishment and Social Structure* (New York, 1939); D. Melossi and M. Pavarini, *The Prison and the Factory: Origins of the Penitentiary System* (London, 1981); and M.R. Weisser, *Crime and Punishment in Early Modern Europe* (London, 1981).

magisterial sentencing policy.[58] As Cameron has pointed out, there was great variation in work experience throughout the country: not everyone who was committed to bridewell was put to labour due to over-crowding, lack of equipment and insufficient skills.[59] However, many inmates in the Glasgow bridewell were employed in spinning yarn, weaving, tambouring, cutting corks, clipping muslin and picking oakum.[60] In the Edinburgh bridewell, a treadmill and machinery for making corks was introduced in the early 1820s.[61] Magistrates in Edinburgh even joked about the labour expected in bridewell as they imprisoned offenders. In 1832, for instance, John Cameron, a magician, was sentenced to time for breaking a pane of glass in a 'gentleman's area' on George Street, Edinburgh. The magistrate joked: 'Can you do any thing on the treadmill? It is very good exercise.'[62] That bridewells were closely linked to the local economy was illustrated in *The Seventh Report of the Committee of the Society for the Improvement of Prison Discipline, and for the Reformation of Juvenile Offenders* in 1827. After noting that the total cost to the public of running the bridewell for the County of Lanark and the City of Glasgow for the year 1825–1826 was £934 after income and expenditure had been accounted for, the bridewell's annual report noted that 'the expense to the public this year has been unavoidably increased [it had been £593 the previous year], in consequence of the great difficulty in procuring profitable employment, and the unprecedented low prices received for labour'.[63] It was a revealing insight that raised the possibility that local demand for the products produced by bridewells might affect which of the convicted individuals magistrates would send to bridewells.

As in Glasgow, inmates in Edinburgh were entitled to a share of the earnings procured from bridewell labour after maintenance costs had been accounted for.[64] According to evidence given by Sheriff Duff to the 1826 Prison Inquiry, prisoners in the Edinburgh bridewell received one third of the profit to which their labour had contributed on liberation, one third 6 months after liberation, and another third after 12 months if they had 'behaved well during that time'.

---

[58] 'Report from the Select Committees on the State of Prisons in Scotland', p. 20.

[59] Cameron, *Prisons and Punishment in Scotland*, pp. 58–9.

[60] Professor Garscombe, *The Contrast: or Scotland as it was in the Year 1745, and Scotland in 1819* (London, 1825), p. 299. For more see ibid., p. 58.

[61] 'Report from the Select Committees on the State of Prisons in Scotland', p. 13.

[62] *Caledonian Mercury*, 20 August 1832.

[63] *The Seventh Report of the Committee of the Society for the Improvement of Prison Discipline, and for the Reformation of Juvenile Offenders* (London, 1827), p. 222.

[64] Sheriff Duff believed that in Glasgow prisoners received the whole of the profit of their labour after deductions for maintenance and expenses and claimed the total revenue raised was substantial. When asked if the income paid for prisoners' aliment, he replied: 'In the Glasgow bridewell, they do more than pay the expense of the aliment. They [profits from bridewell labour] are also considerable in Edinburgh, but they [the prisoners] go there to help to defray the expense of the establishment.' 'Report from the Select Committees on the State of Prisons in Scotland', p. 20. A similar point was made in ibid., p. 218.

He also, though, pointed out that 'these last two were seldom applied for', thereby ensuring that the bulk of revenue could be defrayed for the upkeep of the bridewell or wider civic purposes.[65] As such, the income that convict labour generated in the bridewell was a subject closely monitored. In May 1823, *The Scotsman* reported on a police meeting in the city in which the reported business of the court from February to April included 142 people sent to the lock-up house, and 329 to bridewell:[66]

> The Commissioners, we understand, are to institute an inquiry whether the inhabitants, who pay for supporting those who are sent from the Police Court to Bridewell, have allowed them a rateable share of the proceeds of the labour of the criminals. This is a matter of some importance; but as the Magistrates are now acting (cordially it is hoped) along with the Commissioners of Police, we have no doubt that the matter will be settled amicably.[67]

The *First Report of the General Board of Directors of Prisons in Scotland* in 1840 concluded favourably on the state of bridewell compared to ordinary prisons, implying that this arose in part because they were organised for profit:

> Bridewells were in a different situation from the common prisons. The sentence of imprisonment in them carried along with it a power to treat the prisoner according to the rules of the establishment which imply labour. From this cause, probably, as well as from the management of such prisons being more carefully and recently regulated, the discipline and good effects of the bridewells have been in general comparably superior to those of the other prisons.[68]

Fiscal considerations, it seemed, were never far away from magistrates' thoughts when handing down sentences.

It has also been widely recognised that gender was an important variable in determining judicial judgements on punishment.[69] As Garland has pointed out, female offenders 'are dealt with in gender-specific ways which reflect traditional conceptions of the female role and its pathologies',[70] while ideals of, and attitudes towards,

---

[65] 'Report from the Select Committees on the State of Prisons in Scotland', p. 20.

[66] *The Scotsman*, 28 May 1823.

[67] Ibid.

[68] *First Report of the General Board of Directors of Prisons in Scotland* (London, 1840), p. 11.

[69] For an invaluable collection on this, see Margaret L. Arnot and Cornelie Usborne (eds), *Gender and Crime in Modern Europe* (London, 1999). See also J.M. Beattie, 'The Criminality of Women in Eighteenth-Century England', *Journal of Social History*, 8/4 (1975): pp. 80–116; J.M. Beattie, *Crime and the Courts in England, 1660–1800* (Oxford, 1986); and Shani D'Cruze and Louise A. Jackson, *Women, Crime and Justice in England since 1660* (Basingstoke, 2009), pp. 122–42.

[70] Garland, *Punishment and Modern Society*, p. 202.

masculinity have played a key role in influencing changing prosecution and sentencing patterns.[71] However, while acknowledging that gender mattered, the precise ways in which it impacted on punishment have been contested in recent years. A plethora of studies of the eighteenth- and nineteenth-century courts in England have argued that justices treated female offenders more harshly than male offenders on account of the fact that their law breaking offended middle-class expectations of femininity.[72] Others, however, paint a more varied and nuanced picture of gendered sentencing patterns that gives greater attention to different judicial outcomes for specific crimes and offences,[73] with some scholars contending that far from female offenders being handed down harsher sentences than men, women actually received more lenient penalties for certain offences, especially property crimes.[74] The investigation by Barry S. Godfrey, Stephen Farrall and Susanne Karstedt into assault in late Victorian and Edwardian England, for instance, found that 'local magistrates directed their

---

[71]　See, for instance, Martin J. Wiener, 'The Victorian Criminalization of Men', in Pieter Spierenburg (ed.), *Men and Violence: Gender, Honor and Rituals in Modern Europe and America* (Columbus, 1998), pp. 179–231; and Wiener, *Men of Blood*.

[72]　Lucia Zedner, *Women, Crime and Custody in Victorian England* (Oxford, 1991); D'Cruze, *Crimes of Outrage*; and Shani D'Cruze, 'Sex, Violence and Local Courts: Working-Class Respectability in a Mid-Nineteenth-Century Lancashire town', *British Journal of Criminology*, 39/1 (1999), pp. 39–55. Modern studies include Frances Heidensohn, 'Women and the Penal System', in Allison Morris and Loraine Gelsthorpe (eds), *Women and Crime: Papers Presented to the Cropwood Round Table Conference* (Cambridge, 1981), pp. 125–39; Frances Heidensohn, 'Feminist Perspectives and their Impact on Criminology and Criminal Justice in Britain', in N. H. Rafter and F. Heidensohn (eds), *International Feminist Perspectives in Criminology* (Buckingham, 1995), pp. 63–85.

[73]　Peter King has suggested that women may have been subject to harsher treatment than men in some instances, but not all. In Cornwall between 1737 and 1821, he argues, 'women [convicted of assault] were nearly twice as likely to be given direct prison sentences as men'. However, he identifies the courts' comparatively lenient treatment of female offenders for other crimes and 'the almost complete abandonment of the public punishment of women' in the early nineteenth century. Peter King, *Crime and the Law in England, 1750–1840: Remaking Justice from the Margins* (Cambridge, 2006), pp. 6 & 255–78. See also Peter King, *Crime, Justice and Discretion*, pp. 259–96. Drew D. Gray found, in his study of the summary courts in eighteenth-century London, that women convicted of assault were also likely to be imprisoned or have their cases remitted to a higher court. Drew D. Gray, *Crime Prosecution and Social Relations: The Summary Courts of the City of London in the Late Eighteenth Century* (Basingstoke, 2009), pp. 108–9. For an overview of female experience, see Mary Bosworth, 'Confining Femininity: A History of Gender, Power and Imprisonment', *Theoretical Criminology*, 4/3 (2000): pp. 265–84.

[74]　See, for instance, Peter King, 'Gender, Crime and Justice in Late Eighteenth and Early Nineteenth-Century England', in Arnot and Usborne (eds), *Gender and Crime in Modern Europe*, pp. 44–74; Beattie, *Crime and the Courts in England*; Robert B. Shoemaker, *Prosecution and Punishment: Petty Crime and the Law in London and Rural Middlesex, c.1660–1725* (Cambridge, 1991); and J.I. Kermode and Garthine Walker (eds), *Women, Crime and the Courts in Early Modern England* (London, 1994).

efforts of "civilising" lower-class communities at "dangerous masculinities", and deemed assault committed by women as less important in this task'.[75] Similarly, Andrew Davies, in his study of gang culture in late Victorian Manchester, concluded that women convicted of gang-related violence received lighter sentences than men.[76] This pattern reflected, in many ways, the courts' growing preoccupation with curbing the rougher elements of working-class masculinity and punishing male violence in late Victorian England.[77] This has been accredited in Malcolm Feeley and Deborah Little's study with partly contributing to the decline in female criminal prosecutions in the second half of the nineteenth century.[78]

Unfortunately, it is extremely difficult to ascertain with any degree of certainty the impact of gender bias on sentencing patterns for the Scottish police courts. While statistics on the punishment administered by magistrates is available on an annual basis from mid-century, the absence of court records over the same period makes it impossible to ascertain how far 'contextual' factors influenced sentencing patterns. As a number of criminologists have pointed out for modern studies, while bland statistics might portray the image of gender bias in sentencing, they can also disguise the fact that gendered differences might be indicative of the strength of evidence, the levels of violence administered, previous convictions, and so on. Indeed, Susanne Karstedt and others have argued that 'gender-related' associations rather than 'gender bias' explain gendered sentencing patterns; that is, women received more lenient sentences because they were less likely to use excessive violence, less likely to have offended in the past, and more likely to have family commitments than male offenders.[79] Moreover, the importance to judicial outcomes of an offender's

---

[75] Godfrey, Farrall and Karstedt, 'Explaining Gendered Sentencing Patterns for Violent Men and Women in the Late Victorian and Edwardian Period', p. 45. They show that once contextual factors that influenced judicial decision-making are accounted for (such as the severity of the offence, strength of evidence) men were more likely to receive a harsher punishment than women.

[76] Andrew Davies, 'Youth Gangs, Masculinity and Violence in Late Victorian Manchester and Salford', *Journal of Social History*, 32/2 (1998): pp. 349–69; and Andrew Davies, '"These Viragoes are No Less Cruel than the Lads": Young Women, Gangs and Violence in Late Victorian Manchester and Salford', *British Journal of Criminology*, 39/1 (1999): pp. 72–89.

[77] For more on this, see Wiener, *Men of Blood*; and McLaren, *The Trials of Masculinity*.

[78] Malcolm Feeley and Deborah Little, 'The Vanishing Female: The Decline of Women in the Criminal Process, 1687–1912', *Law and Society Review*, 25/4 (1991): pp. 719–57. However, Peter King has challenged this argument, arguing that spatial variations and geography complicate the pattern of female crime which he claims exhibited much continuity over the eighteenth and nineteenth centuries. King, *Crime and the Law in England*, passim.

[79] See, for instance, Susanne Karstedt, 'Emancipation, Crime, and Problem Behaviour of Women: A Perspective from Germany', *Gender Issues*, 18/3 (2000): pp. 21–58; and D. Farrington and A. Morris, 'Sex, Sentencing and Reconviction', *British Journal of Criminology*, 23/3 (1983): pp. 229–48.

performance and appearance in court and, in particular, the level of deference they afforded to the sitting justice has led Kathleen Daly to suggest that conclusions about the relationship between sentencing and gender can only be satisfactorily achieved through courtroom observation.[80] Nonetheless, sentencing statistics can still prove useful, especially when used with newspaper trial reports which, for all their weaknesses, provide illuminating insights about how magistrates perceived female and male offenders. Moreover, the punishments which magistrates administered can, when examined in alliance with media reports, reveal much about the importance of how magistrates saw their role in the wider community, and how this affected the decisions they made. Sentencing patterns in the Glasgow and Edinburgh police courts reveal notable gender variations in the way in which offenders were dealt with by magistrates – albeit with significant variations between the types of punishments, and the crimes, offences and contraventions to which they related.

Although it has been recognised that women who did not conform to the Victorian ideal of womanhood could be harshly treated by the courts, those scholars who argue that justices in England took a tougher stance against male violence in the late Victorian period point to the harsher sentences that men received relative to women for similar offences.[81] On first observation, women in Scottish police courts appear to have been treated more leniently, too. As Tables 7.7 and 7.8 show, women convicted of assault in the Glasgow Police Court were more likely to be admonished and more likely to be fined than men. They were also most likely to be admonished for drunk and disorderly conduct.[82] The 1880 Edinburgh police returns paint a similar picture.[83] Moreover, they show that the women were

---

[80] Kathleen Daly, *Gender, Crime and Punishment* (New Haven, 2004). Some studies have attempted to account for wider 'contextual' factors, but, as indicated in the main text, this is not possible for the Scottish police courts given the huge gaps that exist in police court records and the selective and biased nature of trial reporting. See, for instance, Godfrey, Farrall and Karstedt, 'Explaining Gendered Sentencing Patterns for Violent Men and Women in the Late Victorian and Edwardian Period', pp. 696–720.

[81] See, for instance, Wiener, 'The Victorian Criminalization of Men', pp. 179–231; Wiener, *Men of Blood*; and Godfrey, Farrall and Karstedt, 'Explaining Gendered Sentencing Patterns for Violent Men and Women in the Late Victorian and Edwardian Period', pp. 696–720.

[82] Of the 1,272 people admonished for being drunk and incapable in the Glasgow Police Court in 1880, 929 were women, despite the fact that more than twice as many men had been apprehended and convicted for this offence. ML, *City of Glasgow Police Criminal Returns for the Year Ending 31st December 1880*, p. 15.

[83] Of the 160 women apprehended for simple assault in Edinburgh during 1880, 150 were convicted (94 per cent). Only 4 per cent of those convictions were admonished, but 17 per cent were cautioned. Almost half were fined (49 per cent) and 29 per cent were imprisoned. By comparison, less than 1 per cent of men were admonished and only 5 per cent of men were put under caution. The majority of men (63 per cent) were fined. ECL, *Return of Crimes and Offences Reported, Persons Apprehended and Cited, and Miscellaneous Returns Connected with the Police, for the Year Ending 31st December 1880*, Table 2.

Table 7.7   People Convicted for Simple Assault in Glasgow Police Court who were Admonished, 1860 to 1890[†]

	1860	1871	1880*	1890
Population	395,303	477,732	511,415	565,839
Male	55 out of 1,331 (4%)	856 out of 11,175 (8%)	917 out of 12,899 (7%)	1,397 out of 14,959 (9%)
Female	34 out of 423 (8%)	701 out of 4,212 (16.5%)	1,023 out of 7,127 (14%)	985 out of 7,512 (13%)

*   Also included eight boys who were whipped.

Note for Tables 7.7 to 7.10: The 1860 and 1871 returns record simple assault on its own. In 1880 and 1890, it was recorded alongside disorderly conduct (although separate from drunk and incapable).

†   ML, *The Number of Persons taken into Custody by the City of Glasgow Police and the Results for the Year Ending 29th September 1860*, pp. 6–7; ML, *City of Glasgow Police Criminal Returns for the Year Ending 31st December 1871*, pp. 16–17; ML, *City of Glasgow Police Criminal Returns for the Year Ending 31st December 1880*, pp. 14–15; and ML, *City of Glasgow Police Criminal Returns for the Year Ending 31st December 1890*, pp. 14–15.

Table 7.8   People Convicted for Simple Assault in Glasgow Police Court who were Fined, 1860 to 1890

	1860	1871	1880*	1890
Population	395,303	477,732	511,415	565,839
Male	837 out of 1,331 (63%)	5,764 out of 11,175 (52%)	7,442 out of 12,899 (58%)	8,712 out of 14,959 (58%)
Female	317 out of 423 (75%)	2,690 out of 4,212 (64%)	4,271 out of 7,127 (60%)	5,022 out of 7,512 (67%)

Note: The police records do not record the sums raised through fining or forfeited bail pledges according to gender or offence.

more likely to receive a lesser fine than men. Eighty-one per cent were fined amounts under 20s., compared with 43 per cent of men who paid fines. These figures may have reflected their lesser ability to pay larger sums, or the severity with which their violence was perceived (see Table 7.9).

However, while there were aspects of penal policy that suggest that women received milder punishment than men, any claim to judicial leniency for women needs to be qualified. Although a greater percentage of women were fined for

Table 7.9		Edinburgh, Women's Fines and Imprisonment for Simple Assault, 1880†

FINES	Number of women (% of total fined or imprisoned respectively)	
Under 5s.	1	(1%)
From 5s. to 10s.	13	(18%)
From 10s. to 20s.	44	(61%)
From 20s. to 40s.	13	(14%)
From 40s. to £5	1	(1%)
£5 and above	0	
Total number of women fined	72	(63% of all women fined or imprisoned)
IMPRISONMENT		
Under 3 days	0	
From 3 to 10 days	7	(16%)
From 10 to 20 days	19	(44%)
From 20 to 30 days	8	(19%)
From 30 to 60 days	7	(16%)
60 days	2	(5%)
Total number of women imprisoned	43	(37% of all women fined or imprisoned)

† ECL, *Return of Crimes and Offences Reported, Persons Apprehended and Cited, and Miscellaneous Returns Connected with the Police, for the Year Ending 31st December 1880*, Table 6.

simple assault than men, this seems to have been because they were more likely than men to turn up in court to be fined in the first place. As Table 7.10 reveals, men were much more likely than women in Glasgow to forfeit their pledges, by way of penalty, by not appearing before the judicial bench.[84] When the disproportionate number of men to women who did this is added to the numbers fined, then men were more likely to have their cases settled by financial penalty than women. In 1871, for instance, 9,829 of 11,175 men who were convicted of simple assault (88 per cent) were either fined or forfeited their pledge compared with 3,355 of 4,212 of women (80 per cent). Magistrates' willingness to accept bail pledges was to some degree shaped by pragmatic necessity: it is inconceivable that a small number of lay magistrates could have dealt with such a huge volume of courtroom hearings or trials. Nonetheless, the readiness with which they allowed men charged with violence to escape coming before the bench for formal judicial censure makes questionable the notion that the courts were overly preoccupied with reforming the rougher features of working-class masculinity.

Table 7.10   People Convicted of Simple Assault in Glasgow Police Court who Forfeited Bail, 1860 to 1890

	1860	**1871**	**1880**	**1890**
Population	395,303	477,732	511,415	565,839
Male	375 out of 1,331 (28%)	4,065 out of 11,175 (36%)	3,444 out of 12,899 (27%)	4,343 out of 14,959 (30%)
Female	59 out of 423 (14%)	665 out of 4,212 (15.5%)	680 out of 7,127 (10%)	1,026 out of 7,512 (14%)

Perhaps more significantly, women convicted of simple assault were more likely to be imprisoned than men. As Table 7.11 shows, it was extremely rare for men convicted of this offence in the Glasgow Police Court in the late nineteenth century to be imprisoned. In 1880 and 1890, twice as many women relative to the number convicted were imprisoned for simple assault than men. In Edinburgh too, in 1880,

---

[84]   In 1860, for instance, more than half of the men convicted for offences in the Glasgow Police Court had their pledge – most commonly given for petty thefts, breach of the peace and assaults in lieu of court appearance – forfeited for not showing up in court. For women, it was less than one third. By the end of the century, the disparity was even greater. Whereas one third of men forfeited their bail money by way of penalty, the corresponding figure for women was just one in 10. It seems likely that women were less able to produce the funds required to post bail or pledges in the first place and thus, were liable to other kinds of punishments even for the same offences. See note (†) in Table 7.7 for references.

Table 7.11   People Convicted of Simple Assault in Glasgow Police Court who
were Imprisoned, 1871 to 1890†

	1860	1871	1880	1890
Population	395,303	477,732	511,415	565,839
Male	64 out of 1,331 (5%)	490 out of 11,175 (4%)	1,085 out of 12,899 (8%)	507 out of 14,959 (3%)
Female	13 out of 423 (3%)	156 out of 4,212 (4%)	1,153 out of 7,127 (16%)	479 out of 7,512 (6%)

Note: The police records do not record the amount of days women and men were imprisoned for assault or, indeed, for any other crime or offence.

† ML, *The Number of Persons taken into Custody by the City of Glasgow Police and the Results for the Year Ending 29th September 1860*, pp. 6–7; ML, *City of Glasgow Police Criminal Returns for the Year Ending 31st December 1871*, pp. 16–17; ML, *City of Glasgow Police Criminal Returns for the Year Ending 31st December 1880*, pp. 14–15; and ML, *City of Glasgow Police Criminal Returns for the Year Ending 31st December 1890*, pp. 14–15.

women were more likely to be imprisoned than men, albeit as a smaller proportion of the total (29 per cent of women convicted of simple assault on others, compared to 25 per cent of men).[85] These figures may have reflected an understanding that women's capacity to be punished in economic terms was less than that of men and, in reverse, that the absence of a male breadwinner from the home through imprisonment was a more serious economic impediment to a household than the loss of a female member. Yet the length of women's imprisonments were comparatively shorter than those of men, suggesting that their violence was perhaps not seen as equally dangerous to that of men. Sixty per cent of women who were imprisoned were held for periods of up to 20 days, whereas only 48 per cent of men were. It is unclear how strongly this data echoed social assumptions that female assaults and disorderly conduct were more dangerous and in need of penal correction than non-normative behaviour, or simply reflect men and women's different capacity to cover financial punishments. What is clear, though, is that historiographical assumptions about how the courts treated men and women need to recognise the complex array of social, moral and fiscal considerations of which concern with working-class young male violence was just one.

---

[85]   Of the 185 women apprehended and brought to court for assault, 53 were imprisoned. The corresponding figures for men were 735 and 180. ECL, *Return of Crimes and Offences Reported, Persons Apprehended and Cited, and Miscellaneous Returns Connected with the Police, for the Year Ending 31st December 1880*, Table 2.

Although records for the first half of the century do not record the specific offences for which offenders were imprisoned, it appears as though women were generally more likely to suffer this fate at the hands of magistrates than were men. A snapshot of a month of imprisonments at the Glasgow Police Court in 1829, as presented in the *Police Reports*, highlights the clear distinction between the sexes with regards to imprisonment in bridewell, and compared to gaol. In Table 7.12, women represented on average just under one quarter of the total population in gaol in any one week. However, within bridewell they dominated the population. Women represented on average 60 per cent of those imprisoned there. As Shani D'Cruze and Louise Jackson have pointed out, bridewells had always been concerned with disciplining women's sexuality, and lewd women were always vulnerable to be imprisoned in them.[86] Moreover, those with needlework skills are likely to have been in particular demand, for reasons outlined above.[87]

A similar pattern continued in the second half of the century. Table 7.13 demonstrates that between 1852 and 1890 women were more likely to be imprisoned for crimes, offences and contraventions, as well as imprisoned more often than any other form of punishment for these less serious offences, than men. The police court in Edinburgh imprisoned proportionately more of the female criminal offenders (74 per cent) than male (61 per cent), a pattern that is also observable in the Glasgow data where 54 per cent of men convicted of crimes were imprisoned and 67 per cent of the women in the sampled years between 1852 and 1890. For offences and contraventions, the disparity between male and female experiences of imprisonment was just as evident. From 1852 to 1871 (the 1880 data is not used here because the returns included only information on offences, not contraventions), just 9 per cent of men convicted in Edinburgh Police Court were imprisoned, but 25 per cent of the women. In Glasgow, this was paralleled: 3 per cent of men convicted were imprisoned and 4 per cent of women. Unlike the first half of the century, most of those imprisoned would have been housed in new purpose-built prisons rather than bridewells, with the latter either closed down following the birth of the new penitentiaries and other forms of bureaucratised disciplinary regimes or, in some cases, expanded to become the main local prison.[88] Of course, whether these returns represented a real difference in the treatment of male and female offenders is impossible

---

[86]   D'Cruze and Jackson, *Women, Crime and Justice in England since 1660*, p. 131.

[87]   The development of such skills for female prisoners was a particular concern of penal reformer Elizabeth Fry. Ibid., p. 133.

[88]   In Aberdeen, in 1842, the bridewell became the 'West Prison'. See Cameron, *Prisons and Punishment in Scotland*, p. 152. Joanna Innes claims that in England, 1865 was a watershed as gaols and bridewells were amalgamated to form local prisons, a development which marked the dissociation of bridewell project. Joanna Innes, 'Prisons for the Poor: English Bridewells, 1555–1800', in Francis Snyder and Douglas Hay (eds), *Labour, Law and Crime: An Historical Perspective* (London, 1987), p. 109.

Table 7.12   Showing Percentage of Men and Women under Restraint in Glasgow Gaol and Bridewell, July to September 1829[†]

	27–31 July	1–7 August	8–14 August	15–21 August	22–28 August	29–4 Sept
	Numbers Under Restraint (Men, Women)	Numbers Under Restraint (Men, Women)	Numbers Under Restraint (Men, Women)	Numbers Under Restraint (Men, Women)	Numbers Under Restraint (Men, Women)	Numbers Under Restraint (Men, Women)
In Bridewell	132, 185	139, 209	136, 185	148, 183	131, 174	110, 193
In Gaol	76, 20	81, 24	84, 24	84, 24	77, 24	74, 25
Total under restraint	413	453	429	439	406	302

[†] *Police Reports*, 1 August 1829, p. 34; 8 August 1829, p. 48; 15 August 1829, p. 54; 22 August 1829, p. 70; 29 August 1829, p. 74; and 5 September 1829, p. 96.

Table 7.13   Number of Imprisonments for Crimes, Offences and Contraventions, Edinburgh and Glasgow, 1852 to 1890[†]

Imprisoned	Edinburgh: 1852	Edinburgh: 1859	Glasgow: 1860	Edinburgh: 1868	Glasgow: 1871	Edinburgh: 1880	Glasgow: 1880	Glasgow: 1890
Crimes	629 Men Convicted (295 imprisoned or 47%)	292 Men Convicted (199 imprisoned or 68%)	708 Men Convicted (470 imprisoned or 66%)	421 Men Convicted (244 imprisoned or 58%)	1469 Men Convicted (824 imprisoned or 56%)	381 Men Convicted (277 imprisoned or 73%)	1843 Men Convicted (992 imprisoned or 54%)	1527 Men Convicted (623 imprisoned or 41%)
	400 Wmn Convicted (265 imprisoned or 66%)	185 Wmn Convicted (136 imprisoned or 73%)	728 Wmn Convicted (562 imprisoned or 77%)	218 Wmn Convicted (158 imprisoned or 72%)	951 Wmn Convicted (624 imprisoned or 66%)	171 Wmn Convicted (146 imprisoned or 85%)	748 Wmn Convicted (495 imprisoned or 66%)	550 Wmn Convicted (326 imprisoned or 59%)
Offences and Contraventions	5133 Men Convicted (364 imprisoned or 7%)	4808 Men Convicted (548 imprisoned or 11%)	15744 Men Convicted (182 imprisoned or 1%)	6146 Men Convicted (468 imprisoned or 8%)	24515 Men Convicted (717 imprisoned or 3%)	4573 Men Convicted* (1180 imprisoned or 26%)	28293 Men Convicted (1396 imprisoned or 5%)	33486 Men Convicted (659 imprisoned or 2%)
	4518 Wmn Convicted (518 imprisoned or 11%)	4381 Wmn Convicted (1323 imprisoned or 30%)	3276 Wmn Convicted (77 imprisoned or 2%)	4767 Wmn Convicted (1579 imprisoned or 33%)	9896 Wmn Convicted (287 imprisoned or 3%)	3759 Wmn Convicted* (1623 imprisoned or 43%)	14945 Wmn Convicted (1265 imprisoned or 8%)	17101 Wmn Convicted (529 imprisoned or 3%)

* Offences only, Contraventions not listed

Note: A number of convicted offenders had their sentences delayed or forfeited their bail pledges which explains the disparity between convictions and punishments recorded in Tables in 7.6, 7.13 and 7.14.

[†] ML: *The Number of Persons taken into Custody by the City of Glasgow Police and the Results for the Year Ending 29th September 1860* (Glasgow, 1861), pp. 6–7 & 18; ML: *City of Glasgow Police Criminal Returns for the Year Ending 31st December 1871* (Glasgow, 1872), pp. 16–17 & 29; ML: *City of Glasgow Police Criminal Returns for the Year Ending 31st December 1880* (Glasgow, 1881), pp. 14–15; and ML, *City of Glasgow Police: Criminal Returns for the Year Ending 31st December 1890*, pp. 14–15 & 26; Edinburgh Central Library (ECL): *Return of Crimes, Offences and Contraventions, and of Drunkenness, within the Bounds of Edinburgh Police. Prepared by the Superintendent for the Commissioners of Police* (Edinburgh 1855), passim; ECL: *Report and Returns as to Crimes, Offences, and Contraventions, and to Cases of Drunkenness, within the Police Bounds of the City of Edinburgh, during the Last Six Years. Prepared for the Magistrates and Council, by Thomas Linton, Superintendent of Police* (Edinburgh, 1860), pp. 18 & 27; ECL: *Report and Returns as to Crimes, Offences, and Contraventions within the Limits of the Police of the City of Edinburgh. Prepared for the Magistrates and Council by Thomas Linton, Superintendent of Police, 1868* (Edinburgh, 1869), pp. 18 & 33; ECL: *Return of Crimes and Offences Reported. Persons Apprehended and Cited, and Miscellaneous Returns Connected with the Police, for the Year Ending 31st December 1880* (Edinburgh, 1881), Tables 2 & 3.

to say. Statistical returns were influenced to a large degree by the ability of the people convicted to pay a fine, and women were often in a more financially vulnerable position than men. Indeed, Jones's study of the summary courts in nineteenth-century Wales has shown that about half of the inmates in the local gaols and correctional facilities were there because they were not able to pay the fines the courts had imposed.[89] In addition, magistrates throughout the century had always been more inclined to imprison those deemed to be prostitutes, and this policy appears to have escalated in the second half of the century. In his 1869 annual returns, Thomas Linton, Superintendent of the Edinburgh Police, attributed a short-term fall in the amount of revenue raised through police fines, from £5,806 in 1866 to £5,474 in 1868, to the fact that from July 1867 those classified as prostitutes were sentenced to summary imprisonment, whereas before that date most had been fined.[90] National and local police legislation in Glasgow in the second half of the nineteenth century also gave the police and the courts wider powers to remove those deemed to be prostitutes from streets and brothels and to incarcerate them in local gaols.

As Table 7.14 suggests, admonition was used much less in Edinburgh for crimes than in Glasgow. On average about 8 per cent of those convicted were admonished across the second half of the century in Edinburgh, whereas in Glasgow verbal censure was used more often, on average for 19 per cent of those convicted. While the overall proportion of men and women admonished in Edinburgh was relatively similar, in Glasgow the differences were more striking, with far fewer women admonished for crimes than men (in 1880 as many as 26 per cent of convicted male criminals were admonished compared to just nine per cent of women). Glasgow's figures may reflect gender assumptions that female criminality was far more shocking than that of men, assumptions that would render admonition an insufficient consequence.[91] However, there is a danger of overstating this. Not only does it not explain why these ideologies did not also apply in Edinburgh, it also belies the influence of youth crime which had a significant bearing on admonition figures recorded in the criminal returns. Glasgow's overall differential was, to a large extent, indicative of the gender breakdown of the crimes prosecuted. Admonitions for crimes were nearly always reserved for crimes against property committed without violence, and malicious crimes against property (classified as fire raising and malicious mischief). While women were not noticeably underrepresented for

---

89   Jones, *Crime in Nineteenth-Century Wales*, p. 234.

90   ECL, *Report and Returns as to Crimes, Offences, and Contraventions, within the Limits of the Police of the City of Edinburgh, Prepared for the Magistrates and Council, by Thomas Linton, Superintendent of Police, 1868*, p. 13.

91   See, for instance, Beattie, 'The Criminality of Women in Eighteenth-Century England'; Carolyn A. Conley, *The Unwritten Law: Criminal Justice in Victorian Kent* (Oxford, 1991); and Deirdre Palk, 'Private Crime in Public and Private Places: Pickpockets and Shoplifters in London, 1780–1823', in Tim Hitchcock and Heather Shore (eds), *The Streets of London: From the Great Fire to the Great Stink* (London, 2003), pp. 135–50.

Table 7.14   Number of Admonitions for Crimes, Offences and Contraventions, Edinburgh and Glasgow, 1852 to 1890[†]

Admonished	Edinburgh: 1852	Edinburgh: 1859	Glasgow: 1860	Edinburgh: 1868	Glasgow: 1871	Edinburgh: 1880	Glasgow: 1880	Glasgow: 1890
Crimes	629 Men Convicted (116 adm. 18%)	292 Men Convicted (12 adm. or 4%)	708 Men Convicted (67 adm. or 9%)	421 Men Convicted (39 adm. or 9%)	1469 Men Convicted (364 adm. or 25%)	381 Men Convicted (5 adm. or 1%)	1843 Men Convicted (488 adm. or 26%)	1527 Men Convicted (525 adm. or 34%)
	400 Wmn Convicted (88 adm. or 20%)	185 Wmn Convicted (8 adm. or 4%)	728 Wmn Convicted (47 adm. or 6%)	218 Wmn Convicted (12 adm. or 5%)	951 Wmn Convicted (209 adm. or 21%)	171 Wmn Convicted (1 adm. or 1%)	748 Wmn Convicted (68 adm. or 9%)	550 Wmn Convicted (129 adm. or 23%)
Offences and Contraventions	5133 Men Convicted (1675 adm. or 33%)	4808 Men Convicted (958 adm. or 20%)	15744 Men Convicted (1422 adm. or 9%)	6146 Men Convicted (964 adm. or 16%)	24515 Men Convicted (3213 adm. or 13%)	4573 Men Convicted* (164 adm. or 4%)	28293 Men Convicted (3576 adm. or 13%)	33486 Men Convicted (4620 or 14%)
	4518 Wmn Convicted (1741 adm. or 38%)	4381 Wmn Convicted (724 adm. or 16%)	3276 Wmn Convicted (456 adm. or 14%)	4767 Wmn Convicted (425 adm. or 9%)	9896 Wmn Convicted (2023 adm. or 20%)	3759 Wmn Convicted* (255 adm. or 7%)	14945 Wmn Convicted (2893 adm. or 19%)	17101 Wmn Convicted (3354 adm. or 20%)

*Offences only, contraventions not listed

Note: A number of convicted offenders had their sentences delayed or forfeited their bail pledges which explains the disparity between convictions and punishments recorded in Tables in 7.6, 7.13 and 7.14.

† ML: *The Number of Persons taken into Custody by the City of Glasgow Police and the Results for the Year Ending 29th September 1860* (Glasgow, 1861), pp. 6–7 & 18; ML: *City of Glasgow Police Criminal Returns for the Year Ending 31st December 1871* (Glasgow, 1872), pp. 16–17 & 29; ML: *City of Glasgow Police Criminal Returns for the Year Ending 31st December 1880* (Glasgow, 1881), pp. 14–15; and ML, *City of Glasgow Police: Criminal Returns for the Year Ending 31st December 1890*, pp. 14–15 & 26; Edinburgh Central Library (ECL): *Return of Crimes, Offences and Contraventions, and of Drunkenness, within the Bounds of Edinburgh Police, Prepared by the Superintendent for the Commissioners of Police* (Edinburgh 1855), passim; ECL: *Report and Returns as to Crimes, Offences, and Contraventions, and to Cases of Drunkenness, within the Police Bounds of the City of Edinburgh, during the Last Six Years, Prepared for the Magistrates and Council, by Thomas Linton, Superintendent of Police* (Edinburgh, 1860), pp. 18 & 27; ECL: *Report and Returns as to Crimes, Offences, and Contraventions within the Limits of the Police of the City of Edinburgh, Prepared for the Magistrates and Council by Thomas Linton, Superintendent of Police, 1868* (Edinburgh, 1869), pp. 18 & 33; ECL: *Return of Crimes and Offences Reported, Persons Apprehended and Cited, and Miscellaneous Returns Connected with the Police, for the Year Ending 31st December 1880* (Edinburgh, 1881), Tables 2 & 3.

admonitions relative to charges for the former crime, they were for the latter. In 1890, for instance, the Glasgow police returns show that women accounted for 119 of 456 admonitions for crimes against property committed without violence (26 per cent) compared with just ten out of 189 admonitions for malicious crimes against property (5 per cent).[92] The latter were, as studies have shown, more likely to be committed by young boys, suggesting that there might have been a youth element to the pattern of admonitions. Thus, while gender may have influenced judicial thinking to some extent on admonitions for criminal charges in Glasgow, it was but one of a multiple range of considerations that also included wider concerns for child welfare (see Chapter 2 of Volume 2 for more on the courts' role in treating child offenders) and the fiscal and civic priorities of magistrates.

Overall, it is extremely difficult to gauge exactly how far gender influenced sentencing patterns in Scottish police courts. While the experience of punishment for men and women differed, it is not possible to conclude with any degree of certainty that women were treated more leniently or harshly than men.[93] Magisterial decisions were informed by a wide range of factors, from practical considerations to social and cultural assumptions about male and female, young and old, native and foreign, first-time and recidivist offenders. Traditional concepts of male and female roles undoubtedly shaped the framing of local laws that could impact upon sentencing patterns, such as the tough measures taken against female prostitution, as well as the representation of those convicted in trial reports. However, the fact that magistrates in many, if not most, cases gave the offender the option of either paying a fine or going to a local bridewell or gaol illustrates that magistrates were not always the prime variable in determining gendered sentencing patterns – it was sometimes influenced by the situation of the offenders or, rather, the economic and social circumstances in which they found themselves. Differences in the punishments received by men and women for similar crimes, offences and contraventions were to a large extent the product of economic and fiscal realities – in other words, gender-related, rather than gender-specific, biases. In so far as women were more likely to be imprisoned it had, with the notable exception of prostitution, less to do with gender and more to do with their financial circumstances. While magisterial mores and values were, undoubtedly, important in shaping the judicial treatment offenders faced, it is worth noting that there were concerns in the media about the inconsistent way in which magistrates were applying the law in the late nineteenth century. They were not all following the same course of action. Nor should this come as any great surprise, given the absence of full-time, permanent, stipendiary magistrates for much of the nineteenth century and the fact that lay magistrates would typically serve for just a few years before leaving office. Magistrates, as councillors and

---

[92]   ML, *City of Glasgow Police Criminal Returns for the Year Ending 31st December 1890*, p. 13.

[93]   A similar point is made by D'Cruze and Jackson, *Women, Crime and Justice in England since 1660*, p. 141.

members of various local police, improvement and welfare boards, had many roles to fill, all of which were likely, at some point, to have shaped sentencing policy. Fiscal penalties were always going to be attractive in an era when judicial duties were balanced with civic ones – and when cash-strapped local authorities were preoccupied with urban improvement initiatives. It meant that gender, social and moral imperatives always had to be balanced with fiscal ones.

III. Patriarchs and the Press

Magistrates attached considerable significance to their own status and authority when administering justice and handing down punishments. In giving evidence to the 1839–1840 Law Inquiry James Clerk, Town Clerk of Irvine, suggested that

> were magistrates enabled more speedily, and less expensively, to try and punish minor offences in their own bounds, it would tend greatly to establish and strengthen their authority, and would be a powerful means of keeping down crime in their respective jurisdictions, and at much less trouble and expense than at present, both to parties concerned and to the public at large.[94]

Often, the attitude of the convicted played an important part in the sentence they received. If they were respectful of magistrates' authority, punishments were sometimes lessened. In 1832, the unstamped periodical *The Police Intelligencer* reported on a number of attacks on Police and Board of Health officials who had attempted to take cholera patients to the hospital. In passing sentence, Bailie Crichton made a point of noting that the contrition shown by the offenders had been key to their lenient punishment:

> The Magistrate said that such conduct as the defenders had been guilty of could not be tolerated. Nothing could be more absurd … [than] … ignorant, misled and ungrateful wretches attempting to frustrate the attempts of the humane exertions of the Managers of the Board of Health to allay that direful enemy which so deeply interests every individual. He intended to punish the defenders severely as an example to others, but as they had shewn some contrition for what they had done, he would fine them in the lowest possible sum, five shillings.[95]

On the other hand, lack of respect for the decisions made by magistrates in police courts was always punished strongly. In 1825, an Irish porter was charged with annoying passengers outside the Star Hotel in Princes Street, Edinburgh, and was fined 5 shillings. The *Caledonian Mercury* reported that

---

[94] 'Fourth Report by Her Majesty's Law Commissioners, Scotland, 1839', pp. 185–311.
[95] *Police Intelligencer*, 11 April 1832.

he 'threw down a shilling, and protested against the decision, displaying at the same time great insolence to the Court'. The Magistrate responded by increasing the fine to half a guinea and depriving him of his badge and means of employment.[96]

Police courts provided an opportunity to judge the status of governing men as useful, authoritative operatives of public service – and, more specifically, a way for magistrates to display their value to the community.[97] As such, magistrates were keen not just to chastise offenders, but also to provide advice and guidance to 'deserving' recipients. The media provided many examples, however unrepresentative they might have been of regular practice, of how magisterial paternalism could operate to 'save' women, youngsters and the vulnerable from themselves. Judges were shown to weigh the possible damage of punishments for these offenders against their future potential. In 1885, Charles Stewart, a 16-year-old labourer, stole manure and bags of bones from a stoneware merchant to purchase whisky and drink it with his friends in a nearby field. After he pleaded guilty in the Aberdeen Police Court, the bailie reflected that

> the charge was a very serious one, but he was very unwilling to send the boy to prison. Perhaps this might have been a boyish prank, or perhaps it might have been more than that; but in any case, the parent of the boy (who was in Court) could hardly be doing his duty to his family when a thing of this kind happened. Under the circumstances, however, he would take it upon him, although he was, perhaps, hardly justified, to impose a fine, which would be 10s, the alternative to be seven days' imprisonment.[98]

As William Davie, Assessor of the Glasgow Police and Burgh Courts, informed the 1839–1840 Law Inquiry, magistrates often used their judicial authority to ensure that juvenile delinquents were not imprisoned in the tolbooth or bridewell in order to safeguard their well-being and stop them mixing with hardened criminals.[99] In their own mind, procurators and

---

[96]   *Caledonian Mercury*, 4 April 1825.

[97]   See the report by the *Aberdeen Journal* in 1840 of those offences which had come before the Banff Police Court since its creation and their disposal, discussed in Chapter 6. *Aberdeen Journal*, 30 December 1840.

[98]   *Aberdeen Weekly Journal*, 10 March 1885.

[99]   He said magistrates opted for this course 'to advert to the great want of the means of punishing juvenile offenders, or persons guilty of a first and venial offence, other than by confinement in the Tolbooth or Bridewell. The magistrate has no power to award punishment by confinement in lock-up rooms in, or connected with, the Police Buildings. This is a very serious desideratum, the effect of which must be, either impunity on the one hand, or too severe, and, therefore, unjust punishment on the other. A medium course is frequently adopted, that of remanding a party (which the Police Act authorises, for further examination) and delaying sentence till another diet, at which he is brought up and discharged; the confinement which

magistrates were not only administrators of justice, but also patriarchal guardians of social welfare – a role which took on increasing importance for the image of magistrates in an era of increased media reporting of judicial decisions.[100]

In some instances, judicial discretion was used to publicise magistrates' decisions to take a tough stand against certain forms of behaviour that threatened public safety,[101] or to protect deserving and vulnerable groups from the harsher penalties that a higher court could impose.[102] Procurators and magistrates sometimes dealt with cases that should legally have been tried in a higher court in order to ensure that the offender received a more moderate punishment than would have been imposed on conviction by the higher court. Magistrates were sometimes more lenient when they knew that an offender had two previous convictions, choosing to send them to reformatories rather than remit them to a higher court. Moreover, procurators on occasion undervalued stolen items in order to keep the case within the remit of the court and the level of punishment low if the defender was deemed to be worthy of the court's protection. Cases such as these were often published in the press, seemingly as a sign of the system's clemency – even though this might not always have been the motive of the fiscal or the magistrate. A case in which the female defender pleaded guilty to keeping a gold watch for herself to pawn illustrates the point. In 1880, the *Aberdeen Weekly Journal* reported the following from the fiscal of the Aberdeen Police Court:

> taking the most favourable view of this case, the woman's own admission, it was found that she went away and, without the least attempt to restore the watch to the owner, proceeded to convert it to her own use. Technically, the fiscal had charged her not with any breach of honesty; but he did not think there was much difference.

The report went on:

---

he has, in that way, intermediately undergone, being implied as punishment for the offence'. 'Fourth Report by Her Majesty's Law Commissioners, Scotland, 1839', pp. 326–7.

[100]　Ibid.

[101]　In 1865, John Simpson was charged with careless driving, in which a young girl was thrown down and seriously injured. 'Bailie Adamson referred to the frequency of accidents in the streets by reckless driving, and observed that it was necessary for the public protection that such cases as the present should be severely punished. Bailie Robb concurred, and pronounced sentence – a fine of 40s. or, failing payment, 14 days' imprisonment.' *Aberdeen Journal*, 22 November 1865.

[102]　'Fourth Report by Her Majesty's Law Commissioners, Scotland, 1839', p. 327.

Mrs Donaldson said she had been told the watch was not worth anything, only 15s. The Bailie said that anybody who looked at it would see it was worth six times that sum. But as the Fiscal was inclined to take the most merciful view, he would modify the fine to 10s, with the option of 7 days' imprisonment. For himself, he thought there was little to be said on her behalf, and, if it had not been for the Fiscal, he would have been more severe.[103]

It was an approach which spoke volumes about how public men within the police court structure viewed their role as civic and community leaders and not merely enforcers of the law. They used their discretionary powers of punishment as a vehicle for promoting themselves as paternal figures and protectors of the vulnerable, reflecting their well-developed sense of their role as agents of pastoral care and welfare for the offenders under their supervision. However, as Volume 2 will show, its use was severely restricted to a small group of 'worthy' recipients. Those who disappointed magistrates by their recidivist behaviour would rarely be offered further assistance. Indeed, as returns evidence makes clear, some of the cities' most vulnerable populations were more often made scapegoats for the protection of the greater majority than they were protected from the force of punishment by kindly magistrates.

In recording the sentences that were handed down by magistrates in trial reports, and the reaction of the convicted, the media allowed readers to make judgements about the appropriateness of judicial practices and decisions. Sometimes reports served to highlight how the accused could play to the galleries in an attempt to show contempt for authority and to send out their own moral messages about the 'caring' nature of magisterial justice. In April 1832, Bailie Crichton examined the case of Catherine Sutherland for drunkenness in the Edinburgh Police Court, and advised that she should be placed in the house of refuge. Sutherland, fearful of catching cholera, cried out: 'Catherine – I ken I'll catch the Cholera, and they are sure to kill me. Nabody escapes them!' Serjeant Ferguson subsequently took hold of her by the arm to lead her away, which provoked Catherine to exclaim: 'Puir thing, I'm just led like a lamb to the slaughter [great laughter].'[104]

On some occasions the press was critical, or published the views of others who were critical, of the punishments magistrates handed out. These typically involved cases in which magistrates were deemed to have been too lenient in punishing particular offenders. In May 1825, the *Caledonian Mercury* reported a correspondent's complaint about 'inadequate punishment frequently awarded in the police court for atrocious crimes'. In the case in question, in which the accused had hit a man on the head with a stone to the effusion of blood and received 14 days' imprisonment, the correspondent argued that 'in England the latter crime might have been punished by death, and that at least it was deserving of a good

---

[103]   *Aberdeen Weekly Journal*, 8 March 1880.
[104]   *Police Intelligencer*, 12 April 1832.

whipping'. There was also criticism that magistrates valued private property over public safety. In a letter to the editor of the *Caledonian Mercury* in 1825, 'R.B.' complained that:

> It would appear that, in the judgment of the [Edinburgh] Police Court, the crime of maltreating a horse, and of course the value of its life, is somewhat more than quadruple the enormity of abusing a human being, and his or her life proportionally of less value. In proof of this, I refer you to two decisions reported in your paper of yesterday, immediately following one another. A fellow is fined a guinea, (most justly certainly) for abusing his horse; – immediately after, a fine of *five shillings* is levied from three blackguards, (each to be sure) for maltreating a poor girl, it is no matter what she was – had she not belonged to the human species, the punishment it would appear would have been more severe.[105]

In 1844, the *Dumfries and Galloway Standard* ridiculed the low level of punishment levied by the Dumfries Police Court when it reported that Mary Moffatt, who had been convicted of striking Mary-Ann McKain to the effusion of blood, was sentenced to pay 5s., or face gaol for ten days. Moffatt remarked: 'That's not much.' Moreover, it was reported that McKain assisted her to pay the fine.[106] While the *Standard* used the case to illustrate the court's ability to impose order on the masses, it also hinted at other codes of conduct and honour within the offender's own community about who was at fault (Moffatt had claimed provocation) – regardless of what the magistrate imposed. The *Caledonian Mercury* offered a more explicit criticism of the courts in 1855, when an Irish man received a fine of 2 guineas or 30 days' imprisonment for smashing a glass window in Edinburgh, commenting: 'we wish we could have added that the imprisonment was to be spiced with hard labour.'[107]

Criticism that magistrates were being too harsh towards offenders was recorded much less frequently in the mainstream media and was, as Chapter 2 has discussed, much more likely to occur in the late nineteenth century to add weight to the newspaper campaigns for a stipendiary magistrate. In general, dissent was more likely to be expressed in other forms of media. In 1885, the *Thistle or Detective* wrote sympathetically of a case in Dundee in which

> a poor labourer who was starving was sent to prison for forty days for stealing three apples ... Bailie Hunter was the 'administrator of justice' in this case and I think his action exhibits clearly how totally unfit those nobodies, who aspire to the dignity of an unpaid Bailie, are to mete out the laws.[108]

---

[105]   *Caledonian Mercury*, 13 June 1825.
[106]   *Dumfries and Galloway Standard*, 17 July 1844.
[107]   *Caledonian Mercury*, 31 August 1855.
[108]   *The Thistle or the Detective*, no. 24, vol. II (New Series), 17 September 1885, p. 1.

For the most part, though, the mainstream media recorded their approval of the punishments magistrates administered. Sometimes it was recorded explicitly. In 1842, the *Scotch Reformers' Gazette* reported that: 'On Monday, in the Police Court, a half-denuded fellow, with a most sinister expression of countenance, was placed at the bar' charged with disorderly conduct. 'He was most deservedly fined in 10s. 6d.'[109] In other cases, approval was implied. In 1842 the same newspaper published the case of a boy who was charged with stealing a quarter of a pound of sugar from a grocer's shop. The trial reporter made a point of noting that

> up to the present act, not the slightest charge could be preferred against him. His mother, a respectable-looking person, appeared in Court, crying bitterly, and Bailie Leadbetter, after a humane and judicious admonition, dismissed the case.[110]

These were the kinds of people who were deemed worthy of the court's protection, and – in the way it was reported – the journalist was happy to ensure that readers were made aware that the 'humane' magistrate could be relied upon to provide it. Periodicals even went so far as to record the voices of courtroom personnel to justify what might have appeared to readers to have been harsh punishments. In 1829, *Police Reports* published the case of an 80-year-old man, John Burd, who was sent to bridewell for the maximum length of 60 days for being drunk and disorderly in the shop of Mr Kelly, spirit dealer. On hearing the sentence, the accused said: 'stop a wee, Bailie, and ca canny friend.' He was, it was reported, 'taken away by force'. What is interesting here is that Captain Graham who led the police prosecution subsequently mentioned that the old man was more 'rogue than fool' and had been repeatedly in the office and allowed to go away on promises of amendment.[111] In publishing this remark, the newspaper was alerting readers to the mercy that the court had shown to the offender previously.[112]

That the mainstream media was largely sympathetic to magisterial sentencing policy is further illustrated by the publicity it gave to bailies' opinions on this matter. The media frequently reported cases in which the magisterial voice was recorded expressing frustration with the limited powers at their disposal. In 1825, for instance, a woman, 'an old offender' who was convicted of child stripping,

---

[109]   *Scots Reformers' Gazette*, 8 October 1842.

[110]   *Scots Reformers' Gazette*, 26 November 1842.

[111]   *Police Reports*, 10 July 1829, p. 22.

[112]   Indeed, the periodicals sometimes specifically used the word mercy in their coverage. In the case involving William Callander, slater, charged with stealing a quantity of lead from the roof of Mr Lang's foundry, the *Police Reports* noted that 'This man has been repeatedly before the Court, and often in Bridewell, for similar charges, and mercy has often been extended to him, on account of his wife, and young family. So many repeated warnings and slight punishments, proving in the end ineffectual; it was judged expedient at this time, to send him and the lead to the Chamber, where a precognition was taken; and he will be tried next circuit, and is fully committed for that purpose.' *Police Reports*, 27 July 1829, p. 27.

'a theft of a most base and unfeeling description', was sentenced to 60 days in bridewell by the Edinburgh magistrate who 'regretted that it was not in his power to inflict a more severe punishment'.[113] Similarly, in 1829, two men guilty of breach of the peace, and suspected of attempting a riot, were berated by the magistrate who said he

> was sorry that the powers vested in him by the Police Act allowed him only to pronounce on them a sentence of 60 days imprisonment and hard labour at Bridewell. Had it been possible, he should have been glad to have given them six months; but he hoped that the present sentence would teach others that they were not to escape such conduct with impunity.[114]

In choosing to record the voice of the magistrate in such a way, the newspaper absolved him of any possible criticism from those who might have sought a tougher penalty. He could, in other words, be relied upon to do what was within his power to punish offenders to the maximum the law allowed. The press also published the views of high court judges to add further weight to this view. In 1823, in a case before the High Court of Justiciary, a carter was charged with careless driving and culpable homicide, having killed a man with his loaded cart. He was imprisoned for 9 months. The judge, Lord Gillies, opined:

> He was sorry to observe that the punishments inflicted by the Magistrates in the Police Court were inadequate to repress the offence; these punishments he was disposed to consider as nothing but a mere farce. He observed, in some of the papers, a report of a conviction of a carter for crushing a child through negligence, whereby its life was endangered; and for this offence was only fined the paltry sum of 10s. His Lordship trusted that those who had the administration of the Police would take some effectual steps to repress this crime. The Lord Justice Clerk concurred with Lord Gillies in thinking that the punishments awarded by the Police Magistrates were not likely to remedy the evil. He trusted that the observations of the Court would be attended to by those whose duty it was to regulate the Police of the city.[115]

The above example shows that magisterial sensitivity to how they were judged through the media was well founded, as High Court judges were forming judgements about summary justice in part through police court trial reports.

Thus, although options for punishing offenders in police courts made allowance for substantial discretion by the magistracy, the mainstream media fulfilled an important role in representing the punishments that were administered. In publicising instances in which magistrates were constrained by legislative

---

[113]   *Caledonian Mercury*, 24 November 1825.
[114]   *Aberdeen Journal*, 23 December 1829.
[115]   *The Scotsman*, 16 July 1823.

guidelines, media reports helped to some extent to absolve bailies from criticism. Moreover, the media could play a significant part in punishing those who appeared before magistrates. As the next section explores, simply appearing in court as the accused could, even for those who were acquitted or had their cases dismissed, be a sentence in itself as it ran the risk of unwanted publicity and the shame that often accompanied it.

IV. Naming and Shaming

Shame was an important part of judicial censure in pre-modern society. Community-sanctioned shaming punishments, such as public whipping or the burning of effigies, were designed not only to humiliate and damage the reputation of offenders who had violated local standards and customs, but also to serve a wider social and judicial purpose. They publicised scandal, served as a warning to others, and sought to police the morals and behaviour of the wider community.[116] Crucially, popular participation in administering 'rough music' – a folk practice highlighted by E.P. Thompson in which humiliating punishments were administered by local people against those who had violated community standards – helped to legitimise the workings of the criminal justice system and to buttress the social order.[117] Shaming rituals were especially important, as Thompson and others have pointed out, in maintaining discipline and promoting harmonious social relations in pre-industrial society where law enforcement and judicial provisions were underdeveloped or absent.[118]

However, scholars have noted that concerns with street disorder, changing attitudes towards the use of public streets, and growing revulsion to displays of violence rendered shaming punishments less effective and less acceptable in the late eighteenth and early nineteenth centuries. According to Shoemaker, many members of the public in London lost interest in rituals that damaged people's reputations, which made it 'much more difficult for shame and public humiliation to work as a form of punishment'.[119] Instead, the printed word became increasingly important in shaping reputations.[120] Gossip and social networking continued to be

---

116   Nash and Kilday, *Cultures of Shame*, p. 10.

117   E.P. Thompson, 'Rough Music: le charivari Anglais', *Annales*, 27/2 (1972): pp. 285–312; and E.P. Thompson, *Customs in Common* (New York, 1991), p. 530.

118   There is evidence also that shaming rituals continued in some ways throughout the nineteenth century. See, for instance, Nash and Kilday, *Cultures of Shame*, ch. 2; and Conley, *The Unwritten Law*, p. 23.

119   Shoemaker, 'Streets of Shame?', p. 233. See also Shoemaker, 'The Decline of Public Insult in London', pp. 97–131.

120   Ibid. Moreover, as Donna Andrew has shown, the middling ranks in the second half of the eighteenth century were more likely to use printed advertisements in local newspapers than insults to attempt to shape people's reputations. Donna T. Andrew, 'The

important mediums for damaging a person's character,[121] but in the larger cities, and among the middle ranks in particular, popular culture was becoming increasingly dependent upon the printed word for the transmission of news.[122] As Jürgen Habermas has argued, the press became a crucial component for representing socially damaging forms of behaviour in modern civil society.[123] In the nineteenth century, the press, in the words of Nash and Kilday, 'played an important role in the formation, articulation and sustenance of values associated with cultures of shame'.[124] In the media reports of Scottish police court trials, shame was often used in order to convey wider social, cultural and moral messages. The Edinburgh *Police Intelligencer* and Glasgow *Police Reports* both applied social and cultural norms to protect the reputations of some courtroom participants by withholding names in trial reports, while 'naming and shaming' others.[125] Below, it is argued that these media reports became an important, if informal and highly selective, form of judicial censure in the way that they sought to ridicule, humiliate and embarrass those brought before magistrates.

Simply appearing in court as the accused could, it was perceived, damage a person's reputation, social standing and future career paths, especially for those drawn from the middle and upper classes. In 1877, *The Dundee Courier and Argus and Northern Warder*, in defending the use of discretionary justice to protect the future well-being of young first-time offenders, noted: 'it should be remembered that the public appearance of such individuals before the Police Court might not improbably lead to social ruin, and an amount of ulterior suffering out of all

---

Press and Public Apologies in Eighteenth-Century London', in Norma Landau (ed.), *Law, Crime and English Society* (Cambridge, 2002), pp. 208–29.

[121] Ellen Ross, 'Survival Networks: Women's Neighbourhood Sharing in London before WW1', *History Workshop: A Journal of Socialist and Feminist Historians*, 15 (1983): pp. 4–27.

[122] Shoemaker, 'The Decline of Public Insult in London', pp. 97–131.

[123] Jürgen Habermas, *The Structural Transformation of the Public Sphere: An Inquiry into a Category of Bourgeois Society*, trans. Thomas Burger (Cambridge, 1989, first published 1962); and Jürgen Habermas, 'The Public Sphere: An Encyclopaedia Article', in Chris Greer (ed.), *Crime and Media: A Reader* (London, 2010), pp. 11–19.

[124] Nash and Kilday, *Cultures of Shame*, p. 139. See also Gail Savage, 'Erotic Stories and Public Decency: Newspaper Reporting of Divorce Proceedings in England', *Historical Journal*, 41/2 (1998): pp. 511–28; and Kristine Ottesen Garrigan, *Victorian Scandals: Representations of Gender and Class* (Columbus, 1992). Moreover, D'Cruze has shown that 'in regard to cases of physical and sexual violence, newspaper reporting ... fuelled the gossip and discussion that was not only a pleasurable leisure occupation but also attributed judgements about the respectability of the parties involved'. D'Cruze, *Crimes of Outrage*, p. 178.

[125] Susan Broomhall and David G. Barrie, 'Making Men: Media, Magistrates and the Representation of Masculinity in Scottish Police Courts, 1800–1833', in David G. Barrie and Susan Broomhall (eds), *A History of Police and Masculinities, 1700–2010* (London, 2012), pp. 72–101.

proportion to the nature of their offence.'[126] Defenders, too, were acutely aware of the shame that a courtroom appearance could entail and sometimes sought to hide their appearance. In 1831, *The Police Intelligencer* reported on the case of an 'old acquaintance' charged with breaking into the shop of a spirit dealer and stealing £4 or £5 in silver and copper, who:

> Either from modesty or to prevent the auditory from recognizing him ... placed his hat immediately before his face, covering the whole with the exception of one eye, which he no doubt considered necessary to guide him to the bar. Although he thus contrived to hide his features, we could perceive that Sir John was blushing like dewy morn' to find himself in such an awkward predicament. The hectic flush even suffusing that part of his neck which was uncovered; and we doubt that had his bosom been bare, the same delicious appearances would have been also apparent.[127]

As Jennifer S. Davis has argued, abused wives could use police courts as a strategy to shame abusive husbands by exposing their conduct to judicial, public and, sometimes, media scrutiny.[128] Others used the courtroom as a place to criticise their enemies publicly.[129]

Shame was an important part of the discourse of the courtroom and the way it was represented in the media. On some occasions, editors offered their own moral opprobrium as a supplement to the court ruling or when one was not recorded by the magistrate. In 1829, John Brownlie, the author of the *Police Reports*, commented that John Carslaw had been charged with 'beating and abusing his wife' in a 'most shameful manner'.[130] On other occasions, reports specifically highlighted magisterial criticism of behaviour that was deemed to be disgraceful and dishonourable. Indeed, the frequency with which the magisterial voice was recorded alluding to the shame that the accused should feel for their indiscretions points not only to the continuing belief in media and judicial public penance as a form of discipline, but also to the reciprocal relationship and shared values that existed between bailies, journalists and editors. The 1829 *Police Reports*, for

---

[126] *The Dundee Courier and Argus and Northern Warder*, 31 August 1877.

[127] *Police Intelligencer*, 28 September 1831.

[128] Davis, 'A Poor Man's System of Justice?', p. 321. See also D'Cruze, *Crimes of Outrage*, p. 70.

[129] In 1855, the *Aberdeen Journal* reported a fight between two women that brought them to the Edinburgh Police Court. The Magistrate enquired of the complainer (who had a child in her arms) whether she had a husband, – a question which was answered in the negative. 'She can do without ane', said the old lady – 'she'll may be tell you that she has six bairns.' The complainer then cried out, 'you old jade, would you have better proof that I'm no the bad woman you call me?', 'Satisfied with the triumph she had obtained over the complainer's character, the defender heard with great complacency the judgement of the Court, ordaining her to pay five shillings of damages.' *Aberdeen Journal*, 10 October 1855.

[130] *Police Reports*, 10 July 1829, p. 21.

instance, published the following case in which a mother was questioned about the behaviour of her daughter, who had been charged with stealing three handkerchiefs from a shop:

> Superintendant: 'Your daughter's cloke is very convenient in secreting stolen goods.'

> Magistrate: 'Are you not ashamed to train up your child in such a detestable manner? Both you and her must go the Bridewell for 6 weeks.'[131]

In publishing selective comments from magistrates, such reports gave resonance to the moral opprobrium contained within the media coverage and helped to create the impression that bailies and the periodical spoke with the same voice, especially when magisterial condemnation of offenders was accompanied by press disapprobation.

Magistrates and the media appear to have worked together to publicise deviant behaviour that offended the Church of Scotland's strict moral code. Press reports were particularly concerned with exposing sexual indiscretion and highlighting magistrates' criticism of it. Those found guilty of associating with 'loose women' were sometimes singled out as having brought shame on themselves and, in some cases, their families. In 1829, for instance, William Trevan, who was charged with lounging at half-past one o'clock in the morning with a prostitute on a stair at St Andrew's Square, 'was ordered [by the magistrate] to go away and think shame of himself'.[132] What is particularly interesting about such judicial and media condemnation is that magistrates were seeking public penance from offenders: they were expected, as the above example reveals, to feel shame themselves. It was a system of control that was very much in keeping with the internalised, self-reinforcing notions of godly discipline in pre-modern Scotland and was further proof of the ways in which police courts, and the media, helped to propagate religious values and practices at a time when many churches were struggling to do so in rapidly expanding Scottish cities in the first few decades of the nineteenth century. Indeed, the tone of trial reports could, on occasion, appear almost confessional; offenders lamented their behaviour and following a rebuke from the magistrate promised not to repeat it.[133] In 1831, for instance, *The Police Intelligencer* reported the case of a 'respectable-looking' woman who 'thanked the Magistrate, and promised that she would take his advice and be more circumspect in future' after he dismissed her for being drunk and disorderly.[134]

---

[131] *Police Intelligencer*, 20 October 1831.
[132] *Police Reports*, 15 August 1829, p. 50.
[133] D'Cruze makes a similar point. D'Cruze, *Crimes of Outrage*, p. 169.
[134] *Police Intelligencer*, 23 September 1831.

It was the possibility that courtroom participants would have their indiscretions revealed in the local press that, arguably, made shaming such a potent form of punishment. Indeed, the chances of being publicly exposed in print resulted in some offenders attempting to withhold their identities[135] or giving false names in court.[136] Although impossible to prove conclusively, the tendency of magistrates to deliver what was akin to a religious form of censure suggests that they were acutely aware of the shaming potential of the press and utilised it as an informal judicial resource in order to get their message across to the widest possible audience. The editor of the *Police Reports*, intriguingly, appears to have used the threat of being 'named and shamed' to shape the future behaviour of both the accused and the complainer. In 1829, he published the case of 'a married man of rather superior appearance' who charged a prostitute with stealing two shillings from him in a house:

> 'Do you really wish to persevere in your case.'
>
> Accuser: 'I do.'
>
> Magistrate: 'you must give proof.'
>
> Accuser: 'I have none. I will swear she took the money.'
>
> Prisoner: 'Deed, Bailie, I have two shillings of his, but he gave it to me as a present, and he kens himsel what for.'
>
> Magistrate: 'you say you are married.'
>
> Accuser: 'I am.'
>
> Magistrate: 'have you a family.'
>
> Accuser: 'I have.'
>
> Magistrate: 'do you really not think shame of yourself, look at that woman, and consider where you are now...'

Significantly, Brownlie ended his commentary with the following: 'This accuser's name will be inserted if ever he again appears on a similar charge.'[137] It was a comment that spoke volumes about the shaming and disciplinary power of his periodical. Similar sentiments about the shaming impact of trial reports were expressed in the mainstream press. In 1833, the *Aberdeen Journal* reported: 'In the Police Court, on Monday, a young man was charged with exercising the functions of the canine species, and biting and severely wounding a woman! in a pub fight. ...Out of pity, we do not give his name, nor any more particulars.'[138] There were also instances in which the convicted pleaded with the magistrate to

---

[135]　See, for instance, the 'old man, who would not tell his name, ... brought into the office in the early morning, charged with being drunk and disorderly'. *Police Reports*, 10 July 1829, p. 22.

[136]　In the case involving William Trevan, charged with lounging with a prostitute in a public place, it was reported that the accused gave a false name. *Police Reports*, 15 August 1829, p. 50.

[137]　*Police Reports*, 5 September 1829, p. 92.

[138]　*Aberdeen Journal*, 22 May 1833.

keep their name out of the press – a fact which adds further evidence to suggest that magistrates were able to, or that people thought that they were able to, influence trial reports and use them as an extra-judicial resource when it suited. In 1890, for instance, the *Aberdeen Weekly Journal* picked up a story from the Banff Police Court, in which it was reported that:

> an inhabitant of the burgh who is not a stranger at the bar of justice, but who has the misfortune to possess a sobriquet, appealed to the Bailie to use his influence with the reporters to keep the obnoxious nickname from appearing in print. The reason he gave was that 'he was as much entitled to his proper name as any other decent man who appeared before his Honour.'[139]

The fact his name and nickname were withheld suggests his appeal was successful.

Editors had much discretion when it came to the identity of courtroom participants. While some defenders were named, others were identified only by their sex, occupation, status, appearance, age, nationality or criminal past (typically only one or two of these).[140] Of the 252 people charged in the Edinburgh Police Court who had their cases covered in *The Police Intelligencer* between 18 August 1831 and 22 October 1831, 153 (61 per cent) had their names revealed and 99 (39 per cent) did not (see Table 7.15).[141] Similarly, in the *Police Reports'* coverage of

Table 7.15   People Accused Named and Not Named in *The Police Intelligencer* Trial Reports, 18 August 1831 to 22 October 1831[†]

Number	Named	Not Named
252 (127 Males) (125 Females)	153 (59 Males) (94 Females)	99 (68 Males) (31 Females)

Note: Figures for Table 7.15 (and Table 7.16 below) relate only to those cases (which represented the vast majority) in which the specific number of persons on each charge was recorded in the trial reports. The few instances in which it was stated that 'a group' or 'a number' of people were charged have not been included as the numbers involved are not known. However, not only was it unusual for this to be recorded, such cases were usually given very little coverage in the periodicals.

† *Police Intelligencer*, 18 August 1831 to 22 October 1831.

---

[139]   *Aberdeen Weekly Journal*, 23 October 1890.

[140]   See, for example, 'A Young Tailor', *Police Intelligencer*, 27 October 1831; 'A Gigantic Hibernian Cobbler', *Police Intelligencer*, 27 October 1831; and 'A Little Pickpocket', *Police Intelligencer*, 1 November 1831.

[141]   *Police Intelligencer*, 18 August 1831 to 22 October 1831.

Table 7.16   People Accused Named and Not Named in *Police Reports*
Trial Reports, 6 July to 15 August 1829†

Number	Named	Not Named
255 (181 Males) (74 Females)	149 (103 Males) (46 Females)	106 (78 Males) (28 Females)

† *Police Reports*, from 6 July 1829 to 15 August 1829, pp. 5–56.

Glasgow Police Court trials published between 6 July and 15 August 1829, 149 accused (58 per cent) were named and 106 (42 per cent) were not (see Table 7.16).[142]

It was, however, rare for the accused who were named to have their addresses revealed (house numbers were never included), which should caution against overstating the capacity of readers to put a face to a name in what were large, populous cities. Of 100 people charged in the Edinburgh Police Court who were named in *The Police Intelligencer* between 18 August and 28 September, only nine reports made reference to the defender's street/court, nine to their stair/close, and four to their district; 18 made no reference to the addresses of the accused at all (which was the norm for the vast majority of cases recorded in Glasgow's *Police Reports*).[143] Indeed, the fact that *The Police Intelligencer* chose to specifically identify so few general places of residence suggests that naming and shaming of individuals in the majority of cases selected for publication was not the overriding concern of trial coverage, except perhaps in cases involving sexual morality (see below). *The Police Intelligencer* was much more likely to reveal the location in which an alleged offence had taken place than the address of the defender, accounting for the remaining 60 persons whose names had been published. Many of these reports concerned property crimes against shopkeepers, reflecting the periodical's interest in letting middle-class readers know about theft in their area; but they also included a large number of named locations of disorderly houses and brothels, which was testament to the periodical's fascination with illuminating the darker and seedier side of Edinburgh life. It was also indicative of how trial reports often reflected, and to some degree reinforced, wider police and civic priorities and initiatives aimed at controlling unruly properties, rowdy behaviour and public space.

However, although the capacity for those named who had their neighbourhoods withheld to be identified was somewhat limited, the fact that editors chose to withhold the names, and protect the reputations, of some people testifies to the capacity of readers within limited catchment areas and specific social circles

---

142   *Police Reports*, from 6 July 1829 to 15 August 1829, pp. 5–56.
143   *Police Intelligencer*, 18 August 1831 to 28 September 1831.

to be able to identify the people profiled. Besides, the actual number of people who would have had their identity exposed in *The Police Intelligencer* is likely to have been far higher than the above figures suggest.[144] The periodical often made a point of identifying the specific location of 'unruly and immoral' houses, leaving readers in that community in little doubt as to the identity of those who lived there.[145] The location of brothels was commonly published even when the names of those charged were not recorded, such as the case of 'CYPRIANIC ROBBERY' in which 'two girls belonging to Lucky Brown's establishment, North Grey Close, were charged with theft'.[146] Indeed, the preference for including the addresses of houses of ill-repute is likely to have been of significance in tarnishing the reputation of communities and neighbourhoods and, in all likelihood, helped to reinforce public perceptions of social and spatial boundaries in Scottish cities.

Editorial decisions over whether or not to publish the identities of the accused might, in some instances, have been influenced by practical considerations, such as the business of the caseload on a given day and word constraints (when, for instance, dealing with a number of people on the same charge, such as drunk and disorderly conduct). Sometimes reports gave only the nationality of the accused, not because the editor wanted to protect them, but because it reinforced stereotypes as to their perceived criminality. This was especially common for Irish defenders.[147] There was even the odd occasion when the journalist made a note that he had not been able to hear the accused's name, which suggests that the journalists for *The Police Intelligencer* and *Police Reports* gained their information from attending court in person rather than second-hand from court books as some journalists mid-century appear to have done.[148]

What is significant is that guilt was by no means the determining factor in editors' decisions to publish a person's identity. Of the 153 persons who were charged in the Edinburgh Police Court and named, 95 (62 per cent) were convicted; the others were either dismissed, remanded or had their cases remitted to a higher court. Similarly, of the 149 persons named in the Glasgow Police Court, 91 were convicted (61 per cent). In the vast majority of cases, selection decisions were determined by the social, moral and cultural values of editors, with perhaps some input and influence from magistrates. In *The Police*

---

[144] See, for instance, the report concerning noisy neighbours. *Police Intelligencer*, 20 August 1831.

[145] *Police Intelligencer*, 9 September 1831. See also ibid.

[146] *Police Intelligencer*, 9 September 1831.

[147] See the report of an Irish woman charged with assault, for attempting to stab policeman. *Police Intelligencer*, 22 August 1831.

[148] Sometimes the journalist felt the need to explain why he was not sure of the accused's name. For example, 'A very pretty and handsome young lady, but whose name as true and genuine reporters of the misdeeds committed in this ancient city, we did not catch, but it appeared to us to sound something like Mrs Adanlong, was charged with using very abusive and offensive epithets to a Mrs Drummond, residing in Queen Street, a gentleman's lodging house keep, a middle aged matron.' *Police Intelligencer*, 8 October 1831.

Intelligencer, female defenders were more likely to be named. Three quarters of the 125 women who were charged in the trial reports were identified by name, compared with less than half of the 127 men (see Table 7.15).[149] It was a similar situation with the *Police Reports* although the gender differential was much smaller, which reflected the Glasgow periodical's fascination with reporting on 'immoral' offences involving certain types of men and women (see Table 7.16). Of the 181 male defenders who were recorded, 103 (60 per cent) were named and 78 (40 per cent) were not. The corresponding percentages for female defenders were 62 per cent and 38 per cent (of the 74 women recorded).[150] Both periodicals also appear to have been more likely to identify by name repeat offenders, although the selective nature of court reporting and the absence of comparative court records makes it impossible to establish this conclusively. Nonetheless, the fact that editors sometimes threatened to reveal the identity of offenders if they came before the court again indicates that at least some first-time offenders were given greater protection from editors than repeat ones. Periodicals, in keeping with pre-modern forms of punishment, were especially concerned with identifying certain offenders as criminally deviant, which could have had a long-lasting impact on their reputations long after their sentences had been served or fines paid.[151]

Both periodicals displayed a keen interest in protecting the identity and reputation of men of a certain social standing.[152] Occupational profiles, allied with press assumptions about, and descriptors of, appearance often determined whether identities were revealed. Indeed, some people whose names were withheld were identified only as 'respectable looking', illustrating the importance of appearance, dress and demeanour for media coverage.[153] Safeguarding the career paths of young professional men was of particular concern. In 1829, the *Police Reports* published the case of two 'dandy clerks' charged with fighting on the streets on Sunday morning who were not only sent on their way by the magistrate, but who had their reputations protected by the journal, which warned that 'if these two dandies again appear in the

---

[149]   *Police Intelligencer*, 18 August 1831 to 22 October 1831.

[150]   *Police Reports*, from 6 July 1829 to 15 August 1829, pp. 5–56.

[151]   For more on pre-modern forms of punishment and the labelling of offenders as criminally deviant, see Shoemaker, 'Streets of Shame?', p. 232.

[152]   For studies on the intersection of newspaper reporting, policing, and legal and extra-legal forms of punishment – and, in particular, how the press protected the reputation of white men involved in lynching in America – see Bryan Wagner, *Disturbing the Peace: Black Culture and the Police Power after Slavery* (Cambridge, 2010); Philip Dray, *At the Hands of Persons Unknown: The Lynching of Black America* (New York, 2007); and Grace Elizabeth Hale, *Making Whiteness: The Culture of Segregation in the South, 1890–1940* (New York, 1999).

[153]   See the case of four 'respectable looking men' charged with being drunk and disorderly. *Police Reports*, 15 August 1829, p. 54.

office, their names will be inserted in the Reports'.[154] The periodical also often hid the identity of men employed in the trades, perhaps reflecting their importance within the city's municipal sphere of governance. Businessmen nearly always had their names withheld. In 1831, *The Police Intelligencer* published the case of 'A grocer of considerable note, residing in the [affluent] new town, [who] was charged with committing a breach of the peace by spitting in the face of a wine and spirit merchant, residing in Broughton Street.'[155] In the same year it revealed, under the heading 'FRACAS EXTRAORDINARY', that 'a celebrated auctioneer and his assistant, were charged with assaulting and striking a person who calls himself a master upholsterer, in a public house'.[156] Professionals who defrauded their employers,[157] and senior military personnel involved in drunken assaults, also usually had their names withheld.[158] The latter were frequently brought before magistrates, reflecting the high number of soldiers stationed in Scotland's capital and their tendency for alcohol-fuelled violent behaviour. Moreover, there were even instances in which the periodicals went out of their way to show extenuating circumstances that led to charges being levelled against 'respectable' men in the first place. In 1831, *The Police Intelligencer* reported:

> The natural son of a noble Lord was charged with assaulting and striking a boy about half his own size, residing at the Water of Leith. The cause of complaint was as natural as the defender. The sum and substance is this: – The complainer had, without cause or provocation, called the noble Lord's son a b____d b____h! The defender's hair stood on end, and without the least hesitation, struck the complainer a severe blow on the face, which grounded the present complaint.[159]

Although stopping short of actually stating so, there was an assumption that the complainer got what he deserved in the altercation.[160]

---

[154] *Police Reports*, 14 August 1829, p. 32.
[155] *Police Intelligencer*, 22 August 1831.
[156] *Police Intelligencer*, 2 September 1831.
[157] See, for instance, the report about 'A CLERK ON THE RAMBLE: An elderly man of rather decent appearance, clerk to a respectable merchant tailor, was charged with a breech [*sic*] of trust by taking from his master's counting room the sum of £5, 8s., and appropriating part of the sum to his own use.' The charge was dismissed, the magistrate finding that the clerk did not take the money with the intention of stealing it. *Police Intelligencer*, 19 August 1831.
[158] In 1831, a sergeant belonging to the light company was convicted in the Edinburgh Police Court of being drunk and disorderly and striking two women. He was fined a guinea but had his name withheld. *Police Intelligencer*, 20 August 1831.
[159] *Police Intelligencer*, 2 September 1831.
[160] Similar protection was often afforded to policemen. In 1831, *The Police Intelligencer* reported the case of 'two police officers' convicted of assaulting and striking

Social background also mattered when it came to protecting women's identity, at least for women who conformed to middle-class ideals of femininity. When women from middle-class backgrounds were brought before the court, the media drew on the words of magistrates to highlight how unusual and out of character it was, which in the eyes of the editor might have helped to justify withholding the defender's identity. For instance, *The Police Intelligencer* reported without comment that the magistrate had dismissed without investigation the case of one 'well dressed and respectable looking elderly woman' who had been found drunk and disorderly in the High Street, after hearing of her previous reputation for good conduct.[161] The press, in mirroring the views and values of magistrates, also saw it as their duty to protect the reputations and futures of young women who were deemed worthy. *The Police Intelligencer* reported the case of an unnamed girl, a milkmaid, who was charged with stealing money that had been entrusted to her by Mr Ramsay, cowfeeder, in the following manner:

> A decent looking man, her father, and a woman, stepped forward to the bar, when the poor girl, in a paroxysm of insensibility, clung to the woman and cried bitterly. The court, and particularly, the worthy Magistrate, seemed to feel intensely for the situation of the poor girl and her parents. When the agitation and seeming penitence of the defender had subsided, the Magistrate warned her father to keep a strict look out after his daughter, who did not seem to be yet lost to the better feelings of rectitude and virtue.[162]

The combination of the parent's 'respectable' background, the accused's vulnerability and remorse, and the sympathy of the 'worthy' magistrate was enough to ensure that the latter's identity was not exposed in print.

Even a woman's attractiveness could influence journalistic and editorial decisions. In 1832, *The Police Intelligencer* reported the case of 'a young beaux [*sic*], dressed in the military academy uniform, quite smart, and a young Belles [*sic*], dressed in silk of Lincoln green, who simpered and smiled as she skipped to the bar', who were charged with 'stealing a black cloth vest, from a lockfast trunk, in the duty house corner of the North Bridge'. The report went on: 'This was a strange case, alleged to have been committed by such a fashionable and sprightly couple, caused many a neck to be stretched and many a mouth to gape amongst the auditory, to witness the result of the inquiry.' Significantly, it ended with the

---

a lad with their batons and otherwise maltreating him. Not only were their names withheld, but the periodical's commentary began by stressing that they 'have hitherto born a good character in the establishment'. Exactly how the journalist knew this is not known, although it points to the possibility that he was reflecting uncritically, as with other reports, the view of the magistrate in court. *Police Intelligencer*, 31 August 1831.

[161] *Police Intelligencer*, 23 September 1831. See further discussion of this case in Chapter 2.

[162] *Police Intelligencer*, 27 September 1831.

following remark: 'We was [*sic*] happy to learn that the supposed theft turned out to be a frolic, although one of a very dangerous nature. Dismissed, not guilty.'[163] Not only did the journalist take the unusual step of stating how pleased he was that the accused had been dismissed, his decision to take the equally unusual position of recording 'not guilty' after 'dismissed' (the overwhelming majority of reports simply stated 'dismissed') removed any blemish on the defenders' characters that might have been implied by their appearance in court.

Such protection, though, did not extend to 'deviant' women who, in the editors' eyes, were in need of correction. For all their proposed gallantry towards the vulnerable and 'decent' in society, and women in particular, it is evident that the media extended this only to certain individuals. Jess Williamson and Ann Findlay, described as 'dashy Cyprians' (slang for prostitutes), had their names exposed in *The Police Intelligencer* for being drunk and disorderly and using wicked and obscene language in a public place. So, too, did the vast majority of females identified as prostitutes. The report on Williamson and Findlay went on: 'the most superb dressed was fined 10s, and the other 5s.'[164] Although an attractive appearance could sometimes be a signifier of respectability in itself,[165] for women labelled as prostitutes it could be a sign of their 'always-ready sexualised femininity'.[166] Moreover, as Melanie Tebbutt has shown, the naming and labelling of a woman as a prostitute, or any questioning of her sexual morality, had the potential to do great damage to her reputation. A woman's sexual conduct, allied with her capacity to maintain a clean household, was a major arbiter of her standing within her own community.[167]

Yet there was a double standard in the periodicals' exposé of immoral behaviour. While they were particularly concerned with revealing the identities of women they perceived to be lewd and licentious, their male 'clients' in the majority of cases had their names withheld. On occasion, the media even expressed sympathy for men for having fallen into such 'bad' company. In a case involving 'Walker, prostitute, charged with stealing a pair of boots and spurs from a man' in 1829, the *Police Reports* revealed the name of the woman charged with theft but not the complainer and lamented: 'It was a shame for him, a married man, and the father of no less than ten children, to be drinking with a common prostitute.'[168] Also in 1829, the same periodical reported the case of an 'old grey headed sinner,

---

[163]   *Police Intelligencer*, 4 September 1832.

[164]   *Police Intelligencer*, 12 September 1831.

[165]   The trial examined in note 164 makes this point.

[166]   D'Cruze, *Crimes of Outrage*, p. 143.

[167]   Ibid., ch. 6; Melanie Tebbutt cites Glasgow reminiscences of the 'slitter in every close' whose 'dirty home implied a certain sexual laxity'. Melanie Tebbutt, 'Women's Talk? Gossip and "Women's Words" in Working-Class Communities, 1880–1939', in Andrew Davies and Stephen Fielding (eds), *Worker's Worlds: Cultures and Communities in Manchester and Salford, 1880–1939* (Manchester, 1992), p. 83.

[168]   *Police Reports*, 6 July 1829, p. 6.

once a respectable tailor, who could hardly stand on his legs at the bar, was charged with keeping a common bawdy-house, a house the harbour of the dissolute and disorderly, in High Street, and in the immediate neighbourhood of Mr Forrest, [Police] Commissioner'. It went on: 'The Magistrate found the complaint sufficiently proven, and observed, that it was a shame and disgrace for an old man like him on the verge of the grave, to keep a common brothel.'[169] The proximity of the defender's house to that of the local police commissioner might well have played a part in the editor's decision to publish the magistrate's chastisement of the accused, but the latter's identity was safeguarded all the same. Despite Brownlie's self-proclaimed desire to use the *Police Court* reports to expose immorality, it was the behaviour of certain sections of society that most interested him.

The protection of anonymity was not extended to working-class men to anywhere near the same extent as those from the middle classes. As with working-class women, editors were less concerned with respecting the lives and reputations of men from poorer backgrounds. The lives and experiences of society's underclass were not, in the eyes of editors, private, but rather a form of amusement. In his 'Secret Memoirs', the Glasgow policeman Samuel Rodger alluded to the class bias that existed not just in bringing people before the courts, but also in the way that trial proceedings were represented. Reporting on how a closed court had been held for 'a young swell' who had 'committed one of the most immoral acts which is possible for a man to commit in the presence of ladies', Rodger pointed out how young middle-class men often escaped being brought before the police court and the fascination journalists had in reporting the crimes and offences of the lower orders:

> Now just you compare this with the way the case would have been conducted if it has been a young workman who had went up to a big swell's window and done what this fellow did. Why, he would have been tried in open court with 4 or 5 newspaper reporters taking down every word as minutely as possible, and in little more than 24 hours, this young man's name and everything about him and what he had done would be read over at least half the English speaking world. The swells, after reading it in their morning paper would shrug their shoulders and say, "O, these horrid drunken working men".[170]

---

[169]   *Police Reports*, 10 July 1829, pp. 18–19.

[170]   Rodger also noted that, after being apprehended and escorted to the police station, 'instead of being locked up and brought before the court in the usual way, he [the accused] was allowed to leave [the police office] on depositing a pledge of two guineas. A special court was held with closed doors and the magistrate did not insist upon the young swell being present, but allowed the case to be tried by proxy, the father appearing in place of the son. He was only fined in the two guineas as left at the time of the apprehension.' 'The Secret Memoirs of Samuel Rodger (1846–1901) The Glasgow Teetotal Bobby', produced at the People's Palace Museum, Glasgow Green, to accompany the exhibition 'Scotland

His comment highlighted not just the role of the media in shaming individuals, but also its capacity to reinforce perceptions of class boundaries and the potential damage that naming and shaming could have on certain social groups. While being exposed in print could damage people from all walks of life, the selective nature of reporting suggests that editors and journalists believed that it was the middle classes, and middle-class males in particular, who had the most to lose from being named and shamed. Respectability, in other words, was in the eyes of the media more important to the middle classes, or those who aspired to become so, than it was for the lower orders who had no dignity to lose. Indeed, there were even suggestions in the media's coverage of the accused's demeanour and behaviour that some of the lower orders wore a courtroom appearance as a source of pride and badge of honour. Whether this was a view shared by those who had to endure being interrogated by procurators and magistrates, and the punishment which in most cases would come their way, is of course impossible to determine.[171]

For those suspected of crimes perceived as being particularly heinous, punishment could involve community as well as judicial sanction. Child stripping was one such crime, of which there had been 309 recorded reports to police in Glasgow in 1880.[172] Periodicals always identified by name those – invariably, in the reports, women – accused of stripping children of their clothing. Inflammatory language was often deployed, which left the reader in little doubt as to the shameful and odious nature of the crime. In 1831 *The Police Intelligencer*, under the title 'CHILD STRIPPER', described Janet Fraser as 'one of these despicable and half-hearted women, charged with stealing several articles of dress from a little girl, in a close or common stair'.[173] The following year it reported that 'Mary Stodart, a noted child stripper, was charged with the cruel and petty act of stealing a pair of shoes from a child's feet, at the Old Buildings, Castle Hill.' Despite being found innocent, the report left the reader in little doubt as to the accused's character and presumed guilt. It commented: 'A little girl who had charge of the girl, said that the prisoner took off the shoes for the purpose of cleaning them. Unfortunately, the proof was not sufficiently strong to convict the hard hearted monster, and she was consequently dismissed.'[174] Reports sometimes went to great lengths to portray

---

Sober and Free' marking the 150th anniversary of the temperance movement in Scotland, by kind permission of William Rodger, grandson of Samuel Rodger, pp. 1–2.

[171] Although the media stopped short of articulating this, the manner in which it highlighted the accused's lack of contrition and sarcastic response are likely to have helped forge in the minds of readers the impression that a courtroom trial was anything but a harrowing and humiliating experience for certain members of the community. See, for instance, the case of William McKinnon, Michael Collins and two other unnamed boys, charged with pick-pocketing, 'who, when placed at the bar, displayed a good deal of levity'. *Police Reports*, 14 August 1829, p. 52.

[172] ML, *City of Glasgow Police Criminal Returns for the Year Ending 31st December 1880*, p. 6.

[173] *Police Intelligencer*, 9 September 1831.

[174] *Police Intelligencer*, 4 October 1832.

the accused not only as sub-human, but also to convey the community response to such deviant behaviours. In 1829, the *Police Reports* published the following case:

> Ann Stewart, an old offender, was charged by Peter McGregor, No.12 Brunswick Place, Hugh Gilmour, John Boyle, Hugh Kilgour, and Richard McCall, weavers, Woodside, with stripping the clothes of an interesting looking boy, of four years of age, named Francis, son of William Walker, collier, residing in Gorbals, in the rope-work entry, Stockwell Street, Glasgow, on the 20th July. Mr. McGregor (whose dwelling-house is in the rope-work entry,) while at dinner, saw the prisoner from his window, stripping the child, and called the other accusers to his assistance, and she was apprehended in the act. The case was remitted to the council chamber for trial, as one of an aggravated description.[175]

Naming and portraying working-class women in such ways brought with it the potential for punishment as significant, if not more so, than the court could administer – namely, the wrath of, and potential alienation from, the local community. As Ellen Ross, Anna Davin, W. Hamish Fraser and others have shown, neighbourhood support was an important survival strategy for working-class women,[176] and a woman's reputation within her own community often determined her access to support networks. Indeed, as D'Cruze has pointed out, 'women, especially in the lower courts, were operating within an extension of the public arena of neighbourhood as well as within the institutional framework of the law'.[177] Crimes such as child stripping could be perceived as crimes against both femininity and the community if committed by women, and could, crucially, lead to a woman being ostracised and denied access to financial and child support on which many depended. Media coverage, in other words, raised the possibility of vigilante justice. In her study into the workings of the Victorian criminal courts in Kent, Carolyn Conley has argued that the police and magistrates often turned a blind eye to those who were guilty of extracting their own justice against those who had violated accepted community norms: 'in cases where the target of rough music brought charges, J.P.s usually announced that such conduct was disgraceful and could not be tolerated, and then dismissed the case for lack of evidence that anyone had been annoyed or dismissed.'[178] Given their shared values with magistrates, editors are unlikely to have condoned – and there is no evidence that they did –

---

[175] *Police Reports*, 1 August 1829, p. 29.

[176] Ross, 'Survival Networks', pp. 4–27; Anna Davin, *Growing Up Poor: Home, School and Street in London 1870–1914* (London, 1996), pp. 57–62; W. Hamish Fraser, 'The Working Class', in W. Hamish Fraser and Irene Maver (eds), *Glasgow, Volume II: 1830 to 1912* (Manchester, 1996), p. 302; and D'Cruze, *Crimes of Outrage*, pp. 60–62.

[177] D'Cruze, *Crimes of Outrage*, p. 169.

[178] Conley, *The Unwritten Law*, p. 23. This challenges the view of Robert D. Storch, who argued that the new police and magistrates were ruthless in their attempts to suppress traditional forms of community justice and self-policing. Robert D. Storch, 'The Policeman

physical acts of aggression against perpetrators of deplorable crimes that might have followed the publication of such trials. Nonetheless, in the manner in which they reported some offences as being abhorrent, and in exposing the identities of those involved, the media provided a mechanism for informal community action outwith the judicial sphere. And, importantly, the fact that journalists chose to portray offenders in such a negative way suggests that vigilante justice through community alienation might have been their intention.

Of course, in such, crowded, close-knit, poor communities, word of mouth and gossip rather than the media appears to have been the principal means of communicating information.[179] Glasgow's overcrowded, high-density tenement housing stock, in particular, made it extremely difficult for much of working-class domestic life not to be public.[180] Nonetheless, as our Introduction argues, the periodicals were not beyond the reach of large sections of the working class. Indeed, one trial report could help to extend the reach of information to a wide range of people given the propensity for information to be verbally exchanged in working-class communities.[181]

It was not only, though, the media's capacity to reveal the names of the accused and their alleged offences that had the potential to humiliate and embarrass. So, too, did the way in which court appearance was represented. As Chapter 4 has shown, the media often recorded courtroom personnel mocking and ridiculing the background, intelligence and speech of defenders, which, significantly, was often accompanied by an equally damning commentary from journalists and editors that effectively amounted to character assassination. In 1831, *The Police Intelligencer* published the following trial report:

> DAFT BOBBY NAPIER – This eccentric, who seems to be a compound of idiot and knave, his tattered habiliments and long bare legs exciting pity, but his physiog at the same time indicating a degree of cunning and roguishness according with the wickedness of his exploits, was yesterday placed at the bar, charged with striking Mrs Rae, turnkey to the Police Office. Sentenced to sixty days in bridewell.[182]

The appearance of the accused was often ridiculed. Indeed, some reports gave more attention to how the accused looked than the details of the case. In 1831, *The Police Intelligencer* described Jean Miller, charged with being drunk and

---

as Domestic Missionary: Urban Discipline and Popular Culture in Northern England, 1850–80', *Journal of Social History*, 9/4 (1976): p. 490.

179   Tebbutt, 'Women's Talk?', pp. 49–73.

180   Fraser, 'The Working Class', p. 302. Glasgow had amongst the most overcrowded housing in western Europe. See W. Hamish Fraser and Irene Maver, 'The Social Problems of the City', in Fraser and Maver (eds), *Glasgow*, pp. 363–78.

181   Ross, 'Survival Networks', p. 10.

182   *Police Intelligencer*, 18 August 1831.

disorderly, as 'a termagant of an obnoxious appearance'.[183] In the same year, it described John Todd, under the heading 'QUEER DANCING MASTER', as being

> dressed in a Galashiels light blue coat, minus the elbows and one of the flaps of the tail, a broad brimmed glazed sailor's hat, a vest and inexpressibles originally black, but now brown with age, a pair of Shetland hose, with clogs on his feet, the soles of which was at least one inch thick, was charged with keeping a dancing school, to the annoyance of his neighbours.[184]

Such depictions served to highlight the poverty and personal flaws of the accused. It left them exposed to embarrassment and ridicule and, in some cases, such as that involving John Todd, it had the potential to damage their modest means of making a living. *The Police Intelligencer* even ran a series of court reports under the heading 'MUTCH JOHN'S BALL' – a satirical and fictional reference to dancing parties and balls in brothels in Edinburgh – in which the accused in entering court were mockingly represented as entering a social function.[185] It reported: 'We find that it will be impossible to furnish our Readers with the names and designations, with a short sketch of the whole motley group who attended the late grand LET OFF all at once, but we will now and then introduce them by degree.'[186]

The Police Intelligencer also frequently referred to the accused, especially poor, working-class women, by nicknames even when their names were known. 'Craw' was an especially common colloquialism given by journalists and editors to women who spoke too much, and 'blackguard' a common title for young men perceived to be involved in immoral and criminal activities.[187] Indeed, in the case of 'Mary Martin an African Black … better known by the name of Blackie, and Margaret Campbell, alias spunkie, alias Craw' *The Police Intelligencer* continued to use those nicknames for the women, rather than their actual names for the rest of its description of the case:

> Blackie – She ca' d me a black B___! and I cried craw, craw!
> Superintendant (to Blackie) – You are much more like a craw than her.

---

[183]   *Police Intelligencer*, 15 June 1832.

[184]   *Police Intelligencer*, 1 November, 1831.

[185]   For more on 'Mutch John's Ball', see William Tait, *Magdalenism: An Inquiry into the Extent, Cause and Consequences of Prostitution in Edinburgh* (Edinburgh, 1840), p. 137.

[186]   *Police Intelligencer*, 22 October 1831.

[187]   The periodical reported 'George Paterson, a well known black guard, was charged with assaulting Jean Johnstone, alias Yankie, his fancy wife, in the stair leading to the Equitable Loan Company of Scotland. Yankie stated that she was pulling Paterson by the tail of the coat in order to get him advised home, when he turned round and knocked her head against the wall. Magistrate (to Yankie) – What business had you with him? Are you any relation to him? Yankie – He's my lad!' *Police Intelligencer*, 20 August 1831.

> Witnesses being called in, the Magistrate found it difficult to decide which of
> the craws were most to blame; but as the public did not seem to have been much
> disturbed by the crow fight, he was pleased to dismiss the case, without caging
> the craws.[188]

Although both women were later dismissed of the charges of fighting with each
other, the tone of this presentation was one of ridicule at two squabbling poor
women. The use of nicknames in such a manner helped to make the accused,
and sometimes complainers, caricatures for their readers, promoting a kind of
Dickensian fictionalisation of the lives of society's 'underbelly': they became
almost make-believe characters, displaced from the real world of the middle-class
readership. Moreover, such portrayals helped readers to form a judgement not just
about the guilt of the accused, but also their criminal pasts. In 1831, *The Police
Intelligencer* referred to Tom Innes, charged with 'wickedly and feloniously
attacking a gentleman belonging to Leith, in Prince's Street', as 'Gallows Tom',
leaving the reader with little doubt as to his recidivism or where, in the journalist's
opinion, he was headed.[189] Even women's hairstyles could carry with them a
criminal association. Their shortly-cropped hair was sometimes highlighted in the
press as a sign of guilt, since it denoted a previous stay in the bridewell. When
Bell Boyd appeared in the Edinburgh Police Court charged with breaking window
panes, the *Intelligencer* opined: 'Poor Bell complains that her hair is never allowed
to grow longer than the bridewell crop, and we believe never will, until she gives
up her evil ways and mends her manners.'[190] Indeed, the periodical developed a
reader history with Boyd which publicised her criminal past and made her life akin
to a comic character in a soap opera. In September 1831, it reported:

> This infatuated individual, who has seen better days, as many of our readers are
> aware of, and who has been confined in Bridewell a dozen of times in the court
> of the last two years, and above 60 times during her life, has at length reconciled
> her mind to become an inmate of that excellent Institution, the Magdalane
> Asylum.[191]

On 27 October 1831, it reported: 'Bell Boyd back again. Charged with breaking
window panes.'[192] A few weeks later, the periodical even covered her trial in the
local sheriff court. It reported that 'Bell Boyd, who is perhaps one of the best
customers to the glaziers, who was ever known to perform at an illumination
night, or any other mob, or city riot is back for glass breaking again.'[193] These

---

[188] *Police Intelligencer*, 19 August 1831.
[189] *Police Intelligencer*, 10 November 1831.
[190] *Police Intelligencer*, 27 October 1831.
[191] *Police Intelligencer*, 30 September 1831.
[192] *Police Intelligencer*, 27 October 1831.
[193] *Police Intelligencer*, 1 December 1831.

reports appeared in the press (and in the court, it seems) as little more than amusement for readers, rather than as a matter of real women's lives and legitimate social tensions. In Boyd's case, as with other women from a similar social background, shaming does not necessarily seem to have been the main function of trial reporting, as the way in which her charges were presented made her appear to be incapable of feeling opprobrium. Nonetheless, even if a person's shaming was not always the main intention, the damage such reports could do to reputation is likely to have been significant.

As Chapter 6 emphasised, the media frequently highlighted previous convictions as a signifier of guilt and to impugn the character of the accused. Significantly, trial reports did this even when charges were dismissed. Bess McAlpin, charged with robbery, was described as 'the Chieftainness of the Edinburgh Thieves';[194] Bell Holland, charged with stealing a £1 note from the pocket of 'an unwary wright whom she had untrapped', was characterised as 'a pretty successful cyprianic thief, who generally prowls about the Grassmarket';[195] and George Sutherland, charged with stealing 11s., 6d. from a grocer's till, was described as a 'a sly old fellow'.[196] Despite there being insufficient evidence against all three defenders to secure convictions, their reputations were tarnished, regardless, by the way their past indiscretions and characters had been portrayed. The reader was left in little doubt that the accused had, in *The Police Intelligencer*'s eyes at least, been fortunate not to have been found guilty.

The media, therefore, acted as a form of judicial censure in exposing the people whom it believed were guilty but had escaped conviction. Editors applied their own assumptions about judicial outcomes and guilt, and by association, the character of the accused, regardless of the court's findings. Doing this gave them some form of power and adjudication over the accused and served as a continuation of pre-modern forms of community shaming in that it did not necessarily require formal judicial sanction. It was, though, a form of reporting that was very much class-specific. While working-class defenders who were acquitted were often named, middle-class ones nearly always had their identities protected. The media, in other words, was happy to condemn and punish irrespective of judicial judgements, but less so social ones. The sanctity of character was every bit as important, if not more so, in media circles as it was in judicial ones.

Damaging someone's reputation through public shaming was not the only similarity between media reporting of police court trials and pre-modern principles of punishment. The media's decision to identify, or not, courtroom participants reflected its own moral, cultural, civic and even comic imperatives, but it was also, significantly, designed to serve as a warning to others. As earlier chapters have shown, Brownlie used the *Police Reports*

---

[194]   *Police Intelligencer*, 29 September 1831.
[195]   *Police Intelligencer*, 18 August 1831.
[196]   *Police Intelligencer*, 29 August 1831.

to 'warn others'.[197] *The Police Intelligencer* also published trial reports with the specific purpose of warning both the wider community about possible dangers and potential criminals about the penalty that awaited them if they broke the law,[198] as did *The Detective* which claimed that 'Our intention is the exposure and suppression of crime in every possible shape, and we only give publication to those acts which will be warnings to other people similarly tempted.'[199] Moreover, as with pre-modern forms of punishment, the periodicals relied upon public participation, in this case its readership, to help get their message across, the effect of which was reinforced by the media's references to the gasps, cheers and murmurs of the gallery. It was also a system of 'punishment' that was based on discretion – although in this instance it was the editor and not the magistrate who decided who was to be selected for exemplary public shaming.

Having said that, the impact of trial reports on an individual's reputation was potentially much longer-lasting and wider-ranging than pre-modern forms of shaming given the diffusion of newspapers in the nineteenth century and the permanence of the printed word. Whereas pre-modern forms of shaming rituals were localised, the rise of the national press – and the exchange of information between newspapers – meant that individuals could have their names blackened in print throughout the country, which the press would often worsen by highlighting past indiscretions. More importantly, media shaming represented a switch in the balance of those who could humiliate and those who could not. Whereas in the eighteenth century, the 'rough music' of pre-

---

[197]   *Police Reports*, p. 1. See also the warning about brothels in the following report, which was given extensive coverage, in which a ship's captain, Jeremiah Snooks, was violently assaulted in a disorderly drinking den and brothel: 'From what has been disclosed in this case, men ought to be on their guard against attending brothels; they are sufficiently blackened, whether married or unmarried, by going there, without running the risk of being murdered by house bullies; indeed, if they met with a misfortunate there, to disable them, or otherwise incapacitate them from lawful pursuits, few would have compassion for them. … there are many, too many, married men seen in disorderly houses, for neither more nor less than sensual purposes, and keeping up a correspondence with prostitutes, disgraceful to morality, and injurious to the constitutions of their offspring; yet those very men, outwardly, walk in a very superior sphere, and in society their company is courted by the unsuspecting, sober, and well-thinking classes.' Significantly, it stopped short of naming who these men were who walked in this 'superior' sphere. *Police Reports*, 1 August 1829, p. 27.

[198]   See, for instance, the case of James Cook, charged with stealing a pawnbroker's duplicate for a pair of blankets from the house of a young widow. *The Police Intelligencer* reported: 'The circumstances attending this case requires it to be recorded at length, as it may be of use to the community to guard against such a rascally conduct as that of which the prisoner is proved to be guilty.' It went on to quote the magistrate as saying: 'although it was the prisoner's first offence of the kind it was his duty to make him an example to others.' *Police Intelligencer*, 18 August 1831.

[199]   *The Detective*, no. 6, vol. I, 16 May 1885, p. 14.

industrial punishment described by Thompson required a degree of community participation for shaming to be effective, in the nineteenth century it could be done by journalists – albeit with the involvement of a reading public – writing a few words or pressing a few typewriter keys. The media in this era might, as Habermas has argued, have formed an important role in shaping the democratic administration of society and served as an important instrument for the formation of public opinion. But, when it came to moulding the reputations of those tried in police courts, it was a role confined to just a few privileged men.[200] The 'rough music' of community sanction might have lingered into the nineteenth century and beyond, as Conley has claimed, but when it came to smearing reputations, it was journalists and editors who were often calling the tune.[201]

V. Conclusion

Magistrates' wide-ranging judicial and civic roles ensured that many sentencing decisions would be determined on a discretionary, individual, basis rather than according to a uniform formula. The moral, social and cultural values of both the convicted and the magistrate all had a role to play in determining the outcome of judicial sentencing and the framing of police legislation on which decisions were loosely structured. So, too, did magistrates' position in local government and their own perceived role as paternal protectors of vulnerable groups. The civic magistrates who staffed the benches of Scotland's police courts had to balance a burgeoning caseload, and limited penal and human resources with which to deal with it, with the wider needs of the community and civic governance. While, at various points, the police and procurators might have targeted certain social groups and forms of behaviour, the need for magistrates to raise funds for wider civic improvements and balance budgets always made financial penalties an attractive option and somewhat blunted attempts to tackle the rougher elements of male working-class masculinity or, indeed, other forms of behaviour, through tougher punishments. As in the eighteenth century, punishment was also important to the status, position and authority of governing men. Although by no means as dramatic as the discretionary powers exercised by the ruling elite, and the paternal bonds it reinforced, as Douglas Hay has argued for indictable property offences in pre-industrial England, the discretionary powers of punishment at magistrates' disposal were important to how they viewed themselves, and, as importantly, how they wanted others to view them.[202]

---

[200]   Habermas, *The Structural Transformation of the Public Sphere*. See also Habermas, 'The Public Sphere', pp. 11–19.
[201]   Conley, *The Unwritten Law*, p. 23.
[202]   Hay, 'Property, Authority and the Criminal Law', pp. 17–63.

The media was not only largely supportive of magisterial sentencing but also punitive in its reporting – reinforcing, contextualising and justifying magisterial punishments, whilst offering its own form of censure in trial reports. In publicising sexual indiscretions and other forms of immorality, the media played an important part in the disciplinary culture of nineteenth-century society – and one akin, in terms of potential impact on the offender, to that of a Church of Scotland kirk session. The media functioned in the judicial sphere as a disciplinary resource through its shaming potential and was an important commentary on and resource for magisterial sentencing. Trial reports supported the workings and judgements of magisterial sentencing decisions by complementing judicial condemnation of behaviour for which the offender was expected to feel shame. Moreover, they helped to establish boundaries for what was acceptable and unacceptable behaviour by highlighting the ways in which those who transgressed them would be disciplined and, in publishing calls for wider-ranging punishments, publicised debates about appropriate punishments.

Conclusion

Police courts, and the manner in which laws were administered in them, represented the social, political and conceptual conflicts of the new urban world that was developing at this time. They were a product of, and had to adapt to, new concerns, crimes and raised expectations of comfort and security that stemmed from conglomeration in cities. The manner in which the law was administered, though, was steeped in tradition and the governing principles of Scottish civil society.[1] In 1875, the *Dundee Courier* captured the degree of autonomy enjoyed by Scotland's civic justices:

> Scotch Bailies and their Assessors have always been allowed to do very much as they like in the Police Courts, until many of them seem to act as if they thought the suggestions of their own unaided and in general uneducated judgement were the direct inspiration of Themis.[2]

Themis, the organiser of human affairs who protected custom, tradition, and social order, sometimes acting upon the whim of the gods, was an accurate reflection of the kind of community-oriented justice delivered by magistrates firmly bound to their neighbourhoods. While, for the most part, magistrates stayed within the legal remit of their judicial powers, judgements were often informed by social, moral and ethnic bias and by the belief that flexible, common-sense justice was preferable to uniformity in legal practice and procedure. It was a system of law enforcement that was indicative of the fact that the men who governed Scottish cities, despite pioneering civic initiatives and leading commercial enterprises,[3] retained the pastoral and parochial mentalities of the Established Church and the social values of the pre-industrial town and village. In other words, they knew what was best for their community and could vouchsafe for its people.

Procurators and clerks of court may have had some oversight over the actions of the bailies, but in general individual magistrates had remarkable scope to apply their own ideas to court practice and people's lives. Potential for conflict between them was somewhat reduced both by the fact that magistrates appointed the

---

[1] For more on civil society and its impact on policing in Scotland, see David G. Barrie, 'Police in Civil Society: Police, Enlightenment and Civic Virtue in Scotland, 1780–1833', *Urban History*, 37/1 (2010): pp. 45–65.

[2] *Dundee Courier*, 3 August 1875.

[3] W. Hamish Fraser and Irene Maver, 'Tackling the Problems', in W. Hamish Fraser and Irene Maver (eds), *Glasgow, Volume II: 1830 to 1912* (Manchester, 1996), pp. 394–440.

former and by their shared social and cultural mores. The advent of stipendiary magistrates placed bailies under scrutiny that they had not experienced previously and encouraged media outlets to take a more critical stance about the decisions of individual magistrates. Yet, here too, criticism applied to one individual 'bad apple' tended to suggest the general 'good character' of the rest of the magistracy. For the most part, the concept of the civic magistracy was supported because it was perceived as being an essential component of how Scottish civil society was governed. As the discourse surrounding the introduction of the stipendiary magistrate in Glasgow in the late nineteenth century highlighted, the British government's attempts to impose greater central control over Scottish affairs was regarded as a threat to local autonomy and the power, status and influence of a small group of elite men – just as the proposed introduction of elected police commissions had been in the first few decades of the century.

The constitutional framework of police courts reflected not just Scottish civic governance and magistrates' own values and interests concerning what constituted the common good, but also the latter's wider role in the community and the function that these courts were designed to serve. They were, in keeping with the wide meaning of 'police' in nineteenth-century Scotland, just one part of a broader municipal sphere – a sphere in which magistrates fulfilled many civic duties in different branches of local government. Although centres of justice, police courts could not be divorced from local government or the public servants who staffed them. As civic rather than stipendiary justices, magistrates had to balance judicial decisions with civic ones, a consideration that had significant implications for how the law was enforced and for how historians understand theories of punishment at a summary level. Sentences were determined not just by the nature of the crime, offence or the profile and gender of the convicted, but also often by practical and fiscal realities, by magistrates' role as civic leaders, by how they saw their role in the community, and by their preoccupation with their image in the media.

The multi-faceted role of magistrates, courtroom officials and, indeed, the police itself meant there was often much overlap between public men and the offices they staffed – a peculiar arrangement that had significant implications for police–judicial relations. The relationship between magistrates, the police and other branches of public life was complex and by no means clear cut. Indeed, at times, it could be hostile – especially prior to the incorporation of elected police commissions, around mid-century, when magistrates and elected commissioners frequently clashed on a range of civic issues. Although magistrates served as *ex-officio* police commissioners throughout the century, at no point did they command a majority presence on either elected police commissions or watch committees. Magisterial capacity to formally direct police policy had to be made with the support of a majority of fellow commissioners, which in the fractious years that pre-dated burgh reform in 1833, in particular, was by no means always forthcoming. As has been argued elsewhere, chief constables in Scotland gained greater autonomy over police affairs from council watch committees as the second half of the nineteenth century progressed, which further reduced magistrates' capacity to direct police business on a day-to-day basis.[4] Moreover, the large number of cases that were dismissed pre-trial, especially in police courts' formative years, suggests that the police and magistrates were not always working to the same script. Within the police itself there was often, as studies have shown, tension between senior officers and beat constables, with the latter adopting a pragmatic approach to law enforcement and turning a blind eye to certain behaviours that had the potential to inflame social tension.[5] Nineteenth-century policing was always a balancing act between what senior police officers desired, and what officers on the ground thought was practical and were capable of enforcing.[6]

Having said that, the fact that civic magistrates never severed their links with the police, continued to appoint chief constables and burgh procurators, and never in most towns introduced a stipendiary magistrate – who, significantly, did not serve as a police commissioner – meant that there was never a complete separation between the judiciary and the police. While magisterial power and authority over police affairs might have fluctuated throughout the century, there is little doubt that at certain points they were able to direct police affairs – even, in some instances, losing public office after serious disturbances had failed to be effectively checked. As has been shown throughout this analysis, there were enough recorded instances of magistrates directing senior police officers to deploy their officers at certain events to apprehend certain persons, or to take specific actions, to show that the police were not completely independent from the judiciary at a summary level. A more in-depth investigation of police–fiscal–magisterial relations at an institutional and civic level would certainly produce greater results than was uncovered in a study such as ours which focused mainly on courtroom discourse. Indeed, such a line of inquiry would help to address an important area of criminal justice history that has not received the attention it deserves. However, in so far as courtroom evidence can illuminate this topic, it suggests many shared interests, values and mores between magistrates and senior police officials. Often, they were recorded

---

[4]   See, for instance, David G. Barrie, 'Anglicisation and Autonomy: Scottish Policing, Governance and the State, 1833 to 1885', *Law and History Review*, 30/2 (2012): pp. 478–9.

[5]   Moreover, officers on the ground were by no means always guaranteed to share the same values as senior officers and local justices, although they were, in theory at least, expected to enforce the policies of senior police officials. For more on the complex relationship between police personnel, and the challenges involved in untangling this, see Mark Finnane and Stephen Garton, 'The Work of Policing: Social Relations and the Criminal Justice System in Queensland 1880–1914: Part I', *Labour History*, 62 (1992): p. 54. As David Taylor has argued, although police were given a mandate to prevent crime, the constable on the beat often took a pragmatic approach to policing, turning a blind eye to certain behaviours such as drunkenness or prostitution that might adversely impact on social relations in certain communities. David Taylor, *The New Police: Crime, Conflict and Control in Nineteenth Century England* (Manchester, 1997), p. 5.

[6]   For more on the complex relationship between police governing structures and the social context in which they operated, see Mark Finnane, *Police and Government: Histories of Policing in Australia* (Oxford, 1994).

in the press mocking the accused and casting aspersions as to their character. Perhaps more tellingly, police officers, journalists and members of the public were all recorded at various times alluding to the intimate relationship that existed between magistrates and the police. While this speaks to public perceptions, the fact that such comments were drawn from a cross-section of society, from people who experienced police and magisterial justice first-hand as defenders, witnesses and courtroom reporters, suggests it was not without foundation. At the very least, it is likely to have influenced how some sections of society viewed, and used or otherwise, the police and the courts.

Although media evidence projected stylised voices of various types of accused, victims and witnesses (very much according to preconceived middle-class notions), the reality was that the structure of the Scottish police court limited the capacity of the majority of its legal participants to discuss and negotiate competing views, ideals and identities from positions of any strength. The discretion that procurators fiscal and magistrates wielded in the courtroom created different dynamics about justice for adversaries to those seen south of the border for much of the nineteenth century, although the police take-over of prosecutions in England in the second half of the century might have brought the Scottish and English systems more into line with each other. Courtroom personnel were certainly attentive to influences both in and out of the court (not least those generated by the civic elite and mainstream media), and certainly exposure to the 'problems' of the working classes affected both the perception of crime and suitable punishments for offenders. In these respects, the police court may well have been the most responsive of all contemporary courts, especially as magistrates had more flexibility than higher court justices to match outcomes to their perceptions of need. However, magisterial responses to the voices and experiences of working-class interlocutors before them rarely resulted in judgements that favoured the socially disadvantaged in urban society.

Although the willingness of certain sections of the lower orders to use police courts to settle disputes and seek justice should caution against overstating the extent to which they were an ideological tool of the propertied class, the manner in which they functioned, and the way in which police law was constructed and evolved, makes it impossible to divorce them from wider institutional developments designed to discipline and control urban populaces through bureaucratic and repressive means.[7] Many of these new institutions, such as police forces, industrial schools and prisons, developed within the remit of the criminal justice system, but there were also other, older, institutional pillars within Scottish society with which the police courts worked in tandem. Police court justices sought to provide moral leadership akin to kirk session elders and poor law officials – both of whom were managing rapidly changing dynamics in expanding urban environments. The role of magistrate was one that was similar to a new pastor of an urban meta-

---

[7]   See, for example, Michel Foucault, *Discipline and Punish: The Origins of the Prison* (London, 1978).

parish in that he served as a social and moral missionary to urban populations. The construction and expansion of police law in the nineteenth century gave magistrates scope to intervene in the regulation of people's lives in a hitherto unprecedented manner. Statutory local laws were elevated to central importance in the running and structuring of the built environment and it was through police courts that magistrates were able to enforce them. Indeed, while scholars have identified the criminal law and the higher courts in the eighteenth century as a principal means by which society was ordered and structured,[8] in the nineteenth century it was the relatively mundane police laws and police courts that were at the forefront in empowering some, disempowering others, and in fashioning the nature and perception of urban communities. Higher courts, of course, continued to occupy a place of central importance within the criminal justice system. But, in terms of the volume of people they prosecuted, the manner in which they filtered and processed cases, and in their capacity for extending the judicial reach, authority and status of magistrates, police courts were increasingly playing an integral role in the everyday functioning of the judicial system, civic governance and urban society.

While the remit of police courts grew over the century, the social profile of the convicted offender changed very little. Working-class people remained both the imagined and actual focus of most of the courts' work. Despite being grounded in Enlightenment ideals of improvement and the common good,[9] the overwhelming majority of police laws that were prosecuted were designed to control the behaviour of the urban masses and impose a greater level of public order, with the issues that brought the middle class to court – not least smoke pollution – being much less vigorously pursued.

Jennifer S. Davis, in her study of the London police courts, has argued that as the second half of the century progressed the working class became less willing to use police courts as centres of conflict resolution or support, instead viewing them increasingly as part of a bureaucratic police machine.[10] As their counterparts

---

[8] E.P. Thompson, for instance, argued for eighteenth-century England that 'the law was elevated during this century to a role more prominent that at any other period in our history'. E.P. Thompson, *Customs in Common* (New York, 1991), p. 34. For the importance of the criminal law in eighteenth-century Scotland in empowering the Scottish legal profession, see Peter Stein, 'Law and Society in Eighteenth-Century Scottish Thought', in R. Mitchison and N.T. Phillipson (eds), *Scotland in the Age of Improvement* (Edinburgh, 1970), pp. 148–68; Nicholas Phillipson, 'Lawyers, Landowner, and the Civic Leadership of Post-Union Scotland', *Judicial Review*, 97 (1976): pp. 97–120; and John Stuart Shaw, *The Management of Scottish Society, 1707–1764* (Edinburgh, 1983).

[9] For more on the Enlightenment ideal of improvement and its influence on the built environment, see Charles McKean, 'Improvement and Modernisation in Everyday Enlightenment Scotland', in Elizabeth Foyster and Christopher A. Whatley (eds), *A History of Everyday Life in Scotland, 1600 to 1800* (Edinburgh, 2010), pp. 51–82.

[10] Jennifer S. Davis, 'A Poor Man's System of Justice? The London Police Courts in the Second Half of the Nineteenth Century', *Historical Journal*, 27/2 (1984): p. 333.

in Scotland became increasingly consumed with cases of drunk and disorderly conduct, vagrancy, prostitution, and public order offences, and as the summary powers of sheriff courts increased, there were reports that the more respectable members of society sought to distance themselves from these courts. Whether this was reflected among the lower orders is difficult to say. Although significant numbers continued to press charges through the fiscal's office for crimes and offences, their capacity for using police courts to settle personal disputes in an informal manner – itself somewhat contained and restricted by the public prosecutor who determined whether a case could be brought to court or not – appears to have diminished as the century went on. Higher conviction rates, allied with a reduction in the proportion of cases that made it to court in which no proceedings were taken, suggest that the police, and burgh procurators, had become more preoccupied with, and skilled in, filtering out weak cases. And, more importantly, they indicate that the role of the courts was increasingly to administer justice formally rather than settle disputes informally and impart magisterial counsel. What is more certain is that the huge volume of Scots who were prosecuted in the late nineteenth century points to the resistance among large sections of the Scottish urban population to 'civilising' processes and to the persistence of rougher aspects of culture and behaviour.

Drawing conclusions about what prosecution patterns reveal about how far sections of the lower orders had become reconciled to the advent of the policed society, and what this might suggest about the perceived legitimacy of the law, is far from easy. The urban masses' relationship with the police and the courts was often ambiguous, fickle and fraught. Of fundamental importance to this was the role of the public prosecutor – both in the form of the burgh fiscal and the police. Prosecution was a discretionary instrument of power that not only impacted upon the masses' day-to-day lives,[11] but also is likely to have influenced their perception of the police and the courts. On the one hand, the role of the police in prosecuting cases in the public interest and the willingness of magistrates to hear and, in some cases resolve, working-class grievances might have helped to reduce suspicion towards the legal system and encourage others to use it. On the other hand, the huge number of police-led prosecutions for 'victimless' offences is likely to have turned people against the police, exposing what they perceived as the latter's inherent class bias. Besides, seeking legal redress through police courts did not necessarily mean acceptance of the law or unconditional support for the workings of the judicial system. Legal redress for many people is likely to have been a last resort and one that was designed primarily to meet specific individual needs.[12]

The mainstream media consulted in this project had an important role in representing the work of police magistrates. Press reports were, on occasion,

---

[11]   Douglas Hay and Francis Snyder, 'Using the Criminal Law, 1750–1850: Policing, Private Prosecution and the State', in Douglas Hay and Francis Snyder (eds), *Policing and Prosecution in Britain, 1750–1850* (Oxford, 1989), p. 47.

[12]   Jennifer S. Davis, 'Prosecutions and their Context: The Use of the Criminal Law in Later Nineteenth-Century London', in ibid., p. 419.

critical, condemning what editors perceived as a lack of judicial action over particular categories of crimes and offences, or what journalists observed in court of the way magistrates dealt with particular offenders before the bench. Police-produced returns provided grist to the mill of media campaigns that pinpointed specific offences, the types of punishments, or the level of funds raised through the work of the police court. In another way, the provision of the auditory in the courtroom also allowed the media a seat to witness the everyday workings of police court justice, for better or worse. Their insights into the actual practice of justice revealed for readers far and wide the fallibility of human nature – demonstrated by the displays of the accused, witnesses and even on occasion, magistrates themselves. By and large, though, the mainstream media, in its coverage of police court trials, projected a positive image about magisterial justice and law and order issues. Media concerns about public safety and crime were much more likely to be found in wider news reports rather than trial reports, and often had a political inflection in seeking to undermine those in civic administration. Critical commentary about courtroom convictions, punishments and workings was striking because it was relatively rare – and typically, manifested itself when the press believed it was protecting a wider common good rather than the rights of specific individuals.[13] Indeed, criticism on specific judicial judgements concerning the urban masses was conspicuous by its absence. Even the 'radical' era of unstamped periodicals did little to challenge the authority of the courts and likely contributed more to opening up access to a sensationalised version of the same representation of the courts' work to a wide popular readership. Magisterial concern about the representation of courtroom trial reports in certain newspapers in the mid-century suggest that the rise of the Sunday 'tabloids' might have been more critical of the courts, and the personnel in them, although this would require further investigation; but the mainstream media studied in this project certainly helped to legitimise magisterial justice throughout the nineteenth century. Indeed, the supporting manner in which the media recorded the voice of magistrates, and the way it highlighted the 'character' of offenders in order to help convince readers that convictions and punishments were just, suggest that the courts and the mainstream media were working to a similar agenda – an agenda based upon shared social and moral values.

As has been demonstrated throughout this study, magistrates and senior police officers were preoccupied with both their own public image and that of the court at large. Their relationship with the media was in many respects a symbiotic one: it was, on the one hand, in the interests of the civic elite that the court was bestowed with the public authority that justified its close supervision of urban landscapes and peoples, and validated it as a legitimate source of justice to the right kind of complainer. As a result, police court personnel were aware of the importance of the press gallery and, in all likelihood, engaged in a close dialogue with media outlets to supply and project an image of an efficient, effective and just form of order to

---

[13] Explored further in Volume 2.

urban societies. Threats to reveal in the press the identities of offenders convicted of embarrassing offences testifies at the very least to a contemporary perception about the nature of this relationship and magistrates' capacity to direct it. Indeed, this was a relationship that became ever more important as the century progressed with press coverage of police court trials helping to further distance ordinary people from the courtroom itself, thereby giving the media an important function in conveying the message from the magistrate's bench. On the other hand, the media was dependent upon magistrates permitting them access to the court and court books in order to satisfy the growing thirst among the reading public for sensational and amusing trial reports. Unflattering or inaccurate coverage could, after all, result in court personnel threatening to deny journalists access to the sources of information they needed. Moreover, the selective reporting of court cases helped editors such as Brownlie to further their own moral campaigns and exploit the behaviour of the urban masses for commercial gain.

In his influential study, Jürgen Habermas argued that the media in the nineteenth century became a central component of the public sphere.[14] Newspapers, he wrote, functioned as an instrument of debate, helping to form public opinion, shape perceptions and define sub-cultures. In its coverage of police court trial reports, the mainstream media in Scotland fulfilled a similar function, assuming a level of importance that transcended the mere representation of how the courts dealt with petty criminals and offenders. It took on an informal judicial role that embedded it as an instrument of law and order – sometimes working with, and sometimes independently of, magistrates in naming those convicted of 'shameful' crimes and offences and in sending out warnings about the dangers of a range of activities it regarded as immoral. Although the media's selective coverage could be unrepresentative of the reality of court practice, it was nonetheless important in showcasing the kinds of debates that were occurring within the court about what the city was, what it should and could be, who was to protect it, and what to do when this did not occur.

Perhaps the media's most important role, though, was the constraining influence it could have on magistrates. Despite being largely supportive, media reports forced some magistrates, it seems, to live in a constant state of anxiety from the court reporter and their own media representation – and offered some written, albeit highly selective, form of trial proceedings in a system in which court transcripts were sacrificed in the name of efficiency. While bailies, as the *Dundee Courier* in the introduction to this conclusion suggested, enjoyed a capacity for independent direction in administering the law in police courts, it always had to be balanced by concerns about their own media representation. In the courtroom, it seemed, the journalist's pen could be as mighty as the sword of justice on which it reported.

---

[14]   Jürgen Habermas, *The Structural Transformation of the Public Sphere: An Inquiry into a Category of Bourgeois Society* (Cambridge, 1989, first published 1962); and Jürgen Habermas, 'The Public Sphere: An Encyclopaedia Article', in Chris Greer (ed.), *Crime and Media: A Reader* (London, 2010), pp. 11–19.

Selected Secondary Reading

An extensive secondary literature has been referenced throughout and need not be listed in full here. What follows is a selective list of key studies for further reading.

Books

Barrie, David G. and Broomhall, Susan (eds), *A History of Police and Masculinities, 1700–2010* (London: Routledge, 2012).

Barrie, David G., *Police in the Age of Improvement: Police Development and the Civic Tradition in Scotland, 1775–1865* (Cullompton: Willan Publishing, 2008; reprinted, London: Routledge, 2012).

Beattie, J.M., *Policing and Punishment in London, 1660–1750: Urban Crime and the Limits of Terror* (Oxford: Oxford University Press, 2001).

Beattie, J.M., *Crime and the Courts in England, 1660–1800* (Oxford: Oxford University Press, 1986).

Brown, Callum G., *The Social History of Religion in Scotland since 1730* (London: Methuen, 1987).

Cameron, Joy, *Prisons and Punishment in Scotland* (Edinburgh: Canongate, 1983).

Conley, Carolyn A., *The Unwritten Law: Criminal Justice in Victorian Kent* (Oxford: Oxford University Press, 1991).

D'Cruze, Shani (ed.), *Everyday Violence in Britain, 1850–1950: Gender and Class* (London: Pearson Education, 2000).

D'Cruze, Shani, *Crimes of Outrage: Sex, Violence and Victorian Working Women* (London: UCL Press, 1998).

Devine, T.M. and Wormald, Jenny (eds), *The Oxford Handbook of Modern Scottish History* (Oxford: Oxford University Press, 2012).

Devine, T.M., *The Scottish Nation: 1700–2000* (London: Penguin, 2000).

Devine, T.M. and Jackson, Gordon (eds), *Glasgow, Volume I: Beginnings to 1830* (Manchester: Manchester University Press, 1995).

Emsley, Clive, *The English and Violence since 1750* (London: Hambledon, 2005).

Emsley, Clive, *Crime and Society in England, 1750–1900*, 3rd edn (Harlow: Pearson Longman, 2005).

Farmer, Lindsay, *Criminal Law, Tradition and Legal Order: Crime and the Genius of Scots Law, 1747 to the Present* (Cambridge: Cambridge University Press, 1997).

Foucault, Michel, *Discipline and Punish: The Origins of the Prison* (London: Penguin, 1991 edn; first published Paris: Gallimard, 1975).

Fraser, W. Hamish and Maver, Irene (eds), *Glasgow, Volume II: 1830 to 1912* (Manchester: Manchester University Press, 1996).

Godfrey, Barry and Cox, David J., *Policing the Factory. Theft, Private Policing and the Law in Modern England* (London: Bloomsbury, 2013).

Gray, Drew D., *Crime, Prosecution and Social Relations in London: The Summary Courts of London in the Late Eighteenth Century* (Basingstoke: Palgrave Macmillan, 2009).

Griffiths, Trevor and Morton, Graeme (eds), *A History of Everyday Life in Scotland, 1800 to 1900* (Edinburgh: Edinburgh University Press, 2010).

Habermas, Jürgen, *The Structural Transformation of the Public Sphere: An Inquiry into a Category of Bourgeois Society* (Cambridge: The MIT Press, 1989, English edn; first published in Frankfurt am Main: Suhrkamp, 1962).

Harris, Bob, *Politics and the Rise of the Press: Britain and France 1600–1800* (London: Routledge, 1996).

Hay, Douglas and Snyder, Francis (eds), *Policing and Prosecution in Britain, 1750–1850* (Oxford: Clarendon Press, 1989).

Hay, Douglas, Linebaugh, Peter, Rule, John G., Thompson, E.P. and Winslow, Cal (eds), *Albion's Fatal Tree: Crime and Society in Eighteenth-Century England* (London: Pantheon, 1976).

Jones, David J.V., *Crime, Protest, Community and Police in Nineteenth-Century Britain* (London: Routledge and Kegan Paul, 1982).

Kilday, Anne-Marie, *Women and Violent Crime in Enlightenment Scotland* (Woodbridge: Boydell Press, 2007).

King, Peter, *Crime and the Law in England 1750–1840: Remaking Justice from the Margins* (Cambridge: Cambridge University Press, 2006).

King, Peter, *Crime, Justice and Discretion in England, 1740–1820* (Oxford: Oxford University Press, 2000).

Knox, W.W.J., *Industrial Nation: Work, Culture and Society in Scotland, 1800–Present* (Edinburgh: Edinburgh University Press, 1999).

Lemmings, David (ed.), *Crime, Courtrooms and the Public Sphere in Britain, 1700–1850* (Farnham: Ashgate, 2012).

Leneman, Leah and Mitchison, Rosalind, *Sin in the City: Sexuality and Social Control in Urban Scotland 1660–1780* (Edinburgh: Scottish Cultural Press, 1998).

Maver, Irene, *Glasgow* (Edinburgh: Edinburgh University Press, 2000).

McGowan, John, *Policing the Metropolis of Scotland: A History of the Police and Systems of Police in Edinburgh and Edinburghshire, 1770–1833* (Musselburgh: Turlough Publishers, 2010).

McLaren, Angus, *The Trials of Masculinity: Policing Sexual Boundaries, 1870–1930* (Chicago: The University of Chicago Press, 1997).

Miller, Wilbur, *Cops and Bobbies: Police Authority in New York and London, 1830–1870* (Chicago: The University of Chicago Press, 1977).

Miskell, Louise, Whatley, Christopher A. and Harris, Bob (eds), *Victorian Dundee: Image and Realities* (East Linton: Tuckwell Press, 2001).

Shoemaker, Robert B., *Prosecution and Punishment: Petty Crime and the Law in London and Rural Middlesex, c.1660–1725* (Cambridge: Cambridge University Press, 1991).

Taylor, David, *Hooligans, Harlots, and Hangmen: Crime and Punishment in Victorian Britain* (Santa Barbara: Praeger, 2010).

Waddy, H.T., *The Police Court and its Work* (London: Butterworth, 1925).

Whatley, Christopher A., *Scottish Society 1707–1830: Beyond Jacobitism, Towards Industrialisation* (Manchester: Manchester University Press, 2000).

Wiener, Martin J., *Men of Blood: Violence, Manliness and Criminal Justice in Victorian England* (Cambridge: Cambridge University Press, 2004).

Wood, John Carter, *The Shadow of Our Refinement: Violence and Crime in Nineteenth-Century England* (London: Routledge, 2005).

Zedner, Lucia, *Women, Crime and Custody in Victorian England* (Oxford: Clarendon Press, 1991).

Articles

Barrie, David G. and Broomhall, Susan, 'Public Men, Private Interests? The Origins, Structure and Practice of Police Courts in Scotland, 1800–1833', *Continuity and Change*, 27/1 (2012): 83–123.

Barrie, David G., 'Naming and Shaming: Trial by Media in Nineteenth-Century Scotland', *Journal of British Studies*, forthcoming at time of publication, 54/1 (2015).

Barrie, David G., 'Anglicisation and Autonomy: Scottish Policing, Governance and the State, 1833 to 1885', *Law and History Review*, 30/2 (2012): 449–94.

Barrie, David G., 'Police in Civil Society: Police, Enlightenment and Civic Virtue in Scotland, 1780–1833', *Urban History*, 37/1 (2010): 45–65.

Broomhall, Susan and Barrie, David G., 'Changing of the Guard: Governance, Policing, Masculinity and Class in the Porteous Affair and Walter Scott's *Heart of Midlothian*', *Parergon: Journal of the Australian and New Zealand Association for Medieval and Early Modern Studies*, 28/1 (2011): 65–90.

Davis, Jennifer S., 'A Poor Man's System of Justice? The London Police Courts in the Second Half of the Nineteenth Century', *Historical Journal*, 27/2 (1984): 309–35.

Davis, Michael T., 'Prosecution and Radical Discourse during the 1790s: The Case of the Scottish Sedition Trials', *International Journal of the Sociology of Law*, 33/3 (2005): 148–58.

Devereaux, Simon, 'The Fall of the Sessions Paper: The Criminal Trial and the Popular Press in Late Eighteenth-Century London', *Criminal Justice History*, 18/1 (2002): 57–88.

Donnachie, Ian, '"The Darker Side": A Speculative Survey of Scottish Crime during the First Half of the Nineteenth Century', *Scottish Economic and Social History*, 15/1 (1995): 5–24.

Godfrey, Barry S., 'Changing Prosecution Practices and their Impact on Crime Figures, 1857–1940', *British Journal of Criminology*, 48/2 (2008): 171–89.

Gray, Drew D., 'The People's Courts? Summary Justice and Social Relations in the City of London, c.1760–1800', *Family and Community History*, 11/1 (2008): 7–15.

Hughes, Annemarie, 'The "Non-Criminal" Class: Wifebeating in Scotland, c.1850–1949', *Crime, Histoire & Sociétés/Crime, History & Societies*, 14/2 (2010): 31–54.

King, Peter, 'The Summary Courts and Social Relations in Eighteenth-Century England', *Past and Present*, 183/1 (2004): 125–72.

Morgan, Gwenda and Rushton, Peter, 'The Magistrate, the Community and the Maintenance of an Orderly Society in Eighteenth-Century England', *Historical Research*, 76/191 (2003): 54–77.

Philips, David, 'The Black Country Magistracy, 1835–60: A Changing Elite and the Exercise of its Power', *Midland History*, 3/3 (1976): 161–90.

Riggs, Paul T., 'Prosecutors, Juries, Judges and Punishment in Early Nineteenth-Century Scotland', *Journal of Scottish Historical Studies*, 32/2 (2012): 166–89.

Shoemaker, Robert B., 'The Old Bailey Proceedings and the Representation of Crime and Criminal Justice in Eighteenth-Century London', *Journal of British Studies*, 47/3 (2008): 559–80.

Smith, Bruce P., 'The Presumption of Guilt and the English Law of Theft, 1750–1850', *Law and History Review*, 23/1 (2005): 133–72.

Storch, Robert D., 'The Policeman as Domestic Missionary: Urban Discipline and Popular Culture in Northern England, 1850–80', *Journal of Social History*, 9/4 (1976): 481–509.

Swift, Roger, 'The English Urban Magistracy and the Administration of Justice During the Early Nineteenth-Century: Wolverhampton 1815–60', *Midland History*, 17 (1992): 75–92.

Book Chapters

Barrie, David G., 'The Birth of Modern Policing in Britain, 1750–1829', in Gerben Bruinsma and David Weisburd (eds), *Encyclopedia of Criminology and Criminal Justice* (New York: Springer, 2014).

Barrie, David G., 'Urban Order in Georgian Dundee, c.1770–1820', in Charles McKean, Bob Harris and Christopher A. Whatley (eds), *Dundee: Renaissance to Enlightenment* (Dundee: Dundee University Press, 2009).

Barrie, David G. and Broomhall, Susan, 'Policing Bodies in Urban Scotland, 1780–1850', in Susan Broomhall and Jacqueline Van Gent (eds), *Governing Masculinities: Regulating Selves and Others in the Early Modern Period* (Farnham: Ashgate, 2011).

Broomhall, Susan, and Barrie, David, G., 'Making Men: Media, Magistrates and the Representation of Masculinity in Scottish Police Courts, 1800–1833', in David G. Barrie and Susan Broomhall (eds), *A History of Police and Masculinities, 1700–2010* (London: Routledge, 2012).

Carson, K. and Idzikowska, H., 'The Social Production of Scottish Policing, 1795–1900', in Douglas Hay and Francis Snyder (eds), *Policing and Prosecution in Britain, 1750–1850* (Oxford: Clarendon Press, 1989).

Crone, Rosalind, 'Publishing Courtroom Drama for the Masses, 1820–1855', in David Lemmings (ed.), *Crime, Courtrooms and the Public Sphere in Britain, 1700–1850* (Farnham: Ashgate, 2012).

Crowther, M.A., 'Crime, Prosecution and Mercy: English Influence and Scottish Practice in the Early Nineteenth Century', in S.J. Connolly (ed.), *Kingdoms United? Great Britain and Ireland since 1500: Integration and Diversity* (Dublin: Four Courts Press, 1999).

Davis, Jennifer S., 'Prosecutions and their Context: The Use of the Criminal Law in Later Nineteenth-Century London', in Douglas Hay and Francis Snyder (eds), *Policing and Prosecution in Britain, 1750–1850* (Oxford: Clarendon Press, 1989).

Gatrell, V.A.C., 'Crime, Authority and the Policeman–State', in F.M.L. Thompson (ed.), *Cambridge Social History of Britain, 1750–1950* (Cambridge: Cambridge University Press, 1992).

Godfrey, Barry S., 'Sentencing, Theatre, Audience and Communication: The Victorian and Edwardian Magistrates' Courts and their Message', in Benoît Garnot (ed.), *Les témoins devant la justice* (Rennes: Presses universitaires de Rennes, 2003).

Hay, Douglas, 'Property, Authority and the Criminal Law', in Douglas Hay, Peter Linebaugh, John G. Rule, E.P. Thompson and Cal Winslow (eds), *Albion's Fatal Tree: Crime and Society in Eighteenth-Century England* (London: Pantheon, 1976).

Kilday, Anne-Marie, 'Contemplating the Evil Within: Examining Attitudes to Criminality in Scotland, 1700–1840', in David Lemmings (ed.), *Crime, Courtrooms and the Public Sphere in Britain, 1700–1850* (Farnham, Ashgate, 2012).

Knox, W.W.J. and McKinlay, A., 'Crime, Protest and Policing in Nineteenth-Century Scotland', in Trevor Griffiths and Graeme Morton (eds), *A History of Everyday Life in Scotland, 1800 to 1900* (Edinburgh: Edinburgh University Press, 2010).

Morris, R.J., 'Urbanisation and Scotland', in W. Hamish Fraser and R.J. Morris (eds), *People and Society in Scotland, Volume II: 1830–1914* (Edinburgh: John Donald, 1990).

Nenadic, Stana, 'The Victorian Middle Classes', in W. Hamish Fraser and Irene Maver (eds), *Glasgow, Volume II: 1830 to 1912* (Manchester: Manchester University Press, 1996).

Wiener, Martin J., 'The Victorian Criminalization of Men', in Pieter Spierenburg (ed.), *Men and Violence: Gender, Honor, and Rituals in Modern Europe and America* (Columbus: The Ohio State University Press, 1998).

Glossary

Assessor
A writer to the Signet (legal practitioner/solicitor) who would provide legal advice in court if requested

Bailie (also spelt 'baillie')
See also 'magistracy' and 'magistrate'
A senior magistrate, second in rank to the Lord Provost. Often the terms 'bailie' and 'magistrate' were used interchangeably. Not to be confused with the late nineteenth- and early twentieth-century weekly magazine, *The Bailie*, which provided a satirical look at Glasgow's public life and the people in it

Burgess
Freeman of a town, often restricted in Scottish burghs primarily to merchants and craftsmen or to those who performed public service, and who enjoyed trading privileges within the burgh. Their political privileges were removed with the reform of local government in the 1830s and their exclusive trading privileges abolished as the century progressed

Burgh
A town or city

Burgh Court
A magistrate's court. Its powers were gradually overtaken by police courts (which had wider summary powers than burgh courts) in the nineteenth century. Like police courts, dealt mainly with minor crimes. They had slightly stronger powers of punishment than police courts, but not as strong as sheriff courts. All cases were heard before a magistrate, not a jury

Chief Constable
See also 'superintendent'
Senior police officer appointed either by police commissioners and/or, local justices and senior legal officials to manage police affairs. 'Superintendent'

was the preferred title for the senior police officer in Scotland for much of the nineteenth century

Clerk (burgh or town) Municipal officer, often with legal training, who would assist magistrates in court on specific points of law

Complainer Complainant

Court of Session Scotland's most senior civil court

Dean of Guild Court Enforced building regulations and settled trade disputes. Staffed typically by the head of the guild or merchant company. Under Scots law the dean of guild was also a magistrate

Defender Defendant/panel

High Court of Justiciary *See also* Justiciary Court
Scotland's senior criminal court. Dealt with serious criminal charges. Also, the court of appeal against police court judgements. Staffed by legally trained judges

Justice of the Peace Court A local summary court with similar powers of punishment to police courts, although dealing mainly with petty offences outside the burgh boundary. Staffed by lay magistrates and justices

Justiciary Court A senior circuit court (north, west and south) which, along with the High Court of Justiciary (Edinburgh), dealt with the most serious crimes in Scotland in the early nineteenth century

Kirk Session The lowest court of the Presbyterian Church but one that dealt with a wide array of behavioural offences. The session was made up of the local minister, elders and deacons. The court's main role was to enforce godly discipline

Lord Advocate The Government's chief legal representative in Scotland

Lord Provost Chief magistrate

Magistracy	In Scots constitutions, the magistracy consisted of the Lord Provost and bailies/magistrates. Typically, bailies/magistrates would serve for a few years depending on what the council set before submitting themselves for re-election or standing down
Magistrate	*See also* 'stipendiary magistrate' Legal guardians of Scottish communities; would sit in police and burgh courts and possessed *ex-officio* representation on police commissions. With the exception of Glasgow's stipendiary magistrate (*see* below), all magistrates were civic magistrates; that is, lay magistrates, elected by, and from among, town councillors, who up until burgh reform in 1833 were appointed by local merchant and trade guilds. After 1833, councillors were elected by male householders of property valued at £10 a year annual rental
No proceedings	Charges withdrawn by the public prosecutor (police/procurator fiscal) before trial proceedings commenced or an adjudication by the court was reached
Panel	Defender/defendant
Police Commissioners	In the first half of the nineteenth century, typically, a body of men elected by qualified ratepayers to manage police affairs. As the century went on commissioners were increasingly appointed from among councillors and magistrates (the latter of whom enjoyed *ex-officio* representation on police commissions throughout the century)
Procurator Fiscal	Scotland's public prosecutor. Most towns would employ their own burgh procurator fiscal to lead criminal prosecutions, but as the century progressed the police often served as public prosecutor for less serious crimes and the majority of offences and contraventions (with police-led prosecutions being brought in the name of the procurator fiscal for the common good)
Sheriff Court	Civil and criminal court with stronger powers of punishment than police and burgh courts but lesser

	powers than Justiciary courts. Dealt with solemn and summary criminal cases. Staffed by legally trained sheriffs
Solemn Procedure	Criminal trials carried out before a jury
Stipendiary magistrate	Legally trained, full-time, salaried magistrate, first appointed in Glasgow in 1876
Superintendent	*See* definition for 'Chief constable'. Contemporary sources in Scotland, especially up to the mid-nineteenth century, often used the term 'superintendant' rather than 'superintendent', reflecting the word's French origins
Writer	Legal practitioner

Index

Bold page numbers indicate figures, *italic* numbers indicate tables.

Police Courts in Nineteenth-Century Scotland, Volume 1

Printed in Great Britain
by Amazon